Modern Philippines

MODERN PHILIPPINES

Patricio N. Abinales

Understanding Modern Nations

BLOOMSBURY ACADEMIC
NEW YORK · LONDON · OXFORD · NEW DELHI · SYDNEY

BLOOMSBURY ACADEMIC
Bloomsbury Publishing Inc
1385 Broadway, New York, NY 10018, USA
50 Bedford Square, London, WC1B 3DP, UK
29 Earlsfort Terrace, Dublin 2, Ireland

BLOOMSBURY, BLOOMSBURY ACADEMIC and the Diana logo are trademarks of
Bloomsbury Publishing Plc

First published in the United States of America by ABC-CLIO 2022
Paperback edition published by Bloomsbury Academic 2025

COVER PHOTOS: Kayangan Lake, Philippines. (Alexey Kornlyev/Dreamstime.com);
The Filipino eagle. (Smithore/Dreamstime.com); Karekare, a Filipino dish (Griffinyx/
Dreamstime.com); Banaue rice terraces, Philippines. (Kobby Dagan/Dreamstime.com

Bloomsbury Publishing Inc does not have any control over, or responsibility for,
any third-party websites referred to or in this book. All internet addresses given
in this book were correct at the time of going to press. The author and publisher
regret any inconvenience caused if addresses have changed or sites have
ceased to exist, but can accept no responsibility for any such changes.

Library of Congress Cataloging-in-Publication Data
Names: Abinales, Patricio N., author.
Title: Modern Philippines / Patricio N. Abinales.
Description: Santa Barbara, California : ABC-CLIO, [2022] | Series: Understanding
modern nations | Includes bibliographical references and index.
Identifiers: LCCN 2022008079 (print) | LCCN 2022008080 (ebook) |
ISBN 9781440860041 (hardcover) | ISBN 9781440860058 (ebook)
Subjects: LCSH: Philippines—Encyclopedias.
Classification: LCC DS654 .A25 2022 (print) | LCC DS654 (ebook) |
DDC 959.9003—dc23/eng/20220216
LC record available at https://lccn.loc.gov/2022008079
LC ebook record available at https://lccn.loc.gov/2022008080

ISBN: HB: 978-1-4408-6004-1
PB: 979-8-7651-4112-0
ePDF: 978-1-4408-6005-8
eBook: 979-8-2161-1868-8

Series: Understanding Modern Nations

To find out more about our authors and books visit www.bloomsbury.com
and sign up for our newsletters.

CONTENTS

SERIES FOREWORD

We live in an evolving world, a world that is becoming increasingly globalized by the minute. Cultures collide and blend, leading to new customs and practices that exist alongside long-standing traditions. Advancing technologies connect lives across the globe, affecting those from densely populated urban areas to those who dwell in the most remote locations in the world. Governments are changing, leading to war and violence but also to new opportunities for those who have been oppressed. The *Understanding Modern Nations* series seeks to answer questions about cultures, societies, and customs in various countries around the world.

Understanding Modern Nations is geared toward readers wanting to expand their knowledge of the world, ideal for high school students researching specific countries, undergraduates preparing for studies abroad, and general readers interested in learning more about the world around them. Each volume in the series focuses on a single country, with coverage on Africa, the Americas, Asia and the Pacific, and Europe.

Each country volume contains 16 chapters focusing on various aspects of culture and society in each country. The chapters begin with an Overview, which is followed by short entries on key topics, concepts, ideas, and biographies pertaining to the chapter's theme. In a way, these volumes serve as "thematic encyclopedias," with entries organized for the reader's benefit. Following a general Preface and Introduction, each volume contains chapters on the following themes:

- Geography
- History
- Government and Politics
- Economy
- Religion and Thought
- Social Classes and Ethnicity
- Gender, Marriage, and Sexuality
- Education
- Language
- Etiquette
- Literature and Drama
- Art and Architecture

- Music and Dance
- Food
- Leisure and Sports
- Media and Popular Culture

Each entry concludes with a list of cross references and Further Readings, pointing readers to additional print and electronic resources that might prove useful.

Following the chapters are appendices, including "A Day in the Life" feature, which depicts "typical" days in the lives of people living in that country, from students to farmers to factory workers to stay-at-home and working mothers. A Glossary, Facts and Figures section, and Holidays chart round out the appendices. Volumes include a Selected Bibliography, as well as sidebars that are scattered throughout the text.

The volumes in the *Understanding Modern Nations* series are not intended to be comprehensive compendiums about every nation of the world, but instead are meant to serve as introductory texts for readers, examining key topics from major countries studied in the high school curriculum as well as important transitioning countries that make headlines daily. It is our hope that readers will gain an understanding and appreciation for cultures and histories outside of their own.

PREFACE

Modern Philippines has two sets of audiences in mind. The first is high school students and first-year college students interested in the country. The second audience is the teachers who have been teaching or are planning to teach about the Philippines and who may need a stand-alone textbook or a supplement to what they are using.

Either way, the intention is to introduce as much *vital information* about the Philippines and Filipinos in a compact but substantive set of 16 chapters. This is done by assigning each chapter a theme, broken into an overview and several entries. Each entry contains a brief description of the topic and ends with a list of suggested additional readings and thematic connections with other chapters' entries.

The first few chapters of the book look into the topography, history, economics, and politics of the Philippines. The next few chapters cover social relations, ethnoreligious identities, and gender relations. The last few chapters deal with the arts and culture, including culinary practices and forms of leisure. These categories were inspired by other country studies that ABC-CLIO has produced and by what I considered specifically crucial in understanding the modern Philippines.

Each chapter has a set of entries based mainly on their importance to Filipinos and scholars of the Philippines. These are people, events, institutions, places, and practices that Filipinos encounter, experience, adore or criticize in their daily lives. These are also issues that they cite when explaining the history of the country, its politics, and such questions as "How did the Philippines change from the second most-promising economy after World War II to the 'poor Man of Asia'?" or "Why are the eight million Filipinos living abroad the 'New Heroes of the Republic'?" These are also the topics that concern scholars of the Philippines, which they closely study to understand the different cultural, economic, political, religious, and social patterns that appear to be distinctively Filipino.

The *Modern Philippines* does not pretend to cover all these topics, but it hopes to stir readers' curiosity by including a list of suggested additional readings per entry. Some of the books and articles listed can be accessed through libraries, but I also tried to find web-based sources accessible to readers *for free*.

A friendly critic questioned me about the book's value given that there is *Wikipedia*, which is perhaps the most popular source of information today, particularly for young people. She also added that *Wikipedia* has a distinct advantage due to the ease with which a reader can update the entry. My reply to her was that when a reader looks at the interconnections between chapters and between entries, they may be able to discern the patterns that interest scholars (as mentioned in a previous paragraph). More importantly, by the time they finish reading the book, a reader can imagine the "big picture" of the modern Philippines and situate the entries from the different chapters. If you like, this context or framework is of little concern to *Wikipedia* contributors.

Not everyone will like the way it is organized, and a close reader will find lapses. It was not easy to write this encyclopedia. It forced me to get off my comfort zone and plunge into areas I initially knew very little about. I had to learn new literature, and the bibliography will attest to this. And it took me some time to complete this project. And I would not have done it without the assistance and advice from the ABC-CLIO staff. I wish to thank Kaitlin Ciarmiello, ABC-CLIO's former senior acquisitions editor for geography and world cultures. Later, Erin Ryan, Nicole Azze, and Kousalya Devi Khrisnamoorthy took over and *patiently* guided me in completing the process. They held a steady hand as I struggled with entry selection and kept alert when I slipped into my comfortable Filipino English.

Angela Marie Amoroso Abinales was born in the Philippines, the adopted daughter of an Italian American mother and a Filipino father. Before moving to Hawaii, she spent her early childhood years in Japan and Washington, DC. It was a hard move because her mother passed away in 2011. But we are now in a place where there is much diversity and where she felt very comfortable as a Filipina-American. Hawaii has helped her cope with what happened. She now considers the islands her home, a third-culture young adult who has finally settled down. She is the perfect "first audience" of *Modern Philippines*.

It is to her that I dedicate this book.

INTRODUCTION

In 1991, the Filipino director Manny Reyes came out with the film *Dreaming Filipinos*. The movie revolves around Paul Gabriel, a Filipino who was born in the United States but grew up in the Philippines. Paul is in his last semester as a college student and plans to return to the United States after graduation. However, Paul's plan encounters a snag: his history professor tells him that he will only allow him to graduate if he can answer the question "What's wrong with the Filipino?" Paul grudgingly seeks out relatives, a family friend, and even a courtesan for answers. This leads to several engaging conversations. What gets Paul his passing grade is an uncle turning the table around and suggesting that maybe the question should be posed to the Americans, not to Filipinos. Paul migrates but is unhappy in the United States. The movie ends with him going back to the Philippines after two years as a green card holder and visibly happy.

Dreaming Filipinos was hardly a top grosser; I believe it did not even reach the theaters. But it reflected two contrasting trends of that time. First, Paul was no different from many other Filipinos wanting to become Americans. Second, the United States to Paul, his contemporaries, and those before him was the Land of Opportunity, where they would find gold. In 1980 there were 501,000 migrants; by 1990, this nearly doubled to 913,000. This rise would continue, and in 2018 the U.S. Census Bureau reported 2,014,000 Filipinos (Gallardo and Batalova 2020). Yet, by going back "home," Paul also reaffirmed the power of Filipino nationalism, which at that time was at an all-time high, as Filipinos were still savoring the ouster of the dictator Ferdinand Marcos and the abrogation of a 45-year-old military agreement that allowed the Americans to establish bases in the country.

There were also signs that these trends were changing. The number of Filipinos leaving for work (not migration) rose fast—214,590 in 1980 to 837,020 in 1999. Their destinations were the Middle East and East Asia, where countries like Saudi Arabia and Japan filled gaps in their employment. Overseas Filipino workers (OFWs) remitted US$421,000 back to their families in 1980; by 1990, this had gone up to US$1.18 million and would not stop climbing. In 2020 OFW remittances had reached US$33.1 billion, contributing 9.2 percent of the gross domestic product and raising the Philippines' foreign reserves to a high of US$109.8 billion (*Bangko Sentral ng Pilipinas* 2020). The United States was not the source of gold anymore. There were other new lands of opportunity open to Filipinos and Filipinas aspiring for a better life for their families (That said, Filipino Americans still accounted for the most significant percentage of overseas remittances, estimated at US$12 billion in 2020).

In the United States, Filipino migrants still comprise the majority population, and a high percentage of them (71 percent) applied for naturalization (as against 51 percent of the total immigrant population), in the 1980s. However, beginning in the 1990s, the percentage of U.S.-born Filipinos grew, and by the second decade of the 21st century, parity was achieved by these two groups. The Pew Research Center has this pegged at 50:50 (Budiman 2021).

These metamorphoses have spawned the term "global Filipino" to describe the lives of not just one diaspora (the United States) but of several other diasporic settlement zones the world over. I will leave it to readers to explore the many ways in which scholars explain the term. Still, I would also like to tease out a couple of observations that may be pertinent to the purpose of this collection, particularly on the issue of nationalism.

First, fidelity for the nation has changed in meaning since the time of Paul and his respondents. *Dreaming Filipinos'* nationalist message echoed the prevailing popular ideal: loving the Philippines meant fighting for its future and defending it against challenges in situ. You can never love it from afar; being a real Filipino meant setting up your roots there. A decade later, that was not the case anymore. Nationalism was not anymore circumscribed within the Philippines. It has "traveled out" with the OFWs whose locations have forced them to relate with other nationalities, including those of the host countries. They cannot help but *compare themselves* and discover (or, some argue, rediscover). Some look at religion, social norms, cultural practices, and cuisines.

Others recall Philippine history or become involved in politics, albeit from afar. And to silence skeptics from Paul's era, the Philippine government has already declared the OFW the "new heroes of the nation" (Franco 2015). It has gone out of its way to assure them that they will attain the middle-class status they have been aspiring for so long. OFWs have graciously reciprocated. Once the Philippine Congress passed an Overseas Filipino Voting Act, the registration of OFW voters steadily rose (Abad 2021). They also had become increasingly involved in political affairs back home.

Second, when Filipino migrants who have switched their citizenship to America are also predisposed to integrating themselves into the culture of their new country, the beneficiaries have been their children (Yu-Wen and Meekyung 2008). Yet, many among the immigrants still claim loyalty to the "old country." As one respondent informed a researcher, "My brain is enticed to the United States, but my heart remains here" (Seki 2012, 196). Others have returned home to retire (Pido 2017). These sentimental attachments have invariably roused the interests of their progenies. With American society becoming more ethnically diverse, the latter have become more curious about the Philippines. Their curiosity ranges from food to history, from performances to the nation's politics. The scholar Benedict Anderson calls this "long-distance nationalism" (Anderson 1992).

Third, the United States and the Philippines had had a long history since the 20th century, when the former ruled over the latter for 40 years. This history was characterized by brutal confrontations, political accommodations, economic challenges, educational attainment, and complex cultural interaction. As a result, Filipino-American relations become frayed at times, but they have never been severely threatened or undermined for the most part. With the rise of China today, the United States has more reason to reinforce ties with old allies like the Philippines. As a result, interest in the Philippines among policymakers, policy analysts, and students of American international relations and Asian politics is expected to grow.

The *Modern Philippines* has this "audience" in mind and aims at introducing them to some of the essential features of the country. The 16 chapters of this book are organized such that some basic features associated with the geography, history, politics, and economy of the country are covered in the beginning chapters. The remainder of the book focuses on language, religion, and socioeconomic status issues. There is a chapter that looks at, among other things, the changing nature of Filipino families as more of their kin seek jobs abroad. Other chapters discuss the value that Filipinos place on their education, their etiquette, the novels they read, the music they listen to, the architecture they gaze at, and the dances they relish. There is also a chapter on food, which is the most popular way Filipinos develop and nurture friendships, and another on sports—one of the activities that unite an often-divided nation.

This is not a comprehensive compilation, and neither does it justice to the topics and their often-complex histories. But I hope that our audiences' interest in the Philippines can induce them to persist in their effort to understand the country and its people, using *Modern Philippines* as their guidepost.

Further Reading

Abad, Michelle. 2021. "OFW Groups Call for Extension of Overseas Voting Registration Period." *Rappler*. October 13. https://www.rappler.com/nation/elections/overseas -filipinos-groups-call-extensions-voting-registration-period/

Anderson, Benedict. 1992. "Long-Distance Nationalism: World Capitalism and the Rise of Identity Politics." In *Wertheim Lecture*. Amsterdam: Centre for Asian Studies Amsterdam.

Bangko Sentral ng Pilipinas. 2020. "Overseas Filipinos' Cash Remittances, by Country, by Source for periods indicated, in Thousands US dollars." *Statistics – External Accounts*. https://www.bsp.gov.ph/Statistics/External/Table%2011.pdf?

Budiman, Abby. 2021. "Filipinos in the U.S. Fact Sheet." *Pew Research Center*. April 29. https://www.pewresearch.org/social-trends/fact-sheet/asian-americans-filipinos-in -the-u-s/

Franco, Jean Encinas. 2015. "Overseas Filipino Workers (OFWs) as Heroes: Discursive Origins of the 'Bagong Bayani' in the Era of Labor Export." *Humanities Diliman* 12, no. 2 (December): 56–78.

Gallardo, Luis Hassan, and Jeanne Batalova. 2020. "Filipino Immigrants in the United States." *Migrant Policy Institute*. July 15. https://www.migrationpolicy.org/article/ filipino-immigrants-united-states-2020Ban

Pido, Eric J. 2017. *Migrant Returns: Manila, Development, and Transnational Connectivity.* Durham, NC: Duke University Press.

Seki, Koki. 2012. "Difference and Alliance in Transnational Fields The Pendular Identity of the Filipino Middle Class." *Philippine Studies: Historical and Ethnographic Viewpoints* 60, no. 2 (June): 187–221.

Yu-Wen, Ying, and Meekyung Han. 2008. "Parental Contributions to Southeast Asian American Adolescents' Well-Being." *Youth and Society* 40, no. 2: 289–306.

PHILIPPINES

CHAPTER 1

GEOGRAPHY

OVERVIEW

The Philippines is an archipelago in the western end of the Pacific Ocean. With a total land area of 116,518 square miles and a length of about 1,150 miles from the north to the south, it is part of what scholars call the Southeast Asian maritime region along with Indonesia, Singapore, and Timor-Leste. The archipelago has 7,107 islands of varying sizes, the 2 largest being Luzon in the north and Mindanao in the southeast. In between are a group of islands collectively known as the Visayas. The Philippines has no contiguous border with any other country; its nearest neighbors are Vietnam to the west, Southern China to the northwest, Taiwan to the north, the Malaysian state of Sabah to the southwest, and Indonesia to the south.

The Philippines mostly comprises mountain ranges, with some narrow coastal plains and valleys. The land is volcanic, the riverine systems extensive; "inland seas" surround the islands, while three "outer seas" define the archipelago's contours. The landscapes and the seascape endow the country with abundant natural and mineral resources. Rice, corn, sugarcane, tropical fruit, and various types of vegetables are grown in the plains and hills, while more than 2,400 fish species inhabit the 640,000-mile territorial waters, making the Philippines one of the world's richest fishing zones. The mountain ranges are rich in flora and fauna as well as rainforests, although unrestrained logging has reduced the forest cover to only 10 percent of the total land area.

As mentioned earlier, three "outer seas" surround the Philippines. In the northwest part of the Pacific Ocean lies the Philippine Sea, which extends as far as the Japanese islands of Okinawa, Kyushu, and Shikoku in the north, the North Mariana and the Federated States of Micronesia and Palau in the east, and the Caroline Islands in the southeast. The Philippine Sea has a depth of 19,700 feet and a total surface area of about 40,000 square miles (3 percent of the Pacific region).

The floor of the Philippine Sea consists of geographic faults and fractured zones arising from regular plate tectonic activity. Isolated volcanic mountains called table mounts (or guyots) are found on the ocean floor. The Philippine Sea is also home to the two deepest channels in the world—the Philippine Trench and the Mariana Trench. It has more than 500 kinds of hard and soft corals and a rich variety of fish species ranging from bottom feeders like tuna to mobile sharks and whales and the Japanese eel (which spawns in the area). This diverse ecosystem is the result of the Pacific North Equatorial Current, a warm undercurrent that flows through the north of the Philippines to the south of Japan and back.

In the southwest and south-central side of the Philippines is the Celebes Sea (Laut Sulawesi to the Indonesians), which is located in the western Pacific Ocean, with the Sulu archipelago to the northwest, the island of Mindanao to the north, and the Indonesian island of Sulawesi to the south. It has a total surface area of 110,000 square miles and a depth ranging from 13,000 feet to 20,406 feet (half the sea is 13,000 feet deep). There are volcanoes in the sea's northeastern portion.

The International Hydrographic Organization (IHO), a consultative and technical organization established in 1921, considers the Celebes Sea an extension of the waters of the East Indian Archipelago. Like the Philippine Sea, it has a vibrant ecosystem that is home to different species of corals and a wide range of fish, including the yellowfin tuna. It is, therefore, a rich fishing ground and an ocean "small enough" for luxury cruises. The Celebes Sea is the natural border between the Philippines, the Malaysian state of Sabah, and Indonesia. This border was formalized between Indonesia and the Philippines on May 23, 2013, wherein both countries agreed to respect each other's exclusive economic zones.

Finally, west of the Philippines is the South China Sea (its Chinese name is Nan Hai), which has an area of 1,423,000 square miles, a maximum depth of 16,457 feet, and an underwater plain with a depth of 14,100 feet. There are deep troughs at the eastern, southern, and northwestern edges of the sea. The equatorial current and run-off water from the lands surrounding it have kept the water warm around this "basin," allowing for varied marine life to thrive. Geologists also believe that beneath its ocean floor are some of the largest, if not the largest, oil and natural gas reserves.

The South China Sea connects East and Southeast Asia and the Pacific Ocean. It links up with the Taiwan Strait to the north, while in the Luzon Strait, it joins with the Pacific Ocean. In its southern part, the South China Sea functions as a channel that joins western Indonesia, Borneo, and Sumatra, and in its farthest reach, the Strait of Malacca and the Indian Ocean. These distinct features have made the South China Sea one of the world's most vital trading passages for China, Japan, Korea, and other countries on the western edge of the Pacific, with key markets mainly in the Americas and Europe. Some 130,000 cargo ships pass through Singapore and the South China Sea each year, bearing some of the critical needs of East Asian economies. Two-thirds of South Korea's energy supplies, 80 percent of Japan's, and 39 percent of Chinese oil requirements go through this sea.

Eight channels, twelve straits, and four passes are the natural boundaries between islands and the "larger" Visayan Sea that adjoins the Cebu, Leyte, Masbate, and Panay Islands. Among these is the Inland Philippine Sea. Further offshore is a series of trenches, the most famous of which is the Philippine Trench (alternately called the Philippine Deep, the Mindanao Trench, or the Mindanao Deep), an abyss that runs down through the east coast of Mindanao. In 1945, the American explorer ship *Cape Johnson* pinged the trench, recording a depth of 34,440 feet.

As an archipelago, it is but natural for the Philippines to have bays as part of island coastlines. There are 310 listed bays of various sizes across the country, 3 of which are famous for different reasons.

Port of Manila at Manila Bay. (Richie Chan/Dreamstime.com)

Perhaps the most well known of these is Manila Bay, which is a natural harbor for ships and an important national port for passengers and cargo from different parts of the islands and from abroad. The second is Subic Bay, which was known as the largest naval base in the United States outside the American mainland. After the Americans left in the early 1990s, it has been transformed into an export processing zone and ship repair dockyard. The third is Sarangani Bay, which has become famous as a landing point for tuna caught in the Celebes Sea.

The Philippines sits on the westernmost part of the so-called Ring of Fire, a horseshoe-shaped chain of oceanic trenches that runs from the southern tip of Latin America up through the western side of Central America, the United States, and Canada, crossing in Alaska into Vladivostok, Japan, Taiwan, and the west side of the Philippines, and then turning east, cutting through Bougainville and Tonga. There are 450 active and dormant volcanoes in these trenches, and 90 percent of volcanic eruptions and 81 percent of earthquakes in the Asia Pacific region occur in this area.

Most of the 50 volcanoes on the Philippine side of the trench are dormant, but seismologists continue to warn that these could erupt anytime. Such was the case in 1991 when Mount Pinatubo, a long inactive volcano, erupted, spewing gas and rocks and triggering mudflows of pyroclastic material and water across several provinces north of Manila. This lahar (Indonesian for flowing lava) also forced the United States to close its air force base in the province of Pampanga. The Mount Pinatubo eruption is recorded as one of the most massive volcanic eruptions of the 20th century.

The Philippine islands' mountain ranges are, therefore, the dryland upper extensions of these volcanoes. At the foot of these mountain ranges are flat spaces that extend to the coastline, while valleys or plateaus can be found in between the mountain ranges. Most of the major mountain ranges are concentrated in the islands of Luzon and Mindanao. The former has 11 of these, running north to south and west to east, while the latter has 3 that are located mainly in the southwest and central parts of the island. The Visayas has one mountain range—the central Panay Island range. These ranges are interspersed with smaller ridges.

The more famous of these ranges are associated with mountains that exude a dramatic appearance. The Sierra Madre, the mountain range running from the east and southeast of Luzon is not as well known as Mount Mayon, an active volcano with a "perfect cone" located on the southeastern tip of the range. The same is true of Mindanao's Apo-Talomo range, which many are unfamiliar with unless mentioned in connection to Mount Apo, its easternmost elevation that is also the highest summit in the country.

These mountain ranges are found all over the country. They are the watersheds where myriad streams and rivulets flow to the lowlands and out into the sea. The largest rivers are also the most important because food-producing areas rely on their water. These waters of the Cagayan, Agno, and Pampanga Rivers nourish the sugar and rice lands of central Luzon. The Agusan River, flowing out of the inner marshlands, is the largest river of Mindanao; it sustains the fertile valleys in central Mindanao and the lowlands of the east coast where rice, coconut, and other fruit crops are cultivated. The Rio Grande de Mindanao, whose waters come from the marshes of central Mindanao, maintains the rice and coconut production in the area. The Agusan and the Rio Grande Rivers also function as trade and travel routes between the coastal towns and cities and hinterland areas.

Finally, two more rivers elsewhere in the Philippines are worth mentioning. The first is the Pasig River, which cuts across an urban metropolis. It is an important nexus for the movement of goods from factories on the eastern shorelines of Metropolitan Manila and farm produce farther upriver. The Pasig, however, is severely polluted and its marine life virtually nonexistent. The second is Palawan Island's Subterranean River, whose many underground tributaries flow out to the ocean. This river has been converted into a national park and was designated a World Heritage Site by the United Nations Educational, Scientific, and Cultural Organization (UNESCO) in 1999.

There are 64 lakes of different sizes and depths throughout the archipelago; all but 13 are sections of tectonic plates, lava flows, thermal chasms, and the tops of volcanoes. Half of these lakes are located in Luzon; 26 are in Mindanao, 14 in the Visayas, and 8 in the Sulu archipelago. The largest of these lakes is the 356-square mile Laguna de Bay and the second largest is Lake Sultan Alonto (commonly known as Lake Lanao) in central Mindanao (131 square miles). The deepest of these lakes teem with freshwater marine life—fish, shellfish, and bivalves—that communities catch in the wild or farm. Other lakes have also become tourist attractions, notably Taal Lake, which lies south of the national capital.

These lakes mitigate the tropical temperatures by absorbing "excess" heat, which, according to scientists, is crucial in slowing down climate change and environmental decay. The burgeoning communities around these lakes and the unregulated construction and operation of factories have polluted them. Inadequate monitoring facilities have also allowed nonindigenous fish species to invade lakes like Laguna de Bay. Limited environmental supervision and improper, if not altogether absent, waste management facilities have allowed effluents to be dumped into Laguna de Bay, causing health problems that affect the most vulnerable, namely, children.

See also: Chapter 4: Overview; Agriculture; Industry.

Further Reading

Boquet, Yves. 2015. *The Philippine Archipelago*, n.p. New York: Springer.

Central Intelligence Agency. 2022. *The World Factbook—East and Southeast Asia—Philippines* (February 14). https://www.cia.gov/the-world-factbook/countries/philippines/

Coursey, Oscar William. 2008. *History and Geography of the Philippines*. Charleston, SC: Bibliobazaar. 180 pp.

Goldoftas, Barbara. 2006. *The Green Tiger: The Cost of Ecological Decline in the Philippines*. New York: Oxford University Press.

Hobel, Robert, and Laurie Rosenbaum. 1979. *The Philippines*. Bern, Switzerland: Kummerly and Frey.

Macclintock, Samuel. 2012. *The Philippines: A Geographical Reader-Classic Reprint*. London: FB&C Ltd.

Nance, John J. 1977. *The Land and People of the Philippines*. Philadelphia: Lippincott.

Nickles, Greg. 2002. *Philippines—the Land*. New York: Crabtree Publishing Company.

Administrative Regions

Today there are a total of 187 administrative regions throughout the Philippines. The largest of these is unquestionably the 16 cities that are administratively under the Metropolitan Manila Development Authority (MMDA). Similar superordinate bodies had been set up in the cities of Cebu, Cagayan de Oro, and Davao, and in the provinces just north of Manila as well as in the Muslim provinces of Mindanao Island. Planning for these regional bodies, however, has not been that well organized. Metropolitan Cebu, for example, did not have a functioning coordinating body as late as 2004.

The MMDA and ARMM (now replaced by the Bangsamoro Autonomous Region in Muslim Mindanao, BARMM) are the most important of all these regions, the former because it was the first and oversaw the cities and municipalities of the national capital and the latter as a result of efforts to bring peace in the war-torn area. The MMDA succeeded an earlier agency that President Ferdinand E. Marcos created through Presidential Decree 824—the Metropolitan Manila Commission (MMC), whose creation had been justified as urgent on account of population growth and hence the need for an agency to coordinate projects that cut across local governments.

The decree gave the MMC the authority to "perform general administrative, executive and policy-making functions" over 4 cities, 13 municipalities, and 1 province. It could impose taxes and take control of infrastructure development and repair as well as formulate development plans for the entire region. The MMC had practically taken over the powers and responsibilities of the cities, municipalities, and the province of Bulacan, causing much resentment among the latter's officials. This would partly explain why some of these cities became centers of protests against President Marcos (Chapter 3).

In January 1990, Marcos's successor, President Corazon Aquino, replaced the MMC with the Metropolitan Manila Authority (MMA) and gave the mayors the power to elect from their ranks the chairman (Mr. Marcos had appointed his wife, Imelda as MMC governor). Unlike its predecessor, the MMA had considerably less powers and a budget based on the contributions of the cities, which would use their power over the MMA's purse to defy or exact concessions from the latter.

In 1995, Congress passed the Republic Act 7924 creating the MMDA, with its head appointed by the president from all the mayors of a now-expanded metropolis. The MMDA had a governing board led by the mayors of the cities and municipalities, with the heads of the tourism, public works, budget, housing, and the national police departments as nonvoting members.

The MMDA's powers had also been considerably clipped. Like the MMC, MMDA could plan and implement metropolis-wide programs and projects and set out policies, standards, and procedures for the delivery of essential services within and across cities. It could perform all these functions without necessarily seeking the approval of the member cities. However, local governments also had an effective countermeasure to these powers in a law, which restored their autonomy. Hence, the MMDA could not plan for and regulate targeted urban growth centers unless it received permission from the cities.

Moreover, Congress removed the MMDA's taxation authority and did not include it in the distribution of the IRA. For its operations, MMDA depends on financial support from the cities—a power that the latter often uses to limit the MMDA's influence. The national government is therefore left with no choice but to provide the services the MMDA could not deliver because of financial constraints.

Today the MMDA's primary responsibility has been reduced to crafting one traffic scheme after another in a vain effort to resolve Metropolitan Manila's horrendous traffic problem, as well as flood control and sewage management—the other major problem that hounds the MMDA to this day.

If the MMDA was conceived in response to urban blight, the government created ARMM on August 1, 1989, in response to the demands of the country's Muslim minority for an autonomous regional body that would superintend the development programs of provinces and cities where Muslims are the biggest ethnic group. However, more importantly, ARMM was supposed to become the mechanism for an Islamic form of governance to be practiced.

The government had been aware of the demands of Filipino Muslims and their grievance that they had been left behind as the country moved forward economically. However, it took a rebellion to finally get Manila's full attention on them. For the first time in their history, different Muslim ethnic groups banded together to form the Moro National Liberation Front (MNLF), launching an all-out war to separate the islands of Mindanao, the Sulu Archipelago, and Palawan from the Philippines body politic. The MNLF justified its rebellion on two grounds: the alleged "genocide" perpetrated by the government and the Christian majority against Muslims and the fact that Muslims never considered themselves as part of the Philippines.

The top divisions of the Armed Forces of the Philippines (AFP) were sent to the south to quell the rebellion. The AFP also sought out the help of Muslim governments to broker peace talks with the MNLF. The negotiations fell through during the government of Mr. Marcos, and the peace agreement was signed when President Corazon Aquino replaced the former. Among other things, both sides agreed to the creation of a regional body that will oversee the Muslim provinces, and on August 1, 1989, Congress passed Republic Act 6734, creating ARMM.

The government held a plebiscite in 13 provinces and 10 cities where residents were asked whether they would join the ARMM. Only 4 provinces—Lanao del Sur (except Marawi City), Maguindanao, Sulu, and Tawi-Tawi—elected to do so. ARMM was officially inaugurated on November 6, 1990, with a land area of 10,415 square miles, with a population of 3.2 million (2010), and with Cotabato as the capital. It has jurisdiction over 2 cities, 116 municipalities, and 2,490 villages. The regional government consists of a regional governor and vice governor, and members of a regional assembly; all these positions are filled through elections that take place one year after the general elections.

The governor and vice-governor each have a three-year term and may be reelected for two more successive terms. The governor is directly under the supervision of the president of the Philippines and heads an executive council that includes the vice-governor and three deputy regional governors, each representing Christian, Muslim, and non-Muslim Indigenous communities. ARMM also has a legislative assembly composed of three members per congressional district and sectorial representatives of the three major ethnoreligious groups in the region—both three-year terms that can be extended for another two. The assembly can pass laws that relate to revenue generation; it can also legislate on issues about the Sharia, the religious law governing Muslims. But the assembly cannot legislate on matters of national significance: foreign affairs, national defense, the postal system, fiscal and monetary policies, citizenship, general audit, maritime and air transport laws, and patents, trademarks, and copyright issues.

These limited institutional powers have caused intermittent tension between the regional body and the national government. ARMM officials have complained that while the regional government can collect taxes, the law does not allow them to tax potentially significant sources of largesse: real estate and the capital gains tax. The income derived from the mining of gold and copper, as well as harvests from fish and marine resources, accrue to the national government. In a region that is one of the most impoverished in the country, this economic handicap makes ARMM utterly dependent on the national government. Indeed, 98 percent of ARMM's operating costs come from the national government.

Manila's control of ARMM is not only financial; it is also political. The law gives Congress the sole power to determine when regional elections can be held. Between 1991 and 2011, the legislature postponed ARMM elections eight times for many reasons—from preventing poll violence between rival families to supporting ARMM politicians, to interdicting the illicit sector that has become a threat to public order. At the other end, ARMM's capacity to govern has been compromised because the IRA for cities and municipalities still flow directly to them. These cities and municipalities could, therefore, resist pressure from ARMM.

One of the provisions of the peace negotiations between the Moro Islamic Liberation Front (MILF), a rival of the MNLF, and the Philippine government was to replace ARMM with another regional body with relatively expanded powers. The national government would retain its foreign policy, national defense, and monetary powers, but share power with the regional body over criminal justice, environmental protection, economic development, trade and investments, and education and control over the resources of the Muslims' "ancestral domain." This regional body would also share supervisory powers with Manila over cities and municipalities. In early 2019, the Philippine Congress passed the Bangsamoro Organic Law, but two years later President Rodrigo Duterte signed an amendment providing for a three-year interim period before the holding of elections for a *Bangsamoro* Parliament. Overseeing the transition would be a Bangsamoro Transition Authority, which has executive and legislative power (Engelbrecht 2021).

See also: Chapter 2: Muslim Separatism. Chapter 3: Overview; Elections; Federalism.

Further Reading

Ali, David Aba. 2007. "Regional Development in the Philippines: The Case of the Autonomous Region in Muslim Mindanao (ARMM)." PhD diss., University of Western Australia School of Earth and Geographical Sciences.

Choguill, Charles L. 2001. "Manila: City of Hope or a Planner's Nightmare?" *Built Environment* 27, no. 2 (January): 85–95.

Co, Edna A. 2013. *State of Local Democracy in the Autonomous Region in Muslim Mindanao*. Quezon City: University of the Philippines National College of Public Administration and Governance and the Philippine Center for Islam and Democracy.

Jimenez, Benedict. 2009. "Anatomy of Autonomy: Assessing the Organizational Capacity and External Environment of the Autonomous Region in Muslim Mindanao." *Asian Politics and Policy* 1, no. 2 (April): 282–306.

Shatkin, Gavin. 2000. "Obstacles to Empowerment: Local Politics and Civil Society in Metropolitan Manila, the Philippines." *Urban Studies* 37, no. 12 (November): 2357–2375.

Climate

The Philippines is located in the tropical zone and, as such, has only three seasons—wet, dry, and arid (summer). The rainy season begins around June and usually lasts until October, although the southern part of the country continues to experience rains well into January. The monsoon rains come between May and October at an average of about 197 inches in the mountainous areas and 39 inches in the lowlands. The summer season officially starts in late April and ends in September, but there is considerable overlap between these seasons. A dry season can, therefore, last until November, and the rainy season can begin as early as July or August.

The weather is affected mainly by the monsoon, which, in turn determines the direction of the currents. At the end of the summer, these current flows from the Java Sea to the South China Sea, going up north to the Taiwan and Luzon Straits. During winter, the monsoon comes from the northeast and dumps between 80 and 120 inches of rain, and at their strongest, before they develop into typhoons.

The Philippine Atmospheric, Geophysical, and Astronomical Services Administration (PAGASA) classifies typhoons into several categories depending on the speed of their "sustained winds." From 1947 to 2016, the Philippines had been hit by 21 of the strongest typhoons that moved from the central Pacific Ocean toward China. The strongest of them was Haiyan, which wreaked havoc across the Visayas regions during November 6–9, 2013, killing 6,300 people and costing the government more than US$1.8 billion.

The radical changes in surface ocean temperatures are popularly known as El Niño and El Niña. Peruvian sailors are said to have first referred to the seasonal warm ocean current that runs from the coast of Peru and Ecuador around Christmas to the western parts of the Pacific Ocean as El Niño ("the boy-child," which is how the baby Jesus is often called). This weather condition has had far-reaching effects on the ocean (among them the radical change in fishing patterns) and on agricultural cycles as well.

In the Philippines, El Niño has disrupted the clockwork of the rainy season or terminated it prematurely, disrupting planting-and-harvesting schedules. In 2016, El Niño badly affected food stock supplies in the southern Philippines, prompting peasants to march and demand for relief from the government. This protest had ended in violence, with several peasants killed and wounded by police fire. The government promised to address the incident and went on to enforce improvements in the delivery of emergency rice and food products to farms affected by El Niño but stopped short of prosecuting anyone involved in the violence.

La Niña habitually follows El Niño, and the cooling of the ocean triggers heavy rains and typhoons (hurricanes). This happens mainly in the central and eastern Pacific regions, although the phenomenon is now recurring in Brunei, Indonesia, Malaysia, and the Philippines between the last months of the year and the first months of the next. In the Philippines, the provinces facing the Pacific Ocean—from those in the Cordillera region in the north, Samar and Leyte provinces in the Visayas, and the entire eastern Mindanao—are the most affected by La Niña. Rice and corn lands suffer from long periods of drought caused by El Niño, which are then followed by floods from the heavy rains caused by La Niña. Farmers have never been able to restore the original and full productivity of the land.

See also: Chapter 4: Agriculture.

Further Reading

Algue, Jose. 1904. *The Climate of the Philippines*. Washington, DC: Department of Commerce and Labor Bureau of the Census.

Cuevas, Sining C. 2017. "Institutional Dimensions of Climate Change Adaptation: Insights from the Philippines." *Climate Policy* (April 24): 499–511.

Hilario, Flaviana, Rosalina de Guzman, Daisy Ortega, Peter Hayman, and Bronya Alexander. 2009. "El Niño Southern Oscillation in the Philippines: Impacts, Forecasts and Risk Management." *Philippine Journal of Development* 36, no. 1: 9–34.

Republic of the Philippines, Atmospheric, Geophysical and Astronomical Services Administration. 1978. *The Climate of the Philippines*. Quezon City: PAGASA Publication Section, Climatological Division.

Van Klinken, Gerry 2020. "Typhoon Disaster Politics in Pre-1945 Asia: Three Case Studies." *Disaster Prevention and Management* 30, no. 1 (July 20). https://www.emerald.com/insight/content/doi/10.1108/DPM-01-2020-0027/full/html

Luzon

Luzon is the biggest island of the Philippines, with a total area of 42,458 square miles. It has two major mountain chains—the Cordillera Central in the northernmost part of the island and the Sierra Madre, which runs from the north to the center of the Pacific coast side. Luzon protrudes southeast toward the Pacific, with the Sierra Madre mountain range running down southeast into the tip of the Bicol peninsula, home of Mayon Volcano, which is famous for its near-perfect cone. At the end of the peninsula is a rugged coastline of gulfs and bays. There are two smaller mountain ranges in the west—the Zambales Mountains and the Caraballo Mountains on the southern tip of the Cordillera Central. The Zambales Mountains made international headlines in 1991 when one of its dormant volcanoes, Mount Pinatubo, erupted and devastated the area surrounding it, forcing the United States to close Clark Air Force Base, one of its major military facilities in Asia.

In the middle of the island is a plain that stretches about 150 miles from north to south and 50 miles from east to west. Called the "Central Plain of Luzon," it is the country's largest rice-producing area and also has the second-largest number of sugar plantations. It extends down south where it meets with Laguna de Bay, the country's largest lake that, in turn, connects Mounts Makiling and Banahaw, two elevations that Filipinos associate with stories and creatures from the precolonial and colonial pasts. To the south of Laguna de Bay is a smaller lake (Taal), which is also the crater of the dormant Taal volcano.

Several smaller islands are adjacent to Luzon. At the northern tip are the Batanes and Babuyan island groups. The former is composed of 14 islands of different sizes, with a total area of 84.56 square miles; these are the most proximate to Taiwan. Their topography is rugged and rocky owing to their volcanic origins. There is very little agriculture in the islands, and many rely on communities in the main Luzon Island for food and other domestic needs. Five islands and ten islets constitute the Babuyan group, and these have the same topography as the Batanes islands. South of Luzon are the islands of Palawan, Mindoro, Catanduanes, Marinduque, Romblon, and Polillo.

Polillo is located in the central-eastern part of Luzon and has a total land area of 237.6 square miles. Hilly and mountainous, Polillo allows only for limited and often unprofitable cultivation of coconut and rice. It is more known for its pristine beaches and has lately become a favorite among young local and foreign tourists seeking out-of-the-way beach sanctuaries.

East of Mindoro is Marinduque, an oval-shaped and hilly island with an area of 367.79 square miles. Its highest peak is Mount Malindig, a dormant volcano that has become a regular destination for amateur mountain climbers. Marinduque is also famous for complex cave systems and subterranean rivers that run through these caves. Rice and coconut farms are scattered all over its hilly geography, and there are also quite a few cattle ranches. Underneath its mountains, Marinduque has a rich trove of iron ore and copper.

Palawan Island is a narrow mountainous stretch facing the South China Sea. It has an area of 4,706 square miles and has become quite famous for its relatively untouched shorelines and a diminutive but rich rainforest. In the past, Palawan was a backpacker's mecca, but it has since become a popular tourist destination as well as a retirement haven for families weary of urban life.

The Mindoro islands comprise an area of 4,082 square miles—a roundish island group that has a mountain chain with a coal-rich core extending into broken-coast plains. Mindoro is known as one of the transit points for tourists traveling to the small island of Boracay (which lies southeast of Mindoro). Boracay is the top tourist draw in this area since its "discovery"—again by backpackers—in the 1970s.

Finally, Catanduanes island lies in the east-central part of Luzon. It has an area of 550 square miles, and except for a lowland area on the southeast coast, it is mostly hilly. Coconut farms of various sizes are the main economic activity of Catanduanes communities.

See also: Chapter 3: Overview; Federalism.

Further Reading

Alencon, Ferdinand Philippe Marie d'Orleans. 1986. *Luzon and Mindanao.* Manila: E. Aguilar Cruz.

U.S. Defense Mapping Agency. 1980. *Luzon.* Washington, DC: Hydrographic/Topographic Center.

Mindanao

Mindanao is the second-largest island of the Philippines and is located south of the archipelago. It borders the Malaysian state of Sabah and is a day's travel from western

Indonesia through the Celebes Sea. Mindanao has an area of 37,657 square miles, and its topography consists mainly of mountain ranges, bays, gulfs, rivers, peninsulas, plateaus, and valleys.

Many presume that because Mindanao is smaller than Luzon, it is less significant politically and economically. This wrongheaded notion has, in turn, influenced how Filipinos—especially those from Luzon and the Visayas—regard Mindanao's politico-economic value. The fact is, Mindanao has a much larger land area than 125 countries, among them the Netherlands, South Korea, the Czech Republic, Hungary, Austria, and Ireland. Mindanao's natural resources far exceed those of East Asian countries. Mindanao's image as a frontier remains prevalent. It is a land that offers the "promise" of prosperity to those who will move there. What also persists is its reputation for being a violent, unstable part of the Philippines dominated by rebels, terrorists, and warlords.

Mindanao's mountain ranges include 52 inactive volcanoes (some of which are islets surrounding Mindanao). The highest of these dormant volcanoes are Mount Apo (9,724 feet) and Mount Talomo (9, 491 feet) in the southeastern part of the island called the Davao region; Mount Ragang (9,236 feet) and Mount Kitanglad (9.478 feet) in central Mindanao; Mount Malindang (7,956 feet) on the northwestern side of the island; and the North Mountain (7,162 feet) in the southern peninsula of Zamboanga.

Unlike Luzon, Mindanao has extensive flatlands whose soil is kept fertile by swamps, lakes, and river systems. Corn, rice, hemp (abaca), coffee, bananas, pineapples, mangoes, and coconuts were grown traditionally by both smallholders and plantations in these areas. Arable lands expanded further after timber companies cleared much of Mindanao of its rainforests. The fabled richness of its lands had prompted a succession of Philippine governments to encourage Filipinos in the central and northern parts of the country to move to Mindanao, the "Land of Promise." Migration started slowly in the decades before World War II but accelerated postwar when families trying to escape poverty and desiring to own lands moved in considerable numbers to Mindanao. By the 1960s, over a million Filipinos had settled in this Land of Promise—it was the most significant demographic shift in Philippine history.

Mindanao's rugged and narrow coastlines allow for abundant marine life to thrive. Coral reefs and tiny islets are a common sight all around the island, making inland fishing one of the most common sources of livelihood. A few miles off the northeastern Mindanao coast is the Philippine Deep, an ocean trench reaching down 34,696 feet, the third-deepest after the Mariana and Tonga trenches. Finally, the Celebes Sea, which is the natural border between the Philippines and Indonesia, is a fishing ground rich in tuna and other deep-sea fish. It has been extensively fished since the second decade of the 20th century, and this protracted harvesting has led environmentalists and fishery experts to warn that the deep-sea marine life in the area is fast being depleted.

Upland plateaus, located mainly in the center of the island, comprise the third major topographical feature of Mindanao. Like the plains, these plateaus have incredibly fertile soil where pineapple and other crops for export are cultivated by agro-corporations led by the American agriculture firm Del Monte. Besides being the location of Mindanao's largest lake, Lake Lanao, these plateaus also have deep canyons with spectacular waterfalls. One of these, the Maria Cristina Falls, has become an essential source of hydroelectric energy.

See also: Chapter 2: Overview; Muslim Separatism. Chapter 4: Overview; Agriculture; Industry. Chapter 6: *Bangsamoro* Identity.

Further Reading

Alejo, Albert, ed. 2005. *Annotated Bibliography of Mindanao Studies*. Davao City: Mindanao Studies Consortium Foundation.

Alencon, Ferdinand Philippe Marie d'Orleans. 1986. *Luzon and Mindanao*. Manila: E. Aguilar Cruz.

Growth with Equity in Mindanao. 1999. *Mindanao: An Island Economy with a Global Outlook*. Davao City: Growth with Equity in Mindanao Program. CD ROM.

"Mindanao." 2016. *Hutchinson Unabridged Encyclopedia with Atlas and Weather Guide*. Boston, MA: Helicon.

Tiamson, Alfredo T. 1970. *Mindanao-Sulu Bibliography*. Davao City: Ateneo de Davao University.

Natural Resources

Its extensive coastlines, vast plains, plateaus, and mountain ranges have endowed the Philippines with rich natural resources that give the country some advantage in the global trade of these commodities. In recent decades, however, overexploitation of some of these geological and oceanographic assets has created some serious environmental and economic problems.

With territorial waters that cover 644,791 square miles, the Philippines has some of the richest fishing grounds in the Pacific Ocean. An estimated 2,400 fish species live in these waters, and fishers classify 65 of these as having commercial value. Different varieties of crabs also thrive in the waters, especially in the inner seas; southeastern Mindanao and the Sulu Archipelago are known for bountiful beds of seaweed and thousands of mollusks that produce pearls. Freshwater fish like catfish and silver perch can also be caught in rivers and lakes, and in places like Laguna de Bay, milkfish, tilapia, and carp are farmed to supply markets mainly in Metropolitan Manila.

The world's smallest freshwater fish, the dwarf pygmy goby (*Pandaka Pygmea*), can be found in the rivers of Camarines Sur. Scientists fear that the *Pandaka Pygmea* has all but gone extinct as its habitat becomes more and more polluted. The smallest clam (*Pisidium*), one of the biggest quahogs (*Tridacna gigas*), and the Conus gloriamaris shell can also be found in Philippine waters.

These ocean ecosystems, however, are in danger. Overfishing and destructive fishing techniques like dynamite fishing have taken a toll on fish catch, while pollution and climate change have destroyed coral reefs and, with them, the abundant life dependent on the richness of these structures. Coastlines are not exempt from the devastation either. Some 70 percent of mangrove forests—areas that host different fish species and serve as natural protection against erosion by waves and winds—have been destroyed by shrimp farming.

At the beginning of the 20th century, almost the entire Mindanao Island and the mountain ranges in Luzon and the Visayas—or 45 percent of the country's land—were rainforests. Sheltered in the tree canopies were 657 kinds of birds, from the rare Philippine eagle and the *paboreal*, a local peacock pheasant found in Palawan Island, to six of the world's nine rackettails. These forests are also home to different animal species like the tarsier, one of the smallest primates in the world found in Southeast Asia, and the mouse deer.

The rich upland ecosystem, however, is fast disappearing. Rapid commercial lumber operations and the clearing of lowlands for export agriculture or settlement have severely reduced forest cover. By 1950 forested lands had declined from 70 percent to 50 percent. This reduced further to 25 percent in the 1980s, to 20.2 percent in 2000, and 1.98 percent by 2005. Between 1990 and 2005, the Philippines lost 32.3 percent of its forest cover (about 3,412,000 hectares).

One major consequence of this forest denudation is soil runoff. The degradation of watersheds has allowed soil sediments to flow freely downriver, clogging dams and irrigation systems, which also leads to more flooding in lowland communities.

Strategies for land recovery (including reforestation) have not been effective; in fact, it became more difficult for these programs to be implemented as the population in these now-opened upland areas increased (between 1960 and 1987, for example, David Kummer wrote that upland population reached a high of 18 million). Moreover, deforestation has also put an end to timber profitability. In 1995, the gross domestic product share of forestry was 0.3 percent. Today, even if forest products are included under agriculture, hunting, and fishing, this combined total is only 1.1 percent.

The Mines and Geosciences Bureau (MGB) estimates that 30 percent of the country's land area contains about 21.5 billion tons of metal and 19.3 billion tons of non-metal mineral deposits (asbestos, clay, guano, asphalt, sulfur, talc, silicon, phosphate, marble, and several others). The Philippines holds 11 percent of the world's nickel deposits and also has significant deposits of gold, silver, iron, and copper. The total value of these deposits is said to be about US$840 billion.

The Philippines has an estimated 21.5 billion metric tons of metal deposits and 19.3 billion metric tons of nonmetal deposits under mountain ranges, hills, and gorges. It ranks second in terms of gold reserves, holding an estimated US$1.4 trillion worth of the metal. Manganese, silver, iron ore, nickel, and copper are also mined extensively in the country.

In April 2017, the Philippines' Department of Environment and Natural Resources (DENR) reported that the 2016 gross production value of these mineral resources was US$2.3 billion, down from US$924.9 million in 2015, and US$1.19 billion in 2014. The country also has an abundance of marble, lime, and cement and substantial deposits of asbestos, guano, asphalt, sulfur, and silicon.

Environmental groups have long protested what they call the adverse impact of mining, leading to the ban of mining activities in July 2012 by President Benigno

Aquino III. His successor, President Rodrigo R. Duterte, also responded to popular pressure by auditing the mining sector, which resulted in the suspension of 20 mining operations for environmental violations. The debate regarding this matter continues as of this writing, both within and outside of government.

The New York–based Revenue Watch Institute produces an annual Resource Governance Index (RGI) and ranks countries based on four criteria: the strength of institutions and the legal setting in relation to resource management; the effectiveness of the report system of governments; quality control in the production process; and safeguards to prevent if not minimize environmental problems. Of the 58 countries with abundant national resources surveyed, the Philippines ranked 23rd. The rankings are based on the accessibility of mining data, problems in the remittance of revenues to local governments, and less transparency at the local government level. RGI believes that the Philippines has done well in these areas, although there is room for improvement.

See also: Chapter 4: Overview; Agriculture; Industry.

Further Reading

Asian Development Bank. 2008. *Republic of the Philippines: Preparing the Integrated Resources and Environmental Management Sector Development Program—Financed by the Japan Special Fund.* Manila: Asian Development Bank.

Garrity, Dennis P., David M. Kummer, and Ernesto S. Guiang. 1993. "The Philippines." In Committee on Sustainable Agriculture and the Environment in the Humid Tropics, Board on Agriculture and Board on Science and Technology for International Development (eds.), *Sustainable Agriculture and the Environment in the Humid Tropics,* 549–624. *Sustainable Agriculture and the Environment in the HUMID Tropics.* Washington, DC: National Research Council.

Magdaraog, Gregorio. 1998. *Environment and Natural Resources Atlas of the Philippines.* Quezon City: Environmental Center of the Philippines Foundation.

Natural Resources Management Center (Philippines). 1986. *Guide to Philippine Flora and Fauna—Volumes 1–13.* Manila: Republic of the Philippines Ministry of Natural Resources and the University of the Philippines.

Natural Resources Management Center (Philippines). 1990. *Philippines Regional Natural Resources Atlas—Volumes 1–2.* Quezon City: Republic of the Philippines, Department of Environment and Natural Resources, Natural Resources Management Center, and Information Systems Management Division Cartographic Unit.

Salita, Domingo. 1974. *Geography and Natural Resources of the Philippines.* Quezon City: University of the Philippines System, College of Arts and Sciences.

Population

As of April 26, 2017, the Philippine population had reached 103,758,420, and the number continues to increase. Filipinos now comprise 1.38 percent of the total world population. The Philippines ranks 13th on the list of countries by population. Its population density is 902 people per square mile in a land area of 115,133 square miles. As of mid-2017, there were already 757,036 births as against only 211,465 deaths. Despite these uneven figures, the rate of population growth went down considerably from 2.22 percent in 2000 to 1.55 percent in 2010 and 1.48 percent in mid-2017.

The male-female ratio is about even: 51,955,246 males (50.1 percent) to 51,647,941 females (49.9 percent). Almost half of this population (46,543,718 people) now lives in urban areas (44.8 percent) and the rest in the countryside. The top 10 largest cities are Metropolitan Manila (12.8 million population), Cebu (2.9 million), Davao (2.5 million), Cagayan de Oro (1.3 million), Angeles (1.13 million), Iloilo (946,146), Naga (799,955), Bacolod (791,019), Baguio (611,316), and Batangas (550,725).

There are six major ethnolinguistic groups in the country, the largest being the Tagalogs (28 percent of the population), who live mainly in Metropolitan Manila and the provinces around the capital. The second-largest group (20.7 percent) comprises people who speak Bisayan—the primary language of the central Visayas and large portions of Mindanao Island. The third-largest ethnolinguistic group (9 percent) is made up of the Ilocanos, who inhabit most of northern Luzon. The western Visayas group of islands are populated by the Hiligaynon (7.5 percent), while in southeastern Luzon, Bikolanos (6 percent) are the main ethnolinguistic group. Coming in last are the Warays (3.4 percent), who live in the eastern Visayan island of Samar and on the east side of neighboring Leyte.

The Philippines has an extremely young population, a feature that it shares with other developing societies. The median age is 24.4 years old, and when further broken down in terms of age structure, 34.6 percent are under 15 years old, 61.1 percent are between 15 and 64 years old, and 4.3 percent are above 65 years old. Life expectancy is 71.7 years (68.7 for males and 74.7 for females). Two figures complicate the age structure: the ratio between the workforce and the unemployed (63.7 percent), and child dependency, or those under 15 (56.7 percent). Both are relatively high and put some constraints on workforce productivity.

See also: Chapter 4: Overview; Overseas Filipino Workers; The Service Sector. Chapter 7: Generational Changes; History of the Family Unit; Parent-Child Relationship. Chapter 9: Overview.

Further Reading

Achacoso-Sevilla, Luningning. 2003. *The Ties That Bind: Population and Development in the Philippines*. Makati City: Asian Institute of Management Policy Center.

Kinsella, Kevin G. 1984. *Detailed Statistics on the Urban and Rural Population of the Philippines, 1950–2010*. Washington, DC: Center for International Research, U.S. Bureau of Census.

Population Center Foundation. 1975. *Initiatives in Population: Quarterly Magazine of the Popular Center Foundation of the Philippines*. Makati City: Population Center Foundation.

Porter, Gareth, and Delfin J. Ganapin. 1988. *Resources, Population, and the Philippines' Future: A Case Study.* Washington, DC: World Resources Institute.

Provinces

The Philippines is organized into provinces, cities, municipalities, and towns called barangay. As of March 2017, there were 81 provinces, 145 cities, 1,490 municipalities, and 42,036 barangays across the country. Luzon has the most number of provinces (38), followed by Mindanao (23), the Visayas (15), and the Autonomous Region in Muslim Mindanao or ARMM (5).

The Local Government Code of 1991 laid out the following criteria for an area to qualify for provincial status. First, the proposed province must show an ability to raise an annual income not less than US$500,000, which needs to be certified by the Department of Finance (DoF). Second, the area must be at least 200,000 square kilometers (77,220 square miles) of contiguous land. A province can also be created out of two islands with chartered cities. Finally, the territory must have at least 250,000 inhabitants. Acts of Congress create provinces formally approved by the president and affirmed by a plebiscite of the population of the area. The Supreme Court, however, can overturn the law, as was the case with regard to Dinagat Province, which the Supreme Court declared illegal because it did not fulfill one of the requirements.

Provincial governments consist of a governor, a vice-governor, and a provincial board, and all serve three-year terms. The provincial board also includes the elected heads of the association of village councils, the city and town councilor's league, and the youth council, who serve as ex-officio members. The number of elected board members is based on the province's income. The average income is computed every four years and is the basis for classifying provinces between first and fourth class.

Policy development and the implementation of projects with a nationwide reach (infrastructure, defense, land reform) remain in the hands of executive departments. Functions relating to the delivery of "basic services"—that is, agriculture research, land and water conservation, disease and drug treatment, health and day care centers, social services, care for the elderly, juvenile reform, and drug rehabilitation—were devolved and are now in the hands of local governments. Funding these activities are local taxes and the so-called internal revenue allocations (IRA) due to the provinces, cities, municipalities, and villages. Local governments can also apply for grants and loans from banks and other lending institutions, as well as foreign aid agencies, to finance their projects, subject to the approval of the Department of Budget and Management (DBM).

The national government also sets aside lump sums from the state budget for the provinces under the category "Priority Development Assistance Funds" (PDAF). These are funds of executive departments that local governments and legislators can request to finance development programs for their respective constituencies and to supplement

Table 1.1: PROVINCES (BY ISLAND GROUP), POPULATION, AREA, CAPITAL

Province	Population	Area (square miles)	Capital
Luzon			
Abra (1846)	241,160	1,608.21	Bangued
Albay (1574)	1,314, 826	994.51	Legazpi
Apayao (1995)	119,184	1,704.00	Kabugao
Aurora (1979)	214,336	1,215.19	Baler
Bataan (1754)	760,650	530.11	Balanga
Batanes (1783)	17,246	84.56	Basco
Batangas (1581)	2,694,335	1,204.53	Batangas City
Benguet (1966)	791,590	1,091.35	La Trinidad
Bulacan (1578)	3,292,071	1,079.58	Malolos
Cagayan (1583)	1,199,320	3,589.11	Tuguegarao
Camarines Norte (1920)	583,313	895.78	Daet
Camarines Sur (1579)	1,952,544	2,122.42	Pili
Catanduanes (1945)	260, 964	575.13	Virac
Cavite (1614)	3,678,301	607.79	Imus
Ifugao (1966)	202,802	1,014.76	Lagawe
Ilocos Norte (1818)	593,081	1,338.96	Laoag
Ilocos Sur (1572)	689,668	1,002.32	Vigan
Isabela (1856)	1,593,566	4,793.43	Ilagan
Kalinga (1966)	212,680	1,247.59	Tabuk
La Union (1850)	786,653	578.27	San Fernando
Laguna (1571)	3,035,081	740.49	Santa Cruz
Marinduque (1920)	234,521	367.79	Boac
Masbate (1901)	892, 393	1,603.01	Masbate City
Mountain Province (1846)	154,590	832.97	Bontoc
Nueva Ecija (1801)	2,151,461	2,220.60	Palayan
Nueva Vizcaya (1839)	452,287	1,535.01	Bayombong
Occidental Mindoro (1950)	487,414	2,264.76	Mamburao
Oriental Mindoro (1663)	844,059	1,636.45	Calapan
Palawan (1902)	1,104,585	6,575.61	Puerto Princesa
Pampanga (1571)	2,609,744	796.32	San Fernando
Pangasinan (1580)	2,956,726	2,104.65	Lingayen
Quezon (1901)	2,122,830	3,501.79	Lucena
Quirino (1966)	188,991	897.10	Cabarroguis
Rizal (1853)	2,884,227	460.21	Antipolo
Romblon (1901)	292,781	592.07	Romblon
Sorsogon (1894)	792,949	818.15	Sorsogon City
Tarlac (1873)	1,366,027	1,179.00	Tarlac City
Zambales (1578)	823,888	1,479.09	Iba
Metropolitan Manila	12,877,253	246.55	Manila

(continued)

Table 1.1: PROVINCES (BY ISLAND GROUP), POPULATION, AREA, CAPITAL (CONTINUED)

Province	Population	Area (square miles)	Capital
Mindanao			
Agusan del Norte (1907)	691, 566	1,369.45	Cabadbaran
Agusan del Sur (1970)	700,653	3,856.98	Prosperidad
Basilan (1973)	459,367	512.45	Lamitan
Bukidnon (1917)	1,415,225	4,053.53	Malaybalay
Camiguin (1966)	88,478	91.87	Mambajao
Cotabato (1914)	1,379,747	3,478.36	Kidapawan
Davao de Oro (1998)	736,107	1,729.65	Nabunturan
Davao del Norte (1967)	1,016,332	1,323.16	Tagum
Davao del Sur (1914)	2,265,579	1,779.00	Digos
Davao Occidental (2013)	316,342	835.31	Malita
Davao Oriental (1967)	558,958	2,192.92	Mati
Dinagat Island (2006)	127,152	400.13	San Jose
Lanao del Norte (1959)	1,019,013	1,606.16	Tubod
Lanao del Sur (1914)	1,045,429	1,495.33	Marawi
Maguindanao (1973)	1,473,371	2,373.19	Buluan
Misamis Occidental (1929)	602,126	793.52	Oroquieta
Misamis Oriental (1901)	1,564,459	1,368.47	Cagayan de Oro
South Cotabato (1966)	1,509,735	1,709.97	Koronadal
Sultan Kudarat (1973)	812,095	2,045.70	Isulan
Sulu (1917)	824,731	617.92	Jolo
Surigao del Norte (1901)	485,088	761.75	Surigao City
Surigao del Sur (1960)	592,250	1,904.53	Tandag
Tawi-Tawi (1973)	390,715	419.85	Bongao
Zamboanga del Norte (1952)	1,011,393	2,808.93	Dipolog
Zamboanga del Sur (1914)	1,872,473	2,283.47	Pagadian
Zamboanga Sibugay (2001)	633,129	1,392.96	Ipil
Visayas			
Aklan	574,823	679,656	Kalibo
Antique	582,012	1,015.70	San Jose De Buenavista
Biliran	171,612	206.95	Naval
Bohol	1,313, 560	1,842.68	Tagbilaran
Capiz	761,384	1,001.80	Roxas City
Cebu	13,710,671	2,062.55	Cebu City
Eastern Samar	467,160	1,782.70	Borongan City
Guimaras	174,613	236.24	Jordan
Iloilo	2,384,415	1,959.84	Iloilo City

(continued)

Table 1.1: PROVINCES (BY ISLAND GROUP), POPULATION, AREA, CAPITAL (CONTINUED)

Province	Population	Area (square miles)	Capital
Visayas			
Leyte	1,977,768	2,524.01	Tacloban City
Negros Occidental	5,556,397	3,090.70	Bacolod City
Negros Oriental	1,354,995	2,092.90	Dumaguete City
Northern Samar	632,379	1,426.63	Catarman
Southern Leyte	421,750	695.55	Maasin City
Western Samar	780,481	2,335.16	Catbalogan City

Source: Mapa 2019.

provincial budgets, revenues from local taxes, and the IRA. The PDAF and the IRA have become controversial issues affecting the relationship between executive and legislative bodies and local governments. Presidents are known to have withheld the release of the IRA to punish local governments that are under the control of political opponents or used the fund as an enticement for the latter to switch political loyalties. The officials' ability to govern had also come into question when they were accused of looting PDAF funds on behalf of their allies (Abinales and Amoroso 2017: 315-318).

See also: Chapter 3: Overview; Elections; Federalism; Political Clans.

Further Reading

Abinales, Patricio N., and Donna J Amoroso. 2017. *State and Society in the Philippines*. 2nd ed. Lanham, MD: Rowman and Littlefield.

Coronel, Sheila S. 1996. *Patrimony: 6 Case Studies on Local Politics and Environment in the Philippines*. Pasay City: Philippine Center for Investigative Journalism.

Coronel, Sheila S., and Jose F. Lacaba, eds. 1995. *Boss: 5 Case Studies of Local Politics in the Philippines*. Pasig City: Philippine Center for Investigative Journalism; Quezon City: Institute for Popular Democracy.

Fragmentation vs. Consolidation: The Case of Philippine Local Governments. 2005. Pasay City: Local Government Foundation; Makati City: Konrad Adenauer Stiftung.

Mapa, Claire Dennis S., ed. 2019. *2019 Philippine Statistical Yearbook*. Manila. Philippine Statistical Authority.

Pimentel, Aquilino Q. 2007. *The Local Government Code Revisited*. Manila: Philippine Normal University.

Tapales, Prosperina Domingo, Jocelyn C. Cuaresma, Wilhelmina L. Cabo, Celenia J. Jamig, and Zita Concepcion P. Calugay. 1998. *Local Government in the Philippines: A Book of Readings—Volume 1–2*. Quezon City: University of the Philippines Center for Local and Regional Governance and the National College of Public Administration and Governance.

The Sulu Archipelago

The last and smallest chain of islands is located in the southwest of the archipelago, extending from the edge of the East Malaysian state of Sabah. The Sulu archipelago is named after the sea in which it is located—the Sulu Sea. It consists of three island provinces—Basilan, Sulu, and Tawi-Tawi—and several islets that surround them, with a total land area of 1,571 square miles. The islands consist of dormant volcanoes and limestone-covered coves and small bays with thriving offshore coral structures. The archipelago's deeper waters consist of submarine ridges that were the result of tectonic movements at the sea bottom. Geographers believe that the similarity between the Sulu archipelago's topography and that of Borneo suggests that the former was once a land bridge that connected these two places. The sea ridges were the lowland and the islands the mountain areas.

Sulu is the only island that sustains an agricultural economy, with the land growing coconut, fruits, and rubber. However, rice production is limited, so the staple is shipped from Mindanao or smuggled out of Sabah. The other islands are mainly mountainous, with much of the upper terrain comprising rainforests, which have been, ironically, preserved by the constant state of war. The main economic activities in these islands are fishing and the collection of marine resources like mother-of-pearl, sea cucumbers, and corals. Turtle shells and eggs are harvested in the small Turtle Island. The prolonged war in the south has prevented the archipelago from becoming a prime deep-sea fishing ground.

Of all the island groups in the Philippines, the Sulu archipelago may be considered as having the "oldest" history for several reasons. First, it is home to the Tausugs, a Muslim ethnic group that has been connected with the rest of maritime Southeast Asia and southern China since the 12th century. The main

Tausug children in the Sulu Archipelago harvesting sea urchins during low tide. (Kksteven/Dreamstime.com)

towns of the archipelago had also become important ports of trade between the rest of the maritime Southeast Asia region and China. The rest of the archipelago consists of "minor ports" that were treated as backwaters by the sultanates, the authorities that governed these ports. This position was reversed after Spain, and then the United States, came to colonize the Philippines.

See also: Chapter 2: Muslim Separatism. Chapter 5: Islam. Chapter 6: *Bangsamoro* Identity.

Further Reading

Afable, Patricia. 2013. *Philippines: An Archipelago of Exchange.* Arles: Actes Sud; and, Paris: Musee du quai Branly.

Allied Forces, Southwest Pacific Area. 1945. *Sulu Archipelago* (Philippine Series). Brisbane: Allied Geographical Section.

Burbridge, Frederick William. 1980. *The Gardens of the Sun, or a Naturalist's Journal on the Mountains and in the Forests and Swamps of Borneo and the Sulu Archipelago.* London: J. Murray.

Editors of *Encyclopedia Britannica*. Last modified 2020. "Sulu Archipelago: Archipelago, Philippines." Accessed July 4, 2017. https://www.britannica.com/place/Sulu-Archipelago

Orosa, Sixto Y. 1970. *The Sulu Archipelago and Its People—Updated and Enlarged.* Manila: New Mercury Printing Press.

Republic of the Philippines, Bureau of Agriculture. 1922. *Mindanao, and the Sulu Archipelago: Their Natural Resources and Opportunities for Development.* Manila: Bureau of Printing.

Spoehr, Alexander. 1973. *Zamboanga, and Sulu: An Archeological Approach to Ethnic Diversity.* Pittsburgh: University of Pittsburgh Department of Anthropology.

The Visayas

A group of islands located in the central part of the country comprises the Visayas region, so named after the primary language of the communities in the area (Visayan). The islands, from the east to the west, are Samar, Leyte, Bohol, Cebu, Negros, Panay, Masbate, and Romblon. Altogether, the Visayan islands have a total area of 27,607 square miles. The islands are hilly and mountainous, although Panay and Negros have vast plains where food crops (rice, bananas, and root crops), nonfood produce (tobacco and abaca), and export crops (sugarcane) are grown. There are also rich fishing grounds in the straits that separate these islands.

Bohol (land area: 1,492 square miles) is a roundish limestone-covered island with a volcanic core. Bohol is famous for a cluster of hills in its western area with near-perfect conical shapes. Brown in color (because of their dryness), people have come to

The Chocolate Hills of Bohol Province. (Tommyandone/Dreamstime.com)

call them "chocolate hills." To the west of Bohol is Cebu island (land area: 1,909 square miles), a 122-mile-long island with a narrow coastline and divided in the middle by a series of hills with rich deposits of coal, copper, and gold. The lowlands are few and small and can only produce limited amounts of corn, tobacco, sugarcane, and root crops. Corn is the staple food since rice is "imported" from other islands (including Mindanao) or from abroad. Coral reefs and small islets surround Bohol; some of them are often accessible by foot during low tide.

East of Bohol is Leyte (land area: 2,785 square miles), which shares similar features—high mountains whose streams flow into rolling plains, and coastal areas where communities plant food (rice and corn) and cash crops (bananas, coconut, hemp, sugarcane, and tobacco). Manganese is mined in the mountains while there are sandstone and limestone quarries around the island. In November 2013, super typhoon Haiyan severely damaged much of Leyte, where rehabilitation efforts continue to this day.

Northwest of Leyte is the v-shaped Masbate Island (land area: 3,269 square miles), much of which is grassland, making it ideal for livestock production. Gold is mined in the north of the island while copper deposits are extracted in the southeast. A deep gulf southwest of the island allows for ample commercial fishing.

Negros (land area: 4,907 square miles) is a boot-shaped island west of Cebu. A mountain ridge divides it from north to south and is famous for an active volcano, Mount Canlaon (8,086 feet), which forms part of the ridge. The other volcanoes are dormant and have small lakes. The plains on the eastern coast of the island are irregular and fragmented. With rice or corn produced only in limited quantities, communities on the east coast are engaged in salt production. The western part has some of the largest lowland areas of the country, extending 100 miles parallel to the shorelines. The Philippines' most extensive sugar plantations and mills can be found in the northern and western parts of the lowlands. The rest is planted with bananas, corn, coconuts, mangoes, and rice. Mining companies extract copper, gypsum, coal, and rock phosphates from the island's mountains.

Panay Island (land area: 4,446 square miles) is the westernmost island of the Visayan group. It has its share of river systems, mountain ranges, and hills, and a vast lowland running from north to south, including deltas located in the south. Its main economic activities are fishing, coal, and copper mining, and rice and sugarcane production.

North of Panay is Romblon (area: 32 square miles), which consists of strips of coastal plains and low hills. Coconut, hemp, and rice are its main crops, while marble is quarried in a small, hilly part of the island. Romblon also lies strategically in a strait that serves as the central passageway for interisland ships traveling between Luzon and the rest of the archipelago.

See also: Chapter 3: Overview; Federalism. Chapter 4: Overview; Agriculture. Chapter 9: Overview; National Language Debate. Chapter 11: Vernacular Literature.

Further Reading

An Annotated Bibliography of Selected Visayan Studies Collection. 1980. Cebu: University of the Philippines in the Visayas, Visayan Studies Collection.

Bryant, P. L. 1916. "The Visayas and Zamboanga." *Mid-Pacific Magazine* 12, no. 2 (August 1): 183–186.

Hester, Evett Dorell, and Paul S. Lietz. 1962. *Alzina's Historia de Visayas: A Bibliographical Note.* Manila: Bibliographical Society of the Philippines.

CHAPTER 2

HISTORY

OVERVIEW

The first humans supposedly walked across land bridges that connected the Philippine archipelago to mainland Asia around 30000 BCE, followed by a second wave of seaborne migrants that came at about 6000–5000 BCE. The latter did not stop in the Philippines but continued on to Borneo, New Guinea, and Australia. Some scholars suggest that it was communities coming from China via Taiwan that pushed out toward Sumatra (around 3000 BCE) and Java (around 2000 BCE), and New Guinea (1600 BCE) before reaching Hawaii, Easter Island, and Madagascar around 1500 BCE. From 221 BCE onward, trade linked the Philippine archipelago to imperial China, the Ryukyu Kingdom (Okinawa), and Japan, and by 500 CE, to India and as far away as Greece. Trading ports sprouted in strategic points where families under the leadership of a strongman traded—among other things—rhinoceroses' horns, beeswax, birds' nests, tobacco, metals, salt, and spices. The communities in these ports were part of a cosmopolitan world that was maritime Southeast Asia. The Spanish thus did not "discover" the Philippines. They simply added themselves as minor players in this thriving regional economy.

Three Spanish ships landed in Cebu Island in 1521, but it was not until 1542 that the Spanish claimed the archipelago on behalf of the Empire, naming it the Philippines after then-prince Philip II of Spain. The colonizers established a permanent settlement in Maynilad (Manila), and in 1572, they set up a galleon trade between China and Mexico, with Manila as the transshipment port for silk and porcelain from China and silver from Mexico. Spain, however, only had control over half of the archipelago. For most of the Spanish era, the Muslim sultanates in Sulu and Maguindanao held power in the southern Philippines enjoying a robust trading relationship with port cities in China to the north, the Malay Peninsula in the west, and Java in the south. But once the British and the Dutch established firm control over Malaya and Java, respectively, the sultanates were relegated to being minor players in the Southeast Asian maritime trade and the balance of power began to favor the Spanish.

The galleon trade ended in 1815 and the independence of the Spanish colonies in Latin America in 1820 forced the Spanish to look for alternative sources of revenue, and they tapped products like coffee, hemp, rubber, and sugar—raw materials needed by Europe, which was in the process of industrializing. The development of export agriculture was spearheaded by Spaniards who were born in the Philippines, and by *criollos*, the children born of Spanish or Chinese men's unions with natives. As these groups began to accumulate wealth, they also sought social status, sending their sons to seminaries and schools, to the consternation of Spanish priests who felt threatened by this new elite. These educated *ilustrados* (the enlightened) began demanding recognition and reforms of the colonial state, eliciting fierce resistance from the friars. There were two outcomes of this conflict. The first was the launching of a propaganda war in Europe where *ilustrados* wrote about abuses in the colonies to convince Madrid to implement reforms. The second was the formation of the underground group *Katipunan* (The "Supreme, Most Noble Association of the Children of the Nation" Kataastaasan, Kagalanggalangang Katipunan ng Mga Anak ng Bayan, or, in Spanish, Suprema y Venerable Asociacion de Los Hijos del Pueblo). Led by the autodidact Andres Bonifacio, the *Katipunan* began secretly organizing chapters in Manila and nearby provinces, to prepare for a grand uprising that would end Spanish rule. When it launched its uprising on August 23, 1896, it already had about 40,000 members. The revolution spread throughout the rest of the colony, especially after the *Katipunan*'s main inspiration, the writer Jose Rizal, was executed by the Spanish.

While fighting was going on, the *Katipunan* held its first open congress where factional conflict ensued. Bonifacio was demoted as a leader, and when he defied the new leadership under Emilio Aguinaldo, he was arrested and together with his brother executed upon Aguinaldo's orders. Within the year, Aguinaldo signed a truce with the Spanish and agreed to go into exile to Hong Kong, giving historians the first hint of the ability of the emerging Filipino elite to compromise their principles. Filipino resistance, however, continued and by 1898, with support from the Americans, Aguinaldo returned to assume leadership of the revolution. The Americans ended Spanish rule by prevailing over a sham battle to take over Manila which excluded Filipino forces. Aguinaldo declared Philippine independence on June 12, 1898, and by September the First Republic had formed its new legislature.

The republic was short-lived with the onset of the Philippine-American War. The war was declared formally over after Aguinaldo was captured. Not everyone surrendered: up until late American colonial rule, there were still many groups (smaller and disparate) that vowed to oppose the new colonizers. The granting of Philippine independence by the Americans in 1946 was not really full independence as the United States continued to control the Philippine economy, protect the Filipino elite's domination, and influence, if not determine, the directions of Philippine foreign policy. Hence what Bonifacio and the *Katipunan* started remains to be accomplished. Nationalist intellectuals call this the legacy of an "unfinished revolution."

The United States set up a civilian-run administration in the central and northern Philippines and an army-administered authority in the Muslim south. These parallel approaches to state-building had an unintended consequence. In the former, Filipino participation expanded, but in the latter, the U.S. army nurtured anti-Filipino sentiments among Muslims, which would affect majority-minority relations thereafter. The Americans promised to teach Filipinos democratic politics as a prelude to the granting of independence, and by 1913, Filipinos were the majority in all but two of the colonial offices. Filipinization, as the Americans called it, reached its apex with the establishment of the Commonwealth of the Philippines in 1930, with Manuel L. Quezon as president. The Commonwealth was to be the forerunner of the Philippine republic but its march was disrupted when Japan invaded the Philippines during World War II.

The Americans returned in 1945, and a year later they granted independence to the Philippines. The leaders of the new republic were immediately confronted by the challenges of postwar rehabilitation, a communist threat, and widespread corruption. The trade and investment treaties with the United States were disadvantageous to a war-torn economy, but the Philippines was given preferential treatment to export sugar to the former. However, imports outpaced exports thereby draining the national reserves, and Filipino industries could not compete with foreign (i.e., American) corporations. The government then tried to correct the imbalance by imposing tariffs on imports and levying taxes on exports to protect local industries. This produced mixed results.

The government also faced the challenge of a communist uprising north of Manila and was only able to defeat it after the U.S. Central Intelligence Agency reformed the Philippine military. The anti-communist campaigns forced the government to implement reforms. Ramon Magsaysay, a former anti-Japanese guerrilla, was elected president (he was the seventh president of the Philippines) to slay the dragon of corruption. But he never had a chance to do so; he was killed in a plane crash in 1957. Finally, to ease the pressure on land (one problem exploited by the communists), the government encouraged migrants to settle in frontier Mindanao; between 1946 and 1960, more than 1 million Filipinos settled in Mindanao. In the 1960s, however, the strain of coexistence between Muslims, migrants, and indigenous communities after the demographic landscape also changed, leading to interethnic tensions and family conflicts over land ownership.

The import-substitution program boosted Filipino manufacturing but allowed corruption when politicians squeezed industries for bribes. Exchange controls and tariffs were eventually abolished, the foreign investors were invited back to the country. The government was also able to put its act together, launching an integrated development plan and passing the first ever land reform law to alleviate rural poverty and correct inequitable access to land. Implementation, however, became the biggest problem; only 3 of the 26 economic development bills passed Congress while the land reform program was limited to rice and corn lands.

President Ferdinand E. Marcos improved on his predecessors' economic development program by giving his technocrats more power to shape policy and involving the Armed Forces of the Philippines (AFP) in his economic agenda. Once he consolidated power, however, Marcos turned the military into his own de facto private security force and used development funds to build his own network of supporters among provincial governors, city mayors, and former members of the House of Representatives. He and his family then proceeded to plunder the economy. This and the uninhibited pillaging of state funds turned Marcos into a polarizing figure. Two years after being reelected, Marcos declared martial law and ruled for another 15 years.

His hold over power began to decline in 1983 as the opposition became bolder amid a serious economic crisis brought about by excessive borrowing, poor export revenues, and corruption. In 1986, Marcos was forced out of power by the combination of a failed military coup and a successful nonviolent uprising.

Presidents Corazon C. Aquino and Fidel V. Ramos were left with the economic mess and a highly politicized society, and it was only in the mid-1990s that stability and growth returned. Filipinos had made sure that dictatorship would not return, embedding the new Constitution with provisions that made it difficult for any president to repeat what Marcos had done, and decentralizing some of the powers of the national government and delegating them to the provinces and cities. The result was a more expanded democracy but also the return of the political families that ruled these localities. A new set of actors entered the political arena and made their presence felt: movie and television stars, and sports personalities. Thus, between 1998 and 2003, the entertainment industry contributed one president, one vice president, six senators, five congressmen, and several provincial governors, city mayors, vice mayors and council men and women to the political arena.

Philippine-American relations also changed when the Philippine Senate rejected the renewal of a military bases agreement, and for nearly a decade the two stood apart from each other. Full military ties were restored in 2000, and since then, U.S. troops have been involved in joint exercises with their Filipino counterparts. U.S. special forces also assisted Filipino troops in going after local terrorist groups. The acceleration of state corporations' privatization, the abolition of tariff, and the ending of monopolies in shipping, telecommunications, and banking had the economy moving forward again. The remittances of overseas Filipino workers—which was growing by the billions—further accelerated the growth.

President Fidel V. Ramos moved to arrest the economic slide. After he signed peace agreements with rebellious officers and the separatist Moro National Liberation Front (MNLF), Ramos focused on the power-shortage crisis and proceeds with the privatization of state corporations and the sale of government lands. Ramos reformed the tax system and abolished tariffs to attract more foreign investments. He also put an end to preferential treatments given to rich families, and deregulated shipping, telecommunications, and banking businesses to end the monopoly of a few families. Privatization earned the government US$12 billion, erasing the budget deficit, and new businesses such as those in the electronics industry improved the economic standing of exports.

When the 1997 Asian financial crisis hit Southeast Asia, the Philippines was the least affected partly because it was at the bottom of the rung of Southeast Asian economies. But this came at a cost. To get Congress's support, Ramos had to augment discretionary funds that the president gives Congress. This pork barrel allocation, ostensibly for countryside development, rose to a high US$1 billion in 1997, with Ramos admitting that at least 20 percent of the amount lined politicians' pockets. The benefits did not trickle down to the poor; in fact, the income gap had worsened. Controversies also hounded Ramos as his term ended, including an attempt to change the Constitution so that he could extend his term (presidents only have one six-year term per the 1987 Constitution). In 1988, the people voted an aging movie star and former city mayor and senator into office as the 13th president.

President Joseph E. Estrada won not only because people remembered him for his action movies but also because he ran at a time when the economy was emerging from the Asian crisis, posting a 3.4 percent growth. But his popularity dipped after he terminated peace talks with the Moro Islamic Liberation Front (MILF) and ordered an all-out military assault of its camps. Then, investigative journalists uncovered secret bank accounts linking Estrada and his men to a national numbers game. Finally, a provincial governor and former close friend revealed that he had given Estrada US$13.6 million (US$1: P29.47) as payoff so he would be allowed to continue running his illegal numbers game. The accusation led the House of Representatives to file an impeachment case against Estrada, which the Senate, acting as the tribunal, moved to hear.

The proceedings, however, were cut short after a coalition of elite groups, middle-class associations, and communists calling for another peaceful popular uprising to oust Estrada received support from the senior leadership of the AFP. This new development forced Estrada to quit. He was later arrested and detained on plunder charges. In 2004, the Global Transparency Report listed Estrada as one of the most corrupt leaders of the world, having amassed a sum of US$78–80 million in his short stint.

President Gloria M. Arroyo, who had the second-longest term after Marcos (she completed Estrada's term and then successfully ran for president again), was severely challenged by military coups, impeachment threats, revelations of corruption in her administration, the inability of the police to stop the kidnapping of Chinese Filipinos by criminal gangs, and the quashing of the Abu Sayyaf, an Islamic terrorist group. In 2004, Arroyo was accused of colluding with a senior election commissioner to manipulate votes to defeat her presidential rival. She withstood these attacks because she had the loyalty of Congress and local governments who were only too eager to receive the development funds she offered them. In two midterm elections (2004 and 2007), Arroyo maintained a majority in the House of Representatives, which helped scuttle repeated attempts (from 2005 to 2008) by her opponents to impeach her. She pardoned Estrada in 2007 and added his followers to her coalition.

The AFP remained loyal to Arroyo and protected her when junior officers mutinied in 2003 and 2007. In exchange, she kept the military budget substantial and, more importantly, did very little to prevent assassination teams purportedly organized by the military to eliminate communist cadres. In 2006 alone, 320 suspected communist cadres were among the 801 victims of extrajudicial killings and 206 disappeared while allegedly under military custody. Some 23 journalists were also killed during Arroyo's term, making the Philippines the second most-dangerous country for journalists after Iraq.

Arroyo joined President George W. Bush's "War on Terror," sending a small contingent of troops to Iraq. In exchange, American military assistance rose considerably; joint exercises by the two armies became routine, and U.S. special forces assisted the AFP's antiterrorist campaigns. Under Arroyo, the economy continued to expand (GDP growth rate was 5 percent in 2006 and 7 percent in 2008). The peso's value vis-à-vis the U.S. dollar increased by 20 percent, as new industries like business process outsourcing (customer service) and the remittances of overseas Filipino workers bolstered the economy. Growth, however, did not trickle down; on the contrary, the poverty incidence remained high.

Toward the end of her term, Arroyo tried to extend her presidency by changing the Constitution, but this unraveled when the media uncovered corruption in the Department of Agriculture, in which an official had diverted fertilizer funds to Arroyo's election campaign. There were also reports of the bribe a Chinese company paid to senior public servants to approve its tender to modernize the country's telecommunications system. Then in 2009, an Arroyo ally and his private army gunned down 58 people who were part of a convoy escorting a wife on her way to register the candidacy of her husband, who was a rival of Arroyo's partner, for governor. Public outrage over what came to be called the Maguindanao massacre forced Arroyo to arrest the warlord and his family and drop any bid to extend her term beyond 2010.

When Benigno S. Aquino III, former President Aquino's son, sought the presidency in 2010, he made two promises: to hold the Marcos family accountable for its misdeeds when they were in power, and to cleanse the government of corruption. He had President Arroyo arrested and jailed for corruption, an ironic twist of fate for the latter. With the help of legislative allies, Aquino also successfully impeached the Chief Justice of the Supreme Court and forced the resignation of the Ombudsman, two Arroyo allies. Aquino failed to recover the Marcos billions and bring the family to justice after the Supreme Court opposed his executive actions. His anti-corruption campaign, however, gained ground, and the Philippines' ranking in terms of transparency rose from No. 121 in 2006 to No. 95 in 2015. The economy rebounded to a 7 percent GDP growth and in 2013, the country's profile changed from being a borrower to that of a lender, committing US$1 billion to the International Monetary Fund (IMF).

Like his predecessors, Aquino used the presidential development fund to reach out to the legislature and local governments, and they rewarded him by promptly switching sides, deserting their erstwhile patroness, President Arroyo. And like previous presidents, Aquino was stumped by the problem of inequality. While unemployment and underemployment decreased, the income gap worsened. The income of the wealthy tripled from P630 billion when Aquino came to power to P2.2 trillion on the eve of the end of his term—a 250 percent increase. The elites and political opportunism were, yet again, alive and well.

If the Maguindanao massacre was Arroyo's undoing, a botched antiterrorist operation in which 44 members of the police Special Action Force (SAF) were killed by MILF forces turned the public against Aquino. In 2016, Filipinos voted Rodrigo R. Duterte to the presidency. Duterte, who at the time was the mayor of Davao City in southeast Mindanao, defeated Aquino's anointed successor by 5.84 million votes. Duterte campaigned on a single issue—the eradication of a supposed drug menace that was eating away at the social fabric. Duterte pointed voters to his accomplishments as city mayor, claiming that Davao was now "drug free" after he and his men liquidated heads of syndicates, pushers, and even drug addicts. The war was brutal, but when he left office Davao was one of the safest cities of the country. He also tapped into popular resentment against the elite and proclaimed himself the people's champion who understood what voters wanted because, like them, he spoke the unrefined language of the streets.

A year after his election more than 10,000 suspected drug addicts and pushers had been killed in extrajudicial killings by assassination teams that were allegedly from a special police group or assassins hired by the police. Duterte had also repeatedly and openly threatened to end the Philippines' relationship with the United States, saying it was time for the country to adopt an independent foreign policy. He had cursed at President Barack Obama while questioning the latter's right to weigh in on the issue of human rights violations in his administration. Duterte went on to visit the People's Republic of China and the Russian Federation to propose new alliances with these two superpowers. Finally, he dropped the Philippines' territorial claim on the West Philippine Sea and allowed China to continue building bases to bolster its alleged sovereignty over the resource-rich zone.

Had these controversial acts been committed by any of Duterte's predecessors, there would most certainly have been passionate criticism from Filipinos who are pro-American (84 percent, according to a 2015 Pew Research survey), anti-Chinese, and anti-communist. But none of it seems to have dented Duterte's approval ratings, which have remained in the high 80s, with his supporters keeping up a zealous defense of their president with vicious attacks on opponents via social media. As expected, the pro-Aquino legislature and the majority of provincial governors and city mayors have since switched sides. The military defended its professionalism from being politicized, but lower- and middle-level officers and their men and women have rallied behind a president who apparently addressed their urgent needs. Under a new leadership consisting of officers Duterte had once worked with, the police force swore its allegiance to him.

At the start of his second year in office, Duterte had to deal with an attack by members of the Islamic State of Iraq and Syria (ISIS), with the support of armed followers of a former mayor and a suspected head of a drug network, on the Muslim city of Marawi in Mindanao on May 23, 2017. Duterte placed the entire Mindanao Island under martial law, with the support of Congress. At some point, the anti-American nationalist Duterte was compelled to seek the help of the United States. Marawi was finally liberated on October 23, at the cost of the complete destruction of the city and the displacement of more than 40,000 residents. Duterte's violent rhetoric, the extrajudicial killings, and Islamic terrorism in the south have all had a negative effect on the economy. In fall 2017, the Philippine peso was tagged the worst-performing Asian currency and economists say this will continue until the end of the year. This never improved since then. The peso sank to a 13-year low of P52.43 to the US dollar in 2018, and dropped further to P50.82 by the dollar in 2021. As of February 2022, it had gone down further to P51.42: U$1 (Karunungan 2022).

See also: Chapter 2: Communism; Extrajudicial Killings (EJK); Marcos Dictatorship; Muslim Separatism; People Power Revolution. Chapter 3: Overview; Civil Society

Organizations; Elections; Federalism; Martial Law; Political Clans; Post-Marcos Philippines; Relations with the People's Republic of China; Relations with the United States; Warlords. Chapter 4: Overview; Crony Capitalism; Overseas Filipino Workers; Chapter 8: The University of the Philippines.

Further Reading

Abinales, Patricio N., and Donna J. Amoroso. 2017. *State and Society in the Philippines.* 2nd ed. Lanham, MD: Rowman and Littlefield.

Agoncillo, Teodoro. 2005. *Revolt of the Masses: The Story of Bonifacio and the Katipunan.* New Edition. Quezon City: University of the Philippines Press.

Agoncillo, Teodoro. 1997. *Malolos: The Crisis of the Republic.* Quezon City: University of the Philippines Press.

Constantino, Renato. 2010. *A History of the Philippines: From the Spanish Colonization to the Second World War.* New York: Monthly Review Press.

"Filipinos Like the US Even More Than Americans Do—Pew Research." 2014. *Rappler.* April 22. Accessed June 12, 2019. https://www.rappler.com/nation/56085-philippines-usa-pew-research

Joaquin, Nick. 1983. *The Aquinos of Tarlac: An Essay on History as Three Generations.* Manila: Cacho Hermanes Publications.

Karunungan, Lilian. 2022. "Philippine Peso Drops Past 51 Barrier for First Time since 2020." *Bloomberg* (January 3). https://www.bloomberg.com/news/articles/2022-01-04/philippine-peso-drops-past-51-barrier-for-first-time-since-2020.

Komisar, Lucy. 1987. *Corazon Aquino: The Story of a Revolution.* New York: George Braziller.

Nadeau, Kathleen M. 2008. *The History of the Philippines.* Westport, CT: Greenwood.

Rodao, Florentino, and Felice Noelle Rodriguez, eds. 2002. *The Philippine Revolution of 1896: Ordinary Lives in Extraordinary Times.* Quezon City: Ateneo de Manila University Press.

Thompson, Mark, and Eric Batalla. 2018. *Routledge Handbook on Contemporary Philippines.* Milton Park, Abingdon, Oxfordshire: Taylor and Francis.

TIMELINE[1]

Year	Events
618–906	Philippine-Chinese trade during the reign of the Tang Dynasty.
982	*Mai* (most likely the name Chinese traders gave to Mindoro Island) export goods to Canton, China.
1001	*Butuan*, a trading port in northeastern Mindanao Island, sends tribute mission to China.
c. 1275	Arab missionaries bring Islam to the Sulu archipelago.
1368–1424	Sulu Sultanate sends six missions to China.
c. 1450	Sayyid Abu Bakr establishes the Sulu Sultanate.
1521	Portuguese captain of a Spanish fleet, Ferdinand Magellan, lands in Cebu.

1525	Arab missionary Sharif Muhammad Kabungsuwan converts the Maguindanaos to Islam.
1542	The Spanish name the islands *Las Islas Filipinas* to honor Philip II of Spain.
1571	Spanish conquistador Miguel Lopez de Legazpi conquers *Maynila*.
1572	Galleon trade between Mexico and China commences with Manila as a transshipment point.
1594	Philip II assigns religious orders to specific regions of the Philippines.
1599	Muslim sultanates conduct slave raids in the central Philippines.
1603	First Chinese uprising against the Spanish.
1609	Spanish decree to conscript labor for public works and naval workforce.
1611	The University of Santo Tomas is founded.
1619–1671	Kachil Kudarat, the greatest of all Muslim sultans, rules Maguindanao.
1621	First revolt against the Spanish in the central Philippines.
1635–1639	The Spanish finally defeat Muslim sultanates; set up garrisons in Sulu.
1639	Chinese revolt in Manila and its environs to protest conscript labor.
1642	Sultan Kudarat defeats the Spanish.
1645	Kudarat signs peace treaty with the Spanish; the Dutch help the Sulu Sultanate attack the Spanish garrison in Sulu.
1656	Kudarat goes to war against the Spanish, attacking the central Philippines.
1660	Revolts break out in provinces north of Manila.
1663	The Spanish abandon their Mindanao garrison to move troops back to Manila in anticipation of an attack by a Chinese "pirate" named Koxinga.
1700	Sulu and Maguindanao sultanates fight over control of Mindanao.
1719	The Spanish return to Mindanao.
1737	The Spanish and Sulu Sultanate sign a peace treaty.
1739	First road system connecting Manila to northern Luzon completed.
1744–1745	The Spanish regime rocked by revolts near Manila and in the central Philippines.
1747–1756	Spanish and Sulu Sultanate return to war.
1764	Another peace treaty signed between the Spanish and Sulu Sultanate.
1762	The British occupy Manila, sparking revolts in provinces north of Manila.
1764	After the British and the Spanish signed a peace treaty in 1763, the Spanish launch counterattacks against rebels and expel Chinese who joined the revolts.
1781	The first cotton and tobacco farms established.
1785	The Spanish form the Royal Company of the Philippines which would oversee the production of export crops like tobacco and sugar.
1789	The Spanish put village chiefs directly under the authority of town mayors to weaken the political influence of religious orders.
1805	Spanish governor of Zamboanga signs a new treaty with Sulu Sultanate.
1807	Spanish deserters revolt in Ilocos province in northern Luzon.
1810	Spanish parliament grants the Philippines representation in the assembly.

1811	Philippines has its first newspaper (the *Del Superior Gobierno*); colony sends its first representative to the Spanish parliament.
1815	Galleon trade ends.
1827	Spanish fleet attacks Sulu Sultanate but was repulsed.
1834	Royal Company of the Philippines abolished; American trading companies set up offices in Manila and Philippine ports are opened to international trade.
1836	Spain signs a commercial treaty with the Sulu Sultanate.
1837	Philippine representation to the Spanish Cortes revoked; colonies now to be governed by "special laws."
1847	Two more newspapers founded—the *La Estrella de Manila* (The Star of Manila) and the *Diario de Manila* (Manila Newspaper); the office of *gobernadorcillo* becomes elective.
1849	A Spanish decree requires colonial residents to acquire Spanish surnames.
1851	The Spanish regime go to war again against the Sulu Sultanate and defeat the latter.
1853	A British company establishes Manila office to trade in sugar and hemp.
1856	British consul sets up sugar plantations in the Visayas.
1863	The Spanish mandate the establishment of a public school system.
1868	The Spanish create the Civil Guards, the precursor of the police.
1872	Sailors in a naval base south of Manila mutiny; colonial officials use it as an excuse to execute three priests accused of subversion.
1873	More ports opened to global trade.
1880	The Spanish abolish tobacco monopoly.
1882	First Filipino-Spanish newspaper established; Jose Rizal leaves for Spain.
1887	Jose Rizal publishes *Noli Me Tangere* (Touch me Not), which the Spanish declare as antipatriotic and heretical.
1888	Filipino students in Spain publish the *La Solidaridad* to convey their fight for reforms in the colony.
1891	Jose Rizal publishes his second novel *El Filibusterismo* (The Subversive); the Spanish retaliate by expelling his family from the land estate they were leasing.
1892	The *Katipunan*—the first nationalist organization—set up in Manila.
1896	*Katipunan* discovered forcing its leaders to launch their uprising; Rizal is executed.
1897	Factional fighting in *Katipunan* leads to ouster and execution of founder Andres Bonifacio and elevation to power of Emilio Aguinaldo, who signed a peace pact with the Spanish and went on exile to Hong Kong, but rebellions continue.
1898	United States declares war on Spain and goes to Manila with Aguinaldo.
1899	Aguinaldo is sworn in as president of the First Philippine Republic; the Philippine-American War breaks out.
1900	War spreads across the Philippines; Philippine forces break up, and members of President Aguinaldo's cabinet surrender and collaborate with Americans.

1901	Aguinaldo is captured; President William McKinley establishes a civil government in the Philippines; Filipino leaders found the *Nacionalista* Party.
1902	President Theodore Roosevelt declares that the Philippine "insurrection" is over; U.S. Congress passes Philippine Bill 1902 establishing the colonial state.
1903	The United States establishes the Moro Province to be governed by the army.
1904	First convention of provincial governors is held in Manila.
1907	Election to the Philippine Assembly; Manuel Quezon and Sergio Osmena emerge as new leaders; the last of the Filipino revolutionaries, Macario Sakay, is hanged on charges of sedition and banditry.
1908	University of the Philippines is established.
1909	The United States allows limited free trade between itself and the Philippines.
1911	Filipino-controlled Philippine Assembly clashes with American-dominated executive body, the Philippine Commission.
1912	Democrats win U.S. elections and President-elect Woodrow Wilson implements Filipinization of the colonial state.
1916	President Wilson signs Jones Law, which grants Philippine independence once the colony is completely stabilized; a Senate and a House of Representatives replace the Philippine Assembly.
1917	*Partido Democrata* becomes the opposition party.
1919	Filipino leaders send the first "Philippine independence mission" to the United States to negotiate terms of independence.
1922–1926	General Leonard Wood, former governor of the Moro, returns as governor general, promises to reverse Filipinization, and gets into political battles with Filipino leaders. This was only resolved when Woods died while undergoing surgery.
1930	Peasants protest Filipino leaders' compromises over independence; the Communist Party of the Philippines is established.
1934	U.S. Congress approves the Tydings-McDuffie law granting Philippine independence after a 10-year transition.
1935	The Commonwealth of the Philippines is established with Manuel Quezon as president and Sergio Osmeña as vice president.
1937	Filipinos are granted the right to vote.
1939	Commonwealth legislature creates a Department of National Defense in response to a "Japanese threat."
1941	Quezon and Osmeña reelected in second general elections under the Commonwealth; Japanese army invades the Philippines.
1943	Japanese puppet Philippine republic is inaugurated.
1944	Commonwealth president Manuel L. Quezon dies of tuberculosis in New York; U.S. forces return to the Philippines.
1946	The United States grants independence to the Philippines with Manuel L. Roxas as president.

1947	Military and economic treaties are signed by the Philippines and the United States; main provisions include free trade, unhampered operations by American companies in the Philippines (including the right to remit profits), and also maintenance of the colonial era military bases; agreements pass in the Philippine Congress after left-leaning members of the House of Representatives are expelled on false charges of election fraud.
1948	Communist Party of the Philippines launches a series of attacks with the end goal of seizing power.
1949	Free trade between the United States—with its booming economy—and the war-devastated Philippines places the latter's economy on a downward spiral; the United States agrees to allow the Philippines to impose import and exchange controls to limit the entry of imports, to give domestic manufacturers the chance to grow with no U.S. competition, and to regulate the outflow of U.S. dollars.
1950	American economic mission recommends that the Philippine economy diversify; Central Intelligence Agency operatives assist the Philippine military in defeating the communist uprising.
1953–1954	Communists are defeated; the reformist Ramon Magsaysay becomes president.
1954	Philippines joins the Southeast Asia Treaty Organization.
1956	Philippine Congress makes the teaching of the life and works of the national hero Jose Rizal a compulsory college course.
1957	President Magsaysay dies in a plane crash; Congress passes the Anti-Subversion Law that outlaws the communist party.
1958	President Carlos Garcia launches import-substitution industrialization under his First Filipino Policy, aiming to replace imported manufacturing goods with goods produced by Filipino industries.
1959	The United States and the Philippines renegotiate military treaties, reducing the 99-year bases agreement to 25 years.
1960	The International Rice Research Institute is established in Manila with funds from Ford and Rockefeller Foundations.
1962	Diosdado Macapagal defeats Carlos Garcia for the presidency and lifts import and exchange controls.
1963	President Macapagal revives Philippine claims to Sabah causing tensions with Malaysia; he also signs the Agricultural Land Reform Code, which abolishes tenancy and replaces it with leasehold arrangement to benefit small farmers.
1964	The communist party revives its network, with students from the University of the Philippines and the Lyceum of the Philippines being among its recruits.
1965	Ferdinand Marcos defeats President Diosdado Macapagal; as president-elect, promises that "this nation will be great again"; breaks promise not to send Filipino troops to Vietnam, deploying a small contingent of the military's Engineering Battalion as an ally of the United States.
1966	The Asian Development Bank sets up its headquarters in Manila.

1967	Government troops massacre members of a religious sect as they marched toward the presidential palace; the communist party forms the coalition Movement for the Advancement of Nationalism (MAN); the Philippines joins the Association of Southeast Asian Nations.
1968	Twenty-eight Muslim trainees are killed in a secret government camp; they were supposed to infiltrate and destabilize Sabah, thereby putting the Philippines in a better position to assert its claim of the Malaysian state; student radicals break away from the communist party, declare that it had ceased to be the vanguard of the revolution, and form a "re-established" Communist Party of the Philippines (CPP) inspired by Chinese leader Mao Tse Tung; CPP vows to renew the armed struggle against the government which the older party abandoned.
1969	President Marcos is reelected in the most violent and fraudulent national elections ever; Marcos bankrupts the government by using revenues for campaign.
1970	Students protest and clash with the police and the military in the first three months of the year; this would be known as the "First Quarter Storm" of the 1970s, and many students join the CPP.
1971	A special CPP team bombs a political rally of anti-Marcos politicians to force President Marcos to crack down on opponents and polarize politics and push moderate anti-Marcos forces to the communist side.
1972	President Marcos declares martial law and places the Philippines under "constitutional authoritarian" rule; Muslim students get the support of Libya and Malaysia and establish alliances with politicians to form the Moro National Liberation Front (MNLF), an armed force dedicated to the separation of Mindanao, the province of Palawan, and the Sulu archipelago from the Philippines.
1973	MNLF engages the Armed Forces of the Philippines (AFP) in battles all over Muslim Mindanao; over 30,000 people arrested by the government by the end of the year; a new constitution is "ratified" by hastily set up "citizen's assemblies"; the older of the two communist parties surrenders to Marcos and the "re-established."
1974	The Catholic Bishops Conference of the Philippines appeals to Marcos to end martial law.
1975	The Philippines and the People's Republic of China formalize diplomatic ties; China stops supporting the CPP; the MNLF war worsens as estimated 500,000 people displaced and 50,000 total casualties.
1976	The MNLF and the Philippine government declare a ceasefire and start negotiations over the issue of Muslim autonomy.
1977	Top CPP leaders, including founding chairman Jose Maria Sison, are arrested even as first communist-led urban protests break out in schools and factories. The first batch of Filipinos leaves to work in the Middle East.

1978	Marcos holds sham elections for a new legislature; CPP establishes its first legal front organization, the National League of Filipino Students, which was later renamed League of Filipino Students (LFS); the sugar industry experiences near-collapse when global prices go down leaving the country with millions of pounds of unsold sugar.
1979	The Philippines and the United States amend the military bases agreement requiring the bases to fly the Philippine flag; noncommunist groups stage bombing in Manila.
1980	CPP establishes its other legal organization, the labor federation May 1 Movement (*Kilusang Mayo Uno*, KMU), which stages protests together with the LFS; top anti-Marcos foe, former senator Benigno Aquino Jr., is released from jail and flown to the United States for a heart bypass surgery; Aquino decides not to go home and becomes involved in the anti-Marcos groups in the United States.
1981	Marcos "formally" lifts martial law; the economy is shaken by a businessman's decision to flee the country and not pay a US$100 million debt. The number of Filipinos working abroad begins a steadily climb.
1982	Anti-Marcos politicians form a coalition even as the government closes two small opposition newspapers.
1983	Senator Aquino decides to return to the Philippines and is assassinated at the airport. Massive protests break out across the country over the Aquino assassination.
1984	In the second national legislative elections, 53 anti-Marcos politicians win seats in the 183-seat assembly. A commission set up by Marcos to investigate the Aquino assassination concludes it was a military plot and indicts AFP chief of staff General Fabian Ver. The Philippine economy is in a tailspin, and the Central Bank reserves are good for only a month's expenditures. Businesses of cronies and relatives of the Marcoses collapse one after another. The International Monetary Fund and World Bank promise to extend new loans to the government if President Marcos agrees to introduce reforms.
1985	Junior officers organize the Reform the AFP Movement (RAM); Marcos surprises everyone by calling for snap presidential elections and the opposition rallies behind Aquino's widow, Corazon ("Cory") as its candidate.
1986	The CPP announces it is boycotting the elections. Marcos cheats heavily to win the elections sparking more protests. An attempted coup by RAM fails, and when officers retreat to a military camp to await a full government attack, a "people power" of over a million surrounds the camp acting as a de facto defensive shield. On the third day of the standoff, the air force declares its support for the rebels and bombs the presidential palace. Senior advisers of President Ronald Reagan convince Marcos to leave the palace and accept exile to Hawaii. Corazon Aquino assumes the presidency, sets up a constitutional commission, and opens negotiations with the MNLF and the CPP. RAM attempts to overthrow President Aquino.

1987	The CPP withdraws from peace talks with the government while RAM continues to overthrow President Aquino. Aquino orders a plebiscite to approve the new Constitution, then holds elections for the new bicameral Congress, provincial, city, and town positions.
1988	The Philippine and U.S. governments begin negotiations over a new military bases agreement. Internal dissensions and bloody purges weaken CPP. The Moro Islamic Liberation Front (MILF) declares itself as the new vanguard of Muslim separatism after accusing the MNLF of abandoning the struggle.
1989	Former president Marcos dies in Hawaii. The last RAM coup attempt almost succeeds until the United States shows its official support of President Aquino by ordering two of its fighter planes to fly over Manila. President Aquino signs into law the creation of an Autonomous Region in Muslim Mindanao (ARMM), which consists of five provinces with Muslim majorities.
1991	The eruption of a dormant volcano effectively closes the adjacent U.S. Clark Field Air Force Base. The Philippine Senate rejects the new treaty, which could have extended the American military presence for another 10 years. U.S. military forces begin to withdraw from the Philippines. President Aquino allows the Marcos family to return to the Philippines. Mrs. Marcos is charged with plunder.
1992	Fidel V. Ramos succeeds Corazon Aquino as president. Ramos reunifies AFP by welcoming back the RAM coup plotters and pro-Marcos officers and repeals the Anti-Subversion Law to reopen peace talks with the communists. There was a surge in the kidnapping of wealthy Filipino Chinese by rogue police officers, drug syndicates, and former communists during Ramos' term.
1993	Ramos achieves partial success in reforming a corrupt police force and instituting a "population control" program despite the opposition of the Catholic Church. His most important accomplishment was deregulating the communications and travel industries and boosting government coffers with the sale of military lands. Global businesses predict the Philippines to be the next Asian economic tiger.
1995	The execution by the Singaporean government of a Filipina worker sparks nationwide protests and strains Philippine-Singapore relations. This does not have an effect on the continuing rise in the number of Filipinos leaving the country for work abroad. The Abu Sayyaf, an Islamic terrorist group, joins forces with some MILF commanders to attack a town in southwestern Mindanao. The government prevents a plot by Islamic terrorists to blow up American airlines as they crossed the Pacific Ocean.
1996	The government signs a peace agreement with the MNLF. It makes an exception to the law governing ARMM by appointing MNLF chairman Nur Misuari its governor.

1997   The Asian economic crisis shatters dreams of the Philippines as the next Asian economic tiger. The Philippines, however, suffers the least among the Southeast Asian countries because it is at the bottom of the pile. Ramos's attempt to change a constitutional provision that would allow him to run for reelection fail. The MILF parades its 14,000 fully armed forces.

1998   Senator Joseph Estrada, a former movie action star, succeeds Ramos as president in a landslide election.

1999   American troops return to the Philippines with the first joint military exercise between the two countries since 1992.

2000   The Abu Sayyaf kidnaps 21 tourists in a Malaysian resort. An ally of President Estrada becomes a whistleblower and exposes the president's involvement in a nationwide illegal lottery network. The House of Representatives impeaches Estrada, but his allies in the Senate block the proceedings that follow.

2001   "People Power II" forces Estrada to resign. Vice President Gloria M. Arroyo takes over and orders Estrada's arrest on charges of corruption and plunder. Abu Sayyaf kidnaps an American missionary couple and their Filipino companion. U.S. intelligence units assist AFP troops in rescue operations, but the husband dies in the firefight.

2002   Arroyo declares her support for President George W. Bush's War on Terror. She promises to build "a strong republic" to overcome the problems of the country.

2003   President Arroyo issues an executive order approving a "visiting forces agreement" with the United States. She decides to run for president and is challenged by a popular aging action movie star, Fernando Poe Jr.

2004   Arroyo wins a full term after receiving 1 million votes from the ARMM, which was then under the control of a brutal warlord clan. U.S. military continues antiterrorism training of AFP military to pursue Abu Sayyaf.

2005   The Philippine Center for Investigative Journalism releases tape of President Gloria Arroyo conversing with a senior election official on the alleged rigging of the 2004 elections, causing a cabinet crisis. Four U.S. Marines are charged with raping a Filipina, jeopardizing Philippine-American ties.

2006   President Arroyo repeals the death penalty and introduces a value-added tax (VAT) bill aimed at simplifying tax collection.

2007   One of the four marines charged with raping of Filipina is found guilty but placed under the custody of the American embassy. Former president Estrada is also found guilty but granted a presidential pardon. The economy experiences a 7.8 percent gross national product growth, first since 1977.

2008   President Arroyo tries to move forward with peace talks with MILF but is derailed by a Supreme Court decision declaring a provision granting MILF right over the ancestral domain unconstitutional. Imelda Marcos is acquitted of 32 counts of illegal money transfers.

2009	Former president Corazon Aquino dies of lung cancer and thousands attend her funeral; 58 people, including 31 journalists, are massacred by a warlord and his armed men forcing President Arroyo to declare martial law and arrest the warlord and his sons. Aquino's son Benigno III is elected president.
2011	Senate hearing reveals massive corruption inside the AFP, with senior officers receiving as much as US$3.3 million in "retirement gifts," and AFP chief of staff commits suicide. Government arrests former president Gloria Arroyo for allegedly sabotaging the 2004 elections while the chief justice of the Supreme Court is impeached by the House of Representatives for "betrayal of public trust."
2012	President Aquino III signs the Cybercrime Prevention Act and a Reproductive Health Bill. Chief justice of the Supreme Court is found guilty by Senate and removed from office; former president Gloria Arroyo is granted bail. Philippine government signs the first provisions of a "Framework Agreement on the *Bangsamoro* (Moro Nation)" as the first step toward the creation of a new autonomous regional body to replace ARMM.
2013	President Aquino III signs the Human Rights Victims Reparation and Recognition Act to compensate human rights victims of the Marcos dictatorship. Millions protest the misuse by politicians of a Priority Development Assistance Fund (PDAF) as journalists expose the businesswoman who masterminded a scam costing the government US$439 million.
2014	The Philippine government and MILF sign the last provision of the "Framework Agreement on the *Bangsamoro* (Moro Nation)" creating the *Bangsamoro* (Moro Nation). Philippine government recovers US$58.3 million from secret Swiss account of former president Ferdinand Marcos after a Singapore court rules that it belonged to the Philippine government. A Senate committee recommends filing plunder charges against four senators involved in the PDAF scam. Former president Arroyo is cleared in a corruption case involving the use of agricultural funds for the elections. The Philippines and the United States sign an "Enhanced Defense Cooperation Agreement" (EDCA) that allows American forces access to Philippine bases while joint military exercises between the two countries continue.
2015	Forty-four members of a special unit of the police are killed in a botched attempt to capture a Malaysian terrorist in Mindanao.
2016	House of Representatives refuses to support the "Framework Agreement on the *Bangsamoro*," while Supreme Court affirms the legality of the EDCA. The Permanent Court of Arbitration supports the Philippines position against China over an area of the West Philippine Sea that the latter claimed as its territory. Mayor Rodrigo R. Duterte wins the presidency and promises to implement the Reproductive Health Law; also announces a "War on Drugs," and an end to the "special relationship" between the two countries.

2017	Over 7,000 people, many of them from low-income families, are killed by the police and hired assassins on suspicion of being drug distributors or users. Public outcry forces Duterte to suspend his "War on Drugs" temporarily. Duterte declares martial law in Mindanao in response to terrorist attacks in towns around Mindanao; the House of Representatives investigates former president Benigno S. Aquino III and his budget secretary over the use of a controversial anti-dengue medicine; the Supreme Court sits as Presidential Electoral Tribunal to oversee the recounting of votes for the vice president position based on a petition by losing candidate Ferdinand Marcos Jr. He had contended that he won over Congresswoman Leni Robredo. Supreme Court removes the chief justice based on the accusation of the solicitor general that she misreported her assets and liabilities. Eleven mayors killed after being suspected by the government to be involved in drug syndicates. Anti-graft court convicts Imelda Marcos on seven counts of graft; Mrs. Marcos automatically appeals.
2019	Plebiscites in Muslim provinces ratify the *Bangsamoro* Organic Law that created the Bangsamoro Autonomous Region (BAR) to replace the ARMM; 20 people killed in a terrorist bombing of a Catholic Church; chief executive officer of the e-newsmagazine Rappler arrested for cyber libel; President Duterte withdraws the Philippines from the International Criminal Court to protest its investigations of state's extrajudicial killing of suspected drug users and distributors.
2020	Philippine government sends official notice terminating the Visiting Forces Agreement with the United States. Congress begins to deliberate over the franchise renewal of the multimedia network ABS-CBN Broadcasting Company after President Duterte accuses it of bias; Bureau of Customs reports that over US$370 million has been illegally moved to the Philippines with the collaboration of military units and the airport police; President Duterte signs a law giving him additional powers as the number of Filipinos affected by the COVID-19 disease rises. As of July 16, 2020, 38,450 Filipinos were reported to display symptoms associated with COVID-19, the highest in Southeast Asia.

Communism

Communism continues to be a major actor in the Philippines at a time when the ideology has ceased to be a major influence in global politics. The Communist Party of the Philippines (CPP) is one of two remaining communist parties in the world. Unlike the Communist Party of Nepal, however, the CPP has retained its guerrilla army (the New People's Army, NPA), has successfully had its leaders elected to the House of Representatives, and has had its ideas positively shape public debates and the decisions of presidents, senators, and other officials.

The CPP began as a rival to another communist party, which used the Filipino name Partido Komunista ng Pilipinas (PKP). The PKP was established by trade unionists and students on November 7, 1930. The American colonial government prosecuted the PKP but eased up and allowed it to organize again on the eve of World War II. The PKP then formed a guerrilla army that fought the Japanese. In the postwar period, however, the government again declared it as illegal and a threat. The PKP's response was to order its guerrilla army to attack government troops. Their successes on the battlefield created a panic that the PKP would soon be knocking on the gates of Manila. PKP leaders were likewise caught in the hype and began believing that they could seize state power.

The PKP's optimism proved short-lived. The United States sent military and civilian operatives to retrain and improve the Philippine Army, help organize front organizations among workers and peasants to rival those that the communists formed, and support the successful campaign of a pro-reform presidential candidate who vowed to end government corruption. At the other end, the PKP had overstretched its military force and fissures had developed in its leadership; this resulted in some laying down their arms and accepting the government's amnesty offer. After the military captured its senior leaders, the others went deep underground.

In the early 1960s, however, the PKP saw a chance to revive the organization when it was presented with a new pool of recruits. These were students who had become radicalized by the United States' war in Vietnam and the role played by the Philippine government in this war through the American military bases located in the country. These students were also attracted to the enthusiasm shown by their fellow students in communist China who seemed to be keeping the fire of the revolution alive through the passionate criticism of their leadership. In 1964, the PKP recruited these students and the result was the formation of the Nationalist Youth, which was then assigned the responsibility of recruiting more young people to the PKP.

This political marriage, however, did not last long. Nationalist Youth chairman Jose Maria Sison volunteered to write a history of the PKP and came out with a report that was extremely critical of the way the senior cadres ran the party. The latter, however, regarded his demand for a thorough reassessment as a threat to their control. Sison was expelled, but instead of accepting the decision he fought back, declaring the PKP dead and declaring that it was time to "re-establish" the communist party.

On December 28, 1968, Sison and his student comrades formed the Communist Party of the Philippines, which distinguished itself from the PKP by expressing its allegiance to Marxism-Leninism-Mao Tse Tung Thought. It chastised the PKP for abandoning the armed struggle and vowed to make that its priority, inspired as it was by what Mao Tse Tung did in China. The CPP vowed to form a "New People's Army" (NPA) to distinguish its armed force from the older and now compromised "People's Army." The NPA was to do the fighting in the rural areas, first as a guerrilla force and then, if it continued to succeed, as a conventional army which would attack the national capital. The CPP relied on the energy and passion of its student recruits to grow the guerrilla army, trade unions, and peasant groups to back up the NPA. It tapped on student anger against "U.S. imperialism" and President Ferdinand Marcos to stage street demonstrations—some of them ended in violence and provided more recruits whose encounters with the police convinced them to join the NPA or to join a communist underground network.

The CPP then sought arms from China and made a daring grenade attack on a rally by anti-Marcos politicians campaigning for the Senate. As Sison had predicted, when Marcos blamed the CPP no one believed him; the public instead pointed a finger at the president. When Marcos suspended the writ of habeas corpus (the right of a detained person to be present in court), the CPP got more new members. The plan to bring guns from China failed, and Marcos would use this, the grenade attack, and the increasing violence on the streets to declare martial law on September 21, 1972.

Martial law crippled the CPP with the arrests of top leaders and the deaths of others, especially those who had joined the NPA. A group inside the PKP urged its leadership to unite with its younger rival in resisting martial law. The PKP responded by having the latter executed, before surrendering to Marcos. By 1975, however, the CPP showed that it was able enough to ride the storm and renew its organization. The separatist rebellion of the MNLF drew the complete attention of the military and gave the NPA some breathing room to recover. At the end of the decade, the NPA had established 30 guerilla zones of varying sizes from where it could launch its ambuscades. In the cities, the CPP had set up front organizations in universities, factories, and plantations. The estimated total CPP force had reached 30,000, half of these with the NPA; it supposedly had a mass base of 1 million supporters and sympathizers. The CPP showed off its new-found strength in 1980 by inviting local and foreign media to one of its guerrilla zones for a press interview. All these audacious moves began to worry the United States, which in turn started to pressure the Marcos government to ease its restrictions and allow an anti-communist opposition to grow.

Ferdinand Marcos, president, 1964–1986, with American president Lyndon Johnson. (Library of Congress)

The CPP reached out to these anti-communist forces, which consisted of politicians, noncommunist left-wing groups, business groups, and nationalists, but their "united front" never lasted because of a tendency to control the alliance. The CPP believed that since it had the numbers and since it represented the masses, it was the natural leader of any coalition. Hence, no anti-Marcos united front with noncommunist forces lasted. This imbalance turned against the CPP's favor in 1983 when the assassination of former senator and top Marcos opponent Benigno Aquino Jr. angered the middle classes and made them join the ranks of the anti-communist groups. The CPP could still ignore these newly politicized groups because it had the NPA. The CPP's political standing further suffered when it boycotted the 1986 elections and stayed away from the People Power Revolution that ended the dictatorship of President Marcos and put President Corazon C. Aquino in power. The CPP's misfortunes did not stop there. In 1987, CPP leaders panicked when rumors spread that the military had successfully infiltrated the organization. In the ensuing investigation, suspects were tortured and even executed. When these became known, public support further went down, for this time the vanguard of the poor appeared to be no different from the military it was fighting. The CPP split into several factions and was hardly a political force after that.

In 1991, however, Jose Maria Sison's faction was able to regain control of the leadership, expel and eliminate leaders of the rival faction, and win over NPA units that had survived the splits. The CPP began its slow recovery but was never able to regain its old strength. Its city organizations were constrained by military assassinations, while the NPA had difficulty recovering its old bases because of unrelenting military attacks. However, the CPP did succeed in forming its party-list organization which was able to get its candidates elected in several elections in the House of Representatives (see Chapter 3). There were several attempts to negotiate peace with the government, beginning with President Aquino; under President Rodrigo R. Duterte, the CPP was even able to negotiate a couple of senior positions. All these fell through, however, and the CPP returned to vowing to overthrow the government.

The CPP is now more than 50 years old, and the question is, how has it been able to survive when other communist parties have collapsed? Observers point to a weak Philippine state whose corrupt and inefficient military could not put the party down. The second reason is that real political power is in the hands of provincial and regional clans, which often have a pragmatic opportunistic relationship with the NPA—the former pay revolutionary tax to the latter in exchange for the votes of the guerrillas' peasant supporters. The CPP's coffers are therefore constantly full, and the leadership continues subsidizing the NPA—the most important of the party's organizations.

See also: Chapter 3: Overview; Armed Forces of the Philippines; Civil Society Organizations; Elections; Martial Law; Political Clans; Post-Marcos Philippines; Presidential Emergency Powers; Relations with the People's Republic of China; Relations with the United States; Warlords. Chapter 4: Overview; Agriculture; Crony Capitalism; Economic Assistance; Land Reform. Chapter 9: National Language Debate. Chapter 11: Overview; Filipino Novels in English; Chapter 13: Nationalist and Political Music.

Further Reading

Abinales, Patricio N., ed. 1996. *The Revolution Falters: The Left in Philippine Politics after 1986*. Ithaca: Cornell University Press.

Jones, Gregg. 1989. *Red Revolution: Inside the Philippine Guerrilla Movement*. New York: Routledge.

Richardson, Jim. 2011. *Komunista: The Genesis of the Philippine Communist Party, 1902–1935*. Quezon City: Ateneo de Manila University Press.

Rutten, Rosanne, ed. 2008. *Brokering a Revolution: Cadres in a Philippine Insurgency*. Quezon City: Ateneo de Manila University Press.

Extrajudicial Killings (EJK)

EJK is short for "extrajudicial killing," a term that is associated with the anti-drug campaign of President Rodrigo R. Duterte. After he repeatedly declared that those involved in the trade and consumption of illicit drugs like methamphetamine do not deserve their day in court but should just be killed instead, bodies began to appear on the streets of the Philippines' major cities. Witnesses reported that the killings were mainly committed by a team of two people riding on a motorbike. There were also cases, however, where police raids ended up with a target—be it a drug user or the local dealer—dead. The police justified these killings by alleging that the victim/suspect resisted arrest despite the police issuing an arrest warrant and pleading with them to surrender. The police called the procedure tokhang, which is the merger of the first two syllables of two words, toktok (knocking) and hangyo (request or plead).

By the end of 2019, over 14,000 people have been killed by tokhang, 90 percent of them from poor communities. Duterte produced a list of drug suspects which included several mayors and local officials, judges, and even police officers. Senator Leila de Lima was imprisoned on charges that she was in the pocket of drug syndicates. Duterte's critics, however, described this as presidential vendetta against de Lima. No judge had been prosecuted; only three policemen had been indicted and two mayors executed for allegedly resisting arrest. The president appeared to encourage the killings by repeatedly declaring that he would defend those who were party to the assassinations, especially policemen.

Duterte's association with EJKs was not new. When Duterte was mayor of Davao City in southern Philippines, he was accused by human rights groups of being party to such killings. During her time as chief prosecutor, Leila de Lima (who later became senator) had the mayor investigated. Davao allegedly became the "safest city in the Philippines" through a systematic elimination of drug addicts and petty criminals by the "Davao Death Squad," which operated out of the mayor's office. The investigations ceased once Duterte became president.

Duterte bristled at the condemnation by local and international human rights groups and expressions of concern by Western governments over this so-called worsening culture of impunity. He accused these groups of interference and a lack of concern for the general welfare of Filipinos. He questioned the sincerity of Western governments when, in fact, their own histories had episodes of violence against their people. Duterte was especially incensed at President Barack Obama and threatened that the Philippines would withdraw from its alliance with the United States and enter a new one with the People's Republic of China. In the last months of 2017, Duterte announced the suspension of the anti-drug war and ordered the police to scale down their operations. The break in the campaign was short-lived. In 2018, the police announced that it was renewing its raid and also stated that their teams would be bringing Bibles and rosaries aside from their guns. This turned out to be just a mere publicity stunt.

See also: Chapter 2: Overview; Marcos Dictatorship; Chapter 3: Overview; Armed Forces of the Philippines; Martial Law; Political Clans; Warlords.

Further Reading

Coronel, Sheila. 2017. "Murder as Enterprise: Police Profiteering in Duterte's War on Drugs." In Nicole Curato (ed.), *A Duterte Reader: Critical Essays on Rodrigo Duterte's Early Presidency*, pp. 167–198. Quezon City: Ateneo de Manila University Press.

Human Rights Watch. 2007. "Scared Silent: Impunity and Extrajudicial Killings in the Philippines." Accessed May 12, 2019. http://www.hrw.org/reports/2007/06/27/scared -silent

Marcos Dictatorship

For 15 years, President Ferdinand E. Marcos ruled the Philippines under what he called "constitutional authoritarianism"—it was essentially a dictatorship. Marcos was the 10th president of the Philippines, the first to be reelected, and the first to extend his presidency by placing the country under martial law. He first justified martial law as the only way to save the republic from an avaricious oligarchy and the violent extremism of the CPP. Thousands were arrested as constitutional rights were suspended. Marcos staged a fake plebiscite to claim that Filipinos supported the continuation of martial law because this time, the goal was for a "New Society" to be born out of and to replace the decaying old order.

The dictatorship managed to consolidate its control over most parts of the country, except for the Muslim regions of the southern island of Mindanao. There an armed group calling itself the Moro National Liberation Front (MNLF) launched a series of attacks on cities and military camps. It announced the start of an armed revolution that would separate Mindanao, Palawan Island, and the nearby Sulu archipelago from the Philippines and form a Bangsamoro (Moro People) republic. Marcos was forced to divert over 70 percent of government troops to fight the MNLF. This enabled a fledgling CPP to strengthen itself and expand its guerilla army and underground network to other parts of the Philippines.

The Marcos dictatorship is also associated with what political scientists call "patrimonial plunder" by Marcos, his family, and the cronies of the Philippine economy. Martial law in the Philippines had become synonymous with crony capitalism, a practice where the president handed out choice businesses to his cronies to monopolize, and when these failed, bailed them out with public funds. Opponents claimed that the Marcoses stole over US$5 billion (US$11.3 billion in 2018 rates) from government coffers, international aid, and public and private credits. An enduring symbol of this corruption is the profligate lifestyle of First Lady Imelda Romualdez Marcos, her global shopping sprees of fine jewelry, historical paintings, and luxury apartments on a whim, and, especially, her 30,000-shoe collection. Only a small portion of the stolen billions has been recovered by government after Marcos was ousted in 1986.

Plunder, the failure of Philippine exports to capture critical markets abroad, the servicing of a national debt that was running out of control, and a consistent inability to collect taxes caused the economy to tailspin by the early 1980s. Marcos tried to prevent any further loss of legitimacy by holding national elections to determine if Filipinos still wanted him to be president. This use of elections to justify the continuation of the dictatorship had become standard practice up until 1984 when Filipinos did vote for some anti-Marcos politicians in the rubber-stamp legislature. Marcos faced his most severe crisis after the assassination of Benigno Aquino Jr., his chief rival, as Aquino was deplaning at the national airport.

Then in 1985, Marcos abruptly declared that he would be holding a snap election to once more feel the public pulse. Aquino's widow, Corazon, challenged him and formed a coalition of different anti-Marcos forces. As expected, Marcos cheated, but he also caused a firestorm with Aquino calling for nationwide disobedience campaigns and disgruntled military officers mobilizing to launch a coup. In what would become known as the People's Power Revolution, these two forces coalesced and ousted Marcos on February 25, 1986, formally ending his dictatorship. Marcos was exiled to Hawaii where he died three years later. The legacies of his dictatorship remain, as evidenced by the unrelenting corruption in government, the political resurrection of the Marcos family, the continued domination by certain cronies of significant sectors of Philippine business, and the failure to recover much of the stolen billions. The biggest irony of all is that Ferdinand Marcos Jr. was not only elected to the Senate but also nearly won the vice presidency in the 2016 elections.

See also: Chapter 3: Overview; Martial Law; Political Clans; Post-Marcos Philippines; Presidential Emergency Powers; Relations with the United States; Warlords. Chapter 4: Overview; Agriculture; Crony Capitalism; Economic Assistance; Industry; Land Reform; Overseas Filipino Workers; Taxation. Chapter 6: Elites. Chapter 13: Nationalist and Political Music.

Further Reading

Mijares, Primitivo. 1976. *The Conjugal Dictatorship of Ferdinand and Imelda Marcos.* Quezon City: Ateneo de Manila University Press. http://rizalls.lib.admu.edu.ph:8080 /ebooks2/Primitivo%20Mijares.pdf

Robles, Raissa. 2016. *Marcos Martial Law: Never Again*. Manila: Filipinos for a Better Philippines.

Muslim Separatism: Update on BARMM

Muslim separatism was the slogan used by Muslim activists and those who argued for the separation of Mindanao, the Palawan Island, and the Sulu archipelago from the Philippine body politic. They presented an alternative history for Mindanao which told of how Muslim-controlled areas had kept their independence from Spanish colonialism and were only forced to become part of the Philippines after the Americans successfully subjugated rebellions by Muslim communities. Even then, their ideologues argued, these Muslim zones were only artificially integrated into the national territory. The republic showed very little concern for the social welfare of the country's largest minority group. What the government did was turn Mindanao into a destination point for settlers from the central and northern Philippines desiring to own a piece of land; land was supposedly widely available across Mindanao, which was touted as the country's most extensive and abundantly endowed land frontier.

Muslim activists and scholars attributed the decline in the Muslim population and the widespread poverty in the Muslim regions to these two processes. As the settlements grew, conflict over land ownership between settlers and Muslims heated up. Settler leaders now challenged the preeminence of Muslim elites in elections. Hostilities between armed vigilantes from both communities also became more frequent. The breaking point came when President Ferdinand E. Marcos abandoned the past policy of state disinterest toward an active national government presence in Mindanao's economic development. Muslims, however, saw this as a deliberate attempt by the government to come to the aid of the settlers.

Muslim student activists warned that this alliance between the government and anti-Muslim groups was just the start of a genocidal campaign to exterminate Muslim society and culture. They called for the formation of an organization to resist this assault on their community (ummah) and finally separated the never-integrated historic Muslim territories of Mindanao, Sulu, and Palawan. Their call fell on receptive ears: anti-Marcos Muslim politicians, leaders of the different Muslim ethnic groups, the Libyan president Muammar Gaddafi who was convinced of the genocide argument, and the Malaysian government which had not forgiven Marcos for attempting to infiltrate a special military unit whose mission was to carry out destabilization operations in Borneo (see Chapter 3). The Federation of Arab States and the Organization of Islamic Conference (OIC) likewise expressed solidarity with the plight of the Muslims in Mindanao.

The result was the organization of the Moro National Liberation Front (MNLF) under the leadership of Nurallaji "Nur" Misuari, a University of the Philippines graduate who was influenced by the nationalist and radical groups in the state university.

Misuari appropriated the term "Moro," which was once the derogatory name used by the Spanish to describe Muslims. With Libya and Malaysia providing the weapons and military training, and the politicians and ethnic leaders mobilizing their followers, the MNLF launched a series of attacks on cities and military camps in the Muslim provinces, turning the Muslim zones in Mindanao into a battleground for the next three years. In 1977, however, successful Philippine diplomatic sorties to Libya and OIC, MNLF battlefield losses, and the decision of the MNLF's political allies to abandon the MNLF after accepting a Marcos offer that allowed them to keep their local power weakened the rebellion.

Splits in the leadership also affected the MNLF's military capacities. Leaders of an ethnic group—the Maguindanaos—broke away and formed the Moro Islamic Liberation Front (MILF). Its founding chairman, Salamat Hashim, accused Misuari of abandoning Islamic principles in favor of the Marxist-nationalist ideology he had learned as a University of the Philippines student, of corruption when it came with the resources the MNLF received from abroad, and of excluding other leaders—like Salamat—in negotiations with the Philippine government. Salamat's Islamic foundation was stronger than Misuari's—he had been educated at Egypt's Al-Azhar University, where he had written a dissertation on the plight of Filipino Muslims. On his way back to the Philippines, he set up offices in Pakistan and through them sent his comrades to Afghanistan to join the mujahideen resistance to the Soviet occupation and to gain military experience. The MILF core group was formed in late 1977, but the organization formally announced its presence in 1984, after Libya and Malaysia began to distance themselves from the MNLF, which continued to split further into more factions after Salamat left the organization.

By the late 1980s, the MILF had some camps in central Mindanao and a 14,000-strong armed force led by veterans of the Afghan war. While it strictly adhered to Islamic principles (religious advisers sat alongside military commanders), its approach to the Philippine government was surprisingly pragmatic. Throughout the 1990s, it avoided encounters with government troops while its leadership repeatedly reached out to the state. The MILF's first and only major battle against the Armed Forces of the Philippines (AFP) happened in 2000, when President Joseph Estrada attempted to distract public attention from reportage of the corruption in his administration. Estrada used a clash between rival clans as a pretext to order an all-out assault on MILF camps; the camps were easily overrun, but this failed to break the MILF. After Estrada was ousted (see People Power), his successor President Gloria Arroyo opened negotiations with the MILF. Three years later, in another instance of its pragmatist politics, Salamat, the head of an Islamic armed group, wrote to President George W. Bush to ask that the United States join Malaysia as mediator between the MILF and the Philippine government. Bush agreed and sent mediators, although Salamat could never see this unusual partnership work, dying from complications of a heart ailment soon after sending the letter.

In 1996, Misuari signed a peace agreement with President Fidel Ramos and was appointed governor of the Autonomous Region of Muslim Mindanao (ARMM). Misuari's term left much to be desired. He squandered resources with his constant domestic and international travel, often with a large entourage. Instead of trimming the ARMM personnel, Misuari just added another layer, appointing his followers to new positions alongside the old. Instead of learning the art of governing after over a decade of fighting the government, Misuari was drawn more to the perks of being a head of state—the travel, the posh accommodations, and the consorting with national and international VIPs. By the end of his term, two other factions had seized control of the leadership and marginalized him. Misuari had tried several times to rouse his remaining followers to wage war, but without the support of the other factions, they failed.

During their peace talks, the MILF and President Gloria Arroyo rushed an agreement over how to go about developing the natural resources in the so-called Muslim areas, but this was declared unconstitutional by the Supreme Court and opposed by Congress. A more careful and better-planned negotiation with President Benigno S. Aquino III moved the peace process one small step forward with better-defined points of agreement over natural resources development, the MILF's demobilization, and a step-by-step establishment of a new autonomous region that would replace the existing one.

On July 26, 2018, President Duterte signed the Bangsamoro Organic Law, creating the Bangsamoro Autonomous Region in Muslim Mindanao (BARMM), which replaced the ARMM. A two-part plebiscite held on January and February 2019 ratified the new regional body, and the Commission on Elections approved the holding of elections to the BARMM legislative assembly. Duterte and other national leaders regard BARMM not just an attempt to improve the practice of regional autonomy, but hopefully as a testing ground for a shift to a federal form of government in the future.

See also: Chapter 3: Overview; Armed Forces of the Philippines; Federalism; Martial Law; Political Clans; Post-Marcos Philippines. Chapter 5: Overview; Islam. Chapter 6: Overview; *Bangsamoro* Identity.

Further Reading

George, T. J. S. 1980. *Revolt in Mindanao: Rise of Islam in Philippine Politics*. Kuala Lumpur: Oxford University Press.

Hutchcroft, Paul D. 2016. *Mindanao: The Long Journey to Peace and Prosperity*. Pasay City: Anvil Publishing.

McKenna, Thomas M. 1998. *Muslim Rulers and Rebels: Everyday Politics and Armed Separatism in the Southern Philippines*. Berkeley, Los Angeles, and London: University of California Press. https://publishing.cdlib.org/ucpressebooks/view?docId=ft0199n64c& brand=ucpress

Vitug, Marites, and Glenda Gloria. 2000. *Under the Crescent Moon: Rebellion in Mindanao*. Quezon City: Institute for Popular Democracy and Ateneo School for Social Policy.

People Power Revolution

The People Power Revolution was a 4-day period in 1986 that ended the 15-year dictatorship of President Ferdinand E. Marcos. It began on February 23 as a coup attempt by officers who were disgruntled by the corruption of the dictatorship and organized the Reform the Armed Forces of the Philippines Movement (RAM). RAM would also become the weapon of factions inside the government opposed to the political ambitions of First Lady Imelda R. Marcos, who regarded herself as successor to her ailing husband. The coup attempt happened amid a political crisis just after the snap elections where Marcos altered the voting tabulations to show that he won against his rival Corazon C. Aquino. Aquino responded by calling for nationwide civil disobedience to protest the manipulation of election results. It was amid this furor that RAM sent an attack force to capture the presidential palace and have Marcos and family arrested, unaware that a mole had already reported their plan to the president. The arrest of this raiding team prompted the rest of the group to retreat to two military camps together with their leading supporters, Defense Secretary Juan Ponce Enrile and the military's vice-chief-of-staff General Fidel V. Ramos. There they waited for the government to attack, which they also promptly announced on the radio.

Upon hearing of the rebels' broadcast, Jaime Cardinal Sin, the head of the Catholic Church, urged Filipinos to go to the camps to support the rebels. By the morning, there were half a million people who were blocking a portion of the Epifanio de Los Santos Avenue (EDSA), the main artery that ran across north-central to south-central Manila. At about the same time, Marcos had flown in the Marines from the southern Philippines; they were deployed just outside the camps, awaiting orders to assault RAM. The latter consolidated its position by moving all its forces to one camp, while the crowd had grown to over a million. For the next two days, there was a tense impasse where several attempts by the Marines to start the assault were thwarted by a mass of people putting themselves in front of bayoneted units and tanks, imploring the government troops with prayers, flowers, and pleas. Fearful of the civilian collateral damage that an attack could result in, and some seriously bothered by their conscience, Marine commanders aborted the assaults and then just refused to follow any succeeding orders from pro-Marcos generals and the president himself.

What broke the impasse was the defection of two major armed services to the rebel camps. The first was the national police force which was once led by Ramos, and the second was the air force. RAM would use its new-found airpower to intimidate Marcos with a couple of bombs targeted at Malacanang, the presidential palace, while police units withdrew to allow more protesters to join the crowd in EDSA as well as to start surrounding Malacanang. Other military units that did not take sides eventually joined the rebels.

On February 25, Corazon Aquino took her oath of office as the 11th president of the Philippines. Marcos tried to hold his inauguration on the same day, but its media coverage was abruptly cut off by RAM rebels who had captured a major government television station. An emissary of American president Ronald Reagan then called Marcos to inform him that it was time to go. A few hours later, helicopters from the American air force base in Clark Field, north of Manila, landed on the presidential grounds to transport Marcos, his family and close cronies, millions of dollars and an inordinate amount of jewelry to the base. Military transport planes then took them to Hawaii. In the Philippines, RAM and Aquino's coalition agreed to set up a revolutionary government as a transition to the full restoration of constitutional democracy.

People Power was used a second time to force President Joseph E. Estrada to step down from power. Estrada was elected as the 13th president of the country in 1998, winning over his opponents by one of the largest margins in Philippine election history. His administration became notorious for its corruption and a marked absence of presidential leadership. Estrada's lifestyle of long nights of drinking with cronies, his propensity to appoint family and friends to cash-rich government agencies, and his decision to launch a major military offensive against the MILF brought about protests in the cities. An attempt by Estrada to muscle into the illegal numbers game of a provincial governor led this erstwhile ally to expose official corruption. Anti-Estrada forces in the House of Representatives moved to impeach the president, and the resolution was sent to the Senate where it was debated before a decision was made. In one crucial session, pro-Estrada senators successfully prevented prosecutors from revealing an alleged bank account where the president stashed his share of the numbers

Remembering the 1986 People Power Revolution. (Klodien/Dreamstime.com)

game. This prompted massive protests in Manila that brought together anti-Estrada politicians (including Vice President Gloria M. Arroyo), members of the business elite, professionals, church people, and the communist party. This coalition was enough to convince the military leadership to withdraw its support for the president and shift their allegiance to Arroyo. The day after, on January 20, 2001, Estrada resigned from office and was promptly arrested under orders by Arroyo on charges of corruption.

People power has been praised across the world as a model for a nonviolent way of removing autocrats and unpopular presidents. Admirers have even pointed to such events as the 1987 Palestinian intifada against Israel, the 1989 student protests at Tiananmen Square in China, and the 1989 student-led protests in Burma, Warsaw (Poland), Prague (then Czechoslovakia), and Berlin as having been inspired by what happened in the Philippines. As presidents Corazon C. Aquino and Gloria M. Arroyo began to govern, there was also evidence that Filipinos benefited very little from these bloodless revolutions. The elites had, in fact, reclaimed their control of the major levers of government while consolidating further their domination of towns, cities, and provinces that were mostly unaffected by the political changes in the capital. While there was indeed some breakthrough in terms of organizing the poor and the powerless—via nongovernment associations, civil society groups, and party-list organizations—their numbers (there were between 249,000 and 497,000 such organizations in 2004, according to the Asian Development Bank) were not enough to expand social policies that would correct income inequalities, reduce the power of the elites, and make rituals like elections genuinely reflective of the popular will. By the second decade of the 21st century, People Power had ceased to be celebrated as instances where ordinary Filipinos had effected historic changes to their politics. Now, it is just one of many annual government ceremonies where pomp takes precedence over substance.

See also: Chapter 3: Overview; Armed Forces of the Philippines; Civil Society Organizations; Elections; Martial Law; Political Clans; Post-Marcos Philippines; Presidential Emergency Powers; Warlords. Chapter 4: Overview; Crony Capitalism. Chapter 6: Overview; Elites; The Poor. Chapter 15: Nationalist and Political Music.

Further Reading

Claudio, Lisandro. 2014. *Taming People's Power: The EDSA Revolutions and Their Contradictions*. Quezon City: Ateneo de Manila University Press.

De Dios, Aurora Javate, Petronilo Daroy, and Lorna Kalaw-Tirol, eds. 1998. *Dictatorship and Revolution: Roots of People's Power*. Manila: Conspectus.

Hau, Caroline S., and Paul S. Manzanilla, eds. 2016. *Remembering/Rethinking EDSA*. Pasay City: Anvil Publishing.

CHAPTER 3

GOVERNMENT AND POLITICS

OVERVIEW

The Philippines is a republic that has a presidential form of government and consists of three interdependent but also autonomous branches: the executive, the two-chamber legislature, and the judiciary. The description of this presidential government, its organizational structure and the responsibilities of the branches, and the rights and responsibilities of citizens, among other things, are enshrined in a Constitution that was approved through a plebiscite in 1987.

The president and vice president are the two top officials of the executive branch. They are elected by popular vote. The president has a six-year term and cannot run for reelection, while the vice president can run for one more term, albeit not immediately after their first term is over. Unlike in the United States where the election of a president automatically hands the vice presidency to their running mate, in the Philippines the vice president may come from another party or could be someone running as an independent. A person can be placed in the position of vice president as long as they get the highest number of votes in the vice presidential election. To become president or vice president, a person must be born in the Philippines. The presidential candidate has to be at least 40 years old and should have resided in the country for at least 10 years before declaring their candidacy.

The Constitution grants the president extensive powers. Under the current structure, the president has authority over 20 departments, 57 government corporations, 39 councils and commissions, and several other bureaus and agencies. In 2010, the national government employed a total of 834,327 personnel, while another 94,759 personnel worked in government corporations. An independent Civil Service Commission—composed of presidential appointees in office only for a single nonrenewable term—helps the president oversee the executive branch. The presidency has direct control over the military under the principle of civilian supremacy. While mayors have authority over their police forces, the president is still able to wield influence on the agency via the head of the Philippine National Police, which is under the Department of Interior and Local Government.

The other powers of the president include being able to grant amnesty and negotiate treaties, although these cannot be completed without the concurrence of Congress. This watchdog role of the legislature is not only with regard to how presidents form their cabinets. The president may declare martial law but must inform Congress within 48 hours of this decision, and Congress can revoke the declaration by a simple majority vote. The Supreme Court could also review, validate, or invalidate the declaration.

The 1987 Constitution was drafted soon after President Corazon Aquino came to power. Some of its provisions were written—by those delegated to draft the Constitution—with the dictatorship of President Ferdinand Marcos in mind. The framers of the Constitution made sure that there were limits to presidential power. For example, a president's spouse cannot hold any government position and the office must inform the public if the president is seriously sick. The president cannot own companies that have businesses with the government and must ensure that military personnel come from all provinces and cities. These provisions are clearly in response to the abuse of power during martial law. The obligation to inform the public when a president is ailing ensured that the secrecy behind Marcos's illness would not be repeated, while the proportional representation of provinces in the Armed Forces of the Philippines (AFP) was written to avert the favoring of AFP officers from the president's home province and region, which happened during Marcos's administration.

The Philippines is divided into provinces, cities, municipalities, and villages (barrios, now formally called barangays). In terms of their structure, and in terms of the positions and responsibilities of executive officers at the provincial, city, municipal, and village levels, they are more or less a replica of the national government. A law that returns 40 percent of what the local governments collected back to their coffers. This was followed by a1991 Local Government Code that devolved certain offices of the national government to these regional governments had enhanced the latter's power. These laws were again the offshoots of the framers of the 1987 Constitution wanting to make sure that power came from the people.

The major urban centers in the Philippines have grown tremendously after 1975 to the extent that adjacent cities have been integrated into metropolitan areas, and a commission charged with supervising public activities that cannot anymore be handled by each city (e.g., traffic management).

Like the United States, the Philippines has a bicameral legislature—the 292-seat House of Representatives (Lower House) whose members represent districts of provinces, and the Senate (Upper House) whose 24 members are elected on a nationwide basis. Twenty-five Lower House seats, however, are allotted to party-list organizations that ostensibly represent the marginalized and underrepresented sections of society. Senators are elected for a term of six years and can only be reelected for one more term. Members of the House have three-year terms and can run for three consecutive terms. Half of the members of the 24-person Senate are elected every election.

A speaker leads the House while the Senate has a president. Both come from the majority party or party coalition. Congress proposes laws and those that pass both houses go to the president for their signature. The House and the Senate also have the power to conduct hearings and investigations in aid of legislation, impeach executive officials including presidents, and prepare the annual national budget. The Senate has the sole right to ratify international treaties.

The third branch of government—the judiciary—consists of the Supreme Court (one chief justice and 14 associate justices, all appointed by the president), the courts of appeals, the regional trial courts, and the municipal courts. There are also special courts that cover appeals courts and a People's Advocate court that, together with the Office of the Ombudsman, deal with criminal and civil cases involving government officials. There is also a court of tax appeals and there are Sharia courts (district and municipal) for the Muslim provinces. All judges are appointed by the president with no legislative confirmation; they are assured the security of tenure until their retirement at the age of 70 and the court's fiscal autonomy. Justices can only be removed by impeachment. The military has its own judicial system and a judge advocate general as the prosecutorial body and military tribunals overseeing cases.

The lower courts and regional courts decide on criminal and civil cases, and decisions are reviewed by a court of appeals. The Supreme Court is the final arbiter of cases submitted to the court of appeals, especially in the matter of the sentencing of those guilty. The Supreme Court also has the power to review international treaties, executive agreements, and presidential decrees and ordinances. It oversees the bar examination and also disciplines lawyers.

As of early 2018, the Congress had approved the US$70.65 billion budget of President Rodrigo R. Duterte, which was 11.6 percent more than that of his predecessor President Benigno S. Aquino III and considered the highest budget proposed by any president. It represented 21 percent of the country's gross domestic product for 2018. The budgetary allocation for the national government has not changed since 1986, when the military-biased budget of President Ferdinand Marcos was changed by his successors to one that served social welfare. Thus, the following departments had received the largest portions of state largesse: the Department of Education (US$10.4 billion), followed by the Department of Public Works and Highways (US$8.7 billion), the Department of the Interior and Local Government (US$2.84 billion), the Department of Defense (US$42.63 billion), and the Department of Social Welfare (US$2.46 billion).

Presidents, however, have priority projects, and in Duterte's case it was the "War on Drugs" and peace talks with rebel groups. The Office of the President's intelligence and confidential funds increased by 400 percent from the previous administration (US$9.6 million in 2016 to US$48 million in 2017) while the Office of the Presidential Adviser on the Peace Process's budget jumped by 950 percent (from US$14.7 million in 2016 to US$55.6 million in 2017). Unfortunately, Duterte's two campaigns yielded largely negative results. His campaign promise to eliminate the drug trade in his first six months in office never happened, leading him to lament that the drug scourge would outlast him. The peace talks with the Muslim separatist group Moro Islamic Liberation Front proceeded at a slow pace, but negotiations between the communists and the government broke down—President Duterte labeled the Communist Party of the Philippines a terrorist organization while the latter tagged him a fascist.

Other programs, however, seemed to be moving ahead. The government's universal health care program that specially targeted indigent patients moved forward during Duterte's first year in office, from US$3 billion to US$3.4 billion. Then in 2019, he signed the Universal Health Care Act guaranteeing all Filipinos equal access to afford-able health care, including free consultations and laboratory tests (Ranada 2019). The Department of Education's budget was increased from US$9 billion in 2016 to US$12 billion in 2017. The department's Commission on Higher Education also received a 234 percent increase in its budget (from US$107.6 million to US$359 million) as Duterte made true his promise of a tuition free education in state universities and colleges (Ranada 2017).

See also: Chapter 2: Overview; Communism; Marcos Dictatorship; Muslim Separatism; People Power Revolution. Chapter 4: Crony Capitalism; Land Reform.

Further Reading

Bacungan, Froilan M. 1983. *The Powers of the Philippine President*. Quezon City: University of the Philippines Law Center.

Coronel, Sheila, Yvonne T. Chua, Luz Rimban, and Booma Cruz. 2004. *The Rulemakers: How the Wealthy and the Well-Born Dominate Congress*. Manila: Philippine Center for Investigative Journalism.

Ranada Pia. 2017. "Duterte Signs Law for Free Tuition in State Colleges." *Rappler* (August 4). https://www.rappler.com/nation/177661-duterte-signs-law-free-tuition-state-colleges-universities/

Rood, Steven. 2019. *The Philippines: What Everyone Needs to Know*. New York and London: Oxford University Press.

Armed Forces of the Philippines

The Armed Forces of the Philippines (AFP) was formed in December 1935 with an organizational structure similar to that of the U.S. Armed Forces. It was immediately tested in World War II where—despite its inexperience—it slowed down the Japanese advance across Southeast Asia. In the postwar period, the AFP sent contingents to join the American-led United Nations Command that fought in Korea, and later, a small engineering battalion to Vietnam. But the AFP was mainly an internal defense force, suppressing a communist uprising in the 1950s, and then a separatist rebellion by the Moro National Liberation Force (MNLF) in Mindanao in 1975. After the war with the MNLF receded, the AFP launched counterinsurgency operations against the Communist Party of the Philippines (CPP). The AFP also fought the Moro Islamic Liberation Front (MILF) in 2000, when President Estrada ordered an all-out attack to destroy the MILF camps. The AFP overran the camps but withdrew once peace negotiations started under President Arroyo.

The AFP was designed as a professional, apolitical organization like its model, the U.S. Army. It changed in the mid-1960s when President Marcos turned it into a partner in his development agenda and used some of its units to wrest control of provinces and cities once under his political opponents. The AFP became Marcos's most valuable instrument during martial law, and it was its wars against the MNLF and the CPP that politicized the AFP. Officers began to attribute their failure to defeat the communists to corruption in the military leadership and to Marcos's turning the AFP into his private army. The more the army committed human rights abuses, the more the pro-Marcos generals looted military resources leaving the corps with inadequate support in its war against insurgents, and the more divided the organization became. In early 1981, young officers formed the Reform the AFP Movement (RAM) to pressure President Marcos to step down.

RAM, however, was not interested in removing politics from the organization. It staged several coups, first against Marcos and then against President Aquino. While the coups failed, they turned the AFP into a political player. They forced governments to abandon programs that the military deemed pro-communist. RAM signed a peace agreement with President Ramos, and its senior leaders shifted to electoral politics. Gregorio Honasan, the founder of RAM, was the most successful among the former coup plotters; he was repeatedly voted to the Senate.

Young officers continued to use extralegal means to exert pressure on governments. Too numerically weak to stage coups, these officers mutinied to try to force President Arroyo to resign. These rebellions failed and, like their RAM seniors, these officers ran for office. One of them, Antonio Trillanes, ran for senator for two terms.

After 9/11, the AFP had been actively pursuing the terrorist group Abu Sayyaf in southern Mindanao, together with U.S. forces that had been allowed to return to the Philippines under a new Enhanced Defense Cooperation Agreement (ECDA) signed by both countries. When China began modifying bases in coral reefs in the West Philippines into naval bases to assert its sovereignty, President Aquino III embarked on a modernization campaign to bring in weapons for external defense. Notwithstanding his anti-American, pro-Chinese position, President Duterte did not stop military modernization nor did he end the bilateral exercises between American and Filipino troops.

See also: Chapter 2: Overview; Communism; Marcos Dictatorship; Muslim Separatism; People Power Revolution.

Further Reading

Berlin, Donald. 2008. *Before Gringo: History of the Philippine Military, 1830 to 1972*. Pasay City: Anvil Publishing.

McCoy, Alfred W. 1999. *Closer Than Brothers: Manhood in the Philippine Military Academy*. New Haven and London: Yale University Press.

Yabes, Criselda J. 2009. *Boys from the Barracks: The Philippine Military after EDSA— Updated Edition*. Pasay City: Anvil Publishing.

Association of Southeast Asian Nations

The Philippines is one of the founding members of the Association of Southeast Asian Nations (ASEAN), an organization committed to the greater integration of the region's economy and to the fostering of political-military, educational, and cultural cooperation. ASEAN was formed on August 8, 1967, by Indonesia, Malaysia, the Philippines, Singapore, and Thailand and later expanded to include Brunei, Cambodia, Laos, Myanmar, and Vietnam. In 2017, the applications of Timor-Leste and Papua New Guinea for admission to the ASEAN were being deliberated by its members.

Its membership in ASEAN does not mean that the Philippines has no problems with its neighbors. Its territorial dispute with Malaysia over the Philippine claim that Sabah is its territory remains unresolved. The Philippines based its claim on the 1903 treaty between the Sultan of Sulu and the British East India Company where the sultan was paid 5,000 Malayan dollars a year for the leasing of Sabah by the Company. The smaller islands were also leased for 300 Malayan dollars a year. Forty-three years later, in 1946, the British government announced that it had annexed North Borneo and hence it was now a British colony. The Philippine government protested the proclamation citing the 1903 treaty.

After World War II, when the British government ceased paying the heirs of the Sultan of Sulu the agreed-upon compensation, the sultan appealed to the Philippine government for help. Congress responded by passing Republic Act 3046 on June 17, 1961, that showed the baseline of the Philippine territory. The new Malaysian government recognized the sultan's claims and agreed to remit US$1,710 annually to the sultan's heirs. The Philippines and the sultan referred to it as "rent," but the Malaysian government called it "cession payment."

President Diosdado Macapagal ratcheted up tensions by declaring that the Philippines was going to claim full sovereignty over Sabah because the republic was, to use Macapagal's term, the "successor state" to the sultanate after the heirs of the Sultan of Sulu renounced their claims on the territory. Macapagal broke off diplomatic relations with Malaysia after Sabah was included in the independent Federation of Malaysia. Malaysia's position was strengthened when a United Nations mission to Borneo reported that the majority of people in Sabah favored joining Malaysia. Diplomatic ties were restored in 1963, but the Sabah claim was unresolved.

Malaysia, however, accepted a compromise by acknowledging that the inclusion of Sabah to the federation would not prejudice the Philippine claim. The de facto truce did not last long. In 1968, the Philippine Congress passed Republic Act 5446, amending the previous law and formally declaring that the Republic of the Philippines had acquired dominion and sovereignty over Sabah. Both countries severed diplomatic ties again in 1968, but this time with little prospects of resolution. Shortly after, President Ferdinand Marcos was exposed for secretly organizing a team of Muslim commandos whose mission was to infiltrate Sabah and foment unrest that would then, by some miracle, convince the communities in Sabah to break away from the Malaysian federation and join the Philippines. Once exposed, Marcos ordered the training camp's closure and the execution of the trainees. One trainee managed to escape from the island, and after contacting an opposition senator, offered to testify against Mr. Marcos.

Malaysia reacted by offering the Muslim separatist group, MNLF, training camps in Sabah. Once the MNLF went to war against the Philippine government, Malaysia transported arms to the rebel groups. Malaysia also facilitated the travel of elite MNLF units that would train in Libya, the other major supporter of the Muslim rebellion. The two countries only resumed diplomatic ties in 1989, three years after the fall of Mr. Marcos.

The Philippines quietly continued to assert its sovereignty over Sabah and the outlying islands but stopped short of revisiting the tensions of the late 1960s. In 2002, the International Court of Justice (ICJ) ruled in favor of Malaysian sovereignty in two islands. The Philippine Supreme Court's rejoinder upheld the Sabah claim, but Malaysia responded by saying that henceforth Sabah was a nonissue and therefore nonnegotiable. Nur Misuari, the founding chairman of the MNLF, charged Malaysia in the ICJ, but Malaysia refused to take part in the proceedings.

On February 11, 2013, about 200 armed men landed in the town of Lahad Datu in southeastern Sabah, announcing that they were the army of Sulu's Jamalul Kiram III, the current claimant to the Sulu Sultanate which included Sabah. Malaysian security forces clashed with the group, killing 56 of the sultan's followers, 10 from the Malaysian police, and 6 Malaysian civilians caught in the crossfire. The claim was again shelved after Malaysia was invited to be one of two international mediators (the other being the United States) in the peace negotiations between the Philippine government and another Muslim armed separatist group, the Moro Islamic Liberation Front (MILF).

See also: Chapter 2: Overview; Communism; Muslim Separatism.

Further Reading

Abad, M. C. 2011. *The Philippines in ASEAN: Reflections from the Listening Room.* Pasig City: Anvil Publishing.

Banloi, Rommel. 2010. *The Philippines in ASEAN at Forty: Achievements, Challenges, and Prospects in Regional Security Cooperation.* Boca Raton, FL: Auerbach Publications.

Noble, Lela Garner. 1982. *Philippine Policy towards Sabah: A Claim to Independence.* Tempe, AZ: University of Arizona Press.

Civil Society Organizations

Civil society organizations (CSOs) are the contemporary versions of voluntary and charity groups which serve communities in various capacities. The first CSOs were the cofradias—brotherhoods that were established by Spanish friars to assist them in their proselytization. Then the American colonial government passed a law allowing residents to form nonprofit organizations. In the early years of the republic, nonprofits took the lead in building rural cooperatives, mutual aid societies, and worker and farmer associations. Their activities ranged from promoting livelihood projects, alternative accessible education, community health, and sustainable development to lobbying and protesting to defend communities or to express their disagreement with state policies.

Under martial law, CSOs were one of the several legal institutions that the opposition used to oppose President Marcos. The communists were especially adept at building one CSO after another, not only for these to become instruments of propaganda but also to provide legal cover for their underground organizing. Noncommunist groups eventually caught up with their radical rivals after the assassination of former senator Benigno Aquino Jr. in 1983 created a huge pool of potential supporters. They eventually became the core supporters of the presidential campaign of Corazon C. Aquino. During her presidency, Aquino moved to institutionalize CSOs as part of the political process. Article 2 of the 1987 Constitution enshrines "non-governmental, community-based or sector organizations that promote the welfare of the nations," while Article 8 requires the government to "respect the role of independent people's organizations." Finally, Article 13 instructs the state to pass laws that require government offices to seek CSO inputs "at all levels of social, political and economic decision-making." Congress supplemented these constitutional provisions by passing laws such as the 1990 Cooperative Code that promoted community cooperatives, and the 1992 Women in Development and Nation Building Act to encourage and formalize women's organizing.

CSOs strengthened their bargaining position by forming the Caucus of Development NGO Networks (CODE-NGO) in 1991 to expand CSO influence. The laws, the CODE-NGO, and the party-list system helped create a brushfire of CSO organizing. The relationship between CSOs and political leaders oscillated between close partnership and outright hostility. We have already mentioned President Corazon Aquino's close relationships with CSOs. This was also the case with her son Benigno S. Aquino III, who worked closely with CSOs in promoting transparency and accountability in government. CSOs were said to be the critical game-changers that won Fidel V. Ramos the presidency when it seemed like political parties were abandoning him. Presidents Estrada and Arroyo sought CSO support, but the concordat never lasted as CSOs became the fiercest critics of high-level corruption in these presidents' administrations.

In 2004, the Asian Development Bank reported that there were between 249,000 and 497,000 registered CSOs in the Philippines, making the country host to the largest number of CSOs per capita in Asia. This showed how much of the popular politics that was inspired by the People Power Revolution had dissipated. These numbers, however, are not good indicators of CSO success in mobilizing the poor and the marginalized.

See also: Chapter 2: Overview; Marcos Dictatorship; People Power Revolution.

Further Reading

Clarke, Gerard. 1998. *The Politics of NGOs in Southeast Asia: Participation and Protest in the Philippines*. New York: Routledge.

Clarke, Gerard. 2013. *Civil Society in the Philippines: Theoretical, Methodological, and Policy Debates*. Milton Park, Abingdon, Oxfordshire: Taylor and Francis.

Rivera, Rosa Maria V. 2003. *Managing Risk and Sustainability on Microfinance: War and Its Impact on Microfinance Clients and NGOs in the Philippines*. The Hague, the Netherlands: Institute of Social Studies.

Elections

Since 1992, national and local elections are held every third year on the second Monday of May, and these rituals of popular expression are supervised by a Commission on Elections (COMELEC). Registered voters must be at least 18 years of age and must have lived in the country for at least a year. A special election for local youth councils allows those between 15 and 18 years of age to vote. Unlike in the United States, Philippine parties have no primaries. Political parties chose a candidate from their ranks or invite outsiders as guest candidates. Party loyalties are not robust, and it is not unusual for candidates to switch parties to run for office. For example, six candidates switched parties to win the presidency (Manuel L. Roxas, Ramon Magsaysay, Ferdinand E. Marcos, Fidel V. Ramos, Joseph E. Estrada, and Gloria M. Arroyo). Party-switching often continues even after elections, with successful congressional or senatorial candidates joining the legislative majority.

On election day, voters write down the names of their preferred candidates on ballots that are then collected and polled by Boards of Elections (often comprising public school teachers drafted for this purpose). The counted ballots are then sent to the city or municipal Boards of Canvassers, which then prepare a Statement of Votes and a Certificate of Canvass of total votes that will be sent to a National Board of Canvassers that reaffirms their validity and proclaims the winners. In 2010, elections became automated with 92,500 voting machines operating across the country.

Special elections are held when general elections are delayed or when there is a vacated seat in Congress, the presidency or the vice presidency. The government can also hold referenda and plebiscites to revise and amend the Constitution, approve or reject legislation, and abolish local governments and autonomous regions. Local officials can be subjected to recall by 25 percent of registered voters of that district. Voters could likewise organize "people's initiatives" to amend or revise the Constitution. For this to happen, at least 12 percent of registered voters must sign the petition, with 3 percent of these voters coming from a legislative district.

When it comes to the extensive revision or wholesale replacement of the Constitution, the process goes through two stages. The first is for the president to call for delegates to a constitutional convention, with Congress deciding on how many delegates should be elected for each district. So far, the country has had four constitutional conventions. In 1986, President Corazon C. Aquino did not go the convention route but instead formed a 48-person constitutional commission to change what was called "the Marcos Constitution." The drafts of the constitutions of 1934, 1971, and 1986 were subjected to a plebiscite and formally passed by three-fourths majority.

The administration of President Benigno Arroyo III published a revised and expanded version of the Philippine Electoral Almanac, and in the section on presidents, it produced the following interesting points. Ten of the presidents had come from Luzon (Manuel V. Quezon, Elpidio R. Quirino, Ramon Magsaysay, Diosdado Macapagal, Ferdinand E. Marcos, Corazon C. Aquino, Fidel V. Ramos, Joseph E. Estrada, Gloria M. Arroyo, and Benigno S. Aquino III), two from the Visayas (Sergio

Osmeña and Carlos P. Garcia), and only one from Mindanao (Rodrigo R. Duterte). Before 1986, seven of the successful presidential teams had candidates who represented the two major regions of the country: one came from Luzon and the other from the Visayas. The combination, however, changed in 1986, with all the presidents and vice presidents coming from Manila. In 2016, Duterte became the first candidate from Mindanao to be elected president, but it is most likely that his case is an exception rather than an indication of a new trend. Two women became presidents (Corazon C. Aquino and Gloria M. Arroyo), and four children of former presidents were themselves elected to the highest national office.

Elections were first introduced in 1786 when the Spanish gave local town elites the right to vote for their municipal officials. The Americans expanded suffrage in 1902 when wealthy educated men were allowed to vote at the municipal and provincial levels; and from 1907 to 1915, they were allowed to elect members to the Philippine Assembly. A House of Representatives was established in 1916 as the lower body of the assembly, and its members were elected by popular vote. In 1935, women were allowed to vote for the first time.

Filipinos always suspected that President Marcos was manipulating elections, plebiscites, and referenda during martial law. Ironically, it was also such kind of elections that proved to be Marcos's undoing, when his call for snap elections in December 1984 became the catalyst for the 1986 People Power Revolution that ousted him. Communists have also tried to delegitimize elections as nothing but a conflict between elites, with the majority having no say in their outcomes. Filipinos, in turn, have repeatedly rebuked communist entreaties and gone to the polls. However, the electoral choices of Filipinos can be unusual. Take the Senate, for example. In the early years of the republic, those elected were politicians with a legal background, exceptional skills, and even principles. There were occasional instances when nonpoliticians, such as movie stars, were elected, but they were a minority. In the 1980s, however, the composition of the Senate became more mixed. Politicians with principles remained, but there was also an influx of nonpoliticians like movie stars, television and sports figures, former police officers, and military officers. Whether this change in the Senate's composition has affected presidential and legislative agenda remains a question that needs studying.

See also: Chapter 1: Administrative Regions. Chapter 2: Overview; Marcos Dictatorship; People Power Revolution.

Further Reading

Arguillas, Carolyn, Yvonne Chua, and Luz Rimban. 2011. *Democracy at Gunpoint: Election-Related Violence in the Philippines.* Makati City: Asia Foundation.

Franco, Jennifer Conroy. 2001. *Elections and Democratization in the Philippines.* New York: Routledge.

Philippine Center for Investigative Journalism. 2012. *Elections Special: The History of Philippine Elections.* Manila. Video File.

Federalism

The idea of federalism has been proposed by political leaders as an alternative to the presidential system. Critics of the latter argue that the failure of the economy to achieve a breakthrough and the failure of politics to be genuinely democratized has a lot to do with power being too concentrated on the top (i.e., the presidency and its executive offices) and the use of natural resources—from money to commodities to people's expertise—being dominated by the national capital, Manila. They argue that by shifting to a federal form of government, these imbalances can be corrected. Granting political autonomy to the provinces and cities by devolving certain functions of the national government (such as health, social welfare, education, among others) to the local level makes government much closer to the majority of Filipinos while also improving the administrative ability of provincial and city governments tremendously. Whereas in the past people only encountered faceless bureaucrats coming to the capital or administrators from outside of town assigned to a locality with very little knowledge of the place, devolution and autonomy enable them to experience what it is like to be governed more closely. Such ties also mean that people can monitor government projects and make political leaders accountable for failures or problems in their administration. Not all national government functions would be moved to the local level; national defense and foreign policy will remain in the national capital.

Federalism advocates point to the rebellion of the MNLF and the MILF and the subsequent concession by Manila to grant Muslims some degree of autonomy as evidence of the regressive effects of a powerful presidency. The state was forced to fight a war against a force that wanted to separate the southern parts of the country because they were never really Philippine territory, and when the fog of war cleared, had to agree to some form of Muslim autonomy. They argue that these confrontations can be avoided in the future by a federal system of government.

Critics of federalism claim that while the presidency is indeed a powerful office, real political power resides in the provinces and cities where political dynasties have long reigned supreme. Local elites use their access to a province's resources (land, minerals) to take control of elections and keep local administration firmly in the hands of the family and their allies. These families use "guns, goons, and gold" to bribe and convince voters to keep them in power. Once their control of provincial or city government is consolidated, these families elect members to the House of Representatives and protect their interests in the national capital. Critics of federalism have repeatedly pointed out the many instances in which Congress has stymied executive programs, especially those like land reform where the promotion of the welfare of the rural poor often threatens the landed estates of the elites.

They argue that federalism is not the answer; what will enhance democracy and enable Filipinos to contribute to economic development is a political project to end, if not weaken, the power of local elites. This project can mean voters being able to send a qualified and pro-people candidate to local and congressional office. An alternative also creates opportunities for dynamic groups like the entrepreneurial middle class and the ambitious poor to become active contributors to and beneficiaries of the local economy. To the argument that the current system gives too much power to the presidency and the national capital, these critics answer by pointing at how the 1987 Constitution has provided Congress and the Supreme Court enough authority to check the executive.

In 2017, President Rodrigo R. Duterte urged Congress to move forward with his proposal for a federal system, insisting that this was the best way to solve the conflict in Mindanao. In early 2018, he formed a presidential commission consisting of political leaders, jurists, and academics that would deliberate on the best way for the country to switch systems with minimum disruption to governance.

See also: Chapter 1: Provinces; Administrative Regions. Chapter 2: Overview; Muslim Separatism.

Further Reading

Araral, Eduardo, Jr., Paul D. Hutchcroft, Gilberto M. Llanto, Jonathan E. Malaya, Ronald U. Mendoza, Julio C. Teehankee. 2018. *Debate on Federal Philippines: A Citizen's Handbook*. Quezon City: Ateneo de Manila University Press.

Miral, Romulo E. M. 2017. "Federalism Prospects for the Philippines." *Philippine Institute for Development Studies Discussion Paper Series*. Manila. https://econpapers.repec.org/paper/phddpaper/dp_5f2017-29.htm

Martial Law

If there was ever a presidential reign that had the most profound impact on modern Philippine society, it was President Ferdinand E. Marcos's 15-year one-man rule. On September 21, 1972, Marcos announced that he was placing the country under martial law to neutralize right-wing and left-wing threats and to deal with growing violence in Muslim Mindanao. Over 30,000 were jailed in the first months. Most Filipinos acquiesced to martial law, seeing it as a chance for the country to stabilize. The only exceptions were the Muslim areas where the separatist armed MNLF waged war against the AFP.

On September 21, 1972, Marcos declared martial law to allegedly neutralize the threats coming from oligarchs, communists, and Muslim separatists. He closed Congress, schools, and media establishments and sent military teams to arrest over 30,000 of his opponents. He broke up the communist network in the cities and drove what remained of the movement's ranks to the countryside.

Anti-Marcos Muslim politicians and students, however, were not easily silenced. They joined the MNLF either as allies or as its members. Some were sent to Libya and Malaysia for military training, and, upon their return, were assigned to command and lead MNLF assault teams. Malaysia supported the MNLF to show its displeasure over Marcos' revival of the Philippines' Sabah claim and his attempt to train a special unit that would infiltrate Sabah and commit acts of sabotage. Libyan leader Muammar Gaddafi got behind the secessionists after being convinced that the Marcos government was committing genocide against Muslims in Mindanao. In 1973, MNLF forces began attacking several towns in the Muslim areas, and the Philippines experienced its second conventional war after the Japanese occupation. The war died down three years later, following peace talks brokered by Libya, but it also never went away. In 1977, the Moro Islamic Liberation Front (MILF) was formed after a split in the MNLF.

Early in his administration, Marcos had pushed an ambitious national economic development plan that opened the economy to promote what economists then called "nontraditional exports" (fruits, fish resources, and Filipino labor). He also launched a massive infrastructure program to connect the entire country. He succeeded in the first— there was rapid expansion of export crop agriculture via joint ventures between Filipino and foreign corporations, and the export of Filipino labor continues to this day. The promised modernization, however, never happened.

The Marcos-era land reform program had been no different from Macapagal's, targeting rice and corn lands but not export crops and real estate. Export agriculture brought in new revenues, but it hardly benefited communities where the plantations were located. In fact, the spread of banana and pineapple lands came at the expense of food crops. Marcos had also invited foreign corporations to help speed up the country's industrialization program (always considered a sign of modernization), but foreign manufacturers only shared technology on ancillary components to industrial products and not the core machinery. Car parts would be branded "Made in the Philippines," but the engine—the most critical component—remained American or Japanese made.

Economic development at the time was also debt-driven and justified as a means to jump-start pioneer industries. The surge in exports compensated for this liability and enriched the public coffers. By the late 1970s, however, exports floundered (sugar prices, for example, collapsed in the global market), and the government had to rescue faltering crony firms, forcing Marcos's economic managers to borrow more money. At the start of the early 1980s, the government was not only compensating for the disparity in exports and imports or coming to the rescue of crony corporations, it was also borrowing money to cover loan payment obligations. The total external debt had by then reached US$24.4 billion, forcing the Marcos government to admit to the International Monetary Fund (IMF) and the World Bank that it could not pay its debts on time.

But it was cronyism that was the bane of Philippine modernization. Marcos bequeathed to family and cronies some of the most critical and well-funded projects in nuclear energy, infrastructure, transportation, pharmaceuticals, mining, and consumer service. The government centralized the production and marketing of the coconut and sugar industries under the guise of rationalizing these traditional exports and making them more competitive in the global market. In reality, these were given as booties to close associates and kin who went on to use the revenues to expand their private businesses, leaving very little to sugar and coconut farmers. By the 1980s, famine was endemic, and poverty had worsened in the coconut and sugar industries. One day, a Chinese businessman with connections to Marcos's cronies fled the country, leaving about US$5 billion in debt.

Then, on August 21, 1983, Marcos's chief rival, former senator Benigno Aquino Jr., was assassinated by his police escort at the airport tarmac. This sparked massive protests, and the country defaulted on its debts a month after. Around 56 percent of the gross domestic product now went to paying debts (it was only 35 percent in 1980), forcing Marcos's technocrats to plead for emergency loans from the World Bank and commercial banks. Then, the chairman of the Philippine Central Bank was exposed as having manipulated the figures to give the IMF the impression that the government still had money in reserve. The economic outlook had gone from bad to worse.

The pressure on Marcos to step down had intensified, with the U.S. Congress and many European nations joining in. After overcoming its early setbacks, the Communist Party of the Philippines (CPP) was now a national threat, as the communists drew in thousands who were victims of military abuses and other human rights violations. Even the anti-communists in the anti-Marcos opposition had warmed to the idea of allying with their radical rivals to oust Marcos. Finally, the AFP, which was once Marcos's most reliable support base, began to fragment. Middle-level officers formed the Reform the AFP Movement (RAM) and demanded an end to institutional corruption.

Then, to everyone's surprise, Marcos announced a snap presidential election to prove he still had Filipinos' loyalty. The various opposition groups unified under Aquino's widow, Corazon ("Cory") Aquino, who submitted her candidacy. Marcos cheated his way to victory, but two weeks after he was proclaimed the winner, RAM staged a coup. It was aborted, but the coup plotters were saved when more than one million people took to the streets to carry on protesting, which in effect protected the military camps where soldiers had retreated. After a three-day impasse, military units switched sides and the People Power Revolution sent Marcos and his family to their Hawaiian exile.

See also: Chapter 2: Overview; Communism; Extrajudicial Killings; Marcos Dictatorship; Muslim Separatism; People Power Revolution. Chapter 4: Crony Capitalism; Land Reform; Overseas Filipino Workers; Taxation.

Further Reading

De Dios, Aurora Javate, Petronilo Daroy, and Lorna Kalaw-Tirol, eds. 1998. *Dictatorship and Revolution: Roots of People's Power.* Manila: Conspectus.

Hutchcroft, Paul D. 1998. *Booty Capitalism: The Politics of Banking in the Philippines.* Ithaca and London: Cornell University Press.

Thompson, Mark. 1995. *The Anti-Marcos Struggle: Personalistic Rule and Democratic Transition in the Philippines.* New Haven and London: Yale University Press.

Political Clans

Scholars studying Philippine politics agree that real power is in the hands of political families. The first generation emerged out of the late Spanish period, where they were overseers of the friar-owned land estates that produced food and export crops. While some joined the nationalist revolution, the majority joined the Americans and ran for local offices and the Philippine Assembly in 1906. These clans dominated colonial politics and continued to be influential in the postwar period as they held control in the provinces by keeping the offices within the family. Provincial politics is, therefore, a musical chair where children or spouses take over the post once the senior patriarch or matriarch reaches their term limit.

After the war, however, a new elite emerged. They were former guerrilla fighters who used the weapons they had amassed during World War II to set themselves up in their political "bailiwicks," in provinces and towns where no clans were in power. Fluent in the argot of their home regions, they assured their constituents that they would represent "their interests" in the legislature and the executive. They presented themselves as the mediators between national politicians and their local constituents. They consolidated, defended, and expanded their power by controlling local elections using goons with guns to physically intimidate voters and their rivals or buying electors' votes.

The old and new elites coexisted with one another and formed coalitions, often short-term, to win in elections. The alliances often revolved around party-mates offering each other the votes of their ethnolinguistic constituents. Successful presidential teams were the results of these linguistic coalitions working successfully, while senatorial teams consisting of candidates coming from different dialects also had better chances of winning.

During martial law, the relations between the prewar and postwar political clans broke down as President Marcos centralized power, weakened the clans using the AFP, and installed his network of allies, many of them postwar strongmen like him. Some of these disenfranchised families formed loose anti-Marcos associations, while others withdrew to ride out the authoritarian storm. Once Marcos was ousted and President Corazon C. Aquino restored democratic politics, the clans reclaimed control of the local governments and the legislature. A new generation of political

Joseph Estrada (center), from action movie star to president (1998–2001). (Department of Defense)

families rose, consisting of cronies and supporters of President Marcos and a few coming from the entertainment industry. Like the postwar clans, they relied on their access to the resources of elective offices, but some began to rely on their links with illicit sectors where profits from drugs, arms trade, and human trafficking were relatively high.

Filipinos began to be exposed to the culture of local politics with the election of Joseph Estrada, a former action movie star whose main political experience was being mayor of a small municipality in Manila. Estrada treated the presidency like he was running a small town, together with his clique of kin and sidekicks. President Rodrigo Duterte also brought to the presidential palace the roughness of local politics that included its crass argot. Estrada's wife, mistress, and sons followed him, and the clan now has significant clout in national politics (his two sons are in the Senate). Duterte ruled Davao City for 23 years and when he became president, the Duterte family's control of their home city never diminished. His daughter, who was elected mayor in 2016, ran as vice president in 2022. Her youngest brother was the vice mayor, while another brother was elected to the House of Representatives.

Political clans have shown so much resilience that it is hard to imagine a Philippine system without them.

See also: Chapter 2: Overview; Marcos Dictatorship; Chapter 4: Overview; Land Reform; Chapter 6: Elites.

Further Reading

Coronel, Sheila. 1998. *Pork and Other Perks: Corruption and Governance in the Philippines*. Manila: Philippine Center for Investigative Journalism.

Coronel, Sheila S., and Jose F. Lacaba, eds. 1995. *Boss: 5 Case Studies of Local Politics in the Philippines*. Pasig City: Philippine Center for Investigative Journalism; Quezon City: Institute for Popular Democracy.

McCoy, Alfred W., ed. 2009. *An Anarchy of Families: State and Family in the Philippines*, 548 pp. Madison, WI: University of Wisconsin Press.

Post-Marcos Philippines

Presidents Corazon C. Aquino and Fidel V. Ramos were left with an economic mess and a highly politicized society. It was only under Ramos that the economy turned, with its persistently negative growth steadily turning positive. This involved reducing the government's involvement in the economy, which was quite pervasive in the Marcos period. State corporations were privatized, and the government increased its financial reserves by selling off government lands. Ramos also pushed further to liberalize the economy, that is, to open more areas to foreign investments, promote joint ventures between Filipino and non-Filipino firms, and to expand incentives like reduced taxes to multinational corporations already operating in the country. Ramos also continued to encourage Filipinos to seek employment abroad as their remittances began to comprise the largest percentage of the national revenue. The presidents who followed Ramos continued what Ramos started even if they disagreed with one another politically.

Thus one major feature of the post-Marcos political landscape is this consistency in government efforts to enhance the Philippines' participation in the globalization process.

Politically, each president left their mark on the democratic system. Corazon Aquino restored constitutional politics and fundamental freedoms (press, assembly, right to vote) and recognized the need to empower the poor and the marginalized through the party-list system and closer government–civil society collaboration. However, "Auntie Cory," as she was popularly known, also presided over the resurrection of the political clans as the centers of power in the regions outside the capital. These families reclaimed their control of local offices (city mayor, provincial governor, etc.) as well as the Lower House of Congress. In power, these families supported a watered-down version of President Aquino's land reform program, turned offices devolved from the national government to the local governments into their sources of spoils, and captured the 40 percent of tax revenues returned to the local government under the new tax system—and used these to advance their interests. Joseph E. Estrada received one of the highest percentages of popular votes as a candidate but wasted his political capital by acting unpresidential—for example, having nightlong drinking binges with friends and cronies. He was also exposed by a former ally as involved in the illegal numbers game. He was later forced to resign by an army-backed popular uprising. President Gloria M. Arroyo promised a "strong republic" that would pursue an economic development agenda for the benefit of all Filipinos and not just for the affluent few.

In fact, there was a discernible pattern where there was economic growth at one end while Philippine democracy kept repeatedly

Gloria Macapagal Arroyo, 14th President of the Philippines (2001–2010), daughter of Diosdado Macapagal, the 9th President. Arroyo's past positions include Senator (199–1998), Vice President (1998–2001), Secretary of National Defense (2006–2007), and Speaker of the House of Representatives (2018–2019). (Mario Soriano/ Dreamstime.com)

floundering at the other. Presidents Ramos and Gloria M. Arroyo pushed for revisions to the Constitution to extend their hold on the office beyond the six-year, one-term limit, and President Rodrigo Duterte promised to form a constitutional commission to advance administrative decentralization by changing the prevailing system into a federal form of government. President Ramos found a way to work with political families wherein he looked the other way when their plundered state resources in exchange for their support for his economic development programs. President Arroyo did something similar, gaining the support of the political families by doling out development funds ostensibly for the needs of their districts, which often ended up in the family coffers. This tactic unfortunately worked against Arroyo's favor when her stature was compromised after a political clan loyal to her was implicated in the massacre of 58 people in Muslim Mindanao.

President Benigno S. Aquino III was able to fulfill part of his promise to end government corruption and received praise from foreign governments and international economic institutions like the World Bank for having reduced this problem significantly. Aquino III, however, was also criticized for only targeting his family's enemies and Arroyo's officials. Like Arroyo, his reputation suffered at the end of his term after he gave a tepid response to the death of 44 law enforcement officers in a botched raid to arrest an Islamic terrorist. His seeming apathy and his anti-corruption crusade had the inadvertent consequence of the public seeing Aquino III's administration as designed to protect the elite.

Rodrigo R. Duterte won the May 2016 presidential election by portraying himself as the anti-elite candidate who would also deal with what he claimed was the country's main scourge—drug addiction. Duterte had been unrelenting in his anti-drug campaign: in its November 22, 2021 issue, the *Economist* presented a table of casualties given by different international and national organizations (the Philippine Drug Enforcement Agency) as shown in Table 3.1.

Human rights advocates have repeatedly criticized Duterte, but his popularity remained at a high 83 percent. His economic managers had not deviated from the liberalization policy that President Ramos started.

TABLE 3.1: DUTERTE'S DIRTY WORK: PHILIPPINES, CIVILIAN DEATHS FROM THE WAR ON DRUGS (ESTIMATES FROM SELECTED INVESTIGATIONS)

Organization	Deaths	Date
International Criminal Court	12.000–30,000	July 2106–March 2019
United Nations Office of the High Commissioner for Human Rights	8,663	July 2016–June 2020
The Armed Conflict Location and Event Data Project	7,742	January 2016–November 2021
ABS-CBN Investigative and Research Group	6,840	May 2016–June 2021
Philippine Drug Enforcement Agency	6.201	July 2016–September 2021
Dahas database	3,891	July 2016–June 2021

Source: Armed Conflict Location and Event Data Project (*The Economist* 2021).

See also: Chapter 2: Overview; Extrajudicial Killings (EJK); Marcos Dictatorship

Further Reading

The Economist. 2021. "Daily Chart: How Many People Have Been Killed in Rodrigo Duterte's War on Drugs?" (November 22). https://www.economist.com/graphic-detail/2021/11/22/how-many-people-have-been-killed-in-rodrigo-dutertes-war-on-drugs

Eder, James F., and Robert L. Youngblood. 1994. *Patterns of Power and Politics in the Philippines: Implications for Development.* Tempe, AZ: Arizona University Program for Southeast Asian Studies.

Kerklviet, Benedict J., and Resil B. Mojares. 1992. *From Marcos to Aquino: Local Perspectives on Political Transition in the Philippines.* Honolulu, HI: University of Hawaii Press.

Thompson, Mark, and Eric Batalla. 2018. *Routledge Handbook on Contemporary Philippines.* Milton Park, Abingdon, Oxfordshire: Taylor and Francis.

White, Lynne, III. 2014. *Philippine Politics: Possibilities and Problems in a Localist Democracy.* London and New York: Routledge

Presidential Emergency Powers

The power of the president to declare martial law is a provision embedded in the 1935 and 1987 Philippine constitutions. It is regarded as a temporary measure that a president can invoke as commander-in-chief of the AFP in case of an invasion or a rebellion that could threaten the nation. Under martial law, a president can suspend the privilege of the writ of habeas corpus (the right of an arrested person to be presented to the courts). The writ has been suspended 14 times—the first on January 31, 1905, when American governor general Luke E. Wright declared a state of emergency in the provinces of Cavite and Batangas to crush Filipino forces. Then, between 1939 and 1941, the legislature granted President Manuel L. Quezon emergency powers to prepare for war. This was followed by a formal declaration of martial law—the first ever—once Japanese forces invaded the Philippines. President Jose P. Laurel, of the puppet republic set up by the Japanese, also declared martial law in September 1944 as Allied forces advanced toward Manila. After the war, President Elpidio R. Quirino suspended the writ of habeas corpus when there was news that the CPP's guerrilla army was threatening the capital.

All these were proclamations of short duration, with the executives mentioned cognizant of their temporary nature. President Ferdinand E. Marcos, however, interpreted the martial law provision differently. He warned that a communist insurgency and an Islamic rebellion and a plot by oligarchs was threatening the stability of the republic, prompting him to declare martial law. A few months later, Marcos had changed the narrative, and a new theme had supplanted the threats. This time, martial law had an indefinite timetable, and its lifting was contingent on how fast the government could build a "New Society" to replace the oligarchic old. This pretext would last for 14 years until Marcos was overthrown in 1986.

President Corazon C. Aquino placed the country under a de facto state of emergency twice—first in August 1987 and then in December 1989—to push back several coup attempts by the military. The threats notwithstanding, President Aquino had already legitimized her government with the drafting of a new Constitution—the so-called "Cory Constitution." Still, 48 hours after declaring martial law, the president must submit a report to the joint houses of Congress which may, in turn, either approve or revoke the proclamation. If approved, martial law is not to exceed 60 days.

President Gloria M. Arroyo availed of the state of emergency provision twice. The first time was when she ordered the military to suppress what she considered a rebellion by the allies of the former ousted president Joseph E. Estrada in May 2001. The second time was on December 4, 2009, when she placed the province of Maguindanao under martial law after the massacre of 59 people by the warlord Andal Ampatuan. This allowed the military to raid Ampatuan's well-defended palatial homes, arrest some of his followers and other family members, and confiscate his vast collection of high-powered weapons. A week later, Arroyo lifted martial law. Finally, in May 2017, President Rodrigo R. Duterte proclaimed martial law for the entire island of Mindanao, supposedly to contain Islamic terrorism after members of the Middle Eastern group ISIS attacked and occupied the Muslim city of Marawi. Duterte asked for an extension after the 60-day limit expired and Congress approved the president's request.

See also: Chapter 2: Overview; Communism; Extrajudicial Killings; Marcos Dictatorship; Muslim Separatism; People Power Revolution.

Further Reading

Abueva, Jose V. 1999. *The Making of the Filipino Nation and Republic: The Pamana Series*, 1078 pp. Quezon City: University of the Philippines Press.

Rosenberg, David, ed. 1979. *Marcos and Martial Law in the Philippines*. Ithaca and London: Cornell University Press.

Relations with Japan

Japan considered the Philippines to be part of a larger Southeast Asian world. The ties between the two countries went back as far as the Spanish period, when Manila was sending missionaries to Japan in the 16th century and as many as 3,000 Japanese settled outside of Manila. The beginnings of a robust trade in the mid-17th century were cut off once Japan decided to isolate itself from the outside world. There was also a series of revolts in Manila, which the Japanese led or participated in.

Japan returned to the Philippines in 1941 as an occupation army. The military established a puppet government and revived Philippine nationalism under the guise of its dream of creating a "Greater East Asia Co-Prosperity Sphere." This regime was short-lived as the United States liberated the Philippines in three years. Diplomatic relations between Japan and the now-independent Philippine republic were established in 1956 as part of the postwar reparations agreement. Japanese investments rose since then, despite the absence of any trade agreement. That agreement was only signed in 1975.

Japanese investments and development funds are now an enduring presence in the Philippines, and the Philippines is a destination for Japanese tourists. Not everything has gone smoothly though. Philippine civil society groups have demanded that Japan apologize for allowing its army to keep Filipinas as "comfort women" during World War II. The Japanese government has still resisted pressure to recognize this issue and pay restitution for the women's enslavement. By the 1980s, another social problem affecting Japanese-Philippine relations was the growing number of Filipinas being recruited into Japan's seamy entertainment districts as demand for bar girls rose. Civil society groups condemned this exploitation of Filipinas who were now derisively called Japayuki, which was a metaphor for a courtesan. Japanese men were also facing difficulties finding a spouse with Japanese women becoming more focused on their occupation. The only option open to them was to seek what the local media called "mail-order-brides," and many of them would come from the Philippines. Scholars from both countries have shown how these marriages have changed the nature of Filipino and Japanese families. Filipinos refer to their children now as Japinos (fusing of the syllables "Jap" and "inos") while a new term has become part of the Japanese language: *hafu*, which is an adaptation of the word "half."

Japan's support for the Philippines has mainly been economic, with much of its loans and related funds devoted primarily to infrastructure development. Starting 2008, however, Japan has played an increasingly important role in helping the peace negotiations between the MILF and the Philippine government move forward. It has assisted in the training programs that would help MILF guerrillas transition into administrative positions, provided support to MILF communities needing immediate assistance, and joined an international monitoring team that prevents hostilities from breaking out or keeps them to a minimum.

In 2016, Japan broadened its support to the Philippines, signing an agreement to provide the latter with defense equipment and technology to help President Benigno S. Aquino III's plan to modernize the external defense capabilities of the AFP. Japanese warships also made frequent goodwill visits to the Philippines.

See also: Chapter 2: Overview. Chapter 4: Economic Assistance.

Further Reading

De Castro, Renato Cruz. 2009. "Exploring a 21st-Century Japan-Philippine Security Relationship: Linking Two Spokes Together?" *Asian Survey* 49, no. 4 (July): 691–715.

Setsuho, Ikehata, and Lydia Yu-Jose. 2003. *Philippine-Japan Relations*. Quezon City: Ateneo de Manila University Press.

Van De Haar, Edwin. 2011. "Philippine Trade Policy and the Japan-Philippines Economic Partnership Agreement (JPEPA)." *Contemporary Southeast Asia: Journal of International and Strategic Affairs* 33, no. 1: 113–139.

Relations with the People's Republic of China

The South China Sea's importance has been underscored of late because different countries are claiming sovereignty over the area. The issue has to do mainly with which country has sovereignty over a set of reefs as well as over the Spratly and Paracel islands between Vietnam and the Philippines. Seven countries have staked their claim over this expanse: Brunei, Indonesia, Malaysia, the People's Republic of China, the Republic of Taiwan, the Philippines, and Vietnam. Another group of countries led by the United States, India, and Japan wants the area to remain part of international waters, given that a significant chunk of the global trade goes through it.

The economic interests behind each country's claim are quite clear: the region accounts for 8 percent of the world's fish catch, and everyone believes that besides natural gas, there is between 11 billion and 17.7 billion tons of crude oil beneath the ocean floor. Around 1947, Nationalist China had first laid claim to the area, drawing an imaginary nine-dash line that covers most of the South China Sea. When the communists defeated the nationalists and established the People's Republic of China, the new regime picked up the claim.

Southeast Asian countries shortly made their claims to parts of the South China Sea. Some worked alone, but there were instances where these countries negotiated. In the 1970s, the Philippines and Vietnam staked their claims in the area, and in the 1980s, the Chinese followed suit. Thus, between 1973 and 1982, tensions flared up after the United Nations Convention on the Law of the Sea (UNCLOS) approved the 200-nautical-mile zone. This time, China's claim overlapped with the exclusive economic zones of Brunei, Indonesia, Malaysia, the Philippines, Taiwan, and Vietnam. These countries then asserted their claims on the Chinese-claimed territory, to which China responded with belligerence, refusing to participate in any arbitration and demanding that the United States and Japan distance themselves from the parties. The latter has responded by reiterating that the South China Sea is in international waters and demanding that China not impede the freedom of navigation across this basin. These countries backed up their claims by sending their naval fleets to the area and conducting regular surveillance of Chinese activities.

In 2012, Chinese boats evicted Filipino fishers from the area and went on to build bases in the islands and set up a blockade to keep Filipino fisherfolk out of the zone. Chinese militarization picked up speed after an international tribunal ruled in favor of the Philippine claim. Refusing to recognize the court's decision and calling it illegal, China hastened its military buildup in the area. Former president Benigno S. Aquino III moved to modernize the country's external defense, but President Rodrigo R. Duterte reversed everything by distancing himself from the United States while reaching out to China. In early 2020, Duterte appeared to create the possibility of a full break when he ordered the termination of the Visiting Forces Agreement with the United States.

See also: Relations with the United States. Chapter 1: Overview. Chapter 2: Communism.

Further Reading

Baviera, Aileen. 2000. *Comprehensive Engagement: Strategic Issues in Philippines-China Relations*. Quezon City: Philippine-China Development Resource Center.

Haberer, Claude. 2009. *Between Tiger and Dragon: A History of Philippine Relations with China and Taiwan*. Pasay City: Anvil Publishing.

Rabena, Aaron. 2018. "The Complex Interdependence of China's Belt and Road Initiative in the Philippines." *Asia and Pacific Policy Studies* 5, no. 3 (September): 683–697.

Relations with the United States

Two different threads define Philippine-U.S. relations. The first and dominant thread is the United States turning a blind eye to the corruption and repressiveness of Filipino elites because of its strategic interest in maintaining its power and hegemony in the Asian region. The second and weaker thread refers to attempts by American and Filipino reformists to correct the power imbalances in the Philippines.

There were two instances where these threads intersected with each other with varying results. Shortly after the Philippines was granted its independence, on July 4, 1946, the new republic faced the threat of a communist uprising that was instigated by police attacks on members of the Partido Komunista ng Pilipinas and the removal of communist representatives in the House of Representatives. With the constabulary— the agency whose primary assignment was maintaining domestic stability— experiencing difficulty quelling the rebellion, the public turned against President Elpidio Quirino whose alleged corruption accounted for the government's inability to quell the rebellion. This worried the United States' Central Intelligence Agency (CIA), Filipino professionals, church people, and noncommunist trade unions and peasant associations. In response, these groups put up Quirino's defense secretary Ramon Magsaysay as their presidential candidate, cultivating his image as a "Man of the People" who would stop the communists and cleanse the government of its corruption. Magsaysay won the elections while successfully ending the communist uprising with assistance from the CIA.

Unfortunately, Magsaysay was not able to accomplish his reform promises because of his untimely death. The reformist coalition he formed, however, persisted, developing free elections campaigns, sponsoring reformist candidates in the legislature, and filling up the gap in worker and peasant organizing after the coalition's communist rivals were destroyed. The coalition's position, however, weakened when American policymakers decided that security considerations were more important than internal reforms as the United States ratcheted up its involvement in the Vietnam War. This thread dominated Philippine-American relations for the next two and a half decades.

The second time these two threads intersected was in the mid-1980s, when American officials worried about the stability of President Marcos's regime. The U.S. State Department and several senators began pushing for democratic reforms and support for the kinds of groups in the Philippines that constituted Magsaysay's mass base. This moderate coalition was the vanguard in the ouster of Marcos and the installation of Corazon Aquino as president, and it had the support of pro-reform American leaders who successfully convinced pro-security colleagues, including President Ronald Reagan, that American security interests would be better served under a democratic regime than an authoritarian one. They were wrong. Aquino was committed to the alliance, but her supporters in the Senate were not. In September 1991, senators voted not to renew the military bases agreement. The United States responded by cutting aid to the Philippines drastically. The reformist thread prevailed, but this time at the expense of security.

Philippine-American relations underwent a revival with the rise of Islamic terrorism, after a terrorist attempt to plant bombs in American planes going back to the mainland was foiled in Manila. These ties were further strengthened when American and Filipino forces worked together to rescue an American missionary couple kidnapped by Islamic terrorists. Presidents Arroyo and Estrada followed this up by pushing for a new visiting forces agreement in 1999; this was signed during Estrada's term. In 2000, the first joint military exercises were staged. American special forces were also sent to the Philippine south to help Philippine forces defeat Islamic terrorist groups. In 2014, President Benigno S. Aquino III signed the Enhanced Defense Cooperation Agreement (EDCA) allowing Americans to operate inside Philippine bases, in response to the growing tensions with China. President Rodrigo R. Duterte consistently attacked the U.S. government over its alleged interference in his drug war and declared his plan to ally with China and Russia. The Philippine military, however, continued to maintain strong ties with the United States, while a significant majority of Filipinos (92 percent) remained pro-American. In this last episode, the two threads appeared to have fused together as the feature of 21st-century Philippine-American relations.

See also: Chapter 2: Overview; Marcos Dictatorship. Chapter 8: Overview; Bilingual Education; History of Education; Textbooks; The University of the Philippines. Chapter 9: Overview; Carabao English; English; National Language Debate. Chapter 11: Filipino Novels in English. Chapter 12: Overview; Bungalows; Modern Architecture. Chapter 15: Baseball; Basketball; Boxing. Chapter 16: Overview; Comics/*Komiks*; Film; Television.

Further Reading

Karnow, Stanley. 2010. *In Our Image: America's Empire in the Philippines.* New York: Ballantine Books.

McCoy, Alfred W. 2009. *Policing America's Empire: The United States, the Philippines and the Rise of the Surveillance State.* Madison, WI: University of Wisconsin Press.

McCoy, Alfred W. 2016. "A Rupture in Philippine-U.S. Relations: Geopolitical Implications." *Journal of Asian Studies* 75, no. 4: 1049–1053.

Warlords

Warlords are politicians in small towns and cities who use the threat of violence to keep themselves in power. They rely on their armed retinue (also called private armies) to guarantee compliance, fend off rivals, and maintain a stable environment for their benefit. Official security forces like the police or army can neutralize or eliminate private armies but are often prevented from doing so by a warlord's alliances with national politicians. Warlords give a national politician his or her victory during elections by manipulating results in their areas or intimidating the electorate to vote for the favored national candidates. Those who win reward warlords with appointments to national offices and prevent the police and the army from dismantling their private armies.

There were towns where warlords dominated during the American colonial period, but it was only after World War II, with thousands of available guns and a new republic formally establishing its various representative offices (from the presidential down to the town mayor level) that warlords became a widespread phenomenon. Warlords got themselves elected to local offices and using these positions expanded their influence in the community, protected by followers supplied with the excess weapons. They then offered their services to national politicians or forged alliances with other warlords and political families offering them a solid voter turnout in their favor in exchange for spoils and protection.

One of the favorite political phrases among Filipinos is "guns, goons, and gold" (also known as the "Three Gs") and this refers to the way politicians use their private armies and the wealth they acquire from corruption as well as their involvement in legal and illegal businesses. The "Three Gs" enabled politicians like Ferdinand Marcos and Gloria Arroyo to amass the votes that propelled them to the presidency. In Marcos's case, his warlord allies gave him a 100 percent election victory in the 1969 presidential elections which historians describe as one of the dirtiest and bloodiest in postwar history. Gloria Arroyo won the 2004 presidential election based on the one million votes she received from the Autonomous Region for Muslim Mindanao (ARMM), which was then under the brutal control of the warlord Andal Ampatuan who was said to have a 2,400-strong militia armed with the most sophisticated of small arms. Ampatuan and his sons were implicated in the massacre of 58 people, including the wife of a political rival, in November 2009. They were detained (and Ampatuan died from cancer) but the family still retained its power in its locality.

One of Marcos's warlord supporters, former provincial governor Luis Singson, benefited from martial law and survived the fall of Marcos by defeating any attempts by presidents Corazon Aquino and Fidel V. Ramos to dislodge him from his rural power base. He did this by keeping his coterie of armed men intact while reviving an illegal numbers game. President Joseph E. Estrada politically resurrected Singson and even allowed him to expand his illicit network. When Estrada turned against him, Singson accused him of trying to take over his numbers game, and this became the basis for the president's impeachment and eventual forced resignation. Under President Arroyo, Singson was allowed to keep his turf and was even able to get a son elected to the House of Representatives.

The "Three Gs" have had a long history in postwar Philippine politics. There have been efforts to expose their deleterious effects on the polity. There are those who contend that changing the system of government could resolve these problems, but their critics equally insist that administrative restructuring will yield no long-term positive results unless the power of warlords is eliminated.

See also: Chapter 2: Overview; Marcos Dictatorship; People Power Revolution. Chapter 4: Crony Capitalism.

Further Reading

McCoy, Alfred W., ed. 2009. *An Anarchy of Families: State and Family in the Philippines.* Madison, WI: University of Wisconsin Press.

Sidel, John T. 1999. *Capital, Coercion and Crime: Bossism in the Philippines.* Stanford: Stanford University Press.

Teehankee, Julio C., and Cleo Ann A. Calimbahin. 2020. "Mapping the Philippines' Defective Democracy." *Asian Affairs: An American Review: Special Issue of Democratization in East Asia* 47, no. 2 (April): 97–125.

CHAPTER 4

ECONOMY

OVERVIEW

The Philippines is the 34th largest economy in the world and the 13th largest in Asia in terms of the gross domestic product (GDP). In Southeast Asia, this emerging market—as multilateral aid agencies and international financial networks describe the country—is the sixth richest, after Singapore, Brunei, Indonesia, Malaysia, and Thailand. In 2017, the country's purchasing power was US$878.980 billion. Economists also describe the Philippines as a "newly industrialized country" (NIC) based on the commodities it has been producing. Semiconductors, electronic products, shipping and transport equipment, and industrial minerals like copper are now the top products, displacing agriculture which was once the primary source of revenues.

The modern Philippine economy can be traced back to the late Spanish colonial period. Before the Spaniards came to occupy the archipelago, there was no unified economy. Instead, different port cities traded with China and kingdoms in mainland Southeast Asia, selling to these markets a variety of products that ranged from birds' nests (for a Chinese soup recipe) to gold nuggets. But once the Spaniards consolidated their rule, they established a new trading network that linked China and Mexico with Manila as the transshipment port. From 1565 to 1815, Chinese silk was purchased with Mexican pesos in Manila and loaded into galleons that crossed the Pacific Ocean for Mexico.

In the late 1700s, however, all this changed once the "Industrial Revolution" forced Spain to integrate itself into a global market dominated by England, turning the Philippines into an agricultural export economy that traded hemp (abaca), coffee, tobacco, and sugar—all raw materials needed by British industries. The galleon trade was abolished and Spain opened the colony to global trade. The importance of land for the export sector altered social relations. The Spanish religious orders that owned most lands lacked the skills to manage the farms; they ended up leasing the lands to Spanish and Chinese *mestizos* who turned out to be exceptionally good managers.

After the Spaniards were overthrown in 1896, this colonial economy continued under American rule, although this time the raw material products were increasingly exported to the United States and, to a certain extent, an industrializing Japan. On the eve of World War II, the colony was the second richest in Asia, with a per capita GDP of US$1,033, second only to Japan (US$1,135).

The Americans granted the Philippines its independence on July 4, 1946, and the new republic faced its first most pressing challenge of postwar rehabilitation. The U.S. and Philippine governments signed an economic agreement where the United States offered a postwar aid package of US$800 million, but only if the Philippines provided preferential tariffs for American imports, pegged the peso to the U.S. dollar, imposed no restrictions on currency transfers from the Philippines, and gave American citizens and corporations equal rights as their Filipino counterparts. The last provision required amending the Philippine Constitution which limited foreign ownership, but for this amendment to pass Congress, President Manuel A. Roxas got his Congressional allies to oust six leftist and two nationalist representatives on charges of electoral fraud in the 1946 elections. Congress passed the act and in a nationwide plebiscite on March 11, 1947, 79 percent of voters ratified the amendments.

Trade between a largely untouched United States and a war-devastated Philippines was one-sided. A trade deficit quickly developed as revenues from cheaper agricultural exports were unable to compensate for the amounts paid for more expensive manufacturing imports. Only sugar grew because of a guaranteed U.S. market. This imbalance caused a crisis that prompted the Philippine government to impose restrictions on the dollar remittances and imports and launch an import-substitution program where locally manufactured goods would replace the costly imports. Imports fell by 40 percent between 1949 and 1950, and by the end of the 1950s, domestic manufacturing was contributing 7.7 percent to the gross national product. The Philippines and the United States also revised the Bell Trade Act in 1955, abolishing American authority to control the dollar-peso exchange rate, and extended the quota privileges of sugar exports to the United States but reaffirmed American parity rights. The outline of an industrial sector was becoming discernible.

Unfortunately, import substitution could not be sustained. Import costs continued as the purchases from abroad—of oil, and of machinery and equipment to replace aging ones—continued to drain dollars. Domestic manufacturing's growth rate declined from a high 12 percent in 1950 to 7.7 percent at the end of the decade, while the GNP growth fell from 6.2 percent to 4.9 percent. The economy had slowed down, and it did not help that the government's standing had suffered after a series of exposes by the media and political opposition to corruption in the allocation of licenses. President Diosdado P. Macapagal removed most tariffs on import, devalued the peso to rejuvenate trade and attract foreign investments, and created opportunities for the agricultural sector to seek new markets abroad. These measures had very little effect as imports remained a drain, reaching a high 17 percent of the GNP at the end of Macapagal's term. President Ferdinand E. Marcos's approach to the problem was to open the economy further, signing an Industrial Incentives Act in 1967 that removed the 40 percent restriction on foreign ownership for pioneer industries such as new export crops, marine resources, and industrial joint ventures.

More importantly, Marcos turned his attention to rural poverty, implementing the "Green Revolution," a project of the Ford and Rockefeller Foundation and the International Rice Research Institute (IRRI) to increase the yield of food crops through hybrid seeds. The country attained self-sufficiency in rice production in 1968. Marcos thus skirted the politically incendiary issue of land reform through this technological innovation. Yet, despite the Investments Act and Green Revolution, economic progress remained limited. It took some time for the new export crops to attain projected earnings, and a hostile Congress stymied efforts by Marcos's technocrats to modernize the economy by ending the monopoly of the sugar industry by a few families and increasing indirect taxation that was biased against the poor. It did not help that the government continued to be plagued by weak tax collections and corruption. At the end of Marcos's first term, the deficit reached 1.13 billion pesos.

As Marcos started his second term in 1969, there was already growing political turmoil over corruption in high places and the rise of student protests. Foreign capital began to hedge its bets and investments that had reached US$20 million before 1968 went down drastically to US$8 million. Inflation also began to rise erratically, abetted by Marcos's bankrupting of the national coffers to finance his reelection. A series of climatic disasters combined with the economic crisis that ensued, forcing Marcos to devalue the peso again to make the country attractive to foreign investments. This move only aggravated the situation as incomes plunged and the prices of goods, especially imports like cars, household products, and crucial components of industrial enterprises, went up. When the political opposition doubled down, Marcos responded by declaring martial law in 1972, citing the crisis and the existence of left-wing and right-wing threats to the republic.

Marcos now ruled by decree, and one of his first moves was "Operation Land Transfer," which ordered landlords with lands over 1.75 acres to break these up and allow the government to distribute them to tenants. Marcos created super agencies headed by U.S.-educated technocrats that oversaw government investments in strategic sectors of the economy—oil, power, mass transportation, agricultural modernization. Between 1972 and 1976, therefore, the share of public-sector investments in the overall investments went up to 6.5 percent from a low 2 percent.

With peace and order restored under martial law, the GDP grew from P55 million when martial law was declared to P193 million. There was a US$10 million surplus in the balance of payment as export revenues exceeded import costs for the first time in postwar Philippine history. This, however, did not last long: imports again prevailed over exports, and a decline in global demand for sugar in 1978 destroyed the industry, with devastating consequences on sugar land communities. "Operation Land Transfer" was only partially successful as landlords resorted to various measures to prevent distribution—from converting their rice lands to other crops, replacing tenancy agreements with leasehold contracts, to using the local police to harass tenants. Beneficiaries of the program also found themselves increasingly indebted as the cost of fertilizer and pesticide inputs for "Green Revolution" rice rose. By 1980, there were already signs that food self-sufficiency was coming to an end.

The foundations of Marcos's development plan turned out to be flawed. The GDP did grow, but only because the regime borrowed heavily from multilateral lending sources and commercial banks to finance its development program. The rise of the external debt was phenomenal: from US$3.75 million in 1974 to US$10.7 million in 1975, to US$17.25 million in 1980, to US$24.81 million in 1982, US$25.41 million in

1984, and US$28.18 million in 1986, when Marcos fell from power. Again, even as the government hoped that exports could compensate for the deficit, many domestic corporations were tipping over, especially those owned by cronies and relatives of Marcos who had benefited from preferential treatment. When these crony corporations—many of which were monopolies of critical industries like coconut and sugar—began collapsing, the government bailed them out by absorbing their debts and thus increased general indebtedness. Marcos then resorted to short-term, high-interest loans to pay off these debts or their interests, which only worsened the deficit. Finally, there were mis-priorities in infrastructure development—including the edifices that First Lady, Imelda Marcos, ordered built to showcase the achievements of the new order—which turned out to be wasteful fiascos. For example, Mrs. Marcos's arts and cultural centers provided glitter, but their activities hardly reached the majority of Filipinos.

The economy reached its nadir in 1983 when the assassination of Marcos's principal opponent, former senator Benigno Aquino Jr., led to foreign investors fleeing the country. The GDP dropped to 1.8 percent and then to -7.3 percent in 1983 and 1984 respectively. To prevent further disaster, the government again resorted to short-term loans. Between August 1983 and December 1984, these loans totaled US$330 million, rapidly emptying government coffers and forcing Marcos to declare a debt payment moratorium. The country immediately went into recession. This was the first ever recession since 1946.

One outcome was the severe rise in social inequality with the most impoverished 60 percent receiving only 22.5 percent of the nation's income, while the wealthiest 10 percent enjoyed 41.7 percent. The unemployment rate rose from 14.7 percent in 1978 to 24 percent in 1982 and poverty incidence, which was pegged at 41 percent in 1965, became worse, shooting up to 58.9 percent in 1985. What mitigated these instances of poverty were the remittances of Filipinos working abroad, which rose from US$82 million in 1975 to US$384 million in 1978 and then to US$944 million in 1983 before going down to US$300 million between 1984 and 1986. Marcos fell, partly because of the economic mess; and the Aquino assassination delegitimized his regime not only to ordinary Filipinos but also to the business elite.

President Corazon C. Aquino was able to restore some economic confidence. The peso once more became competitive, business confidence gradually returned and investors began to notice the Philippines. The new president's hands, however, were tied up by her promise to be unlike Marcos and to respect the democratic process. For example, the government seized the assets of the Marcos family and their cronies, but its decision to resolve these through the judicial process slowed down, if not put a stop to, the process of recovering these and returning the wealth to government coffers. In 2019, only US$3.16 billion of an estimated US$10 billion of the Marcos's ill-gotten wealth has been recovered by the government.

Persistent threats from anti-government groups, including a series of attempted coups, an earthquake in 1990 and a volcano eruption in 1991 further slowed down the economic recovery. The economic turnaround only began to happen under President Fidel V. Ramos, whose reform program actively promoted trade liberalization, enticing foreign investors to take advantage of a deregulated oil industry, and dismantled telecommunication and airline monopolies. The government invited private companies to build power plants to solve the nation's recurring power crisis, privatized state corporations such as an oil company and a waterworks system, and sold off government assets such as a vast military camp in Manila to fill up government coffers. The 1997 Asian financial crisis, however, almost undid economic growth. After Thai officials decided to delink the baht from the U.S. dollar, investors fled the Thailand stock market, prompting similar withdrawals in other Southeast Asian countries as well as in Hong Kong. The peso depreciated from P29.47 to US$1 to become P40.89 to US$1, while the GDP fell from 5.3 percent in 1997 to 0.5 percent in 1998. It was only after the International Monetary Fund (IMF) and the Japanese government infused over US$110 billion of short-term loans that the Asian economies stabilized.

President Joseph E. Estrada continued the economic liberalization started by his predecessors and gave special attention to the poverty alleviation programs of the Ramos administration. However, Estrada resigned when the military and a coalition of different political groups threatened to overthrow him on charges of corruption (see chapters on History and Politics). Hence, the political scandal and subsequent firestorm overshadowed the modest economic accomplishments.

It was under President Gloria M. Arroyo that the Philippines experienced its most sustained growth. The GDP rose from 2.8 percent in 2001 to 6.6 percent in 2004, and reached a high 7.6 percent at the end of her term. The main drivers for this were remittances by overseas Filipino workers and by Western business companies outsourcing their customer services to the Philippines where wages were cheap and employees spoke fluent English. President Arroyo's deft handling of the value-added tax (VAT) and its electronic equivalent (e-vat) allowed the government to increase tax collection and stem the regressive impact of tax evasion. By 2008, the country's monetary reserves were enough to cover 10 months of national expenditures and reduce the foreign debt from 58 percent in 2008 to 45 percent in 2009. The rebound was so impressive that the Philippines became a lender, contributing US$125 million to the IMF and helping European economies recover from their crises. This contribution increased to US$251.5 million under President Benigno S. Aquino III. Not even a temporary slip of 3.6 percent of the GDP in 2011, resulting from the flooding in Thailand and the tsunami in Japan affecting Filipino manufacturers, could stop the progress. The Philippines easily jumped back to a growth of 7 percent because of the factors mentioned above.

Yet, growth did not come without blemish. In her last year of office, Arroyo was accused of corruption in relation to the awarding of a US$329 million construction deal where the Chinese telecommunications corporation ZTE would merge with the government-owned National Broadband Network (NBN) to improve the Philippines' communications capacity. Due to intense public pressure, Arroyo canceled the deal, but the courts indicted her nevertheless. The charges were dismissed in 2016 by the special court, which has jurisdiction over criminal and civil cases involving government officials.

The GDP experienced its fastest growth since 1970 reaching a high 6.2 percent at the end of his first year. A major earthquake (7.2 in magnitude) and a super typhoon affected the country in 2013, forcing the government to lower the GDP to 4 percent, but it easily bounced back to 6.9 percent in 2014, the highest ever in the country's history. Inflation was kept under check by strong foreign reserves, the steady flow of remittances, and the increasing profitability of the business processing outsourcing (BPO) sector. Improved earnings raised consumer spending (P9.154 trillion to the P12.642 trillion GDP, or 72.4 percent of the GDP) and led to a decline in the unemployment rate from 7.3 percent in 2010 to 5.8 percent at the end of Aquino's term. The World Economic Forum ranked the Philippines 57th in terms of global competitiveness when President Aquino III ended his term. The rank went down to 64th in 2019, in President Duterte's second year then rose to 52nd again in 2020. The international watchdog Transparency International also noted that in terms of its corruption perception index (CPI), the Philippines was ranked between 33rd and 35th among the 101 countries with corruption problems (Transparency International 2021).

The Philippines was competitive globally, but it was not conducive to do business in. In a survey of 189 countries, the World Bank graded the Philippines poorly, bringing down its ranking from 86th in 2014 to 95th in 2015. Unemployment had gone down, but underemployment remained high. When Aquino stepped down, 18.7 percent of the labor force were working in occupations below their level of qualification or doing part-time work. Finally, the poverty rate only slightly declined during Aquino's term—from 26.6 percent to 26.3 percent in 2009—but this was enough for the Social Progress Index Global Survey to praise the Philippines for promoting fundamental freedoms and providing access to a college education as well as information technology.

President Duterte's economic policies were no different from that of his predecessor. He picked up from where they left off—continuing the tax reform program, enhancing government support to agriculture, fast-tracking the infrastructure program that President Benigno S. Aquino III started, and further opening the economy to global trade. But Duterte would also leave his own mark: he enhanced the poor's access to higher education by doing away with tuition in the state colleges and universities; he signed into law a national health insurance program, and institutionalized the popular conditional cash transfer program for the poor, that was started under President Arroyo and continued by President Aquino, by making it a part of Department of Social Work and Development's annual budget. Duterte also vowed to bring down poverty by 7.2 percent. Despite the tensions caused by Duterte's controversial "War on Drugs" campaign, the World Bank predicted that the 6.8 percent GDP would not be affected given that remittances and BPO profits had reached US$50 billion. COVID-19, however, put a stop to this progress. The 6.1 percent GDP growth in 2019 was followed by a 9.5 percent contraction of the GDP, which was the worst in the Southeast Asian region (Guido, 2021). This negative growth was the first one since 1999 (Mendoza 2021).

The oversupply of money had led to higher consumer demand in early 2017, which, in turn, caused inflation as the prices of goods and services rose. The government estimated that inflation would be between 2 percent and 4 percent in 2018, but in the first quarter of the year, it had already reached 4.2 percent. Inflation had also depreciated the value of the peso vis-à-vis the U.S. dollar, but the government remained hopeful that the decline would stimulate purchases by overseas workers who would find Philippine products now cheaper.

Foreign direct investments had increased to 6.6 percent in 2017, but the Philippines fared badly in comparison to other Southeast Asian states. About US$5.9 billion was invested in Thailand, US$4.4 billion in Malaysia, and US$1.6 billion in Vietnam, but only US$592 million in the Philippines. Duterte had also borrowed US$ 180 billion worth of loans from China and Japan to pursue his "Build, build, build" infrastructure program. There remained the trade deficit which had reached a record high of US$4.02 billion in December 2017 as the US$4.72 billion export revenue was offset by the doubling of imports to US$8.74 billion. When Aquino ended his term, there was a US$600 million surplus in the government coffers. Duterte turned this into a US$100 million deficit after his first year. The government's chief economist described all this as a manageable transition that still had a lot of glitches.

See also: Chapter 2: Overview; Marcos Dictatorship; People Power Revolution. Chapter 3: Martial Law.

Further Reading

Asian Development Bank. 2007. *Philippines: Critical Development Constraints*. Manila: Asian Development Bank. https://www.adb.org/sites/default/files/publication/29274/cdc-philippines.pdf

Balisacan, Arsenio M., ed. 2003. *The Philippine Economy: Development, Policies, and Challenges*. Oxford and New York: Oxford University Press.

Balisacan, Arsenio M., and Hal Hill. 2007. *The Dynamics of Regional Development: The Philippines in East Asia*. Cheltenham, UK: Edward Elgar.

Mendoza, Ronald U. 2021. "The Philippine Economy Under the Pandemic: From Asian Tiger to Sick Man Again?" *Brookings* (August 2). https://www.brookings.edu/blog/order-from-chaos/2021/08/02/the-philippine-economy-under-the-pandemic-from-asian-tiger-to-sick-man-again/

Paqueo, Vicente B., Aniceto C. Orbeta Jr., and Gilberto M. Llanto, eds. 2017. *Unintended Consequences: The Folly of Uncritical Thinking*. Quezon City: Philippine Institute for Development Studies. https://pidswebs.pids.gov.ph/CDN/PUBLICATIONS/pidsbk2017-unintended_fnl.pdf

Transparency International. 2021. "Corruption Perception Index." https://www.transparency.org/en/cpi/2021?gclid=CjwKCAiAsNKQBhAPEiwAB-I5zefdOrhnsvEVgC-GnQiG_Fzpt4x2mREkKDN9fhd9m70qfpRRDKh8WxoCsBcQAvD_BwE

Agriculture

Philippine agriculture is divided between food crops (rice, corn, coconut) and export crops (sugarcane, fruits, vegetables). The country is the eighth largest rice producer worldwide, but on several occasions, it has had to import this essential commodity when typhoon-induced flooding, pest infestation, and poor government planning affected production.

In the 1970s, the Green Revolution program, which introduced genetically modified high-yielding rice varieties, allowed the Philippines to achieve self-sufficiency. This marked improvement happened even as the total acreage for rice shrank because more farms were shifting to the more profitable export crops or converting into real estate properties. In the 1980s, rice production slowed, but it was not until 1995 that a food crisis arising from government mismanagement forced the country to import. Regaining rice self-sufficiency remained elusive in the first decade of the 21st century as a growing population put pressure on a topography that had no major river deltas like in Vietnam and Thailand. Dwindling rice lands raised rice prices, leading to inevitable shortage as production could not cope up with demand and rice hoarding became rampant. In 2014, for example, agricultural officials admitted that the rice harvest of 19.3 million metric tons could only feed 96 million Filipinos out of a total population of 100 million. The government had no choice but to import from countries like Vietnam and Thailand. With climate changes being unpredictable as ever, there was no guarantee that self-sufficiency could last. In 2016, a long drought attributed to the phenomenon El Niño damaged 100 percent of all crops in the southeastern part of Mindanao Island.

Corn (*maize*) is both a food crop and a source of animal feed. Farmers grow rice and corn twice a year, and in Mindanao, farmers attempt to plant a third cycle if the weather permits. The crop had been growing at the rate of 1.7 percent from 1980 to 2000 but began to decline due to climate change. Improved technology reversed the decline but this was only temporary as weather changes would negate the progress. Agriculturists, however, are hopeful that because the plant needs less water, and the government has introduced hybrid varieties, corn will be able to withstand the effects of climate change.

Sugar is the oldest of the export crops and grown in large estates across the country. Over 50 percent of these estates can be found in the central-western part of the archipelago, 20 percent are in Mindanao, and 17 percent in Luzon, with the rest distributed in the eastern Visayas. Its beginnings go back to the 1860s when the Spanish government opened the colony to global trade. Production expanded under American rule, especially after the Philippines was guaranteed a share in the U.S. market. This preferential treatment continued in the postwar period and ended in 1974, and sugar's status diminished after this particular arrangement ended.

President Ferdinand E. Marcos tried to offset this by placing the production and sale of sugar under one corporation, arguing that this could make sugar more competitive since the Philippines—the ninth largest producer in the world—could dictate the price as a single merchant instead of several competing private enterprises. A Marcos crony was put in charge of setting up the monopoly but he badly miscalculated when he delayed the release of Philippine sugar to the world market in order to get the best price. This manufactured scarcity led to the collapse of the industry, with hundreds of warehouses full of unsold sugar. The sugar-producing provinces suffered

Tropical hilltop, Southern Philippines. (Hugo Maes/Dreamstime.com)

considerably and communities dependent on the product experienced the most severe famine ever since the immediate postwar period. Sugar never recovered from this crisis. When Marcos fell from power, the growth was a negative 68.1 percent. In the 1990s and 2000s, only during two years was there positive growth, the rest was all negative. In the second decade of the 21st century, sugar exports never went beyond 2 percent.

The Philippines remains the world's largest producer of coconut and 25 percent of total agricultural lands are planted with this crop. A quarter of the rural population (about 0.5 million) work in the industry, a majority of them tenants working for absentee landowners on a piece-rate basis instead of a daily wage. In 1973, Marcos attempted to deal with the constant fluctuation in coconut prices by creating a super-agency, the Philippine Coconut Authority (PCA), with the power to impose a levy on copra and coconut-made goods. The PCA then used the levy to fund the development of hybrid varieties that could withstand pestilence and yield more nuts and to buy out privately owned coconut mills to merge production and marketing. PCA purchased a bank that acted as the depository of the levy money that coconut farmers could ostensibly tap when needed. It was, however, the cronies of Marcos—who controlled the PCA—who took advantage of the levy money, using it to diversify their businesses. One crony used coconut funds to buy the country's top beer firm.

The monopolizing of the industry to protect the Philippines' domination of the market failed in the 1980s when world coconut prices fell. When the United States brought in a requirement that products with saturated fat had to carry warnings of its

Drying Manila Hemp. (Nathan Allen/Dreamstime.com)

possible deleterious effect on people's health, the price dipped further. Poor farmers lost the most, facing radical decline in incomes but continuing to pay the levy. The big planters were the least affected because of their control of funds. In 1985, the government was finally forced to break up the monopoly when the IMF made it a precondition for extending financial support to an increasingly unstable Marcos government. The ouster of Marcos completely privatized the industry and this appeared to bode well for the coconut industry. By the 1990s, the industry's annual growth rate had risen to 6.5 percent, higher than that of its nearest competitor, Indonesia.

The Philippines is the largest producer of hemp (abaca), controlling 87.4 percent of total world sales (Ecuador is second, with 12.5 percent). Hemp plantations are found in the Bicol region, located southeast of Manila. The demand for the crop has been consistently high, but its profitability is limited as demand for its main competitor, plastic, is greater. Yet, 42 percent of Philippine abaca is sold to Britain and 37.1 percent to Germany. Processed abaca is turned into cordage and this is mainly sold to the United States. Finally, there are the fruit crops. The Philippines is the third-largest exporter of pineapple and one of the top three banana-producing countries worldwide. Demand for these fruits grew in the 1970s after Japan opened its economy to these commodities, followed later by the Middle East. Production was given an added boost when Hawaii-based fruit companies moved to Mindanao because of cheaper labor. Mindanao is an ideal place to grow them given that it is rarely hit by hurricanes and its lowlands are ideal for plantation agriculture. Today, the export crops benefit tremendously from the growing Chinese market.

See also: Chapter 1: Natural Resources. Chapter 2: Overview; Marcos Dictatorship. Chapter 6: Overview; The Poor.

The Green Revolution in the Philippines. (Rockefeller Foundation)

Further Reading

Alarde-Regalado, Aurora, and Cynthia Hallare-Lara. 1992. *A Profile of the Philippine Rice Industry*. Quezon City: Philippine Peasant Institute.

Billig, Michael S. 2003. *Barons, Brokers and Buyers: The Institutions and Cultures of Philippine Sugar*. Honolulu, HI: University of Hawaii Press.

Hallare-Lara, Cynthia. 1992. *A Profile of the Philippine Corn Industry*. Quezon City: Philippine Peasant Institute.

Crony Capitalism

Crony capitalism was a notorious practice of former President Ferdinand E. Marcos, who gave preference to his family and friends when it came to government project contracts, industrial investments, and corporate credits. This was not with regard to mere spoils. These privileges were extended with the end that Marcos's cronies would establish monopoly control over a host of industries ranging from gambling to labor export, crop export, food and beverages, and the power sector. A presidential decree would then protect these crony industries by providing them with tariff and tax protection as well as sole import rights. All crony corporations, except the coconut and tobacco monopolies, collapsed as their owners looted their enterprises and mismanaged them. One classic example was the construction of a nuclear power plant that was supposed to boost the country's competitiveness by providing affordable electricity. The $2.3 billion plant had to be mothballed because of cost overruns and structural issues. The crony who brokered the deal with the American corporation Westinghouse was not only bailed out by the government after it experienced liquidity problems (the Central Bank advanced P1.2 billion), he also got to keep his commission of $40 million. Another example was the sugar industry, where another crony was given monopoly control.

Local companies—especially those owned by Marcos's cronies—were collapsing, prompting the government to come to their rescue by infusing funds to keep them running. At the end of the year, the government's Philippine National Bank (PNB) and the Development Bank of the Philippines (DBP) had poured in a total of 9 billion pesos on 122 corporations. These rescues bankrupted the DBP, forcing the government to doctor its financial statements to hoodwink its foreign creditors. It did so by listing noncash incomes like property assets as profits. The PNB still had some liquidity in it, but its overdue loans totaled 21.9 billion pesos, which constituted 42 percent of loans outstanding. When Marcos fell from power, the so-called nonperforming assets, which government financial institutions held after taking over the debts of crony corporations and businesses critical to the economy that had collapsed, reached P1.113 billion or almost 20 percent of the GNP.

The downfall of crony capitalism was massive, such that the government had to set up a P1.5 billion industrial rescue fund that crony-owned corporations could draw from to maintain their liquidity. Then, in 1980, a series of events practically bankrupted the economy. First, global oil prices and interest rates went up, making production doubly expensive. Second, a commercial bank collapsed exposing how fragile the financial sector had become. Then in January 1981, a Chinese Filipino businessman fled the country leaving US$80 million of debts that his company owed local banks including the PNB and instigating a general capital flight, and investment houses experienced a severe hemorrhage of funds. In fact, two of the largest firms closed while the government had to acquire six banks that experienced critical liquidity problems. In 1983, these banks held only 8 percent of the total bank assets, but their share of the total bank debts was a high 24.3 percent.

See also: Chapter 2: Overview; Marcos Dictatorship; People Power Revolution. Chapter 3: Martial Law; Political Clans; Post-Marcos Philippines.

Further Reading

Kang, David C. 2002. *Crony Capitalism: Corruption and Development in South Korea and the Philippines*. Cambridge: Cambridge University Press.

Manapat, Ricardo. 1990. *Some Are Smarter Than Others: The History of Marcos' Crony Capitalism*. New York: Aletheia Publications.

Economic Assistance

The Philippines has been a recipient of aid from other countries since its independence in 1946. This assistance has been provided for various reasons—military upgrade, peace and postwar rehabilitation, emergency support and, most important of all, economic growth and poverty alleviation. Two countries have been the major donors— the United States and Japan. American assistance is often explained as arising from "special relations" between the two countries that date back to the colonial era, which has been reinforced by the two countries' collective experience in World War II and them being allies during the Cold War. Japanese assistance began as part of the war reparations for the occupation of Philippines during World War II. Later on, European countries and Australia also became involved in extending aid to the Philippines, mainly focused on humanitarian projects.

Foreign assistance comes in different forms. There are the outright grants that the above-mentioned countries and three international organizations (the Asian Development Bank, the International Monetary Fund, and the World Bank) give to the Philippines. Others come in the form of loans with reasonable interest rates or lines of credit which the Philippine government can then use to purchase equipment and services related to economic development. In 2015, the Asian Development Bank was the highest aid donor putting in $803 million to support infrastructure development, disaster prevention, and educational reforms. The second most-significant source of assistance was the World Bank, contributing $356 million to finance rural infrastructure and jump-start anti-poverty programs, people's empowerment, and disaster risk management. The bank has until recently been the biggest contributor to the government's "conditional cash transfer program" aimed at providing extra monies to help 4.4 million poor Filipinos to overcome poverty gradually. In 2015, the World Bank also committed a total of US$500 million to help the Philippine government in the rehabilitation of communities hit by Typhoon Haiyan.

In 2014, the Japanese government extended US$238 million in soft loans (70 percent), technical cooperation (20 percent), and grants (10 percent) for infrastructure upgrade, natural disaster preparation, and climate change monitoring. Closely following Japan was the United States with US$236.9 million, mainly in grants aimed at fast-tracking development cooperation to increase investments, economic competitiveness, environmental protection, and peace and stability in Mindanao and the southern Philippines. Australia (US$65 million), France (US$57.5 million), the European Union (US$33 million), Germany (US$12.9 million), and Canada (US$11.6 million) devoted their assistance programs to poverty alleviation and post-typhoon rehabilitation. Parts of the aid from Australia, European Union, and Germany went to the rehabilitation of communities affected by the separatist wars in Muslim Mindanao.

Note that all of the figures cited pertained to aid before Rodrigo R. Duterte came to power. After he became president, Duterte did not show any restraint in expressing his contempt for the United States and the European Union after they criticized the extrajudicial killings associated with his anti-drug war. While his relationship with Japan remained stable, as a sign that he was weaning the Philippines away from its dependence on Western aid he sought help from China, which promised US$24 billion to help build a railway system across the country. However, as 2018 was winding down, there was no visible indication that China had started to release the funds.

See also: Chapter 2: Overview; Marcos Dictatorship. Chapter 3: Overview; Armed Forces of the Philippines; Post-Marcos Philippines; Relations with the United States.

Further Reading

Kang, Hyewon. 2010. *The Philippines' Absorptive Capacity for Foreign Aid*. Manila: Philippine Institute for Development Studies.

Reyes, Romeo A. 1993. *Absorptive Capacity for Foreign Aid: The Case of the Philippines*. Manila: Philippine Institute for Development Studies.

Industry

Philippine industry does not have a robust industrial base like South Korea or Japan. Among small and medium industries (less than 100 workers), the top ones are furniture, chemical processing, publishing, primary metals (e.g., processed iron), and beverages. Not that there were no attempts to establish an industrial base similar to Japan's and South Korea's. In the early postwar years, the Philippines was mainly an agricultural country. There were industries, but these were few in number and often tertiary industries that provided auxiliary parts.

In the early 1950s, the government imposed import controls to stop the hemorrhage of dollars paid for imports and to create a favorable climate for Filipino manufacturing to grow. Soon, a manufacturing sector comprising of small- and medium-sized factories producing textiles, paper (and paper products), chemicals, nonmetallic mineral products, and small machineries began to appear. With foreign competition limited by tariff and export restrictions, Filipino manufacturing grew 12 percent per annum, a rate that was only reproduced 60 years later.

This domestic capitalism stopped growing in the second half of the decade, when dollars began to leave the country as domestic industries had to purchase new equipment and even raw materials from abroad. These firms could do so only by requesting dollar allocation from the Central Bank. These requests became an opportunity for corruption as corporations competed for the allocation by bribing finance officials or the officials gave the allocation to the highest bidder and were assured of a certain percentage. These two factors caused the economy to contract and by the end of the year, there was pressure on the government to end the tariff on imports and currency control.

Import substitution was abandoned as a policy in the early 1960s, and the economy was opened again to foreign investments. The return of foreign competitors did not displace Filipino industries. In fact, they stood their ground and even in the pharmaceutical industries, which Western transnational corporations dominated, United Laboratories, a local corporation, was able to maintain its market share. President Ferdinand Marcos then shifted economic policy completely and launched an export-oriented industrialization program by turning the Philippines into a desirable place for foreign investments. Tax breaks, unhampered remittance of profits, and a docile work force were just some of the perks given to transnational corporations. In the mid-1970s, joint ventures between Filipino corporations and Japanese and American firms began to be formed in the automotive, mining, textiles, electronics, synthetic fiber, telecommunications, and high technology industries, and in export crops and fishing.

Some of the joint ventures, however, were not really designed to help the country develop an industrial base. Foreign firms that transferred operations to the Philippines were not actual industrial plants. In the transportation sector, for example, what was described as "industries" were mere assembly plants where bodies of cars were installed after the engines—the center pieces of automobiles—were imported from either Germany, Japan, or the United States. With Filipino participation in the production of vehicles only minimal, the only way the country could truly benefit from this profitable enterprise was to control the processing and distribution of a motor vehicle's lifeline—oil. The government purchased the local subsidiary of the Eastern States Standard Oil (ESSO), an American company, and renamed it PetroPhil Corporation. Marcos ran it as a monopoly but President Corazon Aquino privatized Petro-Phil as part of her promise to restore free market competition and remove government involvement in the economy.

However, privatization had its limits. For example, not all state-owned enterprises had been turned over or sold to the private sector. As of 2016, there were still 144 government-owned and controlled corporations (GOCCs) that had investments in power, infrastructure, communications, social services (including housing), and water and land resources. Government agencies also continue to be a significant player in the infrastructure and energy sectors through its "build-operate-transfer" (BOT) programs. Under this arrangement, private corporations are offered franchises to design, construct, and operate an infrastructure program. They have to raise funds for the project but are also allowed to keep the profits from its operation. After a period, the project will be turned over to the government without any cost to the corporation.

In the first decade of the 21st century, the industrial sector's value-added contribution to the economy hovered between 33 and 34 percent of the GDP, while the contribution of agriculture was around 14 percent of the GDP. It was the service sector that was growing the fastest, increasing its share to over 50 percent during the same period. In 2017, the service sector's share was up to 57 percent of the GDP, while agriculture's contribution dropped to 9 percent. As of December 2009, there were 37 projects being operated as public-private enterprises, 17 in energy, 4 in transportation, 3 in information technology, 5 in water supply and sewerage, 5 in public market management, and one each in health, real estate, and public housing. Foreign investors participated in 17 of these projects, although they faced problems arising from inefficient planning, government regulations, and legal issues relating to revenue generation.

It is unclear if the country will ever experience economic takeoff and become a fully industrialized economy. The Philippines may not be able to produce its own car but if it succeeds in attracting industries that produce the secondary components to do so in the country, it could use this seemingly minor cog to firm up its role in the overall global production of the automobile.

See also: Chapter 2: Overview; Marcos Dictatorship; People Power Revolution. Chapter 3: Relations with Japan; Relations with the United States.

Further Reading

Aldaba, Rafaelita M. 2013. "Twenty Years after Trade Liberalization and Industrialization: What Has Happened and Where Do We Go from Here." *Philippine Institute for Development Studies Discussion Paper Series No. 2013-21.* March. https://dirp3.pids.gov.ph /ris/dps/pidsdps1321.pdf

Kuo, Cheng-Tian. 1995. *Global Competitiveness and Industrial Growth in Taiwan and the Philippines.* Pittsburgh: University of Pittsburgh Press.

Yoshihara, Kunio. 1986. *Philippine Industrialization: Foreign and Domestic Capital.* Cambridge: Oxford University Press.

Land Reform

Land has always been an extremely politicized issue, the result of a few families owning thousands of hectares of lands worked by tenants and farmworkers under a sharing arrangement that favors the owners and impoverishes the latter. In the 1890s, Filipinos who joined the nationalist revolution that overthrew the Spanish regime did so because they were exploited and oppressed in these estates. When the Americans replaced the Spaniards, one of their first moves to win over the Filipinos was to break up the friar estates and distribute them among their tenants. During the American period, nationalist and radical groups were able to make their presence felt in the political arena by including the land question as their mobilizing issue. A rallying call of a peasant uprising north of Manila in the 1930s was to end feudalism and to fight for national independence. When Filipino leaders took complete control of the colonial state with the establishment of the Commonwealth, President Manuel L. Quezon promised a "Social Justice" program that included land distribution to neutralize the uprising. He was intensely opposed by a Philippine Assembly that was dominated by landlords and their representatives and allies.

Four years after Philippine independence, a communist-led rural rebellion threatened the young republic. Even the Americans who actively intervened to help the Philippine government defeat the rebellion admitted that unless this inequitable land-tenure system was resolved, peasants will remain attracted to communism. When an

American economic mission essentially repeated what their colonial predecessors did with the friar lands, calling for a nationwide land reform program, the landlord-dominated Congress accused its members of proposing "communistic" ideas.

It was President Ramon D. Magsaysay who first submitted a detailed land reform program that decreed that lands above 14 hectares be subdivided and distributed to tenants at cost. Congress successfully blunted this by raising the exemption to 300 hectares for individually owned lands and 600 hectares for those owned by corporations. Moreover, land reform could only move forward if the majority of the tenants filed a petition in support of it. The only concession Congress allowed was full expropriation and distribution in areas where there was justified agrarian unrest. Faced with this overwhelming legislative resistance, Magsaysay and the Americans shifted tactics, sending community development workers to organize peasants to nurture new leaders who would challenge the political bosses of their localities. When Magsaysay died in an airplane crash, so did the community development experiment.

The second attempt to push for a land reform program was by President Diosdado Macapagal, who promised 400,000 tenants that they would get their lands and the rights of agricultural workers would be recognized. To ensure the success of the program, Macapagal created a new bank specifically for the rural workforce, offering credit, technical and marketing advice, and a legal defense office. Congress once again weakened the bill, introducing amendments like exempting a landowner who ejected their tenants or turned them into wage workers. The legislature also narrowed the land reform areas to rice and corn lands, excluding lands planted with coconut and sugar. The reason here was that these were export crops and critical to government revenue generation. Finally, their control of the budget enabled Congress to reduce the allotments for the support offices. Macapagal retreated.

President Ferdinand E. Marcos's initial venture into land reform also met legislative resistance. What he did, however, was to strengthen social welfare programs (including agricultural development) with the aid of the military (via activities like "civic action") and led by American-educated technocrats who were given a free hand in crafting policies and implementing them. When Marcos declared martial law in 1972 and placed the country under the rule of constitutional authoritarianism, he launched "Operation Land Transfer" to expropriate lands above seven hectares, compensate landowners in cash, revenues and stocks from the Land Bank, and provide favorable amortization schemes. The program's success was more or less ensured by the "Green Revolution," which doubled rice harvests with the introduction of genetically modified high-yielding varieties (HYVs).

Landlords may have lost their most reliable defenders with the abolition of Congress, but "Operation Land Transfer" had several loopholes that they could take advantage of. Since the program was limited to rice and corn lands, landlords simply converted their lands to other crops, particularly those for export (fruits, and later on, vegetables), or re-registered them as real estate lands. There were reports of landlords denying the new owners access to sources of irrigation, slowing down the transfer process by filing civil and even criminal charges, tampering with hectarage lists, and— much like what happened during the term of President Macapagal—convincing tenants to become leaseholders which thereby exempted the land from being expropriated. Certain landlords also reclassified their tenanted lands into commercial farms, turning their tenants into wage workers, thereby avoiding being subjected to land reform.

It did not help that for the HYVs or "miracle rice" to maintain high productivity, they needed massive amounts of two very expensive inputs— fertilizers and pesticides. The Land Bank helped new owners cover the cost of these inputs, but it also increased their indebtedness.

By 1986, only 800,000 (13 percent) of the 6 million hectares of rice and corn lands had been transferred to former tenants, while 550,000 hectares (9.1 percent) had been converted to leaseholds and therefore exempted from land reform. There were those who benefited from the program, but these were what agricultural experts described as larger tenants who already had political influence at the village level.

In 1988, the restored Congress passed a Comprehensive Agrarian Reform Program (CARP), again in the name of achieving social justice and equity and resolving rural poverty. This time CARP covered all agricultural lands and provided them with institutional support similar to that of the previous programs. Unlike its predecessors which had to be amended or even discarded once a new president was elected, CARP's essential features were never altered by any of the heads of state after 1988. In 1996, however, the government quietly decreased the land reform area from 10.3 million hectares to 8 million hectares for unexplained reasons. Of these 8 million hectares, 7.4 million hectares had been distributed to 4.6 million beneficiaries by 2011. The agrarian office did admit that some 1.5 million hectares of the distributed lands were public lands and that only about 500,000 hectares were private lands voluntarily transferred by their owners.

CARP's difficulties, however, are just part of the more significant problems of Philippine agriculture. In 2005, two economists evaluating the progress in Philippine agriculture listed the following stumbling blocks to its progress: overcentralization and politicization of the bureaucracy, a disorganized framework, lack of coordination, inadequate technical and managerial capability, weak communication lines, corruption, and a limited budget. These are still present as of this writing.

See also: Chapter 1: Natural Resources. Chapter 2: Overview; Communism; Marcos Dictatorship. Chapter 3: Overview; Martial Law.

Further Reading

Borras, Saturnino. 2007. *Pro-Poor Land Reform: A Critique*. Ottawa: University of Ottawa Press.

Monk, Paul M. 1995. *Truth and Power: Robert S. Hardie and Land Reform Debates in the Philippines, 1950–1987*. Monash: Monash University Centre for Southeast Asian Studies.

Putzel, James. 1992. *A Captive Land: The Politics of Agrarian Reform in the Philippines*. Quezon City: Ateneo de Manila University Press.

Overseas Filipino Workers (OFW)

The total number of Filipinos who have migrated to other countries and who are temporarily working abroad is 10.23 million or 11 percent of the total population. The numbers continue to grow—the government's Commission on Overseas Filipinos has reported that about 5,000 Filipinos leave the country every day to migrate or work abroad. Permanent migrants comprise the most prominent number (4.9 million or 48 percent of the total) as against temporary migrants (4.2 million or 41 percent) and those working or living illegally (1.2 million or 11 percent). The most significant number of Filipino migrants are found in the United States (3.4 million), followed by Canada (851,410). Saudi Arabia hosts the most considerable Filipino working force (1.02 million), followed by the United Arab Emirates (679,819), Malaysia (325,089), and Japan (260,553). Males account for 52 percent of OFWs and 47 percent within this group are between 24 and 34 years old.

OFWs and migrants are the primary sources of the Philippines' revenue. In 2017, the government's Central Bank reported that Filipinos remitted US$31.29 billion back home, and as of May 2018, US$132 billion had been sent to local banks, up 4.4 percent from the same month a year earlier. In 2015, the United States was the most significant source of remittances (US$10.3 billion), followed by Saudi Arabia (US$25 billion), the United Arab Emirates (US$1.71 billion), the United Kingdom (US$1.39 billion), Singapore (US$1.17 billion), Japan (US$981 million), Hong Kong (US$694 million), Canada (US$650 million), Germany (US$490 million), and Australia (US$472 million).

The history of Filipino migrant labor can be traced back to the 1900s, with the first Filipinos working in sugar and other agricultural plantations in Hawaii and California. The second wave of Filipinos came to the United States as military personnel during World War II and after. Then in 1965, the United States liberalized the Immigration and Nationality Act, and the number of Filipino immigrants jumped from 2,500 in 1965 to 25,000 in 1970, a 900 percent increase. Moreover, these were not agriculture workers or military families anymore but professionals (doctors, accountants, engineers, among others). In 1990, the number of Filipino Americans was 1.4 million; in 2020, it rose to 2.3 million; and in 2010 it was 3.4 million. By 1918, there were 4.2 million Filipinos, making them the second-largest Asian American community after the Chinese.

In the mid-1970s, a new pathway opened up for Filipinos wanting to leave the country: the Middle East. After the Organization of Petroleum Exporting Countries (OPEC) raised oil prices in the early 1970s, member countries like Saudi Arabia were awash with money to launch a program to diversify their economies and make them less dependent on oil while expanding their capital cities. These Middle Eastern countries, however, lacked the expertise necessary to launch the program and keep it running. It was Saudi Arabia that opened up its economy to foreign workers and the Philippines was one of the first countries to cater to the demand. Demand from the Middle East coincided with the efforts of President Ferdinand Marcos to find new sources of revenue other than mining and the usual exports of sugar, coconut, and food crops. Labor became one of these nontraditional exports, and it continued to expand at a fast pace of 30 percent a year.

Then in the 1980s and 1990s, demand for domestic helps and caregivers rose in places like Hong Kong, Singapore, and Europe, and the boom in mail-order brides and adult entertainment in Japan provided an opportunity for women to go abroad. Today, there is near parity between the number of Filipinos and Filipinas working abroad. In 2017, the Philippine Statistics Authority reported that Filipinas now outpaced Filipinos (53.7 percent and 46.3 percent, respectively). Filipina workers also tend to be younger (25–29 years old) compared to Filipinos (30–34 years old).

Have remittances helped the incomes of the families who sent their kin abroad? The answer is yes and no. Remittance-receiving households earn more from their investments and have a higher savings rate than non-remittance families. In 2006, the average incomes of the former were 37 percent higher than the latter. They could thus spend more for their children's education and family members' health. These families were likewise able to purchase more goods, spend more leisure time, and purchase new homes or renovate existing ones. Finally, OFW remittances have increased the incomes of impoverished families, increasing the possibility that they would be able to get out of poverty. Households that had described themselves as poor pre-migration later reported that they were now better off than their neighbors as a result of the migration experience.

Economists and sociologists have also observed that in most regions of the country, the primary beneficiaries of OFW remittances are those in the urban areas and who come from the middle classes. Their higher incomes, in turn, allow the city and middle-class families to send their children to much better schools (the top private universities or the elite University of the Philippines). The more professional the family, the better their job opportunities and the higher their wages. Moreover, urban families are better informed about job openings than their rural peers, given that the significant placement agencies and government offices in charge of OFWs are located in the cities.

The rural and urban poor do not have such opportunities. Education may likely stop at high school or technical school. They are therefore limited to blue-collar occupations, with lower wages and very little chance of moving up. Their limited resources and distance from the cities reduce their chances of getting regular updates on job opportunities and devoting time to interact with placement agencies and government offices. Finally, needy families go into debt to pay for going to work abroad.

Despite all this, Filipinos continue to go abroad. In 2009, an average of 2,500 flew out of the Manila and Mactan International Airports, with the number reaching 5,031 in 2013 and 6,092 in 2014.

See also: Chapter 2: Overview; Marcos Dictatorship; People Power Revolution. Chapter 3: Overview; Martial Law; Post-Marcos Philippines; Relations with Japan; Relations with the United States.

Further Reading

Ang, Alvin P., Guntur Sugiyarto, and Shikha Jha. 2009. "Remittances and Household Behavior in the Philippines." *Asian Development Bank Working Papers Series No.*

188. December. https://www.adb.org/sites/default/files/publication/28401/economics-wp188.pdf

Burgess, Robert, and Vikram Haksar. 2005. "Migration and Foreign Remittances in the Philippines." *IMF Working Paper* (May 11): 18 pp.

Guevara, Anna Romina. 2009. *Marketing Dreams, Manufacturing Heroes: The Transnational Labor Brokering of Filipino Workers*. New Jersey: Rutgers University Press.

The Service Sector

In the 21st century, the term "industry" became synonymous with the service sector. The sector refers to small and medium businesses contracted by Western businesses to work on the ancillary components of industrial production. They include legal services, accounting and auditing, engineering and computer services, and even business management. The sector also includes enterprises involved in wholesale and retail trade, real estate, food and transportation services, and even education and health. The most popular of these service sector industries are the business processing outsourcing (BPO) companies, which essentially provide customer services for companies abroad.

In 2017, the World Bank described the service sector as the "main driver of growth." It is the biggest of the three main sectors of the economy. The service sector's share of the total GDP is 59.89 percent, with industry a distant second (30.45 percent) and agriculture a poor third (9.66 percent). The service sector is also the country's biggest employer. Of the 40 million Filipinos employed as of mid-2017, 55.4 percent (20.7 million) were in the service sector (as against 26.1 percent in agriculture and 18.5 percent in industry).

OFWs constitute the largest group in the service sector. At the end of 2017, there were 2.3 million Filipinos working abroad, employed in diverse types of work—from managers in Indonesian firms to crew of cargo ships or cruise liners, from oil workers in Saudi Arabia to employees in Israeli fruit farms, and from household staff in Italy and Hong Kong to English teachers in Myanmar and China. In 2017, these service workers sent home US$28.1 billion, which comprised 10 percent of the country's GDP.

The second highest source of revenue in the service sector are the BPOs. The Philippines has the second-largest number of BPO centers in the world, second only to India. Most of these are mainly "call centers" and "non-voice, back-office services," that is, operators who assist customers in various things, from booking air travel to computer repairs. There is, however, a small but growing number of BPOs that deal with high-end work in finance (banking, insurance, and accounting services), human resource management, healthcare, and tourism. In 2017, the BPO centers earned a total of US$24 billion; in 2020 it reached $26.7 billion, despite the COVID-19 pandemic (Gutierrez 2021). The BPOs, together with OFW remittances, have been responsible for the growth of the Filipino middle class, which stood at 41.8 percent of the total population in 2019 (or 4 of every 10 Filipinos).

The middle class has also been responsible for sustaining the third-largest industry in the service sector—the retail industry. The Philippines is ranked 16th among the most attractive retail markets in the developing world. The four largest retail companies are family-owned and provide Filipinos with a variety of items, mainly catering to household needs—from clothes and footwear to food and kitchenware. The largest of these family-owned enterprises is SM Supermalls, which has 70 shopping arcades all over the country plus 7 in China, one of which is the largest in the world. The four largest enterprises combined with a couple of smaller companies employ about 35.3 percent of the total 40 million labor force.

See also: Chapter 2: Overview, Marcos Dictatorship, People Power Revolution. Chapter 3: Overview; Martial Law; Post-Marcos Philippines; Relations with the United States.

Further Reading

Banados, Papias Generale. 2011. *The Path to Remittance: Tales of Pains and Gains of Overseas Filipino Workers*. Singapore: Global Eye Media.

Bird, Miriam, and Ernst Christoph. 2009. "Offshoring and Employment in the Developing World: Business Process Outsourcing in the Philippines." *Employment Working Paper No. 41*. Geneva: International Labour Organization. http://www.ilo.org/wcmsp5/groups/public/---ed_emp/---emp_elm/---analysis/documents/publication/wcms_117922.pdf

Gutierrez, Pia. 2021. "BPO Industry Revenues Hit $26.7-B in 2020, Up 1.4 Percent: IBPAP." *ABS-CBN News* (May 26). https://news.abs-cbn.com/business/05/26/21/bpo-26-7b-revenues-2020-ibpap

Magtibay-Ramos, Nedelyn, Gemma Esther B. Estrada, and Jesus Felipe. 2007. "An Analysis of the Philippine Business Process Outsourcing Industry." *Asian Development Bank ERD Working Paper No. 93*. Manila.

Mitra, Raja Mikael. 2013. "Leveraging Service Sector Growth in the Philippines." *Asian Development Bank Economics Working Paper Series No. 366*. September 6. https://papers.ssrn.com/sol3/papers.cfm?abstract_id=2321536

Patalinghug, Epictetus. 2001. "An Assessment of Market Saturation in the Retail Trade Industry in the Philippines." *Journal of Asian Business* 17, no. 1: 69–88.

Taxation

In Article 6, Section 8 of the Philippine Constitution, the government is mandated to implement a taxation system that is uniform and equitable; and Congress, in turn, is supposed to establish a progressive system of taxation. Republic Act No. 8428 (or the Tax Reform Act of 1997) is supposedly the latest version of this system. Apart from the national government, local government units also have the power to collect taxes by passing local ordinances. The Bureau of Internal Revenue (BIR) collects taxes at the national level, and local taxes are the responsibility of the treasurer's office of provincial, city, and town governments. The types of taxes collected are similar to that of the United States. Filipinos are assessed for their individual, employment, corporate, estate, property, excise, and donor incomes. In 2006, the government introduced the value-added tax (VAT), which is based on whatever value is added as a commodity moves from production to sales.

On paper, the tax structure appears organized, but when it comes to the implementation, taxation has been one of the most irrepressible administrative problems. First, the Philippines has one of the highest tax rates in Southeast Asia. The corporate tax is a hefty 30 percent and has been the cause of many a foreign investor preferring places like Singapore (17 percent), Thailand (20 percent), and Vietnam (25 percent). The value-added tax (VAT) is 25.80 percent of the total tax revenues. This is the highest in Asia where the range is 0–10 percent. Adding to the problem is that there are 59 goods and services exempted from the VAT, which accounts for the low tax revenue from the supposedly most productive sections of the economy. Finally, the income tax rate in the Philippines (32 percent) is the second highest in Southeast Asia, exceeded only by Thailand and Vietnam where the rate is 35 percent.

Second, the BIR has rarely met its revenue target. In the second decade of the 21st century, for example, it managed to collect 9 percent of the total tax revenue targets. BIR officials blame this on the lack of personnel, but it is also the case that tax evasion has always been endemic. Moreover, the collection system is not the progressive system that it is designed to be. For example, between 2010 and 2013, those receiving salaries and wages constituted 60 percent of the total individual incomes but paid 80 percent of all income taxes, while the self-employed and those adept in hiding their incomes shelled out only 20 percent. Tax rates on dividends and capital incomes—usually the primary business activity of the wealthy—are also lower than those for ordinary workers.

Third, the system of collection is byzantine, complicated, and incredibly inefficient. These deficiencies had prompted the international audit firm PricewaterhouseCoopers (PwC) to rank the Philippines 127th out of 189 countries it surveyed. PwC noted that it would take 193 hours for a business enterprise to fill up and accomplish the BIR's 36 requirements. In contrast, Singapore is ranked 5th and only requires 84 hours compliance, Malaysia is 31st at 118 hours compliance, and Thailand is ranked 70th albeit with 264 hours of compliance. These problems were not only the BIR's problems; they were also replicated: 52 of the 80 provinces, for example, have problems collecting education taxes.

On December 19, 2017, President Rodrigo R. Duterte signed the Comprehensive Tax Reform Program (CTRP) that, as per the website of the Department of Finance, aims "to create a more just, simple, and more effective system of tax collection" such that "the rich will have a bigger contribution and the poor will benefit more from the government's programs and services." The law, which is popularly known as the "Tax Reform for Acceleration and Inclusion" (TRAIN), has a series of ambitious goals—with a 7–10 percent growth in "investments" toward attaining these goals. The term "investment," however, is broadly defined and includes "sustainable borrowings" as well as tax and budget reforms. These reforms would hopefully raise another

1.7 trillion pesos over "the current 1.7 trillion pesos" in the long term. The money would fund education (create "a more conducive learning environment with the ideal teacher-to-student ratio and classroom-to-student ratio"), improve health care services, and modernize the country's infrastructure.

Implementation of the tax reforms, however, yielded the opposite results. TRAIN fueled inflation because while it lowered the tax on personal incomes (good for consumers), it raised the tax on fuel and the so-called "sin" products (cigarettes and alcohol). Then global oil prices went up for three reasons. First, OPEC decided to cut production till the end of 2018 to increase its profits. Second, oil production in one of its members—Venezuela—collapsed because of the economic and political crisis that the country is mired in. Third, the decision of President Donald Trump to withdraw from a "nuclear deal" with Iran narrowed the market of the world's fifth largest oil producer. Oil importing countries, including the Philippines, were hit hard by these three issues. The prices of goods and services went up as businesses that rely on fuel— from huge corporations to mom-and-pop stores—were compelled to raise the prices of their goods in order to compensate for higher taxes and cope with the impact of global oil production and trade.

By July 2018, the inflation rate had risen to 5.2 percent, from 4.6 percent two months before. Apart from alcohol and tobacco (the prices of which rose by 20 percent), economists also noted increases in the prices of housing, electricity, gas, and water (4.6 percent), education (4.0 percent), home furnishings and other household equipment (3 percent), transportation (7.1 percent), and communications (0.4 percent). These led to a public clamor for President Rodrigo R. Duterte to suspend TRAIN. Instead of meeting the problem head on, however, Duterte passed on the onus to Congress, saying it is the only government body that is legally allowed to suspend, amend, or modify existing laws.

See also: Chapter 2: Marcos Dictatorship; People Power Revolution. Chapter 3: Martial Law; Post-Marcos Philippines; Relations with the United States.

Further Reading

Alonso y Terme, Rosa Maria. 2014. "What Prevents the Philippines from Undertaking Reform? A Story of the Unravelling State." *International Centre for Tax and Development.* Institute of Developing Economies. January. https://assets.publishing.service .gov.uk/media/57a089d240f0b652dd000412/ICTD-WP16.pdf

Diokno, Benjamin E. 2005. "Reforming the Philippine Tax System: Lessons from Two Tax Reform Programs." *University of the Philippines School of Economics Discussion Papers 0502* (March): 1-27. http://www.econ.upd.edu.ph/dp/index.php/dp/article/view/122/120

Trading Partners

The Philippines exports electrical machinery and equipment, ships (the country is now the fourth largest shipbuilding country in the world), metals and gems, fruits,

Table 4.1: PHILIPPINE EXPORTS

Country/Ranking	Exports (US$)	Percentage of Total Exports
Japan	10.2 billion	16.2
United States	9.2 billion	14.6
Hong Kong	8.6 billion	13.7
China	7.0 billion	11.1
Singapore	3.9 billion	6.1
Thailand	2.6 billion	4.2
Germany	2.6 billion	4.1
South Korea	2.5 billion	4.0
Netherlands	2.5 billion	3.9
Taiwan	2.3 billion	3.6
Malaysia	1.6 billion	2.5
Vietnam	867.2 million	1.4
France	791.5 million	1.3
Indonesia	702.1 million	1.1
Malta	685.6 million	1.1

Source: World Trade Organization. 2018. *World Trade Statistical Review*. https://www.wto.org/english
/res_e/statis_e/wts2018_e/wts2018_e.pdf

timber, medical apparatuses, coconut oil, minerals (like nickel), and clothing accessories. A quarter of exports still go to its traditional trading partners, such as the United States and Japan. The country, however, has diversified its markets, especially increasing trade with neighboring Southeast Asian countries as well as China. The 2017 ranking of countries to which Philippine products were exported is shown in Table 4.1.

The imports consist mainly of mineral ores, iron and steel, oil and petroleum, transport equipment, transport (trucks, vehicle and aircraft parts), food, electronics, industrial machinery, and office machine parts. The Philippines purchases these goods from the countries listed in Table 4.2.

The trade has not been advantageous. In 2017, the country incurred a trade deficit of negative US$35.3 billion, which was up from the US$29.6 billion in 2016. If you break this down per country, the trade deficit with China was the largest (US$10.8 billion), followed by Indonesia (US$6 billion), South Korea (US$5.9 billion), Thailand (US$4.3 billion), Taiwan (US$3 billion), Malaysia (US$2.2 billion), Singapore (U$2.9 billion), Vietnam (US$2.8 billion), Australia (US$1.4 billion) and Saudi Arabia (US$1.2 billion). The deficit with South Korea rose the fastest (up by 66.7 percent), followed by Indonesia (up by 46 percent). The possibility of this deficit being replaced by a surplus is unlikely. Economists regard this imbalance as disadvantageous to the competitiveness of Philippine products, although they also put a positive spin to the problem by recommending that the Philippines could plan strategically as to which countries could yield the best export revenues and which countries' imports can be its priority.

Table 4.2: PHILIPPINE IMPORTS

Country/Ranking	Imports (US$)	Percentage of Total Imports
China	19.4 billion	21.0
Japan	10.1 billion	11.0
United States	7.51 billion	8.1
Thailand	6.7 billion	7.3
South Korea	6.5 billion	7.0
Singapore	5.7 billion	6.1
Indonesia	4.87 billion	5.2
Malaysia	3.19 billion	3.4
Hong Kong	2.62 billion	2.8
Germany	2.18 billion	2.4
Vietnam	1.93 billion	2.1
India	1.60 billion	1.7
Australia	1.39 billion	1.5
France	1.02 billion	1.1
Saudi Arabia	978 million	1.1
Kuwait	907 million	0.98
Italy	678 million	0.73
United Arab Emirates	612 million	0.66
Netherlands	567 million	0.61
United Kingdom	566 million	0.61

Source: World Trade Organization. 2018. *World Trade Statistical Review.* https://www.wto.org/english/res_e/statis_e/wts2018_e/wts2018_e.pdf

See also: Chapter 2: Overview; Marcos Dictatorship; People Power Revolution. Chapter 3: Overview; Martial Law; Relations with the United States.

Further Reading

Cororaton, Caesar B. 2015. "Will the Philippines Benefit from the Regional Comprehensive Economic Partnership?" *Policy Notes No. 2015-23.* November.

Llanto, Gilberto M., and Ma. Kristina P. Ortiz. 2013. "Regional Comprehensive Economic Partnership: Reform Challenges and Key Tasks for the Philippines." *Philippine Institute for Development Studies Discussion Paper Series No. 2013-51.* November.

Manzano, George, and Kristine Joy Martin. 2015. "Implications of a Philippine-US Free Trade Agreement on Trade in Goods: An Indicator Approach." *Philippine Institute for Development Studies Discussion Paper Series No. 2015-42.* September.

Medalla, Erlinda M., and Angelica B. Maddawin. 2015. "Supporting WTO and Pathways to the Free Trade Area of the Asia Pacific (FTAAP)." *Philippine Institute for Development Studies Discussion Paper Series No. 2015-17.* February.

Observatory of Economic Complexity. n.d. *The Philippines.* https://atlas.media.mit.edu/en/profile/country/phl/

Papers 0502. March. http://www.econ.upd.edu.ph/dp/index.php/dp/article/view/122/120

CHAPTER 5

RELIGIONS

OVERVIEW

Religion is an intrinsic part of Filipino life. Christianity is the dominant religion in the Philippines, with 92 percent of Filipinos officially identifying themselves with the religion. Muslims constitute 5.6 percent of the population. Of the remainder, some identify with pre-Christian belief systems, the Chinese practice Taoism, some follow the Sikh religion, some are Hindus, and some are nonreligious.

Among Christians, the majority (82 percent) belong to the Catholic Church, while 11 percent belong to various Protestant groups and local churches. Around the late 1990s, evangelical groups began to attract more Filipinos and in the 2010 census, 11 percent of the population stated that they were members of such groups.

Missionaries introduced both Christianity and Islam to the archipelago, but they soon found themselves incorporating aspects of the precolonial belief systems into these religions to boost their legitimacy among the people. There are ethnoreligious tensions between Christians and Muslims, but compared to Indonesia or Malaysia where these have led to periods of violence, in the Philippines these two religions have learned to coexist with one another. Their leaders have even worked together in pursuit of peace in war-torn Mindanao Island. In the past, it has been the Filipino-established churches that challenged Catholic doctrines as part of their proselytization campaigns. These hardly made a dent on the Catholic Church. Where some change could happen is with the Catholic Church's relations with charismatic evangelical groups. Although the rivalry between these two denominations has not been belligerent, as religious groups gain more membership, there is also a tendency for these Christians groups to examine and explain how they are different from each other (McLoughlin 2015).

Evangelical groups have come at a time when there have been changes in the way Christians, especially Catholics, look at their practice. Filipinos remain conservative on issues like abortion (93 percent are opposed to it), premarital sex (71 percent are against it), and divorce (67 percent against). Weekly church attendance has gone down by half—from 64 percent in 1991 to 37 percent in 2013 (Picardal 2018). Adult Filipinos supported the passage of a Reproductive Health Bill in 2012, and 51 percent of them disagree with the anti-abortion stance of the church establishment. Young Catholic Filipinos, however, claim that their primary religious influences are their families, friends, educators, and Catholic organizations rather than the clergy or the parish (Cornelio 2016, 132–133).

See also: Chapter 7: History of the Family Unit; Parent-Child Relationships; Sexuality. Chapter 10: Fiesta.

Further Reading

Cornelio, Jayeel Serrano. 2016. *Being Catholic in the Contemporary Philippines*. New York: Routledge.

McLoughlin, Scotty. 2015. "The Boundary Indefinite: Schism and Ethics of Christian Strategy in the Philippines." PhD diss., University of Michigan. https://deepblue.lib.umich.edu/bitstream/handle/2027.42/113319/scottmcl_1.pdf

Picardal, Amado. 2018. "Seasonal and Nominal Catholics in the Philippines." *LaCroix International: The World's Premier Independent Catholic Daily*. May 7. https://international.la-croix.com/news/seasonal-and-nominal-catholics-in-the-philippines/7524

Catholicism

Overseeing the 76 million Filipino Catholics is a hierarchy that is a replica of other similar church organizations found internationally. At the top are 82 active archbishops, bishops, and cardinals, plus 43 honorary bishops. The former are appointed by the Pope to oversee dioceses while the latter's selection does not lead to a diocesan appointment. There are 16 archdioceses, 51 dioceses, 7 apostolic vicariates (areas where the church has not yet established a diocese or a parish and headed by a titular bishop), 5 territorial prelates (areas that do not belong to a diocese), and a military ordinariate (the body that attends to the religious needs of the military).

The Pope assigns a bishop or an archbishop to a diocese and oversees all the religious functions of the territory. There is no hierarchical difference between archbishops and bishops, and the only distinction is that the former presides over a larger diocese. Each diocese is autonomous from the other, and each bishop only answers to the Pope, although bishops do coordinate with each other through the Catholic Bishops Conference of the Philippines (CBCP). The other name for the CBCP is the Episcopal Conference, and it is headed by the archbishop of Manila, the largest city of the country. The origins of the CBCP can be traced back to February 1945, when there was a need for coordinated efforts to take care of those imprisoned by the Japanese. The CBCP eventually evolved into its present role which is to formulate church programs, foster harmony among the clergy and laity, and ensure that specific Vatican policies are implemented.

The CBCP's highest policy-making body is the Plenary Assembly, which meets twice a year to lay out the apostolic programs. It has a set of officers that includes a president, vice president, secretary general, and treasurer. The assembly also elects 10 members to a Permanent Council (coming from the three primary island groups) and

Catholic devotees read the pabasa, recounting the Passion of the Christ. (Junpinzon/Dreamstime.com)

the heads of the Episcopal Commissions and other offices that are under the CBCP. The Permanent Council sets the agenda for Conference meetings, deals with the annual budget, releases pastoral letters and CBCP statements, and creates the appropriate Episcopal Commissions for issues the CBCP is concerned with. These will then be approved by the Plenary Assembly.

The dioceses are divided into parishes, each of which is headed by a parish priest who reports to the bishop of the diocese and ultimately the Pope. Each parish has a chapter of the Neocatechumenal Way, whose primary function is to take the lead in the so-called Christian formation programs where members immersed themselves in reading the Bible and listen to the priest's interpretation of God's Word. There are about 25,000 members of this charismatic organization across 700 communities. There are also several "Catholic Charismatic Renewal" movements providing another layer of proselytization in the parishes. These include the Couples for Christ whose members come mainly from the white-collar professions, the Light of Jesus family, the Soldiers of Christ, and the largest of them all, El Shaddai.

Institutional religion, however, has been and continues to be Catholicism. Today, the major religious congregations have missions in the Philippines, and the country has the third-largest number of Catholics worldwide. Filipinos are some of the most devout Catholics, conscientiously following all the rituals associated with the religion (from the celebration of the mass to the commemoration of the different vital stages of the life of Jesus Christ, i.e., from Christmas to his death). Apart from the Crucifixion mentioned above, Filipinos do not just commemorate the official rituals; they create their own rituals like crawling or walking on their knees from a church's door to the altar, praying all the while. Families also hire "prayer ladies" who plead with the sacred on their behalf. Filipinos also revere material presentations of Christ. In Cebu City, located in the central Philippines, devotees from all over the country flock to the Church of the Santo Nino (Church of the Holy Child), where they hear mass but also wipe their handkerchiefs and bandanas on the Child Jesus statue purportedly to be blessed but also to be protected by him. In a town north of Manila, Catholic sinners atone for their sins by re-enacting the suffering and death of Jesus. This includes carrying a stone across the street or whipping themselves bloody, with the enactment culminating in them being nailed to the cross.

The church also has a strong movement that concerns itself with celebrating the holiness of the Blessed Virgin Mary, the mother of Jesus Christ. Mary has her special days—like the Feast of the Immaculate Conception to celebrate the angel's announcement that Mary that she is pregnant with Jesus, and the monthlong Flores de Mayo (where Filipinos shower Mary with flowers). Some groups describe themselves with pride as "Marian devotees," displaying the statues of Mary during town fiestas. There is a more formal "The Legion of Mary," which functions as a lay support group for parishes. So popular has the icon of Mary become that Filipinos now refer to her in the most special terms. They call her their "Mama Mary," and she is as essential a figure in the Catholic upbringing of children as Jesus. Below Jesus and Mary, there are a host of religious individuals who are adopted as patron saints by towns and villages.

Finally, the Catholic Church is one of the largest owners or administrators of private schools. The Philippines has a total number of 225 universities distributed all over the archipelago, of which 72 are Catholic. Of the top 20 institutions of higher learning, 8 are run by religious orders. A notch lower, you have almost the same distribution: 24 of the top 50 high schools are Catholic-managed. It is not far-fetched to argue that one reason behind Catholicism's unchallenged preeminence are these schools. Consider, for example, the following statistics—in the 2016–2017 school year, 18 percent of the 1.3 million secondary school students were in private schools, while 45.8 percent of the 3.5 million students were enrolled in nonstate universities and colleges (Macha, Mackie, and Magaziner 2018).

It is this robust presence through time that has made the church a politically influential social actor ever since the first Spanish conquistadores and religious missionaries arrived in 1565 and turned the small port town of Manila into the colonial capital. Islam had already made some headway with Arab missionaries and Chinese Muslims connecting trading ports like Sulu to China. Once the Spaniards consolidated their presence in the lowland communities of central and northern Philippines, they created a barrier to stop the spread of Islam to the north of the archipelago. Several attempts to set up missions to contain Islam, if not push it out of the archipelago, failed.

In the Spanish-controlled communities, however, Catholicism consolidated its control of people's belief systems. Missionaries took to learning local languages and lived among the people of their parishes and defended them against abuses by Spanish officials. They prohibited precolonial religious practices but also did not put a stop to the indigenization of the Catholic religion, that is, the intermixing of pre-Spanish belief systems with the new monolithic one. To the colonized, the priest was just another "shaman," and their religious icons were the new and more powerful "spirits" which replaced the "gods and goddesses" who ruled their natural surroundings. The missionaries appeared to be aware of this but looked the other way if this synthesis worked toward hastening conversions. What sealed the relationship between the missionaries and the colonized was their defense against Muslim slave raids of communities north of Mindanao.

With nonreligious Spaniards showing very little interest in staying in the Philippines for a long duration, the priests eventually became the real power centers and their parishes the de facto structures that administered the colony. The archbishop of Manila stood in the same pinnacle as the governor general, and there was even an occasion where conflicts at the top led to the death of the governor general in the hands of a mob of clerics. By the late Spanish period, however, the kind of missionaries being sent to the Philippines were no more of the same intellectual caliber and moral rectitude as those who had preceded them. They became the face of the enemy for an emerging middle class as well as peasants toiling in their lands. The national hero Jose Rizal's novels *Noli Me Tangere* and *El Filibusterismo* censored these abusive friars, and the nationalist revolution was sparked by Rizal's death as well as the gravity of friar abuse. This critique of the church by an emerging Filipino elite defined its relationship with society. As Coeli Barry puts it, "the central place of Catholicism in the Philippines [makes it] not surprising that it is implicated in the politics of the country in many different levels" (Barry 2018, 330). After expropriating some church lands to appease Filipinos and encourage them to help them rule the new colony, the Americans made peace with Rome. The Americans did not expropriate additional church properties and neither did they break down its administrative structure.

What the Americans did, however, was to remove the much-despised Spanish clerics and replace them with priests and nuns from non-Spanish European orders, priests from American dioceses as well as Filipino priest. The church was never able to recover the kind of power it had during the Spanish period because Americans abided closely to the separation of church and state (Schumacher 2009, 951–952). It withdrew from the center stage and shifted to exerting its influence through schools and churches, the molding of young minds, and quietly supporting pro-Catholic politicians to defend its interests. This arrangement extended well into the Republican era, where the church helped the government foment an anti-communist sentiment among the populace as propaganda support for government efforts to defeat the Partido Komunista ng Pilipinas (PKP). The church also tried to prevent a law that required the teaching of Rizal's novels in all colleges but was defeated by pro-Rizal forces among the legislators.

In 1959, Pope John XXIII announced the formation of a Second Vatican Council where 2,000 bishops, priests, nuns, and laypersons met between 1962 and 1965, producing a series of documents which included encouraging Catholics to engage in dialogue with other religions and celebrate rituals in the local languages instead of Latin, with the clergy encouraging active participation by their congregations. These doctrinal changes attracted young Filipinos who were inspired by the reformist advo-cacies of then-president Ramon D. Magsaysay, were alienated by the way their leaders conducted their politics (spoils and patronage), and saw the PKP rebellion as the last option taken by impoverished peasants. Two global events became a new inspiration to Vatican II supporters. On the one hand, the growing failure of the United States' war in Vietnam eroded American political and moral standing while making heroes out of the tenacious Vietnamese resistance. On the other hand, there was a growing sociocultural gap between the older generation, which benefited from the global eco-nomic boom after World War II, and their children, who desired greater freedom and autonomy from a life they regarded as too conformist and constricting (especially for women and minorities).

By the mid-1960s, students from Catholic universities and schools had formed "movements" seeking social justice, were volunteering for cleaner elections, and were helping form peasant associations and trade unions. When the new communist party burst into the political arena in the next decade, its cadres flipped some of these reformist societies to the radical side, while others pushed their interpretations of the Vatican II reforms further to justify the fact that they had resorted to arms. The hier-archy, which was initially resistant to Vatican II, now began cherry-picking its doc-trines to put a stop to the radicalization within the ranks while appropriating themes from the reformists and claiming them as its own; this, too, weakened the pro-Vatican II flank. Martial law put a temporary stop to the worsening of these fault lines inside the church.

The church hierarchy was divided on how to engage the Marcos dictatorship. Some bishops supported the new order, while others urged the church to withdraw from politics and concentrate on the spiritual. A smaller group argued in favor of looking at martial law as a challenge to the principles of Vatican II. They would prevail over a new leadership headed by the archbishop of Manila, Cardinal Jaime Sin, who declared that the church would adopt the policy of "critical collaboration" vis-à-vis the Marcos government. The rest of the church supported Sin, but as the regime became more repressive in pursuit of communists, military atrocities turned many of these clerics as well as nuns into passionate human rights defenders. Some of them would join the New People's Army (NPA), but the majority remained suspicious of communist intentions.

The Catholic Church shed its "collaboration" side after the 1983 assassination of the anti-Marcos leader Benigno Aquino Jr., and two years later it was instrumental in supporting Corazon Aquino's electoral challenge of Marcos. Then, when military officers failed in their attempt to overthrow Marcos, the cardinal Sin called on Filipi-nos to protect the former. When Aquino became president, the Catholic Church once more became a major player in national politics but never a dominating one. The leadership used this political capital to rid the church of radical and left-wing influence. In the late 1990s and early 2000s, the church's stature was shaken by a series of sex scandals that had bishops apologizing to the congregation. Even as this was going on, the church joined another uprising that forced the resignation of President Joseph E. Estrada in 2001.

Going against an extremely popular president, however, had its drawbacks. The church's influence on the poor began to wane after it said nothing regarding the police action launched by President Gloria M. Arroyo against pro-Estrada supporters who tried to stage "People Power 3." The latter, many of them coming from poor families, interpreted this silence as a condoning of state violence. The church's standing suffered another blow. While certain bishops and priests were still regarded highly, mainly because of their devotion to human rights, it was clear that this was no more the powerful church of the 1980s. Political leaders took advantage of this weakened position to push for programs the church was opposed to. Such was the case in 2012 when President Benigno S. Aquino III and Congress passed a reproductive rights law despite fervent church opposition. After President Duterte launched his "War on Drugs," the church was unable to mount an effective opposition because it neither had the "people power" nor the institutional cohesion that it once had.

Discussion of the Catholic Church would not be complete without mentioning Jaime Cardinal Sin, the archbishop of Manila and leader of the church. Sin was appointed by the Vatican to the position on March 19, 1974, just after Marcos consolidated martial law. The new head of the Philippine Catholic Church had to navigate an extremely difficult course. There was President Ferdinand E. Marcos worried that the church could become an institutional threat on the one side, while on the other side, an increasingly restive clergy and sisterhood began demanding that the church take a more active stance in defending human rights and the welfare of their congregations. Sin pursued what he called the policy of "critical collaboration." The church would recognize the authority of the new regime and work together with the government on social welfare projects that it deemed would benefit Filipinos. Sin would join the Marcoses in public ceremonies, and the latter would also grace specific church festivities. The church would be critical of the government if it deemed its programs and actions would lead to more suffering. In the early years, Cardinal Sin would express his concerns to Marcos in private. He preferred muted criticism except when the government raided church offices to arrest dissidents seeking sanctuary.

Sin, however, allowed priests and nuns wide latitude in pursuing the "preferential option for the poor" that Vatican II had been promoting. He stopped short of supporting the radicalization of church personnel, which was one of the promises he gave to Marcos to placate his political discomfort. Sin quietly supported the formation of "social action" programs which spread the liturgy, educated people on social justice issues, assisted in livelihood promotion programs among the poor, and protected them from the police and the military. Sin began to be more openly critical of the regime after the 1983 assassination of Marcos-oppositionist Benigno Aquino Jr. Not only were his homilies on current events more critical, he also allowed his priests to use sermons as the platform to proselytize. When Marcos announced a snap presidential election in 1985, Sin persuaded Aquino's widow Corazon to run against Marcos, and then approved church participation in the revival of an election watchdog. Sin's authority and influence reached its fruition in the 1986 "People Power" uprising when he called on Filipinos to protect armed rebels holed up in two military camps.

When Aquino took over the presidency, Sin became one of her closest advisers. This elicited concerns from the Vatican—worried that church politicization had gone too far—but Sin was able to placate the Pope. Sin's star began to dim after he supported the 2001 ouster of President Joseph E. Estrada and denounced the poor's participation in "People Power III," the massive protest over Estrada's ouster which the police and military brutally suppressed. So widespread was the displeasure toward the church that Sin had to apologize publicly. In 2003, Sin had to ask for forgiveness again when a sex scandal wracked the church. Two years later, Sin passed away leaving a church that had lost much of its political luster.

See also: Chapter 2: Overview; Marcos Dictatorship; People Power Revolution. Chapter 3: Overview; Martial Law; Post-Marcos Philippines. Chapter 11: *Noli Me Tangere* and *El Filibusterismo*.

Further Reading

Barry, Coeli. 2018. "Gender, Nation and Filipino Catholicism Past and Present." In Mark R. Thompson and Eric Vincent C. Batalla (eds.), *Routledge Handbook of the Contemporary Philippines*. Oxford and New York: Routledge.

Macha, Wilson, Christopher Mackie, and Jessica Magaziner. 2018. "Education in the Philippines." *World Education News and Reviews*. March 6. https://wenr.wes.org/2018/03/education-in-the-philippines

Robertson, James Alexander. 2018. "Catholicism in the Philippine Islands." *Catholic Historical Review* 3, no. 4 (January): 375–391. https://www.jstor.org/stable/pdf/25011532.pdf

Schumacher, John S. 2009. *Growth and Decline: Essays on Philippine Church History*. Quezon City: Ateneo de Manila University Press.

El Shaddai

El Shaddai (Hebrew for "God Almighty") is a charismatic Catholic movement founded in 1981 by Miguel "Brother Mike" Velarde, a businessman who claimed that while recovering from a heart operation, he was visited by an angel of God who, after speaking to him, led him to his remarkable recovery. God did not just help him heal; the Supreme Being also helped reverse his financial fortune, when, after a "Charismatic Mass and Healing Rally," a group of businessmen advanced Velarde millions of pesos to save his real estate business from bankruptcy. Velarde declared himself a "born again Catholic" and purchased a radio station where every Sunday, from 9:00-11:00 a.m., he ran the program "To God Be the Glory," where he called on Filipino Catholics to confess their sins and return to religion. He later changed the program name to "El Shaddai," became a full-time missionary, and with the support from Catholic foundations, formed the El Shaddai DWXI Prayer Partners Foundation International (DWXI-PPFI). Velarde became the "serving manager" of the Foundation and the leader of the flock. El Shaddai proved to be a successful medium for religious proselytization.

In 1984, over 1,000 people showed up at the radio station when Velarde invited them for a Thanksgiving mass. Many claimed they were cured of their infirmities, and from that time on, thousands went to Velarde's monthly prayer rallies, which moved outside the radio station and into various massive amphitheaters and grandstands all around Manila. He complemented these with his radio program. Today, DWXI is one of the most listened-to stations in the Philippines. The sign of its success has been the increase in El Shaddai membership. In the 1990s, El Shaddai had a million members; today the estimated number has reached 8 million. The movement now has 62 chapters in the Philippines, and also in the Middle East, Europe, Australia, Canada, and the United States.

El Shaddai does not follow a set of religious doctrines in the way that the Aglipayan and Iglesia ni Cristo do. To become a member, however, one must attend a "Catholic-for-Life-in-the-Spirit" seminar where one is required to recite three times a day the "Our Father" (The Lord's Prayer), Psalm 90 (an excerpt of which goes, "Lord you have been our dwelling place throughout all generations. Before the mountains were born or you brought forth the whole world, from everlasting to everlasting you are God."), and Psalm 23 (the famous opening lines of which are: "The Lord is my shepherd; I shall not want. He makes me lie down in green pastures. He leads me beside still waters. He restores my soul. He leads me in the path of righteousness for his name's sake. Even though I walk through the valley of the shadow of death, I will fear no evil, for you are with me . . ."). Would-be members are also encouraged to apply for fellowships sponsored by the El Shaddai foundation and regularly contribute tithes.

Once a member, the person is expected to become a servant-volunteer worker, offering their services for at least three years. They must follow the Catholic Church and El Shaddai and not be involved in any immoral or illegal activities. They must have no pending case in court concerning "moral turpitude," adultery, divorce, malversation of funds and swindling. Moreover, they have to be a member of the foundation for at least three years. Male members who excel become preachers and are trained at a "College of Divine Wisdom" where they deepen their knowledge of the Bible and are trained in evangelization, counseling, and praying. After their training, these preachers are assigned to coordinate organizations of the movement and a whole slew of activities—from outreach programs to organizing liturgical events, extending legal and medical help and helping poor members overcome their fate. An important activity for the members is the "Baptism of Spirit" assemblies (where members are baptized or born again in the water of the Holy Spirit) where religious supplications and songs are combined with statements by witnesses regarding their financial difficulties, marriage problems, employment challenges, and health issues. Velarde either promises a miracle or points to changes in the natural environment (such as rain) as signs of blessings to come.

Velarde makes no claims of giving new interpretations of Catholic teaching; all he did in the monthly rallies was exhort people to pray to the Holy Spirit for spiritual comfort, but more importantly, for real and emotional success. It is not unusual to hear Velarde ask the crowd if they want this or that amenity, or if they want to resolve a marital crisis, pass the exam, or get a job abroad. He reminds his followers that if they put their trust in God, miracles will happen that will bring financial success, improvement in health, and unexpected opportunities that would be extremely beneficial to them. His sermons do include warnings to his followers about corruption and engaging in electoral fraud. Velarde's critics complain that these invocations are distortions of the Catholic Church's concept of a miracle and what the institution wants of its members—spiritual salvation. Church leaders, however, remain close to El Shaddai, with bishops appointed to the position of spiritual directors.

Critics also worry that El Shaddai has a stronger influence than the Catholic Church not merely because of its large membership but also because of the way politicians relate to it. In 1992, there were rumors that El Shaddai was a significant factor in the narrow electoral victory of President Fidel V. Ramos. Velarde also tried to mediate between the rivals, presidents Joseph E. Estrada and Gloria M. Arroyo, in the 2005 elections. This action gave the public a glimpse of the extent to which those who hold political power value El Shaddai. When the organization inaugurated its US$21 million 10-hectare "House of Prayer," Arroyo was one of the guests.

The other issue raised by critics is the handling of the group's finances. Members are expected to contribute 10 percent of their incomes as tithes. These revenues usually go to support the prayer groups, but Velarde reported that half goes to support facilities of the Catholic Church. Velarde has also established the El Shaddai Golden Rule Corporation, a joint stock company that owns and manages a supermarket where members can purchase commodities at a discounted price. Members are encouraged to invest in the company, and the biggest attraction is that since El Shaddai is a religious organization, its incomes are not taxable.

Velarde is now in his early 80s, and there are worries that his successor may not have the same charisma that he possesses. However, members hope that he has set up a strong enough collective leadership (which includes family members) that will ensure the organization's well-being if and when he dies or retires.

See also: Chapter 2: Overview; People Power Revolution. Chapter 3: Overview; Martial Law.

Further Reading

Mercado, Leonardo. 2001. *El Shaddai: A Study*. Manila: Logos Publications.

Wiegele, Katherine L. 2004. *Investing in Miracles: El Shaddai and the Transformation of Popular Catholicism in the Philippines*. Honolulu, HI: University of Hawaii Press.

Iglesia ni Kristo (The Church of Christ)

The Iglesia ni Kristo (The Church of Christ) was founded by Felix Manalo (1886–1963), who claimed that he was the "messenger from God" as foretold by the Bible. Section 2,

Paragraph 7, of the Bible's "Revelation" foretold the coming of an "angel" from the "Far East." Manalo claimed that date was 1914, the year of the Iglesia's founding.

Manalo was raised Catholic but converted to Protestantism after watching an American Protestant missionary getting the best of a Catholic priest in a public debate. Manalo joined the Methodist Episcopal Church in 1904 and attended a Bible school run by Presbyterian missionaries. A decade later, at the age of 26, Manalo decided to join the Seventh-Day Adventists and was ordained a preacher. His new status did not work for him. Manalo spiraled into depression, doubting the existence of God, and was on the verge of abandoning his faith. To overcome this debility, in November 2013, he devoted himself to a close study of Roman Catholicism and the teachings of Adventists while going into seclusion, fasting, and meditating. Seven months later, on July 27, 1914, he founded the Iglesia, together with his first 12 converts, by filing its articles of incorporation with the Division of Archives, Patented Properties of Literature and Industrial Trade Mark.

The Iglesia grew steadily, from 25,000 members in 1935 to 88,125 members after the war and 100,000 members after a decade. It expanded to the American West Coast and Hawaii and to Asia and Europe. In August 2021, the Church had about 5 million members in the country and Iglesia congregations can be found in 158 countries (Mabasa 2021). The Iglesia's remarkable growth has been attributed to Manalo's charisma, talent at arguing, and mastery of the Bible and its many interpretations. A majority of its members are people from poor backgrounds who were promised not only the salvation of their souls but also that the Iglesia would help them secure or keep employment. The fact that Manalo mandated that all church rituals were to be conducted in Filipino was appealing to its members. He and his officials also took the teaching of the church's interpretation of the scripture to its members seriously. This made them feel important and enhanced their sense of community (Sanders 1969, 358).

In a society where Catholics and Protestants knew very little about the Bible (much less read it), Iglesia members pride themselves in being well-schooled in the Scriptures and being able to defend them (Sanders 1969, 206). The Iglesia denies the doctrine of the Trinity and while it recognizes Jesus as "the Son of God," it contends that he was not "God himself" (Introvigne 2006, 293). The Bible is the only source of truth, and members are "drilled in memorizing verses which support the claims of the Iglesia" (Sanders 1962, 9). Members are also made to believe that the Iglesia is the only true church. It regards the Catholic Church and Protestantism as apostasies, that is, false religions that do not recognize that the real Church of Christ that was founded in AD 33 was reborn in 1914. The only way to salvation, therefore, is to leave the other churches and join the Iglesia.

The church claims it is one big family with members calling each other *kapatid* (brother or sister). Iglesia members are organized into groups of eight that function as study groups but also spy on and make sure its members are devoted to the Scriptures and do the duties assigned to them by the Executive Minister. These groups likewise function as the moral police (preventing excessive gambling or drinking, apostasy, and marriage outside of the Iglesia). The other important responsibility of the group is recruitment. According to Albert Sanders, "groups go into homes of friends and neighbors or from home to home in the neighborhood [to educate them on] the errors of the Roman Catholic Church and if Protestants are present, the 'falsehood' of Protestantism" (Sanders 1962, 11). They relish debating in their homes and in public, confident that their Catholic or Protestant opponents will not be able to compete with them when it comes to the Scriptures.

Leadership, however, is exclusive to the Manalos, and to charges that the Church is a family dictatorship, Iglesia leaders point that it was the members who voted their leaders. According to one scholar, "[Manalo] has the final authority on appointments and transfers of members to the administrative staff, of division and local ministries . . . . He prepares the lessons to be taken up in a class by the ministers and also lessons delivered by the ministers during their weekly services" (Reyes-Santa Romana 1955, 340). After Felix died in 1963, his son Erano took over as "Executive Minister" and "Supreme Brother." Erano passed away in 2009, and the current head is his son Eduardo. There is an economic council comprising a general treasurer, an auditor-general, and legal counselors, which oversees the church's finances. There is a Division of Ministers composed of moderators, superintendents, local ministers, deacons and assistant deacons who serve voluntarily. These officials monitor the participation of members in the weekly services, collect members' contributions, report on offenses, and mediate when members come into conflict with each other.

In 2015, the Iglesia administrative council expelled Felix Nathaniel Manalo and Cristina Manalo, brother and mother of current head Eduardo Manalo, revealing for the first time a rift inside the family and the organization. Several ministers were also expelled and even reported that their lives were being threatened. A government investigation cleared the Iglesia, especially after several politicians came to the church's defense. This case also revealed the extent to which the Iglesia wields political influence. The Iglesia has parlayed its extraordinary unity and unquestioned loyalty to the Manalo family into political capital, and it is one of the most sought-after religious groups among politicians because they know that every member will vote for the candidate chosen ("privileged") by the Supreme Brother. There has also been the occasional news of the Iglesia influencing the decisions of political leaders (Sanders 1962, 12–13).

See also: Chapter 2: Overview. Chapter 3: Overview.

Further Reading

Cornelio, Jayeel Serrano. 2017. "Religion and Civic Engagement: The Case of Iglesia ni Cristo in the Philippines." *Religion, State and Society* 45, no. 1 (January): 23–38.

Elesterio, Fernando G. 1988. *The Iglesia ni Kristo: Its Christology and Ecclesiology.* Manila: Ateneo de Manila University, Cardinal Bean Institute, Loyola School of Theology.

Kavanagh, Joseph J. 1995. "The 'Iglesia ni Cristo.'" *Philippine Studies* 3, no. 1 (March 1): 19–42.

Mabasa, Roy. 2021. "Iglesia ni Cristo at 107: Faith Anchored on Values." *Manila Bulletin* (July 28). https://mb.com.ph/2021/07/28/iglesia-ni-cristo-at-107-faith-anchored-on-values/

Reyes-Santa Romana, Julita. 1955. *The Iglesia ni Kristo*. Manila: University of Manila.

Sanders, Albert J. 1962. *A Protestant View of the Iglesia ni Cristo*. Quezon City: Philippine Federation of Christian Churches.

Sanders, Albert J. 1969. "An Appraisal of the Iglesia ni Cristo." In Gerald H. Anderson (ed.), *Studies in Philippine Church History*. Ithaca and London: Cornell University Press.

Islam

Islam arrived in the archipelago in the 13th century through Muslim traders who were also missionaries. This was, however, "not Islam as such but Islam as a form of a state religion with its attendant political and social institutions" (Abinales and Amoroso 2017, 44). The missionaries brought Sufism to the southern Philippines with its belief system that emphasizes an intimate interaction with God through contemplation, prayers, and reading of poems and selections from Islam. The missionaries and those they trained were called *Saik a Datu* (from the Arabic word *shayk*); they were respected for their religious knowledge and sense of piety. They were "men possessing esoteric spiritual knowledge and supernatural powers who shared their knowledge and used their powers to benefit others . . . They were . . . spiritual leaders who were distinguished from others . . . by their spiritual potency and their mode of living" (McKenna 2002, 542–543).

Among the Maguindanaos, there is another religious figure—the *sutti a tau* (*sutti* is from Sanskrit); these were "ascetics known for their ecstatic love of God and their unself-conscious service to others." Unlike the *saik a datus*, however, the *sutti a tau* knew nothing about religion. And while the *datus* and the *sultans* ruled by combining force and charisma, the *sutti a tau* were admired for their "humility, simplicity and (relative) non-violence" (McKenna 2002, 543). That said, even if the *saik a datus* and the *sutti a tau* were the acknowledged spiritual leaders of the community, the *datus* were not without their divine attributes. An American colonial officer observed that "[t]he datu is God's vice-regent's earth. He is of noble birth, and the Prophet's blood runs through his veins. The people owe him allegiance and tribute" (Saleeby 1905, 17). Officials who governed the sultan's districts, collected taxes, mediated conflicts, and mobilized the community for labor or slave raids were also the representatives of Islam. This made it easier for the religion to move northward until it was slowed down and stopped by the Spaniards. The Americans did not interfere with Islamic practices as, unlike the Spaniards, they were able to gain the active support of the sultans and the *datus*. After independence, mutual accommodation was reached by Muslim leaders and the national government, and this was primarily left unbothered until the late 1960s.

Like Catholicism, Islam is also "localized," integrating with the religious beliefs and practices that were indigenous to the southern Philippines. During the Spanish period, Muslims considered the Spaniards as their equals but took exception when it came to slavery. The sultanates raided the Spanish settlements for slaves without providing any

Muslim Mindanao, 1800s. (Wilkes, Charles, *Narrative of the United States Exploring Expedition*, vol. 5, 1845)

religious justification. Slaves, however, were freed if they converted to Islam. Slavery disappeared under the Americans, but other forms of amalgamation between Islam and the distinctive local beliefs and practices continued well into the contemporary period.

For example, Muslims prayed to Allah but also made offerings to the same spirits as the Catholics in the north, and for similar reasons—health, good harvests, and family safety. Community leaders (*datus*) possessed magical charms and amulets to appease these deities and ward off evil spirits, and when celebrating or commemorating, they did not do away with pre-Islamic ceremonies for births, deaths, and rites of passage such as marriage. They were, therefore, spiritual leaders who were distinguished from others, including other *datus*, by their spiritual potency and their mode of living.

Women also had considerably more power under this localized Islam as compared to their sisters in the Middle East. In her study of the Sama—one of the ethnic groups in Muslim Mindanao—Patricia Horvatich observed that the young people interested in Islam trained under "local gurus" who helped them memorize the Koran in Arabic without understanding its content. She noted that the majority of those who began at the first level were girls, and when asked, her respondents explained that "girls are more devout than boys [who] are more concerned with worldly pleasures [such that] most of them neglect the study of Islam." Only when they became fathers did they become interested in Islam (Horvatich 1994, 812–813).

Women who complete the training assume more specific functions like being midwives or supervisors for the burial of women and girls. However, they are also

The Marantao Mosque, Lake Lanao, Lanao del Sur Province. (Alexey Kornylyev/
Dreamstime.com)

charmers who are capable of removing curses and concocting charms. Mothers/wives
are also the main and only mediators when it comes to settling interclan conflict (*rido*).
Once contending families decide that their bloody disputes have reached a limit, the
matriarchs of the two sides meet to negotiate the terms of peace. Thus, Muslim women
may face several restrictions imposed upon them by the religion (like staying behind
the men while praying in the mosque), but they have not been disempowered.

In the early 1980s, however, Muslims who had gone up for higher education, especially in Islamic universities abroad, returned, demanding that their communities act
as "true Muslims" and discard pre-Islamic beliefs. These students found support from
the Moro Islamic Liberation Front whose leadership claimed it was fighting not only
for the separation of Mindanao and the Sulu archipelago from the Philippines but
also for the establishment of an Islamic Bangsamoro Republik (Republic of the Muslim Nation). What has followed is a struggle within Muslim minds between what
Thomas McKenna calls "identity-affirming rituals" (being Muslims) and "un-Islamic
behavior." It is not yet clear which has had the upper hand. And despite the growing
popularity of the hijab, it is not clear as to whether the reformists have prevailed. The
headscarf may indicate that Muslims, especially the young, are more serious in pro-
jecting their Islamic persona (McKenna 1997, 62); the diversity of the hijab's colors,
however, also suggest that—unlike their sisters in the Middle East—there is also a
concern for style, for "looking nice," as it were.

The resolution of this tussle, however, will depend on where Muslim elites will
stake their positions. The legatees of the precolonial and colonial sultanates remain
the principal sponsors of Islamic proselytization. The elites invest in mosques and
act as patrons of Islamic schools (madrasahs), and it is their leadership that has "kept

the Muslims united and spiritually bound together." The Muslim intellectual Alunan Glang added: "So deeply ingrained into the fabric of Muslim life is this institution that the faith and loyalty of the Muslims have withstood the severe vicissitudes of time and change" (as quoted by McKenna 1997, 54). Islamic "reformists," including leaders of the armed separatist groups, have tried to challenge and undermine this authority, but there is no evidence that "folk Islam" is being displaced by "real" Islam.

Not even the coming of ISIS-inspired groups has affected the situation. These groups made headlines when they seized the Islamic city of Marawi, declaring this the first step in establishing a Caliphate in Muslim Mindanao. It took the Philippine military five months for this group could be dislodged. As the battle began to recede, however, a different portrait emerged. The group, which was led by two brothers who were ISIS converts, included members from the moderate Islamic group, the Moro Islamic Liberation Front, armed relatives coming from local political families, and even followers of the brothers' kin who were involved in the drug trade. It also turned out that some of its fighters had joined after being offered a hefty sum. Once the leaders were killed, these combatants also went back to where they came from, some vowing to execute any ISIS leader for tricking them into joining the rebellion. There is indeed evidence of Islamic radicalization, but so far "folk Islam" has continued to be the dominant strand.

See also: Chapter 2: Overview; Muslim Separatism. Chapter 3: Martial Law; Post-Marcos Philippines.

Further Reading

Abinales, Patricio N., and Donna J. Amoroso. 2017. *State and Society in the Philippines.* 2nd ed. Lanham, MD: Rowman and Littlefield.

Horvatich, Patricia. 1994. "Ways of Knowing Islam." *American Ethnologist* 21, no. 4 (November): 811–826.

McKenna, Thomas M. 1997. "Appreciating Islam in the Muslim Philippines: Authority, Experience, and Identity in Cotabato." In Robert Hefner and Patricia Horvatich (eds.), *Islam in an Era of Nation-States: Politics and Religious Renewal in Muslim Southeast Asia.* Honolulu, HI: University of Hawaii Press.

McKenna, Thomas M. 2002. "Saints, Scholars and the Idealized Past in Philippine Muslim Separatism." *Pacific Review* 15, no. 4: 539–553.

Saleeby, Najeeb M. 1905. *Studies in Moro History, Law and Religion. Ethnological Survey Publications* 4, no. 1. Manila: Department of Interior: 107 pp.

Philippine Independent Church (Aglipayan Church)

There are about six to eight million members of the Philippine Independent Church (a.k.a., Aglipayan church), making it the second-largest Christian denomination in the Philippines after the Catholic Church. As of 2017, it had 47 dioceses across the country and in the United States, Canada, and Europe, divided into "three regional conferences." The church is led by an Obispo Maximo (Supreme Bishop), who is supported by a Supreme Council of Bishops that interprets doctrines, prescribes the liturgy, and provides moral and pastoral guidance. The council also oversees three "regional episcopal conferences." The highest governing body, however, is a General Assembly that meets every three years. When the assembly is not in session, an Executive Commission consisting of the Obispo Maximo, a representative of the laity, five bishops, five representatives from the Council of Priests and from the National Lay Council which is the organization of the laity oversees Church activities.

The church was founded by a former Catholic priest, Gregorio S. Aglipay, who joined the nationalist revolution against Spain and was excommunicated for his political involvement. Aglipay responded by declaring himself the "Spiritual Head of the Nation under Arms," and led a campaign to arrest Spanish clergy and take over church properties. In 1902, Aglipay was accepted by labor leader Isabelo de Los Reyes to form the Iglesia Filipina Independiente (Philippine Independent Church, popularly known as "Aglipayans"). The church rituals are an admixture of Catholicism, Masonry, Anglicanism, and eventually Unitarianism. It retained the Catholic "traditional mass" (but allowed this to be celebrated in the vernacular) and adopted the Anglican Book of Common Prayers for important rituals (baptism to funerals) and daily litanies. It also allowed its priests to marry.

In the 1920s, Aglipay traveled abroad and came back a convert of Unitarianism, the religion that said that God did not comprise of three persons—the Father, the Son, and the Holy Spirit—but was only one being and that Jesus was not God but a mere messenger. Aglipay's new theological interpretation led to a schism in 1946 with a faction led by De Los Reyes breaking away and forming its church a year later. After Aglipay died in 1940, his successors discarded all the changes their founder had implemented and joined the American Episcopal Church and the global Anglican Communion. The schism continued well into the 1990s with the last breakaway group forming a Philippine Independent Catholic Church.

Politicians have sought the Aglipayan church continuously for political support, going to the extent of even converting to the religion during an election. Aglipayans, however, have also been involved in progressive and left-wing causes, with claims of preserving the anti-colonialist, nationalist legacy of their founder. A bishop who was a government critic and human rights advocate was assassinated in 2006. There have been several media reports of Aglipayan priests and seminarians disappearing after being accused of being leftists, even to this very day. The church's bishops had publicly supported the passage of a Reproductive Health Bill that promoted sex education and the use of contraception. This was a stand opposite to that of the Catholic Church, which was opposed to the bill.

See also: Chapter 2: Overview.

Further Reading

Binsted, Norman. 1958. "The Philippine Independent Church (Iglesia Filipina Independiente)." *Historical Magazine of the Protestant Episcopal Church I* 27, no. 3 (September): 209–246

Rodell, Paul A. 1988. "The Founding of the Iglesia Filipina Independiente (The Aglipayan Church): An Historical Review." *Philippine Quarterly of Culture and Society* 26, no. 2 (September–December): 210–234.

Scott, William H. 1962. "The Philippine Independent Church in History." *Silliman Journal: A Quarterly Devoted to Discussion and Investigation in the Humanities and the Social Sciences* 10, no. 3: 298–310.

Whitemore, Lewis Bliss. 1961. *Struggle for Freedom: History of the Philippine Independent Church*. Greeenwich: Seabury Press.

Precolonial Religions

Before Christianity, people across the archipelago believed in an array of creatures and spirits that guarded their homes and the natural surroundings; they appeased these "gods" with prayers and rituals. Prosperity meant that these creatures of nature listened to them and were pleased by their supplications. In this belief system, it was women who bridged the world of the humans and the deities. They were the shamans (babaylan, babaylanes in the plural) who conducted seances to enable their fellow villagers to communicate with the spirits. Their closer ties to nature also gave them privileged access to the healing powers of plants and animals, and conversely, their harmful potency. There were male shamans, but they were usually "feminized," that is, they acted, spoke, and dressed like females—villagers treated them as women.

This spiritual capital of the babaylanes accorded them the respect that placed them on the same level as the chiefs. While the Spanish military targeted the latter, the Spanish priests saw to it that the babaylanes were also targeted. It was already unsettling to encounter women who co-ruled with men; their moral standing was a significant obstacle to the conversation. The missionaries zealously destroyed any physical evidence of babaylan power, proclaiming them as heretics and expelling them from their communities. Missionaries took over supervision of children, placing them under the care of the parish. The girls and young women were introduced to an alternative model: the docile, quiet, chaste, sexually repressed, and powerless Mary, mother of Jesus. Henceforth young women had only two options in life—to marry and dutifully serve their husbands or enter the nunnery and become servants of God. On the path to marriage or the monastery they had to be accompanied by countless never-ending prayers and invocations to Jesus, his Father, and the Holy Spirit.

Despite the ferocity of their campaigns, the missionaries were never able to eliminate this deity-driven belief system. The new converts simply or by stealth assimilated practices of the system into their "new Catholic worldview." In this syncretic "folk Catholicism," converts accepted Catholic symbols as evidence of the religion's power to be used, among other things, to protect them from the church's enemy, Satan, and from the older spiteful spirits and giants that resided in the forests. Crucifixes became de facto shields that prevented enemies' spears from penetrating bodies, and the sign of the cross was made to deflect the wrath of the spirits that controlled thunder and lightning. In front of missionaries, new converts professed their obedience to God the Father and Jesus Christ, but inside their homes or in secret places these personalities stood alongside statues of ancestor-spirits, nature-spirits, and deities. Practices like puberty ceremonies likewise persisted (Juergensmeyer 2012, 714).

Babaylan healing practices were passed on to a group of healers who community members sought out to correct their body imperfections and whose expertise lay in determining the medicinal value of herbs. The missionaries were fascinated with the herbalists, collecting as much information as they could and sharing them in Europe. They also appeared to tolerate these two healers mainly because they were never a center of authority as the babaylanes were. There was also a practical reason for this: the missionary promise of spiritual salvation had to be matched by a vow to improve the material condition of those they came to administer. This did not necessarily pull through, but the promise was there. A sparse colonial state that barely had enough resources to support an army had nothing to support medical personnel (vaccination was only introduced in 1800). If the army had their native militia, the missionaries had these herbalists and body healers whose "prestige" (but not power) received a boost from Catholic chants and icons to improve their patients' well-being. These "traditional doctors" persisted way beyond the Spanish era and continue to remain permanent fixtures in the rural areas.

See also: Chapter 1: Overview.

Further Reading

Go, Fe Susan. 1979. "Mothers, Maids and the Creatures of the Night: The Persistence of Philippine Folk Religion." *Philippine Quarterly of Culture and Society* 7, no. 3 (December): 186–203.

Juergensmeyer, Mark. 2012. *Encyclopedia of Global Religion*. Los Angeles: Sage.

MacDonald, Charles H. 2004. "Folk Catholicism and Pre-Spanish Religions in the Philippines." *Philippine Studies* 52, no. 1: 78–93.

McCoy, Alfred W. 1982. "Baylan Animism: Animist Religion and Philippine Peasant Ideology." *Philippine Quarterly of Culture and Society* 10, no. 3 (September 1): 141–194.

Protestants

Protestants constitute about 6 percent of the population, and the denominations range from the Pentecostal and independent churches to evangelical movements. There are supposedly 200 denominations divided among the "ecumenical, evangelical and Pentecostal-charismatic churches, although the lines between these groups are often blurred" (Hwa Yung, 2004, 208). The five most significant of these churches include the Philippine Independent Church, the United Church of Christ in the Philippines (UCCP), the United Methodist Church, the Convention of Philippine Baptists Churches, and the Philippine Episcopal Church (Elwood 1969, 366–367).

Protestantism came to the Philippines on the backs of American troops and colonial administrators, with its missionaries vowing to challenge the preeminence of the Catholic Church they regarded as corrupt and repressive (Anderson 2004, 472). They vowed to replace the church with "the ideas of liberalism and secularism, religious liberty, lay ministry, justice, democracy, public education, equality, and a democratizing religious education: Methodism" (Juergensmeyer 2012).

The different Protestant missions came into a "comity agreement" that divided the Philippines into specific districts and coordinated the mission. They also were able to convince Washington to impose a series of obstacles on the Catholic Church that ranged from breaking up its landholdings to threatening to tax the institution. Finally, on the ground, to embed themselves, the first group of pastors learned the local languages and translated missals and religious texts into these dialects. They received support from public school teachers in the lowland and soldier-administrators in the uplands and the Muslim areas.

This "advantage" did not last. Protestants made inroads among Filipino elites and professionals who saw an opportunity for social and political advancement by converting. However, they were never able to make a dent on the Catholic Church. First, the U.S. government came to an agreement with the Vatican that allowed the Catholic Church in the Philippines to keep its parishes and wealth but replace the despised Spanish clerics with American and non-Spanish priests. Without state support and with their limited resources, the Protestant missions were therefore forced to scale down their goals and focus on two activities—setting up medical and health facilities and establishing schools. The missions set up the Philippine chapter of the Young Men's Christian Association (YMCA) to promote healthy living but also to battle vices like gambling and drinking (which they alleged were promoted by the Spanish Catholics). Education, however, is what the missions became famous for. Among the highly respected private schools in the country are the Protestant-established Brent International School in Baguio City in the north, Silliman University in the central Philippine province of Negros Oriental, and Dansalan College in the Islamic city of Marawi. There are also schools located in the northern Philippines and the interior of Mindanao Island—areas where Catholicism's influence was not as strong and where positive memories of American colonialism remain strong.

Protestants remain a minority in the Republican period. That said, the Philippines among the countries of Southeast Asia, has the most significant percentage of Protestants (24.1 percent), with Indonesia a far second (9.7 percent). Only in Korea are there more Protestants. In recent years, Protestant missions have grown significantly to a point where Singapore, Malaysia, and the Philippines can send their missionaries abroad, including to Europe and the United States (Hwa Yung 2004, 208–209). There are still tensions between Catholics and Protestants (Hwa Yung 2004, 208). These began to subside during the Marcos dictatorship when the National Council of Churches in the Philippines (NCCP) and the church leadership became strongholds as well as havens for priests and pastors opposed to the regime. The ecumenicals are the most militant of the Protestant groups, especially with the World Council of Churches

(WCC) on their side. The blurry divisions between the other Protestants have become a more definitive divide.

Today, Filipinos classify Protestants into the ecumenicals, the evangelicals, and the Pentecostals. The ecumenicals commit themselves to the mission of going back and recovering the apostolic beginnings of the church to be able to function as a good Christian in the modern world. Their evangelical counterparts declare themselves as having been "born again," that is, of having undergone an experience similar to that of Jesus Christ who was crucified and died on the cross but was able to rise and be "born again" the day after his internment. While ecumenicals also claim to find God's words and hands in the daily lives of Filipinos, evangelicals believe that the Bible is the sole source of answers to questions of faith and its propagation. Filipinos refer to Pentecostals more as "charismatics" who claim they can recognize "signs" (including supernatural events) as gifts of the Holy Spirit, the third "persona" in the mysterious triad of God the Father, God the Son (Jesus), and God the Holy Spirit.

Filipino ecumenicals have been involved in political issues, with ministers and members of the UCCP and the NCCP being active in the struggle against the Marcos dictatorship—their churches often became places of refuge for activists and even communist party cadres fleeing from the military and the police. Evangelicals and charismatics avoid politics and keep their distance from political organizations. This is one of the reasons why these groups have become the fastest-growing religious denominations in the late 20th century. Politicians, however, see their potential value as sources of solid blocks of voters. It is not unusual for politicians, therefore, to be present during the weekend ministries of charismatic and evangelical groups.

See also: Chapter 1: Overview.

Further Reading

Anderson, Allan. 2004. "The Future of Protestantism: The Non-Western Protestant World." In Alister E. McGrath and Darren C. Marks (eds.), *The Blackwell Companion to Protestantism*, pp. 468–482. Malden, MA: Blackwell Publishing Ltd.

Elwood, Douglas. 1969. "Varieties of Christianity in the Philippines." In Gerald H. Anderson (ed.), *Studies in Philippine Church History*. Ithaca and London: Cornell University Press.

Hwa Yung. 2004. "The Missiological Challenge of David Yonggi Cho's Theology." *Asian Journal of Pentecostal Studies* 7, no. 1 (January): 57–77.

Juergensmeyer, Mark. 2012. *Encyclopedia of Global Religion*. Los Angeles: Sage.

McGrath, Alister E., and Darren C. Marks, eds. 2008. *The Blackwell Companion to Protestantism*. Malden, MA: Blackwell Publishing Ltd.

Lugo, Luis, Sandra Stencel, John Green, Timothy S. Shah, Brian J. Grim, Gregory Smith, Robert Ruby, and Allison Pond. 2006. "Spirit and Power: A 10-Country Survey of Pentecostals." *Pew Forum on Religion and Public Life* (October): 1–229. http://www.pewresearch.org/wp-content/uploads/sites/7/2006/10/pentecostals-08.pdf

CHAPTER 6

SOCIAL CLASS AND ETHNICITY

OVERVIEW

Precolonial coastal settlements in the Philippines were called barangay, a derivative of the Malay word "balangay," which was the name given to large sailboats that
transported families across islands in search of ideal settlements. A barangay often
consisted of 30–100 families and was divided into several "classes." Governing them
were hereditary "chiefs" (*datus*) whose authority was based on prowess, charisma, and
religion. The *datus* had multiple responsibilities: they led wars as well as diplomatic
expeditions; they mediated intra-community disputes; they acted as patrons of luxury
goods, collected tributes, and oversaw the exchanges of so-called prestige goods.

Both Muslim and non-Muslim barangays used the term *datu*, but Muslims had
two other titles to refer to their chiefs—sultan and rajah. Sultan is an Arabic term that
means "ruler," "authority," or "power," and the position of sultan could be held by
either a man or a woman (sultana). Its preeminence came from the fact that it was
both a secular and a sacred title. Sultans and sultanas were known for their military
and political prowess and claimed to have descended directly from the Prophet
Mohammad. A rajah was of the same status as the sultan when it came to authority
(the female equivalent being *rani* or *rajin*), and the only difference between the two is
lexical. *Rajah* is a Sanskrit word (Sanskrit being an old language of India), while *sultan* is Arabic. *Rajah* is secular while *sultan* is a strange title because its origins are
religious, but in practice chiefs conferred the title tend to known and respected for
their personal charisma, business acumen, and military prowess—all very secular
attributes.

As mentioned earlier, the title *datu* (*datuin* for women), which meant "chief" or
"prince," was not exclusive to Muslims. Communities in the hinterlands of the mountains likewise called their village heads *datus*. Muslim sultans could be called *datus*,
but chiefs who were *datus* at the onset could not become sultans.

Below these chiefs were elites called *timawas* or *maharlikas* who were direct relatives or "fictive kin" who possessed special skills and acted as "personal vassals" to
the *datu*, rajah, or sultan. They participated in the trade and accompanied their liege
into battle, and in exchange, were exempted from providing labor and services. These
"freemen" (as the Spanish chroniclers called them) had a reciprocal relationship with
their chiefs—in exchange for being allowed to till the lands owned by the latter,
engage in trade and accumulate some wealth, they were to serve in the chief's naval

expeditions and provide them security from enemies within and outside the barangay. Their amassed wealth, harvests and slaves, of course, belonged in principle to their *datus*, rajahs, or sultans. Chief-timawa were defined by their body postures (non-elites bowed their heads, twisted or wriggled their bodies as signs of subservience), speech patterns, ornaments (chiefs wore precious stones), and body tattoos.

Slaves comprised the lowest rung in precolonial society, and Spanish chroniclers estimated that at one time a *datu* could own 100–300 of them. People became slaves by heredity (their parents were slaves), due to economic motives (sold to stave off hunger, to get out of or honor debt obligations or to make money), in order to pay for judicial punishment, or because they were captured in slave raids or as part of war booty. Slaves, according to Laura Junker, "were economic commodities to be exchanged or sold at will, like gold, cloves, pearls, or other valuables" (Junker 1999, 137). Slaves, however, retained some degree of economic independence (including being allowed to own lands) and could, in fact, buy back their freedom by paying off their debts or exempting their children from the curse of debt bondage, thereby allowing them to grow up as *timawa*. Slaves could also become free by becoming part of a *datu*'s household, thereby being treated as kin, and thus changing their status into that of a *timawa*.

The almost 300-year war between the Muslim sultanates and the Spanish colonizers primarily revolved around slave raiding, with the sultanates attacking central and northern Philippines to capture slaves and the Spanish defending communities they controlled from these attacks. It was only after the Spanish were able to use steamboats against the sultanates—weakened by the decline of the maritime trade in Southeast Asia and by rivalries—that the "Moro war" began to favor the colonizers. However, it was also through these wars that the Spanish introduced new classifications. While the Muslim sultanates saw these conflicts as principally driven by economic needs, the Spanish regarded these as an extension of their religious war against the Islamic Umayyad Dynasty, which occupied southern Spain until 1492. They referred to the sultanates as "Moros," a derivative of "Moors," the term used to describe their Umayyad occupiers.

What "disappeared" in the midst of all this was the rich culture that the Umayyad dynasty brought to southern Spain, which could have been evidence of a civilized Islamic world. Instead, the Spanish identified the label "Moro" closely with slave raiding and the refusal of the sultanates to convert to Catholicism. From there it was easy to append another label, "backward," to describe the sultanates as well as Islam. When the Americans replaced the Spanish, they adopted the label "Moro" along with all the negative attributes the Spanish had heaped on it. Most American colonial officials believed in the separation of church and state, and one of the reasons they were able to establish a stable regime in Muslim Mindanao was because they kept Islam at arm's length.

The Spanish used geographic location as a social classifier. Villages and towns under their control were mainly located in the lowlands (valleys and plains) while communities that the Spanish had difficulty extending their authority over were located in the uplands. Like "Moro," this topographical grouping acquired a political and cultural meaning. The Spanish began to refer to those in the uplands as *remontados*—people of the mountains. They were considered to be uncivilized, because they were not converted, and as criminals who lived in the highlands to escape prosecution. Backwardness and banditry became synonymous with residing in the impenetrable forests. The Americans replaced the term *remontados* with "people from the boondocks" (from the Filipino word *bundok*, which means mountain), adding to this list of "ungovernable" characters the anti-American revolutionaries who continued to fight against American rule, and, under the republic, communist guerrillas who set up their bases in the area where the state was relatively weak. In everyday life, the term *"taga-bundok"* (from the mountains) now referred to the primitive, the uneducated, and hence, the culturally backward; those from the "modernized" lowland were better educated and hence considered civilized. Politically, to be from the *bundok* meant to be a fugitive from the state or a subversive intent on overthrowing the state.

The Spanish were not interested in assimilating the Muslims and upland communities while the Americans hesitantly pursued integration to keep up with the schedule of turning over governance to the Filipinos as the prelude to full independence. Many colonial officials argued that the "civilization" of these "wild tribes" would still take generations and thus to integrate them was an impudent move as lowland Filipinos could easily edge them out of the political process because they were "minorities." "Integration" was a policy that post-independence governments pursued more earnestly, but again with minimal results. The financial support was inadequate, and agencies in charge had limited funding and were often limited to advisory roles. Religious differences plus the Spanish image of the "savage Moro" came back after independence, particularly after the mass migration of non-Muslim Filipinos to Mindanao. To this very day, a big percentage of Filipinos (40 percent) still regard Muslims as a group that is prone to go "amok," resorting to fanaticism and savagery. Lowland Filipinos still regard upland communities as backward, although among the educated there is a tendency to romanticize these communities as the forefathers of the Filipinos of today.

In keeping with the practice of all European imperial powers, the Spanish called the inhabitants of the archipelago *indios* ("Indians"). This despite religious accounts that recognized linguistic and cultural differences across the colony. Like *taga-bukid* and *moro*, the *indio* was synonymous with backwardness; worse still, they were perpetually trapped in their barbarism and hence never allowed to become civilized. Friars and colonial officials repeatedly reminded *indios* that their rightful place was always with their water buffalos (carabaos) and thus they should stop dreaming about becoming as civilized as the Spanish.

The economic changes in the late 18th century led to the emergence of a new "class" in colonial society, composed mainly of Philippine-born Spaniards (*insulares*) as well as children of mixed unions between Chinese or Spanish persons with *indios*. These mestizos and creoles tore down the crude sociocultural divide between the Spanish and the *indios*. The latter's wealth and education alarmed the Spanish who began caricaturing them as "brutes laden with gold." The cultural clash inevitably turned into a political conflict with the outcome being the nationalist revolution of 1896. Indio and mestizo persisted as categories after the Spanish left. Their attributes—dark and sparse *indios*, pale (with almost Anglo-Saxon skin) and wealthy *mestizos*—are still being used in classifying Filipinos.

The Chinese were the other minority that had a fraught relationship with the Philippine state. Like their counterparts in Southeast Asia, they were "essential outsiders"—hard to be integrated into society because governments suspected them as potential subversives, but also an indispensable group in keeping the internal economy functioning. Intermarriages with Filipinos since the Spanish colonial period led to the emergence of Chinese mestizos who acted as bridges between the government, the Filipino majority, and the other ethnic groups and were also critical in facilitating the integration of the Chinese into Philippine society. Beginning in the middle of the 20th century, the Chinese were as much Filipino as any other ethnic group. It did not come easily, as in the 1980s, the Chinese were associated with "new wealth" and became prey to kidnap-for-ransom gangs. They not only survived this "storm" but also reinforced their being Filipino as evidenced by their refusal to move their families and wealth outside of the country. It was about this period that social acceptance of the Chinese reached a new level with the popularization of the term *Tsinoy* (a wordplay of two monikers that combined the first syllable of *Chino* with the last syllable of *Pinoy*).

During American rule and after independence, social divisions based on wealth began to assume equal, if not more, prominence compared to the distinctions mentioned above. Academics and student activists began to use the term "oligarchy" or cacique to describe wealthy Filipinos who also dominated politics. These terms had been used as far back as when Spanish and American colonial officials and radical labor and peasant organizers and communist guerrillas talked about the Filipino elite. In the middle of the 20th century, however, their use assumed more bellicose turns as student radicals and cadres of a "re-established" communist party ratcheted up their struggle to overthrow the government. Ironically, when Marcos declared martial law, he blamed "oligarchs" and caciques as having forced his hand.

Finally, Filipinos distinguish each other by language. The Spanish never made any effort to unite the disparate communities by introducing a universal language like the French did in Vietnam and the Dutch in Java (now Indonesia). Instead, they preserved the linguistic divide and learned the different languages themselves to be able to communicate with the colonized. It was the Americans who recognized how much of an obstacle this Tower-of-Babel situation was to administrative consolidation. They resolved this by making English the medium of instruction in the colony-wide public school system they set up and at the University of the Philippines, the premier institution of higher learning in the colony. English became the premier lingua franca of the Philippines, the bureaucratic argot and the language for social mobility in an evolving political and economic system.

Encouraging signs began to appear in the 1980s when non-Tagalog communities, especially in the Muslim realms, began to adopt the "national language" as a means to talk to "outsiders," especially the Armed Forces of the Philippines which had kept the majority of its troops in the Muslim areas since 1976. In the last decade of the 20th century, integration moved faster thanks in part to the power of television networks that could broadcast nationwide and expose the provinces and far-flung regions to "national news" as well as to the national language Filipino. There remains some resistance from the provinces. City and provincial governments have taken the lead in preserving and promoting the local languages, devoting resources to compiling dictionaries but it is clear that everyone today can speak Filipino apart from their languages and dialects of birth, and English.

See also: Chapter 2: Overview; Chapter 3: Overview; Federalism; Chapter 9: Overview; Filipino or Pilipino?: Mother Tongue Teaching; National Language Debate.

Further Reading

Filipinas Foundation. 1976. *Philippine Majority-Minority Relations and Ethnic Attitudes: An In-Depth Study*. Makati City: Shell Foundation.

Go, Julian. 1999. "Colonial Reception and Cultural Reproduction: Filipino Elites and United States Tutelary Role." *Journal of Historical Sociology* 12, no. 4 (December): 337–368.

Hau, Caroline S. 2018. *The Chinese Question: Ethnicity, Nation and Region in and beyond the Philippines*. Quezon City: Ateneo de Manila University Press.

Junker, Laura Lee. 1999. "Warrior Burials and the Nature of Warfare in PreHispanic Philippine Chiefdoms." *Philippine Quarterly of Culture and Society* 27, no. 1–2 (March–June): 24–58.

McDonald, Charles J., and Guillermo M. Pesigan (Guillermo Mangubat). 2000. *Old Ties and New Solidarities: Studies on Philippine Communities*. Quezon City: Ateneo de Manila University Press.

Bangsamoro Identity

In 1975, the Moro National Liberation Front (MNLF), a coalition of Muslim student radicals and political elites opposed to President Ferdinand E. Marcos, and their armed entourage launched a series of attacks on towns and camps of the Armed Forces of the Philippines. The MNLF described its attacks as the continuation of the *Bangsamoro's* (Moro Nation's) struggle against colonial forces that had tried to subjugate them since the Spanish era. This time, the opponent was "Filipino colonialism," which, the MNLF alleged, was engaged in a campaign of genocide to erase Muslim identity. While the MNLF lost that war and gradually weakened, the struggle was picked up by the Moro Islamic Liberation Front (MILF). The latter signed a peace agreement in 2019 which included a provision where the Philippine government would recognize and help preserve the *Bangsamoro* identity.

To its advocates, the *Bangsamoro* identity combines the secular nation with religion (Islam) and a Muslim history that is different from national history because it is older than the Philippine nation-state. They point out that the sultanates were already

Flag of the Moro National Liberation Front Bangsamoro Army. (Bumbleedee/Dreamstime.com)

the power centers in Mindanao Island before the Spanish came and that these politico-religious authorities had in fact prevented the former from effectively governing the entire archipelago. The Americans succeeded where the Spanish failed but even after their subjugation the *Bangsamoro* remained united. It returned to war in defense of the Moro identity and culture in the 1970s when Muslims felt threatened by the national government. What the MNLF and the MILF struggle reinforced was the anti-colonial sentiment of the *Bangsamoro* identity. An MILF ideologue (Jubair 2007) would go on to argue that this struggle has become a source of Moro pride because it is one of the longest armed conflicts in the modern era.

The inspirational message of *Bangsamoro*, however, also tends to gloss over differences among Muslims. The first of these differences has to do with the fact that the "Moro nation" is comprised of 13 different ethnolinguistic groups: these are the Maranao, Maguindanao, Tausug, Sama, Sangil, Iranun, Kalagan, Kalibugan, Yakan, Jama Mapun, Palawani, Molbog, and Badjao. The members of these groups are largely Muslim, except for the Kalagan and Palawani who have many non-Muslims among them, and the Badjaos who are generally non-Muslim (Rodil 1993). These groups have their own distinct identities and even languages (Magindanaos, for example, can hardly understand Tausogs). Second, the identity does not erase hierarchy within the community. Moro elites invoke their "royal blood" to separate themselves from the ordinary folks, while economic disparities between elites and ordinary people is very evident in many towns in Muslim Mindanao. There is also a tendency among Moro elites to act like their Christian counterparts when it comes to engaging in the seamier side of politics. The former have been accused of using their positions to enrich themselves and of using being Muslim (not Islam per se) as a political weapon to win votes.

Third, there exists the constant tension between those whose Islam is inspired by countries like Saudi Arabia and Iran and those who see their religion as a philosophy introduced from the outside and then made stronger by its adoption of local practices. One such tension arising from these dual interpretations is the role of women in the community. Those who believe in the preeminence of Middle Eastern Islam tend to devalue women, but those who practice "folk Islam" recognize the power and contributions of women as members and leaders of the *Bangsamoro*. Filipino Muslims also regard this divergence as the local representation of the interpretive and contentious divide between Salafism and Sufism. Salafists argue that a true Muslim is one who literally and strictly follows the teachings of the Koran, the Prophet Mohammad, and the first three generations of Muslims who are believed to have practiced the "most pure" form of Islam. Sufists, however, place more importance on how to become a better Muslim and hence prepare oneself for Heaven. Their inspiration comes from Islam's saints and virtuous leaders, including those in politics. A majority of Filipino Muslims are Sunnis and lean toward Sufism, although younger Muslims coming back from religious schools in the Middle East have been leaning more toward Salafism.

Yet, while there may be more younger Salafists today, there is also a growing number of young Muslims who are interested in the forms that Islamic democracy and Islamic feminism could take. Millennial Muslims differ from their elders over the question of arranged marriages, interreligious personal and marital relationships (in other words, control of their bodies), and, most important of all, polygyny (the right of a Muslim man to have more than one wife). Others are critical of the hierarchical structure of Moro society and affiliate themselves with civil society groups and political movements seeking to restructure power in society for the greater good. Thus the *Bangsamoro* identity has done much to unify Filipino Muslim society, but it has also accentuated the tensions within.

See also: Chapter 2: Muslim Separatism. Chapter 3: Armed Forces of the Philippines; Martial Law; Political Clans; Post-Marcos Philippines. Chapter 5: Islam.

Further Reading

Abinales, Patricio N. 2000. *Making Mindanao: Cotabato and Davao in the Formation of Nation-State*. Quezon City: Ateneo de Manila University Press.

Abubakar, Carmen A. 1989. "Moro Ethno-nationalist Movement." In Kumar David and Santasilan Kadirgamar (eds.), *Ethnicity: Identity, Conflict and Crisis*. Hong Kong: Arena Press.

Che Man, W. K. 1990. *Muslim Separatism: The Moros of Southern Philippines and the Malays of Southern Thailand*. Quezon City: Ateneo de Manila University Press.

Coronel Ferrer, Miriam. 2013. *Costly Wars, Elusive Peace: Collected Articles on the Peace Processes in the Philippines 1990–2007*. Quezon City: The University of the Philippines Press.

Jubair, Salah. 2007. *The Long Road to Peace: Inside the GRP-MILF Peace Process*. Cotabato City: Institute of Bangsamoro Studies.

Rodil, B. R. 1993. *The Lumad and Moro of Mindanao*. London. Minority Rights Group.

Vitug, Marites, and Glenda Gloria. 2000. *Under the Crescent Moon: Rebellion in Mindanao*. Quezon City: Ateneo Center for Social Policy and Public Affairs and Institute for Popular Democracy.

Elites

Like any other society, Filipinos use the word "elite" to describe extremely wealthy and politically powerful families that are educated in the best schools in and outside the country and whose Westernized, cosmopolitan lifestyles are a far cry from that of ordinary Filipinos. Caroline S. Hau came up with 26 English and local words that Filipinos use to describe the elite (Hau 2017). The first group comprises the "old families," whose right to wealth and power can be traced back to the late Spanish colonial era, when Chinese and Spanish mestizo families began to accumulate land for the production of export crops like sugar. Their wealth then enabled them to send their children to Manila and Europe for further education. When the Americans took over, the same landed elite entered colonial politics to defend and advance their economic interests. They would take over the helms of power when the Philippines became independent.

The second group of elites are urban families who cut their teeth in industry and commerce. Some belonged to landlord families but diversified into these new sectors while others became rich through the businesses they established. These elites rose to prominence in the 1950s, under the government's "import-substitution program" that sought to replace imported commodities with locally produced goods. They accumulated part of their wealth via privileged access to government loans and the local licensing of foreign products.

The third group of elites are merchant traders who dominated the local market, peddling goods between the rural and urban areas. The top families in these groups are immigrant Chinese and Chinese Filipinos whose enterprises were initially hampered by government regulations targeting "alien" (read: Chinese) businesses. In the 1970s, however, President Ferdinand Marcos issued a sweeping nationalization decree thereby hastening the integration of the Chinese into Philippine society. By the late 1980s, Chinese families were taking the lead in the establishment of malls and shopping establishments in cities and towns as well as investing in the financial sector and food industries. Today, the biggest banks are owned by Chinese Filipino families, and so are the most successful food establishments, the most famous of which is the fast-food restaurant Jollibee.

The new elites among the non-Chinese include those engaged in real estate and "an expanding range of specialist services like accounting, advertising, computing and market research" (Pinches 1999, 280), and who work as franchise holders and subcontractors in the retail, construction, and recreation industries.

The last group of elites are clans whose preeminence has largely been the result of their involvement in politics. There is greater diversity within this group, with some clans belonging to the old families, others using their state positions to enrich themselves, and still others rising to power through involvement in illegal economic activities. However, they all share something in common—their origins can be traced to their involvement in local politics. Today, there are over 250 such political families controlling critical government institutions like Congress; the election of Mayor Rodrigo R. Duterte to the presidency—a first mayor to ever win the presidency in the history of the country—further cemented the importance of political clans.

The gap between the rich, the middle class, and the poor has always been there, but it has worsened since the start of the 21st century. The failure to close this gap is the result of the influence of the wealthy on powerful state institutions like the presidency and Congress; the failure or inadequacy of government taxation policies and social welfare projects; and corruption. The historian Alfred W. McCoy calls this the "symbiosis of the family's political influence and corporate growth" (McCoy 2009, 159). During several serious economic downturns, the elite were expectedly in a better position to cope with the crisis, but not the poor or even the middle class. Finally, globalization has also been a boon to the Filipino elites, and while there was a notable increase in the income of the middle class brought about by working overseas, this was nothing compared to the surge of elite incomes. In 2009, the average per capita income of the richest 20 percent of Filipino families was roughly US$176,863 (rising from US$85,891 in 2003), while that of the middle class was about US$82,712 (rising from US$55,644 in 2003). On the other hand, the average per capita income of the poorest 20 percent of families was only US$14,022 (compared to US$7,015 in 2003). The variations in the rise of incomes clearly shows how the elite have become richer.

Communists and civil society groups and organizations of the poor have joined with "conservative" institutions like the Asian Development Bank, the World Bank, and the United States Agency for International Development to bemoan this inequality in wealth, power, and status. Some families have responded to these "pressures" by establishing philanthropic foundations (there were a total of 115 in 1997) or supporting existing ones (e.g., the Lion's Club or the Chambers of Commerce). Some of those involved in promoting philanthropy are driven by the (business) fact that poverty deprives them of a dynamic market and a skilled workforce. Poverty is a destabilizing force when it comes to their businesses. Their involvement also suggests what Gerard Clarke and Marites Sison call "a greater commitment to the universalistic values associated with citizenship and state action" (Clarke and Sison 2003, 233).

Unfortunately, all these efforts have done very little to reverse the process and there is no sign that this domination by a small minority of the country's wealth and politics will change radically in the near future.

See also: Chapter 2: Overview. Chapter 3: Elections; Martial Law; Political Clans; Post-Marcos Philippiens; Presidential Emergency Powers.

Further Reading

Akita, Takahiro. 2014. "Structural Changes and Interregional Income Inequality in the Philippines, 1975–2009." *Review of Urban and Regional Studies* 26, no. 2: 135–154.

Albert, Ramon G., Jesus C. Dumagan, and Arturo Martinez Jr. 2015. "Inequalities in Income, Labor and Education: The Challenge of Inclusive Growth." *Philippine Institute for Development Studies Discussion Paper Series No. 2015-01.* January.

Clarke, Gerard, and Marites Sison. 2003. "Voices from the Top of the Pile: Elite Perceptions of Poverty and the Poor." *Development and Change* 34, no. 2: 215–242.

Hau, Caroline S. 2017. *Elites and Ilustrados in Philippine Culture.* Quezon City: Ateneo de Manila University Press.

McCoy, Alfred W., ed. 2009. *An Anarchy of Families: State and Family in the Philippines.* Madison, WI: University of Wisconsin Press.

Pinches, Michael, ed. 1999. "Entrepreneurship, Consumption, Ethnicity and National Identity in the Making of the Philippines' New Rich." In *Culture and Privilege in Capitalist Asia.* New York: Taylor and Francis.

Son, Hyun H. 2008. "Explaining Growth and Inequality in Factor Income: The Philippine Case." *ERD Working Paper No. 120.* Asian Development Bank. August.

Indigenous Peoples (IP)

"Indigenous Peoples" (IP) is the name for 110 ethnolinguistic groups that have lived along the coastal areas, hills, and mountains across the archipelago since before the colonial era. The IP excludes the Muslims, because of their religion, and two Mindanao groups that are classified as a subgroup of Visayans, the second-largest ethnolinguistic group in the country. In Mindanao, IPs are called "Lumad," which is Visayan for "Katawhang Lumad." At the same time, highland communities in northern Luzon Island are referred to as "Igorots." These two categories are further "divided" into several subgroupings based mainly on linguistic differences and geographical locations.

The IPs are originally Austronesians and, despite their many linguistic differences, share the same precolonial belief systems—about spirits representing their natural surroundings and the otherworldly power of priestesses (the "babaylan"), for instance—and fishing and farming practices. Many Filipinos think it is because of their relative isolation from the larger ethnolinguistic groups like the Tagalog and Visayans that IPs remain "backward." Historians, however, think otherwise: highland

IPs had earlier been involved in commercial relationships with lowland groups, and IPs in the Mindanao hinterlands traded with the Muslim sultanates. These corrections, however, are yet to be included in many primary, secondary, and even college textbooks.

In 1986, however, public awareness of the IPs increased thanks to the establishment of associations like the Lumad Mindanao Peoples Federation. The federation's organizers had been defending Lumad rights against then-president Ferdinand Marcos's attempts to exploit their resources and silence their protests. Marcos's partiality toward the use of force to incorporate lands and peoples in his development agenda had subjected IPs to countless episodes of human rights violations. In Mindanao, the violence against IP communities took a turn for the worse when communists began organizing in their areas, inviting more military operations. Lumads who lived outside Muslim zones also became caught in the crossfire between the Muslim rebels and government troops. IPs that did not support the communists or the Muslim separatists and assisted the government to protect their homes became targets of insurgent attacks. After Marcos fell in 1986, the violence came down.

The Igorots of northern Luzon. (Library of Congress)

However, IPs still faced the loss of ancestral domains and the disappearance of their identities. This time the Lumad Federation was not alone in defending IP rights. New alliances like the Coalition for Indigenous Peoples Rights and Ancestral Domains (CIPRAD) emerged, receiving support from the Catholic and Protestant Churches, civic groups like Philippine Association for Intercultural Development, the International Labour Organization (ILO), and the Asian Development Bank.

Through persistent lobbying and an active media presence, these advocates were able to educate Filipinos about the history of Filipino discrimination of IPs. They were also able to tell the stories of the IPs' loss of their ancestral domains, and their displacement in the hands of government and private corporations. The absence of IP histories and cultures in school syllabi and textbooks has threatened their way of life as the younger generations know little about their own people. Environmental problems associated with deforestation and irresponsible mining operations have also added to IP burdens. A decade of campaigning gained tremendous ground with the Philippines passing the Indigenous People's Rights Act (IPRA) and creating the

National Commission for Indigenous People (NCIP) in 1997. NCIP's primary responsibility was to craft policy and implement programs to promote IP welfare.

Crafting policy is one thing; implementing these as programs is another. There were problems like the slow, slapdash, and sometimes corrupt process of certifying IP lands as ancestral domains. Differences over the meaning of the term "ancestral domain" further complicated the classification of these lands. The Moro separatists did not welcome IP participation in the peace process in Mindanao, and it took over 10 years for the government and other civil society groups to get them to change their minds. In northern Luzon and central Mindanao, pro-communist IPs engaged their anti-communist rivals in a propaganda war and legal battles over resources, which often led to violent encounters. After the IPRA turned into law, new communities suddenly declared they too were Indigenous Peoples and thus must also benefit from government and international aid support. Finally, better and safer access to IP areas by scholars also led to more nuanced studies of their everyday lives, including a critical re-examination of concepts like Lumad that, as one anthropologist pointed out, tend to minimize the differences among them (Quizon 2012). Despite these obstacles, IP coalitions, NCIP officers, and organizations extending assistance remain optimistic about the prospects of improving the lives of Indigenous Peoples.

See also: Chapter 1: Administrative Regions; Population. Chapter 2: Communism. Chapter 3: Overview; Federalism.

Further Reading

Acosta, Nereus. 1994. "Loss, Emergence, and Retribalization: The Politics of Lumad Ethnicity in Northern Mindanao (Philippines)." PhD diss., University of Hawaii–Manoa.

Carino, Jacqueline K. 2012. *The Philippines: Country Technical Notes on Indigenous People's Issues*. Rome: International Fund for Agricultural Development (IFAD).

Environment and Social Safeguard Division. 2002. *Indigenous Peoples/Ethnic Minorities and Poverty Reduction in the Philippines*. Manila: Asian Development Bank. June.

Perez, Jose M. 2019. "Greed and Grievances: A Discursive Study on the Evolution of the Lumad Struggle in Mindanao, 2010–2019," *Journal of Ethnic and Cultural Studies* 6, no. 3: 41–52.

Quizon, Cherubim A. 2012. "Dressing the Lumad Body: Indigenous Peoples and Development Discourse in Mindanao." *Humanities Diliman* 9, no. 2: 32–57.

Mestizos

The term "mestizo" refers to Filipinos with fair skin resulting from having one Caucasian parent. For an extended period of time, Filipinos associated mestizo-ness with what is beautiful and gorgeous. This was a popular opinion that, according to the nationalist historian Renato Constantino, was a sign of the "colonial mentality" Filipinos had after being exposed to things American—from the teaching of English in American-built public schools to the popularity of Hollywood movies. Some Filipinos also refer to mestizos using the slang word *kastilaloy*, which comes from the Filipinization of the word *Castilan* and then the adding of the syllable "*loy*" which means "ish." Those who use it often attribute it to the impact of more than 300 years of Spanish rule on Filipino languages.

Yet, the term's origin was not exactly Castilian. "Mestizos" was first used in the late Spanish colonial period to describe children with Chinese ancestry, who were the majority among children with mixed parents (more than 200,000 in the late 19th century). When it came to those of non-Chinese lineages, a qualifier was often added: hence a child of a Spaniard and a Filipino was called "mestizo de Espanol" (Spanish mestizo; about 35,000 in the same period.). Racial lines, however, began to blur once the Chinese mestizo families became wealthy thanks to their role in the development of a market economy that connected the Philippine countryside with the global market dominated at the time by the British Empire.

Wealth enabled the Chinese mestizos to enhance their social status in a way that did not just mimic the Spanish colonial elite. The former did start to dress and act like the Spaniards (some even building Spanish-type homes), but they also did more than that. Mestizos began to intrude into spheres that were once exclusive to the Spaniards. Mestizo families sent their children to seminaries to become priests, and while they initially played second fiddle to Spanish priests in running parishes, they eventually came to run them on their own as the supply of priests from Spain began to dwindle. With their money, mestizo families were also able to pay for their children's education at the Ateneo Municipal—the top Jesuit-run secondary school—and then at the University of Santo Tomas, the colony's institution of higher learning where they took classes together with the kin of Spanish families. The mestizos did not stop there. Some, like Jose Rizal's parents, sent their children to Europe for advanced studies and to also soak the cultures of countries like France and Germany, which these families believed to be superior to that of the Spaniards. Upon finishing, the *ilustrados* (enlightened ones) were expected to return and boost their families' social standing with their new profession and how much of European culture they had come to embrace. Hence, in his novel, *Noli Me Tangere*, Rizal would introduce one of the main characters, Crisostomo Ibarra, by describing how he acted like a German gentleman the first time he joined a dinner at his girlfriend Maria Clara's home.

The dilution of distinctions among mestizos and the gradual association of the term with Spanish was also hastened as Chinese mestizos intermarried with mestizos de Espanol or with Spaniards and other Europeans who migrated to the Philippines once the colony was opened to world trade. By the end of Spanish rule, one had this peculiar contradictory portrait where some of the known Spanish families actually had Chinese mestizo ancestors but had since been either erased or reclassified as Spanish. In their accounts of the Filipino elites, American colonial officials still noted the Chinese mestizo ancestries of many elites, but the children of Chinese and non-Chinese unions had ceased to be referred to as mestizos. They had, according to Caroline Sy Hau, " 'disappear[ed]' into the national term 'Filipino.'" After independence, a new social category would emerge—Chinese Filipinos—which by the late 20th century also had its own pun, *Tsinoy* (see the section on Filipino Chinese in this chapter).

American and Filipino unions introduced a new group of mixed children to Philippine society, and this time even the Spanish tag of the term mestizo also began to disappear, such that by roughly the mid-20th century, mestizo was simply a question of skin color (excepting the occasional use of *kastilaloy*). Excluded from the name were children of African American and Filipino parents, obviously by reason of skin color but reinforced by a latent Filipino racism that came with their Americanization.

See also: Chapter 2: Overview. Chapter 3: Overview.

Further Reading

Hau, Caroline S. 2018. *The Chinese Question: Ethnicity, Nation and Region in and beyond the Philippines*. Quezon City: Ateneo de Manila University Press.

Hau, Caroline S. 2017. *Elites and Ilustrados in Philippine Culture*. Quezon City: Ateneo de Manila University Press.

Jubair, Salah. 2007. *The Long Road to Peace: Inside the GRP-MILF Peace Process*. Cotabato City: Institute of Bangsamoro Studies.

McCoy, Alfred W., ed. 2009. *An Anarchy of Families: State and Family in the Philippines*, 548 pp. Madison, WI: University of Wisconsin Press.

The Poor

The Philippines may have achieved a certain amount of growth, but this appears to have had minimal impact on the Filipino poor. In a 2018 study of the Filipino poor, the World Bank reported that the "Philippines remains among the countries with the highest poverty based on both the US$1.90 a day and US$3.20 a day poverty lines in the region." The bank added: "The pace of extreme poverty reduction in the Philippines averaged 0.9 percentage points per year between 2006 and 2015, less than half the 1.4 points per year decline in the developing world overall" (World Bank 2018, 26). In 2008, out of 82 million Filipinos, 15.3 million (or 18.6 percent of the total) were classified as persistently poor. In 2015, this increased to 22 million out of 102 million (or 21 percent), with 8.2 million of the 22 million (37.2 percent) having incomes that could not cover a family's daily food needs. By 2018, 26 million Filipinos out of a total population of 105 million were tagged poor. This 24 percent had not changed much since 2003, and economists predict that by 2022, one in every five Filipinos will live in poverty.

Eighty percent of the poor live in rural areas, which explains why self-employed fishermen or agricultural workers are the top occupations. Three-quarters of the rural

Metropolitan Manila contrasts. (Sjors737/Dreamstime.com)

poor live in areas that are regularly flooded during the typhoon season. This natural disaster has made it difficult for government and international aid agencies to sustain social welfare and poverty-reduction programs. A substantial number of the rural poor live in Mindanao (two out of five), with 50 percent residing in the Autonomous Region for Muslim Mindanao (ARMM). ARMM has consistently been ranked the lowest on the human development index. More than that, it is also located smack in the middle of what was once a war zone between Muslim separatists and government troops. A tenuous peace now exists in the area after the Moro Islamic Liberation Front (MILF) and the government signed an agreement. ARMM, however, remains unstable because of warlords and political clans and a pervasive illicit trading network (from drugs to home appliances). These volatile conditions are also obstacles to an effective and long-term poverty-reduction strategy.

Urban low-income families may be lesser in number compared to their rural counterparts. However, in major cities, they are the majority. Metropolitan Manila alone has 1.5 million "informal settler families" (World Bank 2018, 43), which constitute 40 percent of the metropolis's population. They work mainly in industries, the service sector, and the informal sector, receiving an average wage of US$1.25 a day. They live on public lands or private lands that the owners have not developed. A dearth of public housing is the main reason for the sprouting and expansion of these urban poor communities.

Moreover, even if a family has been able to claim the land as their own, they still have to deal with a costly and bureaucratic government administrative process.

Living on these lands, families lack access to essential services. Water, for example, is brought in and sold by vendors as water connections are expensive. Septic tanks are rare or badly designed so that residents use rivers and canals to dispose of their waste. As a result, diarrhea is widespread, affecting mainly the children and seniors. In 2009, the Asian Development Bank warned that tuberculosis was on the rise and would most likely also affect the same age groups (Aldaba 2009, 11).

There is also a high incidence of diseases like diabetes, cancer, epilepsy, and heart disease among the rural and urban poor. The cost of medical treatment and the lack of health insurance often deters them from seeking medical help. In 2007, only 11.7 percent of the poor sought treatment in a clinic or hospital, and there is a gradual decline in visits to public hospitals (3.7 percent in 1998 to 3.4 percent in 2007). The poor tend to avoid private hospitals as seen by the sharp decline (6.8 percent) in visits (3.7 percent in 1998 to 2.25 percent in 2007).

Low-income families are large families (the average is six members per household) and have low educational attainment. In 2018, about 60 percent of the household heads had no education, and 40 percent had failed to complete their primary education. Families that can send a child to college are the ones that would most likely escape poverty, but these are rare cases. Furthermore, while the Philippine government has made public education free from kindergarten to 12th grade, low-income families end up withdrawing their children as "expenses for textbooks, school supplies, uniform, lunches, and transportation costs are often a burden they cannot afford" (World Bank 2018, 49). Finally, with an average wage of US$1.25 a day, 70 percent of the income goes for the food, of which the most important is rice. The price of rice in the Philippines has been higher than the world price, so poor households continue to be "more vulnerable to rice price changes" (World Bank 2018, 41).

The gap between the rich and the poor is one of the highest in the world. The top 1 percent of the population owns more than half of the national wealth while the poorest own only 5 percent of the national income. In his first year in office, President Benigno S. Aquino III worked with the World Bank to expand the latter's conditional cash transfer program (CCT). Under the CTT, the government provided money to low-income families with several conditions (for example, requiring children to have regular health examination, and enrolling them in schools). At the end of his term, Aquino III declared that the poverty rate had gone down from 27.9 percent in 2012 to 24.9 percent in 2016. Since then, and up to 2018, the poor's share of total household incomes per capita had stayed at 24 percent.

See also: Chapter 1: Administrative Regions. Chapter 4: Economic Assistance. Chapter 7: Family, Economy, and Politics.

Further Reading

Aldaba, Fernando. 2009. *Poverty in the Philippines: Causes, Constraints and Opportunities*. Manila: Asian Development Bank.

Son, Hyun H. 2008. "Explaining Growth and Inequality in Factor Income: The Philippine Case." *ERD Working Paper No. 120.* Asian Development Bank. August.

Son, Hyun H. 2009. "Equity in Health and Health Care in the Philippines." *Economics Working Paper Series No. 151.* Asian Development Bank. August.

World Bank. 2018. *Making Growth Work for the Poor: A Poverty Assessment for the Philippines.* Washington, DC: World Bank.

CHAPTER 7

GENDER, MARRIAGE, AND SEXUALITY

OVERVIEW

The Filipino family has many of the following features, some of which may not be familiar to many Western, particularly American, families. First, Filipinos are monogamous, and polygamy is only allowed among Filipino Muslims, which is also in accordance with Islamic teachings. That said, some husbands carry on extramarital relations and have "second families"; in such cases, while the mistress and the wife may never meet each other, the former's children are often accepted as part of the legal household.

Filipino families usually consist of multiple households; they comprise of either several families living together, or one family sharing the home with kin and non-kin. In a typical family home, one can find not only the parents and their children but also grandparents (from either side of the family), the siblings of the parents, and the cousins of the children. A married child's family may even move into the family compound, that consists of several apartments allotted to each of the children. Families invest their monies on large areas in urban centers to build these enclosures, both to help the next generation be economically stable as well as keep the clan together. The latter also prefer this option despite the anticipated tensions among in-laws because it is a more economical way of living in places like Metropolitan Manila. The children may also want to be available always to help their parents, reflecting a strong sense of solidarity, with family members providing financial and emotional support to each other or coming together in dire times. To be near is to show their debt of gratitude to what their parents have done for them. Being near to each other means reciprocal visits, reunions, and other family activities that take place quite regularly. As a result, very few Filipinos are empty nesters. This does not mean that this kind of relationship is set in stone. In 2019, a study of the senior generation responded that they want to live independently from their children, "although some said they would like to live near any of their children" (Cruz et al. 2019, xxvi).

Living in the households also are a host of nonrelatives who, depending on their length of stay, are also inevitably considered as members of the family. They are the maids who take care of the domestic chores and thus free the parents and the children to focus on their professions and studies, respectively. House helps often come from outside the cities and apply for work with the family through an agent, or they may also be recommended by the family's provincial relatives. They are usually paid below-minimum wages but share in the family meal and are provided free lodging. The most favorite among the female house helps (someone who has been in the employ of the family for a long period of time) is entrusted with caring for the children. These caregivers (*yaya*) often become the de facto mothers of the children, especially if the parents are full-time professionals. This has certain positive and negative consequences on the household, which will be discussed later in this chapter.

Relations established by marriage (affinal) expand the family network. As the psychologist Rogelia Pe-Pua points out: "When you marry, you also marry your spouse's entire family" (Pe-Pua 1991, 34). When couples marry, they become members of each other's families, and their respective parents call each other *balae* in Filipino, a term that refers to them as coparents of their married progenies (a rough translation of *balae* is "my son's or daughter's parents-in-law"). Siblings from both families also call each other *bilas*, meaning "the brother or sister of my brother-in-law" or "the brother or sister of my sister-in-law."

To the consanguineal and affinal relations is added kinship based on religious rituals. Among Catholics, a baptism or marriage entourage always includes at least two "sponsors," that is, relatives or nonrelatives who are asked to be the spiritual godfathers (*ninong*) or godmothers (*ninang*) of the child or the couple. Their roles are hardly ceremonial: the *ninong* and the *ninang* are supposed to complement whatever advice parents give to their children, and in case something untoward happens to the parents, they are expected to become one of the many surrogate parents the children can seek for succor and guidance.

Many of the terms that Filipinos use in everyday life are related to or framed by the family. This is mainly because an individual's utterances or actions are generally regarded as indicators of whether he or she "has been raised well." A Filipino's frame of reference has and will always be that of the family. A couple of examples are worth citing here. The word "*kapwa*" literally means "both"; if it is turned into a verb, *kapwa* becomes *pakikipag-kapwa*, or "to treat people equally," which is regarded as a traditional family custom. The same applies to the words "*sama*," "*tungo*," and "*ramay*," which mean "together," "toward," and "sympathy," respectively. When transformed into verbs ("*pakikisama*," "*pakikitungo*," and "*pakikiramay*"), they denote supportive customs, which are expected of a family when relating to its members as well as to others.

An individual's "honor" ("*dangal*") is only relevant or appreciated as reflective of the family's rectitude; a person who tarnishes himself ("*walang dangal*") also shames the family. Even communities' actions are seen through the prism of the family. "*Bayanihan*" and "*balikatan*" (shoulder) are understood as households coming together to cooperate or work as a team and to share in shouldering the burden of work. Such associations between social norms and family are not unusual in the Philippines. This is, of course, not unique to the Philippines as the prioritization of the family over the individual is quite pervasive in developing societies.

See also: Chapter 4: Overseas Filipino Workers. Chapter 5: Overview. Chapter 6: The Poor.

Moving around in the rural Philippines. (Filipe Lopes/Dreamstime.com)

Further Reading

Medina, Belen T. 2015. *The Filipino Family*. 3rd ed. Quezon City: University of the Philippines Press.

Pe-Pua, Rogelia. 1991. "Marriage and Responsible Parenthood." In *The Filipino Family and the Nation: A Collection of Readings on Family Issues and Concerns*. Quezon City: University of the Philippines, College of Home Economics.

Perez, Aurora. 1995. *The Filipino Family: A Spectrum of Views and Issues*. Quezon City: University of the Philippines, Office of Research Coordination.

Porio, Emma, Frank Lynch, and Mary Hollnsteiner. 1978. *The Filipino Family, Community and Nation*. Quezon City: Institute of Philippine Culture and the Ateneo de Manila University.

Seminar on the Filipino Family. 1991. *The Filipino Family and the Nation: A Collection of Readings on Family Issues and Concerns*. 1991. Quezon City: University of the Philippines, College of Home Economics

Family, Economy, and Politics

The family permeates all of Philippine life to the extent that the Constitution contains provisions specifically devoted to this "basic social institution." Section 12 of Article 2 states that the state must "strengthen [the] solidarity and actively promote [the] total development" of this "foundation of the nation." This means recognizing and protecting the inviolability of marriage which is, in turn, "the foundation of the family" (Section 2), defending the right of couples "to found a family in accordance with their religious convictions and the demands of responsible parenthood," providing all assistance and care to the children like free public education (Section 2, Article 14), and protecting them "from all forms of neglect, abuse, cruelty, exploitation and other conditions prejudicial to their development" (Section 3.2, Article 15).

A Family Code elaborates on what is in the Constitution and covers garden-variety provisions—marriage procedures (including annulments and voiding of unions), death certificates, the rights of couples and parental responsibilities, and the rights of children, both legitimate and illegitimate. All these secular regulations, however, are anchored in Catholic principles where the priority is keeping the family together. Section 12 of Article 2 of the Constitution mandates the state to "protect the life of the mother and the life of the unborn from conception." There is therefore a de facto prohibition of same-sex parents as well as a woman's right of choice. Abortion is banned and gay marriages tabooed by law. Pro-choice and gay rights activists face an uphill battle in terms of making themselves recognized as legitimate members of society; they may be citizens but their rights as citizens are severely curtailed.

Politics is also driven by family interests. The historian Alfred W. McCoy refers to this system as "an anarchy of families" (McCoy 2009) where political ambitions, alliances, and transactions from the town level to the highest positions of politics are driven and determined by the needs of families. Politicians may form parties or build alliances to win elections but, more often than not, these are formal organizations bereft of real power and under the control of the most powerful of political clans or dynasties. A political clan is often headed by a grand patriarch but it is also not unusual to have the matriarch wield the same authority as her husband.

Families come to power and try to hold on to it by stacking up elective positions with their members. It becomes normal to read in newspapers about the head of the family being in the House of Representatives while the spouse is provincial governor, the eldest child is mayor of the provincial capital or the biggest city, and the second or third child is a member of either the provincial or city council. The Philippines may be formally a democracy, but in truth it is run by political dynasties. Between 1995 and 2007, for example, an average of 31.3 percent of all Congress members and 21.1 percent of provincial governors were replaced by their relatives. In 2012, an estimated 40 percent of all provinces had provincial governors and representatives of the House who were related to each other. By 2014, 50–70 percent of all politicians came from political dynasties.

The economy of the Philippines parallels its politics. Companies large and small are also typically family businesses, with arrangements similar to those in politics. The top two positions of a company are often held by the husband or the wife, while the children start at the bottom, rising through the ranks and learning the tricks of the trade along the way until they reach the board of directors to be assigned major responsibilities in the company. Rarely do families divest themselves of the corporations they own, and even if they did, these are often sold to trusted acquaintances or members of the extended clan. It is to this same group that families recruit "outsiders" to help run the corporations.

See also: Chapter 3: Overview; Martial Law; Political Clans; Post-Marcos Philippines. Chapter 5: Overview; Catholicism.

Further Reading

Aguiling-Pangalangan, Elizabeth. 1995. "The Family under Philippine Law." In Aurora Perez (ed.), *The Filipino Family: A Spectrum of Views and Issues*. Quezon City: University of the Philippines, Office of Research Coordination.

Family Code of the Philippines—Executive Order No. 209. http://www.chanrobles.com/executiveorderno209.htm

McCoy, Alfred W., ed. 2009. *An Anarchy of Families: State and Family in the Philippines*, 548 pp. Madison, WI: University of Wisconsin Press.

Republic of the Philippines. The 1987 Constitution of the Republic of the Philippines. https://www.lawphil.net/consti/cons1987.html

Generational Changes

Demographers have observed that younger couples have eschewed the hitherto popular practice of family dinners as they "do not value the importance of being together in a round table." This is also the case with teenagers who "nowadays prefer to be with their friends rather than having a peaceful pray day with the family" (Fadol 2014). Furthermore, as young professionals begin to amass their own wealth (or grow their savings), the support system provided by the parents has begun to erode and the so-called "intergenerational flow of wealth" has been reversed, with working children giving financial support to their parents. Yet, sociologists note that "respect for elders" remains quite strong among the younger generation, even though the terms of such deference has changed.

Younger Filipinos postpone marriage—the marriage age for men today is 26.5 years old (compared to 24.8 in the 1980s) while that of women is 23.8 years old (22.4 in the 1980s). Young couples who postpone marriage are also inclined to form what sociologists call "non-conventional families." These include same-sex marriages, "childless unions" (i.e., a conscious decision not to have children, which also means there are no grandchildren for their parents to dote on), and single parenting. Cohabitation without marriage, known in local parlance as "living in," has also become popular among younger Filipinos. Whereas earlier they used to get the approval of their parents to marry, 90 percent of today's married women choose their spouses with or without parental approval. In the past, couples whose parents opposed their planned marriage would elope and reconcile with their elders later using the grandchild as the inducement for the relinking. In recent years, parents worry less about their child's partners as more families have come to accept the idea of their daughters marrying late, recognizing that the latter "are making productive contributions to the household for being economically active or being primarily responsible for important domestic chores" (Raymundo 1991, 18).

Families are also realizing that having children would limit a woman's working hours and this would cause tensions because of a decline in family income. Among the consequences is a tendence for more couples to end their marriages by mutual consent, opting not to go through the tedious process of seeking official annulment of the union (Abalos 2011, 2017). These "trends in divorce and separation" (Raymundo 1991, 19) are also being influenced by "education, type of the first union and childhood place of residence." Or as Corazon Raymundo puts it "[f]or a number of [couples], either the experience and/or the unintended consequence like accidental pregnancy has forced them into an early marriage and to a subsequent life of curtailed education, higher number of children, limited opportunities for economic pursuits, a high probability of prolonged patrilocal residence and increased probability of separation" (Raymundo 1991, 19).

This is not to say that the "old" has been completely replaced by something different. Filipinos still prefer the atomic family and marriage (Medina 2015). Extended households still exist in the urban areas, although there is a notable shift in some of its features. For example, these arrangements are more noticeable among those with higher incomes and education, as such households are in a better financial position to assist nonpaying relatives and friends. Siblings or relatives who migrate to the city may also not join in the households of their urban kin but rather form their own, using savings from their incomes to bring in their other siblings (Raymundo 1991, 20). But the change is there, and one of the areas where there is this tug-of-war between old and new is over the raising of children.

Sociologists and psychologists are divided as to what will happen to the Filipino amid this twirl of societal changes. There are those who warn that uncontrolled migration into the cities and continuous search for work abroad would ultimately lead to the family's ruin. Lourdes Lapuz's closing remarks on a panel on the family reflects this uneasiness. She is nostalgic about a time "long ago, hundreds of years ago [when] the family was everything. It was a source of livelihood; the business was right down the stairs. Children followed the occupation of their parents, without asking why. It was where you learn the three R's. You didn't have to go to some great big school somewhere and pay fabulous tuition fees to learn how to read. Religion was taught right there at your parents' home . . . Before, people behaved according to what is traditional and what is prescribed by the culture."

All these things have changed in the last 20 years. Lapuz laments: "[As] I said since the 60s [and] all throughout the 70s and 80s questions kept cropping up. Parents asked, 'What is right now? What should be done?' [translated from Filipino] And the counselor would say: 'I don't know [translated from Filipino]. Define yourself what you want, what you stand for. All I can do is tell you whether it is possible or if it is realistic and perhaps when it is healthy.' By now, anything goes. So long as you can live with it, so long as you can live with yourself, and so long as you can keep the family intact. Thus the family survives, but not so well. It's alive but not doing so well" (Lapuz 1991, 34).

Others, however, accept the new reality and that what is important is to reorient the teaching of "core Filipino values" in schools and religious institutions to "instill in [young Filipinos'] minds of the positive effects in their character development and in their future relationships." Adds Nina Halili-Jao: "Along these lines, the meaning of Filipino families could be extended to be more comprehensive of non-customary families (e.g., single-parent family units, childless couples, living together couples, and same-sex guardians), and receptive to the requests of the changing Philippine society achieved by many components, for example, monetary, social, and political issues, innovative headway, and movement, among different issues" (Halili-Jao 2018).

The discussions continue to the present day. What has changed, however, is the starting point. Whereas in the past the center was the primary family unit, that center is now cluttered with other types of families. Where this will be heading as cities grow and more Filipinos leave remains unclear. One feature, however, is becoming more and more apparent. Thirty years ago, if one landed in Manila International Airport and lined up at the immigration section and happened to be behind a mixed family where one parent was Filipino, one would most likely hear the child speak in an American accent (in most cases, a Californian one). Today, going through the same line, one can hear the same children speaking to their parents in German, French, Italian, Thai, Arabic, Japanese, Malay, and even Chinese. The family then joins the household reunion where the Filipina meets their parents and their siblings who have also been working abroad.

The cousins talk in English and bond over stories where facets of Filipino culture (the mass, the fiesta, food, etc.) seamlessly intertwine with those of foreign culture (Pokemon, Korean-Pop, Hip-Hop, Harry Potter, etc.). The cousins will also get a chance to meet another cousin who is the child of a single aunt, another who is the adopted child of the gay uncle, as well as the love child of an uncle's illicit and failed affair. As they play, the children will be joined by the offspring of the house help, especially the daughter of the *yaya*. Looking over this diverse set of "uncommon families" will be the grandparents, still marveling at how much their household has changed over the years.

See also: Chapter 5: Overview; Catholicism. Chapter 6: Overview.

Further Reading

Abalos, Jeofrey B. 2011. "Living Arrangements of the Divorce and Separated in the Philippines." *Asian Journal of Social Science* 39, no. 6: 845–863.

Abalos, Jeofrey B. 2017. "Divorce and Separation in the Philippines: Trends and Correlates." *Demographic Research* 36, no. 50: 1515–1548.

Fadol, Hans. 2014. "The Alteration of Filipino Family Values." October 6. Accessed February 9, 2019. https://prezi.com/bafx3um0afpm/the-alteration-filipino-family-values/

Halili-Jao, Nina. 2018. "The Evolving Filipino Family Value System." *Philstar Global*. July 29. Accessed February 15, 2019. https://www.philstar.com/lifestyle/allure/2018/07/29/1837596/evolving-filipino-family-value-system

Lapuz, Lourdes V. 1991. "Marriage and Responsible Parenthood." In *The Filipino Family and the Nation: A Collection of Readings on Family Issues and Concerns*. Quezon City: University of the Philippines, College of Home Economics.

Raymundo, Corazon M. 1991. "Demographic Changes and the Filipino Family." In *The Filipino Family and the Nation: A Collection of Readings on Family Issues and Concerns*. Quezon City: University of the Philippines, College of Home Economics.

History of the Family Unit

Before the Spanish arrived in the archipelago and imposed their rule over communities under their control, religion was already a presence in precolonial lives. This came in the form of animistic worship of one's natural environment, associating life with the planting-and-harvesting cycles of important crops, or interpreting natural "signs" as warnings of dire fates or bountiful futures. These religions gave women prominent roles that complemented the "secular" charisma-centered authority of the men. The women were the ones who had the strongest bond with the natural and ancestral spirits that were the friends, guardians, and guides of people. They were the "spirit companions" who mediated between the world of the spirits and that of humans, conveying their messages to one another or interpreting them when needed. These women were called different names (there are at least 37 recorded names from various areas of the country), but the most popular was *babaylan*, roughly translated as "shaman."

The coming of Spanish colonialism also led to the systematic destruction of these animists. Zealous missionaries destroyed the religion of the "heathens" and "unbelievers" as well as the Muslim sultanates of Mindanao. While they largely failed convert the latter, they were able to convert those in the lowlands. As part of the conversion process, representations of precolonial religions were destroyed and replaced by the cross and statues of Jesus Christ, the Virgin Mary, and the saints. The rituals to honor ancestral and natural spirits were replaced by baptisms, communions, prayers, and masses. Monogamous marriage replaced multiple partnerships, and the *babaylan* were condemned as agents of the devil. The role of women was redefined: they were deprived of their spiritual power and from that time on, a woman's life purpose was seen as that of a wife who would serve her husband with unquestioning devotion.

The Americans took over the Spanish and did nothing to alter what the Spanish had done. The Americans protected the Catholic Church and allowed it to recover the influence it lost during the nationalist revolution, and its institutional recovery also included the preservation of its ideas on marriage and family. Neither did the republic change anything; in fact, its leadership enshrined the colonial social creation.

The Indigenous cultures found a way to survive by selectively appropriating this more powerful external force. The Spanish may have mandated monogamous marriages, but the precolonial Southeast Asian practice of bilateral (or bilineal) kinship persists to this day. A child can claim lineage to both mother and father. Moreover, the Spanish-constructed family had placed husbands as heads of families; yet, there are indications that women remain as important as they were in the precolonial era. Filipino families are "male-dominated," but this is often only for the public eye. In private, females are the actual managers of families, albeit in an understated way. The husband is the recognized head of the family, but the wife has authority over money and other domestic functions.

The Filipino family has, of course, been transformed in the late 20th century. One important indicator of this change is the decline in the number of children. In 1972, 72 percent of households were nuclear families; by 1986, this figure had risen to 83.4 percent. In 1973, 9.8 percent of households were headed by women; by 1986, this had gone up to 10.3 percent. In 1973, the fertility rate was 6 percent; this subsequently declined by one percent every 10 years, reaching 3.3 percent by 2008. The causes behind the decline in fertility echo what has been happening in other countries. As more women enter colleges and universities and then join the workforce, the more families postpone having children; even if they do have children, they limit the number to just one or two. As the per capita income has risen, family size has decreased as households try to start saving or increase savings. The rise of one-person households, particularly those headed by women, has also accounted for the decline in the number of children.

As young professionals settle down in their lives, they develop relationships with "non-kinsmen" (fellow workers, classmates, etc.), thereby creating an alternative social network that would compete with the extended family.

See also: Chapter 5: Overview; Catholicism. Chapter 6: Overview.

Further Reading

Go, Stella P. 1993. *The Filipino Family in the Eighties*. Manila: De La Salle University, Social Development Research Center.

Mendez, Paz Policarpio, F. Landa Jocano, Realidad Santico Rolda, and Salvacion Bautista Matela. 1984. *The Filipino Family in Transition: A Study in Culture and Education*. Manila: Centro Escolar University Research and Development Center.

Raymundo, Corazon M. 1991. "Demographic Changes and the Filipino Family." In *The Filipino Family and the Nation: A Collection of Readings on Family Issues and Concerns*. Quezon City: University of the Philippines, College of Home Economics.

LGBTQ

Gender is a determining element when describing the LGBTQ community in the Philippines. The word for "gay" is *bakla* and it refers to gay men who act like women (including being effeminate); "tomboy" is for females who act "butch" and are "constructed as a man trapped in a woman's body" (Tan 2001 as quoted by Tan, 2014, 15).

Filipinos have a complicated relationship with the LGBTQ community, especially with *baklas*. On the one hand, there is widespread recognition of "gender nonconformity." A major reason for this is the ease with which popular media have incorporated gay and tomboy roles in movie and television scripts, even as early as the 1950s. These continued and became more popular in the 1960s, as a youth-driven counterculture led to changes in sexual norms. There emerged, along with radical-speak (Down with imperialism! Onward with the revolution!), a gay vernacular called either "swardspeak," "*bakla*speak" or "*baklese*," which mixed Filipino, English, and Spanish words or syllables. Gay literature and plays also made their appearance in the literary scene.

By the 1970s, gay culture had "seeped" down into towns and villages, which held "Miss Gay Universe" beauty pageants during fiestas, with the support of local officials and major corporations. It was also around this time—the 1980s and 1990s—that lesbians too began to assert their presence. LGBTQ ideas from abroad introduced terms like bisexual and changed how baklas and tomboys dated. Previously, baklas and tomboys dated heterosexuals, but as more LGBTQ literature reached and was read in the Philippines, what "gay" meant changed considerably. More baklas and tomboys now dated people from their sex (Tan 2001).

The 1990s, however, were distinct for the emergence of gay studies and literary writing and LGBTQ participation in the country's thriving protest scene. LGBTQ activists became prominent in anti-state and pro-poor protests, and making pride marches is a normal part of a town's or city's annual activities. A Lesbian Collective sent a delegation to the International Women's Day March in March 1992 (Tan 2014, 16), a historic moment for many tomboys. While keeping a low profile compared to gay groups, lesbian organizations began to be formed in major cities and introduced an anthology of lesbian writings.

The high point of LGBTQ activism, however, came in the first years of the 21st century. On September 1, 2003, LGBTQ activists formed the *Ladlad* Party (*Ladlad* means the literal unfurling of one's cape, and metaphorically the "coming out" of one's LGBTQ orientation). Its founder, Danton Remoto, embodied all these changes in the LGBTQ world. He was (and still is) an academic and a public intellectual, a writer, a novelist, and a gay rights activist. *Ladlad* registered with the Commission on Elections (Comelec) in 2006, but the Comelec denied its application; in 2010, *Ladlad* appealed to the Supreme Court to overturn the Comelec decision. However, the *Ladlad*'s campaign fell short of getting 2 percent of the national vote which was necessary for it to gain a seat in the House of Representatives. In 2021, *Ladlad* had plans to participate in the May 2022 elections.

That said, the LGBTQ community is still the target of hate crimes. It faces challenges from conservative social forces led by the Catholic Church, Christian groups and ministries, and Islamic imams. Radical groups have formally recognized LGBTQ rights, but an attitude of "class-trumps-all-other-identities" persists. What mitigates these anti-gay sentiments is a society that is very tolerant of homosexuality and progressive-minded members of the churches and mosques who recognize and even support the LGBTQ community, even if they draw the line when it comes to same-sex marriage.

See also: Chapter 5: Overview. Chapter 6: Overview.

Further Reading

Austria, Fernando A., Jr. 2013. "Being LGBT: Is It More Fun in the Philippines?" *Social Science Diliman* (July–December): 115–122.

Human Rights Watch. 2017. "'Just Let Us Be' Discrimination against LGBT Students in the Philippines." https://www.hrw.org/report/2017/06/21/just-let-us-be/discrimination -against-lgbt-students-philippines

Remoto, Danton, and Neil Garcia. 2016. *Ladlad: An Anthology of Philippine Gay Writing— Volumes 1–3.* Pasig City: Anvil Publishing Inc.

Tan, David C. 2014. "Being LGBT in Asia: The Philippines Country Report: A Participatory Review and Analysis of the Legal and Social Environment for Lesbian, Gay, Bisexual and Transgender (LGBT) Individuals and Civil Society." Bangkok. United Nations Development Programme, and the United States Agency for International Development: 81 pp.

Tan, Michael L. 2001. "Survival through Pluralism: Emerging Gay Communities in the Philippines." In Gerard Sullivan and Peter A. Jackson (eds.), *Gay and Lesbian Asia: Culture, Identity, Community.* Pennsylvania, PA. The Haworth Press.

Thoreson, Ryan Richards. 2012. "Realizing Rights in Manila: Brokers and the Mediation of Sexual Politics in the Philippines." *GLQ: A Journal of Lesbian and Gay Studies* 18, no. 4: 529–563.

United Nations Development Program. 2014. "Being LGBT in Asia: The Philippines Country Report." https://www.undp.org/content/dam/philippines/docs/Governance /Philippines%20Report_Final.pdf

Overseas Workers and Their Families

More than urbanization and the decline of agriculture, the most profound transformation that the Filipino family has experienced comes from members of the family finding jobs abroad. More Filipinos are leaving the country—4,018 daily in 2019, increasing to 6,092 in 2015—and they have become the main source of income for their families. In the towns and cities, the construction boom of condominiums and new subdivisions is the result of the remittances; the residences of overseas Filipino workers (OFW) have been allotted higher values than those of nonmigrants and enabled their household to move out of poverty (Ducanes and Abella 2008). In the rural areas, OFW money has generated family-run small businesses like money-lending, drug stores, and retail shops, as well as orchards, poultry, and livestock. Others have formed savings and investments with the assistance of nongovernment organizations working for OFW interests (Hosoda 2008). The most popular long-term investment that OFW remittances have made possible is that of children's education, with those completing their tertiary level turning into able entrepreneurs and often improving on the family business (Aguilar 2014).

The OFW phenomenon has changed the composition of the family in several ways. Some scholars describe how the more than 10 million Filipinos working abroad for long durations have left behind "millions of fatherless, motherless or parentless children" to a point where "very often, young children do not even remember their father or mother well enough to feel close." The results are a loss of intimacy or respect, especially toward the absent parents. Instead, children become spoiled, causing disciplinary problems at home and in school, getting into early marriages, or worse, getting "hooked on drugs, alcohol and gambling" (Medina 2015).

Remittances have caused fissures within the family. One of the problems is the bias against women when it comes to sending money home. There is more pressure on wives, mothers, and sisters to remit money and less on husbands and brothers, a disproportionate relationship that is made stark by the fact that women now comprise 60 percent of OFW. Dierdre McKay found out that adult daughters sent 23 percent of remittances compared to only 11 percent sent by adult sons, and that sisters accounted for 16 percent of remittances while brothers only sent 5 percent (McKay 2012). On the one hand, this allows women a chance at asserting a bigger role in the family, but, on the other hand, since this would inevitably undermine paternal authority, the chances of spousal abuse are higher.

That said, while there are stories about spouses breaking up or families splintering because of relatives being OFW, surveys show that the marriages of OFW are "generally resilient and stable" (Medina 2015, 199). These tensions are also mitigated by the extended household. Aunts, uncles, and grandparents come into the picture and take over some of the family responsibilities, particularly child-rearing, when one or both parents are OFWs (Battistella and Asis 2013, 100). The extra help, however, does not mean that family savings go up, as having additional members to help in running the household often proves expensive. They may be unpaid labor but their upkeep—food, clothing, etc.—has to be factored in when the OFW sends remittances. The inability to save may also be the direct outcome of children and stay-at-home relatives deciding to rely completely on OFW remittances for their upkeep. And this becomes doubly problematic when the money from abroad "create[s] a moral hazard problem by inducing disincentives to work among migrant household members" (Medina 2015, 200).

Some Filipinas end up staying away for good because they married foreigners. While these unions have been part of family narratives in the past (especially Filipino-American marriages), in the 1980s, they caught public attention because of the so-called "mail-order bride" phenomenon. These unions were the result of single Japanese men coming to the Philippines to meet prospective brides who they only first "met" through mail correspondences with the assistance of a matchmaker. Soon after, there were also reports of a rise in marriages between Filipina entertainers and their former clients; some of these unions were the outcome of Filipinas going abroad for work to escape the "gendered surveillance and sexual violence" of their families.

Filipinas who worked in Japan as entertainers, for example, admitted going abroad to escape "domineering fathers, community gossip, philandering husbands, and domestic rape." According to the authors of a 2013 Country Migration Report on the Philippines, "For these women migration is not only about economic reasons but active resistance to gender and sexual norms in the Philippines" (Scalabrini 2013, 99). Marriage to Japanese men was also a way of breaking the chains of Filipino male abuse back home. Couples often went through several adjustments in the early years of their marriage, learning to talk to each other, figuring out how to relate to in-laws, and debating proper parental roles when it came to child-rearing. This phase has often provided the fodder for those critical of such marriages on the grounds that Filipinas end up being abused by their Japanese husbands. The few studies on these unions indicate that Filipina wives have a strong influence on their husbands, to the point that the latter "are now critical of the Japanese tradition and norms of patriarchy and racial chauvinism" (Medina 2015, 185).

In the first decade of the 21st century, there were also reports of Filipinas going to South Korea for marriages arranged by "marriage brokers" in both countries. The practice had been banned by the Philippine government through the "Anti–Mail Order Bride Law" that the Congress passed in 1990, but this has not stopped the practice. And this might have to do with the fact that Filipinas are the third most preferred foreign wives, after the Chinese and the Vietnamese. Thus, as of 2011, 7,550 Filipinas have moved to South Korea by virtue of marriage. As expected, there have been language barriers and different interpretations of married life and of the roles of husband and wife. There have also been many instances of domestic violence. Yet, there are also signs that Filipinas are not taking these challenges lying down. They have formed a Filipino-Korean Spouses Association whose objectives include providing prospective wives counsel on how to deal with their husbands—from learning Korean and their husband's culture to "teach[ing] their husbands the Filipino culture, and [knowing] that it is important to show the Korean in-laws that they are willing to work and adapt to Korean ways" (Medina 2015, 186).

See also: Chapter 4: Overview; Overseas Filipino Workers.

Further Reading

Aguilar, Filomeno, Jr. 2014. *Migration Revolution: Philippine Nationhood and Class Relations in a Globalized Age.* Kyoto and Singapore: Kyoto University Press and National University of Singapore Press.

Ang, Alvin P., Guntur Sugiyarto, and Shikha Jha. 2009. "Remittances and Household Behavior in the Philippines." *Asian Development Bank Working Paper Series No. 188.* December. https://www.adb.org/sites/default/files/publication/28401/economics-wp188.pdf

Battistella, Graziano, and Maruka M.B. Asis. 2013. "Country Migration Report: The Philippines 2013." International Organization for Migration and the Scalabrini Migration Center; 291 pp.

Ducanes, Geoffrey, and Manolo Abella. 2008. "Overseas Filipino Works and Their Impact on Household Poverty." *International Labour Organization Working Paper No. 5.* January.

Hosoda, Naomi. 2008. " 'Open City' and a New Wave of Filipino Migration to the Middle East." In Eric Tagliacozzo (ed.), *Asia Inside Out: Changing Times*. Cambridge, MA: Harvard University Press.

McKay, Deirdre. 2012. *Global Filipinos: Migrants' Lives in the Virtual Village*. Bloomington, IN: Indiana University Press.

Medina, Belen T. 2015. *The Filipino Family*. 3rd ed. Quezon City: University of the Philippines Press.

Parent-Child Relationships

The traditional view of children is that of dependents who reciprocate their parents' benevolent support by strongly identifying themselves with the family. Children benefit from the love and the largesse their parents give them and they are, in turn, required to show respect for their elders and to unquestioningly obey their authority. In the hierarchy of siblings, the older children must be ready to make sacrifices for the benefit of their younger siblings, and the latter are supposed to show gratitude by showing respect for and obeying the former. Then, "[a]s children begin to participate in the adult world, they learn further that they can be in harmonious relation with the community by virtue of their kinship ties" (Jocano 1995, 3).

Church and state collaborate to preserve these views of children. The church calls them the "gifts of God" that should therefore be "desired and enjoyed"; it says that children "are born with specific traits [that] no amount of education or training can restructure." The anthropologist F. Landa Jocano continues: "The child is good—that is quiet, industrious, obedient, and so forth—not because of the training he receives at home or in school, but because he is born with good traits already set in him. He is bad—a troublemaker, disobedient, undependable and the like—because he must have inherited bad traits from either of his parents or some of his ancestors" (Jocano 1995, 4). The challenge for parents is how to nurture the innate goodness while suppressing the "bad traits."

The Family Code has partially answered this by giving parents considerable power in rearing their progenies, from "the right to demand from their children respect and obedience," to imposing disciplined guidance as they "instruct and guide [children], keep them in their company to be instructed and guided as much as they can." The Civil Code is more explicit: children must obey and honor their parents, respect grandparents and excel in the education their parents have paid for. In exchange, parents are to provide their children guidance and protection until they are, as adults, capable of moving on their own. This can even go to extremes as the law gives parents even the right to pry into their children's private lives, including opening their correspondences.

In reality, however, caring for children is not the responsibility of the parents alone. Among the nonrelatives living in the household, this is also the responsibility of the nonrelative domestic help. With this "significant set of people" (Pe-Pua 1991, 38) is the childminder (*yaya* in Filipino) who becomes the de facto mother of the children, taking care of their needs. The *yaya* is a boon to the parents, ensuring that they can focus on their profession (and the accompanying rise in incomes) and get some socializing time. The drawback, however, can be distressing to the parents as they discover that their children have more affinity with to their minders. The psychologist Rogelia Pe-Pua shared her own distress and even anger that one of her children would not go to her but instead to the *yaya* who was a virtual grandmother to her children (Pe-Pua 1991, 39). She came to accept this arrangement as part of the family's everyday life. Aside from childcare, household help—including the childminder—are privy to intimate family stories, from fights to other intimate moments. Household help who stay for long periods with families become their confidants; and the family they live with becomes even "more of a family to them than the maid's own family" (Pe-Pua 1991, 40).

Parent-child relationships have also changed profoundly. The first major shift that was observed came in the late 1960s and all throughout the 1970s, resulting from a worldwide "rebellion" by the young against their parents' politics and lifestyle. In the Philippines, government corruption, its support for the war in Vietnam, and the increasing violence during elections combined with the influence of the American "flower power" generation, the spread of rock and roll, the pill, and the women's movement to change young people's consciousness. Martial law temporarily quashed the protests but not the social *and* sexual transformation of the young. The complication of family relations due to urbanization and rapid migration, for example, has sped up the process by which adolescents begin to assert their autonomy or independence from their parents and lean toward their peer groups, which they now seek out as founts of information for how to behave publicly.

Peer pressure now replaces parental diktat as early as 13 years of age, and on issues like sexual relationships, the opinion of close friends prevails over the advice of elders (Ujano-Batangan 2006, 20–22, 26). That said, there are still areas where young Filipinos defer to their parents for counsel; these include education, money and, until the 1980s, marriage. As Theresa Ujano-Batangan put it, "the support, approval and encouragement of parents are still very important to teens who continue to need some measure of adult supervision and concern," especially given that in actual fact "adolescents (still) have sensitive and fragile egos" (Ujano-Batangan 2006, 24).

See also: Chapter 3: Martial Law. Chapter 4: OFW

Further Reading

Jocano, F. Landa. 1995. "Filipino Family Values." In Aurora Perez (ed.), *The Filipino Family: A Spectrum of Views and Issues*. Quezon City: University of the Philippines, Office of Research Coordination.

Pe-Pua, Rogelia. 1991. "Marriage and Responsible Parenthood." In *The Filipino Family and the Nation: A Collection of Readings on Family Issues and Concerns*. Quezon City: University of the Philippines, College of Home Economics.

Republic of the Philippines Department of Justice Special Committee for the Protection of Children. 2006. "Protecting Filipino Children from Abuse, Exploitation and

Violence: A Comprehensive Programme on Child Protection, 2006–2010 (Building a Protective and Caring Environment for Filipino Children)." Department of Justice. December. Accessed September 23, 2019. https://www.doj.gov.ph/files/Filipino _Children.pdf

Ujano-Batangan, Theresa D. Maria. 2006. *Pagdadalaga at Pagbibinata: Development Contexts of Adolescent Sexuality.* Quezon City: University of the Philippines, Center for Women's Studies, and the Ford Foundation.

Sexuality

From the 1980s onward, the sexual behavior of young Filipinos has also caught up with what is now normal in many other developing as well as developed societies: a more liberal view of sexuality and, in particular, premarital sex. According to Medina (2015, 125), "There [has been] an increase in premarital sex among Filipino youth. Comparing the findings of the Youth Adult Fertility Survey in 1994, 2002, and 2013 show[s] that the prevalence of premarital sex activity increased from 17.8 percent in 1994 to 23.1 percent in 2002, and to 32 percent in 2013." In 1982, 12 percent of women between the ages of 12 and 24 had admitted to having premarital sex with at least one partner (Raymundo 1991, 19). In the next decade, the percentage had gone up to 18 percent (with the breakdown being 26 percent boys and 10 percent girls), with "[m]ost of the girls first [having] intercourse with their boyfriends, often at home. Ten years later, the percentage of adolescents having pre-marital sex had reached 47 percent (31.3 for males and 15.7 for females), with the problem of unplanned, forced sexual intercourse (on women) and the non-use of contraceptives persisting" (Natividad and Marquez 2004).

The 1994 edition of the above Youth Fertility Survey, however, contained two disturbing facts. The first was the admission by those surveyed that they did not resort to contraceptive measures in their first encounters. There were stories of unwanted pregnancies, but only in 1977 were social demographers confident in stating that the "proportion of single women who reported a premarital conception was half of the proportion who reported pre-marital sex" (Xenos 1997, 1). The result was that from the 1970s, abortion was widespread, with women resorting to the procedure under unsafe conditions, and seeking the assistance of doctors, nurses, and even practitioners of "traditional medicine." Between 1994 and 2000, the abortion rate was 27 per 1,000 women (aged 15–44) nationwide. The figure hardly changed during this period but if broken down in terms of regions, the largest increase was in the two largest cities of the country: Metropolitan Manila rose from 41 per 1,000 women in 1994 to 52 per 1,000 women in 2000, and Metropolitan Cebu in central Philippines, from 11 per 1,000 women to 17 per 1,000 women. These, however, were estimates as there has been no "large-scale, community-based surveys . . . that might provide a reasonable estimate of the proportion of all women having induced abortions who were hospitalized" (Juarez et al. 2005).

Yet, when asked if they favored premarital sex, the percentage of Filipinos who approved of premarital sex was equally substantial—31 percent among the men and 15 percent of women. There are possible "deterrents" to adolescents publicly accepting premarital sex as the "new normal." The first is the Catholic Church, which could still exert influence on families, including on parents who have accepted that their teenagers would most likely be involved in premarital sex (Collantes 2018). The second deterrent is the women themselves. They tend to underreport their premarital experiences to avoid bringing embarrassment to themselves and the family. Given that their liaisons were spontaneous and unplanned, and given the fact that the women surveyed were often forced by their male partners to have sex, underreporting was the best way of suppressing "evidence."

The third deterrent is the odd attitude of young Filipinos wherein they recognize and accept premarital sex but also try to preserve "traditional family values" by not boasting about their new-found sexual freedom. Adolescents may be more open to such trysts but are also careful that it should not bring shame to the family (Medina 2015). Premarital sex is a private matter and not a family affair up to a certain point. Unwanted pregnancies in women who choose not to marry their boyfriends are considered a blemish to the family name, but once the child is born, his or her being illegitimate becomes a moot issue—the family gives the child the same love and affection as the other children and is also fiercely protective of the child (Medina 2015, 122).

A disturbing fact, however, is that women also reported that they were forced to have intercourse with their partners. In 1983, 12 percent of those asked said that the men never asked for their consent ("Young Adult Fertility" 1996, 150). This became the disturbing pattern confirmed by one survey after another. In 2005, 40 percent of women said that their first sexual experience occurred "against their will" (Natividad and Marquez 2004). Women were not only coerced into sex, they were also forced to perform sexual acts not to their liking. Belen T. Medina's 2008 survey was ominous: "Overall, 53 percent of the women experienced sexual violence in the hands of their current husbands or partners, 13 percent by former husbands or partners, 11 percent by current or former boyfriends, 3 percent by friends or acquaintances, and 2 percent by other relatives. Among the married, the main perpetrators were the current husbands (61 percent) or former husbands (15 percent), while among the never married, the main perpetrators were the former boyfriends (58 percent)" (Medina 2015, 137).

See also: Chapter 5: Overview. Chapter 6: Overview.

Further Reading

Collantes, Christianne F. 2018. *Reproductive Dilemmas in Metro Manila: Faith, Intimacies and Globalization*. Singapore: Palgrave MacMillan.

Gipson, Jessica D., Socorro A. Gultiano, Josephine L. Avila, and Michelle J. Hindin. 2012. "Old Ideals and New Realities: The Changing Context of Young People's Partnership in Cebu, Philippines." *Culture, Health and Sexuality* 14, no. 6 (June): 613–627.

Juarez, Fatima, Josefina Cabigon, Susheela Singh, and Rubina Hussain. 2005. "The Incidence of Induced Abortion in the Philippines: Current Level and Recent Trends." *Guttmacher Institute* 31, no. 3 (September): 140–149. Accessed February 12, 2019. https://www.guttmacher.org/journals/ipsrh/2005/09/incidence-induced-abortion-philippines-current-level-and-recent-trends

Medina, Belen T. 2015. *The Filipino Family*. 3rd ed. Quezon City: University of the Philippines Press.

Natividad, Josefina N., and Maria Paz N. Marquez. 2004. "Sexual Risk Behaviors." In Corazon G. Raymundo and G. Cruz (eds.), *Youth Sex and Risk Behaviors in the Philippines*, pp. 70–94. Quezon City: Demographic Research and Development Foundation and the University of the Philippines Population Institute.

Raymundo, Corazon M. 1991. "Demographic Changes and the Filipino Family." In *The Filipino Family and the Nation: A Collection of Readings on Family Issues and Concerns*. Quezon City: University of the Philippines, College of Home Economics.

Xenos, Peter. 1997. "Survey Sheds New Light on Marriage and Sexuality in the Philippines." *Asia-Pacific Population and Policy*, July, no. 42: 1–4.

"Young Adult Fertility and Sexuality Survey in the Philippines." 1996. *Reproductive Health Matters* 4, no. 8 (November): 150.

Women and Violence

The problems young Filipinas faced when engaging in premarital sex reflect the broader problem of violence perpetrated against women. In 2013, the number of such cases reported to the Philippine National Police was 23,865 (an increase of 49.4 percent from the previous year), which was the highest since 1997 (Medina 2015, 190). Rape was a prominent scourge for young women, with sociologists reporting that those who committed rape were often the closest relatives and acquaintances of these women, and that the offense happened in the homes of the offenders or at the workplace. Their report added that "more than half of the offenders, included kinsmen, close interactors, and strangers used weapon and other devices to intimidate the victim, while suitors, boyfriends, ex-boyfriends, acquaintances, household members and neighbors were not armed. Most incidents happened in places owned or controlled by the offenders, such as the offender's residence or workplace" (Medina 2015, 136).

According to the government's National Statistics Office 2008 survey, women who reported being victims of sexual abuse experienced both physical and emotional pain. Out of the total surveyed, "20 percent of women aged 15–49 had experienced physical violence since they were 15 years old; 14.4 percent of the married women experienced physical abuse; and 37 percent of the separated or widowed women experienced physical violence. Another 8 percent experienced sexual abuse, and 23 percent were hurt by other forms of violence" (Medina 2015, 187). Sixty percent of abused women said they suffered from depression and anxiety, while "33 percent reported physical cuts, bruises, and aches; 10 percent reported eye injuries, sprains, dislocations, and burns;

and 5 percent reported deep wounds, broken bones, broken teeth, or other serious injuries. More than 10 percent of the women claimed that they had tried to commit suicide" (Medina 2015, 189).

It was (and still is) those who were closest to women who abused them. Husbands beat up their wives for allegedly neglecting their children (12 percent), for not asking their permission to leave the home (5 percent), quarreling with them (3 percent), mishandling the cooking (2 percent) and refusing sex (2 percent). Not all the women took their abuse in silence. Twenty-one of the respondents fought back physically, 27 percent lashed back at their abusers verbally, and 18 percent sought help from a diverse group of people—from relatives to the police to nongovernment organizations—to end the violence. That said, 61 percent of the respondents, "especially the older and more educated, the currently married compared to the divorced, separated, or widowed, and those who married only once compared to those who married more than once, claim that their husbands do not display any of the six controlling behaviors" (Medina 2015, 189–190).

Women's ability to resist sexual abuse is further hampered by the lack of institutional support. Women's groups have demanded that political leaders give attention to the problem, but the response has been pitiably lackadaisical. Access to reproductive health services remains very limited despite the passage of a popular Reproductive Health Law in 2012. Conservatives in Congress have made this so by successfully limiting the budget for reproductive health. In 2016, for example, only US$20 million was allotted for reproductive health, which was 0.34 percent of the US$52 billion proposed in the national budget (Geronimo 2016). For women's groups, the struggle for better state support for women's reproductive rights is far from over.

See also: Chapter 5: Overview. Chapter 6: Overview.

Further Reading

Geronimo, Jee Y. 2016. "RH Budget Cut Exposes Problematic Lawmaking in PH." *Rappler*, January 21. https://www.rappler.com/newsbreak/in-depth/119493-reproductive-health-budget-cut-lawmaking

McKay, Deirdre. 2012. *Global Filipinos: Migrants' Lives in the Virtual Village*. Bloomington, IN: Indiana University Press.

Medina, Belen T. 2015. *The Filipino Family*. 3rd ed. Quezon City: University of the Philippines Press.

Pe-Pua, Rogelia. 1991. "Marriage and Responsible Parenthood." In *The Filipino Family and the Nation: A Collection of Readings on Family Issues and Concerns*. Quezon City: University of the Philippines, College of Home Economics.

CHAPTER 8

EDUCATION

OVERVIEW

Filipinos have high regard for education, seeing it as the means of moving forward. For the poor, it is the most accessible pathway out of their dire conditions; for the middle class, it is the road that will lead them to a higher income bracket; and for the rich, a way in which ownership of resources are preserved across generations. Families would be willing to sacrifice in various ways (going into debt; limiting household necessities, forced savings, etc.) just to make sure a child is given the best chance of preparing for college, and then once in college, completing a degree that will be of benefit not only to the child but to the entire family. To be "educated" means to have achieved a certain standing that is a notch or two higher than where one is. Filipinos are fond of saying that someone is smart, competent, caring, thoughtful, and ready to serve their family and community because of their education. In Filipino, they say "*may* (pronounced 'my') *pinag-aralan*."

The Philippine educational system comprises public and private schools for all levels, as well as technical and vocational institutions. There are, as of 2016, 14.9 million children enrolled in primary education, 6 million in the secondary level, and 3.5 million at the college and university levels. In 2013, the government finally implemented a K–12 program which extended primary and secondary education from 10 years to 12 years. This was a significant move because K–12 is what the rest of the world had been implementing. The Philippines was one of three countries that held on to the 10-year school system (the others being Angola and Djibouti), until 2011 when it moved to the universally accepted primary-secondary school program.

Students cannot enter primary school without going through compulsory kindergarten school. The age group at the primary level ranges from 6 years to 11 years. These students get introduced to the core courses: mathematics, English, science, and Filipino (Tagalog). The student also enrolls in music, arts, physical education, and health. When the student reaches 4th and 5th grades, she takes a class on her "mother tongue" (her language of birth other than Tagalog) and another on ethics, values, and character education. In public schools, the latter is mainly a class in civics, while in private schools, especially Christian ones, this course on ethics includes a section on Christian values. Muslim schools (madrassas) teach Arabic and Islamic values, while Chinese schools add Mandarin to the language requirements. In the past, classes could be taught in English or Filipino, but in the late 1980s, the Department of

Typical morning scene in the rural Philippines—schoolgirls heading to their elementary schools. (Passionphotography2018/Dreamstime.com)

Education issued a memorandum requiring that the classes in social studies, physical education, and music be taught in Filipino, while English is to be used for science and technology and livelihood-related classes.

The 1987 Constitution's provision requiring the teaching of "Mother languages" was institutionalized in 1989, adding one more medium of instruction. Thus, it is not unusual for teachers and students to seamlessly shift from one language to another or for teachers to conduct lessons with an admixture of English, Filipino, and the students' mother tongue. Those who pass primary school then take a "National Elementary Achievement Test" (mandated in 2004) to determine a students' aptitude once she enters secondary school. This is not a criterion for accepting or rejecting a student's application but often is used by private schools, together with their examination, to determine whether an application will be accepted or rejected. According to the United Nations Educational, Scientific and Cultural Organization (UNESCO) website, in 2018, there were 2,239,549 Filipino children enrolled at the primary school level.

Education in the secondary school (more known as "high school" in the Philippines) goes from grades 7 to 12. Students continue their education in the courses they took at the primary level, although with more specialized topics (e.g., a humanities course that is centered on 21st century Philippine and world literature, statistical math, and earth science or disaster management). There are also new classes like "Technology and Livelihood Education." This is essential in terms of preparation should a student decide to enter a vocational or technical school after graduation.

Some schools offer elective courses in language training (e.g., Mandarin in Chinese schools), computer technology, and literary writing.

The Department of Education has also introduced programs similar to that of the American "Advanced Placement Programs," where students can take special classes on the core courses as well as in sports, arts, journalism, foreign languages, and vocational-technical education. The Department of Education likewise administers a network of national and regional "science high schools" aimed at enhancing its STEM (science, technology, engineering, and mathematics) program. In these schools, students take advanced classes in mathematics and the sciences, as well as on biology, chemistry, physics, and disaster management. These schools have entrance examinations, and students are required to maintain a certain average grade to be able to continue from one grade to the other. In the 1970s, the government established a special high school for the arts where students who qualify are provided virtually free education. Finally, grade 11 students have the option to add vocational and technical courses in "home" industries (production of household products on a small scale, like dried fruits or specialty ornaments), agriculture, and fisheries. They can opt for a third and fourth year of technical-vocational training after high school but will need to take a "competency" exam beforehand. The UNESCO website lists 8,359,013 Filipinos who are in the secondary school level.

There are 1,943 colleges and universities distributed across the archipelago. Of these, 112 are state universities and colleges, 107 are colleges and universities supported mainly by regional and provincial governments, 14 are individual schools, and 1,710 are private institutions of higher education. The top schools, be they state-run or privately owned, are clustered in and around the capital and the nearby provinces. The most popular degrees are in business, the sciences, education, and the medical profession—all of which can potentially give high returns on family investments in education. In its 2016–2017 annual report, the Commission on Higher Education reported that of the total number of 3,589,484 college students, 70 percent were enrolled in courses relating to business and management, education, engineering, and information technology.

Finally, it is worth noting in this overview that gender distribution in general favors Filipinas over Filipinos. While there is parity between males and females at the primary school level (87 percent male, and 88 percent female), more women (41.1 percent) complete secondary school compared to men (36.4 percent). More women (55 percent) enter college than men (45 percent) and proceed to graduate studies (69 percent and 60 percent at the master's and PhD levels, respectively). When it comes to completion the ratio remains more or less the same: 60 percent of women complete their baccalaureate; 66 percent their master's degree and 62 percent receive their PhDs. The extensive network of schools across all levels helps account for a relatively high literacy rate—96.6 percent in 2015 and 93.3 percent in 2018.

See also: Chapter 4: Overseas Filipino Workers. Chapter 7: Overview; Family, Economy, and Politics; Generational Changes; History of the Family Unit; Overseas Workers and their Families; Parent-Child Relationships; Sexuality.

Further Reading

Institute for Statistics. 2022. "Philippines." United Nations Educational, Scientific, and Cultural Organization. http://uis.unesco.org/country/PH

Licuanan, Patricia B. 2017. "The State of Philippine Higher Education." Philippine Higher Education Conference Private Education Assistance Committee (PEAC). November 28. https://peac.org.ph/wp-content/uploads/2017/12/LICUANAN-Philippine-Education -Conference-ilovepdf-compressed.pdf.

Macha, Wilson, Christopher Mackie, and Jessica Magaziner. 2018. "Education in the Philippines." *World Education News and Reviews*. March 6. https://wenr.wes.org/2018/03 /education-in-the-philippines

San Buenaventura, Patricia Anne R. 2011. "Education Quality in the Philippines." *Philippine Statistics Authority*. https://unstats.un.org/sdgs/files/meetings/sdg-inter-workshop -jan-2019/Session%2011.b.3_Philippines___Education%20Equality%20AssessmentFINAL4 .pdf

Bilingual Education

In 1901, acting on the instruction of President William McKinley to make English the lingua franca of the colony, the Philippine Commission, the governing authority during the early years of American rule, issuing Act No. 74 in 1901, created the Department of Public Instructions whose primary responsibility was to develop and oversee "a comprehensive system of public education," from the elementary level up to higher education, with the establishment of the University of the Philippines. Three years later, the commission issued Act No. 1459 that gave private schools the right to grant diplomas and confer degrees. English was to be the medium of instruction in both public and private schools. The purpose was to make "possible the rapid development of a universal and unified system" that would bring about "national unity" and "nourish a generation of brilliant speakers of intercommunication for all educated Filipinos" (Carson 1978, 40). The value of English as a language of instruction was underscored when in 1913, it also became the official language of all colonial state offices. The linguistic strategy worked. The 1918 census listed 30.4 percent of Filipinos and 16.9 percent of Filipinas as English literate. Twenty years later, the census reported that over a quarter of Filipinos could read and write in English. The Americans, however, continued to caution that while literate in their new language, Filipinos, especially the children, still "do not learn the English language well enough to guarantee facility in its use in adult life, and that college graduates continued to suffer English language deficiency."

These doubts provided an opening to those who insisted that a Filipino language be given equal importance as English. As early as 1904, the Americans also proposed that an Institute of Philippine Languages be created to promote other languages, and in 1907, a course on Tagalog (the base of what would become the national language) was approved to be taught at the Philippine Normal School, a teacher-training institute. The issue was once again taken up in the 1930s when Filipino officials renewed their appeal. This idea, however, never gained traction initially as the use of English continued to be policy even after the Americans had turned the governing of the colony to Filipinos. In 1923, then Senate president Manuel L. Quezon decided "not to disturb the language situation" (Martin 1980, 173). Yet, this did not stop advocates from raising the issue again although this was stymied in the legislature. When he became president of the Commonwealth, however, Quezon did move to establish an official "national language." The 1935 Constitution had a provision requiring the development of a national language, and Quezon issued a December 30, 1937 executive order creating the Institute of National Languages, which would develop a national language based on Tagalog and to be taught as a required course at the high school level as well as in teacher-training institutes. During World War II, the Japanese puppet government expanded this to the elementary schools.

A 1939 survey commissioned by President Quezon still recommended the continued use of English while allowing schools to "experiment" with using local dialects as "a supplementary tool of instruction in geography, history, and other social sciences" (Martin 1980, 240). This appeared to be in response to complaints by Filipino educators that the use of English had marginalized the other "native languages." They added that this would actually have a deleterious effect on the efforts to develop a national language as Filipinos would continue to prefer their languages of birth while learning English. When the Philippines became independent, the new republic retained English as the main language of instruction on the grounds that the Philippines already had 1.3 million children learning English.

Despite the continuation of the English-as-language-of-instruction policy, plus the return of Spanish in the high school and college curricula, provincial public schools started adding the local vernacular (or language of birth) in the grade 1 classes. In 1952, there were 778 grade 1 classes (with 36,672 students enrolled) across the nation conducting this experiment. This was followed by a "companion movement" in 1955 where the "dominant vernacular of the locality" was used as "the language of instruction" for grades 1–2. The Bureau of Education approved the implementation of the program in 12 of the 16 divisions (the public school systems across the country were organized around "divisions" that covered more than two provinces). There is no record of any official evaluation of this experiment, although it is likely that its impact was limited as there were hardly any teaching materials that teachers could use. Moreover, since teachers were now to teach the vernacular, they also could not be moved out of their divisions to others where the local language was different.

From the 1950s to the late 1960s, the push for Filipino as a national language was mainly symbolic—an annual national language week, the renaming of government offices in Filipino, and the use of Filipino in all official correspondence. The 1972 Constitution, approved as soon as President Marcos declared martial law, retained a provision from the 1935 Constitution ordering Congress to "take steps toward the development and formal adoption of a common national language to be known as Filipino." The Board of Education also retained the bilingual program, but increased the number of subjects to be taught in Filipino at the college level. A 1974 Department of Education directive mandated that all public and private institutions of higher education teach 6 units (1 course = 3 units) of Filipino. This would be expanded to 9 units in 1996. At the elementary and high school levels, civics was now to be taught in Filipino, while English continued to be used in mathematics and science.

The experiments with using the vernacular of a place in grade school continued into the independent era, and these were implemented throughout the country. This time local-based studies confirmed that they "had varied yet generally positive results," meaning in these places "children who learned in their mother tongue (Hiligaynon) surpassed English-taught pupils in arithmetic, reading, and social studies, and demonstrated greater emotional stability, extroversion, and emotional maturity." Researchers also found out "that the teaching of the vernacular did not prevent good diction and fluency in English." In Cebu province, "pupils in the experimental schools outperformed the other group in all four areas measured—language, reading, social studies, and arithmetic—but this lead reduced in the upper elementary grades once the MOI switched to English." The study showed that using the mother tongue as medium of instruction yielded "benefits in the first few years, but gains in student performance can be undermined if the mother tongue is removed too early" (McEachern and USAID 2013, 9).

The 1987 Constitution also declared Filipino the national language and officially legitimized the teaching of other Philippine languages and vernacular in its Article XIV which stated that, "The national language of the Philippines is Filipino. As it evolves, it shall be further developed and enriched on the basis of existing Philippine and other languages." The presidents after Marcos promoted further the experiments in trilingual education (English, Filipino, and vernacular) throughout the rest of the 20th century and the first decade of the 21st century. Had bilingual education worked? Three scholars working on education wrote: "Unfortunately, longitudinal data based on stable product assessments of student learning are not available. The absence of data on both student learning and systematic process assessments of the BEP has made it nearly impossible to directly link achievement scores to the Bilingual Education policy alone" (Bautista et al. 2008/2009, 20).

Again, like in the earlier decades, the results were uneven. In certain places, children did better in comprehension tests for English, Filipino, and their mother tongue. Dropout rates declined and so did the number of repetitions, as students learned how to conceptualize more than just go through the traditional rote memorization system. That said, the impact of these projects still remains limited due to the same problems their colonial predecessors had: inadequate teachers' training in the local language, the lack of instructional materials, and the teaching of the vernacular using methods based on the teaching of English. This did not deter the government from pushing for the program. In 2010, a "Mother Tongue Based Language Education" (MTB-MLE) program had formalized *and* institutionalized what were once just trial-runs at trilingual education.

See also: Chapter 9: Overview; Carabao English; English; Filipino or Pilipino?; Mother Tongue Teaching; National Language Debate. Chapter 11: Overview.

Further Reading

Bautista, Ma. Cynthia Rose B., Allan B. I. Bernardo, and Dina Ocampo. 2008/2009. "When Reforms Don't Transform: Reflections on Institutional Reforms in the Department of Education." *Human Development Network Discussion Papers Series No. 2.*

Burton, Lisa Ann. 2013. "Mother Tongue–Based Multilingual Education in the Philippines: Studying Top-Down Policy Implementation from the Bottom Up." PhD diss., University of Minnesota. May. https://conservancy.umn.edu/bitstream/handle/11299/152603/Burton_umn_0130E_13632.pdf

Carson, Arthur L. 1978. *The Story of Philippine Education*, 316 pp. Quezon City: New Day Publishers.

Dawe, Christopher J. 2014. "Language Governmentality in the Philippine Education Policy." *Working Papers in Educational Linguistics (WPEL)* 9, no. 1 (Spring): 62–77.

Madrunio, Marilu Ranosa, Isabel Pefianco Martin, and Sterling Miranda Plata. 2018. "English Language Education in the Philippines: Policies, Problems and Prospects." In Robert Kirkpatrick, ed. *English Language Education Policy in Asia*, Vol. 11. The Netherlands: Springer.

Martin, Dalmacio. 1980. *A Century of Education in the Philippines, 1861–1961.* Manila: Philippine Historical Association.

McEachern, Firth, and United States Agency for International Development (USAID). 2013. "Local Languages and Literacy in the Philippines: Implications for Early Reading Instruction and Assessment." *EdDAta II Technical Assistance and Managerial Assistance.* Task No. 17. Contract Number: AID-4920-M-12-0001. December 31. 78 pp.

History of Education

The religious orders ran schools during the Spanish period, first founding parochial schools, and then *colegios* for boys (equivalent to today's high school) and *beaterios* for girls (pre-convent and secular training). Among the best *colegios* was those managed by the Jesuits where boys took classes in chemistry, English, French, Greek, Latin, literature, mathematics, natural history, philosophy, physics, rhetoric, and science. In 1611, the archbishop of Manila founded the Pontifical and Royal University of Santo Tomas (UST), which was run by the Dominican Fathers. The university's Philosophy and Letters program included cosmology and metaphysics, theodicy, and the history of philosophy. UST also had a four-year medicine program as well as courses on the arts, canon law, civil law, grammar, logic, medicine, pharmacy, philosophy and letters, theology, as well as "vocational courses" that included agriculture, commerce, mechanics, and surveying.

In 1863, the Spanish government issued an education decree that provided free public education for the entire colony, moving the responsibility of running the primary school for boys and girls to the municipal governments. The government also established a normal school to train male teachers. In three years, there were 841 primary schools for boys and 833 for girls. On the eve of the Philippine revolution of

1896, a total of about 135,000 boys and 95,000 girls were attending these schools. These schools took away control over children's education from the friars, and the eagerness with which Spanish and Chinese mestizo families sent their children to these public schools and the Universidad de Santo Tomas further alarmed and angered the religious orders which already felt threatened by these "brutes laden in gold." However, these educational reforms never completely prospered for the simple reason that there were not enough teachers for the planned public schools. The reforms also never had time to prosper: 30 years later, a nationalist revolution weakened Spanish colonial rule, and the Americans ended it.

When the United States took over the colony from Spain in 1898, it installed its own public school system, with soldiers becoming the first teachers as soon as the war against Filipino revolutionaries died down. The Americans opened seven elementary schools amid the war between Filipino nationalist armies and the new colonial power, and by the end of 1899, 4,500 students had already enrolled with 24 teachers overseeing their education. Two years later, the first batch of American women teachers arrived in the Philippines. Popularly called the "Thomasites," after the transport that brought them to the colony, these 1,000 teachers formed the vanguard in implementing the 74th decree of the governing body, the Philippine Commission, which implemented a centralized public school system. The commission created a new regular school, replacing the one established by the Spanish, and this was followed in 1901 by schools of agriculture, trade and commerce, marine aquatic centers, and special education. Finally, the Americans gave young Filipinos the opportunity to study in the United States and come back to augment the teaching force. Act No. 854 by the commission subsidized this program and between 1903 and 1907, a total of 209 received subsidies to study in different schools in the United States.

The first public high schools were set up in 1902, and in 1908, the commission passed a law creating the University of the Philippines (UP), the country's national university. Aware of the linguistic diversity of the colony, American authorities made English the medium of instruction for pragmatic reasons (the teachers did not understand Spanish nor any of the Philippine languages). The impact was exceptional. In 1900, the literacy rate was 19.3 percent; in 1920 it was 35.8 percent; and in 1939, it was 51.1 percent. It never went down after that: 72.05 percent in 1960, 83.40 percent in 1970, 89.27 percent in 1975, and 92 percent in 1983. More than just the numbers, the system "made possible opportunities for upward social mobility in Philippine society" (Casambre 1982, 10). The historian Napoleon Casambre adds: "Although wealth was, and still is, the primary qualification for high social status, educational attainment became the requisite for the strengthening of such status. Moreover, it became an important basis in the recruitment of political leadership" (Casambre 1982, 10).

During World War II, the Japanese military administration introduced the teaching of Nihongo and replaced English with Filipino as the medium of instruction, clearly aiming at legitimizing the new order. This new policy hardly made a dent on the educational system created by the Americans. As soon as the Japanese were ousted, the latter returned with little difficulty. The new republic continued where the Americans left off, with a Department of Education established in 1947, and succeeding regimes introduced reforms after reforms ostensibly to improve the system. In the 1960s, the government began to implement the recommendations of a Presidential Commission to Survey Philippine Education to synchronize education with economic priorities that sought to promote greater Philippine integration in the global economy. American influence continues even today: in 2000, the secretary of education observed that "our military school system inherited from the American colonial period has been modified but little and has substantially maintained its [i.e., the American] structure despite many problems" (Gonzalez 2002, 29).

The most extensive modification came in 1982, when President Marcos integrated formal and nonformal education across levels, forcing colleges and universities to improve by submitting themselves to "voluntary accreditation" in exchange for state subsidies. The 1987 Constitution included a provision that made elementary education compulsory, and Congress followed this up by passing a law that expanded it to the secondary level, albeit not mandatory. In 1990, there was a "trifocalization program" that was to be implemented in the next decade. The educational system was broken into three divisions: the Department of Education was to take charge of elementary and secondary education, while a Commission on Higher Education oversaw colleges and universities, and a Technical Education and Skills Development Authority (TESDA) was given mandate over vocational and technical education. These administrative changes were made alongside another major program to decentralize the system and replace it with "a school-based management approach." Schools were given considerable flexibility with their programs based on government targets.

Additional modifications were made in relation to student competence, with national achievement examinations at the elementary level and refining of college entrance tests. There seemed to be specific positive changes, with the United Nations Economic and Social Organization (UNESCO) reporting significant increases in the functional literacy among those who were to go to college (88 percent in the case of the 15–19 age group, and 91 percent among those in their early 20s). In 2004, concerned that literacy improvements in the primary level were still slight (83.4 percent in 1994 to 84.1 percent in 2003), the Department of Education began using a National Achievement Test that consisted of examinations in English, math, science, and social studies. All 6th, 10th, and 12th grade students for public and private elementary schools were supposed to take the NAT. In 2006, private schools complemented this with their own entrance examinations.

President Benigno S. Aquino III finally brought the Philippines in line with global standards with the K–12 program in 2011. Aquino continued the school-building projects of his predecessor, Gloria M. Arroyo, and between 2010 and the end of his term, the government—with support from the World Bank and countries like the United States and Japan—was able to build 84,479 classrooms and hire an additional 128,000 new teachers. Aquino ended his term with a new education plan to expand literacy to out-of-school youth, reduce dropouts and repetitions, and increase the percentage of secondary school completion. Then in 2017, President Rodrigo R. Duterte signed the "Universal Access to Quality Tertiary Education Act" that mandated free tuition in all state universities and colleges (the new law exempted private schools).

Over 1 million students in 111 state universities and colleges would receive free tuition that totaled US$160 million.

Problems, however, continue to persist, particularly when it comes to student performance. The official primary school entry age is 6 years old, and the Asian Development Bank noted that government statistics showed that between 2002 and 2007, "less than half of 6-year-old children [were] not yet in primary school" and that "63.36% of Grade 1 enrollees [were] older than six years" (Maligalig et al. 2011, 17). In 2010, of the over 13.1 million students enrolled in public elementary schools, 27.82 percent either never attended or never completed elementary schooling, usually due to the absence of any school in their area, education being offered in a language that was foreign to them, or financial distress.

NAT scores remain a problem. The government had set 77 percent performance for primary school students and 65 percent for those in high school. The highest reached in 2015 was 69.1 percent for the elementary students, while it was 49.48 percent among high school students. A 2005 UNESCO survey showed that the 54.7 percent NAT scores "of Grade 6 students were way below the acceptable mastery level of the required elementary competencies." High school students performed much worse, having scored only "45.3 percent in 2005." The report added, "Only about 20% of Grade 6 students, and barely half a percent (0.48%) of high school graduating students had mastery (75–100 percentile score) of the required competencies in their respective level. More than a quarter of elementary students and more than half of high school graduating students were found to have no mastery of basic education competencies. In both levels, the performance level of students was found lowest in science" (Caoli-Rodriguez 2008, 196). The NAT tests percentage score in the last year of high school was only 44.3 percent.

In June 2016, the World Bank report "Assessing Basic Education Service Delivery" reported that increased government spending had led to improvements like a decline in the student-teacher ratio (from 38:1 in 2010 to 29:1 in 2013). The quality of teachers' training, however, remained inadequate. The Asian Development Bank expressed a "worrisome preponderance" over the poor passing rates in the national teachers' examination. Between 2005 and 2015, for example, the percentage never reached even 50 percent (34 percent in 2005 and 43 percent 10 years later). The college statistics were problematic in the first years of the second decade of the 21st century. The Commission on Higher Education reported a drop by 12.7 percent in college enrollments between 2015 and 2017, while the percentage of graduates vis-à-vis enrollment averaged 17 percent. It was only in the school year 2017–2018 that this rose to 24 percent (CHED 2018). It is still not clear if this spike is the result of President Duterte's free tuition program for state schools, but that was most likely a strong incentive. Finally, the personnel needed to ensure a quality education still remain inadequate. In 2017, only 5.2 percent of graduates decided to enter into a master's program and less than 1 percent proceeded to pursue their PhDs.

See also: Chapter 9: Overview.

Further Reading

Bautista, Ma. Cynthia Rose B., Allan B. I. Bernardo, and Dina Ocampo. 2008/2009. "When Reforms Don't Transform: Reflections on Institutional Reforms in the Department of Education." *Human Development Network Discussion Papers Series No. 2.*

Caoli-Rodriguez, Rhona B. 2008. *Insular South-East Asia Synthesis Report: Asia and the Pacific Education for All (EFA) Mid-Decade Assessment.* Bangkok: UNESCO. Accessed April 22, 2019. http://uis.unesco.org/sites/default/files/documents/education-for-all -mid-decade-assessment-for-insular-south-east-asia-en_0.pdf

Carson, Arthur L. 1978. *The Story of Philippine Education.* Quezon City: New Day Publishers.

Casambre, Napoleon J. 1982. "The Impact of American Education in the Philippines." *Educational Perspectives* 21, no. 4 (Winter): 7–14. Accessed April 22, 2019. https:// scholarspace.manoa.hawaii.edu/bitstream/10125/47216/EDPVol21%234_7-14.pdf

Gonzalez, Andrew. 2002. *An Unfinished Symphony: 934 Dats at DECS.* Manila: Andrew Gonzalez.

Institute for Statistics. 2022. "Philippines: Education and Literacy." United Nations Economic and Social Organization (UNESCO) http://uis.unesco.org/en/country/ph?theme =education-and-literacy

Maligalig, Dalisay S., Rhona B. Caoli-Rodriguez, Arturo Martinez, and Sining Cuevase. 2011. "Education Outcomes in the Philippines." *Asian Development Bank Economics Working Paper Series No. 199.* January. Accessed April 22, 2019. https://www.adb.org /sites/default/files/publication/28409/economics-wp199.pdf

Martin, Dalmacio. 1980. *A Century of Education in the Philippines, 1861–1961.* Manila: Philippine Historical Association.

Republic of the Philippines, Commission on Higher Education (CHED). 2018. "Statistics: 2018 Higher Education Indicators." https://ched.gov.ph/wp-content/uploads/2018/07 /Higher-Education-Indicators.pdf

World Bank Group and Australian Aid. 2016. "Assessing Basic Education Service Delivery in the Philippines: The Philippines Public Education Expenditure Tracking and Quantitative Service Delivery Study." Report No. AUS799. June. Accessed April 22, 2019. http://documents.worldbank.org/curated/en/507531468325807323/pdf/AUS6799 -REVISED-PH-PETS-QSDS-Final-Report.pdf

Kindergarten-to-Grade-Twelve Program

The Kindergarten-to-Grade-Twelve Program (or K–12) was finally implemented in the Philippines beginning 2011 and graduated its first 12th graders in 2018. After several decades of relying on the old system of separating primary (K–7) from secondary education (4 years), government leaders and educators finally took seriously a problem that had plagued primary education since the postwar period—student withdrawal from schools before reaching grade 6. A scholar of Philippine education wrote that as far back as 1959, of the 100 students who began grade 1, "an average of only 46 were able to reach Grade 6," leading to "the average annual wastage [of] 11.63 percent of the public school funds" between 1959 and 1963 (Carson 1978, 39–40). Another scholar wrote that during this period, "of the total number of 2,192,900" students of high school age (13–16 years old), "about 1,800,132 or over 82 percent were out of school" (Martin 1980, 348). These problems persisted in the next decades. Only 40.55 percent of children completed their primary education, and 27.55 percent were able to finish four years of high school in the 1960s.

In the 1970s, the figures rose (41.28 percent) but still did not exceed 50 percent. Finally, despite a major overhaul of the educational system during the 15-year rule of President Ferdinand Marcos, the percentage of graduates remained low: between 1975 and 1985, the elementary school graduates rose only by 0.6 percent (from 11.6 percent in 1975 to 12.2 percent in 1985), and secondary school graduates by 0.8 percent (from 19.61 percent in 1975 to 20.46 percent in 1985). Even a few years before K–12 was implemented, the United Nations Economic and Social Office (UNESCO) worried that the Philippines was still "among the countries with decreased net enrollment rate from 1999 to 2006, and with the greatest number of out-of-school children (more than 50,000)." It concluded that the country's "current performance in education [was] not so promising" (Maligalig et al. 2011, 1).

In 1991, a congressional commission on education reforms recommended that the Department of Education, among other things, give "basic education," its "undivided attention," develop "alternative learning modes, especially for literacy acquisition," and require the use of the mother tongue as medium of instruction for grades 1–3 students. These recommendations were part of the reforms the department introduced as part of its "trifocalization" program, which was designed to attain the goals of the United Nation's "Basic Education Sector Reform Agenda." When he became president, Benigno S. Aquino III vigorously pushed for K–12 with these decades-long problems in mind but also cognizant that 21st-century education must include information technology and social media. Department of Education began the program even as it waited for Congress to pass a law legitimizing the program. The legislature finally passed the "Enhanced Basic Education Act" in 2013 which mandated that children must have sufficient time to learn concepts and skills and master their mother tongue to prepare them for the next level. K–12 consists of four phases: phase 1 (Laying the Foundation) requires kindergarten nationwide, phase 2 (Modeling and Migration) where a new curriculum would be followed by all schools for grades 1–10, phase 3 (Complete migration) where grades 11 and 12 (senior high school) would also have their respective curricula, and phase 4 or "completion of the reform."

The first cohort group of the K–12 program graduated in 2018. While it is still premature to evaluate its effectiveness, teachers' groups had already raised concerns about its effectiveness in overcoming the shortcomings of primary and secondary education. The first concern has to do with facilities. Critics have argued that K–12 will not succeed if the facilities are inadequate. There are not enough classrooms, seats and other provisions are not there. In 2014, the government allotted US$1.5 billion for classrooms, but the budget office only released US$65 million, of which only US$38 million was actually used. Others complain that the curricula emphasize science and

Elementary school in Puerto Princesa, Palawan. (Klodien/Dreamstime.com)

technology at the expense of national history and "indigenous knowledge," accusing the government of tailoring the program based on the desire for Filipinos to seek employment or migrate abroad and not on "Filipino values or Asian way of life" (Abu-lencia 2015, 235). These criticisms have some validity when it comes to government funding, although President Rodrigo R. Duterte did increase the allocation for the Department of Education, making it the largest recipient of the national budget. In 2018, for example, education received US$10.99 billion out of a total budget of US$ 74.79 billion. Other than this increase in funds, the government did not respond to the criticism.

Between 1980 and 1990, UNESCO showed a jump of more than 10 percentage points in literacy rates (from 83 percent to 94 percent), and this has remained in the lower 90s since then (UNESCO 2019). Underneath these aggregate numbers are more worrisome figures. The ratio of graduates to enrollments at the elementary level rose gradually—9.43 percent in 1965; 11.6 percent in 1975; and 12.2 percent in 1985. It slowed down further at the secondary level—19.4 percent in 1965; 19.61 percent in 1975; and 20.46 percent in 1985. Other statistics also show cause for worry. In 1990, only 3 out of 10 grade 1 students ever made it to the next grades, and those who dropped out before grade 4 reverted back to illiteracy (Chua 1999). The UNESCO reported that: "The cohort survival rate for both primary and secondary education levels declined from 72.4% to 70% and from 77% to 67.3%, respectively, during the period 2002–2005. This implies that the proportion of those who entered Grade 1 and Year 1 secondary education who get to the last year of the respective education levels is decreasing due to high incidence of drop outs and the relatively declining efficiency of the basic education system" (Caoli-Rodriguez 2008, 195).

The long-term success of the K–12 program also depends on how the government will solve the shortage of teachers. In 1998, the shortage totaled 17,000 teachers, growing to 40,000 in 2000 and 35,000 in 2003. This deficiency was aggravated further by the low quality of their training (Mullis et al. 2004). A former secretary of education lamented that Filipino teachers were ranked "fourth and third to the last respectively among the 41 countries," that took the International Mathematics and Science Studies examination in 1995 and 2000. He added that "few of our English teachers can write English well; many read about Grade 6 level based on teacher scores when we give workshops in reading." Those who taught economics lacked the competence to teach "a modern science which relies heavily on quantitative reasoning and the application of mathematics."

The same education secretary worried that in "our 36,000 public elementary and 4,000 secondary schools, only about 25% of the elementary schools had full-time principals and slightly over 51% of our high schools had full-time principals. The rest were supervised and managed by head teachers or teachers-in-charge." Adding to the problem is the school system's weak administrative structure. There was a shortage of 2 million desks in 1998 despite 500 million pesos allotted from the national budget. The increase in the overall student population and the wear and tear of school equipment mitigated the budget allotment. Thus, in 2001, the schools still lacked the same 2 million desks they needed in 1998.

See also: Chapter 7: Overseas Workers and their Families. Chapter 9: Overview.

Further Reading

Abulencia, Arthur S. 2015. "The Unraveling of K–12 Program as an Education Reform in the Philippines." *Sipathahoena: South-East Asian Journal for Youth, Sports and Health Education* 1, no. 2 (October): 230–240.

Caoli-Rodriguez, Rhona B. 2008. *Insular South-East Asia Synthesis Report: Asia and the Pacific Education for All (EFA) Mid-Decade Assessment.* Bangkok: UNESCO. Accessed April 22, 2019. http://uis.unesco.org/sites/default/files/documents/education-for-all -mid-decade-assessment-for-insular-south-east-asia-en_0.pdf

Carson, Arthur L. 1978. *The Story of Philippine Education*, 316 pp. Quezon City: New Day Publishers.

Chua, Yvonne. 1999. *Robbed: An Investigation of Corruption in Philippine Education.* Quezon City: Philippine Center for Investigative Journalism.

Institute for Statistics. 2019. "Philippines: Education and Literacy." United Nations Economic and Social Organization (UNESCO). http://uis.unesco.org/en/country /ph?theme=education-and-literacy

Maligalig, Dalisay S., Rhona B. Caoli-Rodriguez, Arturo Martinez, and Sining Cuevase. 2011. "Education Outcomes in the Philippines." *Asian Development Bank Economics Working Paper Series No. 199.* January. Accessed April 22, 2019. https://www.adb.org /sites/default/files/publication/28409/economics-wp199.pdf

Martin, Dalmacio. 1980. *A Century of Education in the Philippines, 1861-1961*. Manila: Philippine Historical Association.

Mullis, Ina V.S., Michael O. Martin, Eugenio J. Gonzalez, and Steven J. Chrostowskio. 2004. *TIMSS 2003 International Mathematics Report: Findings from IEA's Trens in International Mathematics and Science Study at the Fourth and Eighth Grades*. Chestnut Hill, MA: International Association for the Evaluation of Educational Achievement (IEQ).

Textbooks

The first textbooks used by the public and private schools were naturally in English. American officials, however, were well aware that while these were "admirable books for use in the field for which they were designed," that is, the American public school system, they were "but wretchedly ill adopted for the instruction of boys and girls in these islands." The director of education, Frank White complained of the "amount and character of material included within their covers which is foreign to the thought and activities of Filipino children." He added: "The primers and the readers have much to say of the changes of seasons of a temperate country, and of fruits and flowers and birds which have never been seen or heard of here; of a home life and social customs which are beyond the experience and comprehension of children of the Tropics."

Moreover, the "arithmetics deal with weights and measures unknown in the Orient; their problems are based on the buying and selling of products in which these pupils have no interest The geographies are descriptive of North America and the States of the Union; they ignore the home of the Filipino and give scant treatment to the Orient in general. The histories deal with America and Europe, making no mention of the Philippine Islands, and little of China, Japan and Malaysia. The text on nature study and plant and animal life tell the children of a vegetation and a fauna which are strange to the Filipino as German script is to a boy or girl in American primary school" (White, Director of Education, 1909–1910, as quoted in Martin 1980, 189–190).

To address this problem, a series of American-authored books on the Philippines were added to the elementary and high school basic textbooks (i.e., arithmetic, reading and language). These covered a diverse set of topics, from Philippine folklore and geography to maps and Philippine history. The first textbooks produced on the islands were *How to Live: A Manual of Hygiene for Use in the Schools of the Philippine Islands* and *The Story of the Philippines for Use in the Schools of the Philippine Islands*. Both were written by Adeline Knapp, who was part of the first group of American teachers aboard the USAT Thomas. Knapp was appointed teacher in May 1901 and wrote these books despite being ill. Then, in 1909, Austin Craig, an American teacher who became an admirer of Jose Rizal, wrote a book about the national hero (*Rizal's Own Story*), which was added as supplementary reading in grade 4. He would follow this up with another biography of Rizal (*Lineage, Life and Labors of Jose Rizal,* published in 1914) for the upper grades (Martin 1980, 198). In 1923, Rizal's two great novels, *Noli Me Tangere* and *El Filibusterismo*, were translated by Charles Derbyshire to be used in junior and senior high school classes.

In 1918, the first two Filipino-authored textbooks were introduced to the elementary schools—Leandro Fernandez's *A Brief History of the Philippines* (written for grade 6) and Camile Osias's *Philippine Readers Series* (released 1918) for grades 1–7. Osias's series became a very important "guide" for Filipinos, as they learned about language, "character-building" (or "the habits which Filipino children ought to form"), "civic spirit and patriotism," as well as "diligence and perseverance," which would enable them to "understand more about life and things" (Coloma 2013, 310).

Textbook publication more than doubled in the third decade of American colonial rule, especially after a fact-finding mission from the United States strongly recommended ending the "bookish and artificial" approach to teaching that was directly the result of the use of American textbooks (Cortes 1993). The result was a panoply of books on basic and "practical" English as well as how to improve one's writing and speaking in English. The new "Modern Arithmetic" textbook was written by a Filipino, and so was a book on Philippine "primary geography." The Bureau of Education also published introductory texts on home economics, wood working, trade, home gardening, and Philippine prose and poetry. Most of the books, however, were focused on citizen's training. Apart from upgrades on the books about Rizal and his works, and the *Philippine Readers Series*, there were new texts on "Philippine National Literature," "Great Filipinos," "Philippine Civics," and "Philippine Government."

Finally, American and Filipino authors cowrote the first textbook on "the Orient." It was clear that by this period, everyone connected to education was focused on preparing young Filipinos for national independence. The books on government were divided into topical chapters like "Law and Justice," "Protection of Life and Liberty," "Finance," "Elections," "Municipalities," "The Executive," "The Legislative Power," and "The Judicial Power." The civics texts included sections on "Community Welfare," "Public Welfare and Charities," "Philippine Ideals," "Great Filipino Leaders," and "Education."

Under the new republic, education officials and political leaders continued the work of their colonial predecessors. It was, however, easier said than done. There were several advances. Basic English and Mathematics texts were regularly updated. There was the institutionalization of the teaching of Rizal's life and works by Congress despite fierce opposition from the Catholic Church. Republic Act No. 1425 (also known as the Rizal Law) made the course on the national hero's life and works a compulsory requirement for college students. New Philippine history textbooks, including those written specifically for Catholic high school, also "considerably toned down, if not eliminated altogether, expressions of anti-Muslim sentiments" (Curaming 2017, 430). By the 1960s, however, this progress had slowed down due to problems with regard to resources, the orientation of textbooks, and corruption.

For one, textbook production and improvement was unable to match the growth in enrollments. Education officials were warning that the ratio of textbooks to students had steadily declined throughout the 1960s, such that in the first study of this issue, educators found out that the ratio of textbooks per student at the primary and high school levels was quite alarming: 1 textbook for 9 students at the primary level; 1 for 11 in the intermediate grades; and 1 for 8 in high school (Carson 1978, 253). The numbers were not the only issue. An education development task force revealed that 67 percent of existing textbooks needed major revisions, with 33 percent of them needing to be discarded and replaced. With all power centralized under his authority, President Ferdinand Marcos launched an ambitious text upgrade program centered especially on the basic courses (English, Filipino, civics, mathematics, and science) and targeting the 22 poorest provinces of the country.

The end goal was to bring the ratio down to the ideal one textbook per student. The World Bank helped by extending a US$120 million loan to help the Philippines develop textbooks for vocational schools in eight years. In its first year of implementation, the first project produced 20 million science, math, and Filipino language textbooks for 1st and 2nd grade students. At the end of the eight years (1984), the Department of Education had put out 94,807,965 textbooks for public elementary and secondary schools and another 38,098,941 for private high schools for a total of 132,906,906 textbooks (Carson 1978, 253). This improved the ratio of the number of students per book to 1:2 (Aprieto 1983, 351–359).

But not for long. A department awash in money due to a larger share in the national budget and constant international support inevitably breeds corruption. The centralization of the approval and evaluation of textbooks to a Philippine Textbook Board in 1984 made plundering more appealing since it was only the people on the top who could be targets or potential coconspirators (Buhain 1998, 82). In 1990, Yvonne Chua, an investigative journalist, exposed suspicious transactions where P383 million out of a total P683 million to be used as security deposit in the commissioning and production of textbooks had never been remitted, while P114 million could not be found (Chua 1999, 146–147).

Between 1996 and 1998, Chua discovered that regional offices of the Department of Education spent P414.4 million to fund 4,858,021 illicitly produced books— broken down to 3,140,794 books (P234.4 million), 139,125 overpriced books (P2.04 million), and 1,578,102 unapproved books (P177.9 million). Private publishers who "won" textbook contracts had to pay off 20–65 percent of the fund. Overpricing and delivering substandard textbooks was pervasive, and so were under-deliveries which ranged from 30 percent to 60 percent of a contract (Chua 1999, 8–9). In 1999, an agent of several book publishers was caught with US$110,000 in bribe money to be used so that these publishers' books would be approved (and the budget released) without pre-auditing (Chua 1999, 18).

Nothing changed in the second decade of the 21st century. The e-magazine *Rappler* reported that the Department of Education procured 15,263,111 textbooks worth US$11.42 million for the 2013–2014 school year. Only 9,691,583 (US$6.95 million) were delivered to division offices nationwide. Monitoring and preventing corruption were becoming doubly difficult when the Department of Education could "barely keep track of its expenditures." A World Bank report admitted that it was "difficult to monitor the actual implementation of specific budget programs and objectives." The report added: "A particular concern, in this respect, is whether and to what extent MOOE (maintenance, operating and other expenditures) appropriations . . . are eventually used for the intended purpose" (as quoted by Chua 1999, 7).

The final and perhaps most profound problem in the production of textbooks, particularly in history and civics, has to do with nationalism. A 2002 UNESCO team of social scientists noted that the social science textbooks were "vague on nationalism" (Gonzalez 2002, 29–30). This criticism was not new. It was raised way back in 1966 by historian Renato Constantino whose essay "The Miseducation of the Filipino" critiqued how Americanization had stunted the growth of Filipino nationalism. Twenty years later, the educator Luisa C. Doronila provided the Constantino argument empirical substance by examining "the discontinuity between the official policy of promoting nationalism and the low level of nationalism among Filipino elementary school children" (Curaming 2017, 419). The government's decision then to increase the number of textbooks written in the national language was warmly received by nationalist educators who regarded this as the first step toward finally breaking down the "colonial mentality" fostered by an American-inspired educational system.

The increase in classes being taught in Filipino may have pleased Filipino nationalists, but it worried government leaders whose idea of greater Philippine integration into the global economy involved sending more Filipinos abroad or expanding the workforce of the business processing companies whose main clients were from the United States and the West. The problem of an inadequate education in English in the 1980s and 1990s continued to hound the government in the new century, prompting President Gloria M. Arroyo to issue a May 17, 2003 executive decree that reiterated the need to teach English as a second language at all levels, its use as a primary medium of instruction for mathematics and science in select primary school grades and at the secondary level. The "return to English" received additional impetus from the efforts of the member nations of the Association of Southeast Asian Nations (ASEAN) to speed up the development of a regional economic zone. It remains to be seen whether future governments can find a lasting resolution to the perpetual problem of lack of teachers training and limited facilities (classrooms) and resources (textbooks, teaching materials, etc.).

See also: Chapter 9: Overview; English; Mother Tongue Teaching; National Language Debate.

Further Reading

Aprieto, Pacifico N. 1983. "The Philippine Textbook Project." *Prospects: Quarterly Review of Education* 13, no. 3: 351–359.

Buhain, Dominador D. 1998. *A History of Publishing in the Philippines*. Manila: Rex Book Store.

Caoli-Rodriguez, Rhona. 2006. "Asia and the Pacific Education for All (EFA) Mid-Decade Assessment: Insular South-East Asia Synthesis Report." United Nations Educational, Scientific and Cultural Organization and the Japan Funds-in Trust. http://uis.unesco

.org/sites/default/files/documents/education-for-all-mid-decade-assessment-for
-insular-south-east-asia-en_0.pdf

Carson, Arthur L. 1978. *The Story of Philippine Education.* Quezon City: New Day Publishers.

Chua, Yvonne. 1999. *Robbed: An Investigation of Corruption in Philippine Education.* Quezon City: Philippine Center for Investigative Journalism.

Coloma, Ronald Sintos. 2013. "Care of the Postcolonial Self: Cultivating Nationalism in the *Philippine Readers.*" *Qualitative Research in Education* 2, no. 3: 302–327.

Constantino, Renato. 1982. *The Miseducation of the Filipino.* Quezon City: Foundation for Nationalist Studies.

Cortes, Josefina R. 1993. *Explorations in the Theory and Practice of Philippine Education, 1965–1993.* Quezon City: University of the Philippines.

Curaming, Rommel A. 2017. "Hegemomic Tool? Nationalism in Philippine History Textbooks, 1900–2000." *Philippine Studies: Historical and Ethnographic Viewpoints* 65, no. 4: 417–450.

Gonzalez, Andrew. 2002. *An Unfinished Symphony: 934 Dats at DECS.* Manila: Andrew Gonzalez.

Grosser, Larry Lee. 1967. "A Content Analysis of Philippine School Textbooks: A Study of Political Socialization and Development." MA thesis, Western Michigan University, August.

Heyneman, Stephen P., and Dean T. Jamison. 1984. "Textbooks in the Philippines: Evaluation of the Pedagogical Impact of a Nationwide Investment." *Educational Evaluation and Policy Analysis* 6, no. 2 (Summer). http://citeseerx.ist.psu.edu/viewdoc/download?doi=10.1.1.898.1486&rep=rep1&type=pdf

Martin, Dalmacio. 1980. *A Century of Education in the Philippines, 1861–1961.* Manila: Philippine Historical Association.

The University of the Philippines

The University of the Philippines (UP) was founded on June 18, 1908, through a law (Act No. 1870) of the first Philippine legislature. Its mission, as laid out in its website, is to provide an "advanced instruction in literature, philosophy, the sciences and arts, and to give professional and technical training" to every qualified student regardless of "age, sex, nationality, religious belief and political affiliation." Filipino and American leaders envisioned UP to be the training ground for the economic, political, and cultural leaders of the colony and the eventual Philippine republic. The university has eight major campuses nationwide, with the largest and main campus located in Quezon City. Its 57 degree-granting units (college, school, institute) offer 246 undergraduate and 362 graduate diplomas. Their foundation is a liberal education program (created in 1959 and revised in 2001) which enables a student to take a series of courses in the humanities, science, mathematics, and the social sciences before going into their field of specialization.

University of the Philippines, Diliman, Quezon City. (Walter Eric Sy/Dreamstime .com)

To enter UP, a student has to pass a rigorous college admission test (UPCAT) that is conducted annually. Only 18 percent of the total number of high school graduates pass UPCAT. This exam has been criticized as favoring students who come from the cities and study in the top public and private schools of these metropolises. The university had responded to such displeasure by introducing a "democratization policy" that ensures that UP students are representative of the general population, including those coming from various parts—urban and rural—of the country. Tuition fees are subsidized by government taxes and are structured in such a way that students from low-income and disadvantaged families do not have to pay tuition and instead receive stipends, scholarships, and employment as student assistants.

The university's highest ruling body is the Board of Regents consisting of representatives from the two houses of legislature, the concurrent secretary of the Department of Education, the head of the Commission on Higher Education, the UP president, the faculty regent, the student regent, a representative of the UP alumni, and three appointees by the president of the Philippines. The Philippine president gets to appoint the UP president who has a six-year term. UP has had 20 presidents, and all save two were Filipinos. As of this writing, the 21st president is Danilo Concepcion, a former dean of the College of Law. The UP Alumni Association was formed in 1913 and a student council followed a year later. Students would have their own paper when the *Philippine Collegian* was established in 1922.

UP prides itself as the country's national university where the country's elite are trained. Its graduates include 7 Philippine presidents, 13 Supreme Court justices, 36 national scientists, and 40 national artists. Its other source of pride is its defense of academic autonomy. UP has defended this principle against more powerful external forces, like the time in 1923 when an angry Senate president Manuel L. Quezon demanded that they discipline the staff of the *Philippine Collegian* for criticizing the his policy. When UP President Rafael Palma refused and invoked the institution's autonomy in defense of the students, Quezon retaliated by using his allies in the Board of Regents to stymie Palma's policies and his legislative allies to investigate UP's finances. Palma resisted as much as he could, finally resigning from UP. The Board of Regents added insult to injury by denying him the gratuity or honorarium he was supposed to receive as UP president.

In the 1950s, Filipino politicians and clergymen accused UP of harboring communists and conducted a witch hunt inside the campus. Students and faculty fought back to defend UP's "academic freedom." From these protests would be emerge the student radicals who would proceed to form a new communist party (see Chapter 1). The other instance where the state interfered in UP's functioning was when President Ferdinand Marcos declared martial law in 1972. Marcos closed UP for several months, and after he ordered the resumption of classes, imposed several restrictions on all university activities, sent military spies to monitor student organizations, and refused calls for a restoration of the university and college student councils. Student activists were initially shaken by martial law, but once they adjusted to the restrictions, they were able to revive political organizing and staged protests soon after.

Activism was at its strongest on the eve of martial law, as UP students and their comrades in other schools protested against the United States' war in Vietnam, while being drawn to a fast-spreading communist underground network. The number of students indulging in such activism, however, has remained small. The majority of UP students kept their distance through even the most politically polarized periods. They were sympathetic but finishing their undergraduate degrees was always priority. They tended to join protests over issues that financially threatened their standing (like the 1977 anti-tuition-fee-increase strikes), but once these were "elevated" into national problems by activists, the students withdraw from the political arena. That said, during critical moments, students do join those on the streets, like in 1986 when Marcos was about to be forced out of the palace by a peaceful "People's Power" mobilization.

From the 1990s to the present, UP has continued to grow and maintain its status as the country's top national school. New colleges were established while old ones were expanded. A campus in Mindanao and an "Open University" were opened in 1995. Relationships with counterpart universities in other countries also expanded during this period, allowing for more student and faculty exchanges and opportunities for joint research. In 2008, President Gloria M. Arroyo signed "The UP Charter" (Republic Act No. 9500) that expanded on the university's general goal laid out in 1908. This mandate was much more explicit. The charter directed UP "to perform its unique and distinctive leadership in higher education and development by taking the lead in setting academic standards and initiating innovations in teaching, research, faculty development in philosophy, the arts and humanities, the social sciences, engineering, natural sciences, mathematics, and technology, and maintain centers of excellence in these disciplines and professions." UP was to become a center for graduate studies as well as basic and applied research.

See also: Chapter 6: Overview. Chapter 7: Overview; Family, Economy, and Politics.

Further Reading

Alfonso, Oscar M., and Leslie E. Bauzon. 1985. *University of the Philippines: The First 75 Years (1908–1983)*. Quezon City: University of the Philippines Press.

Aquino, Belinda. 1991. *The University Experience: Essays on the 82nd Anniversary of the University of the Philippines*. Quezon City: University of the Philippines Press.

CHAPTER 9

LANGUAGES

OVERVIEW

The website *Ethnologue: Languages of the World* (https://www.ethnologue.com/) lists between 182 and 187 languages native to the Philippines, four of which are now extinct. Of all these languages, 170 are mutually unintelligible to one another. Linguists though classify them as belonging to the Austronesian family of languages that include those from Indonesia and Malaysia in the Southeast Asia region; Melanesia, Micronesia, and Polynesia in the Pacific islands; and as far as Madagascar, whose national language Malagasay has features similar to Filipino. Their ancestries, however, are diverse. The lineages of some may be Indonesian or Malaysian, but the histories of others are much closer to those of Polynesians and Micronesians. There are three languages that do not belong to "the family." Chavacano (a Spanish-Portuguese creole language spoken only in three towns), Hokkien (the lingua franca of the Chinese community), and Filipino English.

Of these 182–187 languages, the 2016 census classified ten as major languages based on the number of speakers. These are Tagalog (24,748,230), Visayan (15,810,000), Ilocano (7,016,400), Hiligaynon (5,770,000), Bikol (4,580,000), Waray-Waray (2,560,000), Pampango (1,905,430), Pangasinan (1,162,140), Maguindanaoan (1,100,000), and Tausog (1,062,000). Five are in Luzon Island (Tagalog, Ilocano, Bikol, Pampango, and Pangasinan), two in the Visayas (Cebuano and Hiligaynon), and three in Mindanao (Visayan, Maguindanaoan, and Tausog). These languages have their own "dialects" that are associated with specific subregions or cities and towns. These are often distinguished by their accents and pronunciations as well as word spelling and use.

One possible explanation for these variations is that Filipinos are typically trilingual. They are fluent in their mother tongue (the language they speak at home) and in English and Filipino. With the nationalization of television (see Chapter 16), more Filipinos have become articulate in the national language (Filipino), and those who have been working abroad for an extended number of years have also added their language-of-work to their repertoire.

The Philippines has two official languages—English and Filipino. English is a "holdover" from the colonial period, used by the Americans as a "common language" to unite and better rule a linguistically diverse colony. Filipino is based mainly on Tagalog, which has elicited a lot of protests from non-Tagalog speakers but also inspired others to push for replacing foreign words with their Filipino equivalents,

Table 9.1: LEXICONS

Primitive Austronesian	Filipino	Ilocano	Visayan	English
Abara	Abaga	Abaga	Abaga	Shoulder
Agay	Agaw	Agaw	Agaw	Snatch
Ama	Ama	Ama	Ama	Father
Anaj	Anay	Anay	Anay	Termite
Babaji	Babae	Babai	Babai	Babai
Bavang	Bawang	Bawang	Bawang	Garlic
Hat'ang	Bagang	Bagang	Bagang	Molar
Pilih	Pili	Pili	Pili	Select
Tambak	Tambak	Tambak	Tambak	Pile, heap
Tijan	Tiyan	Tiyan	Tiyan	Stomach
T'ulat	Sulat	Sulat	Sulat	Letter
Valo	Walo	Walo	Walo	Eight
Pat'u paso	paso	paso	paso	Burn

Source: Fullante 1983, 59.

and the teaching of more classes taught in Filipino. What is often glossed over is the fact that Philippine languages, including the national language, continue to be constantly enriched by foreign words and the mixing of local languages and dialects. The archeologist Stephen Acabado writes of how "trans-oceanic exchanges and mobility" between the Philippines and the rest of Asia have enriched Filipino languages with words and phrases from "borrowed South (Indic, Tamil), Southwest (Arabic, Persian), and East (Chinese, Japanese) Asian terms. Of course, Spanish terms are now considered part of our existence." Acabado adds: "What a lot of present-day Filipinos don't know though, is that we have borrowed Nahuatl (the language of the Aztecs) terms including nanay (mother), tatay (father), tiyangge (outside/open-air market) and many more" (Acabado 2020). It is therefore unsurprising these days to hear Filipinos combine mother tongue words and phrases with those from Filipino and English, with some adding a sprinkling of Japanese, Arabic, Thai, Italian, German, Spanish, Hebrew, and Mandarin. One can hear these linguistic "amalgamations" often at arrival or departure lines at airports and even in community corners and small gatherings of families of overseas Filipino workers.

Something similar has also been happening within the country. Internal migration from the rural areas to the cities, or from one province to another, has led to the emergence of pidgin versions of local languages. In the colonial past, settlement zones—such as residents of what is now Davao City—spoke a pidgin language that mixed English, Filipino, Japanese, Spanish, and Visayan. After independence, the Japanese words and phrases gradually disappeared, and the Spanish was indigenized, "creating" a new dialect called "Davao Filipino" which is a mix of Tagalog and Visayan. The Institute of National Languages has also cited "1,000 basic Pilipino words" to show that "Pilipino is 48.2 per cent identical with Cebuano, 46.6 per cent with Hiligaynon; 41.3 per cent with Samar-Leyte; 59.6 per cent with Pampango; 39.5 per cent with Bicol; 31.1 per cent with Ilocano; 29.6 per cent with Pangasinan; 34 per cent with Kiniray-a; and 30 per cent with Tausug" (as quoted by Enaka 2006, 79). Table 9.1, for example, shows just how close the connections between the three top language groups—Filipino, Ilocano, and Tagalog—are to each other as well as to their Austronesian forebears.

This closeness is further confirmed in daily life. Dana Osborne observed, "[d]uring classes, one could hear Ilocano, English, and Filipino spoken in various combinations throughout the day, depending on both predictable and felicitous conditions, including but not necessarily limited to: teacher preference/competency, classroom language assignment . . . perceived linguistic competency of the students by the teacher, topic, time of day, mood of the teacher, among many other factors that shifted daily" (Osborne 2015, 53). All this "intimacy" suggests that Philippine languages will continue to evolve either for the better (more outside words added into the language) or for the worse (disappearance of older Indigenous words caused by popularity of externally introduced words).

See also: Chapter 8: Overview; Bilingual Education; History of Education; Textbooks.

Further Reading

Acabado, Stephen. 2020. "The Bahay Kubo and the Making of the Filipino." *Rappler.* June 26. Accessed June 26, 2020. https://www.rappler.com/move-ph/ispeak/264808-opinion-bahay-kubo-making-filipino

Bao, Maohong. 2015. "The Pluralism of Ethnic Cultures and Inclusive Development in the Philippines." *Suvannabhumi* 7, no. 11: 139–155.

Conant, Carlos Everett. 1909. "The Names of Philippine Languages." *Anthropos* Bd. 4, H. 4: 1069–1074.

Enaka, Hachiro. 2006. "Language Planning and Bilingual Education in the Philippines: A Historical Approach." PhD diss., Merdeka Malang University, Indonesia.

Fullante, Luis Cruz. 1983. "The National Language Question in the Philippines, 1963 to the Present." PhD diss., University of California, Los Angeles.

Larson, Donald N. 1963. "The Philippine Language Scene." *Philippine Sociological Review* 11, no. 1–2 (January–April): 4–12.

Lewis, M. P., G. F. Simons, and C. D. Fennig, eds. 2016. *Ethnologue: Languages of the World.* 19th ed. Dallas, TX: SIL International. https://www.ethnologue.com/about/language-status

McFarland, Curtis D. 1994. "Subgrouping and Number of the Philippine Languages or How Many Philippine Languages Are There?" *Philippine Journal of Linguistics* 1, no. 2 (June–December): 75–84.

Osborne, Dana M. 2015. "Negotiating the Hierarchy of Languages in Ilocandia: The Social and Cognitive Implications of Massive Multilingualism in the Philippines." PhD diss., University of Arizona.

Carabao English

Carabao English (water buffalo English), also called "Bamboo English," is a derogatory term used by Western-educated urbanites to describe the way their less-educated, rural and urban poor countrymen speak the language. For the former, Carabao English is a pidginized version of American English that was popular in the 1970s. It refers to the grammatical mispronunciations, misspellings, and distortions of English words. In Carabao English, there is less concern about sentence organization and meanings of words. What is important is that the words used—even if these are the wrong ones—must be able to convey one's intentions. One thus encounters several examples in which Filipinos impishly play with English words and phrases to catch people's attention and, of course, evoke laughter. The website "More Pun in the Philippines" (https://www.pinterest.com/boldak228/more-pun-in-the-philippines/) gives samples of these hilarious gags, as shown in Table 9.2.

The website also has equally hilarious advertisements and reminders such as the following:

(a) "Government warning: Pls. don't throw your cigarettes end on the floor. The cockroaches are getting cancer"
(b) "Entrance fee!! Daytur (*day tour*), P50.00; Fear (*per*) head, over night—P100.00 fear head by management"
(c) Bathroom sign: "Our aim is to keep this bathroom clean. Gentlemen—Your aim will help, stand closer. It's shorter than you think. Ladies: Please remain seated for the entire performance."

In recent years, Filipino intellectuals have come to the defense of Carabao English, arguing that it is yet another variation of Filipino English, which is also an adaptation of American English. One of the country's top writers, Jose Lacaba,

Table 9.2: MORE PUN IN THE PHILIPPINES

English	Carabao English
Photocopy	Putocopy (*puto* is rice cake)
John Lennon	John Lemon cake store
Living things	*Libing* Things Funeral Parlor (*libing* is to bury)
Facebook	*Facebool* (a stall that sells deep-fried fish cakes)
Brad Pitt	*Bread Pitt* (a small bread store)
James Taylor (the singer)	James Tailor
Wifi	Wi-Pie (a bakery)
Cesar's Palace	Scissors Palace Barbershop
Air Force One	Hair Force One
This is it!	This is Eat! Restaurant

vacillated between being an English language purist and not being one, but admitted that "More often I find myself on the side of the hecklers, hooting off the stage all instances of careless, awkward, inelegant, patently ludicrous, and linguistically incorrect writing" (Lacaba 1995). He had come to recognize that when people use English, it is often to make sense of their own surroundings. He declared: "So, if a sidewalk toy vendor puts up a sign like one I saw a few Christmases ago—*free gift raping*—I will go prescriptive and rap the hand that scrawled the misspelling" (Lacaba 1995).

See also: Chapter 8: Overview; Bilingual Education.

Further Reading

Alegre, Edilberto. 1999. "Pinoy na Pinoy: Spokening English: The Travails of Amboy." *Business World*. June 16. https://advance-lexis-com.eres.library.manoa.hawaii.edu/api /document?collection=news&id=urn:contentItem:3WR8-79V0-00JS-93GN-00000 -00&context=1516831

Lacaba, Jose (a.k.a. Felix Culpa). 1995. "Carabeef Lengua." *Manila Times*. August 3, http:// kapetesapatalim.blogspot.com/2008/11/carabao-english.html

Sison, Shakira. 2014. "Punny Filipino Translations." *Rappler*. April 24. https://www .rappler.com/move-ph/ispeak/56193-punny-filipino-translations

English

The *World Population Review* (2022) lists the Philippines as 5th among the top 10 English-speaking countries in the world, preceded only by India (1.4 billion), the United States (333 million), Pakistan (225 million), and Nigeria (211 million). English became the other lingua franca of the country after the American regime established a colony-wide public school system (see Chapter 8) and made English the medium of instruction (see Overview). English remains an official language despite efforts by nationalists to have it removed from being a language of instruction (see the National Language Debate). This eloquence has been the best advertising tool of the Philippine government to the world when it sends its workers to other countries. In 1992, the government was also able to attract American corporations seeking to move their customer service divisions, getting them to move these divisions to the Philippines where wages were cheaper and the workforce spoke English. Twenty-nine years later, this English-is-an-asset mantra is still how the country offers its working population to the world, although English is now also being used to draw foreign students to the Philippines so they can take advantage of its low-cost education (McGeown 2012).

Cracks, however, are beginning to appear beneath this positive outlook. These come in the form of a declining quality of English. Educators and journalists have warned that students have been failing. In 2006, the polling group Social Weather Station (SWS) reported a decline in the English proficiency of Filipinos. The percentage of Filipinos who could read English went down from 77 percent in 2000 to 65 percent in 2006; also, only 48 percent could write in English in 2006, down from 54 percent in 2000. English speakers also declined from 54 percent in 2000 to 32 percent in 2006. SWS added that at the other end, the percentage of Filipinos who admit they are not competent in English rose from 7 percent in 2000 to 14 percent in 2006 (Araneta and Punongbayan 2006). Conditions appeared to have gone from bad to worse. In 2010, business processing companies were rejecting nine-tenths of applicants from the Philippines (Rapoza 2012) and in 2018, only 7 percent of high school graduates were fluent in English (Jimenez 2018). The effects were alarming, with the *Economist* ("E for English" 2009) warning that the Philippines was losing its edge in the global economy. The Department of Education also expressed concern after the EF English Proficiency Index showed the country's ranking steadily declining from 13th place in 2016 to 20th place in 2019. The undersecretary of education partly blamed the slide on students "having difficulty in handling questions that are of higher cognitive requirements, as well [as] situational or contextual questions" (Calvielo 2020).

How did an official language decline that fast and what were the reasons behind this? The first, and perhaps most important, factor was the constant tension over the relationship between English, Filipino, and the other Philippine languages (see National Language Debate). As mentioned in the Overview, the United States made English the language that would solve the linguistic diversity of its colony. An English-educated Filipino workforce would also fill up the hundreds of positions in the colonial government and a growing private sector. The success in making English a de facto Philippine language received enthusiastic support from Filipino leaders. Rafael Palma, one of the members of the Philippine Commission, the executive body laying down policies, released a circular stating: "I am fully convinced that regardless of what may be the future political status of these Islands the greatest good will come to our people through the medium of a common language" (quoted in Tovera 1975, 44–45). Palma was being too optimistic.

Twenty years later, when the U.S. government set up a survey mission to determine whether the Philippines was ready for independence, its final report on education mentioned how Filipino students were still having a hard time with English: "Out of 1,134 candidates in the tests in letter writing and English composition, 1,114 or 98 percent failed" (as quoted in Tovera 1975, 83). After Filipino leaders had taken control over the government with the establishment of the Commonwealth of the Philippines, the proposals to create a national language alongside English had moved forward with the creation of the National Language Institute in November 1936, ushering a debate over English's perceived dominance and the need to counterbalance this with a national language or the mother tongue (Dekker 2017, 40). When the push for Filipino gradually gained ground after independence, the percentage of Filipinos fluent in English was the same as the percentage of Filipinos fluent in Filipino: 37 percent.

For the next two decades, the debate shifted to how much class time each language should be allotted in primary school and which classes would be taught in English and which ones in Filipino.

It was in the 1950s that the second factor behind the decline of English became apparent. The 1949 report of the United Nations Educational, Scientific and Cultural Organization (UNESCO) and the 1951 Education Committee of the Philippine Congress warned of "a lowering of educational standards [due to] the transfer time allotted to using English to the National Language, the shortage of textbooks and other reading materials, the increase in the number of unqualified teachers, larger classes, and the unavailability of good language models" (Tovera 1975, 121–122). This conclusion was reiterated nine years later by another American economic survey mission worried about the decline of English fluency at the primary level. The mission cited the same deficiency in resources and trained teachers as the reasons behind this deterioration. It also criticized the Department of Education for being remiss in promoting English in schools, pointing out that of the 64 school divisions throughout the country, only 29 had English supervisors.

At around this time, the use of Filipino in homes had risen to 64 percent, outpacing English which was at 51 percent; the literacy rate was 37 percent for Filipino and 29 percent for English. These changes in the percentages enabled a pro-Filipino Board of National Education to order the gradual shift to all-Filipino elementary classes, with the teaching of English moved to the secondary and tertiary levels "provided that (1) there were competent teachers; (2) sufficient reference materials and (3) the students were sufficiently prepared" (Enaka 2006, 128). A Presidential Commission to Survey Philippine Education (PCSPE), formed in 1969 by President Marcos, seconded this proposed move.

Yet this decline in English fluency did not mean Filipinos had completely turned away from English. In 1968, a Ford Foundation–supported survey by the Language Study Center of the Philippine Normal College "showed that teachers and householders (parents) preferred English to be the medium of instruction. Even those whose native language was Tagalog expressed preference for English instruction. Only 2–7 percent of householders would send their children to schools that would use Pilipino as medium" (Tovera 1975, 145). When asked about the reasons for this, the respondents replied that while they recognized the growing importance of Filipino, they still saw English as the language that would advance them or, more importantly, their children, socially *and* economically. This pragmatism became the time-honored response of every Filipino when asked why they still continued to value English. This would also frame the subsequent English-and/or-Filipino debates and the constitutional provisions regarding the national and official languages. The language school Ruanni Tupas aptly summed up the role of English in this way: "English for modernization and Pilipino for nationalism; English for pragmatism, Pilipino for national identity; English for the world, Pilipino for the nation" (Tupas 2015, 593).

The fierce debates among intellectuals over whether English stunted national identity and must be replaced completely by Filipino therefore had very little impact on ordinary Filipinos (Shegina 1988, 59, 60–61, 64, 67, 69–70, 73, 75,77–79). English connected them and their overseas worker relatives to the world, and Filipino boosted national identity when at home. Yet, the meaning of English literacy had changed. On the one hand, when 52 percent of Filipinos claimed in 1980 that they were English-conversant, it did not mean this high percentage was the result of the Philippine government finally addressing the recommendations of the 1949 UNESCO report. There was still a dearth of teachers of English, and students continued to suffer from disorganization in class time allotments (Shegina 1988, 27–30). On the other hand, English did not disappear either. Filipinos continued to speak English but it was no more the English that included interest in literature or improved reading proficiency.

It was an English that was just good enough for a Filipino to engage in everyday conversation. It was the English that an increasing number of Filipinos working abroad needed to communicate with their bosses and fellow expatriates. It was, what academics called, a "fossilized" English (Bolton and Kachru 2006, 449). Basic errors in grammar and sentence structure were the least of its worries. Neither were complicated sentences, full of metaphors and qualifiers, thought to be necessary: all one needed to know was "business English." It was only the elite schools that worried about English; the second- and third-tier schools, concerned mainly with training a workforce for the global market, had no time for nuances.

See also: Chapter 8: Overview; Bilingual Education; History of Education; Textbooks.

Further Reading

Araneta, Sandy, and Michael Punongbayan. 2006. "Poll: Pinoy Proficiency in English Declining." *PhilStar Global*. April 19.

Bautista, Ma. Lourdes, and Kingsley Bolton, eds. 2009. *Philippine English: Linguistic and Literary Perspectives*. Hong Kong: Hong Kong University Press.

Bolton, Kingsley, and Braj B. Kachru, eds. 2006. *World Englishes: Critical Concepts in Linguistics*. London and New York: Routledge.

Dekker, Diane E. 2017. "Finally Shedding the Past: Filipino Teachers Negotiate Their Identities within a New Mother-Tongue-Based Multilingual Education Policy Landscape." PhD diss., University of Toronto.

"E for English: The Cost of Being Tongue-Tied in the Colonisers' Tongue." 2009. *Economist*. June 4.

Enaka, Hachiro. 2006. "Language Planning and Bilingual Education in the Philippines: A Historical Approach." PhD diss., Merdeka Malang University, Indonesia.

Jimenez, Roda S. 2018. "The Decline of English Proficiency in the Philippines." *Sun Star Pampanga*. August 12.

McGeown, Kate. 2012. "The Philippines: The World's Budget English Teacher." *BBC News*. November 11. http://www.bbc.co.uk/news/busines-2066890

Rapoza, Kenneth. 2012. "Countries with the Best Business English." *Forbes*. April 4.

Shegina, Toni Rose Ortiz Luis. 1988. "The Language Controversy and Its Dilemma in the Philippines: A Consequential Result of the Evolution of English." MS Education, University of Southern California.

Tovera, David Garcia. 1975. "A History of English Teaching in the Philippines: From Unilingualism to Bilingualism." PhD diss., Northwestern University.

Tupas, Ruanni. 2015. "The Politics of 'P' and 'F': A Linguistic History of Nation-Building in the Philippines." *Journal of Multilingual and Multicultural Development* 36, no. 6: 587–597.

Valderama, Tita C. 2019. "Pinoy's English Proficiency Declines Sharply." *Manila Times.* November 18.

Filipino or Pilipino?

Within the pro-national language forces, another fissure developed—mainly among academics—over which name that language should adopt: Filipino or Pilipino? The 1971 Constitutional convention proposed changing Pilipino to Filipino. This was made into law in 1973, when President Ferdinand Marcos issues Presidential Decree 155. These acts of state, however, did not put an end to the disagreement but merely stoked the flame of the exchanges. There was a brief moment of official confusion when soon after the release of the 1973 decree, the government directed school authorities to use Pilipino as a medium of instruction alongside English.

Those arguing for a return to Pilipino pointed to the term's historical importance as the anchor from where Filipino was born. Pilipino was the "anti-colonial symbol that would help the country extricate itself from the clutches of American influence" (Guillermo 1985, 72, as quoted in Tupas 2015, 591). To use Pilipino was to struggle against a culture of silence "engendered through English-medium colonial cultural apparatuses and which continued to influence Philippine life even after the Americans 'left' in 1946" (Castrillo 1994, 527, as quoted in Tupas 2015, 591). Using Pilipino was a way of returning to and promoting Indigenous symbols and practices that were popular with the majority of Filipinos.

Those who were pro-Filipino recognized that Pilipino was foundational, but also argued that since then, the borrowing and adoption of foreign words (notably English and Filipino) had changed the original to a form that, among other things, non-Tagalog speakers were able to identify with. These academics also claimed to be as nationalistic as the other side. What distinguished them from the pro-Pilipino group was that they also recognized how much the Tagalog-centered national language had marginalized the other languages. This exclusion puts in question the role of the current national language as a symbol of national unity. In fact, when it comes to the other languages, it is seen as a weapon of "Tagalog imperialism," directed at reducing the number of non-Tagalog speakers to a point where their mother tongues would be effectively silenced. Filipino "on the other hand, has come to represent inclusivity and multilinguality, taking its cue from the spirit of the 1973 Constitution . . . which envisioned a national language . . . that would emerge from all the languages in the Philippines. Thus, the 'f' in it is supposed to represent languages in the country which have the sound /f/, such as in the languages of the Ibanag, Bilaan and Manobo of South Cotabato, thus demonstrating Filipino's willingness to accommodate influences from all languages it comes in contact with. Consequently, 'f' embraces the future and a modern Filipino outlook" (Tupas 2015, 593–594).

Marcos's 1973 decree was therefore a recognition of how far Filipino had traveled in its progress as a national language. While the government did shoot itself in the foot when the bilingual policy brought back Pilipino, the confusion was finally resolved by the 1987 Constitution which made Filipino the national language on the grounds that it was not regionalist and continues to develop by incorporating words, phrases, and metaphors from the non-Tagalog languages.

This seemingly inconsequential debate has gone beyond politics. The Filipino linguist Ernesto Constantino stated that Pilipino and Filipino differed from each other in terms of their "orthography" (spelling), the frequency with which they "borrow" from English, the number of words they borrow from English, and their grammar construction. Filipino does not see any problem in adopting English or Spanish words to add to its glossary. The result is a re-spelling of English or Spanish words to make them sound more Filipino. Moreover, this constant adding of foreign words has helped non-Tagalog speakers appreciate Filipino because of their familiarity with these words. A pamphlet on Filipino, by Constantino, was titled *Ortografi ng Wikang Filipino* (Orthography of the Filipino Language) and inside it one can find words like *debelop* (develop), *linggwa prangka* (lingua franca), and *kompromiso* (compromise) being used unproblematically by the author (Constantino 1996). Not only could a Visayan or Ilocano easily add these words to their respective languages, such words also served as "bridges" into Filipino. Constantino calls Filipino a language of compromises and this gives it a clear advantage over Pilipino.

The reactions to this debate have ranged from indifference to calling it superficial to describing it as symptomatic of the larger issue of English vs. Filipino. The group that has appeared to complain the most comprises of translators and students taking classes where the medium of instruction is Filipino. Scholars of Filipino predict that the distinction will eventually disappear and be replaced by *Taglish*, which is increasingly the language of everyday life.

See also: Chapter 8: Overview; Bilingual Education; History of Education. Chapter 16: Overview.

Further Reading

Castrillo, P. D. R. 1994. "Philippine Political Theater: 1946–1985." *Philippine Studies* 42, no. 4: 528–538.

Constantino, Ernesto. 1996. *Ortografi ng Wikang Filipino*. Quezon City: University of the Philippines.

Guillermo, Ramon G. 1985. "The Temper of the Times: A Critical Introduction." *Philippine Studies* 33, no. 3: 269–276.

Tupas, Ruanni. 2015. "The Politics of 'P' and 'F': A Linguistic History of Nation-Building in the Philippines." *Journal of Multilingual and Multicultural Development* 36, no. 6: 587–597.

Zamora, Neri (compiler). 1995. *A Topical Vocabulary: English, Filipino, Ilocano and Lubuagan Kalinga*. Manila: Summer Institute of Linguistic Inc.

Mother Tongue Teaching

As of early 1904, there were already debates on how best to educate Filipino children. The American colonial regime settled with using English as a medium of instruction. However, American and Filipino education officials were also pushing for "the use of the learners' mother tongue as a supplementary language alongside English as the primary [language of instruction]" (Dekker 2017, 40). Mother tongue education remained popular despite the 1935 Constitution mandating the use of Tagalog as the foundation of a future national language, and education officials continued to push for the former. After independence, mother tongue advocates received support from international agencies. However, no substantial change happened until 1974, when the Department of Education formally announced the creation of a Mother Tongue–Based Multilingual Education (MTBME) (Cardenas 2018). Moreover, it took another 35 years before there was some movement toward its realization.

The Department of Education released Order No. 94 on July 14, 2009, directing the use of the mother tongue as a medium of instruction for kindergarten and grades 1–3. The directive pointed out how "first-language-first" education has been shown to result in high functional literacy. It reiterated how children were able to learn, explain, and express better using their respective languages of birth. The department then designated the following languages for the program: Tagalog, Pampango, Pangasinan, Ilocano, Bicol, Hiligaynon, Waray, Tausug, Maguindanao, Maranao, and Chavacano. Implementation of the program first began in 2012–2013, with a small number of schools in particular provinces; it was then gradually applied across regions where these designated languages were spoken. Only in grade 4 would students be introduced to English and Filipino. Teachers were not supposed to face any difficulty in starting the program. They were supposed to be conversant in the mother tongue and literate in English and Filipino. All that was needed was for the faculty to be taught techniques of linguistic and cultural analysis and to be supported by a panoply of multilingual vocabularies, dictionaries, and grammar manuals. Initial evaluations appeared to be positive (Llaneta 2018).

However, the optimism dissipated fast. First, the allotment of US$50.75 per student turned out to be paltry. The department provided no additional funding for schools to accommodate the program. MTBME thus became an added expense. It stretched school budgets that already covered "a variety of school needs ranging from utilities and communications expenses; payment of salaries for janitorial and security services" (Cardenas 2018, 156–157). Second, the assumption that teachers in these three levels would ease smoothly into mother tongue teaching because they were already fluent was spot-on. What the program's planners failed to factor in was the diversity of student mother tongues. Lisa Ann Burton noted that out of the 170 languages spoken by different ethnolinguistic groups, 50 were spoken in the northern provinces of Luzon Island alone. Burton wrote that it was "not unusual for a teacher to find herself handling a first-grade class in a public school consisting of children from different linguistic backgrounds." She added, "This poses a challenge for the teachers: how do they make sure the students learn when they are not all equally competent in the language of instruction" (Burton 2013, 108).

Finally, there was little room for initiative. The Department of Education favored a top-down implementation of MTBME instead of what Burton called "a two-way collaboration" between education officials at one end and teachers and parents at the other end. The former never considered any parent input, and they expected teachers to comply with directives and implement them without question (Burton 2013, 104). Some teachers responded by mechanically applying what was handed them with very little concern regarding student learning outcomes. Others simply set these procedures aside and continued to teach in English—a move welcomed by most parents who still regarded English as the language of social mobility. Those who decided to use English were not worried about being penalized. Order No. 94 lacked the enforcement mechanism and monitoring system to ensure compliance.

Dana Osborne, who studied the variations of the Ilocano language, noted that 38 years since the government promised to use mother tongue education as the foundational language of instruction, "the contemporary structure in Philippine education, continues to be largely bilingual English-Filipino" (Osborne 2015, 23).

See also: Chapter 8: Overview; Bilingual Education; History of Education. Chapter 16: Overview.

Further Reading

Burton, Lisa Ann. 2013. "Mother Tongue–Based Multilingual Education in the Philippines: Studying Top-Down Policy Implementation from the Bottom Up." PhD diss., University of Minnesota. May. https://conservancy.umn.edu/bitstream/handle/11299/152603/Burton_umn_0130E_13632.pdf

Cardenas, Marilu Nery. 2018. "From Policy to Local Practice: An Implementation Study of the Mother Tongue–Based Multilingual Education in the Philippines." PhD diss., Teachers College, Columbia University.

Dekker, Diane E. 2017. "Finally Shedding the Past: Filipino Teachers Negotiate Their Identities within a New Mother-Tongue-Based Multilingual Education Policy Landscape." PhD diss., University of Toronto.

Llaneta, Celestina Ann Castillo. 2018. "Teaching in Mother Tongues." February 5. https://www.up.edu.ph/teaching-in-mother-tongues/

Mahboob, Ahmar, and Priscilla Cruz. 2013. "English and Mother-Tongue-Based Multilingual Education: Language Attitudes in the Philippines." *Asian Journal of English Language Studies* 1 (October): 1–20.

Osborne, Dana M. 2015. "Negotiating the Hierarchy of Languages in Ilocandia: The Social and Cognitive Implications of Massive Multilingualism in the Philippines." PhD diss., University of Arizona.

National Language Debate

The issue of what language can unify a linguistically diverse Philippines is something that continues to divide Filipinos even today. During the colonial period, the Spanish used the diversity to their advantage to prevent Filipinos from uniting; the friars learned and preached in the vernacular. Among the reforms pushed by ilustrados like Jose Rizal (see Chapter 2) was the compulsory teaching of Spanish in schools. The Americans also became aware of these linguistic differences but made a policy decision opposite to that of the Spanish. They mandated the use of English as the medium of instruction in all levels of the education system thus providing a common language across the archipelago. For the first time, Filipinos with different mother tongues, some of them mutually unintelligible, could communicate with one another.

The 1935 Philippine Constitution declared Tagalog as the basis for the national language, Pilipino, and also proclaimed English and Spanish as official languages. This provision passed after an acrimonious debate with non-Tagalog delegates accusing fellow delegates representing Tagalog-speaking areas of railroading its approval. The *"Tagalistas"* eventually prevailed thanks to the strong institutional support of the newly established National Language Institute which recommended the use of Tagalog as the foundation of the national language because it had a larger group of speakers and a rich literary tradition. The first act of the Institute was to print out a Tagalog-English dictionary and a primer on the national language. It would take decades before what the Institute set out to do showed any sign of advancement, and ironically, this came not through the hands of the government but through the media. Twenty years after the official enshrining of Tagalog as the national language, English was still the medium of instruction at all levels. In 1956, the Board of Education issued a new policy making the mother tongue and English the main languages of instruction in grades 1 and 2 of primary school and then shifting to English alone from grade 3 onward. The doard changed the directive a year after that—it replaced English with Pilipino for grades 1 and 2 and said that English would only be used from grade 3 onward.

The result was near disaster. A survey of the state of Philippine education by an American economic mission reported a decline in the quality of courses being taught in English due to lack of resources, the indifference of teachers now compelled to teach in three languages, the lack of any model to follow, and, most important of all, the introduction of Pilipino (Tagalog was renamed Pilipino in 1959 by the secretary of education). By 1960, the Catholic Education Association of the Philippines, the largest organization of Catholic-run private schools, reported an increase in the number of students who could speak and write in Pilipino in a span of a decade (from 44.4 percent at the start of the 1950s to 64 percent in 1960); during the same year span, the number of those literate in English went up from 39.5 percent to 51 percent. Pro-Pilipino advocates saw this as a sign of progress in the development of the national language, but supporters of English also warned of how much the facility to learn English had declined since less classroom time was devoted to teaching in the language. Those who were fighting for mother tongue–based teaching added their voice, pointing out that the survey of the American mission reported that 57 percent of its respondents favored the teaching of the vernacular with English, while only 6.4 percent thought teaching the vernacular with Pilipino was a sensible idea.

These differences turned the next decade into the "Era of National Language Wars" (Tupas 2003), which saw a repeat of the arguments of 1930, this time played out with more passion, exacerbating "ethnolinguistic animosity" (Tupas 2015, 590) with non-Tagalogs calling Pilipino nothing but a Tagalog imposition aimed at perpetuating its dominance over the other languages and dialects. Their charges even turned semi-conspiratorial, with the warning that "Tagalog imperialism" would also be the Trojan horse that would enable Tagalogs to loot the human and natural resources of the non-Tagalog areas. Pro-Tagalog speakers argued back by repeating the arguments made by the National Language Institute in the 1930s: Tagalog has more speakers and a literary tradition far richer than the other languages. When a constitutional body was convened in 1971 to revise the 1935 Constitution, the most passionate debates were over the national language. Fr. Andrew Gonzalez narrated how "pandemonium reigned in the convention hall [when] non-Tagalogs took exception to what they perceived as high-handedness and questioned, as a point of order, the use of Pilipino . . . (M)any asked for translations, and when non-Tagalogs were recognized, they began speaking in their own vernaculars, adding babel to bedlam" (Gonzalez 1980, 136). The outcome was no different from that of 1935, with a slight modification that would also spur fervent exchanges, albeit this time among academics. Pilipino was changed to Filipino, English remained an official language, and Spanish was still a required course in upper-level high school and in three college semesters.

The debates were more muted after the 1970s. In the 1980s, English advocates gained some headway over the others by arguing that it was the Filipinos' fluency in English that got them jobs abroad. There were also sporadic debates on which language would pair with English should the government finally implement a bilingual policy in schools. In 1991, the government created the Commission on the Filipino Language (*Komisyon ng Wikang Filipino*) to promote and preserve the local languages. The *Komisyon* would do this by publishing dictionaries, teaching manuals, and the works of writers who wrote in their mother tongue. In 1993, the Department of Education finally drew up plans to make a 1974 bilingual education decree work. To balance the teaching of classes in English and Filipino, it ordered primary and secondary schools "to spend more hours in English (50 minutes), Math (20 minutes), Science (40 minutes) and health (40 minutes)" (Shegina 1988, 23). All these proved to be only good on paper—again. For, 11 years later, the department was back to pushing for a series of "multilingual curricula reforms" (Osborne 2015, 19) to boost multilingual education, especially the use of "minority languages" for instruction. It was supposed to finally resolve the problems associated with bilingual education that had dogged the government for over 40 years. Little headway was achieved and 10 years later, the department again issued another order to institutionalize mother tongue–based education, reduce the dominance of English, and push for Filipino as "the sole unifying language of Filipinos" (Dekker 2017, 7).

See also: Chapter 8: Overview; Bilingual Education; History of Education; Textbooks.

Further Reading

Dekker, Diane E. 2017. "Finally Shedding the Past: Filipino Teachers Negotiate Their Identities within a New Mother-Tongue-Based Multilingual Education Policy Landscape." PhD diss., University of Toronto.

Enaka, Hachiro. 2006. "Language Planning and Bilingual Education in the Philippines: A Historical Approach." PhD diss., Merdeka Malang University, Indonesia.

Fullante, Luis Cruz. 1983. "The National Language Question in the Philippines, 1963 to the Present." PhD diss., University of California, Los Angeles.

Gonzalez, Andrew. 1980. *Language and Nationalism: The Philippine Experience Thus Far.* Quezon City: Ateneo de Manila University Press.

Llamzon, Teodoro A. 1968. "On Tagalog as Dominant Language." *Philippine Studies* 16, no. 4 (October): 729–749.

Osborne, Dana M. 2015. "Negotiating the Hierarchy of Languages in Ilocandia: The Social and Cognitive Implications of Massive Multilingualism in the Philippines." PhD diss., University of Arizona.

Shegina, Toni Rose Ortiz Luis. 1988. "The Language Controversy and Its Dilemma in the Philippines: A Consequential Result of the Evolution of English." MS Education, University of Southern California.

Tupas, Ruanni. 2003. "History, Language Planners, and Strategies of Forgetting: The Problem of Consciousness in the Philippines." *Language Problems and Language Planning* 27, no. 1: 1–25.

Tupas, Ruanni. 2015. "The Politics of 'P' and 'F': A Linguistic History of Nation-Building in the Philippines." *Journal of Multilingual and Multicultural Development* 36, no. 6: 587–597.

Spanish and Philippine Spanish

There is hardly any information on how many Filipinos still speak Spanish. The government's decision to use English and Filipino as official languages and, lately, the decree to use the mother tongue in the first years of primary school has practically pushed Spanish into the margins. John Lipski suggests that Spanish speakers live in the big cities and are descendants of the old elites—Spanish and *mestizos*—who rose to prominence in the late Spanish period. Today, at least one of the most senior members of these families has a relative who was born in Spain, and the descendants (Lipski calls them *mestizos*) tend to intermarry and keep to themselves. While the 1935 Constitution still decreed the teaching of Spanish in high school, those who took the required courses were content with having "a degree of passive competence which allows them to grasp the general meanings of Spanish phrases and expressions" (Lipski 1987a, 38). This meant that the Spanish families were further isolating themselves from anyone non-Spanish. They would continue to speak the language as "a source of pride and an unmistakable mark of aristocratic authenticity" (Lipski 1987a, 39). A creole version of Spanish did seep down below and became popular, but oddly enough, it was spoken only in three districts in the entire country. American colonial officials also mentioned "Davao Filipino," a pidgin language in Davao in the southeastern part of Mindanao Island, which was a hodgepodge of English, Filipino, Japanese, Visayan, *and* Spanish. This grew out of a multi-ethnic community where the lives of the people revolved around hemp production. After World War II, Davao Filipino headed to extinction when American forces deported the Japanese community back to Japan and the last of the surviving Spanish and American planters also began to leave or die.

The number of Spanish speakers may have gone down to a speck. The language, however, has contributed immensely to the growth of Filipino. In the 1980s, the National Language Institute claimed that there were around 5,000 Filipino words that came from Spanish. These found their way into the vocabularies of the different languages thanks to over 250 years of Spanish rule (Fullante 1983, 89). Table 9.3 contains a sample of Spanish words that are now part of everyday Filipino.

While the majority are Spanish in origin, the archeologist Stephen Acabado also reminds readers that some of these Spanish words were in fact Nahuatl words. Words like *tatay* (father), *nanay* (mother), and *tiyangge* (open market) came from the precolonial Aztecs and were carried by Mexico-based Spaniards or Mexicans who thought these were Spanish words (Acabado 2020).

Spanish was never taught to the colonized people by the Spaniards; in fact, the friars learned the local languages for proselytization. The Spaniards never believed that the Filipinos were capable of civilization, and only in 1863 was Spanish taught as part of the free public school system. The intellectuals who demanded reforms during that period wrote their essays, propaganda pieces, poems, and novels in Spanish. Spanish was also the official language of the short-lived Philippine republic (see Chapter 2). The Americans replaced Spanish with English but allowed members of the Philippine Assembly, judges, and Spaniards to continue using Spanish. The 1935 Constitution adopted Tagalog as the national language, but also kept Spanish and English as official languages. It was for this reason that the Department of Education required Spanish to be taught in the last two years of high school and for two semesters of college. In requiring Spanish, however, constitutional delegates in charge of language development knew that learning English and Spanish at the same time was an "unbearable burden" (Tovera 1975, 106) for Filipino students.

Table 9.3: SPANISH WORDS IN FILIPINO

Spanish	Filipino	Meaning
Cómo está	Kumusta	How are you?
Silla	Silya	Chair
Cuchara	Kutsara	Spoon
Jueves	Huwebes	Thursday
Jefe	Hepe	Boss, Chief
Ciudad	Syudad	City
Trabajo	Trabaho	Work
Republica	Republika	Republic
Confesar	Kumpisal	To confess
Iglesia	Yglesia	Church
Padre	Padre	Priest
Biblia	Bibliya	Bible
Cuarto	Kuwarto	Room
Siempre	Syempre	Of course
Sigue	Sige	Go ahead

Spanish did not appear as an official language in the 1973 Constitution, but President Ferdinand Marcos issued a decree making it an official language. In 1987, however, because those speaking Spanish had become an insignificant minority, the Department of Education dropped Spanish from the curriculum. In 1990, several writers called for the reinstatement of Spanish but to no avail.

Spanish, however, survived in pidgin form. Chavacano is a Spanish-Portuguese creole language (Perez 2015). It is spoken only in three cities: Cavite City and Ternate City in the province of Cavite, which is located south of Manila, and Zamboanga City in the southwestern tip of Mindanao Island. There are Chavacano speakers in Cotabato City, which is in central Mindanao, but they are very few. The 2015 census listed 450,000 Chavacano speakers in Zamboanga City, 4,000 in Cavite City, and 3,000 in Ternate. Cavite Chavacano and Zamboanga Chavacano are the nearest to Spanish and are often mistakenly called Philippine Spanish. Chavacano first developed in Ternate when Spanish settlers from the Moluccas islands arrived in Manila to be stationed at the garrison defending the colonial capital from Chinese pirates. These reinforcements were already conversing in "Ternateno," a Portuguese-based creole language. They ended up settling in the towns of Tanza and Ternate, and their constant conversations with the locals led to the emergence of Chavacano. Zamboanga Chavacano was likewise born out of the interaction between Spanish troops stationed in a garrison there since 1719 and mercenaries coming from different parts of the colony to support the troops. Chavacano spread to other coastal towns in Mindanao. A creole Portuguese, which was already the maritime lingua franca of the 15th- and 16th-century trade routes connecting Africa, Asia, and Oceania, further enriched Zamboanga's language (Lipski 2009).

Today, Chavacano continues to thrive in Zamboanga, helped in part by a decision taken by the city government, academics, journalists, and civil society groups to preserve it orally and in print form (Chambers 2003). This cannot be said of Cavite Chavacano and Ternate Chavacano, which are now in danger as fewer and fewer people are speaking them, and despite the government's decision to introduce mother tongue–based education in the first two years of primary school, very little has been done to preserve them in print (Perez 2015, 4).

See also: Chapter 8: Overview; Bilingual Education; History of Education.

Further Reading

Acabado, Stephen. 2020. "The Bahay Kubo and the Making of the Filipino." *Rappler*. June 26. Accessed June 26, 2020. https://www.rappler.com/move-ph/ispeak/264808-opinion -bahay-kubo-making-filipino

Chambers, John S. J. K. 2003. *Creoles and Pidgins (Others)*. Zamboanga City: Ateneo de Zamboanga University.

Enaka, Hachiro. 2006. "Language Planning and Bilingual Education in the Philippines: A Historical Approach." PhD diss., Merdeka Malang University, Indonesia.

Fullante, Luis Cruz. 1983. "The National Language Question in the Philippines, 1963 to the Present." PhD diss., University of California, Los Angeles.

Lipski, John M. 1987a. "Contemporary Philippine Spanish: Comments on Vestigial Usage." *Philippine Journal of Linguistics* 18: 37–48.

Lipski, John M. 1987b. "Modern Spanish Once-Removed in Philippine Creole Spanish: The Case of Zamboangueno." *Language and Society* 16: 91–108.

Lipski, John M. 2009. "Philippine Creole Spanish: Assessing the Portuguese Element." *Zeitschrift fur Romanische Philologie* 104: 1–2.

Perez, Marilola. 2015. "Cavite Chabacano Philippine Creole Spanish: Description and Typology." PhD diss., University of California-Berkeley.

Shegina, Toni Rose Ortiz Luis. 1988. "The Language Controversy and Its Dilemma in the Philippines: A Consequential Result of the Evolution of English." MS Education, University of Southern California.

Tovera, David Garcia. 1975. "A History of English Teaching in the Philippines: From Unilingualism to Bilingualism." PhD diss., Northwestern University.

CHAPTER 10

ETIQUETTE

OVERVIEW

Defining what Filipino etiquette is and under what circumstances its various manifestations are practiced is a bit difficult because of the vast number of similarities that can be found in other societies. This does not only pertain to Asian societies but all societies. For example, deference to elders or making a guest "feel at home" applies to communities the world over, perhaps differing slightly in the way it is expressed (hugs in some, bowing in others, or a soft kiss on the cheeks in several societies), but the intentions are the same. This chapter will, therefore, discuss Filipino etiquette while being aware of these similarities.

Learning about etiquette, as the common saying goes, always starts at home. Children learn about social and cultural proprieties from their elders with regard to a diverse set of everyday activities that include welcoming visitors, dining table manners, and proper behaviors during family-centered activities (from baptism to death rituals). These then act as guidelines to how they relate to different kinds of people in the "outside world." Refusal to learn etiquette or repeated violations of family norms could warrant punishment, which could range from a mere censure (scolding) to corporal punishment. The government has passed several measures and regulations to protect children, but the violence perpetrated against them remains high.

Children are expected to treat adults with respect. The most common way for children to show respect is by taking an elderly relative's hand, placing it on their forehead, and saying the Filipino phrase *mano po* ("Can I ask your blessings?"), to which the elder may say "May God have mercy on you" or nod their head. Urban middle class and elite families prefer children giving elders a quick kiss on the cheek, and boys who are older may shake the hands of their father, grandfather or uncle. The children are expected to show eternal gratitude for this intimate tutelage. Such a relationship does have its pitfalls, the foremost of which is of parents and other adults believing that their words or actions are law. Children are not expected to "talk back" or demand a fair discussion over the parental edict; neither are their opinions sought out when the family has to make significant decisions. Adults often justify this as a critical feature of "Filipino culture." Urban and more Westernized families, however, tend to eschew this "top-down" authoritarian relationship and encourage children to put in their two cents worth of an opinion or idea.

Families do not encourage individualist attitudes, although they may publicly take pride in a family member's achievements. Attempts by a member to pursue his interest at the expense of the family are therefore not taken to kindly. It goes to follow that sacrificing for the welfare of the family is a desirable trait. Parents spend most of their incomes on their children's education, and those who find work after graduation are supposed to help with daily household needs and also assist younger siblings (and sometimes even their children) in their educational pursuits.

It is, therefore, not unusual for a visitor to be received by an entire household to show both hospitality and the family's gentility. These seemingly trivial encounters even follow a specific protocol—the father is the first to greet the guest, followed by the mother. Both parents then introduce the children to the visitor who would be expected to show the same deference, removing their footwear when entering homes, and addressing the heads of the household as respectfully as possible.

Among the Tagalogs, greetings and conversations with elders end with the word "po," which is a term of respect. To show deference while greeting someone senior with a "Good morning," Tagalogs say "Magandang umaga, *po*," or when answering the query, "How are you?" (*Kumusta ka pa?*), a younger person would say "Mabuti naman *po*" (I am fine, thank you). The other language groups do not have an equivalent for "po," but conversations are always inclusive. Thus instead of "How are you?" (*Kumusta kayo?*), Visayans would say, "How are we doing?" (*Kumusta kita?*). It is this deference to an elder or a new acquaintance that has led many observers to describe Filipinos as "hospitable" and friendly. For someone to establish an acquaintance with a Filipino, however, one must be able to spot and correctly interpret their body signals.

The smile or the laughter is endemic among Filipinos and can be heard everywhere— during parties and town fiestas, homecomings of the school alumni, or when the overseas worker returns to their family after years of being away. One can hear Filipinos laugh or show broad smiles even in places like cemeteries or churches where solemnity supposedly prevails. That said, one must be aware that the meanings behind these jovial acts change depending on the context. Filipinos laugh over good news, but they also do so—perhaps in a less raucous fashion—during uncomfortable situations. Filipinos may laugh when they are in tight spots that range from the personal (i.e., the defiance of a their parents' wishes) to the political (engaging the police and the military in street battles during political demonstrations), the religious (inserting smiles while imploring God for forgiveness), and the economic (restarting a business venture after its initial failure). To be able to "read" what the smile or the laughter means, one needs to be sensitive to the contexts in which the public jollity happens. Specific body signals also appear to be patently Filipino. Instead of using a finger to point someone in the right direction (which is considered rude), a Filipino uses their mouth for that purpose.

Filipinos do not say "hello," they raise their eyebrows and nod their heads. This same act is also used to express approval or disapproval; one nods one's head up and down to say "yes," and shakes it from left to right and back to say "no." When calling

It's more fun in the Philippines (a slogan from the Philippine Tourism Authority). (Dtiberio/Dreamstime.com)

a family member or friend, Filipinos use the interjection "Pssst!"; while others not familiar with this vocal signal may deem it improper, for Filipinos it is a friendly gesture that signals warmth and generosity. When puzzled by an answer, Filipinos open their mouths. When Filipinos do go verbal to meet and greet, it is not the usual "how are you?" Instead, they ask, "Have you eaten?"—yet another sign of hospitality and friendship. This is, however, one trait that is not uniquely Filipino. Inquiring with people if they have eaten and then even inviting them to one's home is an Asian trait.

When Americans ask "How are you?," it is only a casual remark that does not need a long answer. Filipinos, however, consider the question seriously and can go through a long monologue about how their lives have been either on that day or as far back as a year ago. This stretched-out oration is often a way of overcoming one's awkwardness, but sometimes Filipinos assume the listener is a good friend and unburden their problems—family, or love—on them. Finally, a similar quirk Filipinos have is the habit of answering "no," when they mean "yes," and "yes" when they mean "maybe." Awkwardness is, once again, the main reason for this seeming inconsistency, but it is also a way of assuring the interrogator that in no instance will the friendship or the family be compromised by vague answers. Social harmony (*pakikisama* in Filipino) prevails over disagreements and diminishes tensions.

See also: Chapter 7: History of the Family Unit.

Further Reading

Miranda, Miguel, et al. 2010. "Discovering Emotions in Filipino Laughter Using Audio Features." Paper Delivered at the Third International Conference on Human-Centric Computing, Cebu City, the Philippines. August 11–13. https://ieeexplore.ieee.org /abstract/document/5563313/authors#authors

Rodell, Paul. 2002. *Culture and Customs of the Philippines*. Westport, CT: Greenwood Press.

Clothing

Precolonial clothing reflected the diversity of the cultures of the communities in the archipelago, although they all share an interest in making their costumes as colorful as possible. Women in the lowland communities of Luzon and their counterparts in the highland areas of central Mindanao are known for weaving these attires. Muslims, for example, wore dyed blouses and tunics, ankle-length robes, and tubed blanket wraps called *malong*. The more colorful their attire is, the higher the status of that person and their family. Colors were also worn the most among women in the highlands. The late Filipina art professor J. Moreno quotes an 1889 Jesuit account of women in the Bukidnon highlands of Mindanao which says they derived "great pleasure from choosing colors and designs for their cloths" (Moreno 1995, 17). The colors disappeared when the Spaniards arrived and imposed a bland style that, as Professor Moreno put it, "over-clothed and over shod [Filipinos] completely from head to toe." If they refused to do so, the Spanish priests warned, would mean committing mortal sin. It was from this "morality of clothes" that modern Filipino fashion emerged, first with strong Spanish imprint and further transformed by American influence.

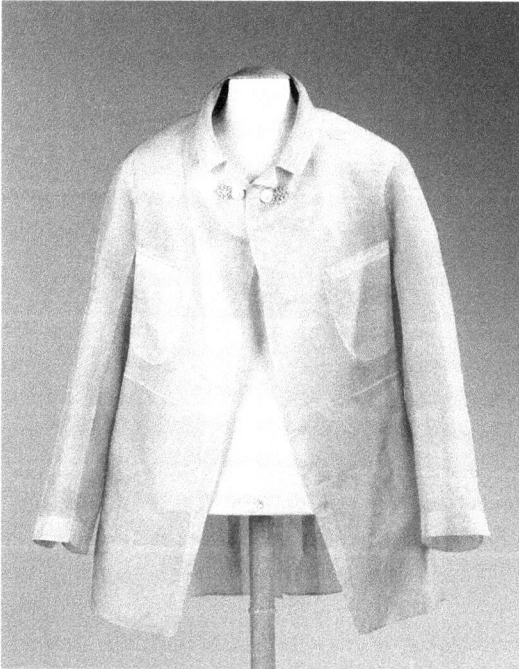

Despite this Westernization, there are several apparels that can be said to be distinctly Filipino. Among the men, the most prominent is the *Barong Tagalog*, a collared, buttoned suit made from the leaves of the pineapple fruit,

Frock coat made from the fiber of a pineapple plant's leaves. Today Filipinos know it more by the local name "Barong Tagalog." (The Metropolitan Museum of Art)

sometimes with elaborate designs. Filipinas also wear a bodice called *"camisa"* (blouse) and a full-length skirt called *"saya,"* both made from the same *"pina"* leaves. Both *barong* and *camisa-saya* underwent some changes during the American period, with the upper part of the *saya* crafted to highlight the body shape or made fuller to conform with the American style. This modified *camisa-saya* would be called *Traje de Mestiza* (the mestiza's dress). Filipinos continued to wear the *barong* during special occasions. The younger generations, however, started wearing the standard coat, suit, and tie introduced by the new colonizers (this would eventually acquire a local name— the *Americana*).

Elite Muslim men also adopted the *Americana*, but the women did not change their garb. Mountain communities in the northern Philippines also supposedly changed their "traditional wear" (loin cloth, bandana for the head, small jacket-like robes) to the *Americana* and the *Traje de Mestiza*. These kinds of clothing continued well into the 1950s when Filipinas began to adopt new styles popularized by American designers like Christian Dior. These included cardigans and floral-printed skirts "raised" as high as the knees. The West's "mod culture" of the 1960s then reached the Philippines, and the following description of this trend by a great Filipino writer aptly captures its appropriation by young Filipinos as well as its indigenization: "Low-waist were the pants when the decade began, but by 1962 the fad was hi-waist (beltline above the navel) and dropped crotch . . . worn with red shirts. Girls looked like astronauts in the pouf hairdos, and wore dresses with plunging backlines . . . [The] later 60s brought in the shirt-jac, the mini, the Beatle hair, the Twiggy haircut, the mau-mau . . . the turtleneck T-shirt in apple green worn with fancy necklaces and pendant, the skin-tight jeans and the coming of the Age of Aquarius" (Joaquin 1990, 329–334).

In the remaining decades of the 20th century until the present, there would be variations of these past styles, although, with the sexualization of media, younger generations were more comfortable with displaying their bodies. This generated some discomfort among the older generation of Filipinos, but there were also movements against body shaming. The global movement of Filipinos either to migrate permanently or to seek long-term employment abroad has led to the dramatic growth of items sent back home by these migrants/workers: used clothes, canned goods, sweets, cosmetics, and essential staple like noodles. Most of these "gifts" are consumed within the household, but the clothes are sold as "second-hand" clothing in flea markets and make-shift street stores. This "new business" has grown popular nationwide, drawing an extensive clientele as the lure of owning imported shirts, dresses, or pants—no matter their condition—is quite attractive to the Filipino shopper (including the urban middle classes) obsessed with American apparel. Buying from these flea markets has become so trendy that it has even forced large shopping malls to come up with their own export surplus sections to compete with their street rivals.

See also: Chapter 13: Overview; Bayanihan Dance Company; History of Dance. Chapter 16: Overview.

Further Reading

Coo, Stephanie Marie R. 2017. "Diverse yet Distinct: Philippine Men's Clothing in the Nineteenth Century." *Suvannabhumi* 9, no. 2 (December): 123–144.

De Las Torre, Visitacion R. 2000. *The Barong Tagalog: Then and Now.* Makati City: Windsor Tower Book House.

Joaquin, Nick. 1990. *Manila, My Manila: A History for the Young.* Manila: Republic of the Philippines.

Moreno, Jose. 1995. *Philippine Costume.* Manila: J. Moreno Foundation.

Pastor-Roces, Marian. 2000. *Sheer Realities: Clothing and Power in Nineteenth Century Philippines.* Manila: Bookmark Press.

Courtship

Traditional Filipino courtship moves through several phases, with the couple assuming specific roles and responsibilities under the close supervision of their parents or other older relatives. The relationship is expected to lead to marriage ultimately. This tradition dates back to the Spanish colonial period when religious orders condemned the independence and power of precolonial women as "satanic" and—using blunt force and the surveillance power of the confessional—promoted a model of the Filipinas as forever immature, submissive, superstitious, and unthinking. She was also expected to be someone who would never question the authority of any male, be he the friar, the father, or the fiancé. The Filipina only had two options in life—either become the dutiful wife of a man or be married forever to God (i.e., spend her entire life as a nun). Men, in return, were supposed to act in a patronizing fashion toward women (under the guise of "chivalry"), although, as husbands, they reserved the right to inflict physical punishment on their wives should this be necessary to keep them acquiescent. This supercilious view is also what informs the courtship process. A Filipino must play on the "childlike" habits of the Filipina to win her heart—she has to be humored, flattered, and admired for her meekness. Since a Filipina rarely left her home (she had to be protected from other lascivious men prowling outside the domicile), the Filipino male became her window to the outside world, explaining to her colonial and global events in parlance "suited" to her level of understanding. The Filipina who defied this caricature was either declared insane or a person devoid of morals—a temptress, or worse, a prostitute.

For most of the 20th century, it was this condescending attitude toward the Filipinas that informed the courtship process. It was always the man who was expected to, as it were, make the first move, regaling the woman with songs and love poems, showering her with gifts, and making sure he remembered all her special days. He did all this while showing deference to her family in order to assure them of his honorable intentions. The woman was expected to be amused at these acts of gentlemanliness but to be so in the most understated way. Being too open about one's appreciation was a sign of someone losing her balance or becoming too aggressive and hence "acting like a man." There were other ways in which a man could court a woman and respect "traditions." He could do so through a friend who acted as the intermediary (a "bridge"), conveying his feelings and giving the woman a brief profile of the potential boyfriend while also acting as his spy. The bridge could also be a family friend who would guarantee a suitor's noble intention.

Once a Filipina said "yes," she was not to entertain any other suitor (lest she, again, be accused of being a flirt). All dates were to be chaperoned, although a woman's family preferred that they spent all their time together at her home, under the watchful eye of parents, siblings, and the house servants. Under no circumstances was premarital sex allowed, and both family and church would make sure that the couple did not fall into such temptation. If ever the couple did end up having premarital sex and the woman became pregnant, both families were expected to move fast to marry them to preserve their reputation. Oddly, this particular restriction was not exclusive to religious and conservative families. The Communist Party of the Philippines also prohibits premarital sex among its members because such affections are believed to exploit women and sully their reputation. In a 1975 memorandum to its members, the party did not only ban premarital sex but also decreed that the relationship must be heterosexual and must end in marriage.

When a couple decides to get married, they are expected to ask for the blessings of the woman's parents. This could be followed by the fiancé's family visiting the home of the bride-to-be, to "formalize" the marriage and discuss various details including how to make sure that kin from both sides are represented. The groom's family will cover the wedding expenses, including a dowry. However, when the groom is not that wealthy, the bride's family is expected to extend some assistance, albeit grudgingly. This imbalance in wealth can be a source of tension, given how closely linked affluence is with social standing. Families often reject children's relationships on the grounds of differing social status. To Filipinos, the hackneyed phrase "Love conquers all" is mainly about defying the rigidness of class differences. A family's inflexibility may force a couple to elope, thereby complicating interfamily relationships. This, however, could be reversed, and reconciliation often becomes possible once a grandchild is born.

Since the 1990s, the Filipinos' views regarding courtship and relationships has changed considerably, mainly because of the nationalization of cable television, the strong sexual content of music videos and social media, and the availability of information regarding reproductive health rights. Cell phones enable young Filipinos to get in touch with each other directly and enter into relationships without necessarily seeking their parents' permission or going through the above courtship rituals. Premarital sex is not taboo anymore. Relationships can be fleeting and, even if serious, do not necessarily end in marriage. This impermanence is reinforced by the growing popularity of online dating websites. The face of Filipino courtship continues to change.

See also: Chapter 7: Overview; Generational Changes; History of the Family Unit; Parent-Child Relationships; Sexuality.

Further Reading

Dobson, Barbara M. 1988. "Like a Thief in the Night: Filipino (sic) Modes of Courtship and Marriage." PhD diss., University of Western Australia.

Vancio, Joseph A. 1980. "The Realities of Marriage of Urban Filipino (sic) Women." *Philippine Studies* 28, no. 1 (March 1): 5–20.

Drinking and Dining

Alcohol consumption among Filipinos is deliberate and well-paced to enliven all kinds of occasions, including stressful situations. Filipinos have a term for such social drinking—*tagay*—which roughly means "let us all drink to that." *Tagay* is a ritual meant to ensure that everyone gets to drink what is being served during the occasion. There are no gender or class distinctions, and the only ones excluded are children and young adults (even the oldest of the elders could join despite their age-related infirmities). Filipinos rarely binge-drink. If they do so, it is often the result of a tragedy (sudden death in the family) or an unfortunate turn of events (a romantic breakup or the loss of a job).

Tagay is for all occasions, including pre-wedding preparations, baptisms, family parties, town *fiestas*, and even wakes. Everyone gets to drink and tell his or her own story to fellow drinkers, and thus the *tagay* could last for days as everyone has a story to share. During such occasions, those drinking organize themselves into a circle, and one is assigned the role of the "gunner." The origins of the term are unclear, but it is likely military, a gunner being the one who supplies the "bullets," which, in this case, is one glass that the gunner fills up and hands to one drinker at a time. The drinker is under no obligation to gulp down the drink, and they can nurse it for as long as they want to or *as long as the conversation is kept lively and exciting*. Introductions, banter, and pleasant mutual entertainment are what *tagay* is all about, with alcohol acting as the icebreaker or the stimulant.

Those who join the *tagay* must then follow certain norms, the first of which is to wait for their turn to be given the drink. Second, under no circumstances will someone be allowed to make the conversation solely about themselves. *Tagay* must be an opportunity for everyone to tell their story. Third, one cannot be forced to drink, and taking a pass is not unusual. All that one needs to do is to either inform the gunner or, if they already have the glass, to put one hand over it and send it back to the gunner, who then throws away the drink, refills the glass, and passes it on to the next drinker. No one considers the disposed-of drink as wasted as it is supposed to be an offering to the devil who is believed to be trying to insert himself in the "session" for malicious purposes. Finally, one can take a "break" from the *tagay*, to rest or to take time to recover, and no one will hold this against the person. Someone who drinks in excess or becomes disruptive is quietly removed from the circle and never invited again until they apologize to everyone.

Finally, *tagay* is not complete without the *pulutan*, a hodgepodge of "finger foods" that range from fruits (green mangoes), vegetables (particularly a local sweet turnip called *singkamas*), peanuts, strips of grilled, broiled or fried meats, and even bizarre appetizers like crocodile meat, iguana, and frog's fried legs. Consuming these small dishes is supposed to "balance" the alcohol that is in the stomach. They keep the conversation going, including the discussions about the type and quality of the *pulutan*.

Tagay, however, is a dying tradition. The karaoke machine has supplanted the gunner as the central figure in community gatherings. The socialization that arises when people face each other in a circle has been supplanted by the singer singing the lyrics on the television screen and drinking their alcohol oblivious of whether the rest of the company is joining in the singing and imbibing or not. Community space has also shrunk, with high-rise apartments and four-lane superhighways displacing neighborhood alleyways and small-town plazas, which are the favored places for *tagay*.

Like *tagay*, dining etiquette involves norms that privilege the family or community (neighborhood) over individual tastes or consumption. Filipinos, like many other Asian societies, do not ask, "How are you?" but "Have you eaten?" The concern is the physical health of the visitor or the "new kid on the block." The latter is expected to demur, then grudgingly accept the offer, accepting a seat at the family table or a community stand set up in a plaza or in the community basketball court during fiestas. Dining tables have the standard utensils *sans* the knife, and sometimes even the chopsticks. It is also not unusual for families and communities to eat with their hands, provided they have been washed with soap and water several times. Filipinos eat with their right hand as the left is considered unclean. There is no clear explanation of how this has come to be. Some regard it as something practical—the right hand is for scooping the food while one uses the left for drinking. Others, however, suggest that this has Islamic origins as the religion regards the left hand as unclean.

Filipinos say grace before their meals. Again, much like the *tagay*, eating is an opportunity for conversation. The hosts could ask the guests questions about their background, their reasons for visiting, and even their plans in life. An exciting conversation inevitably leads to offers of seconds, which a guest must graciously accept. Seating arrangements are similar to that in the West, with the father at the head of the table, the mother to his right, and the guest (or guests) to the left. The seating order in the rest of the table would be based on age, with the eldest and their partner sitting left of the mother or right of the guest, followed by the rest of the siblings. This applies to family dinners as well as when dining outside. All food that is served must be consumed, and a finished meal is indicated by cleaning up one's plate. Among Catholics, wasting a grain of rice is seen as spending some time in Purgatory before being allowed into Heaven. In instances where there are leftovers, guests must take home doggy bags, which Filipinos fondly call "*bring-haus*" (i.e., to bring the food back to one's house). One can *bring-haus* from family gatherings or after dining in public places such as restaurants.

In recent years, mass eating with ones' hands has become popular. The *bodol fight*—a term that was once associated with the military and which comes from the American phrase "kit and caboodle"—consists of placing all the food on a long line of banana leaves, with everyone partaking of the meal using their hands while standing up. Military *bodol fights* start with the highest-ranking officer making the announcement: "Ready on the left, ready on the right! Commence the boodle fight!" In the civilian version, the *bodol fight* starts with saying of grace after which the most senior person invites everyone to "dig in!" Like *tagay*, wolfing down food—be it in an intimate family dinner or in a *bodol fight*—is not looked at kindly. While the hosts may not reprimand the overeating gourmand, it is unlikely that they will be invited again.

The fast-food industry has radically altered these eating patterns. The kitchen used to be the place where a variety of dishes were prepared and cooked and family recipes and lore were passed on from one generation to the next. Now, everyone goes to a MacDonalds' window to order food. Consuming fast food need not be a social affair; one can munch on one's fries and burgers or microwaved television dinner oblivious of anyone else in the room. As "traditional" Filipino dining disappears, it is also likely that the etiquette associated with it will diminish in importance. There is concern over this, especially among the children of Filipinos living abroad who wish to learn, preserve, and recover cultural practices associated with their homeland.

See also: Chapter 14: Appetizers; Drinks.

Further Reading

Bender, Daniel E., and Adrian de Leon. 2017. "Everybody Was Boodle Fighting: Military Histories, Culinary Tourism and Diasporic Dining." *Food, Culture and Society* 21, 1: 25–41.

Fernandez, Doreen G. 2008. *Tikim: Essays on Philippine Food and Culture*. Pasig City: Anvil Publishing.

Low, Kelvin E. Y., and Elaine Lynn-Ee-Ho. 2017. "Eating in the City." *Food, Culture and Society* 21, 1: 2–8.

Salazar, Joseph T. 2012. "Eating Out: Reconstituting the Philippines' Public Kitchens." *Thesis Eleven* 112, no. 1: 133–146.

Fiesta

Each city, town, and village has a patron saint whose birth or martyrdom is celebrated annually with a community-wide *fiesta* (feast). The fiesta is also the way in which Christian Filipinos give thanks for whatever blessings or good fortune their patron saint has bestowed on them. The fiesta's origins date back to the Spanish era, when friars mandated such celebrations as a part of annual church activities. Fiestas continue to be celebrated today for obvious religious reasons.

Fiestas are mostly one-day celebrations, starting with a high mass officiated by the priests of the town, followed by a baptism of newborn babies. In some fiestas, there is even a mass wedding. The religious activities are followed by local government officials raising the Philippine flag in front of the city or provincial building and then

Day 1 of a town fiesta. (Dgmate/Dreamstime.com)

laying a wreath at the statue of the national hero, Jose Rizal. This is followed by a parade across the town where everyone—even the priests and the local officials—marches alongside students and teachers from different schools, professional clubs, and an array of colorfully dressed townspeople. The parade ends back in the town plaza with a musical program. Throughout the day, families open their homes to everyone (even strangers), offering buffets and drinks to guests. A fiesta banquet table's centerpiece is the *lechon*, a whole pig that is slowly cooked under a bed of coal for over eight hours. Dishes like noodle and rice, chicken and fish (fried or stewed), and fruits and vegetables surround the *lechon*, while drinks, mostly soda, are placed in ice boxes on the side. Guests do not just stay in one house; they are expected to visit other homes to continue with the feasting. The day ends with everyone heading to the plaza's open basketball court for the town dance. In addition to all the activities on the day of the fiesta, there is a basketball tournament that runs throughout that week.

The most popular fiesta today is the annual *Sinulog* dance festival in Cebu City, central Philippines. This weeklong celebration is in honor of the city's patron saint, the Child Jesus ("Santo Nino" or Blessed Child), which is supposed to be what the leader of first Spanish expedition to reach the islands gave to the local chief as part of the "peace pact." This fiesta began in 1980 as a small project by the director of the regional office of the then ministry of sports and youth development, where he organized a group of students dressed in Filipino clothes and made them join a religious procession. They distinguished themselves from the rest with their dancing and the use of drums. These were then unusual in a religious procession, which was always solemn. This caught the attention of the Cebu city mayor, who turned it into a festival with the help of the city's elite. A year later, the first *Sinulog parade* was held, where trucks and vans were embellished with different decorations describing the bringing in of the "Señor Santo Niño de Cebu." Three years later, a private foundation took over and turned the parade into a full-blown colorful festival. Since then, every January 19, millions of Filipinos and foreign tourists head to Cebu to celebrate the *Sinulog*. In 2015, a record-breaking 1.8 million visitors joined the festivities. The parade has also been turned into a costume competition. In 2020, 26 contingents joined in the Grand Parade, including a group from South Korea.

See also: Chapter 13: Overview; Chapter 14: Overview; Appetizer; Drinks.

Further Reading

Fernandez, Doreen G. 1989. "Mass Culture and Cultural Policy: The Philippine Experience." *Philippine Studies* 37, no. 4 (Fourth Quarter): 488–502.

Hornedo, Florentino H. 2000. *Culture and Community in the Philippine Fiesta and Other Celebrations*. Manila: University of Santo Tomas Publishing House.

Ness, Sally A. 1995. "When Seeing Is Believing: The Changing Role of Visuality in the Philippines." *Anthropological Quarterly* 68, no. 1 (January): 1–13.

Wendt, Reinhardt. 1998. "Philippine Fiesta and Colonial Culture." *Philippine Studies* 46, no. 1 (First Quarter): 3–23.

Traffic

Metropolitan Manila, with its 17 cities, is considered the most congested city in Asia, with traffic volume far exceeding the capacity of its roads to accommodate all kinds of transportation. Its estimated annual "traffic demand" is 12.8 million trips, resulting from Metropolitan Manila being the country's prime growth center (it accounts for 36 percent of the country's economic output), which is something the megacity's road system has been unable to cope with. Metropolitan Manila has a land area that is only 0.2 percent of the Philippines' total, but this is where 12 million people (18 percent of the total population) live, and where 28 percent of all motor vehicles traverse on a network of only 616 miles of national road, 1,470 miles of smaller local roads, and 1,018 miles of private roads. In August 2019, the government's Land Transportation Office (LTO) estimated that each day 251,628 vehicles are traversing Epifanio de Los Santos Avenue (EDSA), the metropolis's 14.8-mile main artery that was designed to accommodate only 565 vehicles per mile (or 8,362 vehicles for EDSA's total length). However, this figure is only 15.3 percent of the 1,644,932 vehicles plying the entire gamut of Metropolitan Manila roads.

The World Economic Forum's 2012–2013 "Global Competitiveness Report" had ranked the Philippines 87th out of a total of 144 countries whose road systems were surveyed by the organization (it was also 94th in terms of railroads, 112th for airports, and 120th for seaport infrastructure). The Japan International Cooperation Agency

(JICA) estimates that businesses in Manila lost about US$67.2 million daily in 2017, up from US$58.4 million in 2012. This is expected to go as high as US$148 million in 2030, prompting JICA to warn that "if nothing is done, the situation in 2030 will become a nightmare" (ALMEC Corporation 2014, 6). JICA and several development agencies attribute this traffic problem to the failure of the member cities to implement zoning laws or come up with workable urban plans. In the last three decades or so, Metropolitan Manila has profoundly changed thanks to the frenetic construction boom, with shopping centers, high-rise apartments, and gated subdivisions triggered by the remittances of overseas Filipino workers whose families' immediate inclination was to purchase a property.

This transformation is happening in a city that has half a million "informal settlers" comprising 20 percent of Metropolitan Manila's total households, 41 percent of whom live on government-owned land and 34 percent are squatting on private properties. These "informal settlers" are at the losing end when local governments seek to expand their revenue base by leasing public lands to mall companies. The government forcibly relocates them in the outskirts of the metropolis, only to worsen traffic woes as more people now ride the 165 city and provincial bus companies servicing Metropolitan Manila to get to work, further clogging roads already filled with "city folks" doing the same thing. The creation of walled-off, non-accessible elite "villages" has also effectively made traffic flow almost impossible, while middle-class suburbs in the peripheries of Metropolitan Manila have added to the congestion as their residents drive into the city.

What worries city planners and international development agencies further is that this pattern is replicated in other Philippine cities as well. In "Metro Cebu" in the central Philippines, the two-lane roads that are the city's primary arteries now face the problem of accommodating more vehicles in a geographically constricted area also amid a construction boom. The same tell-tale signs are evident in "smaller" cities like Baguio in the north and Cagayan de Oro and Davao in Mindanao Island.

As early as the 1980s, the government had been devising several ways of solving the traffic problem. The Metropolitan Manila Authority, the body coordinating the relationship between the 17 cities, had been using a number coding system to control vehicles traveling Manila's streets, but with limited results. Then in 1999, the government also began constructing a railway system that now has four lines connecting different parts of the city and the national railway that extend to the provinces. The lack of foresight (failure to anticipate how Metropolitan Manila's population explosion could affect railway traffic) and delays in the repair of trains and stations have led to 516 breakdowns in one grid alone in 2017 (or almost 10 a week), up from 441 incidents (or an average of 8.5 percent) in the previous year. As a result, the average number of passengers using the Metropolitan Manila railway system went down from 500,000 per day in the previous five to six years to only 200,000 daily today. When Filipinos now complain of "traffic," they do not only mean hours and hours spent moving from one end of Metropolitan Manila to the other but also the monorail system breaking down because of overcapacity.

Traffic congestion has reached such critical proportions that urban planners have estimated that a Filipino loses nine years of their 40 years of economic life by just being caught in traffic for five to six hours daily ("Manila's Commutes from Hell" 2019). In recent years, urban resentment toward the never-ending failure of the national government to come up with an effective and lasting solution has turned this into a *national* electoral issue. Candidates running for president or senator vow to end Manila's most important problem, only to fail once elected. Like most politicians, of course, presidents and their aides blame someone else for the failure. President Rodrigo R. Duterte and his aides even went one further step backward by denying that a mass transport crisis exists. This contrasts with stories of ordinary Filipinos, like Alejandro Galasao. Galasao is a street sweeper who "navigates a labyrinth of alleys to catch a bus to . . . Manila (18.6 miles away) [and] has to wake up in the middle of the night for a job that does not start until 6am." If Galasao leaves his home "any later than 3:30 am, there is no way he will clock in on time." But he has no choice, as he unhappily told the journalist: "This is the only job I know. Even if I find something else, I doubt I would earn any better. To be honest, there's really not enough time [when I get home] to sleep" ("Manila's Commutes from Hell" 2019).

See also: Chapter 1: Luzon; Administrative Regions.

Further Reading

Abad, Michelle. 2019. "Fast Facts: State of Metro Manila's Public Transport System." *Rappler*. October 10. https://www.rappler.com/newsbreak/iq/242244-things-to-know-about-metro-manila-public-transport-system

ALMEC Corporation. 2014. "Roadmap for Transport Infrastructure Development for Metro Manila and Its Surrounding Areas (Region III and Region IV-A): Final Report Summary." Japan International Cooperation Agency (JICA) and the National Economic Development Authority March.

Boquet, Yves. 2013. "Battling Congestion in Manila: The EDSA Problem." *Transport and Communications Bulletin for Asia and the Pacific*. Combatting Congestion No. 82. United Nations Economic and Social Commission for Asia and the Pacific. https://www.unescap.org/publications/transport-and-communications-bulletin-asia-and-pacific-no-82-combatting-congestion

Gueta, Grace Padayhag, and Lounell Bahoy Gueta. 2013. "How Travel Pattern Changes after Number Coding Scheme as a Travel Demand Management Measure Was Implemented?" *Journal of the Eastern Asia Society for Transportation Studies* 10. https://www.jstage.jst.go.jp/article/easts/10/0/10_412/_pdf

"Manila's Commutes from Hell—A Photo Essay." 2019. *Guardian*. March 8. https://www.theguardian.com/world/2019/mar/08/manilas-commutes-from-hell-a-photo-essay

Miller, Jeffrey M., Primitivo Cal, and Nigel C. Rayner. 2012. *Philippines: Transport Sector Assessment, Strategy and Road Map*. Manila: Asian Development Bank.

CHAPTER 11

LITERATURE AND DRAMA

OVERVIEW

The Philippines has a rich trove of oral and written literary forms. The oral tradition was the most popular during the precolonial period but was displaced once the Spanish introduced formal literacy in their religious litanies, in parish schools, and in the university. Historians and archeologists did find evidence of precolonial writing called "Baybayin," which had evolved from Brahmic scripts (introduced to the islands from India around AD 1000–1200). People used this syllabic, bottom-to-top script to write their personal stories and their poems on palm leaves, bamboo cylinders, and tree barks using a knife or an iron stylus. Much of these writings had disappeared after Spanish missionaries condemned them as "works of the devil" and burned them.

The most dominant literary forms of precolonial Philippines, however, were oral narrations of myths, the adventures of near-God-like heroes, legends of people and places, and fables. These narratives ranged from simple tales to ballads to long epics; they could also be adages and proverbs that advised people on how to behave. They may have been formulaic in their presentations, but the stories could also be theme-based and told using specific, prevalent motifs. Lyrical poems thrived across the archipelago. For example, there were 16 types of songs discovered among the Tagalogs, which were kept alive by their being part of everyday life (from crop planting to boar rowing) and passed on from one generation to another in the form of genealogies and stories of gods and the creation of earth.

The most cited Philippine literary form, however, is the epic. Historians estimate that there were between 100 and 500 of these epics across the archipelago, which were given different names depending on their geographic locations. These were long stories, often chants or verses sung/recited by local bards to an audience. One epic cycle called the Tuwaang, for example, contains 47 songs of over 40,000 lines. These epics spoke of wars, the migration of people, the deeds of heroes imbued with magical powers, and supernatural events. They were also "a repository of law, history and religion, a record of the past and a charter for present and future conduct." Epics, the historian Resil Mojares adds, "placed singer and audience in contact with 'the true and the timeless'" (Mojares 1983, 12).

What gave them their dynamism was that in the process of "singing" them, new stories could emerge which then developed into their own narratives. Tales, epics, and ballads may also be combined, or get "adulterated," resulting in either additional plots and subplots that could enrich the central theme or the emergence of a new narrative entirely unlike the original one. Scholars have also noticed that these precolonial literary forms were able to survive because of their uncanny ability to absorb external influences. Epics from Mindanao Island, for example, were permeated with Islamic themes, while those that continued to be sung in the Spanish colonial era had incorporated Castilian norms or ideas. These narratives were also remarkable for their "high degree of differentiation" (Mojares 1983, 11). There were tales, ballads, epics, and proverbs that were specific to various "classes" in precolonial society, each having that same flexibility and adaptability mentioned earlier, thus ensuring continuing richness.

The Spanish missionaries sought to destroy these symbols of the Devil's work. "Baybayin" was the first to be burned, and the friars replaced the epics and ballads with Christian songs, prayers, and proverbs that were likewise conveyed orally but also made "permanent" with the coming of the printing press. Typography also brought in the European metrical romances together with the religious doctrines and stories of Jesus Christ and the saints. These new literary forms introduced a new worldview (Catholicism), its corresponding values (chastity, anti-materialism, and a life of prayers), rituals (the mass, confessions, fasting, holy days), and new social relationships (powerful men, submissive women). Gradually, the curiosity that informed the incorporation of external ideas or values into precolonial epics was replaced by an unquestioning acceptance of Catholic teachings and practices. The dynamism of precolonial literary forms disappeared, replaced by rote memorization of religious dogma.

The religious orders opposed the teaching of Spanish because they believed that backward "natives" could never learn, much less appreciate, the language of their superiors. There was also fear that if Spanish became the colony's lingua franca, the colonized might soon discover and take advantage of the colonizer's weaknesses. Instead, the friars learned the different Philippine languages and sought to disseminate the Word of God by translating the Spanish original to the local argot. One immediate result was the introduction of the book to Filipinos by the religious-owned printing presses. Between the 1590s and the first years of the 19th century, the Spaniards published 541 books that were religious manuals (*manual de urbanidad*), stories of the lives of saints, or translation guides for missionary work. Most of these were in Tagalog, and the rest were in the Visayan (19), Pampango (13), Ilocano (9), Bicol (5), and Pangasinan (1) languages.

Given the slow pace of the development of Filipino literacy, the four most popular forms were inevitably oral. The first two, the *awit* (song or poem in Filipino) and the *corrido* (an extended story of a person and his adventures), were "metrical romances" that were also either read or sung but, unlike their precolonial counterparts, were preserved through prints. They either came in the form of poetic games of questions and answers (*duplo*), or as dramas (*carillo*) and comedies. The third one was the *komedya* (also called *moro-moro*), which was a staged drama about the religious wars between Catholics and Muslims where, as expected, the Catholics won, and the defeated Muslims converted to Christianity. The *komedya* derived its stories from medieval Spanish ballads, and its theatrical presentation played a big role in Hispanizing mainly the lowland communities. Finally, there was the *pasyon*, which, like the *corrido*, was an extended poem depicting the passion, death, and resurrection of Jesus Christ and was especially recited during the Lenten season.

The missionaries were the principal authors, although by the third decade of colonial rule Filipino parish assistants were also writing their works. In the early 1600s, native poets were contributing to friar-edited *manuales de urbanidad*, and the Filipino writer, printer and publisher, Tomas Pinpin, even came out with his own Tagalog guide to the Spanish language. Pinpin was a defining figure because of his command of Spanish, for despite friar resistance Filipinos managed to learn the colonizers'

Tomas Pinpin, the first Filipino printer. (Walter Eric Sy/Dreamstime.com)

language. Filipinos who adopted the Roman alphabet also came out with their epics, and the most famous of them was the poet Francisco Baltazar whose *awit*, "The History of Florante and Laura in the Kingdom of Albania" (1839), is referred to by scholars as the first written protest against Spanish tyranny.

In the mid-18th century, the economic changes brought about by the Latin American independence movements and the Industrial Revolution, and the assignment of liberal governors to the colony led to, among other things, a flood of newspapers which became the medium for many *ilustrado* criticisms against the religious orders. This "new media" carried manifestoes and articles that parodied the friars and also promoted pro-ilustrado causes like the secularization of the church (and the weakening of the religious orders' control of the parishes), Philippine representation to the Spanish parliament, and allowing the emerging classes a bigger say in colonial affairs. Newspapers diminished the cultural power of the *manuales de urbanidad* that the friar-owned printing presses were churning out. In 1856, the colonial government created a "censor's office that oversaw 13 printing presses, nine bookstores, and 15 newspapers and magazines" (Mojares 1983, 160), but its authority was mostly

The Philippine national hero Jose Rizal.
(Library of Congress)

ineffective. The colony opened to global trade, and no amount of policing could stop the flow of these materials as well as two literary forms that Filipino students studying in Europe brought back with them: the essay and the novel.

The *ilustrados* wrote essays attacking the friars; the most famous of the essays was "La Soberania Monacal en Filipinas" (The Friar Sovereignty in the Philippines) that showed who the real wielders of power in the colony were. Others wrote essays and novels (in the local languages) on Filipino folklore to show that Filipinos had a thriving culture before the Spanish came to the archipelago. One *ilustrado* even wrote *Historia de Filipina*. The most significant of these works, however, were the novels of Jose Rizal—*Noli Me Tangere* (Touch me not) and its sequel *El Filibusterismo* (The Subversive). Both planted the seeds of Filipino nationalism and inspired the Katipunan to launch the first nationalist revolution of Asia.

Under the Americans, journalism grew as the printing press business prospered. Writers continued to write local novels, most of them serialized in newspapers and magazines which many readers followed. The nationalist revolution was still fresh in the minds of many writers, and this could be seen in what they wrote about—independence, instabilities, the rebirth of a nation. They also wrote love stories (short) that were set in turbulent times like the Philippine-American war and their novels addressed poverty, the gap and tensions between the rich and the poor, and even moral issues like prostitution. Their "sense of 'high purpose' [was] expressed in politico-moral and artistic terms" (Mojares 1983, 195), and they endured throughout the American era as peasants and workers protested their condition, their struggles reinforced by the formation of the communist party, and the colony was affected by global economic crises like the Great Depression.

This did not mean that the old forms like the *komedya* of the Spanish era disappeared. Writers who honed their skills in the last years of Spanish rule kept on writing during the American period, continuing to produce *moro-moro* scripts that were about folk religion but also about nationalist issues. These made many of these turn-of-the-century intellectuals jacks of all trades. The Cebuano writer Vicente Sotto, for example, was "a lawyer, libre pensador, publicist, prose fictionist, and politician who read Voltaire, Renan, and Quevedo, and zealously argued for rational, 'scientific' inquiry, and against 'regressive' practices in both religion and the arts" (Mojares 1983, 165–166).

The policy of using English as the language of education and social mobility also introduced Filipinos to American literature. Writers were now reading the works of Henry Wadsworth Longfellow, Walt Whitman, Emily Dickinson, and T. S. Eliot, among others, and by the 1920s they were getting their English writings published. Vernacular literature competed well, so much so that writers celebrated the 1920s as the "golden age" in the first three decades of American rule. There was high productivity. In 1949, the National Language Institute listed a total of 469 Tagalog novels published between 1903 and 1938, while writer Jose Esperanza Cruz cataloged a total of 132 periodicals between 1862 and 1938. These were mostly Tagalog periodicals. Another writer, Leopoldo Yabes, listed 53 periodicals in the Ilocano language and 118 Visayan newspapers between 1901 and 1939. Apart from serializing their stories in newspapers, vernacular writers were also able to keep themselves productive because of their decision to form their organizations. These writers' groups promoted novels and sponsored literary workshops and mutual aid activities.

As English spread, a rift developed between those who wrote in the new language and vernacular writers. The former would be called literati—those who wrote for the elite and the middle class. The latter were known as those who wrote for "those who wear wooden clogs," that is, the poor. The focus of these authors' works also had a hand in this going-of-separate-ways. Many of those who wrote in English became concerned with improving their knowledge of the grammar, rhetoric, and literary styles of their new language. As they gained more access to Western literature, these writers also became more concerned with theoretical sophistication and "pure art," that is, writing for writing's sake. This desire for quality, however, had its limits. Many of the English fictions were "routinized narratives, marked by an exaggeration of sentiment and multiplication of clichés . . . there [was a] fetishization of sentiment, an overexcitement of the emotions [which] harks back to a convention of the corrido . . . but with an empty gesture, deprived of context" (Mojares 1983, 293). A similar process was happening in theater as English plays, the American vaudeville, and the cinema pushed the *komedya* out of "respectable" theaters. The break never healed, and this has become an enduring character of Philippine literature.

The works in the vernacular were described as "cheap, gauche, naïve and provincial" when compared to their English counterparts. According to literary historian May Jurilla, they were lacking in "linguistic artistry, thematic complexity and fullness in characterization" (Jurilla 2006, 124). This was partly true. While there were exceptional writers whose novels talked about the poor and their struggles, the majority of what the vernacular writers "churned out, in general, was fiction that used stilted language, trite themes, and stereotypical characters" (Jurilla 2006, 125). The reason for this was the mass market and the decision to serialize. Vernacular readers did not expect their favorite writers to prod them to look for the "linguistic artistry, thematic complexity and fullness in characterization" in the stories. They wanted stories that

were "cheap, formulaic, and escapist entertainment," mainly about romantic relations. Moreover, it worked. The English writings were left behind ever since the continuation of the metrical romances into the American period and forward. It was the
"novels from the 1920s to the 1940s, comic books from the 1950s to the 1980s, and
romance novels from 1985 to 2000" (Jurilla 2006, 124–125). The vernacular novels
were the "literary best sellers" of the country then, and they remain so even today.

On the eve of World War II, a small group began writing on social issues and
against a looming fascist threat from Japan, Germany, and Italy. Inspired by the "pro-
letarian" writings of Russian authors, these writers also returned to the issues of the
turn of the century, to the questions of nationhood and the regressive impact of
American domination on Filipino identity. They were also critical of their fellow English writers, regarding their works as overly concerned with escapism and aesthetics
and for trying hard to imitate their American/Western mentors. This was, however, a
small cluster of English writers. It was the vernacular authors who led the conversations about the economic and political problems of poor Filipinos. The Japanese
noticed this during World War II and actively endorsed works written in Filipino, in
the hope of getting popular support.

After the war, Filipino graduates who majored in the humanities in American universities introduced New Criticism theory, which had become the most influential per-
spective in the literary field. New Criticism favored stories that were "self-contained,"
and was oblivious to the "realities" around it. Reviewers employing the theory concerned themselves with a close reading of the relationship between a story's ideas and
its forms of expression. They were concerned with aesthetics, not moral or social
issues. This "art-for-art's sake" stream, however, was, in fact, a strawman. It was not an
accurate description of the writers who were said to be icons of Filipino New Criticism.
The authors of the top English novels in the first two decades of the republic were sensitive to a corrupt and repressive political system as well as how economic backwardness and the rule of a small elite had kept the majority weak and powerless. They did
not have the activism of the nationalists of yore, but there was no denying their social
concerns. They wrote about individuals and their sensibilities, but lurking in the background was a flawed Philippine society.

The student protests in the late 1960s did provide a counterfoil to this "decadence,"
with several of the young radical writers coming out with literature similar to the
ones produced by their elders in the 1930s: addressing the poverty, alienation, exploitation, and oppression of the poor. Some stories addressed new subject matters. The
global women's movements inspired authors to write about the problems the Filipina
faced under a corrupt system, while student radicals' near-reverence of the Chinese
leader Mao Tse Tung inspired translations of Chinese plays. Several writers also composed stories about the illusions of upward mobility of the middle class and its role in
the perpetuation of the repressive system. This radical revival could not compete with
the debauchery promoted by cinema and certain magazines. It also had a short shelf
life, for in 1972, when President Ferdinand Marcos declared martial law, the first to be
banned were these leftist writings.

The government created a Ministry of Public Affairs which would supervise all print media. In the name of promoting a new Filipino society, the government also took over and sponsored poetry contests and old plays and promoted the interests of the country's Indigenous communities (especially the Muslims). The revival was not only performative. The First Lady Imelda Marcos built edifices such as a Cultural Center of the Philippines and a Folk Arts Theater and even rebuilt the Manila Metropolitan Theater. Finally, Marcos was aware of how essential writers were in legitimizing (some say deodorizing) martial law. Soon after he declared martial law, he sought out the older, more respected writers by offering them symbolic and monetary largesse. The government created the National Artists Awards in 1973 and conferred this three years later to Nick Joaquin, the country's most famous essayist in English, and then, in 1976, to Carlos P. Romulo, writer, university president and diplomat to the United Nations.

Marcos was less tolerant of the younger, radicalized writers, detaining many and forcing others to the underground, where their writings found space in the pages of communist party newsletters. Some decided to continue fighting as artists, developing ingenious ways to continue opposing martial law. Philippine Education Theater Association (PETA) survived the political exile of its founder and began staging original plays and translations of Western dramas which carried subtle political messages. Others went back to writing in the vernacular, and one of the ironic consequences of martial law was the flowering of regional (i.e., non-Manila) literature. Mindanao authors pooled their works together to publish an anthology that would suggest that there was a distinctive Mindanao literature and not just disparate writings from different parts of the island. These works, however, would not be published till a decade after Marcos fell. The same renewed interest was also being seen elsewhere. Writers produced novels in the Pangasinan language in an effort to preserve the language.

The assassination of a leading Marcos opponent in 1983 fostered a democratic space where more writers became more critical of the regime. This space also rejuvenated and increased the number of readers, who welcomed the alternative press. This surge inspired younger writers to submit their works. This trend continued and even expanded after the fall of Marcos. The press grew from 2 major pro-Marcos tabloids to 19 English and Filipino dailies, inviting more literary contributions. Literary enthusiasm never faltered in the next 14 years. Short stories and novels in the vernacular and English continued to be written, this time encouraged by companies and publishers holding annual book fairs. In the 1980s, the awards were only given to English and Filipino authors.

In the next decade, however, the most prestigious of these book award programs, the Carlos Palanca Memorial Awards (named after the founder of a distillery company), added three other languages for short stories. So productive had writers become that in the 1998 literary contest to celebrate the Philippine Centennial, 350 authors submitted their novels for consideration. The Man Asian Literary Prize received 21 Filipino novels in 2007, 25 in 2008, and 24 in 2009. Literature was given an added boost when the Commission on Higher Education made the teaching of Philippine literature a class requirement. Today, the works of Filipinos living abroad and those who grew up in the diaspora began to appear in Philippine bookstores.

See also: Chapter 9: Overview. Chapter 16: Overview.

Further Reading

Chung, Hernandez Lilia. 1998. *Facts in Fiction: A Study of Peninsular Prose Fiction: 1859–1897*. Manila: De La Salle University Press.

Eugenio, Damiana L. 1989. *Philippine Folk Literature: The Folktales*. Quezon City: University of the Philippines Press.

Jurilla, Patricia May B. 2006. "Tagalog Bestsellers and the History of the Book in the Philippines." PhD diss., School of Oriental and African Studies, University of London. August 30.

Jurilla, Patricia May B. 2016. "Conflicts and Contests: A History of the Filipino Novel in English." *Kritika Kultura* 27: 3–20.

Lacaba, Jose. 2015. "Prometheus Unbound." Martial Law Reminder from *Esquire Philippines*. September 15. https://soundcloud.com/esquire-philippines

Lim, Jaime An, Christine Godinez-Ortega, and Edilberto K. Tiempo, eds. 1995. *Mindanao Harvest 1: An Anthology of Contemporary Writing*. Manila: New Day Publishers and Christian Literature Society of the Philippines.

Lumbera, Bienvenido. 1984. *Revaluation: Essays on Philippine Literature, Cinema, and Popular Culture*. Manila: Bienvenido Lumbera and Index Press.

"Maps of the Philippines." World Atlas. Accessed August 2, 2019. https://www.worldatlas.com/articles/the-countries-that-read-the-most.html

McMahon, Jennifer. 2011. "Excerpt from Dead Stars: American and Literary Perspectives on the American Colonization of the Philippines." *UC Santa Barbara Journal of Transnational American Studies* 3, no. 2: 49–66.

Mojares, Resil. 1983. *Origins and Rise of the Filipino Novel: A Generic Study of the Novel until 1940*. Quezon City: University of the Philippine Press.

Republic of the Philippines, Philippine Statistical Office. 2013. FLEMMS (Functional Literacy, Education and Mass Media Survey Final Report). Manila: Philippine Statistical Office.

Chick Lit

While English literary novels continue to struggle with expanding their audience, this is not the case with the genre that Filipinos refer to fondly as "chick lit" ("chick" being a slang word used in the 1960s to refer to young women). These are works of fiction written by millennials and the generation younger to them and are mainly about women's romantic lives. They tell of the happiness and frustrations women encounter when they fall in love, even as they go through a daily life full of hopes, career problems, the commodities they shop for, the things they do when passing time with friends, and, of course, their relationships with men. Unlike the more conservative romance novels of their parents' time, chick lit does not shy away from talking about body issues, sex, and lately, sexual orientation (a few novels write about LGBTQ relationships).

A chick lit plot often revolves around young women characters who are in full control of their lives and who know what to do with it. They reject people who demand that they "act like women," and they pursue their lives with ambitions while continuing to be mindful of their obligations to help others who are in need. They face challenges from the profession, but, as is often the case, their most significant challenges come from men who neither understand nor appreciate their independence. And these things happen even as these women characters pursue romance and come to terms with their sexuality and individual identity.

All this appears to be nothing new. As one of the older writers put it, the success of chick lit comes from the fact that "Filipinos love reading romance, and Filipinos love writing it." In a way, chick lit has a lot in common with the "gauche" vernacular novels and romantic books produced by American publishers like Mills and Boon (an extremely popular series in the Philippines). What differentiates this genre from vernacular literature and the dollar-dreadful American romances, however, is the importance they give to women's "own voices." Chick lit encourages its women readers to act like the characters they read: to assert their identities and independence with regard to life, but more so, to men (Santiago 2009). Mina V. Esguerra explains the distinction in this manner: "[Chick lit] . . . imagine the careers threatened, recognition withheld, and stories silenced by this environment of disdain. It is also inaccurate because romance books have as a requirement a noble, admirable, and swoon-worthy love interest, and in most of the books, this role will still go to the man. Men are represented in the genre with an optimism that is often criticized as 'unrealistic,' because how dare we expect them to be as noble, as admirable, as capable as romance? What does that tell us when real people see fictional romance heroes as competition, instead of inspiration/aspiration?" (Esguerra and Gonzales n.d.).

The result is a very popular genre. Chick lit authors sign their books for adoring fans who fill up auditoriums. One author whose pseudonym is "HaveYouSeenThisGirL" has reportedly sold over 100,000 copies of her books. The film adaptations of chick lit novels and favorable international reviews have also enhanced their popularity. Chick lit authors scoff at the criticism—usually from established writers—that their works are shallow or not literary at all. Their pointed response is to say that in their stories, "women are main characters [who] can live their lives, get what they want, live their potential without being told to stay home and give up their place for someone else" (Esguerrra 2019). This is precisely the kind of statement that young Filipinas—who are now less constrained by society's conservative norms, who are financially independent of their parents, and who have seen more of the world than their elders—identify strongly with. "Serious" literary writers may hem and haw about the genre's frivolities, but its authors are correct in saying that in the Philippines their writing represents the "21st-century literature in English."

See also: Chapter 9: Overview. Chapter 16: Overview.

Further Reading

Esguerra, Mina V. 2019. "For Those about to Teach 'Chick Lit' in Senior High School (Philippines)." *Wattpad*. May 4. https://www.wattpad.com/445487857-21st-century -literature-philippines-chick-lit-for

Esguerra, Mina V., and Georgette Gonzales. n.d. "12 Essential Romance Books." https:// www.wattpad.com/614617048-21st-century-literature-philippines-chick-lit-12

Prelypchan, Erin. 2004. "Banking on Chick-Lit." *Far Eastern Economic Review* 167, no. 20 (May 20): 56

Santiago, Katrina Stuart. 2009. "The Pinay as Fun, Fearless Female: Philippine Chick Literature in the Age of Transition." *Humanities Diliman* 6, no. 1–2 (December): 58–92.

Filipino Novels in English

The first Filipino novel in English, *The Child of Sorrow*, was published in 1921, and by 2008, there were 240 such novels that had been published. Among the top writers in the postwar period was Nicomedes "Nick" Joaquin who wrote about middle-class Filipinos and their engagements with faiths and other belief systems amid a society that experienced war. Joaquin's protagonists represent a clash of cultures—intellectuals who embody an old, more cultured past against peers who have embraced the modern age. Francisco Sionil Jose's novels are about class conflict and social justice. His most famous one is a five-book saga about a family torn by such battles.

Stevan Javellana uses one of Jose Rizal's characters to build a story about a village before and at the onset of World War II, while Nestor Vicente Madali Gonzalez's novels are about the clash between Filipino and American cultures as personified by Filipinos coming back home. Among the best women writers is Kerima Polotan, whose novels deal with the tradeoffs individuals have to make in life. Critics often describe Polotan's writings as bleak, but one also notices the care she has for her characters. Jessica Hagedorn also writes about class conflict, but through the prism of popular culture (beauty pageants, movie stars) and with the Marcos regime as its setting.

While their interests in Philippine society are varied in focus and even have philosophical differences, these novelists share two things in common. First, their plots revolve around a community and its development or breakdown as a result of conflicting ideas and actions. The lives (and deaths) of their characters are also linked to communities in crisis. Second, these novels are about fissures of various kinds—class, ethnicity, religion, and gender. In the late 20th century, the appearance of novels by Filipino writers in the diaspora has added a new theme—what it means to be a Filipino abroad and what is their relationship with the "homeland." Their different focuses, prejudices, and intentions are also literary reminders of past debates over Filipino nationhood and, with over 8 million Filipinos living abroad, the need for a new way of re-imagining "Filipino-ness."

It is one thing to discuss the brilliance of their works; it is another thing to ask about their readership. Novel production has been inconsistent; between 1945 and

1965, only 25 were published, the average going down to 0.8 a year. High printing cost due to dependence on imports has been the bane of the industry. Government taxation on the imports and the sale of books added more problems resulting in the low quality of book production and cuts in the number of books printed. Moreover, literary pieces were virtually inconsequential in book production. In the 1980s, textbooks, atlases, almanacs, and reference materials constituted the bulk of published books. Literary and scholarly pieces only comprised about 4 percent and 3 percent, respectively. Aggravating all this was the industry's weak distribution system, which meant books were and continue to be concentrated in Manila. In 1948, the Philippines only had 177 bookshops to serve a population of 11 million. Moreover, 124 of these were located in Manila. This trend has never changed since. In 2000, there were 2,000 bookstores nationwide, with 558 based in Manila. The regions outside of the capital averaged about 86 bookstores, and the worst provinces were in Mindanao, where the average number ranged between 9 and 12 per province (Jurilla 2006, 116).

Without a doubt, when the government got involved in boosting the industry, the rise in book production was notable. Writers, however, complained that Filipinos are not drawn to novels. A novel that sold 1,000 copies after three to four years would be considered a best seller (Jurilla 2006, 82). Very often, 95 percent of books are sold in Manila. The provinces would only receive about 5 percent of sales and, because they needed to compensate, would increase the prices of these new editions. State support was inconsistent, but there was some regularity by the 1970s. The Marcos regime formed the National Artist Awards to honor the country's top literary writers. Private foundations also sponsored their own awards ceremonies, giving away money to writers. Finally, universities kept their gates open to novelists, publishing their works. In 1986, this was bolstered by the creation of university presses and the rejuvenation of the printing industry. For the first time since the founding of the republic, Congress passed the Book Publishing Industry Development Act (Republic Act No. 8047).

Yet, novels remain low on a publisher's list, with a maximum of 1,000 copies put out per edition. The reason for this is a limited readership. In a 2003 survey, the poll group Social Weather Station reported that only 9 percent of adult Filipinos read English novels for entertainment while 91 percent read them because these were class requirements. While the Filipinos placed fourth in the World Atlas global survey of the number of hours the citizens of each country spent on reading, in truth, they never were voracious readers. According to Professor Jurilla, "Of the non-school book readers, 76 percent did not borrow their books from libraries. Indeed, the majority of Filipinos . . . [did] not rely on the resources of libraries. Forty-two percent of Filipino adults [were] not even aware if a public library exists in their locality. Fifty-seven percent of Filipino adults prefer to read non-school books in Tagalog (Filipino), 30 per cent in English, and 13 per cent in Cebuano" (Jurilla 2006, 98). The writer Charlson Ong noted with some sadness that a novel in English "that sells a thousand copies in three or four years, itself a rarity, is deemed a best-seller by Philippine standards" (as quoted by Hau 2008, 320).

See also: Chapter 8: Overview. Chapter 9: Overview.

Further Reading

Gonzalez, N.V.M. 1992. *A Season of Grace*. Manila: Bookmark.

Hagedorn, Jessica. 1990. *Dogeaters*. New York: Pantheon Books.

Hau, Caroline S. 2008. "The Filipino Novel in English." In Maria Lourdes Bautista and Kingsley Bolton (eds.), *Philippine English: Linguistic and Literary Perspectives*. Hong Kong: Hong Kong University Press.

Javellana, Stevan. 1947. *Without Seeing the Dawn*. New York: Little, Brown.

Joaquin, Nick. 1966. *Portrait of the Artist as Filipino* (An Elegy in Three Scenes). Manila: Alberto Florentino.

Joaquin, Nick. 2017. *The Woman Who Had Two Navels and Tales of the Tropical Gothic*. London: Penguin Classics.

Jose, F. Sionil. 1962. *The Pretenders*. Manila: Philippine-American Literary House. 1962.

Jurilla, Patricia May B. 2006. "Tagalog Bestsellers and the History of the Book in the Philippines." PhD diss., School of Oriental and African Studies, University of London. August 30.

Pantoja-Hidalgo, Cristina. 2000. "The Philippine Novel in English into the Twenty-First Century." *World Literature Today* 74, no. 2 (Spring): 333–336.

Polotan, Kerima. 1962. *The Hand of the Enemy*. Quezon City: University of the Philippines Press.

Noli Me Tangere and *El Filibusterismo*

The Philippines' national hero, Jose Rizal, wrote the novels *Noli Me Tangere* (published in 1887) and its sequel *El Filibusterismo* (published in 1891) which became the sources of inspiration for the nationalist revolution that began on August 23, 1896. Both revolved around the character Crisostomo Magsalin Ibarra, who we first encounter in *Noli Me Tangere* as a mestizo who was forced to end his extended stay in Europe and return to his Philippine hometown, San Diego. There were two reasons for Ibarra's sudden homecoming: he needed to know the circumstances behind his father's death, and he wanted to propose to his long-time sweetheart Maria Clara.

Ibarra, however, comes home to a town that is entirely under the sway of the Spanish friars. One of them, Padre Damaso, turns out to be the culprit responsible for the father's death. Damaso opposes the marriage between Ibarra and Maria Clara not only because of his lingering animosity toward Ibarra's family (the "sins" of the father naturally tarred the son) but also because, as it turns out, he is the biological father of Maria Clara. Maria Clara was the result of an illicit relationship between Damaso and her mother, although they made it appear that she was the daughter of Pia Alba's husband, Don Santiago de Los Santos. Another friar, Padre Salvi, is against the marriage for far more sinister reasons: his lust for Maria Clara. As one reads through *Noli Me*

Tangere, the reader will gradually discern the plot that the secretive Salvi had concocted to prevent the marriage, destroy Ibarra's reputation, and undermine Damaso's influence over his daughter. There are side stories to these main narratives, and for the most part, the characters in these sidebars are severely compromised. There is Maria Clara's father, who is one of the richest in town, his wealth coming from legitimate business as well as a large share in the sale of opium.

There are others as rich as Kapitan Tiago [the "village philosopher" character in the novel PNA] or connected in various ways to Spanish officialdom, but bereft of moral standing.

Members of the local sodality—an all-women church association that supported the friars—are concerned solely with collecting "indulgences," which points out that people collected through prayer and attending Sunday church. There are also students in the novel, but Rizal writes them as frivolous teenagers who care little about the social problems of the community. The poor in the community are the most abused by the friars. There is a heartbreaking story of a mother, Sisa, whose youngest son was beaten to death by Salvi and eldest son forced to go into hiding, while she—Sisa—is imprisoned on charges of theft that Salvi leveled on her dead son. As a counterfoil, Rizal created the character Elias, a mysterious person who lives on the margins of the community but whose behavior and manner of presenting himself to Ibarra suggests a good upbringing. Another character is called Tasyo the Philosopher for his erudite knowledge of local and global goings-on. Both advise and warn Ibarra about the dangers he faces, although never directly pointing to the friars. However, they are rare and powerless voices and cannot save Ibarra once Salvi's plot comes into play.

Ibarra wants to build a school in honor of his father and as a gift to his fiancée. This dream project never pans out. Ibarra slaps Fr. Damaso when the latter insults his father and is excommunicated. Then a "revolt" breaks out but fails, and those arrested point to Ibarra as their coconspirator. The Spaniards arrest Ibarra but Elias rescues him. He goes to see Maria Clara only to be shocked by her revelation of who her birth father is (Salvi told her after discovering Damaso's letters about her). Ibarra and Elias proceed to get out of the town, but the authorities catch up with them. Elias is fatally wounded, but Ibarra escapes. The town gossip, however, declares him dead. A distraught Maria Clara then forces Fr. Damaso to permit her to enter a cloister. The new head priest of the cloister turns out to be Padre Salvi, and Rizal implies that he repeatedly rapes Maria Clara. At the novel's end, Ibarra returns to exact revenge on those who wronged him.

In *El Filibusterismo*, Ibarra returns to the Philippines after a 13-year absence. He disguises himself as Simoun, a shady and extremely wealthy jeweler who goes around from one town to another to sell his jewels. He also has considerable political clout, having as a close friend and ally the new Spanish governor general. Simoun's real objective is to foment a revolt (he already has amassed considerable firepower), kill everyone responsible for his downfall, and rescue Maria Clara. In order for this revolt-cum-rescue-mission to succeed, Simoun encourages the governor general to use his punitive power in excess and thus anger the population. He then taps on this resentment to recruit people and form an armed force. He does all of this while keeping his disguise. The only person to discover his real identity is Sisa's eldest son, Basilio, who is now a medical student, his education paid for by Maria Clara's adoptive father.

After a few months of planning, Simoun is ready to put his revolt into play. His comrades are supposed to attack the city, while government and church leaders are watching a famous performance. Basilio is supposed to rescue Maria Clara during the attack. This falls through because Maria Clara dies that day, this being the only way she could finally put an end to Salvi raping her repeatedly. Basilio informs Simoun who suffers a breakdown. With no Simoun to lead them, the insurgents do not continue with the rebellion. Basilio is himself compromised when the authorities accuse him of being part of a student group that was using their fight for reforms as a pretext to attack university officials. Simoun, who was plotting another revolt, rescues Basilio who now shares his hatred for those in power.

Simoun's new plot is to explode a nitroglycerin-filled lamp during the reception after the wedding ceremony of the children of the two most influential families. Simoun correctly predicts that government and religious leaders would be at the reception. Simoun will bring the lamp (a wedding gift) and place it in a strategic place where it will wait for a clueless individual who will raise the wick to enhance the illumination, thereby triggering an explosion that will kill everyone. The explosion would be followed by an attack by rebel forces, which, in turn, will be the signal for Basilio and his comrades to distribute firearms to people.

This second revolt also fails after Basilio reveals the existence of the bomb to a friend who is the bride's former lover, who then snatches it from the reception and throws it into the river. Government authorities find out that Simoun is the mastermind, forcing him to seek refuge in a well-respected priest. This does not last, and when word comes that he is to be arrested, Simoun commits suicide. Before he dies, he reveals his true identity to his host, Fr. Florentino. Fearful that the government might confiscate Simoun's jewels (which he brought with him when he escaped), Florentino casts these into the ocean, predicting that when the time comes for people to fight for social justice again, God will guide them to Simoun's treasure.

See also: Chapter 2: Overview. Chapter 6: Overview; Mestizos. Chapter 8: History of Education.

Further Reading

Anderson, Benedict R. O'Gorman. 2003. "Forms of Consciousness in Noli me Tangere." *Philippine Studies* 51, no. 4: 505–529.

Anderson, Benedict R. O'Gorman. 2004. "Nitroglycerine in the Pomegranate." *New Left Review* 27 (May–June): 99–118.

Anderson, Benedict R. O'Gorman. 2006. "Forms of Consciousness in 'El Filibusterismo.'" *Philippine Studies* 54, no. 3: 315–356.

Rafael, Vicente. 2002. "Foreignness and Vengeance: On Rizal's 'El Filibusterismo.'" University of California Center for Southeast Asian Studies. https://escholarship.org/uc/item/4j11p6c1

Vernacular Literature

Novels written in the vernacular languages gained readership by being serialized in magazines published for the principal language groups (Bisayan, Hiligaynon, Ilocano, and Tagalog). This captured audience found the novels entertaining because of their focus on personal relations (particularly love) and fantasy. Students of Philippine literature do point out that there have been several vernacular novels that have been praised by critics because of their timely messages. Among the earliest ones was Franciso Balagtas's 1838 *Florante at Laura* (Florante and Laura), which was an allegory about the Philippines under Spanish rule. It depicts the friendship between a Persian Muslim prince and a Christian Albanian duke, who were both betrayed by their respective usurpers, out to claim the women they love. They, however, prevailed and upon their return to claim their respective thrones, peace reigned in the two kingdoms. Balagtas made compromises in his text by making the sultan convert to Catholicism, but his message was clear—Filipinos of whatever religion could quickly unite were it not for the power of usurpers, that is, the friars.

In 1906, the Tagalog writer and former revolutionary Lope K Santos completed his novel *Banaag at Sikat* (From Early Dawn to Full Light), which he started putting out in parts in 1903 in a labor magazine. It tells the story of two friends, a socialist and an anarchist, who fell in love with women not of their own class (the socialist fell in love with the goddaughter of a cruel landlord who happened to be the anarchist's godfather, while the anarchist was attracted to a "commoner"). The main conflict is between the friends and the cruel landlord-godfather—culminating in the latter's death in the hands of his household help—and it ends with the two friends, having discussed once again their political beliefs, walking into the night to presumably start organizing for the revolution. The novel has been called the "Bible of the working-class Filipinos," and is believed to be a major inspiration in the formation of the Partido Komunista ng Pilipinas.

The big challenge to literature was not from within but from cinema. Two Swiss businessmen first introduced films amid the flames of the nationalist rebellion, and they gradually displaced the *komedya* and *moro-moro* as the primary forms of mass entertainment, and the plaza-showing (and later on the movie house) ran theater owners out of business. The dramas moved to the provinces where the movie industry had yet to expand. While English plays never really received the same public approbation as their vernacular counterparts, they were able to cope with the onrush of movies by finding solace in university theater departments.

The 1960s were associated with two writers. The first was labor leader and socialist Amado V. Hernandez who wrote *Luha ng Buwaya* ("Crocodile Tears," 1962), which is about the struggle of peasants led by a school teacher against landlord oppression. He followed this up seven years later with *Mga Ibong Mandaragit* ("Birds of Prey," 1969) which he described as a sequel to Jose Rizal's *Noli Me Tangere* and *El Filibusterismo*. Its main character is a young intellectual who has just come back from Europe and is being tested about Rizal and his works by an old revolutionary, eventually leading him to search for Simoun's treasure, which he would use to organize Filipinos who fell victim to the American colonial government's industrialization program. The other writer is Edgardo M. Reyes who serialized his novel Sa *Mga Kuko ng Liwanag* (In the Claws of Brightness) in the Filipino magazine *Liwayway* from 1966 to 1967. The novel is about the transformation of a provincial boy into a cynical human being after he moves to "bright" Manila in search of his girlfriend who, he later finds out, has become a victim of human trafficking. The novel was adapted into a movie in 1975, to become one of the first films to subtly rebuke First Lady Imelda Marcos's depiction of Manila as "The City of Man."

The 1980s was the decade associated with Lualhati Bautista who wrote the novels *Dekada '70* (The 1970s Decade, published in 1983), *Gapo* (1988), and *Bata, Bata . . . Pa'ano Ka Ginawa?* (My Child, My Child, How were you made?), which was also published in 1988. *Dekada '70* is about a middle-class family's radicalization under the Marcos dictatorship, with some of its children going to the extent of joining the communists' New People's Army. This book came in the twilight of the Marcos dictatorship when radical writers such as Bautista could not openly write about revolutions and communists, including how such commitments can be a source of tension among presumably apolitical middle-class Filipinos. *Gapo* is a popular abbreviation for the Olongapo City, the site of the American naval base in Subic Bay. The novel's character is an "Amerasian," the child of an American serviceman and a Filipina, and the novel is about the difficulty he and his community confront daily for being under the shadow of the largest American naval base outside of the U.S. mainland. Finally, *Bata, Bata . . .* gives readers an idea of the everyday difficulties that a Filipina activist, who is also a single mother, faces. These authors have inspired younger writers, especially those based in the universities, to write their own stories, ensuring that writings in defense of the poor and about the search for social justice will remain a presence in Philippine literature.

There have not been too many Visayan novels compared to Tagalog, with the best ones written in the American colonial period. The first recorded Visayan novel was Juan Villagonza's *Walay Igsoon: Sugilanong Binisaya* ("No Sibling: A Visayan Story," 1912), which was about two brothers who were orphans and separated from each other by the Spaniards. The separation would take its toll on both—after their reunion, they have never-ending arguments about their different beliefs, the result of them having grown up in separate social classes. The other novels were concerned with the Visayans' fraught encounters with the new American culture. Uldarico Alviola's *Felicitas* (1912) and Vicente Garces *Mahinuklugong Paglubog kang Alicia* ("The Sad Burial of Alicia," 1924) were about marital fidelity, while Angel Enemecio's 1928–1929 serialized novel *Apdo sa Kagul-anan* (The Bitterness of Sorrow) was concerned with how female chastity can be protected. Vicente Rama's *Ang Tinagoan* (The Secret) was about divorce and the need to tolerate this in a Catholic colony. The first Cebuano feminist novel was *Lourdes*, by Gardeopatra G. Quijano (serialized in the magazine *Bag-ong Kusog*, or New Strength), from May 26 to September 23, 1939). It was about women seeking to be educated and trying to overcome household problems. Quijano was a strong advocate of women's autonomy. In the postwar era and even until today, writers continued to serialize their novels in Bisaya magazines, but no one appeared to stand out among the younger novelists.

Ilocano novelists explore similar issues. There were several Ilocano writings in the colonial period, which were mainly about love, religion, and marriage. The exception was Leon C. Pichat's 1935 book *Apay a Pinatayda ni Na Simon?* (Who did kill Don Simon?), which was one of the earliest detective novels in the Philippines. In the 1970s, novels depicting repression and struggle began to appear, its authors affected by the political changes of the era. Juan S. P. Hidalgo's *Saksi ti Kauungan* (Witness to Greatness, 1987) is an anti-colonial novel that explores the need for the "redemption and liberation. . . of the national soul-body" (Galam 2008, 40) but also attempts to extol President Ferdinand Marcos as "the savior and liberator of the nation from colonial perdition" (Galam 2008, 77). Reynaldo E. Duque's *Ankel Sam* (1999) was also openly critical of "U.S. imperialism" and used two historical events where the Ilocanos and another Indigenous community, the Tinggian, defeated efforts by American "colonialists" to impose their presence in the community. Finally, Jose Bragado's *Gil-ayab ti Daga* ("Blazing Land," 1986) is a story about the opposition of an urban poor community to the plans of a powerful businessman to buy their lands.

All in all, it does appear that as long as magazines continue to serialize these vernacular writings, they will continue to be read. However, given that they are a part of print culture, it is not clear as to whether they can survive visual culture.

See also: Chapter 8: Overview. Chapter 9: Overview; Mother Tongue Teaching; National Language Debate.

Further Reading

Banag, Consuelo Cruz. 1970. "A Critical Study of Lope K. Santos' Banaag at Sikat." MA thesis, Centro Escolar University.

Bresnahan, Mary I. 1989. "The Tagalog Literary Tradition in Amado V. Hernandez." *Philippine Studies* 37, no. 1 (March 1): 15–28.

Galam, Roderick G. 2008. *The Promise of the Nation: Gender, History, and Nationalism in Contemporary Ilokano Literature.* Quezon City: Ateneo de Manila University.

Jurilla, Patricia May B. 2005. "Florante at Laura and the History of the Filipino Book." *Book History* 8: 131–196.

Jurilla, Patricia May B. 2006. "Tagalog Bestsellers and the History of the Book in the Philippines." PhD diss., School of Oriental and African Studies, University of London. August 30.

Siapno, Jacqueline. 1995. "Alternative Filipina Heroines: Contested Tropes in Leftist Feminism." In Aihwa Ong and Michael G. Peletz (eds.), *Bewitching Women, Pious Men: Gender and Body Politic in Southeast Asia.* Los Angeles and London: University of California Press.

CHAPTER 12

ART AND ARCHITECTURE

OVERVIEW

ARCHITECTURE

The Filipino architect Leandro Locsin described Philippine architecture as a hybrid of Indigenous styles coming from Malay and Hindu influence mixed with or coexist with those brought in by the Spanish and then the Americans. It is no surprise then to see, in Philippine towns and even small cities, "traditional" homes made of local materials circling the Catholic Church and the compact concrete buildings that the Americans introduced to their colony.

When building homes and edifices, one must take into consideration the nature and climate associated with the Philippines. Torrential rains that last from July to November can cause flooding, while strong winds and rain that regular hurricanes (typhoons) bring demand sturdy structures. Heat is a given in a tropical country like the Philippines. So houses, in particular, need many windows to allow a breeze to pass through and cool the interior. When building a home or an office, one must consider the balance between the healthy rays of the early sunrise and the debilitating heat of the midday sun. Finally, while building homes, one must anticipate the devastating impact of earthquakes caused by the fact that the Philippines is located in the Pacific "Ring of Fire," a horse-shaped basin under the Pacific with constantly moving oceanic trenches and active volcanoes. Precolonial homes were in no position to deal with earthquakes, but they were capable of withstanding rain, wind, and sun.

The origins of these structures, particularly the homes, go back to the precolonial era. In the lowland areas, houses were anchored on hardwood stilts and stood four or five feet from the ground. They were raised in anticipation of flooding but also to provide cover for domesticated chicken and pigs. The floors of these homes were made of bamboo slats that allowed for leftover food to be passed down underneath. The slats also enabled breeze to gush through, and together with the wide window, helped cool the homes, especially during the hot summer. These homes were kept together not by nails (metals were rare) but by a combination of rattan, bamboo, and hemp. As mentioned earlier, the bottom doubled up as a cage for domesticated animals and storage. The roof was made of palms or long dried grass. These homes were one-room rectangular structures, with the kitchen located on the outside where one could cook food over an open fire.

Muslim houses in the southern island of Mindanao were more elaborate than those in the central and northern Philippines. This was primarily because of the influence of Islam. The sides of these homes often included wooden carvings of boats, some copper ornaments, ornate stilts, and a rectangular roof in the middle of the larger roof. These were also the prominent features of mosques and fort encampments (*cotta*) during the period. In highland communities, like in the Cordillera mountains, homes were made out of bamboo or wood with thick thatches of palm. The bamboo floors of those in stilts were more tightly fused to retain heat, while others used the ground soil for the same purpose.

These precolonial structures never disappeared under the Spanish and American regimes. On the contrary, the latter brought in their architectural styles but also had to incorporate the former to be able to deal with the tropical features of the Philippines. This introduction-plus-fusion would be carried well into the Republican period when the Philippines became independent, with precolonial architecture experiencing a renaissance of sorts in the last decades of the 20th century because of a surge in nationalist sentiments and a renewed quest for a "Filipino identity."

Spanish colonialism brought architectural changes to the Philippine lowlands. The colonizers brought with them European architectural styles that were altered in Mexico and Antilles and changed further once introduced to the Philippine setting. The religious orders represented Spanish power (see Chapters 2 and 5), and friar power was, in turn, projected to the colonized via the presence of the church scaffoldings at the center of the town. The most imposing of these structures were made of stone and brickwork with hardwood for posts and for the choir loft above the entrance. Wooden pegs and dovetailed joints connected everything. Not everything in these churches was Spanish or Mexican in origin. The relative unfamiliarity of Filipinos with stone constructions instinctively led them to explore styles they knew. The bricks, which were a mixture of coral lime, clay (loam), and sugar cane juice, were Chinese, and so were the granite lions found outside some churches. The influence of Islam was also evident in the carvings of the church interiors.

The friars built the churches to project colonial and religious power, but these structures also served other functions. They served as courtrooms to hear cases of heresy and subversion and imprison the guilty, schools to teach children the basics of Catholicism, and an evacuation center for victims of calamities like typhoons and earthquakes. People likewise ran to churches for safety in the case of Muslim raids. The bell tower, built a couple of meters away from the main structure, called people to religious services and alerted them of these attacks. These imposing structures thus doubled as fortresses. The basement of the parish house was a mini-warehouse-cum-school. The bell tower mentioned above was constructed a bit further from the main church building so that in the event a strong earthquake broke it down, it would not cause severe damage to the other.

There were two other stone-based structures that the Spanish brought. The first was a wall, which was called *intramuros* (literal translation is "within walls,") that surrounded the colonial capital Manila and smaller forts facing the sea. The other was the so-called *Bahay* (Ba-hai) *na Bato* (stone houses), which were large two-storied homes made of hardwood sitting on a stone or brick-wall foundation. These stone houses had several rooms, of which the largest was the *sala*, the central room surrounded by smaller bedrooms and a kitchen. The ground floor was where nonperishable goods were stored; it sometimes became a stable for horses. The windows were made of wood and conch shells that could be used as glue, chalk, and varnish. There were wide sliding windows that allowed sunshine and gusts of wind to bring in light and cool the interiors, respectively. The *Bahay na Bato* were the residences of colonial officials and private Spanish citizens. However, by the 1860s, these were also built for the rising Filipino middle classes (Chapter 2). Many of these houses have survived to the present time, and the *Bahay na Bato* even served as a model of government public houses.

Cement was introduced to the colony in the last decade of Spanish rule and was then used as building blocks in newly built government offices. These cement blocks were hollow and, when used, were filled with a mixture of sand, gravel, and more cement. Filipinos also tinkered with this new element, with someone known only by name Ermitaño (Spanish for hermit but may also refer to someone living in a section of Manila called Ermita) inventing "a new composite material made of cement and bamboo" (Licio and Tomacruz 2014–2015, 1). This fusion was extensively advertised, but the 1896 nationalist revolution overtook its use. It would be used in the American period.

American *Deco Style*, with its Filipino and Spanish adornments, continued to define Philippine architecture in the postwar period. By the 1960s, the government was hiring architects who were strong advocates of "the Filipino style" for building state complexes like cultural pavilions and convention centers. The *tajuk pasung*, a roofing style that looked like a dragon and was associated with the Muslim ethnic group, the Tausogs, became a prominent feature of these buildings, with their roofs patterned after the *salakot*, a wide-brimmed hat made of palm leave or sugar cane strips. The *Filipinization* of architectural styles was actively promoted by President Ferdinand Marcos and his wife, Imelda, especially after Marcos promised to build a "New Society" under the theme *Isang Bansa, Isang Diwa* (One Nation, One Soul) in 1972. Mrs. Marcos hired the top Filipino architects to build a cultural arts center, a national arts center for the training of young artists, and even a "transfiguration chapel." The most famous of these buildings was the Cultural Center of the Philippines, which Mrs. Marcos announced was a purveyor of the Filipino soul. When an oil crisis hit the world in 1973, Filipino architects used it as an opportunity to design and build energy-efficient structures to help the government and the private sector save money.

The government continued the "Sanitary Barrio" of the American period, creating the People's Homesite and Housing Corporation (PHHC) that designed 240 square meter dwellings attached and divided only by a concrete wall. These affordable homes included two bedrooms, a living room, and full kitchen windows providing ventilation (Santos 1960, 153–154). The "subdivision," which was also an American creation, was the model for "planned [suburban] communities" for the rich and the middle

Weaving traditional Philippine cloth. (Namhwi Kim/Dreamstime.com)

classes. The elite's "parks" were and continue to be enclaves with strictly guarded entrances. Inside are big houses walled-off from each other, in a landscape that looks like the affluent suburbs of American cities. Middle-class "subdivisions" also have secured entrances. However, they tend to be more accessible, and the homes inside vary from apartments to multiroom houses.

As Filipinos working abroad began to remit part of their incomes back to the Philippines in the 1980s, there was a perceptible change in the urban landscape. Builders tapped this new resource to build multifloored "townhouses," offering a variety of domiciles—from studios to three-bedroom apartments. These "starter homes" were hollowed rectangular spaces from whence a new owner could visualize and then construct their interior design. They would become the nucleus around which business enterprises like shopping malls congregated. By the end of the 21st century, these areas became "micro-cities," connected to the rest of the city by roads but also capable of existing autonomously as commercial and residential centers away from the other districts of the metropolis.

Wealthy Filipinos and foreign expatriates were also drawn to these high-rises, and social and class distinctions also became apparent with certain "micro-cities" becoming havens of moneyed families while others were the residences of the new middle class subsidized by remittances. In the former, one could find "modernist" or "neo-modernist" apartments, designed by prominent national and foreign designers. At the same time, the high-rises of the rich tended to look duller, akin to the public housing towers in Hong Kong and Singapore.

The face of Philippine architecture has changed with more "townhouses" and "micro-cities" cropping up all over the country. However, some of the styles introduced as far back as the colonial era persist. The big question is whether the Philippine government has the will to impose stricter urban planning regulations, given the challenges that appear as cities continue to grow and urban space becomes more constricting.

ARTS

Modern Filipino art also evolved from drawing or sketching versions of Western styles to efforts at fusing these with designs from the precolonial era. In many cases, this hybridization was the result of the natural constraints the colonizers encountered. The Spanish missionaries, therefore, had to use Indigenous materials to reconstruct colonial versions of the European basilicas. American colonial officials were equally forced to adjust the inner rooms of government structures and "suburban" homes given the humidity and heat of the Philippines. Filipino artists excelled as students of their colonial mentors, but would also put their imprints on paintings and sculptures. Modernism as an art form had a robust Filipino hue, including the use of designs and sketches associated with this style to broadcast themes critical of Spanish and American colonialism. Many Filipino paintings were modernist in style. In the 1930s and the late 1960s, however, they also became advocates of social realism in order to "expose" the iniquities of Philippine society. They likewise were nationalists who criticized everything Western. There were two periods when defense and promotion of the Filipino "nation" were most intense. The first was when Filipino politicians had seized full control of colonial politics and were pushing the Americans to grant independence. The second was influenced by the global youth protests against "American imperialism" and the brownnosing of the Philippine government to the former's interests.

The nationalist surge was not only exclusive to radicals and nationalist politicians. In 1970, the government also vowed to make it its mission to promote a revival of the arts (including dances, music, and theater) to showcase "the pride of the Filipino." President Ferdinand Marcos and First Lady Imelda Marcos invested in the construction of edifices for this purpose. Theaters and concert halls hosted the performances of Filipino artists, while art schools trained young painters, playwrights, sculptors, and musicians. The government and the private sector collaborated in helping build and maintain museums and acquiring art collections to be displayed in them. Social realism persisted during this period, albeit with its radicalism muted. However, under the Marcoses, abstract art and a new trend called "conceptual art" (an approach that gives more importance to the idea or concept behind a particular work than the completed work itself) also flourished. This mixed bag of artistic styles remains the dominant way in "making art" even today.

See also: Chapter 2: Overview; Marcos Dictatorship. Chapter 3: Martial Law. Chapter 6: Overview.

Further Reading

Art Archive 01: A Collection of Essays on Philippine Contemporary Visual and Performing Arts. 2017. Manila: Japan Foundation. November.

Cabalfin, Edson G. 2008. *Building Modernity: A Century of Philippine Architecture and Allied Arts*. Manila: National Commission for Culture and the Arts.

Cruz, Geoffrey Rhoel C. 2019. "A Review of How Philippine Colonial Experience Influenced the Country's Approaches to Conservation of Cultural Heritage." *Padayomn Sining: A Celebration of the Enduring Values of the Humanities*. Paper Presented at the De La Salle University (Philippines), Arts Congress. February 20–22.

Licio, Gerard, and Mary Delia Tomacruz. 2014–2015. "Infrastructures of Colonial Modernity: Public Works in Manila from the late 19th to the Early 20th Centuries." *Espasyo: Journal of Architecture and Allied Arts in the Philippines* 2014–2015: 125 pp.

Ogura, Nobuyuki, David Leonides T. Yap, and Kenichi Tanoue. 2002. "Modern Architecture in the Philippines and the Quest for Filipino Style." *Journal of Asian Architecture and Building Engineering* 1, no. 2 (November): 233–238.

Santos, Idelfonso P. 1960. "The Development of Philippine Architecture." MA thesis, University of Southern California. January.

Villalon, Augusto. 2001. *Lugar: Essays on Philippine Heritage and Architecture*. New York: Bookmark Publishing.

Bahay Kubo (Nipa Hut)

Four to five decades ago, when asked what epitomized the rural Philippine house, Filipinos would instantaneously say *bahay kubo* (a combination of the Filipino word for house (*bahay*) with the Spanish *cubo* (cube), which was how the house looked). It is usually the ancestral home for many, its ownership passed on from one generation to another. It is also a haven for those seeking safety (e.g., fishermen). Today, couples or families from the city seeking to experience the rusticity of the countryside "vacation" in a bahay kubo.

The bahay kubo is built with flexible but light bamboo tied together by tree vines. Its roof is made from dried coconut leaves or cogon grass. It is raised about three feet to protect the family from floods and pests like snakes, and it is also a place to keep domesticated animals or for storage. Even its stairway can be disconnected. The sliding windows of the bahay kubo are wide to allow for more airflow. There is only one big room on the inside which doubles up as living room and bedroom. There is a back porch where jars containing fresh water are stored.

Not only is the bahay kubo made of local materials (and hence easily replaceable), it is also so light that it can actually be moved from one place to another. All that family and friends have to do is insert four bamboo poles under the hut, crisscrossed, and then lift them. This collaborative endeavor is known as *bayanihan*, which is the Filipino word for working together to promote community solidarity.

With the steady disappearance of bamboo due to over-harvesting and the ready availability of cement, the nipa hut has disappeared from many towns. It can only be

Nipa hut construction. (Dgmate/Dreamstime.com)

found in the outskirts, scattered across rice fields, and at the foot of the mountains. And here is the irony of this architectural structure of domesticity: as it gets pushed further into the countryside, the bahay kubo is increasingly memorialized as an icon of the Filipino soul. One can admire it as "a national symbol, a cultural heritage and a token of togetherness" (Santos 1960, 49). But one cannot build it anymore.

See also: Chapter 11: Overview. Chapter 13: Overview.

Further Reading

Bamboo Houses of the Philippines. http://www.bbc.com/culture/story/20180517-the-bamboo-houses-of-the-philippines

Cabalfin, Edson G. 2020. "*Bahay Kubo* as Iconography: Representing the Vernacular and the Nation in Philippine Post-war Architectures." *Journal of the Society of Architectural Historians, Australia and New Zealand* 30, no. 1: 44–67.

Santos, Idelfonso P. 1960. "The Development of Philippine Architecture." MA thesis, University of Southern California. January.

Bungalows

After World War I, the Americans introduced this single-floor multiroom "comfort" home to "improve" living conditions in towns and cities. The colonial government also recognized that due to economic progress, the "closely knit family unit was becoming more independent in its thinking and in its ways, and was gradually breaking away from the rigid Spanish way of life" (Santos 1960, 98). This anticipation proved to be spot-on. The "tropical bungalow" gained traction. This was interrupted by World War II, but the bungalows were built again after the war as part of the country's recovery. As the economy returned to normal and cities attracted migrants from the rural areas, construction of the bungalow returned in earnest, suggesting the growing acceptance by Filipino families "of the informality and simplicity which marked the new spirit of the times" (Santos 1960, 98).

The bungalow has concrete foundations and walls, galvanized iron for roofing, and interiors made of a lot of hard wood (which also prevents termite infestation). It has no cellars and closets and this is to mitigate dampness and mildew. Instead of having wall paper, the inside walls of bungalows are painted and the basic paint is overlayed with additional decorations. The bungalow has steel window frames that are wide enough for ventilation and sunshine. Behind is a multipurpose yard that alternates as a garden or vegetable plot, the children's play area, and a parking space for the family car.

The Americans prohibited the building of a second floor as this would interfere with plans to set up telephone and telegraph poles and affect movement on narrow streets. This is no more the case today. Recipients of remittances, however, were able to build a second floor and even third floors, thereby adding new rooms and turning their first floors into widened living rooms and kitchens. Land developers have also been purchasing or leasing private lots contiguous to each other to open "subdivisions" for families wishing to have more privacy and set themselves apart from the rest of the town or small city population.

See also: Chapter 2: Overview. Chapter 6: Overview. Chapter 7: Overseas Workers and their Families.

Further Reading

Lorenzo, Clarissa M. 2016. "Filipino Culture of Filling Up Space in a Gated Community." *Social and Behavioral Sciences* 216: 545–551.

Santos, Idelfonso P. 1960. "The Development of Philippine Architecture." MA thesis, University of Southern California. January.

Yamaguchi, Kiyoko. 2006. "The New 'American' Houses in the Colonial Philippines and the Rise of the Urban Filipino Elite." *Philippine Studies* 54, no. 3 412–451.

Burnham, Daniel

Daniel Burnham was a Chicago architect who was famous for, among other things, managing the World Columbian Exposition of 1893 where new versions of "classic architecture" were showcased via the advances in urban technologies, especially electricity. Burnham was also very much involved in modernizing American architecture. The transformation of cities like Cleveland, San Francisco, and Chicago reflected the enthusiasm of his commitment. These cities, especially his hometown Chicago, became the showcases of the "City Beautiful Movement" of the turn of the century, a modernist effort that ran parallel to the rise of Progressivist reforms. His grand ambition to reformat the city earned him the title "Father of the City Beautiful Movement."

In 1905, Burnham was invited to develop a master plan to modernize Manila. This was supposed to run parallel to the other efforts of the colonial regime to prepare Filipinos for self-government. Upon his arrival, Burnham immediately declared his plan to turn Manila into the Paris of the tropics where the hallmarks of American modernity—paved boulevards, waterways, and Greco-Roman government buildings—would seamlessly blend with Filipino and Spanish features. He turned hitherto undeveloped areas outside of Manila into the "suburbs" while preserving the "rusticity" of the Spanish community that the medieval walls of *intramuros* protected.

Burnham conceived of a similar plan for Baguio, a town in northern Luzon which turned into the "summer capital" for the colonial officials escaping the June–August heat. He brought in different styles of American architecture that included hollow blocks and concrete and used local products like the termite-free Philippine hardwood for the new buildings that represented this modernization. He also popularized the mass fabrication of "standard building types" for public housing. He brought the Art Deco and mixed this up with styles associated with the Spanish.

Burnham is also remembered for having designed and built the Manila Hotel in 1909. It was opened on July 4, 1912, to honor American independence. The hotel was built in a reclaimed area adjacent to the Rizal Park, the largest open park of the capital. A little further down lay Malacanang Palace, the official residence of the governor general and later on, the president of the Philippines. General Douglas McArthur used Manila Hotel as his office when President Manuel L. Quezon asked him to form the Philippine Army in 1935.

See also: Chapter 2: Overview.

Further Reading

Boquet, Yves. 2017. "The Growth of Greater Manila." *Philippine Archipelago*. April 22.

Goodno, J. B. 2004. "Burnham's Manila." *American Planning Association* 70, 11: 30–34

Hines, Thomas S. 1972. "The Imperial Façade: Daniel J. Burnham and American Architectural Planning in the Philippines." *Pacific Historical Review* 41, no. 1 (February): 33–53.

Locsin, Leandro V.

If Filipinos are asked who is the greatest Filipino architect, their unanimous answer is Leandro V. Locsin. Locsin was born in 1928. He came from a politically prominent family in a town in west-central Philippines. His education was all Catholic—he went

Evening at the Cultural Center of the Philippines. (Jon Bilous/Dreamstime.com)

to a high school run by the De La Salle brothers from 1935 to 1947 and then studied music in a Dominican university in Manila only to transfer to architecture a year before graduation. He was multitalented—apart from music, he also painted and wrote poetry. His connections in the Manila art scene got him hired in 1953 by one of the richest families to draft a master plan for the part of the city where they lived.

Locsin is credited with steering Philippine architecture away from its "provincial feel" into the modern age and yet retaining much of what was already there. His family background—rich Chinese mestizo political family—made him "aware of the forms and spaces of Spanish-period Filipino architecture" (Paredes-Santillan 2009, 4). Locsin once described the Philippines as a "hybrid culture," which could be both its strength and its weakness. The dominance of Western motif could very well stifle its local counterparts, but Locsin showed that Filipinos could also remold this into a structure that they could admire and identify with.

The most renowned of these fusions is the Cultural Center of the Philippines, a complex of five buildings that the First Lady Imelda Marcos decreed to be built to hype up Filipino culture. The first building Locsin designed and built was a Greek-like amphitheater with a seating capacity of 8,500 that was finished within 77 days, in time for the 1974 Miss Universe contest. The others were built over the next 37 years. Locsin did not live to see the designs of the last two buildings—a Promenade and an Arts Sanctuary Cluster. He passed away in November 1994, but his company continued the work to fruition. In his lifetime, Locsin built "71 residences, 81 buildings and

1 state palace. His major buildings include 9 churches and chapels, 17 public buildings, 4 apartment buildings, 6 hotels and 41 commercial buildings. His largest single work is the palace of the Sultan of Brunei, which has a floor area of 205,200 square meters" (Paredes-Santillan 2009, 4).

See also: Chapter 2: Overview; Marcos Dictatorship.

Further Reading

Paredes-Santillan, Caren. 2009. "A Study in Bipolarity in the Architecture of Leandro V. Locsin," *Journal of Asian Architecture and Building Engineering* 8 (May): 1–8.

Modern Architecture

If the churches symbolized Spanish authority, the legislative and judicial buildings, the post office, and city hall epitomized American colonial rule. These were the structures of civil government that the United States promised to train Filipinos in when it replaced Spain. American colonial officials vowed to replicate the "City Beautiful Movement" that changed American cities from urban landscapes littered with "poor housing, overcrowding, poverty, government corruption, a too-rich mix of nationalities, and seemingly uncontrolled urban growth" into new areas with "public edifices . . . new boulevards and parks" (Morley 2018, 50–51). Some of the leading members of this urban reform movement joined the colonial bureaucracy. They took the lead in "reconceptualizing" Manila and other cities. One of the results was the construction of civic buildings Art Deco style, that is, patterned after Greek and Roman structures.

Concrete had replaced wood as the foundation of the buildings. Early on, the Philippine Assembly, the Filipino equivalent of the American Congress, banned the use of palm as a building material because it was combustible. The Philippines also began to import steel and iron from the United States in significant numbers. In 1902, the value of these materials was US$2million, and this would increase by another US$2 million in the succeeding years. This description of a provincial government building by urban historian Ian Morely was representative of this new architecture: It had a "thirty-nine-meter front elevation and two-story edifice [built] from reinforced concrete, with colonnades on all four light pastel-colored facades, an overall lack of detailing, and a low pitched roof" (Morley 2018, 145). However, such buildings were not just facsimiles of American offices in places like Washington, D.C. The architects retained some of the Spanish features like conch-shell windows that helped cool buildings in a tropical place, and the fondness for detail and high rectangular arches when designing the interior. The first cohort of Filipinos who graduated in architecture likewise included local patterns to make concrete structures more attractive. The Metropolitan Theater of Manila, for example, combined the Greco-Roman style with patterns that showed Filipino imageries of fruits, flowers, and even bamboo.

Not all of the architectural structures introduced by the Americans were designed to project their political power. There were also the edifices to legitimize American rule. The foremost of these was the public school, one-storied, concrete, rectangular wooden structures often built in the town plaza facing the Catholic Church as if to show Filipinos that there was now an alternative secular source of knowledge better than the religious education provided by priests and nuns. The public schools also symbolized the United States' commitment to universal education, an issue that Filipinos fought for during the last decades of Spanish rule. The other visible representation of American benevolence was the "Sanitary Barrio," an urban scheme that separated homes by "subdivisions," with each subdivision having public latrines, baths, and laundry rooms.

The typical home that was built under this new urban scheme was to become the third option to the bamboo huts (of the poor) and the Spanish-type mansions (of the elite). The *tsalet* (from the European chalet) became the "ideal home" of an emerging Filipino middle class. The architects Gerard Licio and Mary Delia Tomacruz describe it as a "modular prototype house [with a] fire-resistive roofing material composed of diamond-shaped shingles molded from a mixture of equal volumes [of] cement, sand, and rice husk and reinforced by woven bamboo" and a floor that was likewise a blend of cement "implanted with . . . woven bamboo" (Licio and Tomacruz 2014, 23). These houses were divided from each other by a concrete wall or open gardens and, with their smooth-looking concrete structure, stood as a contrast to the Spanish *casas* (houses) that, with their stone features, looked rougher and older.

See also: Chapter 2: Overview.

Further Reading

Morley, Ian. 2018. *Cities and Nationhood: American Imperialism and Urban Design in the Philippines, 1898–1916*. Honolulu, HI: University of Hawaii Press.

Painting

The first "paintings" that were discovered in the archipelago were cave drawings of humans, amphibians, and animals. They supposedly represented magical powers and, in the case of the animals, the capacity to heal. There were 127 such drawings discovered, but only 51 were distinct enough for a person to see what they were representing. Archeologists would also discover rare precolonial paintings called *kut-kut* in Samar Island, central Philippines. The *kut-kut* consisted of a wall, plaster, or ceramic with decorative "scratching," which was then painted using a technique called "encaustic painting." This involved heating beeswax, adding colored pigments to it, and then applying this to the scratches. The *kut-kut* was said to be popular in Samar from AD 1600 until AD 1800, after which they disappeared, most likely as a result of the prohibition by Spanish colonial authorities of anything "heathen."

Much like architecture and sculpture, painting during the Spanish colonial period was mostly concerned with the representations of the Catholic religion. Paintings became essential paraphernalia during missions into the hinterlands, but where they were mostly used was as church decorations. Once the Spanish began using more durable materials to construct more towering cathedrals, the demand for painters rose as there were more parts of these large structures—especially the ceilings and additional altars—that needed adorning. These paintings drew a lot from the Baroque style that was popular in Italy, and which was well-suited to the vast interior spaces of cathedrals. The favorite subjects were Jesus Christ, the Virgin Mary, the Apostles, and different saints. Portrait paintings were complemented by religious scenes from both the Old Testament (Adam and Eve in Paradise, or Moses and the Ten Commandments) and the New Testament (the Last Communion of Christ, the Day of Judgment). Scenes from Filipino rural life were also favorites, and images of rivers, mountains, and forests were prominently featured on church ceilings.

The spread of church paintings was the result of some exigency. For one, the Spaniards in the Philippines had a hard time convincing painters from Spain to bring their talents in the farthest colony of the Empire. The only option was to tap local talent, and the Jesuits took the lead by adding painting in the syllabus for would-be-catechists. They were not wrong in their decisions. The friars' Filipino students did many of the interior paintings. Later on, when wealthy Chinese and Spanish mestizo families became interested in art in the 1730s, these Filipino painters began doing portraits for this rising class. In 1823, a newly formed *Academia de Dibujo y Pintura* (Drawing and Painting Academy) established the first formal art school. It closed 10 years later, but when it reopened in 1850, the wealthy Filipinos were already hiring Spanish instructors. Several Filipino artists had also gone to Europe to show their works. The most prominent of these artists were Juan Luna and Felix Resurrection Hidalgo. Their works were prominently displayed in the 1884 *Exposicion Nacional de Bellas Artes* in Madrid.

Murals and historical paintings were the most popular styles during the American colonial period. Filipino painters like Fernando Amorsolo produced warm portraits of rural scenes and the activities of farmers. Critics called these illusions that covered the "real" picture of a countryside wracked by poverty and peasant revolts. Amorsolo's defenders, however, argued that his paintings represented, on the one hand, the desire of Filipinos to "escape from a complicated reality into simplicity," and on the other hand, an attempt at using "traditional folk scenes as an embodiment of the imagined sense of nationhood" (Stancheva 2017). Regardless of who was right, there was no question that Fernando Amorsolo had elevated Filipino paintings to a new level of importance. He would cement his legacy further when the University of the Philippines School of Fine Arts hosted the "Amorsolo school."

Not long after, other styles began to challenge the hegemony of the Amorsolo school. Filipinos like Victorio Edades, who studied in the United States, returned as advocates of modernism, producing abstract works that were innovative when it came to colors, shapes, and lines and experimented with different materials, techniques, and processes. Modernism, which was also driven by social agendas, tended to be critical of the calmness of the Amorsolo school, favoring dynamic scenes and imagining the utopia that Filipinos should aspire to. All this did not mean the end of other, older forms. Classical paintings continued to thrive under the leadership of Guillermo Tolentino. He promoted the style after his return from the art academy of Italy. This time, however, Tolentino and his fellow classicists painted portraits of national heroes and nationalist moments. Finally, social realism, which first made its presence in the late 19th century, began to grow out of the modernist school with illustrators like Jorge Pineda and Jose Periera producing editorial cartoons that were openly nationalist. From this time on, the history of modern Philippine painting would be "marked by the conflict between [conservatives] and the innovative methods of the Modernists" (Stancheva 2017).

In the latter part of the 20th century, social realists who became attracted to communism began to display works that were critical of economic inequalities and repression by the government and laudatory of the "people's resistance." This movement was suppressed in the first years of martial law (Chapter 2), and many of its artists were jailed or killed. However, it was revived once the communist resistance became stronger. Painters used the mural to show the above subjects and also made famous the use of painted effigies of the Marcos dictatorship (often portrayed grotesquely) and the resistance. The nationalist restoration was not exclusive to the radicals. The Marcos dictatorship also avidly promoted Filipino art, depicting the "beauty" of precolonial cultures, with paintings that portrayed the president and Mrs. Marcos as the Filipino Adam and Eve and the Filipinos as their children. These and other similar paintings are plastered on many of the building projects of the regime. At the inauguration of a Philippine Heart Center in 1980, the first things visitors encountered was a mural of Mrs. Marcos that was supposed to be "an allegory of Woman, rendered in warm tropical hues, embodying maternal compassion, healing, and solace" (Quizon 2005, 293).

See also: Chapter 2: Overview; Marcos Dictatorship.

Further Reading

Aldor, Joel Lucky C. 2013. "Look Up: A Study into the Sacred Art of Philippine Church Painting." Presentation at the 8th Biennial National Convention of Church Cultural Heritage Project, Dapitan City, Diocese of Dipolog, Zamboanga del Norte. May 20–23.

Bunoan, Ringo. 2017. "Excavating Spaces and Histories: The Case of HShop 6." In *Art Archive 01: A Collection of Essays on Philippine Contemporary Visual and Performing Arts*. Manila: Japan Foundation. November.

Quizon, Cherubim A. 2005. "Indigenism, Painting and Identity: Mixing Media under Philippine Dictatorship." *Asian Studies Review* 29, no. 3: 287–300.

Stancheva, Yana. 2017. "Five Classics of Modern Philippine Art." *Artdependence Magazine*. November 7. https://www.artdependence.com/articles/five-classics-of-modern-philippine-art/

Sculpture

Precolonial Philippine sculpture consisted of wood carvings of ancestors and the spirits of the natural world. The Ifugaos in the northern mountains of Luzon Island had intricately carved sandalwood figures they called the *bul-ul*, whose roles ranged from protecting rice crops, defending the community from evil spirits, promising good fortune, and promoting fertility. In the southern Philippines, communities had incorporated Islamic imagery, and among the prominent carvings was the *buraq*, which was a statue of a winged animal that was a mix of a mule and a donkey. Islamic folk tales tell the story of the Prophet Mohammad as having ridden on the *buraq* when he traveled across the Islamic world. Spanish colonial sculpture was also heavy on religion. The interiors of churches were adorned with busts and full statues of Jesus Christ, the Blessed Virgin Mary, God the Father, angels, and saints. Sculptors used wood for the bodies and human hair and glass for the head. The attires of these religious figures were made of oil-painted woven textiles called *estofado* (from the word *estofa*, meaning silk that is quilted).

"Classicism," a style that emulated Greek and Roman statues, was the most popular method during the American colonial era. Aside from the monumental structures of government buildings, talented Filipino artists like Guillermo Tolentino carved out figures whose features reminded one of Michelangelo's statue of David. Tolentino, who studied at the Beaux-Arts School in New York City, was famous for sculpting the University of the Philippines' Oblation, a concrete statue of a near-naked man with outstretched arms and passion in his eyes which supposedly showed the UP student's selfless devotion to the nation. The other historic figure Tolentino carved was that of Andres Bonifacio, who led the revolt against Spain in 1896. Tolentino's Bonifacio had this seeming aloofness (a feature of classicism) that quietly evoked the strength, energy, and passion of a nationalist rebel. By the 1930s, however, Art Deco was in vogue, and symbols and styles representing industrialized America began replacing the elegant and romantic styles. This continued into the Republican era, especially alongside architectural shifts that emulated what was happening in the United States.

Filipino sculpture was further enriched in the postcolonial period when Tolentino's student, Napoleon Abueva, became the first to dip into "modernism," a style that combined a wide array of materials—from adobe, marble, and alabaster to bronze, iron, steel, and brass and even palm, bamboo, and local hardwood—for his works. Among his highly regarded works are the towering structure of the Bataan Memorial Cross, a remembrance of the fierce but fatal resistance of Filipino and American forces against the invading Japanese in World War II, a mural on the road to the University of the Philippines that pays tribute to higher education, and different portraits of Mother and Child using the materials mentioned earlier. Abueva became the inspiration for younger sculptors who tried their hands on modernism. For this, he was named "Father of Modern Philippine Sculpture" and given the title of National Artist of Sculpture by the government.

"Social realism" came into vogue in the late 1960s and remained significant for most of the 1970s, as artists grappled with the deepening crisis in Philippine politics, the Vietnam War, and Chinese communism. The first generation of social realist artists produced sculptures depicting peasant exploitation, the oppression of women and children, and the brutal dominance of U.S. imperialism in the Philippines. What was also notable during this period was the rise of women sculptors. Their works included portraits of Filipinas amid their struggles, expressions of sexuality, and dreams of a feminist future.

The nationalism promoted by social realist sculptors also engendered a movement to promote the use of bamboo, rattan, coconut bark and husk, hardwood, and other Indigenous materials in their works. This was not merely about "returning to one's roots" but a commitment toward environmental issues. Their works are prominently displayed particularly in "installation art"—a style that combines different two- or three-dimensional pieces in significant locations or smaller galleries.

See also: Chapter 2: Overview.

Further Reading

Bunoan, Ringo. 2017. "Excavating Spaces and Histories: The Case of HShop 6." In *Art Archive 01: A Collection of Essays on Philippine Contemporary Visual and Performing Arts*. Manila: Japan Foundation. November.

Ito-Tapang, Lisa. 2017. "Visual Arts Activism in the Philippines: Notes on a New Season of Discontent." In *Art Archive 01: A Collection of Essays on Philippine Contemporary Visual and Performing Arts*. Manila: Japan Foundation. November.

Tattoos

Filipinos have rediscovered tattoos and come to celebrate them as yet another expression of Filipino culture. Throughout the second half of the 20th century, the government had been successful in making Filipinos believe that tattoos were the symbols of the criminal underworld. Historians and anthropologists, however, have changed public opinion by showing how tattoos are evidence of the richness of precolonial cultures. They continue to do so, with the help of the Indigenous communities themselves. The latter have become more assertive of their identities and aspirations since the 1970s, when they found themselves caught amid the war between the government and insurgent groups. Today, it is not unusual to see young Filipinos proudly display the elaborate etchings on their bodies.

The local names of tattoos vary. In the northern highlands of Luzon, communities call them *batuk* or *patik* to describe the snake-like or lizard-like pattern or the sound that comes when a tattoo instrument pierces the skin. Filipino tattoos have a rich history that goes back to the precolonial era. Spanish chroniclers wrote about *Las Islas de Los Pintados* (the islands of the painted ones) in their first encounters with communities in the central Philippines. American colonial officials had also detailed the body tattoos of "headhunters" in the mountains of northern Luzon. The Spanish prohibited tattoos in the central Philippines as un-Christian, while the Americans appeared to tolerate them and instead focused on eliminating headhunting, which they deemed as a savage act. Thus, tattoos nearly disappeared in the lowlands and were only revived in the latter part of the 20th century while highland body etchings never really disappeared.

All these communities regard tattoos as important social indicators. They indicate ranks and accomplishments, rites of passage from child to adulthood, and military prowess; they may also be used as talismans or as badges of honor. The body etchings of chiefs displayed a whole panoply of symbols that glorified "military successes and shared pre-war and post-war ritual." They were the "material and ideological means for maintaining and expanding these warrior forces" (Junker 1999, 49) and were akin to today's medals of valor. Tattoos were added on a warrior's hands and wrists to indicate their number of kills. Those with animal figures were said to possess "magical powers while in combat" (Salvador-Amores 2002, 125). To women, they were testimonials of their fertility and marks of beauty. Young women usually got their first tattoo after their first menstruation. Among the Ilubos (in northern Luzon), a female shaman would engrave a tattoo on the forehead, cheeks, and nose of a married or pregnant woman. This was meant to protect her and her children from "evil spirits" of enemies who were killed in combat or in a headhunting expedition. These tattoos were seen as significant deterrents to attempts by dead ancestors to inflict fatal harm on children so that they could accompany their elders to the afterworld.

According to Analyn Salvador-Amores, tattoos were designed "to deceive the malevolent spirits and impede their machinations, and to foster the belief that the [marks] and other rites are effective means of protection" (Salvador-Amores 2002, 113). Finally, tattoos were the emblems of a community's identity and "the collective force of their social group, and a concrete realization of the sense of social unity of the members of the group" (Salvador-Amores 2002, 124). This sense of invincibility extended to their well-being—highland communities believed that tattoos protected them from diseases. A throat tattoo cured goiter, while a snake tattoo fought off cholera and malaria. These tattoos and their value remain strong among the highland communities even today, *sans* the headhunting.

The sun, snake, and crocodile are the favorites for tattoos as they are believed to project different forms of power or represent specific powerful deities. In carving out these symbols, a tattoo artist uses a piece of *calamansi* wood or a piece of a water buffalo's horn with four needles affixed on their sharpened edge. The artist then dips this instrument in a mixture of pigments and resin from a tree and taps it on the skin repeatedly, following a pattern that the artist imagined in their head or roughly sketched on the skin. The tapping is immediately followed by rubbing the wound with soot or charcoal powder to embed the color. An artist often spends days to weeks designing the tattoo since "the four-needle instrument . . . requires 90 to 120 taps per minute to render a design on the skin. The healing process takes one to three months"

(Salvador-Amores 2002, 108). After the tattoo is completed, the artist is paid either in cash or in kind (usually useful possessions like a loincloth or a wraparound skirt).

The persistence of "traditional designs" does not mean that communities have not adjusted to changes. When the Ilubos resisted the communist New People's Army, they marked their "acts of bravery" with body etchings of an eagle, which they copied from an old 1920 Philippine coin. Younger Ilubos and their counterparts in lowland central Philippines tattoo their surnames along with the designs, and the heart or a rose has become a trendy symbol. One unfortunate twist, however, is the disappearance of the traditional ways of etching designs. Many now preferred having their tattoos done with a machine.

See also: Chapter 6: Overview; Indigenous Peoples.

Further Reading

Carbonel, Loneza G., and Janette P. Calimag. 2016. "The Traditional Tattoos of the Philippine Cordillera Region: A Study on Their Differences in Appearance, Causes and Discursive Strength." *International Journal of Advanced Research in Management and Social Sciences* 5, no. 6: 1–8.

Demeterio, F. P. A., III. 2017. "The Fading *Batek:* Problematizing the Decline of Traditional Tattoos in the Philippine Cordillera Region." *Journal of the South East Asia Research Centre* 9, no. 2: 55–82.

Junker, Laura Lee. 1999. "Warrior Burials and the Nature of Warfare in PreHispanic Philippine Chiefdoms." *Philippine Quarterly of Culture and Society* 27, no. 1–2 (March–June): 24–58.

Salvador-Amores, Analyn. 2002. "*Batek:* Traditional Tattoos and Identities in Contemporary Kalinga, North Luzon, Philippines." *Humanities Diliman* 31 (January–June): 105–142.

Salvador-Amores, Analyn. 2014. *Tapping Ink, Tattoing Identities: Tradition and Modernity in Contemporary Kalinga Society, North Luzon, Philippines.* Honolulu, HI: University of Hawaii Press.

Wicker, Lane. 2010. *Filipino Tattoos: Ancient to Modern.* Atglen, PA: Schiffer Publications.

CHAPTER 13

MUSIC AND DANCE

OVERVIEW

Filipino performers are now a significant presence in the "Got Talent" shows in many countries. All one has to do is google a particular country's version of this viral production, and there will always be a Filipino—or someone of Filipino lineage—astonishing the judges. Filipino singers have also become sources of inspiration. Charice Pempengco (a survivor of domestic violence) and Mercelito Pomoy (who was abandoned by his family and grew up homeless) amazed Oprah Winfrey and Ellen DeGeneres, turning these global "cultural icons" into their enthusiastic promoters on the world stage. The 1973 rock band "Journey" underwent a renaissance 34 years later when it introduced a new lead singer, Filipino Arnel Pineda. The group discovered Pineda in a YouTube video that showed him singing at a *Shakey's* restaurant in Manila.

Much of these achievements have to do with Filipinos performing well in theater and in the movies. Filipina Leah Salonga and Filipina American Rachelle Ann Go played the role of "Kim" and "Gigi," respectively, in the Broadway hit "Miss Saigon." Go also played the role of Eliza Schuyler with another Filipina American, Christine Allado, as her sister Peggy in the London edition of the play "Hamilton: An American Musical." Young Americans and Filipinos have also never forgotten how movie and television stars Darren Criss (*Glee* and *The Assassination of Gianni Versace*), Mark Dacascos (*John Wick: Chapter 3*—Parabellum), Liza Lapira (*NCIS* and *Fast and Furious*), Lou Diamond Phillips (*La Bamba*), Shay Mitchell (*Pretty Little Liars*), and Hailee Steinfeld (*The Edge of Seventeen* and *Pitch Perfect*), among many others, have proudly acknowledged their "Filipino heritage." An equally important factor is the significant number of Filipino Americans (4.1 million as of the 2018 census) and the over 10.2 million Filipinos working and living outside of the Philippines.

It is not unusual to hear singing in many districts, cities, towns, and villages of the Philippines, thanks to the karaoke. As a British Broadcasting Company (BBC) writer put it, "it is an understatement to say that Filipinos love karaoke. Almost every Philippine home has a karaoke machine or a Magic Sing microphone. This digital mic turns your television into a karaoke machine. It's almost always a feature at birthday and holiday parties. And scores of bars and restaurants offer karaoke or videoke." The writer added, "even though frequent brownouts plagued the area, the family living in the [bamboo] hut had a karaoke machine because it's just that beloved in the

257

Philippines." She was not just describing karaoke singing in the Philippines, but in the middle of London as well, where migrant workers crooned to the latest Filipino hits that reminded them of home.

Filipino dance companies have also been well received in various global cities where they have been invited to perform. Some Filipino songs and dances have also found their way into American daily life. The most prominent of these is the *tinikling*, a bamboo dance that originated in Leyte Island in central Philippines and is inspired by a local bird called the *tikling*. The *tiklings* are known for their nimbleness as they fly from one branch to another or run through branches to avoid bamboo traps laid out by farmers. The dance emulates these movements with two bamboo poles placed alongside each other, over two pieces of smooth wood at both ends of the poles. Two people rhythmically tap the poles on the wood and then clap them while a guitar and bandurria band plays music. Two dancers—one male and one female—hop into the gap when the poles are "opened" and hop out as they are clapped. As the dance goes on, the tapping becomes faster, and the pair try their best to keep up with the pace. Today, a fair number of American secondary schools from New York City to Ames, Iowa, have made this dance a part of their physical education programs. Doctors have even recommended it as a way of preventing cardiovascular diseases. Gen-X and millennial Filipinos and Filipino Americans have come up with their 21st-century versions of the *tinikling*, the most trendy one being a combination of this "traditional" dance and hip-hop.

See also: Chapter 2: Overview. Chapter 8: Overview. Chapter 9: Overview; English. Chapter 11: Overview. Chapter 16: Overview.

Further Reading

Ang, Gertrudes R. 1978. "The Tinikling as a Literary Symbol of Filipino Culture." *Philippine Quarterly of Culture and Society* 6, no. 4: 210–217.

Cone, Stephen L., and Theresa Purcell Cone. 2016. "Dance in SHAPE America Is Alive and Well!" *Journal of Physical Education, Recreation and Dance* 87, no. 6: 3–4.

Heil, Daniel P., Alona D. Angosta, Wei Zhu, and Rhigel Alforque-Tan. 2019. "The Energy Expenditure of *Tinikling*: A Culturally Relevant Filipino Dance." *International Journal of Exercise Science* 12, no. 4: 111–121.

Lewis, Lisa. 2012. "The Philippine 'Hip Hop Stick Dance.'" *JOPERD* 83, no. 1 (January): 17–32.

Ong, Jonathan Corpus. 2009. "Watching the Nation, Singing the Nation: London-Based Filipino Migrants' Identity Constructions in News and Karaoke Practices." *Communication, Culture and Critique* 2, no. 2 (June): 160–181.

Sood, Suemedha. 2011. "Karaoke in the Philippines." *BBC*. August 12. http://www.bbc .com/travel/story/20110812-travelwise-karaoke-in-the-philippines

Trimillos, Ricardo. 1998. "Filipino-American Youth Performing Filipinicity." *Pahiyas: A Philippine Harvest* 1998: 53–56.

Bayanihan Dance Company

No other group in the Philippines is known for keeping alive the dances of the country than the Bayanihan Dance Company. "Bayanihan" in Filipino means to work together. The group was organized in 1956 by the president of a women's university and was formally introduced to the public a year later. With the help of the Philippine government, it made its international debut at the 1958 Universal Exposition in Belgium. The group has been called "the depository of almost all Filipino dances, dress and songs" (Singapore Embassy, Manila 2015), and its repertoire has ranged from the dances of highland communities to those of the Muslims in the south, and even the "lowland dances" including those that came from the Spaniards. When it performs a dance, the Bayanihan makes sure that the instruments, costumes, and other accompaniments associated with it are also on full display. Its founder, the educator Senator Helena Benitez, describes the Bayanihan as "symbolic of our people and an inspiration and reminder—that our national unity has for its base cultural diversity." She has asked Filipinos for their "sympathetic understanding, sincere appreciation, and a continuous search for beauty and goodness in each of these diverse sectors in order to bind and strengthen our nation" (as quoted by Castro 2011, 101).

The dance troupe pursued the above-mentioned objective in two ways. On the one hand, it made sure its audiences were "a mixed group, ranging from tourists to schoolchildren to socialites [i.e., mothers and daughters of elite families] to international dignitaries and more" (Castro 2011, 66). It does not only perform to these audiences, its members are also the willing teachers of these dances, training and guiding those interested—especially schoolchildren—on how to perform these "folk dances." This way the Bayanihan has positioned itself as the archetype of all Filipino dances and one of the most

Muslim Bamboo Dance. (Jose Gil/Dreamstime.com)

powerful symbols of Filipino culture. On the other hand, the Bayanihan has made performing abroad an integral part of its activities. In so doing it has positioned itself as an unofficial cultural "ambassador of goodwill," whose mission is to show foreigners the richness of the Philippines' diverse culture. The troupe has performed not only in theaters but also on television shows. The fame it "brings home," in turn, has supposedly inspired Filipinos to learn more about their cultures.

This reputation has often led Bayanihan officials to see the group as the inspiration for "other countries to exploit their own folk material for international theater presentation" (as quoted by Castro 2011, 66). The assumption that Filipinos easily identify with the dances has turned out to be a tad overstated. Ethnoreligious differences still persist in the country today, lowland bias toward highland communities remain, and a Westernized Filipino elite tends to patronize Filipino production of American performances. Bayanihan dancers may undertake outreach programs in schools, but hardly any of the students, especially those from the poor families, can afford to watch their performances. All this tends to temper the adulation, but despite these issues, there is general consensus that the Bayanihan has indeed helped "preserve" Philippine dances. The Philippine government has supported the troupe in various ways but it was only in 1998—40 years after it was founded—that Congress passed Republic Act No. 8626 designating the Bayanihan "the national dance company of the Philippines."

See also: Chapter 6: Overview. Chapter 8: Overview. Chapter 10: Overview; Fiesta. Chapter 11: Overview.

Further Reading

The Bayanihan Experience. 1987. Manila: Bayanihan Folk Arts Center.

Bayanihan Philippine Dance Company. 1970. New York: Dunetz and Lovestt.

Castro, Christi-Anne. 2011. *Musical Renderings of the Philippine Nation.* New York: Oxford University Press.

Guillermo, Lourdes E. 1964. "The Bayanihan." *Music Journal* 22, no. 2 (February 1).

Republic of Singapore Embassy, Manila. 2015. "SG50: Singapore-Philippines Cultural Evening in Manila." *Rappler* (August 25). https://www.rappler.com/bulletin-board/103713-singapore-philippines-dance-manila/

Santos, Isabel. 2004. *Bayanihan, The Philippine Dance Company: A Memoir of Six Continents.* Pasig City: Anvil Publishing.

Eraserheads

In 1989, four students from the University of the Philippines (UP)—Ey Buendia, Buddy Zabala, Marcus Adoro, and Raimund Marasigan—formed the band Eraserheads, with the name paying homage to a movie of the same title by iconoclastic director David Lynch. The group was part of the "Pinoy (Filipino) Alternative" movement, a bunch of musicians who found the widespread and dominant pop and rock-and-roll music not to their liking. Many of them were part of a lively underground college rock scene, singing songs that were introspective and concerned with one's anguish; they also sang about transcendent subjects including Mother Earth. Eraserheads' first album, *Ultraelectromagneticpop!* (a play on name of the weapon "ultraelectromagnetic top" used by rival robots in the Japanese anime *Voltes V*), was released in 1993. The songs from this album include "Ligaya" (Happiness), which is about trying to attract someone's attention, "Pop U!" and "Toyang," which are a playful take on an English invective, and the song "Too Young," which is associated with the crooner Nat King Cole. Another song, "Pare ko" (My Dude), became one of the more popular melodies because its lyrics included a commonly used obscenity. The unsuccessful attempt by the association overseeing the record industry to censor the song only enhanced the group's name.

Ultraelectromagneticpop! sold over 300,000 copies and introduced Filipinos to the underground college scene. The band's second album, *Circus* (1994), sold 200,000 copies a month after its release. Like the first one, *Circus* also had its share of controversy. A senator demanded that the song "Alapaap" (Cloud) be banned from being aired, alleging that it was promoting the use of drugs. As with *Ultraelectromagneticpop!*, such controversy helped boost sales, and *Circus* turned platinum. Eraserheads was now a household name; Filipinos had found their "Fab Four" (the Beatles). The band's most iconic song, however, is the 1995 "Ang Huling Bimbo" (The Last Bimbo), which was part of their third album, *Cutterpillow*. It is, as the blogger Retxed Demata narrates, the "story of a boy who would frequently visit a girl's house to learn how to dance. She would teach him numerous dancing techniques, and the boy would always be mesmerized to see her dance the El Bimbo. The boy begins to fall in love with the girl, but as time goes by, they eventually drift apart from one another. As they grow up to adulthood, the boy would hear news about his beloved, she is currently a single mother who works as a dishwasher in a hermitage, but as fate would have it, she would eventually die in a tragic car accident" (Demata 2016). The song closes with a regret that henceforth they could only dance El Bimbo in his dreams. The song's composer and head of the band, Ely Buendia, took the title from the French disco dance, "El Bimbo," and set the story in the 1970s when he was a kid growing up. *Cutterpillow* turned gold, and "Ang Huling Bimbo" would become the greatest Original Pilipino Music (OPM) song of all time.

Eraserheads now has an international audience, composed mainly of overseas Filipino workers (OFWs) and those who had immigrated to the United States and other countries. In March 1997, the band had its first international concert in Singapore, followed by an American tour in the summer. It closed the year by winning the International Viewers' Choice Awards for Asia at the September MTV Video Awards held in New York City. This was the first time a Filipino artist/band had won the award. Two other albums followed *Cutterpillow*, both released in 1997—*Fruitcake*, the group's only English album, and *Sticker Happy* were cut in Manila and New York and released during the MTV awards. Three more albums followed, and in between, the group performed in the Philippines and abroad. Buendia left the group in March 2002, but the other members continued to perform until it was finally dissolved in 2007. In July 2008, however, the group decided to reunite for a Manila concert that drew over 100,000 people. Eraserheads continued to go on worldwide tours for another 10 years, dedicating these to OFWs. In January 2018, Buendia tweeted saying he had graduated. The group's fans interpreted the message as him leaving the group for good. The ride was over.

Students were particularly big fans of Eraserheads, because the band members were like them and understood the ups and downs of campus life, matters related to their friends and lovers, and their struggles. They spoke the language of poor and middle-class students in public schools, and children from affluent families attending high-end private schools admired their rough jargon. However, there was also another distinguishing feature of the band. Eraserheads was formed three years after the fall of the dictatorship of President Ferdinand Marcos and the marginalization of the communist opposition to Marcos. Its members were UP students, but UP was no more the UP of the activists and the radicals.

As historian Lisandro Claudio put it, Eraserheads represented "the changing Pinoy (slang for Filipino) youth culture of the 1990s." He describes Buendia's lyrics as attempting to "seek normality after the politically charged years of dictatorship and resistance." His (Buendia's) UP "was not anymore the UP of communes, rallies, and political discussion groups." It was a UP where one made "fleeting but deep friendships" in dormitories and canteens. In the song "Huwag mo nang Itanong" (Please stop asking), Eraserheads sang about a class field trip to a pencil factory. According to Claudio, in the eyes of the group, the factory was no more "a site of worker alienation but student boredom and a Rorschach test of existential crisis." What made Eraserheads the best of all the OPM groups was its "ordinariness." The band's appeal lay in its songs. These were melodies about everyday life, with lyrics that read like daily conversations of the ordinary Filipinos.

See also: Chapter 2: Overview. Chapter 7: Overview; Generational Changes.

Further Reading

Caruncho, Eric S. 1996. *Punks, Poets, Poseurs: Reportage on Pinoy Rock and Roll*. Pasig, Metropolitan Manila: Anvil Publishing.

Claudio, Lisandro. 2012. "Were the Eraserheads the End of Cultural History." *GMA News Online*. January 1. https://www.gmanetwork.com/news/opinion/content/243261/were-the-eraserheads-the-end-of-cultural-history/story/

Demata, Retxe Bryanne. 2016. "Media Log 1." *E-Portfolio*. August 18. https://shreddingthroughthepages.wordpress.com/blog/

Gabrillo, James. 2018. "*Rak en Rol:* The Influence of Psychedelic Culture in Philippine Music." *Rock Music Studies* 5, no. 3: 1:18.

History of Dance

Filipinos love to dance. In the precolonial era, it was closely related to how communities interacted with spirits in their natural surroundings. The dance was either to reaffirm that connection or an atonement for transgressions committed against nature, or a plea for the spirits' help when communities were at risk. The end goal was to maintain or restore the balance between humans and nature. These spirit-community interfaces were often expressed through incantations/songs and a dance involving the entire community or a select group that addressed the spirits and kept the rest of the community informed.

Other rituals expressed through dances involved courtship and marriage, the celebration of a successful harvest, childbirth, and wars. Among the Bagobos who lived in southeastern Mindanao, one set of dancers acted like hawks preying on the other group that pretended to be baby chickens. Higaonon women in central Mindanao performed a dance called "dugso," to celebrate the harvest, while the Yakan and the Manobos in the southern Philippines imitated fish to celebrate an abundant harvest. In the northern mountains of Luzon, unmarried Kalinga (Ka-ling-gas) women imitated flying birds and bachelors pranced like roosters, either to get each other's attention or to celebrate weddings, a new child, and victories. The Aetas who lived on the foot of these mountains imitated the monkey when they had similar celebratory

The tinikling, a traditional Philippine folk dance. (Michael Edwards/Dreamstime.com)

performances, while T'bolis in central Mindanao imitated lost birds while looking for food or to show off their beauty.

The men of the Subanon (Sub-a-non), who lived on the foothills and mountains of western Mindanao Island, did pantomimes to win over a woman, and Higaonon couples imitated a pair of doves as they danced during the courtship process. The T'bolis' *Kadal Heroyon*, however, was the opposite—performed by young women to signal that they were ready for marriage. In the lowlands, a dance called the *tinikling* mimicked birds pecking on rice stalks, and the Manobos of southeastern Mindanao imitated squirrels, which they regarded as symbols of affection and friendship. As with love, there were also war dances. The Subanons of northwestern Mindanao prepared for war by dancing the *Sohten*. Among the Tausugs in the southwestern part of Mindanao, rival suitors did a war dance to win a woman's heart. The war dance was used differently by the nearby Maguindanaos (Ma-gen-da-nauws), using a wooden shield and swords (metal or wooden) to show their ability to protect their chief, the sultan.

Dances in the precolonial era were often accompanied by rhythmic clapping and percussion instruments (gongs) made out of copper and brass. The Muslims called their instruments *agong* and *kulintang*. The way one presented oneself through dance was also important. Muslim women wore the *malong*, a hand-woven dyed tubular high-waisted skirt, daily. The *malong* also served as a colorful prop when women danced to draw the sultan's attention or to instruct brides-to-be on the different ways it was worn. Kalinga (Ka-ling-ga) women of northern Luzon placed clay pots on their heads as they danced to the beat of a gong. Bamboos and rattan sticks were also frequently used as accompaniments. The Maranaos in central Mindanao were famous for the dance *singkil* (sing-kil), which used bamboos extensively. On the island of Leyte in the central Philippines, farmers clearing the forests to turn them into farmlands, or helping neighbors relocate their bamboo homes, would then be treated by those they helped with a song-and-dance performance called the *Tiklos*. This performance, which was meant to show the value of community, was often accompanied by bamboo flutes and a drum made out of the skin of a wildcat.

These dances survived the attempts of the Spaniards to condemn them as heretical practices, preserved by oral tradition (and secret performances). Many of them were revived during the American colonial period and adopted by modern dance companies in the postcolonial era. When the Spaniards tried to replace these dances with their own, Filipinos, particularly in the lowlands, accepted those cultural impositions and then improvised on them to suit their needs. Filipinos combined movements from the polka and the waltz to come up with a folk dance called the *polkabal*. They adopted the French square dance, improved on it, and came out with the *Surtido Cebuano* in the central Philippines, the *Pasakat* in a province just south of Manila, and the *Rigodon de Honor* and *Maria Clara*, which were performed during formal banquets. The Spanish *fandango* would have its Filipino equivalent in the *Pandanggo sa Ilaw*, a dance where the performers balanced three oil lamps (*ilaw*)—one on their heads, the other two on the back of each of their hands. The rhythmic Aragonese courtship dance *Jota* found its Filipino equivalents in the *Jota Batanguena*

(Ba-tang-gen-ya) and the *Jota Moncadena*, which were performed in the provinces of Batangas and Tarlac, respectively.

Filipinos embraced the Spanish religious stage plays called *Comedia*. Their version, the *komedya*, enthralled audiences with saints and priests fighting "heathens" armed with their amulets and "superstitious" idols. It was the Spanish *Zarzuela*, however, that Filipinos took to heart. This musical theater that turned Greek and Roman mythologies into folk songs and dances (*romanzas*) about Spanish romance was brought to the Philippines in 1878, and the Filipinos wholeheartedly embraced it. They wrote scripts and performed on stage. The Philippine *sarswela* produced plays about saints and stories from the Bible. The most popular of these performances, however, was the *moro-moro*, a depiction of the battles between Christians and Muslims (the Moros), which, as expected, ended with a Catholic victory. The 1896 nationalist revolution that eventually toppled Spain inspired scriptwriters to produce *sarswelas* with nationalist and revolutionary themes. The Americas put a stop to these, and by the end of the first year of their colonial rule, the *sarswela* reversed back to its religious themes. The American vaudeville would later upstage the *zarzuela*, and it would further gradually fade as a result of the movie theater.

Muslim-Christian battles found their way into precolonial dances. The *maglalatik* was a war dance between Christians and Muslims. Coconut shells were harnessed on the bodies of each group, and the battle was enacted by each side striking the shells of the other. The *maglalatik* was performed in town fiestas and religious ceremonies to honor Jesus Christ or the saints. In between celebrations, actors staged the *maglalatik* in people's homes for a fee. Like the *zarzuela*, the *maglalatik* was carried over the American and Republican period, and along the way, its original purpose—depicting a religious conflict—faded.

The Spaniards brought with them instruments and accessories from Europe, which became part of the local argot. They introduced Filipinos to the rondalla, guitar, piano, and violin, which became the standard accompaniments in dances and musical ensembles. Women dancing the *polkabal* or the *rigodon* were expected to wear the *zapatilla* (Spanish for small shoes), wave the *alcamphor* (the scented handkerchief that was a part of the *rigodon*). Spanish dance terms included *Malaguena* (the name of a town in Spain), *Katalona* (a region of Spain), *fandango*, and *La Jota* (the dance). Filipinos enthusiastically embraced the Mexican corrida dance *La Cucaracha* (the cockroach).

The Americans brought in the vaudeville and Filipinos accepted it enthusiastically, and the *bodabil* began to draw crowds away from the *sarswela*. The *bodabil* became the local version of the Broadway shows, and Filipinos began forming their version of folk, Western, and ballroom dances as well as the classical ballet. *Sarswela* actors added the vaudeville to their repertoire and with steamships—and later on airplanes—making travel easier, American, European, and Japanese dance groups and stars came to the theater to perform. Filipinos became adept in mixing local and foreign dances, and in 1939, a Filipino cast performed the first full-length ballet play, *Mariang Makiling*. A group of Filipino vaudevillians even performed a "Manila Cabaret" in the Dutch East Indies (now Indonesia), the British colony of Malaysia, and the Kingdom of Cambodia. Filipinos became the most important conduit of American music and dance in Asia.

The Americans also turned the ballroom from a place where members of high society danced the *rigodon* and the *sarswela* into a popular venue where everyone learned the rumba, ragtime, mambo, tango, as well as the Charleston and the foxtrot from American dancers. Filipinos also danced to the music of famous American jazz musicians like Louis Armstrong and Duke Ellington. By 1908, the largest dance hall, the Santa Ana Cabaret, opened and immediately attracted people from various classes and walks of life. Even students were known to spend their money doing ballroom dancing. The vaudeville, too, could not escape the influence of the ballroom. In 1921, a Cebu theater changed from doing dramas and ballets to circus-like shows that included acrobatics. So popular were dance halls that they became the target of conservative groups, which called them havens of immorality. A writer even wrote a *bodabil* script about a ballerina who became a prostitute after spending time in the ballroom. City governments soon began to regulate ballrooms under the pretext of eliminating immorality and protecting women's "innocence." Women who frequented the ballroom were now being described as people with loose morals and accused of becoming prostitutes. Ballrooms were associated with the "cabarets" in the red-light districts. Ballroom dancing, however, remained popular, and even places like basketball courts would be turned into ballrooms during special occasions.

Yet, like the *sarswela*, the *bodabil* and the ballroom paled in comparison to the crowds that were drawn to the movie theaters.

Filipinos continued to follow dance styles that were popular in the United States: the chicken and twist in the late 1950s and the disco in the 1960s. These were dances first spread through school programs, but once television became part of city life, noontime shows began to feature these different dance styles. Like in the past, a Filipino flare got added to these dances, as "Manila sounds" and "Original Pilipino Music" (OPM) was played on air and as Filipinos formed their rock-and-roll, hard rock, and disco bands. The Village People, one of the icons of American dance music, had their Philippine equivalent in "Hagibis" (Swift); and a group called "VST" became the disco version of the Bee Gees and the Motown group Earth, Wind and Fire, its popularity extending well into the 1980s. Hip-hop came to the Philippines in the 1990s, and before long, Filipino rappers began performing in music bars and on television.

As Filipinos began to excel as copycats of modern American dances, the Philippine government endeavored to "preserve" the dances from the colonial and precolonial periods. The Department of Education encouraged primary and secondary schools to include "traditional dances" in their music and physical education programs, while colleges formed their own "dance troupes" that specialized in dances from the precolonial and colonial periods. Today's Philippine dance scene is an admixture of different styles coming from the United States and older dance styles being kept accessible by the state but lately also by younger Filipinos and the children and grandchildren of Filipinos living or working abroad. Inspired by nationalist themes, they have "modified" dances to create their own versions, such as the hip-hop version of the *tinikling*.

See also: Chapter 10: Overview; Drinking and Dining; Fiesta.

Further Reading

Anderson, Quiliano Nineza. 2015. "Kundiman Love Songs from the Philippines: Their Development from Folksong to Artsong and an Examination of Representative Repertoire." PhD diss., University of Iowa.

Bautista, Regina Angelica. 2017. "Embodied Indigeneity: Translating Tradition for the Philippine Contemporary Dance Stage." MA thesis, York University.

Castro, Christi-Anne. 2011. *Musical Renderings of the Philippine Nation*. New York: Oxford University Press.

Fernandez, Doreen G. 1980a. "From Ritual to Realism: A Brief Historical Survey of Philippine Theater." *Philippine Studies* 28: 389–419.

Ng, Stephanie Sooklynn. 2006. "Filipino Bands Performing in Hotels, Clubs, and Restaurants in Asia: Purveyors of Transnational Culture in a Global Arena." PhD diss., University of Michigan.

Nicolasora, Michelle. 2014. "Kundiman: A Musical and Socio-Cultural Exploration on the Development of the Philippine Art Song." PhD diss., University of Memphis. May.

Villaruz, Basilio Esteban S. 1989. *Sayaw: An Essay on Philippine Dance*. Manila: Sentrong Pangkultura ng Pilipinas.

Villaruz, Basilio Esteban S. 2006. *Treading Through: 45 Years of Philippine Dance*. Quezon City: University of the Philippines Press.

Yagi, Ichiro. 1984. *The Evolution of Dance in Philippine Culture*. Manila: Entrepreneur Trading Corporation.

History of Music

Philippine songs are as rich as the country's print literature. Precolonial Filipinos had a rich oral tradition through which many of their stories were recited and sung. These poems/songs were about their gods and ancestors, their heroes, and their community life. By singing them, these communities were also able to pass the stories from one generation to another. The most popular accompaniment during these musical rituals was a metal gong that is now popularly referred to as the *kulintang*. Muslim Filipinos set them up in a rack while communities in the mountain regions of northern Luzon carry it with them as they sing and dance in circles. The Spaniards suppressed many of these songs—replacing them with Christian hymns—but preserved the *kundiman*, which are gentle love songs that would later become associated with the *harana*, a Mexican-Spanish serenading style that became widely popular among young Filipinos courting each other.

Both *kundiman* and *harana* remain popular to this very day, although the Filipino and Spanish songs have been replaced by American and more contemporary Filipino ballads. Another musical style brought by the Spaniards via Mexico was the *zarzuela*, a lyrical drama that was accompanied by the *rondalla*, a set of string instruments

(Mexican mandolins, bass guitar), and drums. The *zarzuela* gradually faded as a popular musical medium but the adoption of the *rondalla* as part of primary and secondary school activities enabled it to remain popular. Filipino groups outside of the country have even adopted it as a symbol of Filipino music.

Up until the advent of the karaoke, the *harana* was probably one of the most popular ways in which Filipinos sang as a community. In a *harana*, a group of young men would go to a woman's home to serenade her. If she was impressed, the balladeers would be invited into the home for snacks (and playful interrogation by parents); if she found the singing unappealing, either the singing group would find the windows closed on them, or, worse, get drenched by pails of water. The portable karaoke machine, however, has displaced the *harana*, with young Filipinos as well as their elders sitting around the living room or in the backyard to sing mainly American songs all night long. This has strengthened community bonding but at the expense of one of the most romantic pastimes in rural Philippines.

The Americans brought to their Asian colony folk, jazz, rhythm and blues (R&B), and musical stage shows like the vaudeville, which Filipinos enthusiastically adopted and even improved on. By 1912, Filipino jazz bands were doing well on their own, playing not only domestically but also across Asia. A Philippine Constabulary band was also performing in the United States and elsewhere. These overseas entertainers were the forerunners of today's Filipino musicians, playing in practically all parts of the world. Filipinos also showed remarkable talent in emulating American pop stars like Nat King Cole, Perry Como, Bing Crosby, Rosemary Clooney, and Ella Fitzgerald. They would also develop their own versions of pop music, a practice that has become quite pervasive and may be considered now as a matter of habit. In the 1950s, for example, a Filipino band called Rocky Fellers was even able to boost their song "Killer Joe" to 16th place on the American radio charts. The group is now remembered as having laid the groundwork for what people would call Pinoy (slang for Filipino) rock.

In the 1960s, American and British rock-and-roll stars like the Beach Boys, the Zombies, and Simon and Garfunkel had local copycats that went by the name "combos." Given their preference for ballads and pop songs, Filipinos naturally gravitated to the "softer" jazz and the Motown songs of Diana Ross and the Supremes. Even within jazz, the Brazilian band of Sergio Mendez—which plays "cool jazz"—was preferred to the complicated Miles Davis. When Western "heavy rock" and disco became the vogue in the 1970s, Filipinos too came up with their own versions. One of the most famous ones was a band called Juan de La Cruz—a moniker for the "average" Filipino. Filipinos hailed a mestizo named Eddie Mesa as the "Elvis Presley of the Philippines," and there were also balladeers who imitated Frank Sinatra, Tony Bennett, and other crooners.

The radical protests of the late 1960s changed the direction of the music scene. Radicals were resurrecting anti-colonial songs from the revolution for national independence, as well as during the communist-nationalist challenges to government in the 1950s. The classic example of an anti-colonial song that remains popular even today is "Bayan Ko" (My Nation), which was written in 1928 as a *kundiman*, and, according to literature professor Teresita Maceda, "became popular during the struggle for independence" (Maceda 2007, 391). Student activists sang the song during the 1960s before it disappeared during martial law. It "reappeared" in the early 1980s as opposition to the Marcos dictatorship spread across the country, with anti-Marcos forces portraying themselves not only as democrats but also as protectors of the nation. The musicologist Craig Lockard also cites the song "Babaing walang kibo" (Oppressed Women, Unite and Fight) as a melody that was seamlessly passed on from 1940, when it was first sung by communist guerrillas, to the 1960s and 1970s, when students sang it in their rallies.

Those who were less keen on becoming revolutionaries interpreted the protests as a sign that they ought to be "more Filipino" in their compositions (Talusan 2010). President Marcos also promoted this through a decree that required radio stations to play at least three Filipino songs every hour. The government then organized the Popular Music Foundation of the Philippines, which in 1977 held the annual Metro-Manila Popular Music Festival where singers and songwriters competed. The festival came to exemplify what would be called the "Original Pinoy [slang for Filipino] Music" (OPM). It lasted until 1985 and was revived a decade later under a new name—"Metro-pop Song Festival"; it lasted another seven years before it was discontinued for lack of widespread interest. The first groups to respond to the radicals and the Marcos regime were "folk singers," who initially sang Bob Dylan and Peter, Paul and Mary complete with the accents. The disco bands and the crooners immediately followed them. Filipino artists continued to use American singing styles but now sang their own original songs with Filipino lyrics. OPM was here to stay. From the late 1970s through the end of the century, OPM dominated the charts with songs about Filipino pride and love of country, apart from the usual ditties about personal relationships and families. Groups formed by university students spiced up OPM with songs that combined Filipino and English. "Taglish" became the voice of "Manila Sound." Outside the provincial capital, musicians likewise came up with songs in their respective vernaculars. There was even Bisrock, the short-lived Visayan music festival in Cebu City.

Unlike "Manila Sounds," these regional groups did not last long, as they were constrained by linguistic boundaries and lacked the resources that "Manila Sound" had. While the languages they used limited their reach, several bands did manage to break into the national scene with songs about the difficulties of provincial life and about the environment; these songs were also subtle critiques of the Marcos regime. Their national success, however, came with their decision to switch to Filipino. In the 1980s, as the regime weakened, these so-called "ethnic-folk bands" also became bolder in their condemnation of the regime. They would later be joined by pop bands. The term "protest songs" gained traction, particularly after the 1983 assassination of Marcos's political opponent Benigno Aquino Jr. (Maceda 2008).

When new wave, hip-hop, funk, "grunge" music, and "garage rock" became a global phenomenon in the 1980s, the Philippine music scene followed suit. All these genres were brought into the OPM canopy. There were bands that, in the late 1980s and early 1990s, preferred the anti-establishment venues. In such places, away from the purview of the mass media, they played punk and post-punk rock, heavy metal and death metal music. In 2000, younger Filipinos were drawn to hip-hop, reggae, and some R&B; rock and roll was out-staged, but not for long—Pinoy rock and roll returned on the scene with new bands performing in Manila as well as in provincial cities. Certain underground bands did have "conventional" listeners. In 2001, a band called "The Pin-Up Girls" signed a contract with an American record company and their songs were ranked high on several internet radio programs. The internet would increasingly become the outlet for Pinoy "indie" music.

See also: Chapter 2: Marcos Dictatorship; People Power Revolution. Chapter 6: Overview. Chapter 10: Overview; Drinking and Dining; Fiesta.

Further Reading

Buenconsejo, Jose S. 2017. *Philippine Modernities: Music, Performing Arts and Language, 1880–1941*. Quezon City: University of the Philippines Press.

Castro, Christi-Anne. 2011. *Musical Renderings of the Philippine Nation*. New York: Oxford University Press.

CNN Philippine Life Staff. 2017. "The 25 Best Filipino Love Songs of the Last 25 Years." *CNN Life*. February 20. https://cnnphilippines.com/life/entertainment/Music/2019/2/7/filipino-love-songs.html

Fernandez, Doreen G. 1980b. "Philippine-American Cultural Interactions." *University of the Philippines Third World Studies Program Discussion Papers 21*. December.

Fernandez, Doreen G. 1981. "Philippine Popular Culture: Dimensions and Directions. The State of Research in Philippine Popular Culture." *Philippine Studies* 29 (First Quarter): 26–44.

Fernandez, Doreen G. 1993. "Zarzuela to Sarswela: Indigenization and Transformation." *Philippine Studies* 47, no. 3 (Third Quarter): 320–343.

Hila, Antonio. 1989. *Musika: An Essay on Philippine Music*. Manila: Cultural Center of the Philippines.

Maceda, Jose. 1978. "Introduction to Philippine Music." *World of Music* 20, no. 2: 78–81.

Maceda, Teresita. 2007. "Problematizing the Popular: The Dynamics of *Pinoy* Pop(ular) Music and Popular Protest Music." *Inter-Asia Cultural Studies* 8, no. 3: n.p.

Maceda, Teresita. 2008. "Awit, pop, awit protesta." *Lagda*. Centennial Issue (December): 59–78.

Ng, Stephanie Sooklynn. 2006. "Filipino Bands Performing in Hotels, Clubs, and Restaurants in Asia: Purveyors of Transnational Culture in a Global Arena." PhD diss., University of Michigan.

Talusan, Mary. 2010. "From Rebel Songs to Moro Songs: Popular Music and Muslim Filipino Protest." *Humanities Review* 7, no. 1 (January–June): 85–110.

Tiongson, Lito, and Elena Rivera Mirano. 2016. *Musika: A Documentary on the Spanish Influence on Philippine Music*. Manila: Cultural Center of the Philippines. Video.

Kundiman

Kundiman is the linguistic compression of the Filipino phrase *"kung hindi naman"* (if it were not so) and is described as that "pure" Tagalog song that "expresses the lofty sentiment of love, and even heroism in a melancholy mood," as Francisco Santiago, the "Father of the *Kundiman* Song" put it (as quoted by Anderson 2015, iii). Its "inventor" was the composer Bonifacio Abdon, who wrote songs after being inspired by the music of the German composers Robert Schumann and Felix Mendelssohn and the Austrian Franz Schubert.

The *kundiman* has unsurprisingly withstood the deluge of different styles of American music, which became popular thanks to the radio, movie musicals, and television. Young Filipinos danced to the foxtrot, sang like Frank Sinatra, belted out Broadway hits like "New York, New York," and screeched like the Village People. Critics bemoaned the "Americanization" of Filipino culture but tended to portray this as the response of a spellbound generation. This is, however, just half of the portrait. The other side is that Filipinos have adapted the ballads of prominent American crooners and try to imitate them in fine detail or give these songs a Filipino "spin" by exaggerating a lyric or two.

A classic example of such adaptation is Frank Sinatra's "My Way," which is one of the most famous American ballads in the Philippines. It has also become one of the most dangerous because Filipinos have been known to kill each other over it; this is because the song's lyrics, as one Filipino put it, "evoke the feelings of pride and arrogance in the singer as if you're somebody when you're really nobody. It covers up your failures. That's why it leads to fights" (Onishi 2010).

Local composers also continue to come out with their romantic melodies. The most well-known composer was George Canseco whose 1971 *Kapantay ng Langit* (As High as Heaven) became one of the most frequently sung *kundiman* on television, in cultural presentations, and even at street corners where people converge for a drink or two.

The *kundiman's* popularity has ebbed in the era of hip-hop and garage rock, but once in a while, one hears Filipino millennials sing songs of their parents and grandparents in karaoke bars and parties. This suggests that the memory of this style of singing remains alive.

See also: Chapter 10: Drinking and Dining. Chapter 11: Overview; Vernacular Literature.

Further Reading

Anderson, Quiliano Nineza. 2015. "Kundiman Love Songs from the Philippines: Their Development from Folksong to Artsong and an Examination of Representative Repertoire." PhD diss., University of Iowa.

Hila, Antonio, and Ramon Santos. 1994. *"Kundiman." Cultural Center of the Philippines Encyclopedia of Philippine Art.* Vol. 7. Manila: Cultural Center of the Philippines.

Keppy, Peter. 2013. "Southeast Asia in the Age of Jazz: Locating Popular Culture in the Colonial Philippines and Indonesia." *Journal of Southeast Asian Studies* 44, no. 3 (October): 444–464.

Mojares, Resil B. 2006. "The Formation of Filipino Nationality under U.S. Colonial Rule." *Philippine Quarterly of Culture and Society* 34, no. 1 (March): 11–32.

Nicolasora, Michelle. 2014. "Kundiman: A Musical and Socio-Cultural Exploration on the Development of the Philippine Art Song." PhD diss., University of Memphis. May.

Onishi, Norimitsu. 2010. "Sinatra Song Often Strikes Deadly Chord." *New York Times.* February 6. https://www.nytimes.com/2010/02/07/world/asia/07karaoke.html

Pinoy Grooves. 2018. "Music and Magic—I'll Be There/Ain't no Mountain High Enough." December 4. https://pinoygrooves.com/2018/12/04/music-magic-ill-be-there-aint-no -mountain-high-enough/

Quirino, Richie. 2011. *Contemporary Jazz in the Philippines.* Pasig City: Anvil Publishing. 2011.

San Juan, Carolina de Leon. 2010. "From Vaudeville to Bodabil: Vaudeville in the Philippines." PhD diss., University of California, Los Angeles.

Nationalist and Political Music

Filipino nationalism is best expressed through songs that can reach a wider audience. Sacred litanies and rituals, many of which are sung in churches but also in public performances, became the medium to express anti-colonial themes during the Spanish period. In the American era and during the Japanese period, Filipino radicals used songs about independence, landlord exploitation, rural and urban poverty, and the resistance of Filipinos. According to the musicologist Craig Lockard, the communists' anti-Japanese army was also known as the "singing army" for having "utilized varied types of music for recruitment and propaganda as well as for battle hymns" (Lockard 1998, 141). This "people army" sang originals but also translated songs of European communists. They frequently sang the Italian communist song "Bella ciao," which talked about the plight of rice farmers. Anti-Japanese communist guerrillas adopted the melody but changed the lyrics. This time the song told the story of a military encounter with the "fascist" Japanese soldiers. Some of these songs were revised in the independence era, replacing the American "enemy" with the Philippine government. This time, the *"pasista"* was the Filipino soldier or constabulary officer. Student activists in the 1960s also adopted many of these songs as part of their "cultural struggle" against Western (read: American) cultural imperialism and the Filipino "ruling classes."

The *kundiman* evoked not only the romantic feelings of Filipinos but also their heartfelt affection for the nation, especially when defending it against colonialists. The most popular of these nationalist songs, "Bayan Ko" (My Nation), was a composition by Constancio de Guzman that had the lyrics of the great Filipino poet Jose Corazon de Jesus. It was first sung in 1928 just as Filipinos were to take over the reins of the colonial government fully; it became popular again at the height of the student protests of the late 1960s. In the 1970s, when both the government and its radical opponents were trying to show who was the more nationalistic between them, singers composed songs with the *kundiman* as an inspiration. The popular songs that the Marcos regime bandied as representing "Original Pilipino Music" included folk singer Florante's "Ako'y Pinoy" (I am a Filipino) and Heber Bartolome's "Tayo'y Mga Pinoy" (We Are Filipinos), which sought to instill a sense of pride regarding the country and its culture and the need to shed off all vestiges of colonial influence. In schools, nationalist students turned into *kundiman* the 1896 revolutionary hero Andres Bonifacio's *Pag-ibig sa Tinubuang Lupa* (Love for one's Native Land). However, these political *kundiman*-inspired songs were not the only ones being heard on the radio or during school programs.

The absorption of songs from the outside and the resilience of traditional songs are also seen among Indigenous communities. The late musicologist Jose Maceda wrote his thesis on traditional love songs called *bayuk*, where man and woman expressed their love for one another through embellished words and phrases. Muslim communities also absorbed external influences, and one could hear Arab-Islamic melodies sung alongside translations of songs like "Clementine" and "Jack and Jill," which the Americans introduced through the public school system. Scholars have even discovered hybrid tunes where Islamic lyrics were sung using American (and Christian!) melodies like "Battle Hymn of the Republic" and "Glory, Glory Hallelujah." When the Moro National Liberation Front (MNLF) waged its separatist war against the Philippine government (Chapter 2), there were songs extolling their *jihad* (struggle) to defend their communities and religion. When he recorded these songs, the anthropologist Tomas McKenna noticed that a lot of these "new folksongs" adapted the melodies sung by Filipino balladeers (McKenna 1998). When the ethnomusicologist Mary Talusan started listening to the songs of a certain "Johnson" that revolved around the theme of "Islamic renewal," she noticed that the MNLF singer had no problem mixing genres. He wrote in his Maguindanao language, but she immediately recognized the melodies came from Western stars like the Canadian songwriter Bryan Adams, Americans Johnny Cash, Buck Owen, Simon and Garfunkel, and Bobby Vinton, and the famous Filipino balladeer Eddie Peregrina (Talusan 2010). Johnson's songs remain popular to this day.

While love for the nation and "the masses" inform the above songs, the third type of political song is the campaign ditty sung during elections. Filipinos refer to them as "jingles" (obviously from the Christmas song "Jingle Bells"); the Filipino composer George Caparas describes them as "a candidate's musical score [whose] usefulness lies in its being a mnemonic device that compresses name, program, and platform in a two-minute rhyme" (as quoted by Lopez 2019). Journalist Elyssa Lopez regards the "jingles" as an "effective campaign tool especially for a politician who is courting an electorate that loves music and a population that treats singers like they are gods" (Lopez 2019).

More affluent candidates do not merely rely on a 2-minute "jingle." They often pay composers to allow their campaign managers to alter lyrics of popular songs to insert the candidate's name in them. These songs do "stick" in peoples' minds during the campaign season, but they are forgotten after the votes are counted: the "jingles" become YouTube videos, while the political lyrics of the popular ballads are disposed off and forgotten. Journalists call them "iconic" or "memorable," but a quick check on the YouTube websites will show that viewers hardly visit these. In the next election cycle, new "jingles" will be produced and lyrics extolling candidates will be incorporated into the popular songs of the period—and these, like the songs before them, will have a short shelf life.

See also: Chapter 2: Overview; Communism; Muslim Separatism. Chapter 3: Overview; Political Clans. Chapter 5: Overview. Chapter 6: Overview. Chapter 9: Overview.

Further Reading

Lockard, Craig A. 1998. "Philippines: Pinoy, Protest and People Power." In *Dance of Life: Popular Music and Politics in Southeast Asia*. Honolulu, HI: University of Hawaii Press.

Lopez, Elyssa Christine. 2019. "Most Iconic Campaign Jingles in Philippine Elections." *Esquire*. May 10. Accessed April 17, 2020. https://www.esquiremag.ph/culture/most-iconic-campaign-jingles-philippines-a00290-20190510-lfrm

Maceda, Teresita. 2008. "Awit, pop, awit protesta." *Lagda*. Centennial Issue. December.

McKenna, Thomas M. 1998. *Muslim Rulers, and Rebels: Everyday Politics and Armed Separatism in the Southern Philippines*. Berkeley: University of California Press. https://publishing.cdlib.org/ucpressebooks/view?docId=ft0199n64c&brand=ucpress

Talusan, Mary. 2010. "From Rebel Songs to Moro Songs: Popular Music and Muslim Filipino Protest." *Humanities Review* 7, no. 1 (January–June): 85–110.

Overseas Filipino Performers

Filipinos did not only become adept at integrating American music into their cultural context and adapting it accordingly. They also became the most active representatives of American music in Asia. Historical observers have mentioned Filipino brass bands performing in colonial Malaya in the 1890s, French Indochina in the 1900s, India in the 1920s, and Shanghai in the 1930s. On the eve of World War II, Filipino bands were also performing in Guam, Bangkok, Hong Kong, Okinawa, Taipei, and Singapore. In Kuala Lumpur, one of the most popular bands was a nine-member Filipino band, which performed in famous digs like the Great World Cabaret in Singapore and the Lucky Cabaret in Kuala Lumpur.

These bands disappeared during World War II but quickly returned in places like Japan, where Filipino bands played in nightclubs frequented by American soldiers (which soon also attracted Japanese clients). In 1954, a Filipino band playing backup to an American pianist, Larry Allen, distinguished itself by not only playing jazz (which the Japanese were learning very quickly) but also playing cha-cha, rhumba, and tango, among others. By the 1960s, Filipinos had expanded their selections to tango, Latin, and pop music. Club guests could now request Filipino musicians to play jazz; the latter could effortlessly shift between American Top 40 hits, songs sung by American crooners like Frank Sinatra, and even Latin music. In her study of Filipino musicians playing outside of the country, Stephanie Ng notes that "[m]any Filipino bands have a repertoire of over one-thousand songs" (Ng 2006, 90). Their popularity continues to this day, where Filipinos outnumber and outperform other Asian and even American bands in many hotel lounges across Asia. The nine members of a certain Romy Posadas Band used to be the main feature at Bangkok's Raya Hilton, where they played for seven years.

The Filipinos' edge over their Asian competitors was, of course, due to their English eloquence. They were the clear favorites of hotel guests, habitués of ritzy bars, and patrons of high-end restaurants, who were themselves either cosmopolitan locals or Westerners. By the end of the century, Filipino jazz expertise waned, but their proficiency in more "modern" music deepened. Bands were now singing the songs of Frank Sinatra, Elvis Presley, the Beatles, ABBA, Whitney Houston, Celine Dion, and Christina Aguilera. Critics may accuse them of lacking originality, but this has been of no concern to their listeners. Their mimicry, which was once confined to the bars and hotel lounges, is now "out in the open." It is likely to continue with the spread of social media technology.

See also: Chapter 10: Overview; Chapter 16: Overview.

Further Reading

Ackermann, Karl. 1918. "Big in Japan: A History of Jazz in the Land of the Rising Sun." *All About Jazz*. October 29. https://www.allaboutjazz.com/big-in-japan-a-history-of-jazz-in -the-land-of-the-rising-sun-part-1-by-karl-ackermann.php

Barendregt, Bart, Peter Keppy, and Henk Schulte Nordholt. 2017. *Popular Music in Southeast Asia: Banal Beats, Muted Histories*. Amsterdam: Amsterdam University Press.

Fernandes, Naresh. 2015. "The Forgotten Story of a Filipino Swing Musician in 1930s India." *Quartz India*. May 5. https://qz.com/india/398192/the-forgotten-story-of-a -filipino-swing-musician-in-1930s-india/

Keppy, Peter. 2013. "Southeast Asia in the Age of Jazz: Locating Popular Culture in the Colonial Philippines and Indonesia." *Journal of Southeast Asian Studies,* 44, no. 3 (October): 444–464.

Ng, Stephanie. 2013. "Performing the 'Filipino' at the Crossroads: Filipino Bands in Five-Star Hotels throughout Asia." *Modern Drama* 48, no. 2 (April 5): 272–296.

Ng, Stephanie Sooklynn. 2006. "Filipino Bands Performing in Hotels, Clubs, and Restaurants in Asia: Purveyors of Transnational Culture in a Global Arena." PhD diss., University of Michigan.

Yamano, MeLe. 2018. *Theatre and Music in Manila and the Asia Pacific, 1869–1946*. New York and Amsterdam: Palgrave MacMillan and Transnational Theatre Histories.

Singkil

Every troupe has a "traditional" dance in its inventory of dances and this almost always includes the *singkil*. *Singkil* originated from the Maguindanao, the second-largest Muslim ethnolinguistic group in south-central Mindanao, but was appropriated by the neighboring Maranaos who then claimed it as their own. The Maguindanaos translate *singkil* to mean the entangling of dancers with "jewelry and ornament worn on their anklets, while the Maranaos use the word to describe how one gets entangled in vines and stumbles over an uneven surface full of rocks and cut trees." *Singkil* has become recognized as a national dance mainly because the Bayanihan Dance Company has made it one of the high points of its repertoire.

Singkil tells of a hero whose philandering ways worried the fairies so much that they decided to cast a spell on him so that he would only be interested in one princess. The fairies then kidnapped the princess and placed her at a certain spot for the hero to discover. They then caused an earthquake that would force the princess to flee the area, prompting the hero to get her to safety. Their chase takes them through rocks and fallen trees, and it is this pursuit that the *singkil* is all about. One variation of this is where instead of a chase the dance is about the courtship between a prince (the sultan, possibly the hero) and a princess (the Bai Labi), where the former does all he can to get the attention and hopefully the nod of the latter.

In this courtship/chase, the prince and the princess dance through two pairs of crisscrossing bamboo poles which are clapped in by four men, one at each end of the two poles. Both the prince and the princess are elegantly dressed, with the prince waving around a multicolored bright handkerchief while the princess waves an equally multicolored fan with her hand. Sometimes the prince dances with a wooden shield and a Muslim sword called the *kris*, which he waves over his head. Dancing alongside the princess is a maidservant who carries a yellow umbrella to protect the former from the sun. An "orchestra" of different small and big gongs called the *kulintang* provides the melody and the rhythm that accompany the bamboo clapping.

The two step deftly in between each bamboo pair when the pair is separated and then step out as the poles are clapped. They do this as they move around from one pair to another. The prince must do his best to catch the princess's eye, while the latter, who comes from a conservative family, must show her feigned dislike by keeping her chin up (a pose that the Maguindanaos say was adapted from the way the turtle dove raises its head when it feels someone approaching). The clapping starts slow with the princess and her escorts doing the *singkil* first; then it starts to go faster once the prince joins. This is to enhance the tension arising from the meeting of the two and the gradual winning over of the snobbish princess. The princess finally agrees to marry the prince, and their union is celebrated together with the couple's families and their entourages dancing around them.

The Bayanihan has come to represent the *singkil* in its best form. This has opened the dance company to some criticism that its version of the dance has deviated significantly from the Maranao or Maguindanao original. Ironically, it has also been the

Bayanihan that brought the *singkil* to national, and eventually international, attention. This began when two members of the troupe got interested in *singkil* in the 1950s while observing how it was danced by Maranao women. The researchers then created a story line for the dance based on a Maranao epic called the *Darangen*, which is the story of the chase. The Bayanihan performed the *singkil* in 1958, inaugurating what ethnomusicologist Ricardo Trimillos refers to as the "era of dance diplomacy" (Trimillos 1989, 104).

With such theatricalization, local Filipino folk dances that were previously a part of physical education or of social/cultural events of village communities have been recreated into a spectacular theater production and brought to the world as part of a burgeoning national discourse. In 1958, Bayanihan presented a Philippine folk dance production at the Brussels Expo and received international recognition. Bayanihan's success on the world stage made Philippine folk dance, as well as Bayanihan, world famous. Inspired by the company, many folk dance groups, some of which already existed and others that are newly formed, have been to cultural and diplomatic missions abroad. As Trimillos stated, "the Philippine was one of the first Asian nations to use dance as a primary means of establishing international standing" (Trimillos 1989, 104) to project and promote a new, "beautiful" image of the Philippines around the world. This subsequently brought about what Trimillos called an "era of dance diplomacy" in the 1960s and 1970s (Trimillos 1989, 104); this, in turn, reinforced the idea of the Bayanihan's version as representative of this Muslim dance.

See also: Chapter 10: Overview; Chapter 16: Overview.

Further Reading

Ellorin, Bernard Barros. 2016. "Staging Autonomous Ethnicities: The 'Bayanihan Effect' and Its Influence on the Standardization of the Performing Arts from the Muslim Societies of Southern Philippines." *ICTM Study Group on Performing Arts of Southeast Asia: Proceedings of the 4th Symposium*, School of the Arts, Universiti Sains Malaysia, Penang, Malaysia.

Namiki, Kanami. 2011. "Hybridity and National Identity: Different Perspectives of Two National Folk Dance Companies in the Philippines." *Asian Studies* 47: 1–24.

Trimillos, Ricardo R. 1989. "The Changing Context of Philippine Dance Performance." In B. T. Jones (ed.), *Dance as Cultural Heritage*. Vol. 2. Dance Research Annual XV. CORD.

CHAPTER 14

FOOD

OVERVIEW

Food mediates the Filipinos' world. A host welcomes the guest by asking if they have eaten. Meetings have long morning and afternoon breaks where organizers serve a series of snacks. Family members coming home ask the usual "What's for dinner?" After a visit, family friends, friends and other guests are made to take home some of the lunch and dinner meals so that their kin can have a chance to taste the host's food; this, in a way, is also to subtly convey to them what they missed. Doreen G. Fernandez and Edilberto N. Alegre note that when food "talks," it helps one "always say the right thing" (Fernandez and Alegre 1988, 15). When Filipinos celebrate holidays, they are less concerned with what the occasion is all about and more concerned about what food will be served by the host family, or in the case of a town fiesta, the whole community. Identities can be about religion, language, and location, but they are also about the food that families, communities, and regions are known for. When people are asked where they come from, among the subsequent questions will be what food they eat, how these are cooked, and whether these are special cuisines or everyday chow.

One does not enjoy a full meal without rice; rice is what helps "push the food down" (*pantulak ng kanin*). The Filipina food aficionado Gilda Fernando-Cordero has one of the best descriptions of how Filipinos value rice: "Rice is the main bulk of the Filipino meal. The humblest meal is possible with just a cup of rice, a piece of salt, fish and a raw tomato. With a dousing of some meat sauce or some *bagoong*, a cup of rice is lunch or supper" (Cordero-Fernando 1976, 13). Having rice as the foundation also enables Filipinos to have "adventurous palates and consume many items which others, especially Westerners, may fear" (Magat 2002, 71). This culinary intrepidness also helps explain the different delectable blends of Filipino cuisine that most food aficionados ascribe to the Philippines being in food-rich Asia and the country's two colonial experiences. Cordero wrote that "Filipino food was prepared by the Malay settlers, spiced by commercial relations with Chinese traders, stewed in 300 years of Spanish rule and hamburgered by American influence on the Philippine way of life. The multiracial features of the Filipino—a Chinese-Malayan race, a Spanish name, and an American nickname—thusly inform Philippine cuisine, producing dishes of oriental and occidental extraction" (Cordero-Fernando 1976, 9).

The Asian influence is strongly evident in the popular noodle dish, *pancit* (from the Chinese *pian-e-sit*), another dish called *balut* (fertilized duck eggs like that in Vietnam), and the use of coconut oil. The gastronomic outcome of 300 years of Spanish rule links the Philippines to the Latin American colonies through a series of foods with Iberian names (*paella, leche flan,* or *pan de sal*) and ingredients like *tamales* (tomatoes). The Americans brought in the canned milk, and Filipino cuisine was made more pleasurable with the invention of sweets like the *buko* pie (young coconut pie), the adoption of American meals like chicken salad, hamburgers, and French fries, and the introduction of potatoes and mayonnaise. These would develop their own variations as Filipinos cooked and feasted on them. Even the "fast-food" industry which produces standardized fare had to add a Filipino tone to their staples: hence, rice could replace French fries, and banana ketchup was offered alongside tomato ketchup.

If a Filipino was therefore asked by an outsider what exactly is Filipino fare, they would most likely have a hard time answering this question because of the variety of cuisine that she is exposed to. Philippine food ways have always been *mestizo*, that is, mixed and continuously open to further mixing. This is the reason for its popularity; being mestizo is also what makes it delicious. This explains, for example, why Filipino chefs are not finicky about what people may do to the meal they serve. They would gladly set aside their expertise and watch how their cooking is "embellished and enhanced, adjusted and adapted to the individual tastes by means of the . . . dipping sauce. [The Filipino chef] is professing no superiority; the consumer has a part in the creation of the dish just as he has" (Fernandez and Alegre 1988, 14).

However, if pressed for an answer to the question "which is Filipino food?," a Filipino would say, the *adobo*, the *balut*, the *pancit*, the *sinigang*, and the *lechon*.

In Hawaii, every ethnic group knows of each other's cuisine, and with Hawaiian-Filipinos, the first food that comes to mind is *adobo*. The dish is made by marinating pork, chicken, or the combination of these meats with vinegar, garlic, bay leaf (sometimes laurel), and peppercorns. The longer it is marinated, the tastier the *adobo* as the different ingredients are given time to blend. By its name, *adobo's* origins are Spanish as well as Mexican. The Spanish have a pickled dish called *adobado*, from whence came the name *adobo*, but the connections end there. Spanish *adobado* refers to the process of making the pickled dish, while the Filipino *adobo* is the food itself. The Mexican *adobo* consists of different kinds of chilis mixed with garlic, tomatoes, cumin, cinnamon, oregano, cloves, pepper, turmeric, vinegar, lemon juice, and broth. This mixture, however, is a sauce, while the Filipino *adobo* is meat marinated in a mixture of soy sauce, vinegar, peppercorns, bay leaf, and crushed garlic, some for 2 hours, others overnight.

The ideal way of cooking *adobo* is to simmer it. Some Filipinos prefer a "wet *adobo*," that is, having a substantial amount of sauce that, if poured on rice, adds more taste. Others, however, often cook *adobo* till it is dry and crispy, and then fry it in oil. Those who want to cook *adobo* fast do so by adding soy sauce. Mixing in coconut milk gives the *adobo* a different taste. Filipinos do not always use chicken or pork for *adobo*. Coastal communities use squid or shellfish for the meat, and rice farmers, who often find pork or chicken too expensive, make *adobo* out of greens like the ubiquitous and nutritious "swamp cabbage" (*kangkong*). As mentioned, *adobo* is best eaten with rice. If there are leftovers, these are either refrigerated or kept on the pot (in case of "wet adobo"). If this is the meal for the next dinner or lunch, leftover *adobo* is heated up, or in the case of dry *adobo* refried with oil. There is universal agreement among Filipinos that leftover and saved *adobo* comes out tastier than the first time around.

See also: Chapter 10: Overview.

Further Reading

Cordero-Fernando, Gilda. 1976. *The Culinary Culture of the Philippines.* Manila: Vera Reyes Inc.

Daza, Nora, and Michael Fenix. 1992. *A Culinary Life: Personal Recipe Collection.* Pasig City: Anvil Publishing.

Fernandez, Doreen G. 1991. "Balut to Barbecue: Philippine Street Food." *Oxford Symposium on Food and Cookery.* London: Prospect Books

Fernandez, Doreen. 2000. *Palayok: Filipino Food through Time, on Site, in the Pot.* Hong Kong: Bookmark.

Fernandez, Doreen G. 2008. *Tikim: Essays on Philippine Food and Culture.* Pasig City: Anvil Publishing.

Fernandez, Doreen G., and Edilberto N. Alegre. 1988. *Sarap: Essays on Philippine Food.* Manila: Mr. & Ms. Publishing Company.

Magat, Margaret. 2002. "Balut: Fertilized Duck Eggs and Their Role in Filipino Culture." *Western Folklore* 1, no. 1 (Spring).

Sabanpan-Yu, Hope. 2007. "Cebuano Food Festival: A Matter of Taste." *Philippine Quarterly of Culture and Society* 35, no. 4 (December): 384–392*l*.

Valdez, Maria Luisa A. 2014. "Parada ng Lechon in Balayan, Batangas to Honor St. John the Baptist: An Ethnographic Study." *Asia Pacific Journal of Multidisciplinary Research* 2, no. 3 (June): 96–102.

Appetizers

Filipinos love the most unusual of cuisines. *Sisig*, for example, consists of the skin, cartilage, and meat of a pig's head, which are boiled, grilled and fried. The pig's head is first boiled to tenderize it, then stripped out and chopped, and then grilled or broiled or fried. As its sizzles, a cook adds lemon juice, chili peppers, and onions and transfers the mix onto a hot plate. She then cracks a raw egg on top of the meal. The cuisine can be eaten as part of a whole meal, but it is also served as an appetizer in drinking "sessions." Its origins are Spanish and it used to be provincial food. *Sisig's* history dates back to the 17th century, when it was a culinary specialty of Pampanga

Sisig—from Pampanga province street food to high-end Filipino-American restaurant appetizer. (Ppy2010ha/Dreamstime.com)

province. It was first known as a marinade of lemon juice, vinegar, salt, and pepper for unripe mangoes, papayas, or guavas.

The shift from fruits to meat had something to do with the food waste that was coming out of Clark Field, the American air force base. The food waste included pig's head. In keeping with American food habits at the time, the appendages of meat, fish, and even vegetables were disposed of due to the belief that they were unpalatable. Filipinos in neighboring Angeles City seized on this culinary "excess" and turned the pig's head into a savory, quick, food-stall meal. Stall owners then added the hot plate to keep the head hot and warm. *Sisig* came to be when, in 1974, a stall owner, Ms. Lucia Cunanan, experimented with the pig's head, eventually turning out the way of preparing *sisig* that everyone is familiar with now. It was also around this time that the government was vigorously pursuing its infrastructure program to link Manila and the northern provinces, turning places like Angeles City into stopovers. Invariably, travelers found their way to Ms. Cunanan's stall. News spread about this cheap, tasty concoction of pig-head parts doused in vinegar or lemonade, chili peppers, and onions. Within a year or so, *sisig* found its way to Metropolitan Manila; it was first offered in restaurants specializing in Pampanga food and then spilt over to other restaurants.

As *sisig's* popularity spread, the cuisine was inevitably opened to innovations. Today, the meat could come from chicken, squid, tuna, mussels, tofu, ostrich, crocodile, or frog. Some would chop hard-boiled eggs, chicken or pork rinds, and, for the daring, it could be beef's brains, laced not with lemonade or chili but mayonnaise. When the famous chef and gourmand, the late Anthony Bourdain, featured *sisig* in his show, this stall food made of unlikeable animal parts became an international phenomenon. This further whetted local curiosity, and once Filipinos abroad fell for it, *sisig* mutated into yet another culinary symbol of the Filipino heritage. *Sisig's* creator, Ms. Lucia Cunanan, suffered an unfortunate fate when she died under suspicious conditions (some said she committed suicide, others point to her husband as the prime suspect). Today she is enshrined as one of Pampanga province's heroines.

Another Filipino appetizer is *chicharon* (chi-cha-ron)—deep-fried, lightly salted, sometimes-spiced pork rinds. Unlike *sisig*, which seems to be a favorite of Filipinos in Luzon Island, *chicharon* is a nationwide dish. When eaten, the *chicharon* must be dipped into a vinegar-chili or soy sauce-garlic-chili potion. *Chicharon's* provenance is Iberian and one can easily spot its similarity to the Spanish *chicharron* and the Portuguese *torresmo*; but there are also Latin American and Caribbean versions of these delicious crackling rinds in Argentina, Brazil, Colombia, Mexico, Venezuela, Panama, Peru, Belize, and Cuba. Filipinos, however, have—once again—"experimented" with this seemingly simple cuisine, trying it on water buffalo, chicken and tuna skins (purportedly as healthier versions), and on other parts of the pork. A variation called *chicharong bulaklak* (flowered chicharon) is crafted out of the membrane lining in the stomach. These varieties of *chicharon* are sold in stalls and bus terminals and used as garnish in *pansit*. But it will always be regarded as an appetizer that is enjoyed with beer during what Filipinos call their "drinking sessions."

The third most popular of the appetizers is the *kinilaw* (kin-il-laau), a raw fish delicacy that is described as the Filipino version of the ceviche. This dish consists of cubed fresh fish (the most preferred are mackerel, tuna, swordfish, milkfish) mixed with coconut or cane vinegar, along with either lemonade or the juices from lime and a local citrus fruit call *biasong*, tamarind, and a local plum called *sinegwelas* (sin-e-gooey-las). Once all these are blended together, a cook puts in crushed small red-hot chilis, ginger, onions, and pepper. These two sets of combinations are supposed to give the *kinilaw* its tartness. Then, to remove the fish taste in the mix, the grated fruits of the *atuna racemose,* the *heriteria sylvatica* trees, and a young coconut are added. Filipinos say that the *kinilaw* is, in fact, not a raw dish but "cooked" by the vinegar and the spices and fruit nectars that surround it.

In the northern part of Luzon Island, foodies use animal meat, including the skin, in lieu of fish and this is called *kilawin* (kill-a-win). These meats are grilled or boiled rare to medium rare. They are then chopped and transferred into a bowl to be garnished with sliced onion, coconut vinegar, ginger, garlic, bay leaves, and fish sauce. Some Filipino communities prefer their *kilawin* bitter and mix in the bile from the animals gall bladder or squeeze the liquid of the grass in a cow's stomach.

Food scholars and enthusiasts warn their readers not to be deceived by the simplicity of *kinilaw's* preparation. They argue that the dish actually exemplifies what travel writers call "the nuances of Filipino cooking, from its many influences around the world to the melding of contrasting flavors—sourness, sweetness, bitterness" (Cerini 2019). Regions can also be distinguished by how they "cook" their *kinilaw*. Much of this distinction can be traced to the cuisine's long history. In their book *Kinilaw: A Philippine Cuisine of Freshness,* the food writer Edilberto N. Alegre and food historian Doreen G. Fernandez suggest that *kinilaw* is one of the oldest foods in the archipelago based on archeological findings of fish bones and residues of *tabon-tabon* that were dated AD 1200. *Kinilaw,* therefore, can be regarded as "the foundation for understanding Filipino cuisine" (as qouted by Cerini 2019).

See also: Chapter 10: Overview.

Further Reading

Alegre, Edilberto N., and Doreen Fernandez. 1991. *Kinilaw: A Philippine Cuisine of Freshness*. Manila: Bookmark.

Cerini, Mariana. 2019. "It's Kinilaw, the Filipino Answer to Ceviche." *Taste*. July 9. https://www.tastecooking.com/kinilaw-filipino-answer-ceviche/

Desserts

Of the many desserts that are of Filipino origin or local versions of sweets from abroad, two stand out—*leche flan* and *halo-halo*. *Leche flan* is the standard post-meal sweet course that families put out, especially during special occasions. *Leche flan* is the Filipino edition of the French *crème caramel*. However, the name is Spanish in origin (from *flado,* which means custard). It is a milk custard that "sits" on a layer of caramel; it is slowly baked sitting on a pan of hot water or steamed. When served, the host inverts the *leche flan* so the caramel is on top. Food enthusiasts suggest that what makes this dessert distinctly Filipino is the preference for using condensed milk instead of evaporated milk, which thickens the custard. This is where they say that the Americans contributed to the dish: they introduced canned milk, which greatly facilitated the *leche flan's* preparation (uncanned milk deteriorates faster). As expected,

Leche flan dessert. (Junpinzon/Dreamstime.com)

Filipinos experiment with the dish, and the most common variation is adding rinds of lemonade or lime to give the *leche flan* its zest and "brightness."

Following closely behind is *halo-halo* (Filipino for mixed)—layers of yam, roasted rice, starch from the plant *sago*, pieces of *leche flan*, boiled roots, gelatin strips, jackfruit, sweetened beans, and lychees placed at the bottom of a tall glass and then covered with crushed ice, soused with evaporated milk, and topped with a scoop of ice cream. Its origins can be traced back to the Japanese community in the prewar period, whose stalls and restaurants were selling *kakigori*. *Kakigori* was a glass of azuki (mung) beans combined with crushed ice, sugar, and condensed milk. Very few Filipinos had tasted *kakigori* until the Americans built the first ice plant. It was not long before *kakigori* had morphed into *halo-halo*, by the addition of other fruits to the ice and the milk.

Filipinos are fond of *halo-halo* because every time they feast on this dessert, the taste comes out different. There are also regional variations of the dessert. People in the southern Luzon region of Bicol add cheese to *halo-halo*, while in the central Visayas they add water buffalo milk. In northern Luzon, the *Iloko de halo-halo* uses the meat of a young coconut, enjoyed for its mushiness. *Halo-halo* gained international stature when the late Anthony Bourdain described the dessert as "oddly beautiful" when he tasted it for the first time in a Jollibee restaurant.

See also: Chapter 10: Overview.

Further Reading

Besa, Amy, Romy Dorotan, and Neil Oshima. 2014. *Memories of Philippine Kitchens.* Revised and updated. New York: Stewart, Tabori and Chang.

Drinks

A breakfast drink is not always coffee. Filipinos also love to eat their breakfast with *tsokolate* (tso-ko-lah-te), a thick hot chocolate made of 2–3 cacao tablets (*tablea* in Filipino). The cacao beans are picked up from the tree pods and their skins are peeled and then dried under the sun. These dried beans are roasted for about 3–4 hours, ground until the oil comes out, and the now-soft dough is blended with sugar and formed into the *tablea*. Once it is liquefied, the mix is twirled energetically with one's palms using a wooden baton called *batirol* until it becomes frothy. If one does not have a *batirol* (ba-tee-rol), one can boil the cocoa tablets until they dissolve. After the milk and sugar are added, the *tsokolate* is transferred to individual cups and can be drunk like espresso coffee. It also can be used as a dipping cup for pastries, churros, sticky rice, or *pan de sal*. *Tsokolate* has different names based on where the trees grew. In Pampanga province, north of Manila, it is called *suklati* (suk-la-ti), while in Mindanao, people refer to the drink as *sikwate* (sik-wa-te). This hot drink could even be stirred into rice to turn out a favorite breakfast porridge called *champorado*.

The Spaniards brought the cocoa seeds from Mexico and planted them all over the lowlands. Many believe the cacao trees in Batangas, a province south of Manila, produce the best cacao tablets. Their excellence had not changed ever since it was introduced from Mexico in 1665. *Tsokolate's* reputation is not merely because of its taste. Filipinos like the drink because of its place in history. There is a scene in Jose Rizal's *Noli Me Tangere* where a military officer warns a Spanish visitor on what to expect with the parish priest. If the latter "calls to the servant and says 'Juan, make a cup of chocolate, *eh!*' then stay without fear; but if he calls out, 'Juan, make a cup of chocolate, *ah!*' then take your hat and leave on the run." When the visitor thinks the story is a warning that the priest might poison him, the officer replies, "No, man, not at all!. . .'Chocolate, *eh!*' means thick and rich, while 'chocolate, *ah!*' means watered and thin." One who got the latter was of no social or political consequence to the powerful friars. Filipinos who remember this scene by heart also sometimes use the distinction to show the kind of regard they have for people they meet.

Filipinos enjoy their beers and "hard drinks" (gin and rum). However, outside of the big cities, people's favorite is the *tuba* (too-baah). *Tuba* is an Indigenous drink that played a significant role in precolonial animist rituals presided over by priestesses called *babaylan* (bah-bah-ye-lan). The Spanish admired the drink and brought this to Mexico, Guam, the Marianas Islands, and even as far as Australia, where the communities there developed their versions of the brew.

The drink comes from the nectar from the sap of an unopened flower of the coconut tree. Every morning a *tuba* gatherer climbs up the tree with a knife and a bamboo tube whose hollow is used as a container that can hold at most one liter of the sap. He then looks for the unopened flower, cuts its tip, and lets the sap drain into the bamboo container that already has extracts of the bark of a mangrove tree. Filipinos call these extracts *barok* (ba-rouk). He looks for another unopened flower, collecting sap until he fills up the container. Once the sap and the *barok* combine, the fermentation process starts.

Once back down on the ground, the gatherer transfers the mixture into a gallon-size glass or plastic canister. The fermentation usually emits bubbles, and it takes three to four days for these to subside, and the sediment goes down to the bottom. The liquid is then transferred carefully from one container to another through a small hose and left to stand for another four to five days. The decanting is repeated until very little of the sediment is left. The last container is then filled to the brim and covered tightly. The longer the sedimentation process, the higher the alcohol content and the stronger the liquor. This brawny version of the *tuba* is called *bahalina* (ba-ha-lee-na). A *bahalina* that is further distilled turns into a local version of gin, which Filipinos call *lambanog*. If a drinker wants to drink a less potent *tuba,* however, he can drink it as soon as it is brought down from the tree. This "lighter" version is called *mapakla* (ma-pak-la) because of its sharp, sweet taste.

One can drink *tuba* straight or with added ingredients. In the central Philippines, drinkers add raw egg yolk, *tableya* (see *tsokolate*), and milk to come up with a drink called *kutir.* In the southern Philippines, people use saps from different types of palm, instead of the coconut nectar, to produce a *tuba* that is sweet or that emits a foul smell. When asked what to them is the best tuba, Filipinos say that it "depends" on how the *tuba* gatherer "mixes" the sap and the *barok*. However, what makes drinking the *tuba* an adventure as one goes from one part of the country to another is sampling the drink.

See also: Chapter 10: Overview; Drinking and Dining; Fiesta.

Further Reading

Evangelista, Alfredo E. 1973. "Tempered Intemperance: Tuba-Drinking in a Tagalog Community." *Philippine Sociological Review* 21, no. 1 (January): 5–28.

Jollibee

Filipino food has steadily been getting global attention thanks mainly to the positive reviews of celebrity chefs like Anthony Bourdain. It is not, however, the traditional cuisine that have garnered unprecedented international scrutiny; it is the products of the Filipino-owned Jollibee Food Corporation. Jollibee is the largest fast-food chain in the Philippines and is rising fast around the world as well. In November 2019, it had over 1,300 stores across the world, 1,130 of these based in the Philippines and 234 in countries where there is a substantial Filipino population (migrants and overseas workers). The founder of Jollibee is Tony Tan Caktiong, from one of the prominent Filipino Chinese families of Manila, whose first business was an ice cream franchise

Jollibee. (Tupungato/Dreamstime.com)

in 1975. Three years later, upon the recommendation of a management consultant, Caktiong changed strategy and established the corporation with seven branches, all in Metropolitan Manila. By the time McDonald's entered the Philippine market in 1981, Jollibee was ready to compete against the corporate giant. As a brother of Tony Tan Caktong recalls, when friends told him not to compete with a giant like McDonald's, he replied: "Instead of chickening out, we served Chickenjoy!" Fried chicken has always been a favorite "easy-to-make" meal for Filipinos. Chickenjoy prided itself on being able to serve this favorite fast food, clean and with the appropriate accompaniments (rice and tomato ketchup).

Jollibee outsold McDonald's throughout the 1980s serving the above dishes, which the company peddled as fast food but were quintessentially Filipino. It did not help that McDonald's stuck to fried potato instead of adding rice to each menu and selling its burgers at a higher price than the Yumburger (later renamed Aloha Yumburger). By the 1980s, Jollibee had a nationwide presence. It also entered the global market, opening branches in Taiwan in 1986. Jollibee branches opened up in Dubai in 1995, California, Hawaii and Illinois in 1998, New York City in 2009, Singapore in 2013, and Milan (Italy), London (United Kingdom), Kota Kinabalu (Indonesia), Toronto and Winnipeg (Canada) as well as Manhattan (New York) in 2018. Jollibee had also expanded laterally, buying food companies like Red Ribbon (cakes and pastries), Chowking (Chinese dishes), Greenwich (Pizza), and Mang Inasal (chicken rotisserie). It also invested in the Burger King franchises in the Philippines. Outside the country, it owned 47 percent of the Mexican sandwich company Tortas Frontera, invested substantial amounts into food and food preparation companies ($340 million in Asia-Pacific Master, a company producing barbecue pork buns, and Superfood, a Vietnamese noodle shop chain). In September 2018, it entered into a joint venture with the American company Panda Express. It bought another American company, for US$350 million.

Jollibee attracts customers to its menu that, according to one business reporter, is "like a mosaic of different flavors." Its "Aloha Yumburger" is served with a secret sauce, and so is ChickenJoy, a breaded fried chicken that comes with gravy. One can order the fried chicken by itself, but in most cases a customer orders the full meal: ChickenJoy with rice and/or Jolly Spaghetti with a side of banana ketchup. Jolly Spaghetti appears to be no different from Italian spaghetti save that added to its *ragu* sauce are slices of hot dog and ham, which makes it sweet. The other noodle dish is *pancit palabok,* made of thin white noodles covered with shrimps, hard-boiled eggs, and ground pork. There is Breakfast Joy which is corned beef with rice and fried eggs, and finally, the Jollibee version of *Halo-halo.* Of all these products Aloha Yumburger has had a hard time competing with American hamburger chains, but this is balanced out by the high demand for Chicken Joy, which Filipinos outside of the country say reminds them very much of "home."

See also: Chapter 7: Overview. Chapter 10: Overview.

Further Reading

Matejowsky, Ty. 2008. "Jolly Dogs and Spaghetti: Anthropological Reflections on Global/Local Fast Food Competition in the Philippines." *Journal of Asia-Pacific Business* 9, no. 4: 313–328.

Noodles and Bread

Pancit is the Filipino term for noodles, which Chinese settlers brought to the Philippines centuries back. The word comes from the Hokkien (the language of southern China) word *pian-i-sit,* which means "convenient food." Its convenience initially referred to its accessibility to everyone: it was a roadside food that was sold by Chinese peddlers. Eventually it became a regular household cuisine, also available in restaurants (some appropriately called *panciterias*) and food stalls, and serving as the mandatory carbohydrate alongside rice in parties and town *fiestas.*

Pancit is made from four types of flour: wheat, rice, *mung* beans and potato. Rice-based noodles are called *pancit bihon,* while *pancit sotanghon* are made from *mung* beans and potato. These different doughs, in turn, have produced different varieties of *pancit* of which the following are the most popular. The *pancit canton* is a wheat dough that is stir-fried first with ginger and soy sauce and then added in meat (any meat would do) and vegetables. One prepares the thin *pancit bihon* and *pancit sotanghon* the same way. Dry thick rice noodles are immersed in hot water to soften them up and then cooked with shrimp, squid or oysters laced with an orange sauce to produce the *pancit luglog* (*luglog* means "dipped in water").

The other variations of *pancit* are based on geography. For example, the *pancit batil patong,* which is an egg noodle cooked with bean sprouts and water buffalo meat and topped with a fried egg, is associated with the northern Luzon town of Tuguegarao, while the *pancit habhab* (eaten), a meal full of vegetables, comes from the central Luzon province of Quezon. Batangas, a province south of Metropolitan Manila, is known for its *pancit lomi*—a thick egg noodle that is cooked along with pork liver, fish, and quail eggs in a thick broth. The adjoining province of Laguna is famous for its *pancit langlang,* which is also cooked in a broth with onions, pork rinds, and *adobo* meat. Certain regions spice up their *pancit.* In southern Luzon, *pancit* is made hot with chili, while in the west-central provinces, cooks add anchovies, fish paste, or tamarind. Noodles is used less in Mindanao, most likely in deference to neighboring Muslim communities, and in the Muslim provinces, seaweed is added to the vegetable mix. Finally, there are the experimentations: canned tuna instead of fresh meat, and squid ink to produce a "blackened" *pansit.*

Pancit's popularity is due to both practical and philosophical reasons. On the one hand, it is a staple, submerged in broth, that can smoothly absorb the tastes of different vegetable-meat-topping-sauce combinations, and is thus easy to make. On the other hand, Filipinos—like the Chinese—regard the *pancit* as a symbol "of family ties, of long life, of connection" (Palanca 2015, 50). *Pancit* is a sine qua non in birthday parties as family and friends wish the celebrant a long life. It is thus no exaggeration to say that the *pancit* is not just a "complete meal" (Palanca 2015, 5), it is also what keeps Filipino society together.

The other carbohydrate that Filipinos enjoy is the *pan de sal*. Despite its name—"salted bread"—the *pan de sal* is a sweet bun. The initial stage of making the *pan de sal* is no different from how other breads are formed—warmly heated yeast is mixed with flour, sugar, and a dash of salt. The dough is kneaded and sliced into small rolls which would then be sprinkled with bread crumbs. After allowing some time for the rolls to rise further, they are baked in either a wood-fired or electric oven until the outside is brown and crusty.

The bread has a long history. Portuguese traders are said to be the first to introduce the *pan de sal's* precursor, and the Spanish produced it locally as their version of the French *baguette*, using the same wheat that the friars used to make the communion host for their masses. The Americans replaced the Spaniards as the Philippines' colonizer and brought with them cheaper wheat flour, commercial yeast, and canned milk. However, the use of these "new" ingredients yielded a dough that was far softer than the Spanish version of the *baguette*. It was this difference in the texture that gave the *pan de sal* its distinct identity.

Pan de sal is best eaten for breakfast, when it is just out of the oven, hot, crumbly, and crusty. Filipinos dip the bread in coffee or hot thick chocolate and eat it. *Pan de sal* is usually eaten as it is, but there are also times when it is sliced and filled up with accoutrements, from fruit jams, butter or peanut butter to tuna salad, yesterday's *adobo* (heated up or deep fried), corned beef, or a slice of Spam canned meat. Throughout the years, Filipinos have come out with variations of the *pan de sal*, using yam instead of wheat, making doughs out of healthier wheat flour, and making pizza or bagel bites out of the bread. Cooks are also known to replace ice cream cones with *pan de sal*. The *pan de sal* is now considered the Philippines' national bread. It achieved this status because it is eaten by everyone—rich and poor, Muslims and Christians, upland and lowland communities. It is not a special bread but a part of life's daily routine, which further cements its importance to Filipino palates.

See also: Chapter 10: Overview.

Further Reading

Lumen, Nancy Reyes. 2005. "Republic of Pancit." *Philippine Center for Investigative Journalism*. January 2. https://old.pcij.org/stories/republic-of-pancit/

Palanca, Clinton. 2015. *My Angkong's Noodles: A Chinese Filipino Cookbook*. Manila: Elizabeth Gokongwei.

Snacks and Side Dishes

While it has not reached the status of a national dish like *adobo*, *balut* has become one of the most popular snacks of Filipinos. Known as *maodan* ("feathered egg") in China, and *trung vit lon* in Vietnam, *balut* is the embryo of a domesticated duck that has been boiled. Food connoisseur Margaret Magat describes a "good *balut*" is one where the tastes of "the yolk, the white part called *bato* (rock) which is the tough-to-eat albumen, the embryo and some liquid" blend well (Magat 2002, 67). A cracked *balut* loses the liquid and is less palatable; oftentimes it is even spoiled. The liquid is especially necessary because the first step in eating *balut* is opening a small crack on the shell and then sipping the liquid. It is only after the liquid is quaffed completely that the shell is cracked open and the rest of the duck eaten.

Balut production is strictly a small industry. Duck eggs are allowed to develop for 16–20 days before they are boiled. Those that fail to develop are turned into hard-boiled eggs called *penoy*. *Balut*-makers then line up, exposed to the sun for several hours. The eggs are transferred to hatchery-like structures where workers will check each egg to separate the cracked ones and place the "good *balut*" in large cloth sacks where they are to incubate for the next 16–18 days, and where they are checked to see if the embryo and the *bato* are developed. These inspections also allow *balut*-makers to separate the contaminated ones (cracked eggs that are drained of their liquid, or those in which a crack allows water to seep in and taint the permeable membrane). It is easier to spot the spoiled *balut* because they emanate a foul smell.

The good eggs are sold to wholesalers who run a network of street hawkers or who, in turn, sell the eggs to markets and groceries. One of the nightly voices that punctuate the streets is of hawkers shouting "*Balut!*" Customers may range from families wanting to have a midnight snack to men drinking in a small store needing an appetizer, and even men who believe that *balut* is an aphrodisiac that reinforces one's virility. *Balut* is eaten for diametrically opposite reasons: it can be a power bar that gives additional boost to one's working hours but it also functions as a sleeping aid for insomniacs.

Eating the *balut* is a meticulous affair. After gingerly making a small crack on the egg, one carefully breaks the membrane to sip the liquid. The *balut* eater then continues to crack the egg to separate the yolk, embryo and the "hard rock," and adds salt repeatedly while eating the yolk and embryo. *Balut* gourmands say that if one wants the egg's "full taste," they must swallow the embryo as a whole instead of chewing it. One need not eat the *balut* upon purchase and can keep it for two weeks before it is declared old and unconsumable. When refrigerated, the egg can last for a month before the liquid dries out.

The idea that *balut* enhances the sexual process remains popular even today, although there is growing criticism that this only bolsters a double-standard where men get to define sexuality and women's voices are muted if not suppressed. Promoting *balut* as an aphrodisiac only for men is one way in which the skewed, anti-Filipina view of sexuality is reaffirmed. In truth, Filipinas enjoy their *balut* as do Filipinos, and critics have repeatedly cited historical and anthropological studies that point to the egg as "the supreme symbol of fertility, birth and regeneration" (Frazier 1970, 28, as quoted by Magat 2002, 88).

The *lumpia* is the Filipinos' other favorite snack, appetizer, and side dish. This "spring roll" consists of a mixture of chopped vegetables and minced meat (beef, chicken, pork or shrimps) rolled in a wrapper that is made from flour and water, or corn starch, water and eggs, lined in a lettuce leaf. Its culinary ancestry is Chinese: the Fujianese call it *lunpia* while it is called *runbing* in Mandarin. It has "cousins" all over Southeast Asia, resulting from the unremitting flow of Chinese migrants into the region and their subsequent "integration" into Southeast Asian communities as "essential outsiders."

Lumpia is popular because of the ease with which it is prepared. It is generally fried but Filipinos also love eating it "fresh" (with an uncooked wrapper made of white flour and bread) or unwrapped (the Filipino term for this is *hubad*, i.e., naked). Like the *sinigang* and the *tinola*, its meat-vegetable combine is a complete and relatively cheap meal. Like the *balut*, it is easily accessible through street vendors whose makeshift food stalls prepare fried *lumpia* with unceasing regularity. Unlike the egg-appetizer, the *lumpia* can also be served as part of a family meal or a party (where the fresh *lumpia* is a guest favorite).

Filipinos' idea of what a good *lumpia* is has less to do with the meat-vegetable combination or whether it is eaten fresh or fried. The determining factor here is the sauce in which the *lumpia* is dipped. There are four sauces (*sasawan*) that are used for *lumpia*. For the fried *lumpia*, there is the customary vinegar-soy sauce-crushed garlic combination, a blend that Professor Doreen Fernandez argues is what gives *lumpia* its distinct Filipino identity. Another is the same combination sans the soy sauce, and a third is a much thicker one of vinegar, hard-boiled eggs, and onions chopped as finely as possible. For the fresh *lumpia* there is only one sauce and this consists of brown sugar, soy sauce, and corn starch that is heated until the sugar melts, after which mashed garlic is added to it. This said, there are communities that are especially fussy about the *lumpia*. In Negros Occidental, a fresh spring roll must include in the meat-vegetable mix the julienned "heart" of a coconut palm.

See also: Chapter 10: Overview; Drinking and Dining.

Further Reading

Frazier, Greg. 1970. *Aphrodisiac Cookery, Ancient and Modern*. San Francisco: Troubadour Press.

Magat, Margaret. 2002. "Balut: Fertilized Duck Eggs and Their Role in Filipino Culture." *Western Folklore* 1, no. 1 (Spring): 63–96.

Matejowsky, Ty. 2013. "The Incredible, Edible *Balut*: Ethnographic Perspectives on the Philippines' Favorite Liminal Food." *Food, Culture, Society* 16, no. 3: 387–404.

Soups

The three favorite soup dishes are meat, spice, and vegetable broth made tasty by their gingery, tangy, and sour tastes. The most well-liked is the *sinigang* (stewed and pronounced si-ni-gang), a concoction of vegetables, green chili, and meat (beef shank, pork belly, shrimp or fish), with the tangy taste provided by tamarind fruit. One prepares it by first sautéing garlic and onion, then adding the meat, followed by the water (in some cases, the beef or pork meat is often boiled first to tenderize it). Once the mix reaches boiling point, the vegetables and the tamarind are added, with a couple of tablespoons of fish sauce. One then brings down the fire to simmering level until the vegetables have softened up. Before this is served, spinach or "swamp cabbage" is added to it. *Sinigang* is eaten with rice.

Professor Fernandez argues that more than the "overworked *adobo* . . . *sinigang* seems the most representative of Filipino taste." The reason for this, according to this top food scholar in the Philippines, is that Filipinos "like the lightly boiled, the slightly soured, the dish that . . . is adaptable to all tastes (if you don't like shrimp, then bangus, or pork), to all classes and budgets . . . to seasons and availability" (Fernandez and Alegre 1988, 2). Just how good a *sinigang* stew is supposedly depends on just how much sharpness the tamarind brings out. Establishing the tanginess, however, is a subjective matter. The most popular story is supposed to be this exchange where the chef asks a customer if the *sinigang* is "tangy enough," to which the latter responds by saying, "maybe add a little more." What "little" means, however, varies too.

A "milder" cousin of *sinigang* is the *tinola*. The *tinola* must also have slices of green papaya included in the boiling broth, and the *sinigang* needs a long green chili pepper, before both soups are declared ready to be eaten. After five minutes, the soup is taken out of the heat and leafy greens (from bok choy and *kangkong* to spinach leaves) are put into it. After allowing the greens to blend into the soup, *sinigang* and *tinola* are served along with rice. The *tinola* is popular in the central and southern Philippines where it is soured by tomatoes before the other vegetables are added. The tamarind and tomatoes supposedly enhance the taste but also function as preservatives. Their tang may be enhanced by adding green mango, guava, or papaya into the broth. Apart from the tamarind and the tomato, cooks also consider ginger, garlic, and pepper as essential ingredients. Once the stew starts to boil, the cook puts in the vegetables that are the easily available during the season.

Another favorite but "peculiar" food is *dinuguan* (from the Filipino word *dugo*, which means blood). Like *sisig*, *dinuguan* is a stew that consists of the different "discarded" viscera of a pig, cow or water buffalo as well as the animal's blood. A cook starts with minced onion and garlic, after which the innards are added and browned. Once brown, water, bay leaves, and vinegar are added and the mix is brought to a boil, at which stage pepper, green chili, and the blood are put in. The cooking continues for the next 15 minutes, and before serving, sugar, salt, and black pepper are dissolved into the soup. The *dinuguan* is served along with steamed rice cake. Non-Filipinos find the stew repulsive because of the blood and the insides, but Filipinos relish it for the sour taste as well as the fact that it is easier to make (like *adobo*) and can be bought cheap.

These three soups are favorite family dinners because they are easy to make, and because of the mix of meat and vegetables, they are full meals. Filipinos likewise appreciate these soups for their health value. They not only provide the essential natural vitamins a body needs, ingredients like tamarind and ginger also have high antioxidant and anti-inflammatory properties that help a body heal. If Americans serve "chicken soup" to sick family members, Filipino families prepare *sinigang* or *tinola* for kin who are not well. These soups are also considered good indicators of the social ranks that Filipinos assign to each other.

Finally, a feast in the Philippines or in Filipino communities the world over is not complete without the *lechon*. *Lechon* is not strictly Filipino; its name is Spanish, and the variation that reached the Philippines was probably the Mexican variation. However, it is also possible that despite its Spanish name, the *lechon* may be closer to its Asian and Pacific cousins. The slow-roasting of this suckling delicacy is similar to how the Chinese cook *kao ru zhu* (burning pig), the Vietnamese cook *long quay,* the Balinese cook *Babi Guling* in Indonesia, and the Hawaiians cook *kalua* pig.

No one roasts *lechon* on his or her own. Communities and families hire *lechon* "masters" (*lechonero* in the local lingo) who will do everything from the slaughtering of the pig to the laying down of the fully roasted pig on the lunch or dinner table. A master starts early in the morning, slaughtering the pig in a way that allows him to save enough blood for another dish, the *dinuguan*. The *lechonero* then slices the pig and removes the pig's organs that could be added to the *dinuguan* or grilled. The liver is often mashed and cooked in onion, sugar, vinegar, salt, and pepper and made into thick liver sauce. The pig is then placed on a boiling vat, scrubbed until its skin turns white, and skewered using a bamboo pole. The *lechonero* then take out the inner organs, and stuff the now empty body with lemongrass, salt, tamarind leaves, and an herb Filipinos call *tanglad*, to give the stuffed pig a certain fragrance that enhances the meat's taste. After covering the pig's skin with oil to keep it crispy and golden, the *lechonero* puts the skewered pig over a spit of burning coal. It will be slow-cooked for over eight hours, with the *lechonero* rotating it frequently. To relieve the *lechonero* of the tedium, the hosts join him with drinks and appetizers.

The eating begins once the *lechon* is cooked, with some of the guests offering to pinch the crispy skin and take a piece of the exposed flesh. Others then follow suit. In Manila and the surrounding provinces, the meat is dipped in a sauce made up of the organs. Filipinos in central and southern Philippines use vinegar enriched with crushed garlic and chili as their dipping sauce. The diners usually eat as much as they can of the *lechon*. If there are leftovers, these are cooked like *adobo* along with the liver sauce. These could also be deep fried. Both become viands for the next day.

See also: Chapter 10: Overview; Drinking and Dining.

Further Reading

Chan, Bernice. 2019. "The Secrets to Great Lechon—Whole Roasted Suckling Pig That's Virtually a Filipino National Dish." *South China Morning Post.* January 25. https://www.scmp.com/lifestyle/food-drink/article/2108935/secrets-great-lechon-whole-roasted-suckling-pig-thats-virtually

CHAPTER 15

LEISURE AND SPORTS

OVERVIEW

Like the rest of the world, Filipinos love sports. Their love for sports is nurtured by the inclusion of physical education (PE) as part of the academic requirement at all levels of their education. The Americans were the first to institutionalize this requisite. This was part of an effort to wean away Filipinos from cockfighting, a favorite pastime, which the new colonial administrators regarded as a serious vice (as Filipinos bet on two fighting roosters) that had reinforced existing social evils, especially gambling. The first thing the Americans did was to create the position of Playground Director, whose responsibility was to implement the manual *Physical Education, a Manual for Teachers* in Manila. The director and author of the manual, Frederick O. England, defined sports broadly. For elementary students, sports included "marching calisthenics, folk dancing, impromptu games and group athletics," while at the secondary level, he added "impromptu games, group athletics," with "military drill" added only for boys and "folk dancing" only for girls.

The Americans first tested the syllabus in Manila and finding success, made it a colony-wide school activity. The University of the Philippines also became a laboratory of sorts when it created a Department of Physical Education which would "promote, direct, and supervise the physical education and recreation activities of the mass of men and women students attending the institution" (Ylanan and Ylanan 1965, 6). To further encourage Filipino interest in sports, the Americans promoted interschool competitions in the 1920s. This would be formalized a decade later when the Bureau of Education issued a set of guidelines for "mass athletics; intramural and interschool athletics" in 1930 and seven years later placed "physical education . . . on the same level as other subjects." The Bureau also mandated that sports be made into "a curricular subject in the secondary schools." Its grade was "based not only on attendance but in proficiency [and] included in computing [a student's] general average" (Ylanan and Ylanan 1965, 7). From then on, fiesta celebrations were not considered complete if there was no basketball or volleyball game between visiting and local teams. World War II interrupted the development of Philippine sports, but after the war, the new Republic of the Philippines eagerly restored athletics into the curriculum.

In 1951, the Department of Education issued a new *Guide to Physical Education for Secondary Schools* that was more detailed compared to its colonial precedent. Specific sports (some old, some new) were grouped under one category. The new category "gymnastics," for example, included "marching, freehand exercises, light and heavy apparatus (lifting), stunts, tumbling and pyramid building." The "bigger" games were divided into "individual sports" (archery, badminton, handball, and tennis) and "specialized athletics" (baseball, basketball, soccer, softball, track and field, and volleyball). Finally, the manual had a category called "rhythms and dances" that included "foreign folk dance, Philippine folk dance, rhythmic activities, square and round dancing, social dancing, and modern dance" (Ylanan and Ylanan 1965, 8–9). There were some notable changes in some programs, the most serious of which was the gradual disappearance of the once-popular "intercollegiate" "Olympics," where schools from the different regions competed against each other and the winning teams proceeded to represent the country in international competitions. But the foundation laid out by the Americans and expanded by the Philippine government had not been altered.

Filipino fondness for sports, however, rarely translated into great achievements at the international level. The country has been sending its athletes to the Olympic Games since 1924, but has only won a total of ten medals—eight bronzes and two silvers. The last time a Filipino won a medal (silver) was in 1996, and since then no athlete has brought home any medal. A journalist's question was right on the mark: "We aren't short on passion, and neither do we lack talent. So what is it that is making us fail so miserably?" (Gutierrez 2017). The culprit is the government and its lack of interest in supporting sports development on a long-term basis. Athletes have never been provided a healthy diet program and their "physical and mental conditioning" are extremely inadequate due to a lack of facilities. These subsistence and training problems, however, only reflect a more fundamental malaise. The government itself has time and again admitted that sports is not a priority. Poverty, housing, education, and infrastructure are social welfare issues demanding government attention. The budget allocation for sports has been a pittance compared to the funds apportioned to these programs. In 2013, the budget for sports was US$15.7 million while education received US$1.6 billion. Boxer Manny Pacquiao's average net worth has been over US$190 million, making the budget for sport a mere 8.26 percent of his income.

The Philippine Sports Commission (PSC), the government body in charge of sports development, has also been repeatedly criticized for incompetence and corruption. Politics has also repeatedly pushed back any progress in the different programs as they compete over a share of the limited budget. The programs themselves are riven with factional battles over control of their leaderships. Senior officials refuse to give up their seats to a younger generation who could revive lost enthusiasm and pursue new approaches to improve Philippine sports in general. The PSC's corruption and inefficiency are not the only drawbacks. The government agency has constantly been fighting the Philippine Olympics Committee (POC), the private organization authorized by the International Olympics Committee (IOC) to take care of athletes going to the Olympics. The bone of contention revolves around, unsurprisingly, which office controls the money for the Olympics and which has real authority over the athletes.

In 1974, President Ferdinand Marcos created a Department of Youth and Sports Development (DYSD, renamed Ministry of Youth and Sports Development in 1979 when the Philippines shifted to a quasi-parliamentary system). The department/ministry was given the responsibility of developing a sports program that would make the Philippines competitive globally. In 1982, Marcos was forced to restructure a cash-strapped government, and one of the measures taken to save money was to integrate the MYSD into the Ministry of Education. When the 1987 Constitution reverted the country back to a presidential system, the sports program remained part of the Department of Education. The government created a Philippine Sports Program but this was an agency with less resources and lacking the authority that the defunct DYSD had.

In December 2009, President Gloria M. Arroyo signed Republic Act No. 9850 into law, declaring *arnis* the Philippine National Martial Art and Sport as part of her plan to jump-start the sports program. Unfortunately, the noble intentions behind this law as well as other similar decrees never found fruition because of poor implementation. Local governments refused Manila's overtures to co-fund sports programs, arguing that they would rather use their resources for critical social welfare programs. Congress has likewise treated sports development as a low priority area. In February 2016, the House of Representative's Committee on Labor and Employment proposed the creation of a Department of Sports to replace the ineffective Philippine Sports Program. Two years later, the proposal had not moved beyond the creation of a "technical working group" that was supposed to iron out the details of the proposal.

As expected, it is the athletes who have had to bear the brunt of these problems, failing to win in the big game that is the Olympics. Basketball development, for example, suffered between 2005 and 2007 after the IOC suspended the Philippines because of disagreements between the Basketball Association of the Philippines and the POC. Wesley So, who became chess grandmaster in 2007 at the age of 14 (only one of seven in chess history), changed federations seven years later and joined the United States. So blamed his move on the indifference of Philippine chess authorities toward promoting the welfare of its players. Another grandmaster, 44-year-old Richard Bitoon, followed So a year later, requesting permission to move to the American federation for the same reason.

The Philippines was overall champion in the December 2019 Southeast Asian Games held in Manila. However, when it comes to competing beyond in the big games like the Olympics, Filipino athletes still have to make their mark. Efforts by the private sector to help sports achieved some success as shown in the case of soccer. The government's decision to stretch the idea of citizenship allowed players whose parentage is partly Filipino (mother or father) or who are permanent residents of the country to play for the national team. The private sector then helped fund the program. Since then, the Philippines has risen from being a perennial loser to being a major contender in Southeast Asian soccer. The strategy has had limited impact on basketball. The inclusion of Filipino American players raised the team's competitiveness and the national team won gold in the 1985 Asian Basketball Championships. The Philippines remains the top team in Southeast Asia since the early postwar period, but it has never won any gold or silver medal in the Asian elimination rounds in international tournaments sponsored by the *Federation Internationale de Basketball* (FIBA or International Basketball Federation in English), including the Olympics.

Filipinos continue to be proud of their players, but as long as government continues to show limited interest in sports development, the chances of the Philippines becoming a major contender in the Olympics or other global competitions is extremely slim.

See also: Chapter 16: Overview; Television.

Further Reading

Beran, Janice A. 1989. "Americans in the Philippines: Imperialism or Progress through Sport?" *International Journal of the History of Sport* 6, no. 1: 62–87.

Gems, Gerald R. 2004. "The Athletic Crusade: Sports and Colonialism in the Philippines." *International Journal of the History of Sport* 21, no. 1: 1–15.

Gems, Gerald R. 2016. *Sports and the American Occupation of the Philippines: Bats, Balls, and Bayonets*. Lanham, MD: Lexington Books.

Gutierrez, Natashya. 2017. "The Problem with Philippine Sports." *Rappler*. August 16. https://www.rappler.com/sports/10591-the-problem-with-philippine-sports

Ylanan, Reginio R, and Carmen Wilson Ylanan. 1965. *The History and Development of Physical Education and Sports in the Philippines*. Manila: Carmen W. Ylanan.

Arnis

Arnis (also called *eskrima*) is the Philippine version of close-quarter swordplay. The term is an appropriation of the Spanish word *arnis*, which was used to refer to the decorations that Malay strongmen and their followers displayed when they met the Spaniards. *Arnis* is also called by two other names—*escrima*, which is from the Spanish word for fencing, and *kale* (*ka-leeh*), which is a derivative of the Indonesian word *tjakalele* (cha-ka-le-le). Cebuanos from the central Philippines came out with the linguistic blend *kamot* (ka-mot) to mean "hand." At the same time, the Ilocanos of the northern Philippines turned it into a verb (*kali* now meant "to stab"). The Pangasinans, who reside in the regions south of the Ilocanos, shortened the word *Kalinongan* to *kali*, which meant "wisdom."

Men and women play the game. The men are called *arnisador*, and the women, *arnisadoa*. Since the other name for *arnis* is *escrima*, the male fighters may also be called *eskrimador*, and the women, *eskrimadora*. *Arnis* involves two contenders armed with rattan sticks, daggers, spears, or swords. When these weapons are not available, *arnis* fighters also resort to using their arms. This popular sport is not just about the weapons used. The sport is also notable for its choreography, where two fighters

Filipino martial arts. (Innovatedcaptures/Dreamstime.com)

gracefully use force as if they are dancing while thrusting and parrying with their weapons. In *arnis* competitions, fighters are not only judged by the number of hits they inflict on opponents but also for their agility and style. It is, according to Filipino anthropologist F. Landa Jocano, a "complete martial arts system." *Arnisadors* use single-stick techniques (*solo baston*), double-stick techniques (*doble baston*), or a combination of stick and knife (*espada y daga*). They also use a staff and a spear (*sibat*) and are comfortable with using knives (*daga*). Variations of these different techniques can be found across different parts of the archipelago.

There is a consensus that *arnis* was brought to the archipelago from empires that reigned in what is now Indonesia. *Arnis* evolved from an Indonesian martial arts system called *tjakalele* (cha-ka-le-le). The latter, in turn, was a branch of another system, the *pencak silat* (pen-chak-si-lat). What students and practitioners of the sport disagree over is whether *tjakalele* was introduced to the lowland communities of the archipelago by the representatives of the empires or whether it was brought by migrants from Borneo who moved up the archipelago and adapted *tjakalele* to local conditions, leading to the appearance of *arnis*.

What distinguishes *arnis* from other combat sports in the Philippines is the role that spirits and amulets play in the lives of its practitioners. *Eskrimadors* may be confident about their fighting styles. However, they also believe that they have to be ready for the talisman and other "esoterica" that their opponents possess. A good *eskrimadora* or *eskrimador,* therefore, must also come up with their *jujus.* They either wear them as a bracelet or a necklace, or keep them in the pockets of their fighting pants. An *eskrimador* may also seek out the blessings of the community shaman who teaches them different prayers. These *oraciones* are supposed to make them invincible against their opponent's physical and mystical powers and also mend their injuries.

Filipinos see *arnis* as a defensive sport. To prove their point, they cite what happened in the central Philippine island of Mactan when the first expeditionary force led by Ferdinand Magellan tried to subdue the inhabitants. The sparse evidence about that encounter has not prevented Filipinos from arguing that it was the natives' clever use of *arnis* that bested the Spanish and their heavy metal armaments. When the Spanish established their political authority in the lowlands, they banned *arnis.* This deprived communities of their weapons and emasculated the armed entourages of Malay strongmen. Filipinos, however, had found a way to preserve the sport by integrating its different moves into dances and other performances. Even the use of rattan sticks and daggers was incorporated in plays with mock battles, especially the ones that featured Muslim-Spanish encounters.

Arnis was pushed to the margins when American-introduced sports like basketball began to attract Filipinos, although it never disappeared completely. It was played in the provinces and remained popular in areas where there were no basketball courts and town plazas had not been converted into baseball fields. *Arnis* came back into the public eye through the movies. *Arnis* masters became some of the "experts" hired by studios to make fight scenes as realistic as possible. When kung-fu movies became popular in the United States in the 1970s, thanks to action stars like Bruce Lee, it was not long before Hollywood discovered *arnis.* Among the most prominent franchise action movies that have featured *arnis* are *Bourne Identity* (2002), *Taken* (2008), *Quantum of Solace* (2008), and *Fast and Furious* (2015).

Arnis returned to the center of Philippine sport on December 11, 2009, when President Gloria M. Arroyo signed Republic Act No. 9850 declaring it as the "National Martial Art and Sport of the Philippines." Its popularity in the country and abroad has risen further since then.

See also: Chapter 10: Overview. Chapter 15: Overview.

Further Reading

Wiley, Mark V., ed. 2001. *Arnis: History and Development of the Filipino Martial Arts.* Clarendon, VT: Tuttle Publishing.

Baseball

Americans brought baseball (along with basketball) to the Philippines in an attempt to replace "socially immoral" activities like cockfighting wherein Filipinos were known to gamble away even their daily wages. The first game was played by an army regiment and a naval unit. As playing baseball became a frequent activity, American troops formed a league consisting of teams that played three times a week, weather permitting. Some of the teams offered to teach young Filipinos how to play the game. The latter initially expressed indifference, but after a few games, many began "'shagging' foul balls, recovering used balls and creating their bats which they patterned after the broken bats they picked up. The soldiers taught Filipinos the game, and soon teams were formed. Thus began their first English lessons; [the] use of baseball terms such as 'slide,' 'strike,' 'foul ball,' and 'out' became common" (Heiser 1936, 136). In 1901, there were enough teams playing the game for the Americans to form the Manila Bay Baseball League (MBBL), which began as an all-American competition and remained that way until 1912, when the first all-Filipino team joined the league. Baseball's popularity began to challenge the Catholic Church's claims that it was the main crowd puller. Baseball attracted huge numbers at the town plazas, which were adjoined to the Catholic Church, and there was a marked decrease in church attendance during weekend games.

The Americans further boosted baseball's popularity through the public school system where male teachers, "many of whom were former college athletes, introduced baseball in the public schools," and formed teams "under their initiative as extra-curricular activities" (Ylanan and Ylanan 1965, 61). Baseball's popularity grew fast in the provinces as evidenced by the first interscholastic athletic organization formed in 1904, not in Manila but in the Bicol peninsula in southeastern Luzon. Baseball even reached the farthest points of Luzon Island where in Baguio, a mountain town that became the "summer capital" of American officers running away from Manila's heat, a teacher proudly reported that children playing the game had developed a "baseball language" that mixed English with their dialect. So popular had baseball become in 1908 that the government was able to hold the first colony-wide interscholastic competition. In 1909, the Bureau of Education recognized baseball as a sport and extended financial support to school programs. By 1910, there were 482 teams, divided into 37 divisions, playing 1,201 games a year, prompting an American journalist to declare that "[o]verall, the archipelago, from the [headhunters'] village in the mountains to the fishermen's barrio on the coast, baseball diamonds have been laid out, and baseball is being played. Learning to master America's favorite game, the Filipinos eventually started to attract attention from the USA and elsewhere through baseball" (Antolihao 2012, 71). It was from the early "recruits" of these games that the first all-Filipino baseball team was formed, which joined the MBL and then toured Japan and the United States in 1913.

Baseball's reputation continued to grow in the 1920s, with the Philippine Amateur Athletic Federation promoting "indoor baseball" and creating the Philippine Baseball League (PBL) in 1923. This first professional association worked well, with the MBBL and other amateur groups like the Industrial League and the Independent League to promote the game. To sustain public interest, the government facilitated the visits of foreign players to the Philippines, and a team from Waseda University in Japan played friendly games in Manila. Then in 1934, Major League Baseball stars like Babe Ruth, Jimmie Fox, and Lou Gehrig visited Manila and played a series of games against Filipino teams. These visits, however, were the last high point in the story of Philippine baseball. The teams that lost to the MLB stars were the best of the Filipino players, but they were already a dwindling group. Throughout the colony, the quality of the games was declining and along with it, fan interest.

There were several reasons for this gradual decline in baseball. The first was the withdrawal of American teachers once it became clear that Philippine independence was a foregone conclusion. Filipino teams had come to be dependent on their American coaches, who were the most familiar with the sport as Americans considered baseball as a national icon. Filipinos could not seek the coaching services of the American military as it had reduced its presence considerably with the establishment of a local police force and a Philippine Army. American troops had also been confined to military bases, further limiting contact with Filipinos. Thus, the latter were unable to develop their own competent coaches who could step into the shoes of the Americans if and when the Americans left. Second, baseball teams needed space to play, but as towns urbanized and cities became congested, the public space also began to shrink. The plazas were still there, but baseball was not the sole activity anymore: basketball courts and stages for performances had also claimed their plaza space. One option was to set up sports arenas and stadiums, but these were amenities that only the more affluent towns and cities could afford. The schools could have sustained people's fascination with baseball, but public schools had opted for smaller playgrounds to reduce maintenance upkeep or construct more classrooms.

Moreover, baseball never gained traction in the private schools whose administrators never warmed up to the sport, often regarding it as "the game of the masses" in the provincial and rural areas. Baseball was not urbane and middle class enough for these institutions. Finally, Filipinos were never able to match the enthusiasm and dedication of the Japanese with regard to baseball. The latter's commitment to the game was such that Japanese teams dominated the Asian region and were next only to the Americans at the world level. Apart from this, the general lack of interest in Asia with regard to the game also meant that baseball could not produce its heroes and heroines who, in turn, could have inspired Filipinos (Antolihao 2012, 1400). The baseball leagues were the ones that suffered the most because of this decline.

With very few young players coming up from the schools, the MBBL had to rely on aging stars to keep the competition going. There were no fresh faces with better skills to challenge the veterans and animate the fans. Baseball had become a middle-aged man's game. Whatever fire was left in playing baseball was further sapped once Filipinos were drawn to basketball. The Japanese attempted to revive baseball during World War II by organizing games between prominent provincial teams and teams composed of Japanese soldiers. This failed to get fan interest back; instead, baseball was now associated with Japanese military brutality, further tarnishing its declining reputation.

Baseball was finally pushed to the outer recesses of the sports world in the postwar era when Filipinos became avid basketball enthusiasts. The new Philippine government tried to recapture the lost luster by hosting the First Asian Baseball championship in 1954 (the country won gold), but it failed. Since then, the Philippines has never participated in any international competition. Baseball ceased to be a popular sport in

Manila, the capital, although the game was still played in towns in the outer islands, although this too did not last long. In 1979, the MBBL was shut down, followed closely by the most popular of the provincial teams, the Canlubang Sugar Barons. The Philippines has managed to maintain a little league program, which was doing well regionally until the 1992 team was stripped off its title as Little League World Series champions after League officials discovered that the team had violated age and residency rules. The Philippines continued to participate in the League's Asian regional competition but never represented Asia in the World Series after 1992. In 1992, baseball became an official Olympic event, and in 1994, it became an Asian Games event. Japan, Chinese-Taipei, and South Korea dominated the Asian Games while the Philippines hardly figured in the competition. Where the Philippines fared well is in the Southeast Asian region, where the baseball teams of neighboring countries still lagged by decades compared to the Philippine team.

In 2007, to improve the skills of the national team, Philippine sports authorities established the Philippine Baseball League (PBL), which consisted of a mix of corporate-sponsored and school teams. There is still no indication that the PBL has achieved this goal as the Philippines remains unable to break into the sport's elite circle. In 2012, prospects for improving Philippine baseball further dwindled when the game was removed from the list of Olympic games due to its lack of global appeal.

See also: Chapter 10: Overview; Fiesta. Chapter 16: Overview.

Further Reading

Antolihao, Lou. 2012. "From Baseball Colony to Basketball Republic: Post-colonial Transition and the Making of a National Sport in the Philippines." *Sports in Society: Cultures, Commerce, Media, Politics* 15, no. 10: 1396–1412.

Heiser, Victor. 1936. *An American Doctor's Odyssey.* New York: W. W. Norton and Co.

Ylanan, Reginio R, and Carmen Wilson Ylanan. 1965. *The History and Development of Physical Education and Sports in the Philippines.* Manila: Carmen W. Ylanan.

Basketball

Filipinos are so passionate about basketball that they often call it a religion. This strong attachment is the result of history, changes in public space, and the incorporation of the sport into people's everyday lives. As one writer explained to an American visitor, "How could you think of Filipino life without basketball? It's not only a pastime; it's a passion" (Bartholomew 2010, 383–384). Basketball is "religion" to many, and for young men (and increasingly women), an important "rite of passage" to adulthood and even a promising future. Filipinos venerate their favorite players so much that some have parlayed this awe into successful political careers. Basketball gives poor and downtrodden Filipinos a reason to hope. One of the favorite basketball teams is Ginebra San Miguel (Saint Michael's Gin), which was once composed of discards from the other teams but, with sheer determination, was able to win championships. Filipinos associate strongly with Ginebra San Miguel's rise from "rags to riches."

Filipinos play or watch the games wherever there is public space. A sports enthusiast wrote, "No school is so small or obscure that it does not have a team that aspires to local championship at least. In every nook or corner of the archipelago there are ardent basketball fans and wherever there is a vacant lot anywhere, barefooted kids indulge in the sport with the zeal and enthusiasm of true amateurs. In the Philippines, basketball is the sport 'par excellence' " (*The Filipino Athlete* 1935, 4). Seventy-five years later, the American writer Rafe Bartholomew who spent over a year studying Filipino basketball was impressed with how Filipinos took advantage of every available public space to play the game—from the gymnasium where teams battled against each other to the basketball courts built by local governments in public parks, from school grounds to village courts and even building rooftops and street corners. Finally, basketball has turned into a commercial, social, and cultural phenomenon. Bartholomew saw billboards, print advertisements, and television ads all over the country that featured the sport or basketball player endorsing a product such as a beverage or sports apparel. He said that the game was being "used to sell everything from vitamin syrup that is supposed to make kids grow taller and be basketball players to margarine that also somehow purports to make people taller. Basketball gets pimped out for a lot of different causes" (Bartholomew 2010, 383).

American soldiers brought basketball and baseball to their Philippine colony to try to divert Filipinos' attention from cockfighting. It was first played in the YMCA and in the public schools but it did not attract many, perhaps because it was first introduced as a woman's sport. In 1911, the colonial government established the National Basketball Championships that had women's and men's teams. Women's games attracted crowds because of the novelty of the game and also because the players wore bloomers. The Catholic Church condemned this as "immoral" and Catholic and Christian schools did not include the game in their physical education classes. Filipinos became interested in men's basketball after the first Philippine team won gold at the Far Eastern Games in 1913 and 1915.

In 1924, colleges and universities launched the National Collegiate Athletic Association (NCAA) and the sport began to attract a new audience—college students—who rooted for their teams during their annual interscholastic tournaments. When the Olympics added basketball to its list of games in 1936, the colonial government created the Basketball Association of the Philippines (BAP) which joined the newly formed Federation Internationale de Basketball Amateur (FIBA). This spurred universities to form their own University Athletic Association of the Philippines (UAAP) and companies set up the Manila Industrial Commercial Athletics Association (MICAA), which recruited student athletes and also trained players for the Philippine team. MICAA became the face of Philippine basketball for the next 40 years.

The Philippines continued to dominate the Asian Games and its international reputation got another boost when, in 1954, the Philippine team won bronze in the FIBA World Championship, the first ever for an Asian team. It is a record that has never been broken. Lou Antolihao noted that winning "provided the inspiration and gave the impetus that [further] spurred the meteoric rise of basketball as the most popular sport in the Philippines." After this milestone event, the influence of the sport spread from its usual niches (i.e., urban, college, private school, and upper class) to the rest of the population. This development allowed basketball to attract a widespread following from the different sectors of society, turning the Philippines into "one of the few 'basketball republics' in the world" (Antolihao 2012, 1409). In 1975, 10 teams left the MICAA to form the Philippine Basketball Association (PBA), the first professional league in Asia and the second in the world after the NBA.

The PBA is divided into three tournaments ("conferences"): an all-Filipino one, another where each team brings in two "imports" (often American); and a "governor's cup," where winners of the two previous conferences play against each other. These conferences initially attracted the lower and middle classes in Metropolitan Manila. Once television networks were able to extend their reach to the rest of the country, audience interest grew exponentially. In 1981, PBA games were the fifth most-watched television programs, and by the first quarter of the 21st century, 75 percent of Filipinos 18 years and older were following basketball on television. Television made icons of players, with some of them even venturing into films and politics. In the 1990s, the games did not only draw lower- and middle-class Filipinos, but also movie stars, socialites, politicians, and even children of presidents (Antolihao 2009, 136). In 2004, attendance to PBA games reached 132 million in Metropolitan Manila, grossing the association over P16 million.

As basketball gained national prominence, however, the Philippines' global competitiveness declined. Subsequent national teams were never able to replicate the 1954 third place finish. In 1959, the Philippines finished 8th in the FIBA World Championships, 11th in the 1960 Olympic games, 6th in a 1964 pre-Olympic qualifying tournament, and 13th in the 1968 and 1972 Olympics. The Philippines fared better when FIBA founded a regional Asia championship, claiming gold in 1965, 1967, 1973, and 1984 (it won in 1986 but was disqualified), silver in 1965 and 1971, and bronze in 1969. After 1986, however, it failed to earn another medal, sliding to as low as 15th in ranking in 2003.

The Philippines had gradually removed itself from ranks among the best in Asia, despite the Philippine Congress passing a law in 2011 that granted foreign players with a Filipino parent "naturalized citizenship" and the opportunity to play for the country. The last time it reached the top again was in the 2013 FIBA-Asia championships, when a team consisting of professionals and Filipino Americans earned the country a silver medal. When professionals did not join succeeding teams, however, the Philippines once again took a dive—placing 9th in 2016 and 7th in 2017; and in what was its worst outing since 2003, the team lost all its games and placed last in 2019. Today, it is only in the Southeast Asian region that the country has retained the gold.

Ironically, the most serious threat to the PBA is its model and source of inspiration, the NBA. The latter has been expanding rapidly in Asia, stimulated by the Chinese, Japanese, and Philippine markets. Stars like the New York Lakers' Lebron James, the Golden State Warrior's Stephen Curry and Klay Thompson, and the Washington

Wizard's Gilbert Arenas have continued where retired stars like Kobe Bryant had left off, visiting these countries in the off-season. Chinese, Japanese, and Asian American players have also become members of several NBA teams. The PBA has been able to stand on its own despite the NBA's rich resources and famous personnel by buttressing its image as a prime national sport. Filipinos have responded positively, still going to PBA games all over the country in droves and keeping the passion of the game alive.

See also: Chapter 6: Overview. Chapter 10: Overview.

Further Reading

Antolihao, Lou. 2012. "From Baseball Colony to Basketball Republic: Post-colonial Transition and the Making of a National Sport in the Philippines." *Sports in Society: Cultures, Commerce, Media, Politics* 15, no. 10: 1396–1412.

Antolihao, Lou Apolinario. 2009. "Can the Subaltern Play? Postcolonial Transition and the Making of Basketball as the National Sports in the Philippines." PhD diss., National University of Singapore.

Bartholomew, Rafe. 2010. *Pacific Rims: Beermen Ballin' in Flip-Flops and the Philippines' Unlikely Love Affair with Basketball.* New York: New American Library.

The Filipino Athlete. 1935. October 16.

Boxing

Boxing was one of the sports the American army brought to the Philippines in the 1900s, hoping that it could distract soldiers from being mired in alcohol, sex, and tobacco. It found its way to the YMCA in 1909, when three American entrepreneurs who had been running carnivals, circuses, and horse races converted a cockfighting pit into a gym. They invited Filipinos to learn how to box and then held matches featuring Filipino boxers to attract Filipinos and turn them into fans. A sportswriter predicted that the "Olympic Club" could eventually teach "every other Filipino . . . to be a fighter" (Stradley 2008). Filipinos warmed up to the boxing style introduced by the Americans, but the motivation was not just coming from the latter. Filipinos already had their style—"bare-hand fighting" (*suntukan*), which involved two fighters holding their hands high up and then lunging and pummeling each other with punches. Filipinos believe that *suntukan* came out of knife fighting (*kali*) which the Spanish colonizers had banned along with *arnis*. Both sports were forced to go underground and, without their weapons, Filipinos improvised with their hands. When the Americans brought in boxing, Filipinos believed that their boxers could successfully fuse both styles.

And Filipinos responded with enthusiasm. In 1924, one of the gym owners, Frank Churchill, beamed with pride at how "[t]hese boys would storm the club on Wednesday night, begging for a chance to go on. . . . Many of them didn't have enough money to buy an outfit of ring togs, so we always kept a supply of trunks, shoes, etc., available for them. Lots of 'em wouldn't use shoes. They were accustomed to going barefoot, and shoes cramped their style" (Stradley 2008). In 1921, the colonial government legalized boxing "to see the Filipino youth master the manly arts of self-defense—wrestling and boxing" (Gems 2016, 57). It allowed 20-round fights regardless of boxers' weights. The boxing crowds continued to grow.

Then on June 19, 1923, Pancho Villa defeated American boxer Jimmy Wilde and became the first Filipino world flyweight boxing champion. Filipinos celebrated Villa's victory for having placed the Philippines on the international boxing map. Political observers even saw in Villa's feat proof that the Filipinos were now capable of self-government. Villa's fame, however, was short-lived. In 1925, on the eve of a boxing match, he underwent dental surgery and went to the match with a swollen jaw. He lost the match and most likely went into septic shock. He died on the operating table. Filipinos mourned his death but it also inspired a wave of young boxers to come to the United States to fight. They fared relatively well, but no one could match Pancho Villa's prestige until Gabriel "Flash" Elorde placed the country once again on the boxing map 30 years later.

On July 20, 1955, Elorde defeated American boxer Sandy Saddler in a non-title bout in Manila, signaling what Filipinos call Philippine boxing's "second golden age." Five years later, he won the world super featherweight championship belt by knocking out the reigning champion Harold Gomes. The country's new boxing successfully defended his title 10 times, including a first-round knockout of Gomes in their rematch. This remains the record longest reign as a super featherweight (later reclassified into junior lightweight). Elorde became a global celebrity, admired for his modesty, his friendliness (especially toward opponents), and his simple lifestyle. Boxers like Muhammad Ali adopted his footwork, which was derived from the Indigenous *arnis/eskrima*.

Like Pancho Villa, Elorde inspired another wave of young boxers to try their mettle internationally. Twenty of this cohort went on to become world champions. After accomplishing a record of 88 wins (33 by knockout), 27 losses, and 2 draws, Elorde retired in 1967 and became a boxing promoter. On January 2, 1985, Elorde died of lung cancer at the age of 49, most likely due to his turning into a chain-smoker after he retired. On its 20th anniversary, the World Boxing Council named him one of the best junior lightweights in history, and in 1992, he was elevated to the Boxing Hall of Fame.

Thirty-one years after Elorde retired, another Filipino boxer—named Emmanuel "Manny" Pacquiao—achieved global fame. Villa, Elorde, and Pacquiao are the exceptions rather than the norm. The majority of boxers don't even reach the top tier.

See also: Chapter 6: Overview. Chapter 16: Overview.

Further Reading

Barter, Shane Joshua. 2009. "Boxing Day in Cotabato: Notes from the Field." *Explorations: A Graduate Student Journal of Southeast Asia* 9 (Spring): 113–114.

Gems, Gerald R. 2016. *Sport and the American Occupation of the Philippines: Bats, Balls and Bayonets*. Lanham, MD: Lexington Books.

Ishioka, Tomonori. 2012. "Boxing, Poverty, Foreseeability—An Ethnographic Account of Local Boxers in Metro Manila, Philippines." *Asia Pacific Journal of Sport and Social Science* 1, no. 2–3: 143–155.

Stradley, Don. 2008. "A Look at the History of Boxing in the Philippines." *ESPN*. June 24. https://www.espn.com/sports/boxing/news/story?id=3458707

Cockfighting

This seemingly naughty word comes from the word *gamecock*, which in turn was derived from the term "cock of the game" used by the British author George Wilson who wrote the book *The Commendation of Cocks and Cock Fighting* in 1607. The game, however, was not solely British nor was it first "played" in the 1600s.

Scholars claim that the game was played 6,000 years ago, with the first recorded cockfight having taken place in China in 517 BC. From its Asian origins, the game spread across Babylon and Syria, where the fighting cock was revered as a deity. Merchants brought the fighting cocks to Europe, and Romans and Greeks associated them with their gods Apollo, Mercury, and Mars. In the 16th century, the sport was prevalent in France and England, leading to the invention of such English words as "cocky," "cocksure," "cocktail," and "cockpit." In the 1840s, the English parliament declared the game a vice and banned it. However, the edict came too late, as English and French explorers had already brought cockfighting to Africa and the Americas as far back as the 1500s (although archeologists found chicken bones in Chile and Polynesia, suggesting that cockfighting in the Americas may have preceded Europe).

The Philippine edition of cockfighting is called *sabong* and was most likely introduced from China. The chronicler of the first Spanish expedition that reached the islands in the 1620s wrote about having observed cockfighting in a community in northeastern Mindanao. The Spanish colonial regime (Chapter 2) promoted *sabong* so it could raise taxes from the heavy betting that accompanied the game. The Americans were appalled by the blood sport and its lack of morals, banning it and replacing it with the sports they brought from the mainland. The Japanese did likewise, but when the Philippines became independent, so did the national government.

Sabong involves breeding fighting roosters and feeding them with carbohydrates (grained rice or corn), protein (ground meat), vitamins and supplements. They are also vaccinated and sometimes even bulked up through steroids. Poor Filipino breeders get their fowls from "native" varieties, while their wealthier counterparts import their "Texas cocks" from the United States. The former have 2–4 cocks in cages and feed them the sustenance that they can afford, while the latter have at least 200–300 roosters a year that are given a full meal. The cocks are trained for at least two years by being put through "sparring" bouts with other cocks and being made to "exercise" in a larger gated field. Once these are judged as ready, the owners (or their handlers) bring them to the "cockpit," a large dome with rafters surrounding a round or rectangular enclosure where the cockfight happens.

Each rooster will have a 1.5-inch sharp spur or razor blade tied around each other's legs. These blades are covered with a leather wrap, which will be removed when the fight begins. When ready, each handler will bring their cocks into the pit where a *casador* does a final check, which is part of their role as an overall manager. The *casador* also takes the bets of the fowls' owners. There are also other people involved in the game. There is the *manari*—the representative—of each owner, who will make sure the spurs are of the required measurement; a *heeler*, who fixes the blades if they are below the required measurement or wrongly attached; the *sentenciador* (sen-ten-sha-dor), who declares the winner; a *timekeeper;* and *cock doctors* who have the responsibility of treating the wounds of the cocks after the fight.

The most important person in the game is the *kristo* (the bookmaker), who goes around outside the enclosure taking up bets. It is not from the "Son of God" per se that the name comes, but from an action of Christ where he stretched his arms to the public. The *kristo* imitates Christ when he extends his hands to place bets. This remarkable figure can take as much as 50 bets in one fight and remember where the bettors are seated and the amounts they placed (four lifted fingers equal 400 pesos, while the same fingers pointed downward equal 4,000 pesos). After the fight, losers crumple the paper money and throw it to the *kristo* while he hands out the money to the winners. The winners, in turn, tip the *kristo* 10 percent. The procedure is repeated in successive fights until the cockpit closes just before dinner time.

Of all the many portrayals of *sabong*, it was national hero Jose Rizal's description of it in his novel *Noli Me Tangere* that best captures it and is worth quoting despite its length. Rizal writes:

> They advanced slowly, their steps audible on the hard ground; no one in the cockpit spoke or breathed. Raising and lowering their heads as if measuring each other with their eyes, the gamecocks uttered sounds, threatening or perhaps scornful. They caught sight of the razor blades, gleaming with a cold blue light; danger stimulated them, and they approached each other with determination. But a step apart, they stopped, and with fixed eyes lowered their heads and raised their hackles. At that moment blood rushed into their tiny brains, their anger flashed like lightning, and with all their natural courage they hurled themselves impetuously upon each other, beak against beak, breast to breast, steel spur against its fellow, wing to wing: but the blows were parried masterfully, and only a few feathers fell.
>
> They sized each other up again. Suddenly the white cock leaped up, slashing with the deadly razor, but the red cock had bent its legs and lowered its head, and the white cock hit only empty air. As it landed, it turned quickly to protect its back and face the red cock. The latter attacked it furiously, but it defended itself with complete self-control. It was not the favourite for nothing. Everyone followed the ups and downs of the duel with bated breath and one or another involuntary cry. Bloody feathers, both red and white, were littering the pit, but it

was not a duel intended to end at the first drawing of blood; for the Filipino, following the laws of his government, it was a duel that only death or flight could end.

Blood soaked the ground of the pit; the brave encounters were repeated again and again, but victory remained uncertain. At last, in a supreme effort, the white cock hurled itself forward to give a final blow; it nailed its spur in one of the red cock's wings. Where it was caught in the bones; but the white cock had itself been hit in the breast, and the two birds, panting, exhausted, drained of their lives' blood, one joined to the other, were still, until the white cock fell, blood spurting out of its beak, its legs jerking in its last agony. The red cock, bound to it by the wing, remained standing beside it, but little by little its own legs crumpled and its eyes closed. (Rizal, *Noli Me Tangere*, Chapter 46)

It is this bloody nature of *sabong* that has earned the ire of animal advocates. Filipinos, however, have resisted any attempt to reduce or even eliminate *sabong*, with the most unusual of justifications. Some say that it is impossible to oppose *sabong* when politicians are themselves bettors and breeders. Government leaders have even seen it fit to pass a law in support of *sabong* when President Ferdinand E. Marcos issued a decree in 1981, creating the "Philippine Gamefowl Commission" to regulate the industry. President Gloria M. Arroyo abolished the commission in 1993, but its powers were moved to the Games and Amusement Board, which regulates professional sports and "allied activities."

Others use a culturalist argument (*sabong* is inherently Filipino) with a bizarre interpretation of the law. The vice president of the Philippine chapter of the Society for the Prevention of Cruelty to Animals complained that "[o]ur laws protecting animals mainly concern endangered species and bigger animals, like dogs, cats, horses, whale sharks, and monkey-eating eagles" (Watson 2007). There is less sympathy for chickens, which come aplenty and are not big enough. Other Filipinos point to *sabong* as one of the few activities where honesty is the norm. A former secretary of education was asked where he can find honest people, and his answer was quite revealing: "If they want to know if Filipinos are honest, don't go to Malacanang, you'll be disappointed; don't go to Congress, you will be equally disappointed; don't go to the Supreme Court . . . go to the cockpit, and you'll see the Filipinos are basically honest" (Tacio 2017). In *sabong*, bets are honored, and losers pay.

In the end, however, it all comes to money. Today, *sabong* is played in about 2,500 cockpits with over 5 million Filipinos betting and 30 million roosters being killed every year. It is not uncommon to see towns and small cities with three significant landmarks—city hall, the church, and the cockpits. The sport is also a US$300 million industry that has become an international sport, attracting owners and breeders from Kuwait, Malaysia, Indonesia, Taiwan, and especially the United States, where the game is now completely banned. The country now hosts the annual "World Slasher's Cup," a weeklong series of *sabong* averaging 650 matches with the prize money going up as high as US$350,000. Today, the World Slasher's Cup comes second to basketball in national popularity, and it has turned the Philippines into the Mecca of cockfighting.

See also: Chapter 10: Overview.

Further Reading

Anima, Nid, ed. 1973. *Philippine Cockfighting Stories.* Quezon City: Omar Publications.

Davis, Janet M. 2013. "Cockfight Nationalism: Blood Sport and the Moral Politics of American Empire and Nation Building." *American Quarterly* 65, no. 3 (September): 549–574.

Guggenheim, Scott. 1994. "Cock or Bull: Cockfighting, Social Structure, and Political Commentary in the Philippines." In Alan Dunes (ed.), *The Cockfight: A Casebook.* Madison, WI: University of Wisconsin Press.

McCaghy, Charles H., and Arthur G. Neal. 1974. "The Fraternity of Cockfighters: Ethical Embellishments of an Illegal Sport," *Journal of Popular Culture* 8, no. 3 (Winter): 557.

Tacio, Henry D. 2017. "Culture and Arts: This Sport Called Cockfighting." *Edge Davao.* January 31. https://edgedavao.net/culture-arts/2017/01/31/culture-arts-sport-called -cockfighting/

Watson, Paul. 2007. "It's in the Blood." *Los Angeles Times.* June 16. https://www.latimes .com/archives/la-xpm-2007-jun-16-fg-cockfight16-story.html

Pacquiao, Manny

It is said that when the boxer Manny Pacquiao fights, the whole country stops and even the crime rate goes down to zero as both policemen and criminals are glued to the television. Muslims and Filipinos don't trust each other, but when Pacquiao fights, both cheer him on. Shane Barter watched as a "Muslim woman yelped in delight [and a] bearded cleric proclaimed Pacquiao the 'Mexi-cutioner.' The room was packed, the crowd praising Pacquiao's training, skill, and humility. All this time, Abdulaziz's stare did not leave the television. 'Pacquiao,' he said of the Christian boxer, 'is one of us.' For just one hour, these Moros were Filipinos" (Barter 2009, 113). Pacquiao had become an inspiration for your boxers such that in 2012, the country had 5 champions and 36 former champions.

Pacquiao was a cigarette peddler helping his single mother survive the streets when he realized he could do a lot with his fists. He left for Manila—stowing away in a ship—and joined a popular boxing television show *Blow-by-Blow* as a junior fly-weight. He stayed with the show for four years but then, on December 4, 1998, Pacquiao knocked out the Thai boxer Chatchai Sasakil to capture his first world championship. When he lost the crown a year later, Pacquiao moved up to super ban-tamweight and, in June 2001, dethroned the reigning champion, South African Lehlo-honolo Ledwaba, to become the International Boxing Federation's new champion. He defended his crown in 2003 and continued to win the world titles in six other divisions.

In 2010, Pacquiao became the first boxer ever to win six division titles in seven different weight categories of the two boxing bodies, the World Boxing Organization (WBO) and the International Boxing Federation (IBF). Pacquiao's 15-bout winning streak ended in June 2012. He regained his WBO welterweight title in April 2014 but lost twice, once against his No. 1 rival Floyd Merriweather. Pacquiao retired in April 2016 but changed his mind four months later. He lost his WBO belt once again on July 15, 2018. However, a year later, he took away the rival World Boxing Association (WBA) welterweight title.

Pacquiao entered politics in 2007, losing in a mayor's race. In May 2010, he moved to another province and successfully ran for a seat in the House of Representatives. He was reelected in 2013, but in 2016 he decided to run for the Senate. He won. He still has not retired from boxing. He has a record of 57 wins (38 by knockout), 6 losses and 2 draws. He is the oldest welterweight champion in boxing history. In recognition of this impeccable record, the Boxing Writers Association of America named him the "Fighter of the Decade" for the first quarter of the 21st century. Filipinos have also shown their appreciation by giving him different nicknames—"Pac-Man" for "gobbling up" his opponents like the computer game; "The Destroyer" for obvious reasons; and "The Mexican Killer" and "Mexi-cutioner" for having defeated many Mexican boxers (he would disown these names). Since Pacquiao has repeatedly dedicated his fight "to my country," Filipinos have also taken to calling him "The People's Champ" and the "Nation's Fist." The "Pacquiao wave" has rejuvenated Philippine boxing. Among the younger boxers who were inspired by his accomplishments, three have won world titles; two of them have won in several weight divisions just like "The People's Champ."

See also: Chapter 6: Overview. Chapter 16: Overview.

Further Reading

Barter, Shane Joshua. 2009. "Boxing Day in Cotabato: Notes from the Field." *Explorations: A Graduate Student Journal of Southeast Asia* 9 (Spring): 113–114.

Gonzalez, Joaquin Jay, III, and Angelo Michael F. Merino. 2012. *From Pancho to Pacquiao: Philippine Boxing in and out of the Ring*. Minneapolis, MN: Mill City Press Inc.

Plaza to Mall

In towns and municipalities, "downtown" is called the plaza complex. A plaza is a walled square where there is a public park covered with trees and a bandstand. The Spanish introduced the plaza complex. One of the provisions of King Philip II's "Laws of the Indies" was a grid design for the layout of towns and municipalities. Its purpose was to facilitate the concentration of communities that were once spread out all over and difficult to control. All Spanish colonies were to be organized based on this grid. Thus, the plazas in Mexico are strongly identical to those in the Philippines.

The plaza complex is where one finds the two most essential town institutions—the Catholic Church and the local government office (the *munisipyo*)—and the statue of the national hero, Jose Rizal. Plazas also have a stage in the town marketplace, a school, a children's playground, a radio station, and several stores. The local rich also have their family homes around the plaza, and these were two-story residences propped up by large ornamented wooden pillars (Hart 1955, 34). All municipal affairs are held at the plaza. In the early American period, zarzuelas and moro-moro plays (see Chapter 10) were staged in a bandstand, and in the postwar period, these were replaced by musical programs, the performance of the local orchestra, or debating contests. The plaza is also where political candidates rally their followers and reach out to voters. In the adjoining playground, local teams play baseball, basketball, tennis, and volleyball.

As municipalities grow and become more urban, the plaza gradually ceases to be the town center. The church may stay, but the municipal government may move to an area where it can accommodate more residents. The "old families" may also move to a new suburb as downtown traffic becomes more congested, while businesses close and move to the newly constructed mall that is strategically located in the entry point of the municipality. Mass entertainment also ceases to be held in the plaza's stage as people head to the mall to watch movies and croon in the karaoke bars. Ironically, this shift away from the plaza has magnified its quaintness, as residents see the importance of preserving its "culturally valued structures" (Matejowsky 2002, 234). There is now a debate in many communities between architectural conservationists and real estate developers over the fate of their plazas.

In the 1970s, a Filipino crooner translated the lines of the Alan Bergman and Marvin Hamilton song "The Way We Were" into Filipino. One line captured the social importance of the public park. It ran, "We meandered around Luneta Park, without any money." Luneta Park is the most significant public open space in Manila, which gets filled out with families, couples, and friends spending weekend afternoons having picnics, playing games, or simply hanging out observing other people and waiting for the Manila Bay sunset. People still go to Luneta and similar parks in other cities and towns, but their favorites now are the malls. It is estimated that 80 percent of the Filipino population has gone to "shopping centers," with almost half having visited malls more than once. There is every reason to go to shopping centers. They offer comfort (the entire structure is air-conditioned) and security (mall owners have their private security agencies) and are virtually mini-cities. Malls are the enclaves in crowded, dirty cities (Manila has a population of 12 million) where one could, as it were, recover their humanity. As one Manila newspaper puts it, Filipinos regard malls as "safe havens" because they create "a mirage of comfort, security, and affluence" ("Where Do Filipinos Go" 2018) amid a sea of poverty and pollution.

Michael Pinches calls them the "self-contained world of leisure and opulence, away from pollution, grinding traffic and constant reminders of hardship" as well as places that "are so seductive in promoting a life of consumer spending" (Pinches 1995, 12 as quoted by Connell 1999, 433). This description of the Shoemart Megamall, reputedly the largest in Asia, likewise captures what geographers call these "new public spaces." The "Megamall . . . is a six-story building, almost three quarters of a kilometer [0.4 miles] long, with 33 hectares of shopping space; it has twelve cinemas, an ice-skating rink, a ten-pin bowling centre, a pool hall, a fitness centre, amusement arcades, restaurants, specialist stores (such as antiquarian book stores), supermarkets, a church (for Catholic masses), and a food court that can seat 6,000 people" (Connell 1999, 433). The Philippines now has the fourth largest shopping mall in the world. Even the Philippine government has recognized the popularity of malls and has rented space where "satellite" offices of social welfare agencies facilitate applications for social welfare, travel documents, tax submissions, and voter identity cards.

While elites are less likely to fraternize with those who go to the park, their interest in high-end stores that are also found in malls means that they cannot avoid intermingling with the middle classes and the poor who regard malls as the "lifestyle centers" that would bring them the amenities of a "modern" (i.e., American) lifestyle—the latest fashion, music, films, technological paraphernalia, cuisine, and even the most bizarre of fads, skin whitening soap and ointment. With remittances from family members working abroad, these "lower classes" can now afford to spend on some of the commodities that only the rich could purchase in the past.

Malls may have become areas of temporary solace and convenience, but this comes at the expense of the once-popular sites of social recreation—the parks. In Manila, malls have forcefully displaced Luneta Park as the public space for family recreation. Hence, these days, when Filipinos want to invite friends and family to "hang out," they ask them if they are interested in "malling" (i.e., spending their money), instead of spending a pleasant afternoon in Luneta which entails almost no spending at all.

See also: Chapter 4: Overseas Filipino Workers. Chapter 6: Overview.

Further Reading

Connell, J. 1999. "Beyond Manila: Walls, Malls and Private Spaces." *Environment and Planning* 31: 417–439.

Hart, Donn V. 1955. *The Philippine Plaza Complex: A Focal Point in Culture Change*. New Haven: Yale University Southeast Asian Studies.

Joaquin, Nick. 1990. *Manila, My Manila: A History for the Young*. Manila: Republic of the Philippines.

Matejowsky, Ty. 2002. "Globalization, Privatization, and Public Space in the Provincial Philippines." In Jeffrey H. Cohen and Norbert Dannhauser (eds.), *Economic Development: An Anthropological Approach*. Walnut Creek: Altamira Press.

Milgram, B. Lynne. 2012. "Reconfiguring Margins: Secondhand Clothing and Street Vending in the Philippines." *Textile: The Journal of Cloth and Culture* 10, no. 2: 200–221.

Pinches, Michael, ed. 1999. "Entrepreneurship, Consumption, Ethnicity and National Identity in the Making of the Philippines' New Rich." In *Culture and Privilege in Capitalist Asia*. New York: Taylor and Francis.

Rico, Jore-Annie, and Kim Robert C. de Leon. 2017. "Mall Culture and Consumerism in the Philippines." *State of Power*. https://www.tni.org/files/publication-downloads/stateofpower2017-mall-culture.pdf

"Where Do Filipinos Go." 2018. *BusinessWorld*. October 31. Accessed February 16, 2022. https://www.bworldonline.com/where-do-filipinos-go/

Sungka, Sipa, and **Other Traditional Games**

The popularity of the games introduced by the Americans overshadowed several games that were popular in the local streets and the communities. These traditional games have also been given little attention by sports enthusiasts and scholars. Hence, unlike basketball or boxing, the literature on these games is scant and often does not go beyond descriptions.

Filipinos play chess or checkers at the plaza or the barbershops, but inside the house, the favorite game is the *sungka* (song-ka). In *sungka*, two players face each other with a *sungka* board between them. This boatlike board has seven small bowl-like holes carved on both sides and two larger ones carved on each end. Each small hole is filled up with seven small shells called *sigay* (see-guy). The game starts with each player scooping the *sigay* in a bowl at the same time and then putting one on the next one to the left, including into one's large bowl. They do this going around the *sungka* board. If the seventh shell ends up in a small hole that is full of *sigay*, the players scoop the shells in that hole and continue going around the board. However, if the last shell ends up in an empty hole, the player stops while their competitor continues as long as they do not end up in an empty hole.

Sungka is a game of strategy with each player figuring out from which bowl to start so that by the fourth or fifth time they go around the board, they either do not end up in an empty bowl or if they do, they can scoop the shells on their opponent's side. The game usually does not last even 15 minutes, but players and watchers often end up enjoying the game a whole afternoon because of the variations in strategy. *Sungka* remains a popular game—even if it may be played less as Filipinos adjust to the demands of urban life (more work, less play)—and evidence of this is seen in how the *sungka* board occupies an important place in Filipino life. One can find the board filled with *sigay* on the center table of the living room or the veranda; it may also be found on a barbershop bench and or on a small table at the entrance of a public market. The older the board, the more important it becomes as family heirloom.

Sipa ("to kick," or "a kick" in Filipino) is a game where a ball made of either rattan, rubber bands bunched together to form a ball, or a metal disk with a feathery tail made of shredded plastic is kicked around by players either facing each other or

The shell game sungka. (Ravindran John Smith/Dreamstime.com)

formed into a circle. A player can keep the ball to oneself by kicking it upward to land in front of them, or they can kick it upward once and in the second kick direct the ball to another player. The objective of the game is to ensure the ball does not touch the ground, for if it does, the player then removes themself from the game. *Sipa* is an old game, predating the Spanish colonial period, and was extremely popular across the Southeast Asian region (there are versions of *sipa* in Indonesia and Malaysia). Children mainly play it on streets and parks, but the appearance of variants after World War II led to the Philippine government declaring *sipa* a national sport.

One of these variations was primarily responsible for this change in *sipa*'s status. The first is *sipa lambatan* that was "invented" by a Filipino journalist after the war. In *sipa lambatan*, two teams of 1–4 players kick the ball back and forth over a net set up in the middle. The team that allows the ball to touch the ground loses. The game is similar to volleyball and demands the same speed and agility as the latter. *Sipa*'s standing in Philippine sports was further bolstered when another variant, the *sepak takraw*, reached a level of popularity such that those playing it formed clubs, which in turn agreed to coordinate their games by forming the Philippine Amateur Takraw Association (PASTA) that would represent the Philippines in regional *sipa* competitions.

Three games are played at the town plazas during fiestas, Christmas day celebrations, and other holidays. Two of these are games that came from the Spanish (as indicated by their names and how they are played). *Juego de anillo* (ring game) involves a rider who spears off a ring that is hanging from a bamboo arch. Today, the horses have been replaced by bicycles. The other game is called *juego de toro* (bull game); it is a make-shift bullfight with a bull made of paper-mache with a hollowed bottom. A string of firecrackers with just enough gunpowder to make a pop but not harm people is wrapped around the bull. A man slips under the "bull," then someone lights the firecracker. The "bull" then runs fast with people coming after it. The one who can catch the bull before all the firecrackers explode wins the prize. The last of these plaza games is *palo sebo* (*palo* means stick while *sebo* is the Filipino word for oil). It is a game where individual contestants or competing teams try to climb up a greased bamboo pole planted in the middle of a square. Dexterity alone would not get one to the top; improvisation is equally essential. Individual contestants cover their hands and soles with ash for traction. Team members stand on each other's shoulders, doing this while holding on to the pole. This gets repeated until the last to climb reaches the banner. Winners are recognized, but the crowd also cheers for those who failed.

From the games for special occasions, we go on to street games that children love to play. *Patintero* is a two-team competition where, after a coin toss, one team becomes the "the passers" while the other is called "the taggers." The game is played on the ground wherein the children have drawn a rectangular field using charcoal, paint, or chalk. The field must be more or less five by three meters, with four parallel lines drawn inside it. Four "taggers" then position themselves on each of the inside lines to prevent "passers" from crossing from one end of the rectangle to the other. The latter must be able to do this within two minutes, accumulating points as they pass through one line (the first line equals one point and subsequent lines between two and three points).

See also: Chapter 7: Overview; Generational Changes; Parent-Child Relationships.

Further Reading

De Voogt, Alex. 2010. "Philippine Sungka and Cultural Contact in Southeast Asia: Research Note." *Asian Ethnology* 69, no. 2: 333–342

Gabriel, Bernardo A. 1937. "Sungka: Philippine Variant of a Widely-Distributed Game." *Philippine Social Science Review* 9: 1–36.

Panganiban, Teejay D., Rommel P. Manalo, April Kisses S. Polgadno, and Marc John H. Sarmiento. 2019. "Factors Influencing the Sports Involvement of *Sepak Takraw* Athletes in a State University." *PUPIL: International Journal of Teaching Education and Learning.* 3, no. 1: 290–305.

CHAPTER 16

MEDIA AND POPULAR CULTURE

OVERVIEW

The late professor of humanities Doreen G. Fernandez, one of the leading scholars on "Filipino popular culture," explains why it is difficult to pin down what the term exactly means given the sociohistorical diversity of the country. She writes that the Philippines is "a Third World, developing nation; with many indigenous ethnic groups still definitely unurbanized; with a long history of colonization that left behind at least two immediately discernible layers of cultural influence, the Spanish and the American, and a less discernible (being more deeply assimilated) one, the Chinese; in a present socioeconomic state that is still predominantly agricultural, semifeudal (many feudal structures, especially in agricultural practices and related lifestyles continue, barely changed), and neocolonial (dependent on foreign economies, especially through the pervasive presence of multinational corporations)." Fernandez adds: "It is clear that definition of what is popular in the Philippine context can be no easy task" (Fernandez 1981, 26).

Among the three external influences on popular culture, it was the American influence that had the most profound impact. It did not just shape young Filipinos' minds through the education system; it also introduced what Fernandez calls "the structures of mass communications"—films, radio, songs, television. When Filipino entrepreneurs took over this structure, they continued what the Americans had done, although they did introduce more Filipino themes and the Filipino language itself in broadcasting to the people. Filipino popular culture is "heavily American, in that it has absorbed American popular culture as its own." Despite efforts to introduce the Filipino language, popular culture in the Philippines "is still heavily American in influence" (Fernandez 1980b, 3).

The study of popular culture "is comparatively young, having started in the sixties as mass communication research and then getting the attention of literature scholars ten years after." Some social activists asked the questions: who are those who make up popular culture's audience, and for what reasons are they interested in the topic? Others worried about popular culture's literary value: was it "serious literature"? Yet, with the spread of radio and television and film and comics, Fernandez recommends that scholars and writers agree to a "stable definition" of the term starting with the acknowledgment of American influence and then look at how Filipinos adopted the musical, visual, and audio forms coming from the United States to suit their needs.

319

From there, they could turn their attention to resolving other issues like how popular culture can be turned into "a potent force for persuasion and value-building" (Fernandez 1981, 41) for a still-developing society like the Philippines.

The challenge, however, is quite daunting. Radio programs are less concerned with educating their listeners and more engrossed with soap operas, with news that is straight from the newspapers, and talk radio that includes a lot of trash talking. Television is better in terms of discussions on the issues of the day (having 24-hour cable television helps), but the medium's audience still prefers the noontime games-song-and-dance shows, the translated Korean dramas, and the crime segments of news reports. Movies are the least educational for apparent reasons—revenues dictate that scripts are about action, fantasy, and love stories. Some directors produce socially relevant films, but these are a minority.

See also: Chapter 9: Overview. Chapter 11: Overview. Chapter 12: Overview. Chapter 13: Overview.

Further Reading

Fernandez, Doreen G. 1980b. "Philippine-American Cultural Interactions." *University of the Philippines Third World Studies Program Discussion Papers 21*. December.

Fernandez, Doreen G. 1981. "Philippine Popular Culture: Dimensions and Directions. The State of Research in Philippine Popular Culture," *Philippine Studies* 29 (First Quarter): 26–44.

Comics/*Komiks*

The first Filipino comic strip was Kenkoy (Jester) by Antonio Velasquez, whom historians refer to as the Father of the Philippine *komiks*. Velasquez painted the character Kenkoy as a happy-go-lucky, young urbanite who conned people into getting what he wanted. Readers not only enjoyed his antics but also what they called his "pidgin English," where words and phrases were pronounced with an exaggerated Filipino accent. Thus, when he flirted, Kenkoy would not say, "Good morning, Miss Beautiful," but "Gud Morning, Mis Biyutipul." Some historians cite Kenkoy as proof of how much Philippine society had been "Americanized"; others recognized his Western get-ups (Hawaiian shirt, wide pants) but also suggested that Kenkoy may be another version of more than a few rascally sorts from precolonial epics.

The same contrasting views were expressed when it came to new komik characters introduced after 1930. The life and adventures of the hero *Kulafu* were an imitation of *Tarzan* while Dyesebel, a sea siren, was a Filipina mermaid. The 1940 superwoman, Darna, was a lookalike of Wonder Woman while Captain Barbell (introduced in 1963) was the near-perfect replica of Superman (although the artist Mars Ravelo said Captain America inspired him). These figures could also very well represent the heroes of precolonial Philippines—like Labbaw Donggon, an adventurer who fought a lord of darkness for a woman's heart, Tuwaang, a superhero who could ride lightning and fought giants, and Bantugen, a noble and handsome prince who could fly and walk on the water's surface. Some komik writers did mix Western and Filipino stories and themes. One superhero, Flash Bomba (Flash Bomb), was modeled after the American comic book character Flash. However, his enemies included the *tikbalang*, a creature in Filipino folklore who has the body of a human but the head of a horse and hooves for feet.

The borrowing continued in the postwar period, and the appearance of Tagalog *komiks* helped government efforts to spread the Filipino language across the new nation. By the 1970s, Filipino komik writers and illustrators were able to create full story lines of Filipino cowboy movies, television action series, science fiction, jungle adventures, and romances. So popular had the komiks become that in the 1970s, 30–40 percent of young and adult Filipinos had become hooked to the medium. Komiks had done more in spreading the national language, Filipino, than the mandatory teaching of this language in primary and secondary schools.

Some authors continued to promote Filipino characters. Larry Alcala, the "Dean of Filipino Cartoonists," created characters with small-town roots who manage to keep their innocence amid the spread of cosmopolitanism. His characters also impishly mangle English by mixing it with Filipino (Tagalog). Filipinos call the pidgin "Taglish." Komik writers also snuck in political satire that targeted the dictatorship. The author Nonoy Marcelo created the rat "Ichabod" who lived in his community Dagaland (Ratland), where everyone complained about life and their leaders. Through these characters, readers could easily see themselves and their hardship under the Marcos government, and the top rats Ichabod and others interacted with reminded everyone of political leaders.

In the 1980s, the industry began to decline steadily. Several Filipino komik writers and illustrators moved to the United States, accepting offers from American comics companies to work for them. This left a big hole in the production of stories and print. The censorship of popular media during the Marcos dictatorship continued to take a toll on komik production. Those who stayed at home found themselves constricted and became less daring and innovative in producing characters and plots. Blood and gore flew out of the window, and so did several horror movies. They also self-censored themselves through a mutually agreed upon Comics Code. Komiks never recovered even after Marcos fell from power. The Japanese anime came to the Philippines, attracting young Filipinos to characters like *Pokémon* and Sailor Moon at the expense of their former Filipino superheroes.

From the late 1980s, komik production became a small-time affair with writers/illustrators printing for conventions and book fairs. Some wrote their stories in English to reach out to a broader audience. What saved komiks was television. Television networks either contracted komik writers or bought the rights to their work and produced *teleserye* (television series) featuring popular teenage male and female stars. Technological breakthroughs allowed *Captain Barbell* and *Darna* to adorn metallic uniforms and carry superweapons akin to those in Hollywood sci-fi films like *Star Wars* and *X-Men*.

In 2007, the government's National Commission on Culture and Arts initiated a series of programs to bring about a third renaissance of the komiks. It organized symposia and programs for known authors and had their works published as magazines and in the leading newspapers. The commission likewise continued to promote the *teleserye*. The programs never achieved their goals, but because of television, and to an extent movies, komiks continue to be popular fare. As Soledad S. Reyes puts it, "[The] komiks have always communicated with the majority, who knows and speaks the native language. The middle and upper classes have had their own reading fare—from the serious works of Hemingway and Faulkner to kitsch, the best-selling novels, the comic books in English that ranged from the Illustrated Classics to the DC comics strips and the graphic novels, the Mills and Boon romances and their spin-offs (see Chick Lit). But the komiks industry, in engaging the multifarious realities . . . has had the millions as its most enthusiastic patrons" (Reyes 2009, 393).

See also: Chapter 8: Overview. Chapter 9: Overview. Chapter 11: Overview.

Further Reading

Reyes, Soledad S. 1980. "The Philippine Komiks." *Philippines: International Popular Culture* 1: 389–417.

Reyes, Soledad S. 2009. "The Komiks and Retelling the Lore of the Folk," *Philippine Studies* 57, no. 3: 389–417.

Film

Popular culture's oldest medium is film, and the Philippines has one of the oldest film industries in Asia. On January 1, 1897, four French movies were shown in Manila using one of the earliest cameras. Once two Swiss businessmen brought a more advanced model, more films were shown, a couple of them produced locally (short documentaries of Manila street scenes, people, and activities like the fiesta). In 1899, American filmmakers began producing documentary-travelogues of places and people outside Manila. They also highlighted the life of Philippine national hero, Jose Rizal, with the director Albert Yearsley producing the first full-length silent Filipino film, *La Vida de Jose Rizal*, in 1901. By the second decade of the 1900s, however, these historical films were gradually upstaged by entertainment movies, thanks mainly to the decision of Hollywood and New York film companies to open offices in Manila and tap the new market. European films soon followed their American rivals but failed to gain traction as a result of World War I. As these movies gained in popularity, documentary filmmaking was taken over by the colonial government, which began producing films to educate the American public on Philippine affairs.

It was also during this period that Filipinos joined the film world. The most well known of these young filmmakers was Jose Nepomuceno, who set up the film studio Malayan Movies in 1917. Within two years, he released the first Filipino-produced silent movie, *Dalagang Bukid (Country Maiden)*. For the next 42 years (he died in 1959), Nepomuceno produced over 50 films in English, Filipino, and Spanish, with themes that ranged from the superstitious to love, families, religion, and women. One of his masterpieces was the first full movie based on Jose Rizal's novel *Noli Me Tangere*. For this, he became known as "the Father of Philippine Cinema." Nepomuceno's films were a source of inspiration for filmmakers not only in Manila but also in provincial cities like Cebu. In fact, in 1922, three Cebuano filmmakers collaborated to produce the first Cebuano-made movie, *El Hijo Disobiente*.

In the 1930s, after having weathered the competition from American filmmakers, Filipino cinema reached its zenith. Between 1931 and 1941, the four major film studios put out an estimated 334 films, of which 90 percent were in Filipino. Film historians referred to this era as Philippine cinema's "golden age." There were two reasons for this accomplishment. First, there was the appearance of the "talkie" movies, after the successful showing of the American film *Syncopation* in Manila. Manila and Cebu filmmakers were soon making their own "talkies." The second reason was the decision of some directors and producers to come out with political films. Julian Manansala's *Patria Amor (Beloved Country)*, which was critical of the Spanish community, was one example.

Colonial authorities almost censored the movie because of its theme but allowed it to be shown. A film about a fictional young brigand (*Batang Tulisan*) was banned because it portrayed a priest-character as the villain (shades of the friars in *Noli*), a sexual relationship between two 10-year-olds, and the spreading of "subversive ideas" among the young. Both films inspired Filipinos to raise social justice issues and the quest for independence. Finally, scriptwriting replaced the *zarzuelas*, literature, and the dramas, further distancing cinema from these "traditional" forms of public shows and hastening their marginalization. Scriptwriters also sought out stories serialized in the vernacular magazines to come up with a movie version. The advent of the Filipino "talkies" gave scriptwriting an additional boost.

During World War II, the Japanese censored Filipino filmmaking and introduced Japanese films with English subtitles. A Japanese company, Toho Films, produced two movies, one romantic and the other propaganda, that showed the Japanese as liberators. With no movie to show, however, movie theaters reversed into presenting plays. Films returned after the war, and this time the industry was dominated by Hollywood movies. However, the Filipino filmmakers were not easily pushed to the side. They were able to stand their ground, thanks to the emergence of four companies which produced over 350 films a year, second only to Japan in the entire Asia Pacific region. The competition of the so-called Big Four—LVN Pictures, Sampaguita Pictures, Premiere Productions, and Lebran International—brought about the "first golden age of Philippine cinema."

Then the newspaper *Manila Times* added more boost to the film industry by establishing an awards organization that recognized the best films of the year. The *Maria Clara Awards* (named after a character in Rizal's novels) was formed in 1950, but after three years, it was replaced by the Filipino Academy Movie Arts and Sciences (FAMAS), which was the Philippines' version of the Oscar Awards in the United States.

Other developments happened between the 1950s and the 1970s. An independent filmmaking group began to make their presence felt, winning in local and international competitions. Then in 1951, the first Filipino-made full-color movie came out, a breakthrough in Asian cinema.

Filipino filmmakers followed their American counterparts, producing action, adventure, comedy, and romance movies. The reverse did also happen. In 1952, one of the country's top directors submitted his film, *Genghis Khan*, to the Venice International Film Festival, and this inspired a Hollywood company to produce two movies on the Mongol king. That said, studios did produce films about local myths and legends, adaptations of the historic zarzuela and also of the most popular among the widely distributed comics. The trend continued in the 1960s, with yet another production of one of Rizal's novels at one end and Hollywood-type films at the other end. The films produced during this period included those by Gerardo de Leon, like *Huwag mo Akong Limutin* (Never Forget Me) in 1960, *Noli Me Tangere* in 1961, and *El Filibusterismo* in 1962.

These quality films, however, were a trifle when compared to the widespread commercialism of the industry. The large studios collapsed due to unresolved labor-management conflicts and were replaced by smaller studios, which focused on making quick money with films about teenage love, gaudy versions of James Bond, bloodier fight scenes, scripts about rapes and troubled marital relationships (no more the living-happily-ever-after themes), and soft porn. Quality fell by the wayside in the name of quick profit. The industry was littered with badly made movies about guns and cleavages. The turn toward more romantic, bloodier and vulgar raised concerns among Catholics, but it would also be used by President Ferdinand E. Marcos as one of his justifications for declaring martial law. Society had become so corrupted by subversion and smut that it became imperative for the government to impose order by violent means.

One of Marcos's first moves was to control the film industry by releasing a set of guidelines that would be implemented by a newly created Board of Censors for Motion Pictures (BCMP). Soft porn and violent movies were out, replaced by "clean" romance (some films even took out kissing scenes) and movies extolling the services of the police and the military in their fight against criminals and communists. This kowtowing to political restrictions did not last. A couple of young directors skirted the guidelines to produce films about alienation and violence in the everyday lives of the urban poor, women, peasants, and Catholics. Filipinos saw in these films a subtle criticism of Marcos's much-hyped "New Society." Soft porn producers also found a way to bring back their top money-makers but in a subtle way. Women were not outrightly naked, nor were bed scenes allowed. Instead, moviemakers "showed female stars swimming in their underwear, taking a bath in *camison* (chemise), or being chased and raped in a river, sea, or under a waterfall. Such movies were called *the wet look*."

The expansion of this cinematic "democratic space" was aided by two developments in the film industry. The first was the organization of a movie critics' circle by well-respected writers and academics, some close to the Marcos families and others sympathetic to, if not members of, the communist underground. The *Manunuri ng*

Pelikulang Pilipino (Filipino Movie Critics) declared themselves "the champions of the underdog" films (i.e., those that prioritized the artistic over the money) and the "discoverers of new or ignored talents" (Parel 1983, 11). The second development was the attempt by the government to establish the Philippines as an international cinema hub and a laboratory for "experimental films." A group of new producers—mainly Chinese Filipino entrepreneurs—brought back the profitable romance and action movies for the money but also with an eye on competing in international film festivals. Social realist and pornographic directors seized the opportunity to bring back politics and soft porn, respectively, under the guise of experimental films. They were egged on by the *Manunuri*, which sponsored its own "film festival" as an alternative to the government-sponsored Metro-Manila Film Festival. Finally, movie theaters that were once spread out across cities relocated to the mall. From then on, Filipinos did not have to travel a long distance to watch one or two movies, as all theaters were now housed in one structure.

Movie historians described the 1980s as Philippine cinema's second golden age, with an annual average of 2.5 million moviegoers in Metro Manila alone. The Philippines once more rose to the top 10 in global movie production, averaging 300 films a year. This celebration was all the more remarkable because it was during this period that the first two women directors put out their first films, which were highly admired. However, much like the early golden age, the movies produced followed the same story lines—action films, teenage love stories, massacres, and soft porn had come back with a vengeance. Political films likewise remained popular, although directors now turned their attention to the atrocities of the administration of President Corazon C. Aquino. The majority of films, however, had unimaginative, predictable story lines, and the acting was uninspired or overplayed.

The golden age ended in the 1990s, as the Asian financial crisis, high taxes (33 percent of the gross going to the municipal tax, 12 percent to the value-added tax, and another 8 percent to assorted fees), the spread of film piracy, and cable television competition brought the film industry to a near-death situation. Viewership began to decline steadily. Moreover, Filipino filmmakers were still unable to find a way to match the popularity of Hollywood movies. The University of the Philippines Film Institute reported that there were 122 films produced in 1999, but this number declined to 83 a year later, to 80 in 2003, to 56 in 2006, and to 30 in 2007. There was a similar decline in the number of moviegoers. In 1996, a record 131 million went to watch movies. This went down to 80 million in 2003 and further to 63 million in 2004. One of the founders of *Manunuri* called the 1990s the "Decade of the Dying Cinema." The deterioration never let down in the new century. Filipino films comprised 73 percent of total movies in 2000, but by 2009, this was down to 11 percent. There was international acclaim for the works of a group of "indie" (independent) directors, but these movies never did well at the box office. What sold were fantasy-action movies, romantic comedies, and horror flicks.

See also: Chapter 9: Overview. Chapter 11: Overview. Chapter 16: Overview; Film.

Further Reading

De Ocampo, Nick. 2011. *Film: American Influences on Philippine Cinema*. Mandaluyong, Philippines: Anvil Publishing.

Del Mundo, Clodualdo. 1999. "Philippine Cinema: An Historical Overview." *Asian Cinema* 10, no. 2: 29–66.

Guterrez, Jose, III. 2017. "The Realist Cinema of Lino Brocka." *Plaridel* 14, no. 2 (July–December): 169–178.

Lumbera, Bienvenido. 1992. *Pelikula: An Essay on Philippine Film*. Manila: Sentrong Pangkultura ng Pilipinas.

Parel, Tessa O. 1983. "History of the MPC, 1976–1982." In Nicanor G. Tiongson (ed.), *The Urian Anthology, 1970–1979*. Manila: Manuel L. Morato.

Zafra, Jessica. 2020. "The Decline and Fall of the Filipino Movie Industry." *Far East Film Festival 22*. April 24–May 22. https://www.fareastfilm.com/eng/archive/catalogue/2007/il-declino-e-la-caduta-dellindustria-cinematografica-delle-filippine/?IDLYT=31711

Print Media

There are two types of newspapers in the Philippines. The first is the national dailies—that is, the newspapers that have a national distribution network. The second is the community newspapers that are based in the towns and smaller cities in the provinces and cater mainly to the needs of their communities. The most dominant medium is English, with Filipino and the local languages following far behind. The first printed news came out in 1637. It was a "bulletin of fortunate events" (*Sucesos Felices*) in the islands and abroad that the Spanish colonial regime published for the community. The Spanish put out 13 other bulletins from 1690 to 1847 (157 years!). The first daily newspaper, *La Esperanza*, came out in 1846 and since then, Filipinos caught the print media bug. Forty-two newspapers differing in terms of character (some political commentaries, others straight-out bulletins) and year of publication came out until 1899, when the Spanish ceded the Philippines to the United States. This passion for print media continued throughout the American colonial period (48 newspapers in Manila and Cebu, the two largest cities, and 153 in the provinces) and even during World War II, albeit under strict Japanese censorship. The Japanese approved 16 dailies, which the anti-Japanese resistance movements countered with over 137 newsletters.

In the postwar period, until the declaration of martial law in 1972, media researchers counted 26 dailies, 16 periodicals (magazines, or weekly and monthly broadsheets), and 100 community newspapers with a total circulation of 300,000. The Chinese community also had its own 6 dailies written in Mandarin. Despite these big numbers, however, another trend became apparent after 1946: the newspapers with the broadest distribution were controlled by family-owned media conglomerates, which also owned radio and television networks. Martial law closed these newspaper chains and established 2 other newspapers, but in a decade, anti-Marcos media persons established their dailies, which withstood government harassment.

Two years after President Ferdinand E. Marcos fell from power, print media returned with the same energy and flair that it had showed after World War II—13 major dailies were being read by between 600,000 and 1 million readers, and the media directory listed 310 community newspapers, of which 10 were dailies and 220 were weeklies. Pre-martial law newspapers were revived, and new publications also came out, thanks mainly to journalists being freed from the strictures of martial law. However, the democratization of print media, in terms of ownership, never happened; family control of the largest of the broadsheets was there to stay. By 2000, the Philippine Media Factbook listed 475 broadsheets, 45 magazines, and 39 tabloids and comics; 123 of these were in Metropolitan Manila and its surrounding provinces alone.

Filipinos like print media for two reasons. First, it is as accessible as radio and television and often the primary source of news stories at times when the other two spend more time on escapist programs. Second, Filipinos are proud of its long history of resistance to repressive political authority, beginning with the *ilustrados* in the 1860s and continuing with the journalists who became part of the anti-Japanese resistance and then the media persons who bravely opposed martial law. In 1989, the Philippine Center for Investigative Journalism (PCIJ) was established in the name of principled democratic journalism. PCIJ was also supposed to be the foil to print journalism's dark side.

In the 1970s, as part of the effort to boost its image, the Marcos dictatorship began bribing journalists to write stories extolling the virtues of the "New Society." Critics called this "envelopment journalism" (i.e., journalists receiving wads of money in an envelope), which was an impish wordplay on the regime's push for "developmental journalism." The fall of Marcos pushed "developmental journalism" to the margins, but it has since made a comeback as politicians use the same Marcosian tactic to make themselves look honorable and decent to voters. Given the low wages that print journalists receive, it is perfectly understandable why many have been lured back to "envelopmental journalism." The Philippine Press Institute adopted a "Journalists' Code of Ethics" in 1987 to stem this corruption by establishing a code of ethics for journalists and a "school" to hone the skills of young journalists. But these have hardly made a dent in the problem. Eleven years later, in 1998, a PCIJ survey of 100 reporters revealed "that their sources had offered 71 percent. Of these, 33 percent admitted they took the money, with 22 percent keeping the cash for themselves, and 11 percent turning it over to their editors" (Coronel 2001, 118–119).

Newspapers have been one of the "arenas" where political combat has been most fierce. Media owners have used their tabloids to attack those in power, support favored politicians, as well as put down rivals. Governments often try to suppress this defiance by bringing journalists to court, and sometimes arresting or even assassinating them, but these measures have never silenced the print media completely. In fact, "the samizdat tradition" is well ingrained among journalists with the most passionate critics lending advice and assistance to "anti-government groups [publishing] underground papers [and], since the Internet, putting up guerrilla websites" (Coronel 2001, 111).

Filipinos, however, are also drawn to print media for the same reason they like television: tabloid journalism. There are 40 tabloid newspapers in Manila that "offer readers a dizzying assortment of sex, violence, gore, celebrity scandal, strange news, spirited opinion, and personal advice" (Whaley 2012). On any given day, a Manila tabloid will have stories about "a victim of a motorcycle accident, whose head has been severed, lying in a pool of blood on the pavement with no attempt by the publication to mask the gore. Photos of scantily clad men and women and some photos of completely nude women sit alongside columns by priests, senior government officials, and mayors" (Whaley 2012). These tabloids outsell their traditional rivals, but upon closer look, this is not a problem similar to the fate of stage plays and theaters when movies came to the Philippines. The top tabloids are owned by the media conglomerates, and it is an open secret among media people that the former subsidize the national dailies that these conglomerates own. Tabloids have also been the means by which these companies retain a profit from a medium that does not have the same audience reach as television and radio.

It is because of these two reasons that print media in the Philippines has a contradictory image. On the one hand, the international advocacy group Freedom House describes it as one of the "freest press in the world." On the other hand, it is also a blemished Fifth Estate with journalists bought by powerful figures and a style of reportage that favors the vulgar over the factual.

See also: Chapter 2: Overview; Marcos Dictatorship. Chapter 3: Martial Law. Chapter 8: Overview. Chapter 9: Overview.

Further Reading

Committee to Protect Journalists. "83 Journalists Killed in the Philippines." Accessed October 27, 2019. https://cpj.org/data/killed/asia/philippines/

Coronel, Sheila. 2001. "The Media, the Market, and Democracy: The Case of the Philippines." *Public* 8, no. 2: 109–126.

Doyo, Ma. Ceres P. 2019. *Press Freedom under Siege: Reportage That Challenged the Marcos Dictatorship.* Quezon City: University of the Philippines Press.

Gonzalez, Hernando. 1988. "Mass Media and the Spiral of Silence: The Philippines from Marcos to Aquino." *Journal of Communications* 38, no. 4 (Autumn): 33–48.

Lent, John A. 1983. "The Philippine Press at the Advent of the 1980s." *Crossroads: An Interdisciplinary Journal of Southeast Asian Studies* 1, no. 2 (June): 83–93.

Rara, Ma. Cristina Imperial. 2004. "Covering Terror in the Philippines." *Public Policy* VIII, no. 1 (January–June): 79–117.

Sussman, Gerard. 1990. "Politics and the Press: The Philippines since Marcos." *Bulletin of Concerned Asian Scholars* 22, no. 1: 34–43.

Whaley, Floyd. 2012. "Manila's Gory, Sexy Tabloids Outsell Traditional Broadsheets." *New York Times.* June 26. Accessed November 6, 2019. https://www.nytimes.com/2012/06/27/world/asia/manilas-gory-sexy-tabloids-outsell-traditional-news papers.html

Radio

Radio ranks second to television in terms of audience but is first when it comes to the most reliable source of news and entertainment. Philippine Statistical Authority figures show that in 2013, 65.6 percent of the total population relied on the radio for information, with 41.4 percent listening to it at least once a week. There are 1,513 radio stations distributed across the archipelago—416 AM stations, 1,042 FM stations, and 55 community stations (stations with a limited reach like university radio or those run by nonprofit groups). The proliferation of radio stations stands in contrast to their ownership. Three families and the government control the stations with the broadest reach. All but one also own or run television stations.

The first radio stations (three) were set up in June 1922 by an American owner of an electric supply store in Manila. They mainly played music to a tiny audience, as only a few families owned radio sets. In 1924, their 50-watt power was boosted to 100 watts, and Henry Hermann formed the Radio Corporation of the Philippines (RCP) in preparation for expanding his network across the Philippines and connecting it to the United States. In 1929, RCP did open up a station in Cebu City, central Philippines, although Hermann would sell it to another American store owner. The American colonial government would create the Radio Control Board in 1931 to regulate radio, and in 1932, noticing its growing popularity, companies began to buy radio time to advertise their products. Stations held singing contests, and there was even a "Miss Radio of the Philippines" competition. It was also around this time that the first "talk show" appeared in Catholic-owned stations. *Kuwentong Kutsero* (Coachmen's Chat) criticized the government and politics and the immorality of particular Filipino manners. On the eve of World War II, radio personalities competed with movie stars in drawing fans and supporters.

All radio programs were in English, and most shows resembled American shows, even copying sponsorship. These were temporarily stopped during World War II when the Japanese imposed severe restrictions, but after the war, the radio came back. By 1950, 30 radio stations had resumed full operations, aided in part by Filipino companies producing radio sets. More families could now afford a radio as the Filipino brands were cheaper than the imported American radio. Programs were still profoundly American, with stations importing American serials, but one station, DZRH, began adding Filipino shows, including the first soap opera and an action-adventure series featuring a superhero called Kapitan Kidlat (Captain Lightning).

In 1951, an American-owned radio station (DZBB) added panel discussions of controversial topics to its news program, while the Catholic stations revived *Kuwentong Kutsero*. By the end of the decade, stations were using a surefire formula to get listeners' attention. There were a series of romantic soap operas and musical programs, spiced up jokes and commentaries by an emcee usually followed by an oratorical contest. Stations also allotted time for what they called "public service," where listeners could phone in or write about their predicaments and a radio announcer would contact the appropriate government agencies that could help these distraught listeners. There were hourly short news updates and a long one as families started dinner. A soap opera or an hour of new songs often followed, with the night usually ending with "advice-to-the-lovelorn programs" (Fernandez 1981, 34). Stations allotted an hour to religious programs on Sundays and to classical music on the weekends when parents were not at work.

In 1959, with the invention of the transistor—that little switch that could increase electric currents—people in rural areas were able to listen to the radio, and this radically changed things for them; they could not only receive more information, they could also hear pop and classical music and discussions different from the usual rural corner banter. A decade later, the *Economic Monitor* magazine's survey of transistor radio ownership revealed that 62 percent of Filipino households now owned transistor radios. Distribution was still uneven—the farther the province or town was in relation to Manila, the fewer the families that owned radios.

Radio stations continued to grow in the 1960s, although the competition did not lead to more stations opening up. The freedom of radio ended in 1972 when the Marcos regime took over the Chronicle and other media establishments and turned them into de facto state communications agencies. After Marcos fell, the networks were returned to their owners. Radio stations renewed their prime programs with vigor, and in the 1990s, 338 stations reached 78 percent of households across the country. The field came to be dominated by four private corporations and the government broadcasting service. The top two—the Alto Broadcasting System-Chronicle Broadcasting Network (ABS-CBN) and the Global Media Arts (GMA) Network—were multimedia conglomerates operating both radio and television networks and allowing their stars to act in movies. The Philippine Broadcasting Company (PBC) and the Radio Mindanao Network (RMN) were purely radio groups, but the government media agency had radio and television stations to run. This has been the hallmark of Philippine radio ever since.

Despite the dominance of television, radio remains extremely popular. The 1995 survey by the polling group *Media Pulse* showed that 84 percent of households had a radio (the figure was higher in Metropolitan Manila—93 percent) as against 57 percent of households with television. In 2000, radio listeners were still the majority and the *Media Factbook* listed a total of 539 radio stations nationwide; 273 were AM stations and 266 were FM stations; 73 percent of listeners listened to FM, and 27 percent, AM. By 2014, 90 percent of listeners were tuning in to FM stations for the music, and those who listened to AM or community stations did so for the news, public activities, talk shows, and radio drama. There are also "talk radio" segments where commentators engage listeners, who phone in or send letters, in a discussion over political affairs. These talk programs run regularly throughout the year, although their share of radio time may increase during election campaigns.

The media scholar John Lent thinks that these exchanges have made Philippine radio "the freest mass media system in Asia if not the world" (Lent 1968, 176). Others, however, are more skeptical as to whether there is indeed a dialogue going on between commentators and listeners (Mojares 1998). Radios have also been crucial in other ways. In 2013, central Philippines was devastated by one of the strongest typhoons to date. "Disaster radio" was crucial in keeping communications open between towns in the affected areas, disaster assistance agencies, and the general public. Disaster management experts described how, amid the destruction, radio was able "to give general information and demonstrate the capability of officials to manage the situation, to encourage, to promote recovery and foster a sense of hope, and to give practical advice and encourage self-activity" (Hugelius et al. 2016).

Nevertheless, a radio commentator is not always heaped with praise by listeners. These "radio journalists" have also faced threats, and often the intimidation has turned deadly. Of the 83 journalists killed since 1992, 55 worked in radio (Committee to Protect Journalists 2019). Radio commentators are the principal targets because of their "power and influence over thousands, if not millions, of listeners." Prof. Rey G. Rosales adds: "Radio talk shows are often used as an effective medium for millions of listeners to air their complaints about certain public officials, and the shows can exert pressure on government agencies to do something about their sorry state" (Rosales 2006, 148–149). The peril is made worse by radio managers who encourage commentators to use "combative language and aggressive style of commentary, . . . which bordered on name-calling" to increase ratings (Rosales 2006, 249). It is not uncommon, therefore, to see a radio personality carrying weapons or having bodyguards. Journalists have called for the Philippine government to move to end these recurring threats against them, although, given the weakness of the court system, it takes time for these appeals to yield positive results.

See also: Chapter 9: Overview. Chapter 13: Overview.

Further Reading

Committee to Protect Journalists. "83 Journalists Killed in the Philippines." Accessed October 27, 2019. https://cpj.org/data/killed/asia/philippines/

Fernandez, Doreen G. 1981. "Philippine Popular Culture: Dimensions and Directions. The State of Research in Philippine Popular Culture." *Philippine Studies* 29 (First Quarter).

Hugelius, Karin, Mervyn Gifford, Per Ortenwall, and Annsofie Adolfsson. 2016. "Disaster Radio for Communication of Vital Messages and Health-Related Information: Experiences from the Haiyan Typhoon, the Philippines." *Disaster Medicine and Public Health Preparedness* 10, no. 4 (August): 591–597.

Lent, John. 1968. "Philippine Radio—History and Problems." *Asian Studies* (April): 49–60.

Mojares, Resil. 1998. "Talking Politics: The Komentaryo on Cebu Radio." *Philippine Quarterly of Culture and Society* 26, no. 3–4 (September–December): 337–362.

Rosales, Rey G. 2006. "Shooting the Messenger: Why Radio Broadcasting Is a Deadly Profession in the Philippines." *Journal of Radio Studies* 13, no. 1: 146–155.

Social Networking

The existing internet grid in the Philippines has only reached 404,000 of the total population of 101 million, and the average internet connection speed is quite slow—3.5 Mbps (megabits per second) as against South Korea's 29 Mbps. Ownership of desktops and laptops is only 24.3 percent of the total population. This deficit, however, is steadily being reduced thanks to the popularity of mobile phones. In 2017, there were 30.4 million smartphone owners, but by 2021, the number had more than doubled (82 million) Cell phones have allowed one out of five Filipinos access to the internet, to use social message services (SMS or texting), and to connect to social networking sites (SNS). Filipinos send 400 million texts a day (or 124 billion a year); 74.6 million of them have Facebook accounts, 10,200,000 use Twitter, and 17 million posts on their Instagram. Filipinos use social media mainly to make and keep up with friends and be in touch with families. There are 296,000 Netflix subscribers, and 87 percent of internet users watch YouTube and other online videos.

Filipinos are less interested in checking the news via social media, but they actively use it to keep contact and seek help during national disasters. These acts of civic engagement were evident when Typhoon Ketsana hit the country in 2009, followed by Supertyphoon Haiyan which struck communities in central Philippines in November 2013, and the series of earthquakes that hit Mindanao Island in October and November 2019. Social media provided updates on the affected communities to the outside world and helped coordinate delivery assistance apart from raising funds. Observers noted that the civic engagements of volunteers and donors were unusual given how much they personalized their work. Twitter users engaged in civic activities listed the need to express their concerns as their top priority, over everything else including prayer. There were also a high number of tweets concerned with fundraising and volunteer work. Finally, social media had likewise provided a platform for hitherto marginalized groups like upland communities and Muslims as well as OFWs and migrants.

The relationship between social media and politics is a bit complicated. On the one hand, it was a powerful instrument in the effort to unseat President Joseph Estrada in 2000 (Chapter 3). Scholars praised it for its "democratizing" effect on popular mobilization. On the other hand, there is some controversy over the way social media was used in the 2016 campaign of Rodrigo R. Duterte for the presidency. His opponents have accused Duterte of tapping into social media to spread fake news to attack his opponents and, at the same time, motivate the Duterte electorate to go to the polls in huge numbers. Once he became president, Duterte also accused independent journalists of using Facebook and Twitter to expose the failings of government.

See also: Chapter 7: Generational Changes; History of the Family Unit; Parent-Child Relationships. Chapter 8: Overview. Chapter 11: Overview.

Further Reading

Hjorth, Larissa, and Michael Arnold. 2011. "The Personal and the Political: Social Networking in Manila." *International Journal of Learning and Media* 3, no. 1: 29–39.

Komito, Lee. 2011. "Social Media and Migration: Virtual Community 2.0." *Journal of the American Society for Information, Science and Technology* 62, no. 6: 1075–1086.

McKay, Deirdre. 2010. "On the Face of Facebook: Historical Images and Personhood in Filipino Social Networking." *History and Anthropology* 21, no. 4 (December): 479–498.

Rosario-Braid, Florangel, and Ramon R. Tuazon. 2000. "Post-EDSA Communication Media." *Philippine Studies* 48 (First Quarter): 3–26.

Television

The "father of Philippine television" was an American engineer, James Lindenberg, who established the Bolinao Electronics Corporation on June 13, 1946, and then applied for a license to transmit with the newly created Congress. He received the license four years later, but the plan failed to push through as import controls (see Chapter 4) made it difficult to bring in materials from abroad that were needed to build the station. Television arrived in the country when the Alto Broadcasting System (ABS) was granted permission to import 300 television sets from the United States. A transmitter acquired from the Radio Corporation of America (RCA) began broadcasting on October 23, 1953, in Manila and nearby provinces. The Philippines became the first country to have a television network in Southeast Asia and was second only to Japan in Asia.

Then in September 1956, local business people opened the Chronicle Broadcasting Network (CBN) to rival ABS. CBN would buy ABS in 1957, and its owners—sugar barons—revived the name Bolinao Electronics Corporation (BEC) that would be the precursor to the largest multimedia network in the Philippines today, ABS-CBN. When Radiowealth Corporation began manufacturing televisions locally, the new appliance began to be a regular household feature in the urban areas. Within a decade, the number of households owning televisions reached 6,000 (one for every 2,000 households).

The first programs were movies and television series from the United States, and films from different embassies. Among the first American shows aired on local television were *Candid Camera, Father Knows Best*, and *I Love Lucy*. When import controls were partially lifted in 1959, BEC also imported such popular shows as *The Perry Como Show;* the cowboy shows *Tombstone Territory* and *Annie Oakley;* the detective shows *Dragnet* and *Mannix;* the war drama *Combat;* and the medical series *Dr. Kildare*. About the same year, BEC produced its first "public service" program—a reportage of a volcano eruption south of Manila. In November 1953, students from

Vintage television at Crisologo Museum in Vigan City, Ilocos Sur. (Walter Eric Sy/ Dreamstime.com)

the Jesuit school Ateneo de Manila staged *Cyrano de Bergerac* on television. The play inspired the production of regular musical competitions and variety shows. More local shows were produced in the 1960s, including mini-concerts by the country's top chanteuse, dance competitions, and comedy programs. Movie stars recognized the value of television and moved to the new format.

In 1960, three new stations opened to compete with BEC—the Associated Broadcasting Corporation (ABC), the Manila Broadcasting Company (MBC), and the Inter-Island Broadcasting Company. Another company, the Republic Broadcasting System (RBS) which was owned by a former American war correspondent, went on air in 1960 and was the first to sell one-minute advertisement slots to companies. The government also dipped its fingers in the field, establishing the Philippine Broadcasting Service (PBS), which produced educational programs. BEC stayed ahead of the competition by opening the first provincial channel in Cebu City (in the central Philippines), and in Dagupan (a city in the northernmost region of the archipelago). Color television came in 1966 with BEC once again leading the way, adopting the slogan *First in Color Television*. The rest of the stations followed, and by 1971, all television networks were broadcasting in full color.

BEC changed its name to ABS-CBN on February 1, 1967, and continued to expand. By the end of the year, it had added another TV station, making the corporation the largest network of the country. ABS-CBN also had 7 radio stations in Manila, 14 provincial radio stations, 3 affiliate stations, and a newspaper. The other networks adopted the same strategy, and these "tri-media combines" became the standard structure of the industry. ABS-CBN would increase its lead over its rivals by being the first to acquire a cable company and by building a broadcast center that rivaled Japan's NHK (Nippon Hoso Kyokai or Japan Broadcasting Corporation) in terms of equipment and related resources. With its technological superiority, ABS-CBN introduced new programs—a daily drama series (called "soap opera"), the "breaking news" concept, and coverage of international events like the U.S. elections, the historic moon landing, and the Olympic games.

In 1969, television showed its power as an institution when it was used as a campaign weapon by re-electionist president Ferdinand Marcos and his vice president Fernando Lopez (whose family owned ABS-CBN). The alliance did not last, and when Marcos and Lopez became rivals, the latter used ABS-CBN as a de facto propaganda machine to discredit the former. Marcos would retaliate a few years later when, after he declared martial law, the government seized the station and then handed it over to a crony who was a rival of the network. ABS-CBN became KBS (Kanlaon Broadcasting System) and would be instrumental in setting up cable television in the early 1980s. Marcos and his cronies used television to promote their "New Society" and the Marcos family. Marcos also created the Association of Broadcasters of the Philippines, whose role was to police the media. However, the association did something other than play censor; it standardized and promoted the television industry by hosting several awards presentations.

When Marcos fell in 1986, the new government of President Corazon Aquino sequestered the other TV stations, and these would be sold later on to the private sector by Aquino's successors. It retained ownership of the MBS television network. Aquino returned KBS and another station, the Global Media Arts (GMA), to their original owners, with the name KBS changed back to ABS-CBN. In two years, ABS-CBN was again the most-watched television station, followed by GMA. In 1989, ABS-CBN began satellite and international broadcasts, the first for a Philippine station, and had its first competitor in the newly opened Dream Satellite TV, the first direct broadcast satellite television in the country.

Up until the mid-1980s, television was limited to the major cities, but this changed in 1987 when the largest network set up regional programs. Then in 1989, with the adoption of satellite broadcasting, the network—and its rival—were able to broadcast nationwide 24 hours a day the entire week. The percentage of television viewers rose from 48 percent in 1989 to 56.7 percent in 1994. In 2000, the *Philippine Media Factbook* listed the following figures to show how far television had come. Of the total Philippine population of 13.8 million households, 9.8 million (71 percent) have television. Breaking the overall figure further, the *Factbook* shows that Manila has 96 percent of households with televisions; Luzon Island, 73 percent; Mindanao, 63 percent; and the Visayas, 60 percent. Finally, in 2013, four out of every five households owned a television and 81 percent of Filipinos between the ages of 10 and 64 were inveterate television watchers (Philippine Statistical Office 2013, 41). The percentage continued to rise, and in 2016, a private media survey revealed that 96.6 percent of Filipinos were watching television.

New players appeared at the start of the 1990s and well into the new century. These included the first home shopping network, music channels, Christian Evangelist–owned stations, and foremost among them, cable television. Then in the mid-90s, GMA and ABS-CBN set up their international channels to tap the overseas Filipino market. They also became the local franchises of internationally popular shows like *America's Got Talent* and *Who Wants to Be a Millionaire*, and American networks like MTV opened their Philippine branches. Finally, in 2010 the networks also shifted to digital television and high-definition cable thereby expanding their audience base further. The largest of this network, ABS-CBN, was beginning to broadcast in the 17 cities of Metro Manila, and Bulacan and Pampanga provinces. One of the consequences of this "explosion" of television was the decline of the film industry, as more than 50 percent of Filipino viewers shifted to television.

Philippine television did not change its successful news-variety show-soap opera combination. However, while American shows dominated the evening programs in the late 1990s, they found competition in Mexican telenovelas and Korean dramas dubbed in Filipino. The nationalization of television had led to more balanced news reportage, covering both Metropolitan Manila and provincial stories. An unintended effect was the spread of the national language, a goal that the government had not been able to accomplish before. Tagalog became the lingua franca even in the non-Tagalog regions, and the most apt representative of just how far it had been accepted nation-wide was President Rodrigo R. Duterte. Duterte had once expressed his disdain over the language of "imperial Manila," but later in many of his public speeches, he spoke effortlessly in Filipino. And for this, advocates of Tagalog-as-the-national-language have television to thank.

See also: Chapter 9: Overview; National Language Debate. Chapter 11: Overview.

Further Reading

Del Mundo, Clodualdo. 2003. "50 Years of Pinoy TV." *PhilStar*. October 12. https://www.philstar.com/other-sections/starweek-magazine/2003/10/12/223965/50-years-pinoy-tv

Ong, Jonathan Corpus. 2015. *The Poverty of Television: The Mediation of Suffering in Class-Divided Philippines*. London: Anthem Press.

Republic of the Philippines, Philippine Statistical Office. 2013. FLEMMS (Functional Literacy, Education and Mass Media Survey Final Report). Manila: Philippine Statistical Office.

APPENDIX A

A DAY IN THE LIFE

TRAFFIC

Metropolitan Manila traffic is an ordeal unless you live in the enclaves or high-rises of the rich and middle classes. If you do not have a car, you join a long line of commuters waiting for the monorails to take you to the station near your office. With the monorail, you reach your destination faster. Driving a car or taking public transportation, however, is another matter. You look forward to a two-hour grind from home to office, which is only 10–15 miles away. Philippine traffic is the worst in Southeast Asia, and the ninth worst globally, while Metropolitan Manila is the fourth most congested city after Moscow, Mumbai, and Bogota. The national capital's residents lose 257 hours (or 10 days and 17 hours) every year from slow traffic. You increasingly become used to adding another 29 minutes to a 30-minute daytime commute and 38 minutes more when going home in the evening. You are grateful that you have your cell phone to check your social media accounts or listen to music. In the pre–social media age, however, people who took public transport would use the hour-long trip to catch up on their sleep or read about some gossip from the tabloids sold on the streets.

KARAOKE

At the town's fiesta, guests from other towns come to co-celebrate the event. Homes are open for lunch, but as everyone moves to dinner, special guests are invited to stay with the host family for a feast of leftovers. The dinner is the prelude to the last of the day's events: a whole night of karaoke singing. As plates are being removed and alcohol brought out, the hosts also wheel the portable karaoke machine into the living room. The head of the household grabs the mike and belts out their song. The children are next, and there are duets to "A Whole New World" from the *Aladdin* movie, "How Far I'll Go" from *Moana*, and "Let It Go" from *Frozen*. Then it is the guests' turn. And if they happen to be Americans, they are expected to know the lyrics to the songs of ABBA, Celine Dion, Whitney Houston, Frank Sinatra, and the Village People. They must be careful not to sing out of tune or make a mistake with Sinatra's "My Way." The hosts remind them that people get murdered for "mangling" this great song and dishonoring Frank. The singing continues all through the night till early morning.

BASKETBALL AND BILLIARDS

Show a Filipino an open space in the middle of a forested mountainside, a densely packed urban poor community, or an empty lot of middle-class subdivisions, and he will tell you where to mount a basketball post. And once mounted, the game promptly begins. If the field is a half-court, then three-by-three teams compete, but if the space is wide enough for two posts, it is the usual five-team game. The team that reaches 15 points first wins. The game is played loosely, and there is hardly any defense. But in the central and southern Philippines, basketball aficionados put a premium on defense, and everyone abides by the norm "no blood, no foul." If one tires of playing basketball, there is the billiard table. Everyone wants to play like world champion Efren Reyes, called "The Magician" for his incredible shots. The first step is to understand the idea *preparacion* (preparation), which means surveying the lay of the pool table and thinking strategically. One does not hit a ball for the sake of sinking it on the corner pocket. To be like the Magician, one must set up the pool, so you will know which ball goes to which pocket.

"JOKE ONLY"

Walking around Metropolitan Manila is worth it. You see the hilarious names of small shops. There are two laundromats called "Star Wash: Attack of the Clothes" and "Lord of the Rinse" as well as two barbershops—"Hurry Cutter" and "Scissor's Palace." A Chinese restaurant's sign says, "Wok this way," while a local fast-food place proclaims on its entrance the name "SpotiFries." And who does not love to get roasted chicken at "Lord of the Wings" or a skewer or two of deep-fried fish balls from a "Facebool" cart? Famous people's names are appropriated. Thus, there is the egg distributor whose store sign is "Egg Sheehan," a bakery that calls itself "Bread Pitt," a roast chicken place with the name "Kini Rogers," and the soup place "Mami Pakyaw" ("Mami" being the Chinese for noodles). The funeral parlor "Libing Things" ("Libing" being also the term for burial) welcomes clients, while locksmith "Surelock Homes" does home visits. A local businessman vowed to compete with the car company Mercedes Benz by coming out with his own luxury car, "Mercedes Din" ("Din" here means "also"). Finally, McDonald's supposedly threatened a proprietor who put up the sign "Mang (Mister) Donald" to advertise his burger place.

GLOSSARY OF KEY TERMS

Adobo: The most popular Filipino dish to date. Pork or chicken, or a mix of both, is marinated in crushed garlic, peppercorn, soy sauce, vinegar, and bay leaf for at least two hours (some even marinate it overnight) and then slow-cooked until the liquid evaporates. There are several variations to cooking the marinated meat; some fry the meat first before returning it to the sauce and simmering, while others simmer it until the liquid dries out and the meat fries in its oil until it is dry and crispy. *Adobo* is eaten with rice.

Corazon Aquino: Widow of Senator Benigno Aquino Jr. and the most known opposition leader against the dictatorship of President Ferdinand E. Marcos. She opposed Marcos in a "snap presidential election" in 1986, was cheated, but installed to power by a nonviolent people power revolution. Aquino is associated with the return of constitutional democracy after 15 years of dictatorship.

Benigno S. Aquino III: The 15th president of the Philippines and son of Corazon Aquino.

Arnis: A Filipino martial art that uses wooden sticks, which has become increasingly popular in action films like *The Bourne Identity* and *Mission Impossible III* and the fighting sequences of television series like *The Game of Thrones* and *The Daredevil* (2015).

Gloria M. Arroyo: The Philippines' 14th president. She held power for 10 years, from 2001 to 2010, the first four years as vice president, then taking over the position of president after the ouster of Joseph E. Estrada.

Ateneo de Manila University: Founded in 1859 by the Jesuit order as a municipal school; turned into a college from 1901 to 1958 and became a university in 1959. Its most prominent graduate was the national hero Jose Rizal.

Autonomous Region for Muslim Mindanao (ARMM): The regional government created in 1989, consisting of five provinces where Muslims were the majority.

Babaylan: (plural: *Babaylanes*) Men or women shamans from the precolonial period who could communicate with the spirits of nature and the dead and were sought after for advice and healing. Spanish colonial rulers condemned them as heretics but could never eradicate their influence.

Bakla/Baklas: Filipino term for gay men (another name used is *sward/swards*).

Balikatan: (Shoulder-to-Shoulder) The operational name of an annual joint military exercise between the armies of the Philippines and the United States.

Balut: Fertilized duck's embryo; a popular delicacy in the Philippines, Southeast Asia, and South China. The egg is incubated for 14–21 days for the fetus to be formed and then hard-boiled. Filipinos consider it an elixir that gives them strength; older Filipinos call it the local and cheaper version of Viagra.

Barong Tagalog: The long-sleeved dress made of fabric from embroidered abaca (hemp) or pineapple leaves and worn during formal occasions like weddings and official ceremonies.

Bataan Memorial Cross: A memorial shrine for the American and Filipino soldiers who sacrificed their lives during World War II.

"Bayan Ko" (My Nation): A song written by the poet Jose Corazon de Jesus in 1929 protesting American colonial rule, which would be revived by nationalist student activists in the late 1960s, and then by opponents of the Marcos dictatorship in the early 1980s.

Bayanihan: A derivative of the word "bayan" (community or nation), which means to act, work, or play together as one nation or community.

Andres Bonifacio: The founder of the *Katipunan*, the first secret organization Filipinos formed to lead the revolution against Spain. Bonifacio led the tearing of individual tax certificates on August 26, 1896, to signal the uprising. However, he would be ousted in the *Katipunan's* first convention, arrested, and tried for treason but executed upon the orders of the new head of the organization, Emilio Aguinaldo.

BPO: Acronym for business processing outsourcing (BPO), the customer service section of American corporations, subcontracted to Filipino firms to cut production costs.

Chicharon: Deep-fried pork rinds, a favorite appetizer when Filipinos drink socially.

Clark Air Force Base: An air force base built by the Americans in 1903 under a military bases agreement between the Philippines and the United States and turned over to the Philippines in 1991.

Crony Capitalism: An economic arrangement that became popular during the Marcos dictatorship, where the businesses of friends and relatives of the president get special treatment like monopoly of essential industries, privileged access to credits, and special protection from economic regulators.

Datu/Datus/Datuin/Datuins: Malay title for the chief that was once used by precolonial polities but is now generally associated with Muslim communities.

Rodrigo R. Duterte: The Philippines' 16th president, the first mayor to be elected straight to the position and known for his brutal "War on Drugs."

El Filibusterismo: (The Subversive) The second novel of national hero Jose Rizal; explores revolutionary violence as an option in the light of Spanish colonial intransigence.

El Shaddai: ("God Almighty") Charismatic movement formed by a former real estate broker, which became famous for claiming that it could make members rich if they waved their passports in front of their leader during its "prayer rallies."

Enhanced Defense Cooperation Agreement (ECDA): A military agreement between the Philippines and the United States signed on April 28, 2014, allowing American troops to build and maintain their facilities inside Philippine military bases.

Gabriel "Flash" Elorde: The first boxer who won a super featherweight title in 1960 and held the title for seven years.

Eraserheads: Often called "The Beatles of the Philippines," they became the most famous and popular "alternative" Filipino rock band in contemporary history. The band took its name from the David Lynch movie *Eraserhead*. It would be the only Filipino group to receive an award at the 1997 MTV Video Music Awards.

Extrajudicial killings (EJKs): The execution of criminal suspects by police and military authorities without judicial sanction or due process. It became a notorious practice associated with presidents Ferdinand E. Marcos and Rodrigo R. Duterte.

Folk Catholicism: The mingling of pre-Catholic Indigenous practices with Catholic rituals; can be traced back to communities' responses to missionary proselytization. Examples include the cult-like devotion to the Blessed Virgin Mary (or BVM) to wearing amulets embossed with Latin words and the names of Jesus or God (Yahweh), which are supposed to protect people from evil spirits and bullets.

Folk Islam: Teaching from the Koran mixed with the local folk tales, legends, myths, proverbs, and even riddles, believed to be incorporated by Islamic missionaries to reach out to potential converts.

Galleon Trade: Trade between China and Mexico from 1571 to 1814 via Manila, where Chinese traders brought in silk, damask (a glossy fabric), porcelain, gems, and jewelry and gold from China; textiles from India; lacquerware (bowls) from Japan; spices from Southeast Asia; and cinnamon, coconut, and beeswax from the Philippines. These were bought by merchants and loaded into galleons which then headed to Mexico where they would be sold, some in the colony, but mainly to Spain. Chinese traders went home with Mexican silver.

Green Revolution: The introduction of high-yielding rice varieties in Philippine farms to boost production, increase farmers' incomes, and help alleviate rural poverty.

"Guns, Goons, and Gold": The infamous "three Gs" was the way for a local politician to rise to or remain in control of power; the guns in the hands of hired goons to harass voters and the gold as the money used to buy the voters of the electorate.

Halo-Halo: The favorite dessert of Filipinos; it consists of sweetened coconut strips and red and white beans mixed with bananas, lychees, jackfruit, and flan. These would be covered in shaved ice which, in turn, is drizzled with evaporated milk, ice cream, and often rice cereals.

Harana: A popular form of courtship where a man, with the help of his friends, woos the woman by singing in front of her window.

Japayuki: A pejorative term for Filipinas working in bars in Japan.

Nick Joaquin: The Philippines' most brilliant 20th-century writer in English, a novelist, playwright, and biographer of famous Filipinos.

Jollibee: A Filipino food chain whose owners set it up to compete with McDonald's; has since gone global with overseas Filipinos as its primary consumers enjoying its top products, the crispy fried Chickenjoy and its sweet and mayonnaise-laced Yumburger. It is now 107th among the top 300 companies in the world.

Kinilaw: Raw fish mixed with vinegar, tamarind, garlic, and chili and served as an appetizer.

Ladlad: Party The first LGBTQ party-list organization founded on September 1, 2003; planned to campaign for a seat in the House of Representatives in the 2006 elections but was denied registering by the Commission on Elections. This decision was overturned by the Supreme Court in 2010, but the party failed to gain 2 percent of the popular vote needed to win that seat.

Las Islas de Los Pintados: Meaning "The Lands of the Painted Ones."

Lechon: Pig is slow-roasted over charcoal for four to five hours and served as the main dish in family celebrations and town fiestas.

Lumad: This is a term used to refer to non-Muslim Indigenous communities.

Ramon D. Magsaysay: A former provincial governor who became the Philippines' seventh president riding on his image as a reformer; one of the leaders in the successful defeat of a communist insurgency in the 1950s.

Maguindanao Massacre: The killing of 58 people, including 34 journalists, accompanying the wife of a candidate who was going to file his certificate of candidacy, by an armed group led by the son of the incumbent provincial governor.

Mail-Order Brides: Filipinas married to non-Filipino husbands who were first introduced to their husbands by matchmakers who sent the latter the Filipinas' information files by mail.

Marawi City: The town built by Spaniards, then turned into a base camp by American troops, became a city in 1940 and was seized by Islamic terrorists in 2017. The terrorists were ousted five months later by Philippine soldiers at the expense of the city's destruction.

Ferdinand E. Marcos: The 10th Philippine president, the only one reelected, declared martial law before his second term ended and ruled the country for another 14 years as dictator.

Imelda R. Marcos: The flamboyant and controversial wife of President Ferdinand Marcos known for her excessive spending.

Marcos Dictatorship: The 15-year authoritarian rule of President Ferdinand E. Marcos.

Moro Islamic Liberation Front: Rival and successor of Moro National Liberation Front after the latter made peace with the government.

Moro National Liberation Front: Muslim armed force aiming at separating Mindanao, the island of Palawan, and the Sulu Archipelago on the grounds that Muslims were never really part of the Philippine nation-state.

New People's Army (NPA): Guerrilla army of the Communist Party of the Philippines.

Noli Me Tangere: The first novel of national hero Jose Rizal exposed Spanish corruption and exploitation and inspired Filipino revolutionaries, which led to Rizal's execution by the Spaniards.

OFW: Acronym for overseas Filipino workers.

Pan de Sal: Translated "bread of salt"; is the breakfast bread of Filipinos.

Manny Pacquiao: The greatest Filipino boxer to date and considered one of the world's best for winning four world titles in three weight divisions.

Pasyon: A retelling of the last days of Jesus Christ based on a reading of texts written for the occasion.

Philippine Basketball Association (PBA): The first professional basketball association of Asia founded in 1975.

People Power Revolution: The four-day mass sit-down in February 1986 by hundreds and thousands of people in Manila; ended in the ouster of President Ferdinand Marcos.

Pinoy: Slang for Filipino.

Manuel L. Quezon: President of the Philippine Commonwealth, the transition to the establishment of the Republic of the Philippines.

Responsible Parenthood and Reproductive Health Law of 2012: Mandated women's access to health-care issues related to being a future mother.

Jose Rizal: The Philippines' national hero.

Rondalla: A string instrument ensemble that uses flattened plastic or turtle shells to strum the instruments.

Sabong: A blood sport involving game cocks with sharp metal tied to their spurs, which Filipinos consider a weekend pastime.

Sinigang: A tamarind-based pork-cum-vegetables stew.

Sinulog: Annual religious festival held every third Sunday of January in Cebu City in honor of the Child Jesus.

Sisig: Popular appetizer of grilled pig's face and ears, fish flakes, tofu, bits of onions, and chili peppers, sprinkled with lemon juice.

Spratly Islands: Group of small islands in the South China Sea at the center of a territorial dispute between China and several Southeast Asian states.

Subic Naval Base: Former American naval base returned to the Philippines in 1991.

Sultanates: Political structure common in Muslim parts of Mindanao.

Taglish: Daily Manila conversations mixing Tagalog and English.

Tinola: Chicken with ginger and green papaya soup.

Tuba: Wine from the fermentation of a coconut or palm tree sap.

University of the Philippines: The premier state university of the country, established by the Americans in 1908.

University of Santo Tomas: Catholic university founded in April 1611, making it the oldest university in the Philippines and Asia.

War on Drugs: The defining policy of Rodrigo R. Duterte's presidency.

Warlords: The term used to describe politicians who use their private armies to win and control power outside urban centers.

West Philippine Sea: The maritime area west of the archipelago erroneously called the South China Sea. The Philippine government considers this its exclusive economic zone, but China claims sovereignty over it.

FACTS AND FIGURES

Table 1:   GEOGRAPHY

Location	The Philippines is an archipelago located in the western Pacific Ocean to the east of Southeast Asia. Its principal islands are Luzon and Mindanao.
Time Zone	13 hours ahead of U.S. Eastern Standard
Land Borders	0 miles
Coastline	22,550 miles
Capital	Manila
Area	115,831 sq. miles
Climate	The climate in the Philippines is generally hot and humid, although it is cooler in the mountains. Rainfall is frequent. The archipelago is often subject to typhoons.
Land Use	49.44% arable land; 43.01% permanent crops; 36.69% cropland; 5.03% permanent meadows and pastures; 27.77% forest land (2016)
Arable Land	41.5% (2017)
Arable Land Per Capita	0.12 hectares per person (2017)

Table 2:   POPULATION

Population	104,256,000 (estimate) (2017)
World Population Rank	13th (2017)
Population Density	349.7 people per sq. kilometer (2017)
Population Distribution	46.9% urban (2018)
Age Distribution	
0–14 years	33.39%
15–24 years	19.16%
25–54 years	36.99%
55–64 years	5.97%
65 years and over	4.49% (2017)
Median Age	23.5 years (2017)
Population Growth Rate	1.6% per year (2018)
Net Migration Rate	−1.9 (2018)
Languages	Pilipino and English
Religious Groups	Christian (91%)

Table 3:   HEALTH

Average Life Expectancy	69.6 years (2018)
Average Life Expectancy, Male	66.1 years (2018)
Average Life Expectancy, Female	73.3 years (2018)
Crude Birth Rate	23.4 per 1,000 people (2018)
Crude Death Rate	6.1 per 1,000 people (2018)
Maternal Mortality	121 per 100,000 live births (2017)
Infant Mortality	22 per 1,000 live births (2017)
Doctors	1.3 per 1,000 people (2017)

Table 4:   ENVIRONMENT

CO_2 Emissions	1.2 metric tons per capita (2017)
Alternative and Nuclear Energy	20.3% of total energy use (2014)
Threatened Species	783 (2017)
Protected Areas	51,844 sq. miles (2016)
Total Renewable H_2O Resources per Year	4,565 cubic meters, per person, per year (2017)

Table 5: ENERGY AND NATURAL RESOURCES

Electric Power Generation	94,370,000,000 kilowatt-hours per year (estimate) (2017)
Electric Power Consumption	77,790,000,000 kilowatt-hours per year (estimate) (2017)
Nuclear Power Plants	0 (2018)
Crude Oil Production	15,000 barrels per day (2017)
Crude Oil Consumption	398,000 barrels per day (2017)
Natural Gas Production	3,058,000,000 cubic meters per year (estimate) (2017)
Natural Gas Consumption	3,143,000,000 cubic meters per year (estimate) (2017)
Natural Resources	Timber, petroleum, nickel, cobalt, silver, gold, salt, copper

Table 6: NATIONAL FINANCES

Currency	Philippine peso
Total Government Revenues	$49,070,000,000 (estimate) (2017)
Total Government Expenditures	$56,030,000,000 (estimate) (2017)
Budget Deficit	−2.2% of GDP (2017)
GDP Contribution by Sector	Agriculture: 9.6%; Industry: 30.6%; Services: 59.8% (2017)
External Debt	$80,880,000,000 (estimate) (2017)
Economic Aid Extended	$0 (2011)
Economic Aid Received	$283,410,000 (2017)

Table 7: INDUSTRY AND LABOR

Gross Domestic Product (GDP)—Official Exchange Rate	$284,472,000,000 (estimate) (2013)
GDP per Capita	$3,280 (estimate) (2019)
GDP—Purchasing Power Parity (PPP)	$875,572,000,000 (estimate) (2017)
GDP (PPP) per Capita	$8,315 (estimate) (2017)
Industry Products	Textiles, refined petroleum, chemicals, pharmaceuticals, plywood, processed foods, fish, wood products, electronic components
Agriculture Products	Rice, corn, coconuts, sugarcane, bananas, pineapples, mangoes, fish, pigs, buffalo, goats, cattle, eggs, cannabis (illicit)
Unemployment	3.4% (2020)
Labor Profile	Agriculture: 30%; Industry: 16%; Services: 54% (estimate) (2014)

Table 8: TRADE

Imported Goods	Machinery and transportation equipment, basic manufactures, petroleum and petroleum products, chemicals, food and live animals, tobacco
Total Value of Imports	$92,840,000,000 (estimate) (2017)
Exported Goods	Machinery and transportation equipment, clothing, furniture, metals, electronics, textiles, copper, fish, nuts, bananas, sugar
Total Value of Exports	$63,230,000,000 (estimate) (2017)
Import Partners	China 18.1%, Japan 11.4%, South Korea 8.8%, USA 7.4%, Thailand 7.1%, Indonesia 6.7%, Singapore 5.9% (2017)
Export Partners	Japan 16.4%, USA 14.6%, Hong Kong 13.7%, China 11%, Singapore 6.1%, Thailand 4.3%, Germany 4.1%, South Korea 4% (2017)
Current Account Balance	$-2,518,000,000 (estimate) (2017)
Weights and Measures	The metric system is in use

Table 9: EDUCATION

School System	Primary education in the Philippines begins at the age of six and lasts for four years. Early secondary education lasts for two years, followed by four years of upper secondary education.
Mandatory Education	6 years, from ages 6 to 12
Average Years Spent in School for Current Students	13 (2014)
Average Years Spent in School for Current Students, Male	13 (2014)
Average Years Spent in School for Current Students, Female	13 (2014)
Primary School–Age Children Enrolled in Primary School	14,039,867 (2017)
Primary School–Age Males Enrolled in Primary School	7,315,532 (2017)
Primary School–Age Females Enrolled in Primary School	6,724,335 (2017)
Secondary School–Age Children Enrolled in Secondary School	11,346,712 (2019)

Secondary School–Age Males Enrolled in Secondary School	5,603,821 (2019)
Secondary School–Age Females Enrolled in Secondary School	3,685,802 (2016)
Students Per Teacher, Primary School	30.3 (2016)
Students Per Teacher, Secondary School	26.2 (2016)
Enrollment in Tertiary Education	3,563,396 (2016)
Enrollment in Tertiary Education, Male	1,596,629 (2017)
Enrollment in Tertiary Education, Female	1,992,855 (2017)
Literacy	96% (2016)

Table 10: MILITARY

Defense Spending (% of GDP)	1% (2017)
Total Active Armed Forces	153,000 (2017)
Annual Military Expenditures	$3,899,000,000 (2019)
Military Service	Service in the Filipino military is voluntary (2019)

Table 11: TRANSPORTATION

Airports	247 (2013)
Registered Vehicles	7,690,038 (2015)
Paved Roads	28.0% (2016)
Railroads	77 miles (2017)
Ports	Major: 8—including Manila, Cebu, Iloilo, Cagayan de Oro, Zamboanga, General Santos, and Davao

Table 12: COMMUNICATIONS

Facebook Users	62,000,000 (estimate) (2017)
Internet Users	56,956,436 (2016)
Internet Users (% of Population)	43.0% (2019)
Land-based Telephones in Use	4,163,282 (2017)
Mobile Telephone Subscribers	115,824,982 (2017)

APPENDIX D

HOLIDAYS

Holidays, 2022

January 1	New Year's Day
February 1	Chinese New Year
February 25	Commemoration of the People Power Revolution of 1986
April 9	Day of Valor
April 14	Maundy Thursday (part of the Holy Week commemorating the death of Jesus Christ)
April 15	Good Friday (part of the Holy Week commemorating the death of Jesus Christ)
April 16	Black Saturday (part of the Holy Week commemorating the death of Jesus Christ)
May 1	Labor Day
May 2–3	Eid'l Fitr (Muslim Feast of Ramadhan)
June 13	Philippine Independence Day
July 9–10	Eid'l Adha (Muslim Feast of Sacrifice)
August 29	National Heroes Day
November 1	All Saints' Day (Commemoration of saints revered by Filipinos)
November 2	All Souls' Day (Commemorating the memories of those who died)
November 30	Bonifacio Day (Honoring the memory of Andres Bonifacio, founder of the Katipunan, who sparked the 1896 Philippine Revolution)
December 8	Feast of the Immaculate Conception
December 25	Christmas Day
December 30	Rizal Day (Honoring the memory of the national hero Jose Rizal)

SELECTED BIBLIOGRAPHY

Abad, M. C. 2011. *The Philippines in ASEAN: Reflections from the Listening Room*. Pasig City: Anvil Publishing.

Abad, Michelle. 2019. "Fast Facts: State of Metro Manila's Public Transport System." *Rappler*. October 10. https://www.rappler.com/newsbreak/iq/242244-things-to-know-about-metro-manila-public-transport-system

Abad, Ricardo G. 2001. "Religion in the Philippines." *Philippine Studies* 49, no. 3 (September): 337–367.

Abalos, Jeofrey B. 2011. "Living Arrangements of the Divorce and Separated in the Philippines." *Asian Journal of Social Science* 39, no. 6: 845–863.

Abalos, Jeofrey B. 2017. "Divorce and Separation in the Philippines: Trends and Correlates." *Demographic Research* 36, no. 50: 1515–1548.

Abinales, Patricio N., ed. 1996. *The Revolution Falters: The Left in Philippine Politics after 1986*. Ithaca: Cornell University Press.

Abinales, Patricio N. 2020. *Making Mindanao: Cotabato and Davao in the Formation of Nation-State*. Quezon City: Ateneo de Manila University Press.

Abinales, Patricio N., and Donna J. Amoroso. 2017. *State and Society in the Philippines*. 2nd ed. Lanham, MD: Rowman and Littlefield.

Abubakar, Carmen A. 1989. "Moro Ethno-nationalist Movement." In Kumar David and Santasilan Kadirgamar (eds.), *Ethnicity: Identity, Conflict and Crisis*. Hong Kong: Arena Press.

Abueva, Jose V. 1999. *The Making of the Filipino Nation and Republic: The Pamana Series*, 1078 pp. Quezon City: University of the Philippines Press.

Abulencia, Arthur S. 2015. "The Unraveling of K–12 Program as an Education Reform in the Philippines." *Sipathahoena: South-East Asian Journal for Youth, Sports and Health Education* 1, no. 2 (October): 230–240.

Acabado, Stephen. 2020. "The Bahay Kubo and the Making of the Filipino." *Rappler*. June 26. Accessed June 26, 2020. https://www.rappler.com/move-ph/ispeak/264808-opinion-bahay-kubo-making-filipino

Achacoso-Sevilla, Luningning. 2003. *The Ties That Bind: Population and Development in the Philippines*. Makati City: Asian Institute of Management Policy Center.

Ackermann, Karl. 1918. "Big in Japan: A History of Jazz in the Land of the Rising Sun." *All about Jazz*. October 29. https://www.allaboutjazz.com/big-in-japan-a-history-of-jazz-in-the-land-of-the-rising-sun-part-1-by-karl-ackermann.php

Acosta, Nereus. 1994. "Loss, Emergence, and Retribalization: The Politics of Lumad Ethnicity in Northern Mindanao (Philippines)." PhD diss., University of Hawaii–Manoa.

Afable, Patricia. 2013. *Philippines: An Archipelago of Exchange*. Arles: Actes Sud; and Paris: Musee du quai Branly.

Agoncillo, Teodoro. 1997. *Malolos: The Crisis of the Republic*. Quezon City: University of the Philippines Press.

Agoncillo, Teodoro. 2005. *Revolt of the Masses: The Story of Bonifacio and the Katipunan*. New Edition. Quezon City: University of the Philippines Press.

Aguilar, Filomeno, Jr. 2014. *Migration Revolution: Philippine Nationhood and Class Relations in a Globalized Age*. Kyoto and Singapore: Kyoto University Press and National University of Singapore Press.

Aguiling-Pangalangan, Elizabeth. 1995. "The Family under Philippine Law." In Aurora Perez (ed.), *The Filipino Family: A Spectrum of Views and Issues*. Quezon City: University of the Philippines, Office of Research Coordination.

Akita, Takahiro. 2014. "Structural Changes and Interregional Income Inequality in the Philippines, 1975–2009." *Review of Urban and Regional Studies* 26, no. 2: 135–154.

Alarde-Regalado, Aurora, and Cynthia Hallare-Lara. 1992. *A Profile of the Philippine Rice Industry*. Quezon City: Philippine Peasant Institute.

Albert, Ramon G., Jesus C. Dumagan, and Arturo Martinez Jr. 2015. "Inequalities in Income, Labor and Education: The Challenge of Inclusive Growth." *Philippine Institute for Development Studies Discussion Paper Series No. 2015-01*. January.

Aldaba, Fernando. 2009. *Poverty in the Philippines: Causes, Constraints and Opportunities*. Manila: Asian Development Bank.

Aldaba, Rafaelita M. 2013. "Twenty Years after Trade Liberalization and Industrialization: What Has Happened and Where Do We Go from Here." *Philippine Institute for Development Studies Discussion Paper Series No. 2013-21*. March. https://dirp3.pids.gov.ph/ris/dps/pidsdps1321.pdf

Aldor, Joel Lucky C. 2013. "Look Up: A Study into the Sacred Art of Philippine Church Painting." Presentation at the 8th Biennial National Convention of Church Cultural Heritage Project, Dapitan City, Diocese of Dipolog, Zamboanga del Norte. May 20–23.

Alegre, Edilberto. 1999. "Pinoy na Pinoy: Spokening English: The Travails of Amboy." *Business World*. June 16. https://advance-lexis-com.eres.library.manoa.hawaii.edu/api/document?collection=news&id=urn:contentItem:3WR8-79V0-00JS-93GN-00000-00&context=1516831

Alegre, Edilberto N., and Doreen Fernandez. 1991. *Kinilaw: A Philippine Cuisine of Freshness*. Manila: Bookmark.

Alejo, Albert, ed. 2005. *Annotated Bibliography of Mindanao Studies*. Davao City: Mindanao Studies Consortium Foundation.

Alencon, Ferdinand Philippe Marie d'Orleans. 1986. *Luzon and Mindanao*. Manila: E. Aguilar Cruz.

Alfonso, Oscar M., and Leslie E. Bauzon. 1985. *University of the Philippines: The First 75 Years (1908–1983)*. Quezon City: University of the Philippines Press.

Algue, Jose. 1904. *The Climate of the Philippines*. Washington, DC: Department of Commerce and Labor Bureau of the Census.

Ali, David Aba. 2007. "Regional Development in the Philippines: The Case of the Autonomous Region in Muslim Mindanao (ARMM)." PhD diss., University of Western Australia School of Earth and Geographical Sciences.

Allied Forces, Southwest Pacific Area. 1945. *Sulu Archipelago* (Philippine Series). Brisbane: Allied Geographical Section.

ALMEC Corporation 2014. "Roadmap for Transport Infrastructure Development for Metro Manila and Its Surrounding Areas (Region III and Region IV-A): Final Report Summary." Japan International Cooperation Agency (JICA) and the National Economic Development Authority. March.

Alonso y Terme, Rosa Maria. 2014. "What Prevents the Philippines from Undertaking Reform? A Story of the Unravelling State." *International Centre for Tax and Development*. Institute of Developing Economies. January. https://assets.publishing.service.gov .uk/media/57a089d240f0b652dd000412/ICTD-WP16.pdf

Anderson, Allan. 2004. "The Future of Protestantism: The Non-Western Protestant World." In Alister E. McGrath and Darren C. Marks (eds.), *The Blackwell Companion to Protestantism*, pp. 468–482. Malden, MA: Blackwell Publishing Ltd.

Anderson, Benedict, and R. O'Gorman. 2003. "Forms of Consciousness in Noli me Tangere." *Philippine Studies* 51, no. 4: 505–529.

Anderson, Benedict, and R. O'Gorman. 2004. "Nitroglycerine in the Pomegranate." *New Left Review* 27 (May–June): 99–118.

Anderson, Benedict, and R. O'Gorman. 2006. "Forms of Consciousness in 'El Filibusterismo.'" *Philippine Studies* 54, no. 3: 315–356.

Anderson, Quiliano Nineza. 2015. "Kundiman Love Songs from the Philippines: Their Development from Folksong to Artsong and an Examination of Representative Repertoire." PhD diss., University of Iowa.

Ang, Alvin P., Guntur Sugiyarto, and Shikha Jha. 2009. "Remittances and Household Behavior in the Philippines." *Asian Development Bank Working Papers Series No. 188*. December. https://www.adb.org/sites/default/files/publication/28401/economics-wp188.pdf

Ang, Gertrudes R. 1978. "The Tinikling as a Literary Symbol of Filipino Culture." *Philippine Quarterly of Culture and Society* 6, no. 4: 210–217.

Anima, Nid. ed. 1973. *Philippine Cockfighting Stories*. Quezon City: Omar Publications.

An Annotated Bibliography of Selected Visayan Studies Collection. 1980. Cebu: University of the Philippines in the Visayas, Visayan Studies Collection.

Antolihao, Lou Apolinario. 2009. "Can the Subaltern Play? Postcolonial Transition and the Making of Basketball as the National Sports in the Philippines." PhD diss., National University of Singapore.

Antolihao, Lou Apolinario. 2012. "From Baseball Colony to Basketball Republic: Post-colonial Transition and the Making of a National Sport in the Philippines." *Sports in Society: Cultures, Commerce, Media, Politics* 15, no. 10: 1396–1412.

Aprieto, Pacifico N. 1983. "The Philippine Textbook Project." *Prospects: Quarterly Review of Education* 13, no. 3: 351–359.

Aquino, Belinda. 1991. *The University Experience: Essays on the 82nd Anniversary of the University of the Philippines*. Quezon City: University of the Philippines Press.

Araral, Eduardo, Jr., Paul D. Hutchcroft, Gilberto M. Llanto, Jonathan E. Malaya, Ronald U. Mendoza, Julio C. Teehankee. 2018. *Debate on Federal Philippines: A Citizen's Handbook*. Quezon City: Ateneo de Manila University Press.

Arguillas, Carolyn, Yvonne Chua, and Luz Rimban. 2011. *Democracy at Gunpoint: Election-Related Violence in the Philippines*. Makati City: Asia Foundation.

Art Archive 01: A Collection of Essays on Philippine Contemporary Visual and Performing Arts. 2017. Manila: Japan Foundation. November.

Asian Development Bank. 2007. *Philippines: Critical Development Constraints*. Manila: Asian Development Bank. https://www.adb.org/sites/default/files/publication/29274/cdc-philippines.pdf

Asian Development Bank. 2008. *Republic of the Philippines: Preparing the Integrated Resources and Environmental Management Sector Development Program—Financed by the Japan Special Fund*. Manila: Asian Development Bank.

Bacungan, Froilan M. 1983. *The Powers of the Philippine President*. Quezon City: University of the Philippines Law Center.

Balisacan, Arsenio M., ed. 2003. *The Philippine Economy: Development, Policies, and Challenges*. Oxford and New York. Oxford University Press.

Balisacan, Arsenio M., and Hal Hill. 2007. *The Dynamics of Regional Development: The Philippines in East Asia*. Cheltenham, UK: Edward Elgar.

Bamboo Houses of the Philippines. http://www.bbc.com/culture/story/20180517-the-bamboo-houses-of-the-philippines

Banados, Papias Generale. 2011. *The Path to Remittance: Tales of Pains and Gains of Overseas Filipino Workers*. Singapore: Global Eye Media.

Banag, Consuelo Cruz. 1970. "A Critical Study of Lope K. Santos' Banaag at Sikat." MA thesis, Centro Escolar University.

Banloi, Rommel. 2010. *The Philippines in ASEAN at Forty: Achievements, Challenges, and Prospects in Regional Security Cooperation*. Boca Raton, FL: Auerbach Publications.

Bao, Maohong. 2015. "The Pluralism of Ethnic Cultures and Inclusive Development in the Philippines." *Suvannabhumi* 7, no. 11: 139–155.

Barendregt, Bart, Peter Keppy, and Henk Schulte Nordholt. 2017. *Popular Music in Southeast Asia: Banal Beats, Muted Histories*. Amsterdam: Amsterdam University Press.

Barry, Coeli. 2018. "Gender, Nation and Filipino Catholicism Past and Present." In Mark R. Thompson and Eric Vincent C. Batalla (eds.), *Routledge Handbook of the Contemporary Philippines*. Oxford and New York: Routledge.

Barter, Shane Joshua. 2009. "Boxing Day in Cotabato: Notes from the Field." *Explorations: A Graduate Student Journal of Southeast Asia* 9 (Spring): 113–114.

Bartholomew, Rafe. 2010. *Pacific Rims: Beermen Ballin' in Flip-Flops and the Philippines' Unlikely Love Affair with Basketball*. New York: New American Library.

Battistella, Graziano, and Maruka M.B. Asis. 2013. "Country Migration Report: The Philippines 2013." International Organization for Migration and the Scalabrini Migration Center; 291 pp.

Bautista, Cynthia B. 2001. "Composition and Origins of the Middle Class"; "Middle Class Cultures: Glimpses of Lifestyles and Outlooks"; "Middle Class Politics and Views of Society and Government"; and "Images of the Middle Classes in Metro Manila." In Xinhuang Xiao (ed.), *Exploration of the Middle Class in Southeast Asia*. Taipei, Taiwan: Academica Sinica Program for Southeast Asian Area Studies.

Bautista, Ma. Cynthia Rose B., Allan B. I. Bernardo, and Dina Ocampo. 2008/2009. "When Reforms Don't Transform: Reflections on Institutional Reforms in the Department of Education." *Human Development Network Discussion Papers Series No. 2*.

Bautista, Ma. Lourdes. S. 1999. "Bridging Research and Practice in Literacy Work among Minority Language Groups in the Philippines." *Asia-Pacific Education Researcher* 8, no. 2: 111–128.

Bautista, Regina Angelica. 2017. "Embodied Indigeneity: Translating Tradition for the Philippine Contemporary Dance Stage." MA thesis, York University.

Baviera, Aileen. 2000. *Comprehensive Engagement: Strategic Issues in Philippines-China Relations*. Quezon City: Philippine-China Development Resource Center.

The Bayanihan Experience. 1987. Manila: Bayanihan Folk Arts Center.

Bayanihan Philippine Dance Company. 1970. New York: Dunetz and Lovestt.

Bender, Daniel E., and Adrian de Leon. 2017. "Everybody Was Boodle Fighting: Military Histories, Culinary Tourism and Diasporic Dining." *Food, Culture and Society* 21, no. 1: 25–41.

Beran, Janice A. 1989. "Americans in the Philippines: Imperialism or Progress through Sport?" *International Journal of the History of Sport* 6, no. 1: 62–87.

Berlin, Donald. 2008. *Before Gringo: History of the Philippine Military, 1830 to 1972*. Pasay City: Anvil Publishing.

Besa, Amy, Romy Dorotan, and Neil Oshima. 2014. *Memories of Philippine Kitchens*. Revised and updated. New York: Stewart, Tabori and Chang.

Billig, Michael S. 2003. *Barons, Brokers and Buyers: The Institutions and Cultures of Philippine Sugar*. Honolulu, HI: University of Hawaii Press.

Binsted, Norman. 1958. "The Philippine Independent Church (Iglesia Filipina Independiente)." *Historical Magazine of the Protestant Episcopal Church I* 27, no. 3 (September): 209–246.

Bird, Miriam, and Ernst Christoph. 2009. "Offshoring and Employment in the Developing World: Business Process Outsourcing in the Philippines." *Employment Working Paper No. 41*. Geneva: International Labour Organization. http://www.ilo.org/wcmsp5/groups/public /---ed_emp/---emp_elm/---analysis/documents/publication/wcms_117922.pdf

Bolton, Kingsley. 2008. "English in Asia, Asian Englishes, and the Issue of Proficiency." *English Today* 24, no. 2. doi:10.1017/S026607840800014X

Bolton, Kingsley, and Ma. Lourdes Bautista. 2004. "Philippine English: Tensions and Transitions." *World Englishes* 23, no. 2.

Boquet, Yves. 2013. "Battling Congestion in Manila: The EDSA Problem." *Transport and Communications Bulletin for Asia and the Pacific*. Combatting Congestion No. 82. United Nations Economic and Social Commission for Asia and the Pacific. https://www.unescap.org/publications/transport-and-communications-bulletin-asia-and-pacific-no-82-combatting-congestion

Boquet, Yves. 2015. *The Philippine Archipelago*, n.p. New York: Springer.

Boquet, Yves. 2017. "The Growth of Greater Manila." *Philippine Archipelago*. April 22.

Borras, Saturnino. 2007. *Pro-Poor Land Reform: A Critique.* Ottawa: University of Ottawa Press.

Bresnahan, Mary I. 1989. "The Tagalog Literary Tradition in Amado V. Hernandez." *Philippine Studies* 37, no. 1 (March 1): 15–28.

Bryant, P. L. 1916. "The Visayas and Zamboanga." *Mid-Pacific Magazine* 12, no. 2 (August 1): 183–186.

Buenconsejo, Jose S. 2017. *Philippine Modernities: Music, Performing Arts and Language, 1880–1941.* Quezon City: University of the Philippines Press.

Buhain, Dominador D. 1998. *A History of Publishing in the Philippines.* Manila: Rex Book Store.

Bunoan, Ringo. 2017. "Excavating Spaces and Histories: The Case of HShop 6." In *Art Archive 01: A Collection of Essays on Philippine Contemporary Visual and Performing Arts.* Manila: Japan Foundation. November.

Burbridge, Frederick William. 1980. *The Gardens of the Sun, or a Naturalist's Journal on the Mountains and in the Forests and Swamps of Borneo and the Sulu Archipelago.* London: J. Murray.

Burgess, Robert, and Vikram Haksar. 2005. "Migration and Foreign Remittances in the Philippines." *IMF Working Paper* (May 11): 18 pp.

Burton, Lisa Ann. 2013. "Mother Tongue–Based Multilingual Education in the Philippines: Studying Top-Down Policy Implementation from the Bottom Up." PhD diss., University of Minnesota. May. https://conservancy.umn.edu/bitstream/handle/11299/152603/Burton_umn_0130E_13632.pdf

Cabalfin, Edson G. 2008. *Building Modernity: A Century of Philippine Architecture and Allied Arts.* Manila: National Commission for Culture and the Arts.

Cabalfin, Edson G. 2020. "*Bahay Kubo* as Iconography: Representing the Vernacular and the Nation in Philippine Post-war Architectures." *Journal of the Society of Architectural Historians, Australia and New Zealand* 30, no. 1: 44–67.

Calvelo, George. 2020. "DepEd Vows to Address Filipinos' Declining English Proficiency." *ABS-CBN News* (November 27). https://news.abs-cbn.com/news/11/27/20/deped-commits-to-address-filipinos-declining-english-proficiency#:~:text=Over%20the%20past%20years%2C%20the,of%20562%20out%20of%20700

Caoli-Rodriguez, Rhona. 2006. "Asia and the Pacific Education for All (EFA) Mid-Decade Assessment: Insular South-East Asia Synthesis Report." United Nations Educational, Scientific and Cultural Organization and the Japan Funds-in Trust. http://uis.unesco.org/sites/default/files/documents/education-for-all-mid-decade-assessment-for-insular-south-east-asia-en_0.pdf

Caoli-Rodriguez, Rhona B. 2008. *Insular South-East Asia Synthesis Report: Asia and the Pacific Education for All (EFA) Mid-Decade Assessment.* Bangkok: UNESCO. Accessed April 22, 2019. http://uis.unesco.org/sites/default/files/documents/education-for-all-mid-decade-assessment-for-insular-south-east-asia-en_0.pdf

Carbonel, Loneza G., and Janette P. Calimag. 2016. "The Traditional Tattoos of the Philippine Cordillera Region: A Study on Their Differences in Appearance, Causes and Discursive Strength." *International Journal of Advanced Research in Management and Social Sciences* 5, no. 6: 1–8.

Cardenas, Marilu Nery. 2018. "From Policy to Local Practice: An Implementation Study of the Mother Tongue–Based Multilingual Education in the Philippines." PhD diss., Teachers College, Columbia University.

Carino, Jacqueline K. 2012. *The Philippines: Country Technical Notes on Indigenous People's Issues.* Rome: International Fund for Agricultural Development (IFAD).

Carson, Arthur L. 1978. *The Story of Philippine Education.* Quezon City: New Day Publishers.

Caruncho, Eric S. 1996. *Punks, Poets, Poseurs: Reportage on Pinoy Rock and Roll.* Pasig, Metropolitan Manila: Anvil Publishing.

Casambre, Napoleon J. 1982. "The Impact of American Education in the Philippines." *Educational Perspectives* 21, no. 4 (Winter): 7–14. Accessed April 22, 2019. https://scholarspace .manoa.hawaii.edu/bitstream/10125/47216/EDPVol21%234_7-14.pdf

Castro, Christi-Anne. 2011. *Musical Renderings of the Philippine Nation.* New York: Oxford University Press.

Central Intelligence Agency. 2022. *The World Factbook—East and Southeast Asia—Philippines* (February 14). https://www.cia.gov/the-world-factbook/countries/philippines/

Cerini, Mariana. 2019. "It's Kinilaw, the Filipino Answer to Ceviche." *Taste.* July 9. https://www .tastecooking.com/kinilaw-filipino-answer-ceviche/

Chambers, John S. J. K. 2003. *Creoles and Pidgins (Others).* Zamboanga City: Ateneo de Zamboanga University.

Chan, Bernice. 2019. "The Secrets to Great Lechon—Whole Roasted Suckling Pig That's Virtually a Filipino National Dish." *South China Morning Post.* January 25. https://www.scmp .com/lifestyle/food-drink/article/2108935/secrets-great-lechon-whole-roasted-suckling-pig -thats-virtually

Che Man, W. K. 1990. *Muslim Separatism: The Moros of Southern Philippines and the Malays of Southern Thailand.* Quezon City: Ateneo de Manila University Press.

Choguill, Charles L. 2001. "Manila: City of Hope or a Planner's Nightmare?" *Built Environment* 27, no. 2 (January): 85–95.

Chua, Yvonne. 1999. *Robbed: An Investigation of Corruption in Philippine Education.* Quezon City: Philippine Center for Investigative Journalism.

Chung, Lilia Hernandez. 1998. *Facts in Fiction: A Study of Peninsular Prose Fiction: 1859–1897.* Manila: De La Salle University Press.

Clarke, Gerard. 1998. *The Politics of NGOs in Southeast Asia: Participation and Protest in the Philippines.* New York: Routledge.

Clarke, Gerard. 2013. *Civil Society in the Philippines; Theoretical, Methodological, and Policy Debates.* Milton Park, Abingdon, Oxfordshire: Taylor and Francis.

Clarke, Gerard, and Marites Sison. 2003. "Voices from the Top of the Pile: Elite Perceptions of Poverty and the Poor." *Development and Change* 34, no. 2: 215–242.

Claudio, Lisandro. 2012. "Were the Eraserheads the End of Cultural History." *GMA News Online.* January 1. https://www.gmanetwork.com/news/opinion/content/243261/were-the -eraserheads-the-end-of-cultural-history/story/

Claudio, Lisandro. 2014. *Taming People's Power: The EDSA Revolutions and Their Contradictions.* Quezon City: Ateneo de Manila University Press.

CNN Philippine Life Staff. 2017. "The 25 Best Filipino Love Songs of the Last 25 Years." *CNN Life*. February 20. https://cnnphilippines.com/life/entertainment/Music/2019/2/7/filipino -love-songs.html

Co, Edna A. 2023. *State of Local Democracy in the Autonomous Region in Muslim Mindanao*. Quezon City: University of the Philippines National College of Public Administration and Governance and the Philippine Center for Islam and Democracy.

Collantes, Christianne F. 2018. *Reproductive Dilemmas in Metro Manila: Faith, Intimacies and Globalization*. Singapore: Palgrave MacMillan.

Coloma, Ronald Sintos. 2013. "Care of the Postcolonial Self: Cultivating Nationalism in *the Philippine Readers*." *Qualitative Research in Education* 2, no. 3: 302–327.

Committee to Protect Journalists. "83 Journalists Killed in the Philippines." Accessed October 27, 2019. https://cpj.org/data/killed/asia/philippines/

Conant, Carlos Everett. 1909. "The Names of Philippine Languages." *Anthropos* Bd. 4, H. 4: 1069–1074.

Cone, Stephen L., and Theresa Purcell Cone. 2016. "Dance in SHAPE America Is Alive and Well!" *Journal of Physical Education, Recreation and Dance* 87, no. 6: 3–4.

Connell, J. 1999. "Beyond Manila: Walls, Malls and Private Spaces." *Environment and Planning* 31: 417–439.

Constantino, Renato. 1982. *The Miseducation of the Filipino*. Quezon City: Foundation for Nationalist Studies.

Constantino, Renato. 2010. *A History of the Philippines: From the Spanish Colonization to the Second World War*. New York: Monthly Review Press.

Coo, Stephanie Marie R. 2017. "Diverse yet Distinct: Philippine Men's Clothing in the Nineteenth Century." *Suvannabhumi* 9, no. 2 (December): 123–144.

Cordero-Fernando, Gilda. 1976. *The Culinary Culture of the Philippines*. Manila: Vera Reyes Inc.

Cornelio, Jayeel Serrano. 2016. *Being Catholic in the Contemporary Philippines*. Oxford and New York: Routledge.

Cornelio, Jayeel Serrano. 2017. "Religion and Civic Engagement: The Case of Iglesia ni Cristo in the Philippines." *Religion, State and Society* 45, no. 1 (January): 23–38.

Coronel, Sheila S. 1996. *Patrimony: 6 Case Studies on Local Politics and Environment in the Philippines*. Pasay City: Philippine Center for Investigative Journalism.

Coronel, Sheila S. 1998. *Pork and Other Perks: Corruption and Governance in the Philippines*. Manila: Philippine Center for Investigative Journalism.

Coronel, Sheila S. 2001. "The Media, the Market, and Democracy: The Case of the Philippines." *Public* 8, no. 2: 109–126.

Coronel, Sheila S. 2017. "Murder as Enterprise: Police Profiteering in Duterte's War on Drugs." In Nicole Curato (ed.), *A Duterte Reader: Critical Essays on Rodrigo Duterte's Early Presidency*, pp. 167–198. Quezon City: Ateneo de Manila University Press.

Coronel, Sheila S., and Jose F. Lacaba, eds. 1995. *Boss: 5 Case Studies of Local Politics in the Philippines*. Pasig City: Philippine Center for Investigative Journalism; Quezon City: Institute for Popular Democracy.

Coronel, Sheila, Yvonne T. Chua, Luz Rimban, and Booma Cruz. 2004. *The Rulemakers: How the Wealthy and the Well-Born Dominate Congress*. Manila: Philippine Center for Investigative Journalism.

Coronel-Ferrer, Miriam. 2013. *Costly Wars, Elusive Peace: Collected Articles on the Peace Processes in the Philippines 1990–2007.* Quezon City: The University of the Philippines Press.

Cororaton, Caesar B. 2015. "Will the Philippines Benefit from the Regional Comprehensive Economic Partnership?" *Policy Notes No. 2015-23*. November.

Cortes, Josefina R. 1993. *Explorations in the Theory and Practice of Philippine Education, 1965–1993*. Quezon City: University of the Philippines.

Coursey, Oscar William. 2008. *History and Geography of the Philippines*, Charleston, SC: Bibliobazaar. 180 pp.

Cruz, Geoffrey Rhoel C. 2019. "A Review of How Philippine Colonial Experience Influenced the Country's Approaches to Conservation of Cultural Heritage." *Padayomn Sining: A Celebration of the Enduring Values of the Humanities*. Paper Presented at the De La Salle University (Philippines), Arts Congress. February 20–22.

Cruz, Grace T., Christian Joy P. Cruz, and Yashuhiko Saito. 2019. *Ageing and Health in the Philippines*. Jakarta, Indonesia and Quezn City, Philippines. Economic Research Institute for ASEAN and East Asia Demographic Research and Development Foundation, Inc., and Demographic Research and Development Foundation, Inc. 244 pp.

Cruz, Grace T., Elma P. Laguna, and Corazon M. Raymundo. 2001. "Family Influences on the Lifestyle of Filipino Youth." *East-West Center Working Papers*, 108-9 (October).

Cruz, I. R. 1991. "A Nation Searching for a Language Finds a Language Searching for a Name." *English Today 7*, no. 4. doi:10.1017/S0266078400005873

Cuevas, Sining C. 2017. "Institutional Dimensions of Climate Change Adaptation: Insights from the Philippines." *Climate Policy* (April 24): 499–511.

Curaming, Rommel A. 2017. "Hegemomic Tool? Nationalism in Philippine History Textbooks, 1900–2000." *Philippine Studies: Historical and Ethnographic Viewpoints* 65, no. 4: 417–450.

Davis, Janet M. 2013. "Cockfight Nationalism: Blood Sport and the Moral Politics of American Empire and Nation Building." *American Quarterly* 65, no. 3 (September) : 549–574.

Dawe, Christopher J. 2014. "Language Governmentality in the Philippine Education Policy." *Working Papers in Educational Linguistics (WPEL)* 9, no. 1 (Spring): 62–77.

Daza, Nora, and Michael Fenix. 1992. *A Culinary Life: Personal Recipe Collection*. Pasig City: Anvil Publishing.

De Castro, Renato Cruz. 2009. "Exploring a 21st-Century Japan-Philippine Security Relationship: Linking Two Spokes Together?" *Asian Survey* 49, no. 4 (July): 691–715.

De Dios, Aurora Javate, Petronilo Daroy, and Lorna Kalaw-Tirol, eds. 1998. *Dictatorship and Revolution: Roots of People's Power*. Manila: Conspectus.

De Las Torre, Visitacion R. 2000. *The Barong Tagalog: Then and Now*. Makati City: Windsor Tower Book House.

De Ocampo, Nick. 2011. *Film: American Influences on Philippine Cinema*. Pasig City: Anvil Publishing.

De Voogt, Alex. 2010. "Philippine Sungka and Cultural Contact in Southeast Asia: Research Note." *Asian Ethnology* 69, no. 2: 333–342.

Dekker, Diane E. 2017. "Finally Shedding the Past: Filipino Teachers Negotiate Their Identities within a new Mother-Tongue-Based Multilingual Education Policy Landscape." PhD diss., University of Toronto.

Del Mundo, Clodualdo. 1999. "Philippine Cinema: An Historical Overview." *Asian Cinema* 10, no. 2: 29–66.

Del Mundo, Clodualdo. 2003. "50 Years of Pinoy TV." *PhilStar*. October 12. https://www.philstar.com/other-sections/starweek-magazine/2003/10/12/223965/50-years-pinoy-tv

Demata, Retxe Bryanne. 2016. "Media Log 1." *E-Portfolio*. August 18. https://shreddingthroughthepages.wordpress.com/blog/

Demeterio, F. P. A., III. 2017. "The Fading *Batek*: Problematizing the Decline of Traditional Tattoos in the Philippine Cordillera Region." *Journal of the South East Asia Research Centre* 9, no. 2: 55–82.

Diokno, Benjamin E. 2005. "Reforming the Philippine Tax System: Lessons from Two Tax Reform Programs." *University of the Philippines School of Economics Discussion Papers 0502* (March): 1–27. http://www.econ.upd.edu.ph/dp/index.php/dp/article/view/122/120

Dobson, Barbara M. 1988. "Like a Thief in the Night: Filipino (sic) Modes of Courtship and Marriage." PhD diss., University of Western Australia.

Doyo, Ma. Ceres P. 2019. *Press Freedom under Siege: Reportage That Challenged the Marcos Dictatorship*. Quezon City: University of the Philippines Press.

Ducanes, Geoffrey, and Manolo Abella. 2008. "Overseas Filipino Works and Their Impact on Household Poverty." *International Labour Organization Working Paper No. 5*. January.

The Economist. 2021. "Daily Chart: How Many People Have Been Killed in Rodrigo Duterte's War on Drugs?" (November 22). https://www.economist.com/graphic-detail/2021/11/22/how-many-people-have-been-killed-in-rodrigo-dutertes-war-on-drugs

Eder, James F., and Robert L. Youngblood. 1994. *Patterns of Power and Politics in the Philippines: Implications for Development*. Tempe, AZ: Arizona University Program for Southeast Asian Studies.

Editors of *Encyclopedia Britannica*. "Sulu Archipelago: Archipelago, Philippines." Accessed July 4, 2017. https://www.britannica.com/place/Sulu-Archipelago

Elesterio, Fernando G. 1988. *The Iglesia ni Kristo: Its Christology and Ecclesiology*. Manila: Ateneo de Manila University, Cardinal Bean Institute, Loyola School of Theology.

Ellorin, Bernard Barros. 2016. "Staging Autonomous Ethnicities: The 'Bayanihan Effect' and Its Influence on the Standardization of the Performing Arts from the Muslim Societies of Southern Philippines." *ICTM Study Group on Performing Arts of Southeast Asia: Proceedings of the 4th Symposium*, School of the Arts, Universiti Sains Malaysia, Penang, Malaysia.

Elwood, Douglas. 1969. "Varieties of Christianity in the Philippines." In Gerald H. Anderson (ed.), *Studies in Philippine Church History*. Ithaca and London: Cornell University Press.

Enaka, Hachiro. 2006. "Language Planning and Bilingual Education in the Philippines: A Historical Approach." PhD diss., Merdeka Malang University, Indonesia.

Engelbrecht, Georgi. 2021. "The Philippines: Three More Years for the Bangsamoro Transition." *International Crisis Group Q&A/Asia* (29 October). https://www.crisisgroup.org/asia/south-east-asia/philippines/philippines-three-more-years-bangsamoro-transition

Environment and Social Safeguard Division. 2002. *Indigenous Peoples/Ethnic Minorities and Poverty Reduction in the Philippines*. Manila: Asian Development Bank. June.

Esguerra, Mina V. 2019. "For Those about to Teach 'Chick Lit' in Senior High School (Philippines)." *Wattpad*. May 4. https://www.wattpad.com/445487857-21st-century-literature-philippines-chick-lit-for

Esguerra, Mina V., and Georgette Gonzales. n.d. "12 Essential Romance Books." https://www.wattpad.com/614617048-21st-century-literature-philippines-chick-lit-12

Eugenio, Damiana L. 1989. *Philippine Folk Literature: The Folktales*. Quezon City: University of the Philippines Press.

Evangelista, Alfredo E. 1973. "Tempered Intemperance: Tuba-Drinking in a Tagalog Community." *Philippine Sociological Review* 21, no. 1 (January): 5–28.

Fadol, Hans. 2014. "The Alteration of Filipino Family Values." October 6. Accessed February 9, 2019. https://prezi.com/bafx3um0afpm/the-alteration-filipino-family-values/

Family Code of the Philippines—Executive Order No. 209. http://www.chanrobles.com/executiveorderno209.htm

Fernandes, Naresh. 2015. "The Forgotten Story of a Filipino Swing Musician in 1930s India." *Quartz India*. May 5. https://qz.com/india/398192/the-forgotten-story-of-a-filipino-swing-musician-in-1930s-india/

Fernandez, Doreen G. 1980a. "From Ritual to Realism: A Brief Historical Survey of Philippine Theater." *Philippine Studies* 28: 389–419.

Fernandez, Doreen G. 1980b. "Philippine-American Cultural Interactions." *University of the Philippines Third World Studies Program Discussion Papers 21* (December): 13 pp.

Fernandez, Doreen G. 1981. "Philippine Popular Culture: Dimensions and Directions. The State of Research in Philippine Popular Culture." *Philippine Studies* 29 (First Quarter): 26–44.

Fernandez, Doreen G. 1989. "Mass Culture and Cultural Policy: The Philippine Experience." *Philippine Studies* 37, no. 4 (Fourth Quarter): 488–502.

Fernandez, Doreen G. 1991. "Balut to Barbecue: Philippine Street Food." *Oxford Symposium on Food and Cookery*. London: Prospect Books.

Fernandez, Doreen G. 1993. "Zarzuela to Sarswela: Indigenization and Transformation." *Philippine Studies* 47, no. 3 (Third Quarter): 320–343.

Fernandez, Doreen G. 2000. *Palayok: Filipino Food through Time, on Site, in the Pot*. Hong Kong: Bookmark.

Fernandez, Doreen G. 2008. *Tikim: Essays on Philippine Food and Culture*. Pasig City: Anvil Publishing.

Fernandez, Doreen G., and Edilberto N. Alegre, 1988. *Sarap: Essays on Philippine Food*. Manila: Mr. & Ms. Publishing Company

Filipinas Foundation. 1976. *Philippine Majority-Minority Relations and Ethnic Attitudes: An In-Depth Study*. Makati City: Shell Foundation.

The Filipino Athlete. 1935. October 16.

"Filipinos Like the US Even More Than Americans Do—Pew Research." 2014. *Rappler*. April 22. Accessed June 12, 2019. https://www.rappler.com/nation/56085-philippines-usa-pew -research

Fragmentation vs. Consolidation: The Case of Philippine Local Governments. 2005. Pasay City: Local Government Foundation; Makati City: Konrad Adenauer Stiftung.

Franco, Jennifer Conroy. 2001. *Elections and Democratization in the Philippines*. New York: Routledge.

Fullante, Luis Cruz. 1983. "The National Language Question in the Philippines, 1963 to the Present." PhD diss., University of California, Los Angeles.

Gabriel, Bernardo A. 1937. "Sungka: Philippine Variant of a Widely-Distributed Game." *Philippine Social Science Review* 9: 1–36.

Gabrillo, James. 2018. "*Rak en Rol:* The Influence of Psychedelic Culture in Philippine Music." *Rock Music Studies* 5, no. 3: 1:18.

Gaerlan, Barbara S. 1998. "The Politics and Pedagogy of Language Use at the University of the Philippines: The History of English as the Medium of Instruction and the Challenge Mounted by Filipino." PhD diss., University of California, Los Angeles.

Galam, Roderick G. 2008. *The Promise of the Nation: Gender, History, and Nationalism in Contemporary Ilokano Literature*. Quezon City: Ateneo de Manila University.

Garrity, Dennis P., David M. Kummer, and Ernesto S. Guiang. 1993. "The Philippines in Sustainable Agriculture and the Environment in the Humid Tropics." In Committee on Sustainable Agriculture and the Environment in the Humid Tropics, Board on Agriculture and Board on Science and Technology for International Development (eds.), *Sustainable Agriculture and the Environment in the HUMID Tropics*, pp. 549–624. Washington, DC: National Research Council.

Gems, Gerald R. 2004. "The Athletic Crusade: Sports and Colonialism in the Philippines." *International Journal of the History of Sport* 21, no. 1: 1–15.

Gems, Gerald R. 2016. *Sports and the American Occupation of the Philippines: Bats, Balls, and Bayonets*. Lanham, MD: Lexington Books.

George, T. J. S. 1980. *Revolt in Mindanao: Rise of Islam in Philippine Politics*. Kuala Lumpur: Oxford University Press.

Geronimo, Jee Y. 2016. "RH Budget Cut Exposes Problematic Lawmaking in PH." *Rappler*. January 21. https://www.rappler.com/newsbreak/in-depth/119493-reproductive-health -budget-cut-lawmaking

Gipson, Jessica D., Socorro A. Gultiano, Josephine L. Avila, and Michelle J. Hindin. 2012. "Old Ideals and New Realities: The Changing Context of Young People's Partnership in Cebu, Philippines." *Culture, Health and Sexuality* 14, no. 6 (June): 613–627.

Go, Fe Susan. 1979. "Mothers, Maids and the Creatures of the Night: The Persistence of Philippine Folk Religion." *Philippine Quarterly of Culture and Society* 7, no. 3 (December): 186–203.

Go, Julian. 1999. "Colonial Reception and Cultural Reproduction: Filipino Elites and United States Tutelary Role." *Journal of Historical Sociology* 12, no. 4 (December): 337–368.

Go, Stella P. 1993. *The Filipino Family in the Eighties*. Manila: De La Salle University, Social Development Research Center.

Goldoftas, Barbara. 2006. *The Green Tiger: The Cost of Ecological Decline in the Philippines* New York: Oxford University Press.

Gonzalez, Andrew. 1980. *Language and Nationalism: The Philippine Experience Thus Far*. Quezon City: Ateneo de Manila University Press.

Gonzalez, Andrew. 2002. *An Unfinished Symphony: 934 Dats at DECS*. Manila: Andrew Gonzalez.

Gonzalez, Hernando. 1988. "Mass Media and the Spiral of Silence: the Philippines from Marcos to Aquino." *Journal of Communications* 38, no. 4 (Autumn): 33–48.

Gonzalez, Joaquin Jay, III, and Angelo Michael F. Merino. 2012. *From Pancho to Pacquiao: Philippine Boxing in and out of the Ring*. lMinneapolis, MN: Mill City Press Inc.

Gonzalez, N.V.M. 1992. *A Season of Grace*. Manila: Bookmark.

Goodno, J. B. 2004. "Burnham's Manila." *American Planning Association* 70, no. 11: 30–34.

Grosser, Larry Lee. 1967. "A Content Analysis of Philippine School Textbooks: A Study of Political Socialization and Development." MA thesis, Western Michigan University, August.

Growth with Equity in Mindanao. 1999. *Mindanao: An Island Economy with a Global Outlook*. Davao City: Growth with Equity in Mindanao Program. CD ROM.

Gueta, Grace Padayhag, and Lounell Bahoy Gueta. 2013. "How Travel Pattern Changes after Number Coding Scheme as a Travel Demand Management Measure Was Implemented?" *Journal of the Eastern Asia Society for Transportation Studies* 10. https://www.jstage.jst.go.jp/article/easts/10/0/10_412/_pdf

Guevara, Anna Romina. 2009. *Marketing Dreams, Manufacturing Heroes: The Transnational Labor Brokering of Filipino Workers*. New Jersey: Rutgers University Press.

Guggenheim, Scott. 1994. "Cock or Bull: Cockfighting, Social Structure, and Political Commentary in the Philippines." In Alan Dunes (ed.), *The Cockfight: A Casebook*. Madison, WI: University of Wisconsin Press.

Guido, Edson C. 2021. "How the Philippines Can Recover from One of the World's Longest Lockdowns." *Journal of International Affairs* (May 16). https://jia.sipa.columbia.edu/online-articles/how-philippines-can-recover-one-world%E2%80%99s-longest-lockdowns

Guillermo, Lourdes E. 1964. "The Bayanihan." *Music Journal* 22, no. 2 (February 1).

Gutierrez, Jose, III. 2017. "The Realist Cinema of Lino Brocka." *Plaridel* 14, no. 2 (July–December): 169–178.

Gutierrez, Natashya. 2017. "The Problem with Philippine Sports." *Rappler*. August 16. https://www.rappler.com/sports/10591-the-problem-with-philippine-sports

Gutierrez, Pia. 2021. "BPO Industry Revenues Hit $26.7-B in 2020, Up 1.4 Percent: IBPAP." *ABS-CBN News* (May 26). https://news.abs-cbn.com/business/05/26/21/bpo-26-7b-revenues-2020-ibpap

Haberer, Claude. 2009. *Between Tiger and Dragon: A History of Philippine Relations with China and Taiwan*. Pasay City: Anvil Publishing.

Hagedorn, Jessica. 1990. *Dogeaters*. New York: Pantheon Books.

Halili-Jao, Nina. 2018. "The Evolving Filipino Family Value System." *Philstar Global.* July 29. Accessed February 15, 2019. https://www.philstar.com/lifestyle/allure/2018/07/29/1837596/evolving-filipino-family-value-system

Hallare-Lara, Cynthia. 1992. *A Profile of the Philippine Corn Industry.* Quezon City: Philippine Peasant Institute.

Hart, Donn V. 1955. *The Philippine Plaza Complex: A Focal Point in Culture Change.* New Haven: Yale University Southeast Asian Studies.

Hau, Caroline S. 2008. "The Filipino Novel in English." In Maria Lourdes Bautista and Kingsley Bolton (eds.), *Philippine English: Linguistic and Literary Perspectives.* Hong Kong: Hong Kong University Press.

Hau, Caroline S. 2017. *Elites and Ilustrados in Philippine Culture.* Quezon City: Ateneo de Manila University Press.

Hau, Caroline S. 2018. *The Chinese Question: Ethnicity, Nation and Region in and beyond the Philippines.* Quezon City: Ateneo de Manila University Press.

Hau, Caroline S., and Paul S. Manzanilla, eds. 2016. *Remembering/Rethinking EDSA.* Pasig City: Anvil Publishing.

Heil, Daniel P., Alona D. Angosta, Wei Zhu, and Rhigel Alforque-Tan. 2019. "The Energy Expenditure of *Tinikling*: A Culturally Relevant Filipino Dance." *International Journal of Exercise Science* 12, no. 4: 111–121.

Heiser, Victor. 1936. *An American Doctor's Odyssey.* New York: W. W. Norton and Co.

Hester, Evett Dorell, and Paul S. Lietz. 1962. *Alzina's Historia de Visayas: A Bibliographical Note.* Manila: Bibliographical Society of the Philippines.

Heyneman, Stephen P., and Dean T. Jamison. 1984. "Textbooks in the Philippines: Evaluation of the Pedagogical Impact of a Nationwide Investment." *Educational Evaluation and Policy Analysis* 6, no. 2 (Summer). http://citeseerx.ist.psu.edu/viewdoc/download?doi=10.1.1.898.1486&rep=rep1&type=pdf

Hila, Antonio. 1989. *Musika: An Essay on Philippine Music.* Manila: Cultural Center of the Philippines.

Hila, Antonio, and Ramon Santos. 1994. "*Kundiman*." *Cultural Center of the Philippines Encyclopedia of Philippine Art.* Vol. 7. Manila: Cultural Center of the Philippines.

Hilario, Flaviana, Rosalina de Guzman, Daisy Ortega, Peter Hayman, and Bronya Alexander. 2009. "El Nino Southern Oscillation in the Philippines: Impacts, Forecasts and Risk Management." *Philippine Journal of Development* 36, no. 1: 9–34.

Hines, Thomas S. 1972. "The Imperial Façade: Daniel J. Burnham and American Architectural Planning in the Philippines." *Pacific Historical Review* 41, no. 1 (February): 33–53.

Hjorth, Larissa, and Michael Arnold. 2011. "The Personal and the Political: Social Networking in Manila." *International Journal of Learning and Media* 3, no. 1: 29–39.

Hobel, Robert, and Laurie Rosenbaum. 1979. *The Philippines.* Bern, Switzerland: Kummerly and Frey.

Hornedo, Florentino H. 2000. *Culture and Community in the Philippine Fiesta and Other Celebrations.* Manila: University of Santo Tomas Publishing House.

Horvatich, Patricia. 1994. "Ways of Knowing Islam." *American Ethnologist* 21, no. 4 (November): 811–826.

Hosoda, Naomi. 2008. " 'Open City' and a New Wave of Filipino Migration to the Middle East." In Eric Tagliacozzo (ed.), *Asia Inside Out: Changing Times*. Cambridge, MA: Harvard University Press.

Hugelius, Karin, Mervyn Gifford, Per Ortenwall, and Annsofie Adolfsson. 2016. "Disaster Radio for Communication of Vital Messages and Health-Related Information: Experiences from the Haiyan Typhoon, the Philippines." *Disaster Medicine and Public Health Preparedness* 10, no. 4 (August): 591–597.

Human Rights Watch. 2007. "Scared Silent: Impunity and Extrajudicial Killings in the Philippines." Accessed May 12, 2019. http://www.hrw.org/reports/2007/06/27/scared-silent

Hutchcroft, Paul D. 1998. *Booty Capitalism: The Politics of Banking in the Philippines*. Ithaca and London: Cornell University Press.

Hutchcroft, Paul D. 2016. *Mindanao: The Long Journey to Peace and Prosperity*. Pasay City: Anvil Publishing.

Hwa Yung. 2004. "The Missiological Challenge of David Yonggi Cho's Theology." *Asian Journal of Pentecostal Studies* 7, no. 1 (January): 57–77.

Institute for Statistics. 2019. "Philippines: Education and Literacy." United Nations Economic and Social Organization (UNESCO). http://uis.unesco.org/en/country/ph?theme=education-and-literacy

Institute for Statistics. 2022. "Philippines." United Nations Educational, Scientific, and Cultural Organization. http://uis.unesco.org/country/PH

Ishioka, Tomonori. 2012. "Boxing, Poverty, Foreseeability—An Ethnographic Account of Local Boxers in Metro Manila, Philippines." *Asia Pacific Journal of Sport and Social Science* 1, no. 2–3: 143–155.

Ito-Tapang, Lisa. 2017. "Visual Arts Activism in the Philippines: Notes on a New Season of Discontent." In *Art Archive 01: A Collection of Essays on Philippine Contemporary Visual and Performing Arts*. Manila: Japan Foundation. November.

Javellana, Stevan. 1947. *Without Seeing the Dawn*. New York: Little, Brown.

Jimenez, Benedict. 2009. "Anatomy of Autonomy: Assessing the Organizational Capacity and External Environment of the Autonomous Region in Muslim Mindanao." *Asian Politics and Policy* 1, no. 2 (April): 282–306.

Joaquin, Nick. 1966. *Portrait of the Artist as Filipino* (An Elegy in Three Scenes). Manila: Alberto Florentino.

Joaquin, Nick. 1983. *The Aquinos of Tarlac: An Essay on History as Three Generations*. Manila: Cacho Hermanes Publications.

Joaquin, Nick. 1990. *Manila, My Manila: A History for the Young*. Manila: Republic of the Philippines.

Joaquin, Nick. 2017. *The Woman Who Had Two Navels and Tales of the Tropical Gothic*. London: Penguin Classics.

Jocano, F. Landa. 1995. "Filipino Family Values." In Aurora Perez (ed.), *The Filipino Family: A Spectrum of Views and Issues*. Quezon City: University of the Philippines, Office of Research Coordination.

Jones, Gregg. 1989. *Red Revolution: Inside the Philippine Guerrilla Movement*. New York: Routledge.

Jose, F. Sionil. 1962. *The Pretenders*. Manila: Philippine-American Literary House.

Jose, F. Sionil. 1973. *Mass*. Manila: Solidaridad Publishing House.

Jose, F. Sionil. 1973. *My Brother, My Executioner*. Manila: Philippine-American Literary House.

Jose, F. Sionil. 1978. *Tree*. Manila: Solidaridad Publishing House.

Jose, F. Sionil. 1984. *Poon*. Manila: Solidaridad Publishing House.

Juarez, Fatima, Josefina Cabigon, Susheela Singh, and Rubina Hussain. 2005. "The Incidence of Induced Abortion in the Philippines: Current Level and Recent Trends." *Guttmacher Institute* 31, no. 3 (September): 140–149. Accessed February 12, 2019. https://www .guttmacher.org/journals/ipsrh/2005/09/incidence-induced-abortion-philippines -current-level-and-recent-trends

Jubair, Salah. 2007. *The Long Road to Peace: Inside the GRP-MILF Peace Process*. Cotabato City: Institute of Bangsamoro Studies.

Juergensmeyer, Mark. 2012. *Encyclopedia of Global Religion*. Los Angeles: Sage.

Junker, Laura Lee. 1999. "Warrior Burials and the Nature of Warfare in PreHispanic Philippine Chiefdoms." *Philippine Quarterly of Culture and Society* 27, no. 1–2 (March–June): 24–58.

Jurilla, Patricia May B. 2005. "Florante at Laura and the History of the Filipino Book." *Book History* 8: 131–196.

Jurilla, Patricia May B. 2006. "Tagalog Bestsellers and the History of the Book in the Philippines." PhD diss., School of Oriental and African Studies, University of London. August 30.

Jurilla, Patricia May B. 2016. "Conflicts and Contests: A History of the Filipino Novel in English." *Kritika Kultura* 27: 3–20.

Kang, David C. 2002. *Crony Capitalism: Corruption and Development in South Korea and the Philippines*. Cambridge: Cambridge University Press.

Kang, Hyewon. 2010. *The Philippines' Absorptive Capacity for Foreign Aid*. Manila: Philippine Institute for Development Studies.

Karnow, Stanley. 2010. *In Our Image: America's Empire in the Philippines*. New York: Ballantine Books.

Karunungan, Lilian. 2022. "Philippine Peso Drops Past 51 Barrier for First Time since 2020." *Bloomberg* (January 3). https://www.bloomberg.com/news/articles/2022-01-04/philippine-peso -drops-past-51-barrier-for-first-time-since-2020

Kavanagh, Joseph J. 1995. "The 'Iglesia ni Cristo.'" *Philippine Studies* 3, no. 1 (March 1): 19–42.

Keppy, Peter. 2013. "Southeast Asia in the Age of Jazz: Locating Popular Culture in the Colonial Philippines and Indonesia." *Journal of Southeast Asian Studies* 44, no. 3 (October): 444–464.

Kerklviet, Benedict J., and Resil B. Mojares. 1992. *From Marcos to Aquino: Local Perspectives on Political Transition in the Philippines*. Honolulu, HI: University of Hawaii Press.

Kinsella, Kevin G. 1984. *Detailed Statistics on the Urban and Rural Population of the Philippines, 1950–2010*. Washington, DC: Center for International Research, U.S. Bureau of Census.

Komisar, Lucy. 1987. *Corazon Aquino: The Story of a Revolution*. New York: George Braziller.

Komito, Lee. 2011. "Social Media and Migration: Virtual Community 2.0." *Journal of the American Society for Information, Science and Technology* 62, no. 6: 1075–1086.

Lacaba, Jose. 1995. *Boss: 5 Cases of Local Politics in the Philippines*. Manila: Philippine Center for Investigative Journalism.

Lacaba, Jose (a.k.a. Felix Culpa). 1995. "Carabeef Lengua." *Manila Times*. August 3. http://kapetesapatalim.blogspot.com/2008/11/carabao-english.html

Lacaba, Jose. 2015. "Prometheus Unbound." Martial Law Reminder from *Esquire Philippines*. September 15. https://soundcloud.com/esquire-philippines

Lapuz, Lourdes V. 1991. "Marriage and Responsible Parenthood." In *The Filipino Family and the Nation: A Collection of Readings on Family Issues and Concerns*. Quezon City: University of the Philippines, College of Home Economics.

Larson, Donald N. 1963. "The Philippine Language Scene." *Philippine Sociological Review* 11, no. 1–2 (January–April): 4–12.

Lent, John. 1968. "Philippine Radio—History and Problems." *Asian Studies* (April): 49–60.

Lent, John. 1983. "The Philippine Press at the Advent of the 1980s." *Crossroads: An Interdisciplinary Journal of Southeast Asian Studies* 1, no. 2 (June): 83–93.

Lewis, Lisa. 2012. "The Philippine 'Hip Hop Stick Dance.'" *JOPERD* 83, no. 1 (January): 17–32.

Lewis, M. P., G. F. Simons, and C. D. Fennig, eds. 2016. *Ethnologue: Languages of the World*. 19th ed. Dallas, TX: SIL International. https://www.ethnologue.com/about/language-status

Lico, Gerard, and Maria Delia Tomarcuz. 2015. "Infrastrucrutures of Colonial Modernity: Public Works in Manila from the Late 19th to the Early 20th Centuries." *Espasyo: Journal of Philippine Architecture and Allied Arts* 6: 1–25.

Licuanan, Patricia B. 2017. "The State of Philippine Higher Education." Philippine Higher Education Conference Private Education Assistance Committee (PEAC). November 28. https://peac.org.ph/wp-content/uploads/2017/12/LICUANAN-Philippine-Education-Conference-ilovepdf-compressed.pdf

Lim, Jaime An, Christine Godinez-Ortega, and Edilberto K. Tiempo, eds. 1995. *Mindanao Harvest 1: An Anthology of Contemporary Writing*. Manila: New Day Publishers and Christian Literature Society of the Philippines.

Lipski, John M. 1987a. "Contemporary Philippine Spanish: Comments on Vestigial Usage." *Philippine Journal of Linguistics* 18: 37–48.

Lipski, John M. 1987b. "Modern Spanish Once-Removed in Philippine Creole Spanish: The Case of Zamboangueno." *Language and Society* 16: 91–108.

Lipski, John M. 2009. "Philippine Creole Spanish: Assessing the Portuguese Element." *Zeitschrift fur Romanische Philologie* 104: 1–2.

Llamzon, Teodoro A. 1968. "On Tagalog as Dominant Language." *Philippine Studies* 16, no. 4 (October): 729–749.

Llaneta, Celestina Ann Castillo. 2018. "Teaching in Mother Tongues." February 5. https://www.up.edu.ph/teaching-in-mother-tongues/

Llanto, Gilberto M.. and Ma. Kristina P. Ortiz. 2013. "Regional Comprehensive Economic Partnership: Reform Challenges and Key Tasks for the Philippines." *Philippine Institute for Development Studies Discussion Paper Series No. 2013-51*. November.

Lockard, Craig A. 1998. "Philippines: Pinoy, Protest and People Power." In *Dance of Life: Popular Music and Politics in Southeast Asia*. Honolulu, HI: University of Hawaii Press.

Lopez, Cecilio. 1967. "Origins of the Philippine Languages." *Philippine Studies* 15, no. 1: 130–166.

Lopez, Elyssa Christine. 2019. "Most Iconic Campaign Jingles in Philippine Elections." *Esquire*. May 10. Accessed April 17, 2020. https://www.esquiremag.ph/culture/most-iconic -campaign-jingles-philippines-a00290-20190510-lfrm

Lorente, Beatriz P. 2017. "Language-in-Education Politics and Mobile Citizens." In S. Canagarajah (ed.), *Routledge Handbook of Migration and Language*. New York: Routledge.

Lorenzo, Clarissa M. 2016. "Filipino Culture of Filling Up Space in a Gated Community." *Social and Behavioral Sciences* 216: 545–551.

Low, Kelvin E. Y., and Elaine Lynn-Ee-Ho. 2017. "Eating in the City." *Food, Culture and Society* 21, no. 1: 2–8.

Lugo, Luis, Sandra Stencel, John Green, Timothy S. Shah, Brian J. Grim, Gregory Smith, Robert Ruby, and Allison Pond. 2006. "Spirit and Power: A 10-Country Survey of Pentecostals." *Pew Forum on Religion and Public Life* (October): 1–229. http://www.pewresearch.org /wp-content/uploads/sites/7/2006/10/pentecostals-08.pdf

Lumbera, Bienvenido. 1984. *Revaluation: Essays on Philippine Literature, Cinema, and Popular Culture*. Manila: Bienvenido Lumbera and Index Press.

Lumbera, Bienvenido. 1992. *Pelikula: An Essay on Philippine Film*. Manila: Sentrong Pangkultura ng Pilipinas.

Lumen, Nancy Reyes. 2005. "Republic of Pancit." *Philippine Center for Investigative Journalism*. January 2. https://old.pcij.org/stories/republic-of-pancit/

Mabasa, Roy. 2021. "Iglesia ni Cristo at 107: Faith Anchored on Values." *Manila Bulletin* (July 28). https://mb.com.ph/2021/07/28/iglesia-ni-cristo-at-107-faith-anchored-on-values/

Macclintock, Samuel. 2012. *The Philippines: A Geographical Reader-Classic Reprint*. London: FB&C Ltd.

MacDonald, Charles H. 2004. "Folk Catholicism and Pre-Spanish Religions in the Philippines." *Philippine Studies* 52, no. 1: 78–93.

Maceda, Jose. 1978. "Introduction to Philippine Music." *World of Music* 20, no. 2: 78–81.

Maceda, Teresita. 2007. "Problematizing the Popular: The Dynamics of *Pinoy* pop(ular) Music and Popular Protest Music." *Inter-Asia Cultural Studies* 8, no. 3: n.p.

Maceda, Teresita. 2008. "Awit, pop, awit protesta." *Lagda*. Centennial Issue (December): 59–78.

Macha, Wilson, Christopher Mackie, and Jessica Magaziner. 2018. "Education in the Philippines." *World Education News and Reviews*. March 6. https://wenr.wes.org/2018/03 /education-in-the-philippines

Madrunio, Marilu Ranosa, Isabel Pefianco Martin, and Sterling Miranda Plata. 2018. "English Language Education in the Philippines: Policies, Problems and Prospects." In Robert Kirkpatrick (ed.), *English Language Education Policy in Asia*, Vol. 11. The Netherlands: Springer.

Magat, Margaret. 2002. "Balut: Fertilized Duck Eggs and Their Role in Filipino Culture." *Western Folklore* 1, no. 1 (Spring): 63–96.

Magdaraog, Gregorio. 1998. *Environment and Natural Resources Atlas of the Philippines.* Quezon City: Environmental Center of the Philippines Foundation.

Magtibay-Ramos, Nedelyn, Estrada, Gemma Esther B. and Jesus Felipe. 2007. "An Analysis of the Philippine Business Process Outsourcing Industry." *Asian Development Bank ERD Working Paper No. 93.* Manila.

Mahboob, Ahmar, and Priscilla Cruz. 2013. "English and Mother-Tongue-Based Multilingual Education: Language Attitudes in the Philippines." *Asian Journal of English Language Studies* 1 (October): 1–20.

Maligalig, Dalisay S., Rhona B. Caoli-Rodriguez, Arturo Martinez, and Sining Cuevase. 2011. "Education Outcomes in the Philippines." *Asian Development Bank Economics Working Paper Series No. 199.* January. Accessed April 22, 2019. https://www.adb.org/sites/default/files/publication/28409/economics-wp199.pdf

Manapat, Ricardo. 1990. *Some Are Smarter Than Others: The History of Marcos' Crony Capitalism.* New York: Aletheia Publications.

"Manila's Commutes from Hell—a Photo Essay." 2019. *Guardian.* March 8. https://www.theguardian.com/world/2019/mar/08/manilas-commutes-from-hell-a-photo-essay

Manzano, George, and Kristine Joy Martin. 2015. "Implications of a Philippine-US Free Trade Agreement on Trade in Goods: An Indicator Approach." *Philippine Institute for Development Studies Discussion Paper Series No. 2015-42.* September.

Mapa, Claire Dennis S., ed. 2019. *2019 Philippine Statistical Yearbook.* Manila. Philippine Statistical Authority.

"Maps of the Philippines." World Atlas. Accessed August 2, 2019. https://www.worldatlas.com/articles/the-countries-that-read-the-most.html

Martin, Dalmacio. 1980. *A Century of Education in the Philippines, 1861–1961.* Manila: Philippine Historical Association.

Matejowsky, Ty. 2002. "Globalization, Privatization, and Public Space in the Provincial Philippines." In Jeffrey H. Cohen and Norbert Dannhauser (eds.), *Economic Development: An Anthropological Approach.* Walnut Creek. Altamira Press.

Matejowsky, Ty. 2008. "Jolly Dogs and Spaghetti: Anthropological Reflections on Global/Local Fast Food Competition in the Philippines." *Journal of Asia-Pacific Business* 9, no. 4: 313–328.

Matejowsky, Ty. 2013 "The Incredible, Edible *Balut*: Ethnographic Perspectives on the Philippines' Favorite Liminal Food." *Food, Culture, Society* 16, no. 3: 387–404.

McCaghy Charles H., and Arthur G. Neal. 1974."The Fraternity of Cockfighters: Ethical Embellishments of an Illegal Sport." *Journal of Popular Culture* 8, no. 3 (Winter): 557.

McCoy, Alfred W. 1982. "Baylan Animism: Animist Religion and Philippine Peasant Ideology." *Philippine Quarterly of Culture and Society* 10, no. 3 (September 1): 141–194.

McCoy, Alfred W. 1999. *Closer Than Brothers: Manhood in the Philippine Military Academy.* New Haven and London: Yale University Press.

McCoy, Alfred W., ed. 2009. *An Anarchy of Families: State and Family in the Philippines,* 548 pp. Madison, WI: University of Wisconsin Press.

McCoy, Alfred W. 2009. *Policing America's Empire: The United States, the Philippines and the Rise of the Surveillance State.* Madison, WI: University of Wisconsin Press.

McCoy, Alfred W. 2016. "A Rupture in Philippine-U.S. Relations: Geopolitical Implications." *Journal of Asian Studies* 75, no. 4: 1049–1053.

McDonald, Charles J., and Guillermo M. Pesigan (Guillermo Mangubat). 2000. *Old Ties and New Solidarities: Studies on Philippine Communities.* Quezon City: Ateneo de Manila University Press.

McEachern, Firth, and United States Agency for International Development (USAID). 2013. "Local Languages and Literacy in the Philippines: Implications for Early Reading Instruction and Assessment." *EdDAta II Technical Assistance and Managerial Assistance.* Task No. 17. Contract Number: AID-4920-M-12-0001. December 31. 78 pp.

McFarland, Curtis D. 1994. "Subgrouping and Number of the Philippine Languages or How Many Philippine Languages Are There?" *Philippine Journal of Linguistics* 1, no. 2 (June–December): 75–84.

McGrath, Alister E., and Darren C. Marks, eds. 2008. *The Blackwell Companion to Protestantism.* Malden, MA: Blackwell Publishing Ltd.

McKay, Deirdre. 2010. "On the Face of Facebook: Historical Images and Personhood in Filipino Social Networking." *History and Anthropology* 21, no. 4 (December): 479–498.

McKay, Deirdre. 2012. *Global Filipinos: Migrants' Lives in the Virtual Village.* Bloomington, IN: Indiana University Press.

McKenna, Thomas M. 1997. "Appreciating Islam in the Muslim Philippines: Authority, Experience, and Identity in Cotabato." In Robert Hefner and Patricia Horvatich (eds.), *Islam in an Era of Nation-States: Politics and Religious Renewal in Muslim Southeast Asia.* Honolulu, HI: University of Hawaii Press.

McKenna, Thomas M. 1998. *Muslim Rulers and Rebels: Everyday Politics and Armed Separatism in the Southern Philippines.* Berkeley: University of California Press. https://publishing.cdlib.org/ucpressebooks/view?docId=ft0199n64c&brand=ucpress

McKenna, Thomas M. 2002. "Saints, Scholars and the Idealized Past in Philippine Muslim Separatism." *Pacific Review* 15, no. 4: 539–553.

McLoughlin, Scotty. 2015. "The Boundary Indefinite: Schism and Ethics of Christian Strategy in the Philippines." PhD diss., University of Michigan. https://deepblue.lib.umich.edu/bitstream/handle/2027.42/113319/scottmcl_1.pdf

McMahon, Jennifer. 2011. "Excerpt from Dead Stars: American and Literary Perspectives on the American Colonization of the Philippines." *UC Santa Barbara Journal of Transnational American Studies* 3, no. 2: 49–66.

Medalla, Erlinda M., and Angelica B. Maddawin. 2015. "Supporting WTO and Pathways to the Free Trade Area of the Asia Pacific (FTAAP)." *Philippine Institute for Development Studies Discussion Paper Series No. 2015-17.* February.

Medina, Belen T. 2015. *The Filipino Family.* 3rd ed. Quezon City: University of the Philippines Press.

Mendez, Paz Policarpio, F. Landa Jocano, Realidad Santico Rolda, and Salvacion Bautista Matela. 1984. *The Filipino Family in Transition. A Study in Culture and Education.* Manila: Centro Escolar University Research and Development Center.

Mendoza, Ronald U. 2021. "The Philippine Economy Under the Pandemic: From Asian Tiger to Sick Man Again?" *Brookings* (August 2). https://www.brookings.edu/blog/order-from -chaos/2021/08/02/the-philippine-economy-under-the-pandemic-from-asian-tiger-to -sick-man-again/

Mercado, Leonardo. 2001. *El Shaddai: A Study*. Manila: Logos Publications.

Mijares, Primitivo. 1976. *The Conjugal Dictatorship of Ferdinand and Imelda Marcos*. Quezon City: Ateneo de Manila University Press. http://rizalls.lib.admu.edu.ph:8080/ebooks2 /Primitivo%20Mijares.pdf

Milgram, B. Lynne. 2012. "Reconfiguring Margins: Secondhand Clothing and Street Vending in the Philippines." *Textile: The Journal of Cloth and Culture* 10, no. 2: 200–221.

Miller, Jeffrey M., Primitivo Cal, and Nigel C. Rayner. 2012. *Philippines: Transport Sector Assessment, Strategy and Road Map*. Manila: Asian Development Bank.

"Mindanao." 2016. *Hutchinson Unabridged Encyclopedia with Atlas and Weather Guide*. Boston, MA: Helicon.

Miral, Romulo E. M. 2017. "Federalism Prospects for the Philippines." *Philippine Institute for Development Studies Discussion Paper Series*. Manila. https://econpapers.repec.org/paper /phddpaper/dp_5f2017-29.htm

Miranda, Miguel, et al. 2010. "Discovering Emotions in Filipino Laughter Using Audio Features." Paper Delivered at the Third International Conference on Human-Centric Computing, Cebu City, Philippines. August 11–13. https://ieeexplore.ieee.org/abstract/document /5563313/authors#authors

Mitra, Raja Mikael. 2013. "Leveraging Service Sector Growth in the Philippines." *Asian Development Bank Economics Working Paper Series No. 366*. September 6. https://papers.ssrn .com/sol3/papers.cfm?abstract_id=2321536

Mojares, Resil. 1983. *Origins and Rise of the Filipino Novel: A Generic Study of the Novel until 1940*. Quezon City: University of the Philippine Press.

Mojares, Resil. 1998. "Talking Politics: The Komentaryo on Cebu Radio." *Philippine Quarterly of Culture and Society* 26, no. 3–4 (September–December): 337–362.

Mojares, Resil B. 2006. "The Formation of Filipino Nationality under U.S. Colonial Rule." *Philippine Quarterly of Culture and Society* 34, no. 1 (March): 11–32.

Monk, Paul M. 1995. *Truth and Power: Robert S. Hardie and Land Reform Debates in the Philippines, 1950–1987*. Monash: Monash University Centre for Southeast Asian Studies.

Moreno, Jose. 1995. *Philippine Costume*. Manila: J. Moreno Foundation.

Morley, Ian. 2018. *Cities and Nationhood: American Imperialism and Urban Design in the Philippines, 1898–1916*. Honolulu, HI: University of Hawaii Press.

Mullis, Ina V.S., Michael O. Martin, Eugenio J. Gonzalez, and Steven J. Chrostowskio. 2004. *TIMSS 2003 International Mathematics Report: Findings from IEA's Trens in International Mathematics and Science Study at the Fourth and Eight Grades*. Chestnut Hill, MA: International Association for the Evaluation of Educational Achievement (IEQ).

Nadeau, Kathleen M. 2008. *The History of the Philippines*. Westport, CT: Greenwood.

Namiki, Kanami. 2011. "Hybridity and National Identity: Different Perspectives of Two National Folk Dance Companies in the Philippines." *Asian Studies* 47.

Nance, John J. 1977. *The Land and People of the Philippines*. Philadelphia. Lippincott.

Natividad, Josefina N., and Maria Paz N. Marquez. 2004. "Sexual Risk Behaviors." In Corazon G. Raymundo and G. Cruz (eds.), *Youth Sex and Risk Behaviors in the Philippines*. Quezon City: Demographic Research and Development Foundation and the University of the Philippines Population Institute.

Natural Resources Management Center (Philippines). 1986. *Guide to Philippine Flora and Fauna—Volumes 1-13*. Manila: Republic of the Philippines, Ministry of Natural Resources and the University of the Philippines.

Natural Resources Management Center (Philippines). 1990. *Philippines Regional Natural Resources Atlas—Volumes 1-2*. Quezon City: Republic of the Philippines, Department of Environment and Natural Resources, Natural Resources Management Center, and Information Systems Management Division Cartographic Unit.

Ness, Sally A. 1995. "When Seeing Is Believing: The Changing Role of Visuality in the Philippines." *Anthropological Quarterly* 68, no. 1 (January): 1–13.

Ng, Stephanie S. 2013. "Performing the 'Filipino' at the Crossroads: Filipino Bands in Five-Star Hotels throughout Asia." *Modern Drama* 48, no. 2 (April 5).

Ng, Stephanie Sooklynn. 2006. "Filipino Bands Performing in Hotels, Clubs, and Restaurants in Asia: Purveyors of Transnational Culture in a Global Arena." PhD diss., University of Michigan.

Nickles, Greg. 2002. *Philippines—the Land*. New York: Crabtree Publishing Company.

Nicolasora, Michelle. 2014. "Kundiman: A Musical and Socio-Cultural Exploration on the Development of the Philippine Art Song." PhD diss., University of Memphis. May.

Noble, Lela Garner. 1982. *Philippine Policy towards Sabah: A Claim to Independence*. Tempe, AZ: University of Arizona Press.

Observatory of Economic Complexity, n.d. *The Philippines*. https://atlas.media.mit.edu/en/profile/country/phl/

Ogura, Nobuyuki, David Leonides T. Yap, and Kenichi Tanoue. 2002. "Modern Architecture in the Philippines and the Quest for Filipino Style." *Journal of Asian Architecture and Building Engineering* 1, no. 2 (November): 233–238.

Ong, Jonathan Corpus. 2009. "Watching the Nation, Singing the Nation: London-Based Filipino Migrants' Identity Constructions in News and Karaoke Practices." *Communication, Culture and Critique* 2, no. 2 (June): 160–181.

Ong, Jonathan Corpus. 2015. *The Poverty of Television: The Mediation of Suffering I Class-Divided Philippines*. London: Anthem Press.

Onishi, Norimitsu. 2010. "Sinatra Song Often Strikes Deadly Chord." *New York Times*. February 6. https://www.nytimes.com/2010/02/07/world/asia/07karaoke.html

Orosa, Sixto Y. 1970. *The Sulu Archipelago and Its People—Updated and Enlarged*. Manila: New Mercury Printing Press.

Osborne, Dana M. 2015. "Negotiating the Hierarchy of Languages in Ilocandia: The Social and Cognitive Implications of Massive Multilinguialism in the Philippines." PhD diss., University of Arizona.

Palanca, Clinton. 2015. *My Angkong's Noodles: A Chinese Filipino Cookbook*. Manila: Elizabeth Gokongwei.

Panganiban, Teejay D., Rommel P. Manalo, April Kisses S. Polgadno, and Marc John H. Sarmiento. 2019. "Factors Influencing the Sports Involvement of *Sepak Takraw* Athletes in a State University." *PUPIL: International Journal of Teaching Education and Learning* 3, no. 1: 290–305.

Pantoja-Hidalgo, Cristina. 2000. "The Philippine Novel in English into the Twenty-First Century." *World Literature Today* 74, no. 2 (Spring): 333–336.

Paqueo, Vicente B., Aniceto C. Orbeta Jr., and Gilberto M. Llanto, eds. 2017. *Unintended Consequences: The Folly of Uncritical Thinking.* Quezon City: Philippine Institute for Development Studies. https://pidswebs.pids.gov.ph/CDN/PUBLICATIONS/pidsbk2017-unintended _fnl.pdf

Paredes-Santillan, Caren. 2009. "A Study in Bipolarity in the Architecture of Leandro V. Locsin." *Journal of Asian Architecture and Building Engineering* 8 (May): 1–8.

Parel, Tessa O. 1983. "History of the MPC, 1976–1982." In Nicanor G. Tiongson (ed.), *The Urian Anthology, 1970–1979.* Manila: Manuel L. Morato.

Pastor-Roces, Marian. 2000. *Sheer Realities: Clothing and Power in Nineteenth Century Philippines.* Manila. Bookmark Press.

Patalinghug, Epictetus. 2001. "An Assessment of Market Saturation in the Retail Trade Industry in the Philippines." *Journal of Asian Business* 17, no. 1: 69–88.

Pe-Pua. Rogelia. 1991. "Marriage and Responsible Parenthood." In *The Filipino Family and the Nation: A Collection of Readings on Family Issues and Concerns.* Quezon City: University of the Philippines, College of Home Economics.

Perez, Aurora. 1995. *The Filipino Family: A Spectrum of Views and Issues.* Quezon City: University of the Philippines, Office of Research Coordination.

Perez, Jose M. 2019. "Greed and Grievances: A Discursive Study on the Evolution of the Lumad Struggle in Mindanao, 2010–2019." *Journal of Ethnic and Cultural Studies* 6, no. 3: 41–52.

Perez, Marilola. 2015. "Cavite Chabacano Philippine Creole Spanish: Description and Typology." PhD diss., University of California-Berkeley.

Philippine Center for Investigative Journalism. 2012. *Elections Special: The History of Philippine Elections.* Manila. Video File.

Picardal, Amado. 2018. "Seasonal and Nominal Catholics in the Philippines." *LaCroix International: The World's Premier Independent Catholic Daily.* May 7. https://international .la-croix.com/news/seasonal-and-nominal-catholics-in-the-philippines/7524

Pimentel, Aquilino Q. 2007. *The Local Government Code Revisited.* Manila: Philippine Normal University.

Pinches, Michael, ed. 1999. "Entrepreneurship, Consumption, Ethnicity and National Identity in the Making of the Philippines' New Rich." In *Culture and Privilege in Capitalist Asia.* New York: Taylor and Francis.

Pinoy Grooves. 2018. "Music and Magic—I'll Be There/Ain't No Mountain High Enough." December 4. https://pinoygrooves.com/2018/12/04/music-magic-ill-be-there-aint-no-mountain -high-enough/

"Pinoy na Pinoy: Spokening English: The Travails of Amboy." 1999. *Business World.* June 16.

Polotan, Kerima. 1962. *The Hand of the Enemy.* Quezon City: University of the Philippines Press.

Population Center Foundation. 1975. *Initiatives in Population: Quarterly Magazine of the Popular Center Foundation of the Philippines.* Makati City: Population Center Foundation.

Porio, Emma, Frank Lynch, and Mary Hollnsteiner. 1978. *The Filipino Family, Community and Nation.* Quezon City: Institute of Philippine Culture and the Ateneo de Manila University.

Porter, Gareth, and Delfin J. Ganapin. 1988. *Resources, Population and the Philippines' Future: A Case Study.* Washington, DC: World Resources Institute.

Prator, Clifford H., Jr. 1956. *Language Teaching in the Philippines: A Report.* Manila: U.S. Educational Foundation in the Philippines.

Prelypchan, Erin. 2004. "Banking on Chick-Lit." *Far Eastern Economic Review* 167, no. 20 (May 20): 56.

Putzel, James. 1992. *A Captive Land: The Politics of Agrarian Reform in the Philippines.* Quezon City: Ateneo de Manila University Press.

Quirino, Richie. 2011. *Contemporary Jazz in the Philippines.* Pasig City: Anvil Publishing.

Quizon, Cherubim A. 2005. "Indigenism, Painting and Identity: Mixing Media under Philippine Dictatorship." *Asian Studies Review* 29, no. 3: 287–300.

Quizon, Cherubim A. 2012. "Dressing the Lumad Body: Indigenous Peoples and Development Discourse in Mindanao." *Humanities Diliman* 9, no. 2: 32–57.

Rabena, Aaron. 2018. "The Complex Interdependence of China's Belt and Road Initiative in the Philippines." *Asia and Pacific Policy Studies* 5, no. 3 (September): 683–697.

Rafael, Vicente. 2002. "Foreignness and Vengeance: On Rizal's 'El Filibusterismo.'" University of California Center for Southeast Asian Studies. https://escholarship.org/uc/item/4j11p6c1

Ranada, Pia. 2017. "Duterte Signs Law for Free Tuition in State Colleges." *Rappler* (August 4). https://www.rappler.com/nation/177661-duterte-signs-law-free-tuition-state-colleges-universities/

Ranada, Pia. 2019. "Duterte Signs Universal Health Care Law." *Rappler* (February 20), https://www.rappler.com/nation/223942-duterte-signs-universal-health-care-law/

Rara, Ma. Cristina Imperial. 2004. "Covering Terror in the. Philippines." *Public Policy* VIII, no. 1 (January–June): 79–117.

Raymundo, Corazon M. 1991. "Demographic Changes and the Filipino Family." In *The Filipino Family and the Nation: A Collection of Readings on Family Issues and Concerns.* Quezon City: University of the Philippines, College of Home Economics.

Republic of Singapore Embassy, Manila. 2015. "SG50: Singapore-Philippines Cultural Evening in Manila." *Rappler* (August 25). https://www.rappler.com/bulletin-board/103713-singapore-philippines-dance-manila/

Republic of the Philippines, Atmospheric, Geophysical and Astronomical Services Administration. 1978. *The Climate of the Philippines.* Quezon City: PAGASA Publication Section, Climatological Division.

Republic of the Philippines, Bureau of Agriculture. 1922. *Mindanao and Sulu Archipelago: Their Natural Resources and Opportunities for Development.* Manila: Bureau of Printing.

Republic of the Philippines, Commission on Higher Education (CHED). 2018. "Statistics: 2018 Higher Education Indicators." https://ched.gov.ph/wp-content/uploads/2018/07/Higher-Education-Indicators.pdf

Republic of the Philippines, Department of Justice Special Committee for the Protection of Children. 2006. "Protecting Filipino Children from Abuse, Exploitation and Violence: A Comprehensive Programme on Child Protection, 2006–2010 (Building a Protective and Caring Environment for Filipino Children)." Department of Justice, December. Accessed September 23, 2019. https://www.doj.gov.ph/files/Filipino_Children.pdf

Republic of the Philippines, Philippine Statistical Office. 2013. FLEMMS (Functional Literacy, Education and Mass Media Survey Final Report). Manila: Philippine Statistical Office.

Republic of the Philippines. The 1987 Constitution of the Republic of the Philippines. https://www.lawphil.net/consti/cons1987.html

Reyes, Romeo A. 1993. *Absorptive Capacity for Foreign Aid: The Case of the Philippines.* Manila: Philippine Institute for Development Studies.

Reyes, Soledad S. 1980. "The Philippine Komiks." *Philippines; International Popular Culture* 1: 389–417.

Reyes, Soledad S. 2009. "The Komiks and Retelling the Lore of the Folk." *Philippine Studies* 57, no. 3: 389–417.

Reyes-Santa Romana, Julita. 1955. *The Iglesia ni Kristo.* Manila: University of Manila.

Richardson, Jim. 2011. *Komunista: The Genesis of the Philippine Communist Party, 1902–1935.* Quezon City: Ateneo de Manila University Press.

Rico, Jore-Annie, and Kim Robert C. De Leon. 2017. "Mall Culture and Consumerism in the Philippines." *State of Power.* https://www.tni.org/files/publication-downloads/stateofpower2017-mall-culture.pdf

Rivera, Rosa Maria V. 2003. *Managing Risk and Sustainability on Microfinance: War and its Impact on Microfinance Clients and NGOs in the Philippines.* The Hague, the Netherlands: Institute of Social Studies.

Rivera, Temario C. 2001. "The Middle Classes and Democratisation in the Philippines." In Abdul Rahman Embong (ed.), *Southeast Asian Middle Classes: Prospects for Social Change and Democratisation.* Kuala Lumpur, Malaysia. Penerbit Universiti Kebangsaan Malaysia.

Robertson, James Alexander. 2018. "Catholicism in the Philippine Islands." *Catholic Historical Review* 3, no. 4 (January): 375–391. https://www.jstor.org/stable/pdf/25011532.pdf

Robles, Raissa. 2017. *Marcos Martial Law: Never Again.* Manila: Filipinos for a Better Philippines.

Rodao, Florentino, and Felice Noelle Rodriguez, eds. 2002. *The Philippine Revolution of 1896: Ordinary Lives in Extraordinary Times.* Quezon City: Ateneo de Manila University Press.

Rodell, Paul A. 1988. "The Founding of the Iglesia Filipina Independiente (The Aglipayan Church): An Historical Review." *Philippine Quarterly of Culture and Society* 26, no. 2 (September–December): 210–234.

Rodell, Paul A. 2002. *Culture and Customs of the Philippines.* Westport, CT: Greenwood Press.

Rodil, B. R. 1993. *The Lumad and Moro of Mindanao.* London. Minority Rights Group.

Rood, Steven. 2019. *The Philippines: What Everyone Needs to Know.* New York and London: Oxford University Press.

Rosales, Rey G. 2006. "Shooting the Messenger: Why Radio Broadcasting Is a Deadly Profession in the Philippines." *Journal of Radio Studies* 13, no. 1: 146–155.

Rosario-Braid, Florangel, and Ramon R. Tuazon. 2000. "Post-EDSA Communication Media." *Philippine Studies* 48 (First Quarter): 3–26.

Rosenberg, David, ed. 1979. *Marcos and Martial Law in the Philippines.* Ithaca and London: Cornell University Press.

Rutten, Rosanne, ed. 2008. *Brokering a Revolution: Cadres in a Philippine Insurgency.* Quezon City: Ateneo de Manila University Press.

Sabanpan-Yu, Hope. 2007. "Cebuano Food Festival: A Matter of Taste." *Philippine Quarterly of Culture and Society* 35, no. 4 (December): 384–392.

Salazar, Joseph T. 2012. "Eating Out: Reconstituting the Philippines' Public Kitchens." *Thesis Eleven* 112, no. 1: 133–146.

Saleeby, Najeeb M. 1905. *Studies in Moro History, Law and Religion. Ethnological Survey Publications* 4, no. 1. Manila: Department of Interior: 107 pp.

Salita, Domingo. 1974. *Geography and Natural Resources of the Philippines.* Quezon City: University of the Philippines System, College of Arts and Sciences.

Salvador-Amores, Analyn. 2002. "*Batek:* Traditional Tattoos and Identities in Contemporary Kalinga, North Luzon, Philippines." *Humanities Diliman* 31 (January–June): 105–142.

Salvador-Amores, Analyn. 2014. *Tapping Ink, Tattoing Identities: Tradition and Modernity in Contemporary Kalinga Society, North Luzon, Philippines.* Honolulu, HI: University of Hawaii Press.

San Buenaventura, Patricia Anne R. 2011. "Education Quality in the Philippines." *Philippine Statistics Authority.* https://unstats.un.org/sdgs/files/meetings/sdg-inter-workshop-jan-2019/Session%2011.b.3_Philippines_Education%20Equality%20AssessmentFINAL4.pdf

San Juan, Carolina de Leon. 2010. "From Vaudeville to Bodabil: Vaudeville in the Philippines." PhD diss., University of California, Los Angeles.

Sanders, Albert J. 1962. *A Protestant View of the Iglesia ni Cristo.* Quezon City: Philippine Federation of Christian Churches.

Sanders, Albert J. 1969. "An Appraisal of the *Iglesia ni Cristo.*" In Gerald H. Anderson (ed.), *Studies in Philippine Church History.* Ithaca and London: Cornell University Press.

Santiago, Katrina Stuart. 2009. "The Pinay as Fun, Fearless Female: Philippine Chick Literature in the Age of Transition." *Humanities Diliman* 6, no. 1–2 (December): 58–92.

Santos, Idelfonso P. 1960. "The Development of Philippine Architecture." MA thesis, University of Southern California. January.

Santos, Isabel. 2004. *Bayanihan, The Philippine Dance Company: A Memoir of Six Continents.* Pasig City: Anvil Publishing.

Schumacher, John S. 2009. *Growth and Decline: Essays on Philippine Church History.* Quezon City: Ateneo de Manila University Press.

Scott, Margaret. 1989. "Confusion of Tongues: English vs. Filipino in the Language Debate." *Far Eastern Economic Review*, July, no. 6: 44.

Scott, William H. 1962. "The Philippine Independent Church in History." *Silliman Journal: A Quarterly Devoted to Discussion and Investigation in the Humanities and the Social Sciences* 10, no. 3: 298–310.

Seminar on the Filipino Family. 1991. *The Filipino Family and the Nation: A Collection of Readings on Family Issues and Concerns*. Quezon City: University of the Philippines, College of Home Economics.

Setsuho, Ikehata, and Lydia Yu-Jose. 2003. *Philippine-Japan Relations*. Quezon City: Ateneo de Manila University Press.

Shatkin, Gavin. 2000. "Obstacles to Empowerment: Local Politics and Civil Society in Metropolitan Manila, the Philippines." *Urban Studies* 37, no. 12 (November): 2357–2375.

Shegina, Toni Rose Ortiz Luis. 1988. "The Language Controversy and Its Dilemma in the Philippines: A Consequential Result of the Evolution of English." MS Education, University of Southern California.

Siapno, Jacqueline. 1995. "Alternative Filipina Heroines: Contested Tropes in Leftist Feminism." In Aihwa Ong and Michael G. Peletz (eds.), *Bewitching Women, Pious Men: Gender and Body Politic in Southeast Asia*. Los Angeles and London: University of California Press.

Sidel, John T. 1999. *Capital, Coercion and Crime: Bossism in the Philippines*. Stanford: Stanford University Press.

Sison, Shakira. 2014. "Punny Filipino Translations." *Rappler*. April 24. https://www.rappler.com/move-ph/ispeak/56193-punny-filipino-translations

Smolicz, Jerzy, and Illuminado Nical. 1997. "Exporting the European Idea of a National Language: Some Educational Implications of the Use of English and Indigenous Languages in the Philippines." *International Review of Education* 43, no. 5–6: 507–526.

Son, Hyun H. 2008. "Explaining Growth and Inequality in Factor Income: The Philippine Case." *ERD Working Paper No. 120*. Asian Development Bank. August.

Son, Hyun H. 2009. "Equity in Health and Health Care in the Philippines." *Economics Working Paper Series No. 151*. Asian Development Bank. August.

Sood, Suemedha. 2011. "Karaoke in the Philippines." *BBC*. August 12. http://www.bbc.com/travel/story/20110812-travelwise-karaoke-in-the-philippines

Spoehr, Alexander. 1973. *Zamboanga and Sulu: An Archeological Approach to Ethnic Diversity*. Pittsburgh: University of Pittsburgh Department of Anthropology.

Stancheva, Yana. 2017. "Five Classics of Modern Philippine Art." *Artdependence Magazine*. November 7. https://www.artdependence.com/articles/five-classics-of-modern-philippine-art/

Stradley, Don. 2008. "A Look at the History of Boxing in the Philippines." *ESPN*. June 24. https://www.espn.com/sports/boxing/news/story?id=3458707

Sussman, Gerard. 1990. "Politics and the Press: The Philippines since Marcos." *Bulletin of Concerned Asian Scholars* 22, no. 1: 34–43.

Symaco, Lorraine Pe. 2017. "Education, Language Policy and Language Use in the Philippines." *Language Problems and Language Planning* 41, no. 1: 87–102.

Tacio, Henry D. 2017. "Culture and Arts: This Sport Called Cockfighting." *Edge Davao*. January 31. https://edgedavao.net/culture-arts/2017/01/31/culture-arts-sport-called-cockfighting/

Talusan, Mary. 2010. "From Rebel Songs to Moro Songs: Popular Music and Muslim Filipino Protest." *Humanities Review* 7, no. 1 (January–June): 85–110.

Tan, David C. 2014. "Being LGBT in Asia: The Philippines Country Report: A Participatory Review and Analysis of the Legal and Social Environment for Lesbian, Gay, Bisexual and Transgender (LGBT) Individuals and Civil Society." Bangkok. United Nations Development Programme, and the United States Agency for International Development: 81 pp.

Tan, Michael T. 2008. "Survival through pluralism: emerging gay communities in the Philippines." *Journal of Homosexuality* 40, no. 3–4 (October 12): 117–142.

Tangco, Roberto D., and Ricardo Ma. Nolasco. 2002. "'Taglish' Verbs: How English Loanwords Make It into the Philippine Languages." In M. Macken (ed.), *Papers from the Tenth Annual Meeting of the Southeast Asian Linguistics Society*. Tempe, AZ: Arizona State University Program for Southeast Asian Studies.

Tapales, Prosperina Domingo, Jocelyn C. Cuaresma, Wilhelmina L. Cabo, Celenia J. Jamig, and Zita Concepcion P. Calugay. 1998. *Local Government in the Philippines: A Book of Readings—Volumes 1–2*. Quezon City: University of the Philippines Center for Local and Regional Governance and the National College of Public Administration and Governance.

Teehankee, Julio C., and Cleo Ann A. Calimbahin. 2020. "Mapping the Philippines' Defective Democracy." *Asian Affairs: An American Review: Special Issue of Democratization in East Asia* 47, no. 2 (April): 97–125.

Thompson, Mark. 1995. *The Anti-Marcos Struggle: Personalistic Rule and Democratic Transition in the Philippines*. New Haven and London: Yale University Press.

Thompson, Mark, and Eric Batalla. 2018. *Routledge Handbook on Contemporary Philippines*. Milton Park, Abingdon, Oxfordshire: Taylor and Francis.

Tiamson, Alfredo T. 1970. *Mindanao-Sulu Bibliography*. Davao City: Ateneo de Davao University.

Tiongson, Lito, and Elena Rivera Mirano. 2016. *Musika: A Documentary on the Spanish Influence on Philippine Music*. Manila: Cultural Center of the Philippines. Video.

A Topical Vocabulary: English, Filipino, Ilocano and Lubuagan Kalinga. 1995. Manila: Summer Institute of Linguistic Inc.

Tovera, David Garcia. 1975. "A History of English Teaching in the Philippines: From Unilingualism to Bilingualism." PhD diss., Northwestern University.

Transparency International. 2021. "Corruption Perception Index." https://www.transparency .org/en/cpi/2021?gclid=CjwKCAiAsNKQBhAPEiwAB-I5zefdOrhnsvEVgC-GnQiG _Fzpt4x2mREkKDN9fhd9m70qfpRRDKh8WxoCsBcQAvD_BwE

Trimillos, Ricardo. 1998. "Filipino-American Youth Performing Filipinicity." *Pahiyas: A Philippine Harvest* 1998: 53–56.

Tupas, Ruanni. 2003. "History, Language Planners, and Strategies of Forgetting: The Problem of Consciousness in the Philippines." *Language Problems and Language Planning* 27, no. 1: 1–25.

Tupas, Ruanni. 2015. "The Politics of 'P' and 'F': A Linguistic History of Nation-Building in the Philippines." *Journal of Multilingual and Multicultural Development* 36, no. 6: 587–597.

UCAN Directory: Database of Diocese of Asia. http://directory.ucanews.com/congregation /philippines-manila/431

Ujano-Batangan, Theresa D. Maria. 2006. *Pagdadalaga at Pagbibinata: Development Contexts of Adolescent Sexuality*. Quezon City: University of the Philippines, Center for Women's Studies and the Ford Foundation.

U.S. Defense Mapping Agency. 1980. *Luzon*. Washington, DC: Hydrographic/Topographic Center.

Valdez, Maria Luisa A. 2014. "Parada ng Lechon in Balayan, Batangas to Honor St. John the Baptist: An Ethnographic Study." *Asia Pacific Journal of Multidisciplinary Research* 2, no. 3 (June): 96–102.

Van De Haar, Edwin. 2011. "Philippine Trade Policy and the Japan-Philippines Economic Partnership Agreement (JPEPA)." *Contemporary Southeast Asia: Journal of International and Strategic Affairs* 33, no. 1: 113–139.

Vancio, Joseph A. 1980. "The Realities of Marriage of Urban Filipino (sic) Women." *Philippine Studies* 28, no. 1 (March 1): 5–20.

Villalon, Augusto. 2001. *Lugar: Essays on Philippine Heritage and Architecture*. New York: Bookmark Publishing.

Villaruz, Basilio Esteban S. 1989. *Sayaw: An Essay on Philippine Dance*. Manila: Sentrong Pangkultura ng Pilipinas.

Villaruz, Basilio Esteban S. 2006. *Treading Through: 45 Years of Philippine Dance*. Quezon City: University of the Philippines Press.

The Visayas. n.p.: Gale Virtual Reference Library.

Vitug, Marites, and Glenda Gloria. 2000. *Under the Crescent Moon: Rebellion in Mindanao*. Quezon City: Institute for Popular Democracy and Ateneo School for Social Policy.

Wendt, Reinhardt. 1998. "Philippine Fiesta and Colonial Culture." *Philippine Studies* 46, no. 1 (First Quarter): 3–23.

Whaley, Floyd. 2012. "Manila's Gory, Sexy Tabloids Outsell Traditional Broadsheets." *New York Times*. June 26. Accessed November 6, 2019. https://www.nytimes.com/2012/06/27/world/asia/manilas-gory-sexy-tabloids-outsell-traditional-newspapers.html

White, Lynne, III. 2014. *Philippine Politics: Possibilities and Problems in a Localist Democracy*. London and New York: Routledge.

Whitemore, Lewis Bliss. 1961. *Struggle for Freedom: History of the Philippine Independent Church*. Greeenwich, CT: Seabury Press.

Wicker, Lane. 2010. *Filipino Tattoos: Ancient to Modern*. Atglen, PA: Schiffer Publications.

Wiegele, Katherine L. 2004. *Investing in Miracles: El Shaddai and the Transformation of Popular Catholicism in the Philippines*. Honolulu, HI: University of Hawaii Press.

Wiley, Mark V., ed. 2001. *Arnis: History and Development of the Filipino Martial Arts*. Clarendon, VT: Tuttle Publishing.

Wolff, John Ulrich. 1965. "Cebuano Visayan Syntax." PhD diss., Yale University.

World Bank. 2018. *Making Growth Work for the Poor: A Poverty Assessment for the Philippines*. Washington, DC: World Bank.

World Bank Group and Australian Aid. 2016. "Assessing Basic Education Service Delivery in the Philippines: The Philippines Public Education Expenditure Tracking and Quantitative Service Delivery Study." Report No. AUS799. June. http://documents.worldbank.org

/curated/en/507531468325807323/pdf/AUS6799-REVISED-PH-PETS-QSDS-Final-Report
.pdf

World Population Review. 2022. "English Speaking Countries." https://worldpopulationreview
.com/country-rankings/english-speaking-countries

Xenos, Peter.1997. "Survey Sheds New Light on Marriage and Sexuality in the Philippines." *Asia-Pacific Population and Policy*, July, no. 42:1–4.

Yabes, Criselda J. 2009. *Boys from the Barracks: The Philippine Military after EDSA—Updated Edition.* Pasay City: Anvil Publishing.

Yagi, Ichiro. 1984. *The Evolution of Dance in Philippine Culture.* Manila: Entrepreneur Trading Corporation.

Yamaguchi, Kiyoko. 2006. "The New 'American' Houses in the Colonial Philippines and the Rise of the Urban Filipino Elite." *Philippine Studies* 54, no. 3: 412–451.

Yamano, MeLe. 2018. *Theatre and Music in Manila and the Asia Pacific, 1869–1946.* New York and Amsterdam: Palgrave MacMillan and Transnational Theatre Histories.

Ylanan, Reginio R., and Carmen Wilson Ylanan. 1965. *The History and Development of Physical Education and Sports in the Philippines.* Manila: Carmen W. Ylanan.

Yoshihara, Kunio. 1986. *Philippine Industrialization: Foreign and Domestic Capital.* Cambridge: Oxford University Press.

Young, Catherine. 2002. "First Language First: Literacy Education for the Future in a Multilingual Philippine Society." *International Journal of Bilingual Education and Bilingualism* 5, no. 4: 221–232.

"Young Adult Fertility and Sexuality Survey in the Philippines." 1996. *Reproductive Health Matters* 4, no. 8 (November): 150.

Zafra, Jessica. 2020. "The Decline and Fall of the Filipino Movie Industry." *Far East Film Festival 22.* April 24–May 22. https://www.fareastfilm.com/eng/archive/catalogue/2007/il-declino-e
-la-caduta-dellindustria-cinematografica-delle-filippine/?IDLYT=31711

Zamora, Neri (compiler). 1995. *A Topical Vocabulary: English, Filipino, Ilocano and Lubuagan Kalinga.* Manila: Summer Institute of Linguistic Inc.

INDEX

Page numbers in *italics* indicate photos; page numbers followed by *t* indicate tables.

About the Author

Patricio N. Abinales is a professor at the Department of Asian Studies, the University of Hawaii–Manoa, where he teaches Philippine political history, Southeast Asian studies, and Asian food cultures. He grew up in the southern Philippine of Mindanao and was educated at the University of the Philippines, where he worked for nearly a decade before heading to Cornell University to pursue a PhD in Government and Southeast Asian studies. His dissertation was published under the title *Making Mindanao: Cotabato and Davao in the Formation of the Philippine Nation-State* (2001), with an expanded version of the book coming out in 2017. Abinales cowrote, with his late wife Donna J. Amoroso, *State and Society in the Philippines* (2005, 2017), which a Filipino historian described as the definitive textbook on Philippine history for the millennial generation.

www.ingramcontent.com/pod-product-compliance
Lightning Source LLC
Chambersburg PA
CBHW080410270326
41929CB00018B/2968

* 9 7 9 8 7 6 5 1 4 1 1 2 0 *